Grief and Bereavement in Contemporary Society

THE SERIES IN DEATH, DYING, AND BEREAVEMENT
ROBERT NEIMEYER, CONSULTING EDITOR

Beder—*Voices of Bereavement: A Casebook for Grief Counselors*
Berger—*Music of the Soul: Composing Life Out of Loss*
Buckle & Fleming—*Parenting After the Death of a Child: A Practitioner's Guide*
Davies—*Shadows in the Sun: The Experiences of Sibling Bereavement in Childhood*
Doka & Martin—*Grieving Beyond Gender: Understanding the Ways Men and Women Mourn, Revised Edition*
Harris—*Counting Our Losses: Reflecting on Change, Loss, and Transition in Everyday Life*
Harvey—*Perspectives on Loss: A Sourcebook*
Katz & Johnson—*When Professionals Weep: Emotional and Countertransference Responses in End-of-Life Care*
Klass—*The Spiritual Lives of Bereaved Parents*
Jeffreys—*Helping Grieving People – When Tears Are Not Enough: A Handbook for Care Providers, Second Edition*
Jordan & McInotsh—*Grief After Suicide: Understanding the Consequences and Caring for the Survivors*
Leenaars—*Lives and Deaths: Selections from the Works of Edwin S. Shneidman*
Leong & Leach—*Suicide among Racial and Ethnic Minority Groups: Theory, Research, and Practice*
Lester—*Katie's Diary: Unlocking the Mystery of a Suicide*
Martin, Doka—*Men Don't Cry... Women Do: Transcending Gender Stereotypes of Grief*
Neimeyer, Harris, Winokuer, & Thornton—*Grief and Bereavement in Contemporary Society: Bridging Research and Practice*
Nord—*Multiple AIDS-Related Loss: A Handbook for Understanding and Surviving a Perpetual Fall*
Roos—*Chronic Sorrow: A Living Loss*
Rogers—*The Art of Grief: The Use of Expressive Arts in a Grief Support Group*
Rosenblatt—*Parent Grief: Narratives of Loss and Relationship*
Rosenblatt & Wallace—*African-American Grief*
Tedeschi & Calhoun—*Helping Bereaved Parents: A Clinician's Guide*
Silverman—*Widow to Widow, Second Edition*
Werth—*Contemporary Perspectives on Rational Suicide*
Werth & Blevins—*Decision Making near the End of Life: Issues, Developments, and Future Directions*

FORMERLY THE **SERIES IN DEATH EDUCATION, AGING, AND HEALTH CARE**
HANNELORE WASS, CONSULTING EDITOR

Bard—*Medical Ethics in Practice*
Benoliel—*Death Education for the Health Professional*
Bertman—*Facing Death: Images, Insights, and Interventions*
Brammer—*How to Cope with Life Transitions: The Challenge of Personal Change*
Cleiren—*Bereavement and Adaptation: A Comparative Study of the Aftermath of Death*
Corless, Pittman-Lindeman—*AIDS: Principles, Practices, and Politics, Abridged Edition*
Corless, Pittman-Lindeman—*AIDS: Principles, Practices, and Politics, Reference Edition*
Curran—*Adolescent Suicidal Behavior*
Davidson—*The Hospice: Development and Administration. Second Edition*
Davidson, Linnolla—*Risk Factors in Youth Suicide*
Degner, Beaton—*Life-Death Decisions in Health Care*
Doka—*AIDS, Fear, and Society: Challenging the Dreaded Disease*
Doty—*Communication and Assertion Skills for Older Persons*
Epting, Neimeyer—*Personal Meanings of Death: Applications for Personal Construct Theory to Clinical Practice*
Haber—*Health Care for an Aging Society: Cost-Conscious Community Care and Self-Care Approaches*
Hughes—*Bereavement and Support: Healing in a Group Environment*
Irish, Lundquist, Nelsen—*Ethnic Variations in Dying, Death, and Grief: Diversity in Universality*
Klass, Silverman, Nickman—*Continuing Bonds: New Understanding of Grief*
Lair—*Counseling the Terminally Ill: Sharing the Journey*
Leenaars, Maltsberger, Neimeyer—*Treatment of Suicidal People*
Leenaars, Wenckstern—*Suicide Prevention in Schools*
Leng—*Psychological Care in Old Age*
Leviton—*Horrendous Death, Health, and Well-Being*
Leviton—*Horrendous Death and Health: Toward Action*
Lindeman, Corby, Downing, Sanborn—*Alzheimer's Day Care: A Basic Guide*
Lund—*Older Bereaved Spouses: Research with Practical Applications*
Neimeyer—*Death Anxiety Handbook: Research, Instrumentation, and Application*
Papadatou, Papadatos—*Children and Death*
Prunkl, Berry—*Death Week: Exploring the Dying Process*
Ricker, Myers—*Retirement Counseling: A Practical Guide for Action*
Samarel—*Caring for Life and Death*
Sherron, Lumsden—*Introduction to Educational Gerontology. Third Edition*
Stillion—*Death and Sexes: An Examination of Differential Longevity Attitudes, Behaviors, and Coping Skills*
Stillion, McDowell, May—*Suicide Across the Life Span—Premature Exits*
Vachon—*Occupational Stress in the Care of the Critically Ill, the Dying, and the Bereaved*
Wass, Corr—*Childhood and Death*
Wass, Corr—*Helping Children Cope with Death: Guidelines and Resource. Second Edition*
Wass, Corr, Pacholski, Forfar—*Death Education II: An Annotated Resource Guide*
Wass, Neimeyer—*Dying: Facing the Facts. Third Edition*
Weenolsen—*Transcendence of Loss over the Life Span*
Werth—*Rational Suicide? Implications for Mental Health Professionals*

Grief and Bereavement in Contemporary Society

Bridging Research and Practice

Edited by

Robert A. Neimeyer • Darcy L. Harris
Howard R. Winokuer • Gordon F. Thornton

Routledge
Taylor & Francis Group
711 Third Avenue
8th Floor
New York, NY 10017

Routledge
Taylor & Francis Group
27 Church Road
Hove, East Sussex BN3 2FA

Printed in the United States of America on acid-free paper
10 9 8 7 6 5 4 3

International Standard Book Number: 978-0-415-88480-8 (Hardback) 978-0-415-88481-5 (Paperback)

Library of Congress Cataloging-in-Publication Data

Grief and bereavement in contemporary society : bridging research and practice / [edited by] Robert A. Neimeyer ... [et al.].
p. cm. -- (Series in death, dying, and bereavement)
Includes bibliographical references and index.
ISBN 978-0-415-88480-8 (hardcover : alk. paper) -- ISBN 978-0-415-88481-5 (pbk. : alk. paper)
1. Bereavement--Psychological aspects. 2. Death--Psychological aspects. 3. Grief. I. Neimeyer, Robert A., 1954-

BF575.G7G724 2011
155.9'37--dc22 2010044381

Visit the Taylor & Francis Web site at
http://www.taylorandfrancis.com

and the Routledge Web site at
http://www.routledge.com

To Kathy, Eric and Michael,
my witnesses to life's many losses and gains
RAN

To Brad, whose centering presence sustains me,
and to Lauren, who inspires me every day
DLH

To my clients and colleagues who have inspired me
and motivated me to be the best grief professional that I can be
HRW

To my sister, Janice, whose kidney donation
and to my wife, Sally, whose caring nursing and support
made my work on this book possible
GFT

Contents

SECTION II CONTEXTS OF GRIEVING

SECTION III CHALLENGES IN BEREAVEMENT

SECTION IV SPECIFIC POPULATIONS

SECTION V SPECIALIZED THERAPEUTIC MODALITIES

SECTION VI GRIEF IN A GLOBAL PERSPECTIVE

Preface

THE CHANGING GEOGRAPHY OF LOSS

In the late 16th Century, Spanish and Portuguese explorers boldly pushed back the boundaries of the world then known to Europeans, drawing on new maritime and navigational technologies to extend the reach of their growing empires into Africa, Asia, and the New World. Maps drawn in response to the excursions of Magellan, Cabral, and others during this "Age of Discovery" were dense with notations of geographical features and settlements of the coastlines of the recently discovered islands and continents and, for their time, provided remarkably accurate orientation to the changing geography of Iberian interests. Internal features of these same landmasses, however, were conjectural or virtually devoid of notation, representing "dark continents" whose mysterious interiors would only be mapped more accurately in the centuries that followed.

In many respects, 20th Century bereavement studies might be characterized in analogous terms. Like early explorers of the globe, pioneering figures such as Freud and Lindemann fairly accurately mapped the most visible features of grief in its usual symptomatic presentation, sometimes adding elaborate conjectures concerning the internal processes of grieving. By the final decades of the last century, however, many of the latter hypotheses had been called into question by scientific research, and a host of new models drawing on new tools and methods had begun to fill in the contours of their clinical cartography. As the field of bereavement studies enters the second decade of this new Age of Discovery, we as editors agreed it was time to draw together many of these developments in a single authoritative compendium, one designed for a professional as well as scholarly readership.

The partnership that ultimately animated this project arose in the context of our frequent contact and collaboration in a variety of professional contexts, including the *International Work Group on Death, Dying and Bereavement* (IWG), the *Association for Death Education and Counseling* (ADEC), and the *International Conference on Grief and Bereavement in Contemporary Society* (ICGB), organizations in which we have been active for many years. Each of these settings has seen increasing efforts in the last decade to bridge the science and practice of the field of bereavement, as evidenced in the formation of several hybrid work groups on grief, trauma, disaster, war, children's issues, and more in the "summit conference" context of the IWG; in the pursuit of a "Research that Matters" series of featured presentations and organization of a "Bridging" interest group at ADEC meetings; and in the invitation of preeminent international panels of keynote presenters at triennial ICGB gatherings. Given this atmosphere of scientific and applied ferment in the field and a growing enthusiasm for dialogue across the chasm that has traditionally separated scholars and practitioners, we decided it was high time to make a contribution to this effort.

We began by constructing a "wish list" of groundbreaking authors and professionals, those whose pioneering work has begun to change the geography of grief in contemporary culture. Remarkably, nearly all shared our excitement about the project, even in view of the tight schedule imposed on their writing by our plan to have the volume in print in time for the next meeting of the ICGB in Miami in June of 2011. In our letter of invitation to potential authors, we sketched the unusual aim of the book, stressing the central relevance of the "bridging" concept as the *sine qua non* of the endeavor. In part, our letter read:

> Unlike most professional books in which prominent authors propound their own scholarly or applied perspective, we are looking to promote a theme… of meaningful engagement of science and practice with one another. …[In fact], we are hoping to accomplish something similar at the level of each and every chapter in this hefty and authoritative volume. That is, by what we hope will be felicitous match-making between representatives of each community who are passionately engaged with converging concerns (e.g., the relevance of a particular model to clinical practice; family therapy for bereavement; complicated grief; spirituality), we want to do what few professional books actually achieve, namely, bring the best of research-based conceptualization and clinical wisdom to bear on 30 of the most important topics in the field, in a way that is integrated in each contribution.

The publication of the present book more than accomplishes these objectives. In the pages that follow, the reader will encounter the work of 60 preeminent contributors to bereavement research and practice, representing 10 nations, including Australia, Brazil, Belgium, Canada, China, Israel, the Netherlands, Norway, the United Kingdom, and the United States. A unique feature of the book is reflected in our pairing of authors—many of whom had no prior relationship—to ensure that every coauthor team had strong representation of scholarly and applied competencies in the relevant topic, usually by recruiting one well-published researcher, and one well-respected practitioner in each instance, but occasionally inviting two or more scientist-practitioners who were thoroughly "bicultural" in both domains. The result, as we hoped, was a series of thoughtful, readable, and above all practical treatments of a great range of topics in bereavement, every one of which weaves together strands of research and application to construct more robust "blanket" coverage of the field than either perspective could generate in isolation.

What, then, can readers expect to encounter in the chapters that follow? In Section I, *Current Conceptualizations of the Grief Response*, will be found coverage of the most influential and cutting-edge models on the contemporary scene, detailing the role of attachment theory, the Dual Process Model, meaning reconstruction, the Two-Track Model, tasks of mourning, and gender-oriented conceptualizations of grief with rich consideration of their supporting data and clinical implications. Section II considers *Contexts of Grieving* in the intimate crucible of families who have lost children, parents, siblings and spouses, conveying what is known about the risks and resources associated with each, and how they might be approached in therapy. In Section III, the focus is on *Challenges in Bereavement* including substantial coverage of complicated grief, ambiguous loss, nonfinite loss, chronic sorrow, suicide, natural and human-induced disasters, and terrorism. Detailed clinical procedures for addressing each of these difficult forms of loss are provided in each chapter. Section IV gives attention to *Specific Populations* typically marginalized or ignored altogether by dominant institutions including gay, lesbian, bisexual, and transgendered mourners; those who have sustained losses in the context of war and combat; and pet owners who have lost their animal companions. In Section V, *Special Therapeutic Modalities* are outlined and exemplified, offering coverage of family therapy, expressive arts, ritual and legacy work, and hospice interventions that link care of the dying with care of the bereaved. Finally, Section VI places *Grief in a Global Perspective*, taking up issues of culture, technology, social justice, professional ethics, and religion and spirituality. The result is a capstone section that situates the more intimate contexts of individual and family bereavement in a broader contemporary perspective.

What forms of clinical and scientific dialogue can readers expect to find in each of these chapters? The most common is a summary of a research program or theoretical model, which is then illustrated by presentation of a clinical service or case study material that draws on or applies some of its findings or insights. A second collaborative format involves description of a novel evidence-based treatment program, followed by commentary from a practice perspective that supports or extends its various components. A third form of dialogue more closely interweaves the two vantage points as clinical scholars shift repeatedly from the data to their practice implications and back again. And still a fourth entails joint consideration, from a scientific and applied perspective, of a particular problem, controversy, or challenge in the field, performing a more or less literal exchange of counsel from one perspective to the other. What is perhaps most remarkable throughout, in our view, is the consistently respectful tone of engagement between researchers and practitioners, a tone that advances the shared interests of both in understanding the struggles and resilience of bereaved individuals, families, and communities in a way that can make genuine differences in their lives.

As a team of researchers, clinicians, and educators, we are pleased to share with you the dozens of practically useful and carefully constructed maps of the changing geography of grief, which jointly constitute *Grief and Bereavement in Contemporary Society: Bridging Research and Practice*. We hope that these offerings do indeed build a useful bridge into that terrain, one that both clinical and scholarly readers will benefit from traversing.

Robert A. Neimeyer
Howard Winokuer
Darcy Harris
Gordon Thornton

Co-Editors

About the Editors

Robert A. Neimeyer, PhD, is a professor in the Department of Psychology, University of Memphis, where he also maintains an active clinical practice. Since completing his doctoral training at the University of Nebraska in 1982, he has conducted extensive research on the topics of death, grief, loss, and suicide intervention.

Neimeyer has published 25 books including *Constructivist Psychotherapy*, *Grief and Bereavement in Contemporary Society: Bridging Research and Practice*, and *The Art of Longing*, a book of contemporary poetry. The author of more than 350 articles and book chapters, he is currently working to advance a more adequate theory of grieving as a meaning-making process, both in his published work and through his frequent professional workshops for national and international audiences.

Neimeyer is the editor of two respected international journals, *Death Studies* and the *Journal of Constructivist Psychology*, and served as president of the Association for Death Education and Counseling. He was appointed to the American Psychological Association's Task Force on End-of-Life Issues, where he helped implement a research and practice agenda for psychology in this critical area. In recognition of his scholarly contributions, he has been granted the Distinguished Research Award, the Distinguished Teaching Award, and the Eminent Faculty Award by the University of Memphis; elected chair of the International Work Group on Death, Dying, and Bereavement; designated Psychologist of the Year by the Tennessee Psychological Association; made a Fellow of the Clinical Psychology Division of the American Psychological Association; and given both the Research Recognition and Clinical Practice Awards by the Association for Death Education and Counseling.

Darcy L. Harris, PhD, FT, is a professor in the Department of Interdisciplinary Programs at King's University College at the University of Western Ontario, London, Ontario, Canada, where she is the coordinator of the Thanatology program. She also maintains a private clinical practice with a focus on issues related to change, loss, and transition. She serves as a consultant for the Southern Ontario Fertility Treatment program in London, Ontario, as well as a community consultant for victims of traumatic loss.

Prior to her teaching responsibilities at King's University College, Dr. Harris worked as an expanded role nurse in the areas of oncology and hospice care in the

United States for 15 years. She then completed graduate training in counseling psychology and maintained a full-time therapy practice for another 10 years prior to completing her doctoral studies in psychology and thanatology at the Union Institute and University, Cincinnati, Ohio.

Dr. Harris planned and developed the undergraduate degree program in thanatology at King's University College, which provides students from around the world with the opportunity to study about death, dying, and bereavement. She has implemented coursework in thanatology in the specific interest areas of critical theory, social justice, and the exploration of grief after non-death losses. She is also adjunct faculty in the College of Graduate Studies at the University of Western Ontario, and she is on the board of directors for the Association for Death Education and Counseling.

Dr. Harris has written extensively and frequently provides presentations on topics related to death, grief, and loss in contemporary society. Topical areas include the social context of grief in Western society, women's experiences of reproductive losses, shame and social stigma in death and grief, and a recent book that explores non-death and nonfinite loss entitled, *Counting Our Losses: Reflecting on Change, Loss, and Transition in Everyday Life* (Routledge).

Howard R. Winokuer, PhD, is the founder of the Winokuer Center for Counseling and Healing in Charlotte, North Carolina where he maintains a full-time clinical practice. He completed his PhD in 1999 at Mississippi State University where he developed the first course in grief counseling skills. As the founder of TO LIFE, a not-for-profit educational and counseling organization, he was the associate producer of seven PBS specials and helped pilot one of the first teen suicide prevention programs in the Southeast. He has taught numerous courses and been a guest lecturer at many colleges and universities including New York University, Rochester University, The University of North Alabama, Queens University, Appalachian State University, and the University of North Carolina.

Winokuer has conducted workshops and seminars throughout the United States as well as nine foreign countries including programs for St. Christopher's Hospice and St. George's Medical Center, London, England; The National Assistance Board, Barbados; and the United States Embassy, The Hague, Netherlands. He wrote a bi-monthly column entitled "Understanding Grief" in *The Concord Tribune* and hosted a regular radio show on WEGO entitled *Life Talk.* He was a consultant to WBTV, the local CBS affiliate, after the tragedy of 9/11 and has been the mental health "professional on call" for Fox TV's news show "The Edge." In the past year, he has appeared twice on the radio show "Healing the Grieving Heart" and has been interviewed by the *ACA Journal, Counseling Today* as well as in *The Staten Island Advance, The Houston Chronicle, The Charlotte Observer, The Detroit Free Press,* and *The Chicago Tribune.* Winokuer also led an international delegation of funeral directors to Russia and Holland to study death and funeral practices in those countries.

Winokuer has been actively involved in the field of dying, death, and bereavement since 1979. He has presented workshops and seminars to many organizations including The National Funeral Directors Association, The University of

North Carolina's Department of Neurological Surgery, the Tennessee Health Care Association, and Presbyterian Hospital. He also developed the crisis management plan for the Cabarrus County School System, Cabarrus County, North Carolina. Dr. Winokuer has been an active member of The Association for Death Education and Counseling (ADEC) for almost three decades and has served in numerous leadership positions. In his almost nearly thirty years of membership, he has chaired the national public relations committee, co-chaired the 2000 and 2003 national conferences, served on the board of directors, is one of the co-chairs for the 2011 international conference that ADEC is co-hosting with The International Conference on Grief and Bereavement in Contemporary Society, and was the president of the Association for Death Education and Counseling.

Gordon Thornton, PhD, FT, is an emeritus professor of psychology at Indiana University of Pennsylvania where he started teaching the psychology of death and dying in 1975. He has been actively involved in the Association for Death Education and Counseling (ADEC) having served as the association's treasurer and president. He has also served as co-chair of ADEC conferences and as chair of the Credentialing Council for ADEC. He is a Fellow in Thanatology: Death, Dying and Bereavement awarded by ADEC. Since it was established in 1983, he has been actively involved with his local hospice, Family Hospice of Indiana County, as president of the board of directors or chair of the advisory committee. He has presented papers at national and international conferences on a variety of topics in the area of dying, death, and bereavement and has contributed articles to *Death Studies* and the ADEC magazine, *The FORUM*. He is associate editor of *The Handbook of Thanatology*.

Contributors

Carrie Arnold, **MEd**, **CCC**, **RSW,** is an adjunct faculty member at King's University College at the University of Western Ontario in the thanatology program and Department of Psychology. She has co-authored articles on the well-being of adolescent girls and in her clinical practice, specializes in treating adolescents and adults who are experiencing grief and trauma. She is also the founder of *MotherCare London*, an in-home supportive service providing education and resources to mothers regarding the significance and lasting impact of establishing healthy mother-infant bonds.

Timothy S. Ayers received his **PhD** in clinical psychology from Arizona State University. He is an associate research scientist at the Prevention Research Center within the Psychology Department at Arizona State University. Clinically, he is interested in the impact of bereavement on families and the treatment of anxiety disorders in children and adults. His research interests include the assessment of coping and competence in children and adolescents, the development and evaluation of prevention programs for children, and the dissemination of evidence-based practices in natural service delivery settings.

Joy S. Berger, **DMA**, **BCC**, **MT-BC**, is the quality and education researcher for Hosparus, Inc., in Louisville, Kentucky and a music therapy clinical faculty member at the University of Louisville. She was awarded the National Heart of Hospice Psychosocial/Spiritual Caregiver by the National Council of Hospice and Palliative Care Professionals. Dr. Berger is the author of *Music of the Soul: Composing Life Out of Loss,* published in Routledge's Series in Death, Dying and Bereavement.

Paul A. Boelen, **PhD**, works as an assistant professor of clinical psychology at Utrecht University in the Netherlands. He also works as a licensed cognitive behavioral psychotherapist at the Ambulatory Mental Health Care Clinic of the same university. His research focuses on theory, assessment, and treatment of complicated grief in children, adolescents, and adults.

Tashel C. Bordere, **PhD**, **CT**, is an associate professor of child and family development at the University of Central Missouri, where she has developed and taught courses in death, dying, and bereavement and multiculturalism in families. She is a board member of the Association of Death Education and Counseling, past chair of the Multicultural Committee, and is associate editor of *The Forum*. Her research focuses on homicidal death among African American youth, cultural death customs, parenting approaches within context, and cultural sensitivity in research and practice with youth.

Pauline Boss, PhD, is professor emerita at the University of Minnesota; and Fellow, American Psychological Association, American Association of Marriage and Family Therapy, and National Council on Family Relations (past president) and a psychotherapist in private practice. She is also principal theorist in the area of ambiguous loss, a term she coined in 1974. Her research is summarized in the acclaimed *Ambiguous Loss: Learning to Live with Unresolved Grief* (Harvard University Press, 1999). Her most recent book, *Loss, Trauma, and Resilience* (W. W. Norton, 2006), applies the theory with six therapeutic guidelines.

Jennifer L. Buckle, PhD, R Psych, is a clinical psychologist and assistant professor of psychology at Sir Wilfred Grenfell College, Memorial University of Newfoundland, Canada. Dr. Buckle has authored publications and presentations on the grief experience of bereaved parents and the application of qualitative research methods in the study of bereavement. In 2010, Routledge published her book co-authored with Dr. Stephen Fleming entitled *Parenting After the Death of a Child: A Practitioner's Guide.*

Betty J. Carmack. RN, EdD, Professor Emerita University of San Francisco School of Nursing. Dr. Carmack authored *Grieving the Death of a Pet* (2003); has been published in nursing and multi-disciplinary literature; and performed clinical work in pet loss since 1982 with individuals and groups. She is also the primary investigator of *Lived Experience of Pet Loss* and current co-investigator of continuing bonds in pet loss. She received the Delta Society Michael McCullough Memorial Award for "Outstanding Contribution Towards Furthering the Understanding of the Interactions Between People and Companion Animals."

Deborah Carr, PhD, University of Wisconsin-Madison, is professor of sociology at Rutgers University and the Institute for Health, Health Care Policy, and Aging Research. She has published more than 50 articles and book chapters. Dr. Carr has written widely on widowhood, death and dying, and end-of-life decision making. Carr has co-authored or edited six books including *Spousal Bereavement in Later Life* (2006). She is a fellow of the Gerontological Society of America.

Grace H. Christ, PhD, is a professor at the Columbia University School of Social Work in New York City. Previously she was director of the Social Work Department at Memorial Sloan-Kettering Cancer Center. Currently she is a co-founder and chair of the Social Work Hospice and Palliative Care Network. She directed the FDNY-CSU/Columbia University Family Intervention Program for families of firefighters who died in the WTC disaster on 9/11. Dr. Christ has a substantial research record in oncology, palliative social work, bereavement, and disaster response. She has consulted, published and lectured extensively in the United States and internationally.

Amy Yin Man Chow, PhD, MSoc Sc, RSW, FT, has been at Hong Kong University as an assistant professor since 2005. She is a registered social worker with the specialization in bereavement counseling. Dr. Chow is the former director and founder of the first community based bereavement counseling center in Hong Kong, received the *Association for Death Education and Counseling 2005 Cross-Cultural Award* in April, 2005 and was named the CADENZA Fellow in 2008.

Stephen R. Connor, PhD, has worked in the hospice/palliative care movement since 1976 and is senior executive of the Worldwide Palliative Care Alliance. A licensed clinical psychologist, he served for 10 years with NHPCO and focuses on palliative care development internationally as consultant to the Open Society Institute's International Palliative Care Initiative in New York and to Altarum Institute in Washington, DC. He also serves as consultant research director for Capital Hospice in the Washington Area.

Betty Davies, RN, CT, PhD, FAAN, is professor and senior scholar at the University of Victoria, Canada and professor emerita at the University of California at San Francisco. Dr. Davies is the past chair of the International Work Group in Death, Dying and Bereavement. Recently, she received the 2008 Distinguished Career Achievement Award from the Hospice and Palliative Nurses Association and the Canadian Nurses Association Centennial Award. Her extensive research, especially on sibling bereavement, has resulted in numerous publications, including a book *Shadows in the Sun: Experiences of Sibling Bereavement in Childhood.*

Kenneth J. Doka, PhD, is a professor of gerontology at the Graduate School of The College of New Rochelle and senior consultant to the Hospice Foundation of America. A prolific author, Dr. Doka has written 26 books including with Terry Martin *Grieving Beyond Gender: Understanding the Ways Men and Woman Mourn* and more than 100 articles and book chapters. Dr. Doka is editor of both *Omega: The Journal of Death and Dying* and *Journeys: A Newsletter to Help in Bereavement.* He was elected president of the Association for Death Education and Counseling in 1993 and chair of International Work Group on Dying, Death and Bereavement from 1997-1999.

Nigel P. Field received his **PhD** at York University in Toronto, Canada. He currently holds the position of professor of clinical psychology at Palo Alto University in California. He has published extensively on the role of the continuing bond to the deceased in coping with the death of a loved one. More recently, he has extended his program of research to Cambodia in examining loss and trauma stemming from genocide during the Khmer Rouge regime and its effect on second generation Cambodians.

Stephen J. Fleming, PhD, C Psych, is a professor in the Department of Psychology, Faculty of Health, at York University in Toronto, Canada. He has qualified as an expert witness in litigation involving trauma and has served on the editorial boards of the *Journal of Palliative Care* and *Death Studies*. Currently secretary-treasurer of the International Work Group on Death, Dying, and Bereavement, his latest book, *Parenting after the Death of a Dhild: A Practitioner's Guide* (co-author Dr. Jennifer Buckle) was published by Routledge in 2010.

Kathleen Fowler, PhD, FT, is a Professor of Gerontology and Women's Studies at Ramapo College of New Jersey. She is the editor of ADEC's *The Forum*. Dr. Fowler earned her PhD in literature and an MA in thanatology. She teaches a death and dying course and other courses in thanatology such as illness, crisis, and loss. She has published in thanatology, women's studies and literature and is currently working on a book entitled the *Literature of Loss and Grief: Vital Words, Mortal Writers*.

Maria-Helena Pereira Franco has a **PhD** in clinical psychology from Pontifical Catholic University of São Paulo and a post-doctoral fellowship at University College, London. Dr. Pereira is a professor and research advisor in clinical psychology at PUCSP and has been head of the Grief Center since 1996. She is a psychotherapist in private practice and member of Four Seasons Institute of Psychology with a focus on grief and bereavement and the founder and coordinator of a group of psychologists with training for disaster response. She has authored many publications on death, dying and bereavement and is vice-chairperson of IWG International Work Group on Death, Dying and Bereavement.

Louis A. Gamino, PhD, is a diplomate in clinical psychology with Scott & White Healthcare® in Temple, Texas and associate professor of psychiatry and behavioral science, at Texas A&M University College of Medicine. In 2008, Dr. Gamino received the Clinical Practice Award given by the Association for Death Education and Counseling. He is the co-author of two books: *Ethical Practice in Grief Counseling* and *When Your Baby Dies Through Miscarriage or Stillbirth*. In 1997, Dr. Gamino founded the biennial Scott & White Bereavement Conferences. His research is focused on adaptive grieving after loss.

Kathleen R. Gilbert, PhD, CFLE, is a professor of family studies in the Department of Applied Health Science at Indiana University. Her research interests are varied and include loss and bereavement in the family, especially parental bereavement; stress and resilience in the family; the Internet as a tool for coping with loss; and qualitative approaches to grief research.

Linda Goldman, MS, LPCP, FT, NBCC, is a nationally recognized speaker, author and clinician who specializes in children's grief. She is the author of numerous books including *Life and Loss: A Guide to Help Grieving Children (2000, 2nd ed), Breaking the Silence: A Resource Guide to Help Children with Complicated Grief, Raising Our Children to Be Resilient, A Guide to Help Children Cope with*

Trauma in Today's World (2005), and *Coming Out, Coming In: Nurturing the Well Being and Inclusion of Gay Youth in Mainstream Society (2008).*

Roshi Joan Halifax, **PhD**, is a Buddhist teacher, anthropologist, author, and social activist. She has worked with dying people since 1970. She is founding abbot and head teacher of Upaya Zen Center and Institute in Santa Fe, New Mexico. She is a Distinguished Visiting Scholar and Kluge Fellow at the Library of Congress. Author of numerous books, including *Being with Dying: Cultivating Compassion and Fearlessness in the Presence of Death,* she is co-chair of the Lindisfarne Fellows and a board member and Fellow of the Mind and Life Institute. She has been confirmed as a teacher in Korean, Vietnamese, and Japanese Buddhist lineages.

An Hooghe, **MSc**, is a clinical psychologist, marital and family therapist and trainer in family therapy at context at the University Hospital in Leuven, Belgium. As a therapist and researcher she is interested in the topic of loss and grief in families. She is currently working on a PhD study on the sharing of grief in a couple after the loss of a child, at the University of Leuven, Belgium.

Gloria C. Horsley, **PhD**, **MFC**, **CNS**, is a marriage and family therapist and clinical nurse specialist. She is a graduate of the University of Rochester, Syracuse and Holos Universities. She is president and co-founder of The Open to Hope Foundation. Her books include *In-laws: A Guide to Extended Family Therapy* (John Wiley & Sons, Inc., 1995) and *The In-Law Survival Manual* (John Wiley & Sons, Inc., 1996). She is co-author of *Teen Grief Relief,* (Rainbow Books, 2007); *Real Men Do Cry,*(Quality of Life Books, 2008); and *Grief* (Brown Books, 2011).

Heidi Horsley, **MSW**, **PsyD**, is a licensed psychologist and social worker. She is co-founder and executive director for the *Open to Hope Foundation.* She hosts Open to Hope Radio, and is an adjunct professor at Columbia University. Dr. Horsley worked on a longitudinal study for the FDNY-Columbia University Family Guidance Program, providing ongoing intervention to families of firefighters killed in the World Trade Center. She has been interviewed on numerous radio shows and appeared on the national show ABC TV's *20/20.*

William G. Hoy, **DMin**, **FT**, has specialized in issues related to bereavement as a counselor and educator for more than 25 years. With professional experience in church, hospice, bereavement center, and university, he is popular as a conference speaker and presents more than 75 invited continuing education programs and keynote addresses every year. Dr Hoy is active in the Association for Death Education and Counseling, holding the Fellow in Thanatology (FT) designation and teaches in the graduate program in bereavement for Marian University.

John Shep Jeffreys, **EdD**, **FT**, is a licensed psychologist with a practice specializing in grief, loss, and end-of-life concerns; certified group psychotherapist, diplomate in family psychology. He is assistant professor of psychiatry and behavioral sciences at Johns Hopkins University School of Medicine, where he provides seminars on loss, grief, and bereavement for psychiatric residents and medical students; and is affiliate assistant professor of pastoral counseling, Loyola University, Maryland, where he teaches the loss and bereavement course.

John R. Jordan, **PhD**, is a licensed psychologist in private practice in Pawtucket, Rhode Island, specializing in work with survivors of suicide and other losses. He is a Fellow in Thanatology from the Association for Death Education and Counseling (ADEC) and provides training nationally and internationally for therapists, health-care professionals, and clergy. He has published in professional journals and is the co-author of *After Suicide Loss: Coping with Your Grief* and the co-editor of *Grief After Suicide: Coping with the Consequences and Caring for the Survivors*.

Dianne Kane, **MSW**, **PhD**, associate professor at Hunter School of Social Work and assistant director of counseling services for the NYC Fire Department, has co-authored *FDNY Crisis Counseling: Innovative Responses to 9/11 Firefighters, Families, and Communities* and *Healing Together: A Couple's Guide to Coping with Trauma and Post-Traumatic Stress*. Following the loss of 343 FDNY members on 9/11, she expanded the Unit's trauma and bereavement services to the 15,000 member FDNY community, including more than 200 bereaved family members. Additionally, she has assisted the New Orleans Fire Department following Hurricane Katrina and FDNY veterans returning from deployment.

David W. Kissane, **MD**, holds the Jimmie C. Holland Chair in psycho-oncology, is an attending psychiatrist and chairman of the Department of Psychiatry and Behavioral Sciences at Memorial Sloan-Kettering Cancer Center, and professor of psychiatry at the Weill Cornell Medical College. He has researched both cognitive-existential and supportive-expressive group therapy in breast cancer, couples therapy in prostate cancer, demoralization in the medically ill and family-focused grief therapy during palliative care and bereavement. His books include *Handbook of Communication in Oncology and Palliative Care* (2010) and *Family Focused Grief Therapy* (2002).

Dennis Klass, **PhD**, is a retired professor in the psychology of religion. His major research was a two-decade ethnographic study of a self help group of bereaved parents. He then turned his attention to grief narratives in different cultural/religious traditions. He is author and/or editor of 5 books and 50 articles or book chapters. His counseling practice was with difficult bereavements. Dr. Klass lives on Cape Cod where he gardens, golfs, kayaks, and watches the trees grow.

Pål Kristensen, **PsyD**, is a clinician at Community Grief Centre, Bærum, Norway and researcher for the Norwegian Centre for Violence and Traumatic Stress Studies, Oslo, Norway. Dr. Kristensen has conducted studies on the mental health of the bereaved after the 2004 Southeast Asian tsunami. He is also investigating the long-term mental health effects of accidental loss of sons during military service and interventions. He has written numerous articles concerned with disaster and bereavement.

C. Caryn Kondo, **MA in CSoW** from the University of Chicago, is currently the clinical director of Hospice of the Valley's New Song Center for Grieving Children in Phoenix Arizona. Experience includes child life specialist, medical social work in pediatrics, hospice bereavement, child, and family counseling as well as grief support group facilitation for all ages. Her professional passions are children and family grief issues. Special interests include children's developmental issues and grief, suicide effects on schools, self-care, teen perspective on grief, parenting the grieving child, the dying child, and anticipatory grief issues for children.

Jill Harrington-LaMorie, **MSW**, **LCSW**, **ACSW**, is currently the director of professional education at the Tragedy Assistance Program for Survivors (TAPS) and a doctoral student at The University of Pennsylvania School of Social Policy & Practice, Philadelphia, Pennsylvania with a dissertation research focus on military death loss and bereavement. She received her BA in psychology from The Catholic University of America, Washington, DC and her Masters in CSW from Adelphi University, Garden City, New York.

Laura Lewis, **PhD**, **MSW**, is an associate professor of social work at King's University College in London, Ontario Canada. Prior to entering academia, she was a clinical social worker for more than 15 years in a community counseling setting, where she offered counseling to individuals, couples, families, and groups with diverse needs. She has a keen interest in all issues related to bereavement and loss.

Vincent M. Livoti, **PhD**, is a lecturer in the Graduate School of Education at Lesley University, in Cambridge, Massachusetts, where he is also a librarian coordinating the teaching resource collections. He holds an Interdisciplinary PhD in GLBT Studies and presents and publishes his research nationally. This body of work focuses mainly on contemporary depictions of sexuality in multimedia contexts and how these representations inform the construction of youth identities.

Ruth Malkinson, **PhD**, is adjacent senior lecturer at the School of Social Work, Tel Aviv University. She is the director of The Israeli Center of REBT. She is past president of the Israeli Association for Family and Marital Therapy. She specializes in cognitive grief therapy and has co-edited two books on loss and bereavement. Her recent book *Cognitive Grief Therapy: Constructing a Rational Meaning to Life Following Loss* (2007) was published by W W Norton.

Brenda Marshall, **PhD**, is an executive coach, business consultant and founder of The Solacium Group, a management consulting firm that provides support and guidance to grieving senior executives. Brenda's current research interests include narrative inquiry and arts informed approaches to exploring grief and loss both personally and in the workplace. She has presented internationally on adult sibling loss, and has a book on this topic underway.

Terry L. Martin, PhD, is an associate professor of psychology and thanatology at Hood College, Frederick Maryland. He primarily teaches graduate courses in thanatology and professional counseling. He coauthored two books with Ken Doka, and has written numerous chapters and published articles. He is a Licensed Clinical Professional Counselor in Maryland and works almost exclusively with death-related issues. He is married with three children and five grandchildren.

Meghan E. McDevitt-Murphy, PhD, is a clinical psychologist and an assistant professor of psychology at The University of Memphis. She has studied posttraumatic stress disorder in veteran and civilian populations for more than 12 years. She is the recipient of an NIH grant to develop interventions for co-occurring posttraumatic stress disorder and substance use disorders among veterans of the wars in Iraq and Afghanistan.

John L. McIntosh, PhD, is associate vice chancellor for academic affairs and professor of psychology at Indiana University, South Bend; author of many book chapters and professional journal articles; and author, co-author, or co-editor of seven books on suicide including *Suicide and Its Aftermath* (Norton, 1987) and *Grief after Suicide* (Routledge, 2011). He is a past-president of the American Association of Suicidology (AAS), 1990 recipient of the AAS Edwin Shneidman Award (early career contributions in suicidology research), and 1999 recipient of AAS's Roger Tierney Award for Service.

Valarie Molaison, PhD, FT, is a licensed psychologist and fellow in thanatology, death, dying and bereavement who specializes in helping people cope with unexpected stressors. She is currently in private practice and an adjunct clinical associate professor at Widener University. She is a frequent presenter regionally, nationally, and internationally, on topics related to coping with loss and life transition and has written two practical resource books: *School Survival Kit: Helping Students Cope with Grief in the School Setting*, and *Survival Kit for Families: Tools for Healthy Grieving*.

Barbara Monroe, BA, BPhil, CQSW, has been a social worker for more than 30 years. She is chief executive of St. Christopher's Hospice in London, director of the Candle Children's Bereavement Project and was chair of the national Childhood Bereavement Network for 8 years. She is module leader on the St. Christopher's and King's College MSc in palliative care and policy and has lectured and written extensively about psychological and social aspects of palliative care. She sits on a variety of national committees supporting the development of end-of-life care. Ms. Monroe is an honorary professor at Lancaster University and was appointed a Dame in 2010.

Clint Moore III, MDiv, PhD, BCC, FT, is an Episcopal priest in the Diocese of Chicago. Dr. Moore is the clinical ethicist and director of the Center for Clinical Ethics at Advocate Lutheran General Hospital/Advocate Lutheran General Children's Hospital in Park Ridge, Illinois. He provides ethics education for physicians and nurses and ethics consultations around critical decision-making. Dr Moore is a core member of the Palliative Care Consultation Team providing palliative care consultations across the diagnostic and prognostic spectrum. He is a board certified chaplain in the Association of Professional Chaplains and a Fellow in Thanatology.

Wendy Packman, **JD**, **PhD**, associate professor of psychology at Palo Alto University, has studied, presented, and written extensively on sibling bereavement and continuing bonds, the impact of a child's death on parents, and the psychological sequellae of pet loss. She is the primary investigator of an international cross-cultural study examining the continuing impact of a pet's death and she is a co-investigator exploring the use of continuing bonds in pet loss.

Crystal L. Park, **PhD**, is professor of clinical psychology at the University of Connecticut. Her research focuses on coping with stressful events, including the roles of religious beliefs and religious coping, the phenomenon of stress-related growth, and the making of meaning in the context of traumatic events and life-threatening illnesses. She is co-author of *Empathic Counseling: Meaning, Context, Ethics, and Skill* (Brooks/Cole) and co-editor of *The Handbook of the Psychology of Religion and Spirituality* (2nd Edition forthcoming, Guilford).

Colin Murray Parkes, **OBE**, **MD**, **FRCPsych**, is the life president of Cruse: Bereavement Care and emeritus consultant psychiatrist to St. Christopher's Hospice, Sydenham. He has authored books and papers on psychological aspects of bereavement, amputation of a limb, terminal cancer care, and other life crises and is on the editorial board of *Bereavement Care* and *Mortality*. As a consultant following seven major disasters, his recent work is on traumatic bereavements. At the same time, he continues to work on the roots in the attachments of childhood and their relationship to the psychiatric problems that can follow the loss of attachments in adult life.

Susan Roos, **PhD**, **LCSW**, **BCD**, **FT**, is a psychotherapist in private practice in Arlington, Texas. She serves as adjunct faculty at the Union Institute and University as well as the University of Texas at Arlington. As co-chair of the arts committee, she serves on the executive committee of the Dallas Society for Psychoanalytic Psychology and served as the Society's president in 2006-2007. She is an associate editor of *Gestalt Review*. She contributes regularly to professional journals and books on disability, end-of-life, and grief and loss issues. She has authored *Chronic Sorrow: A Living Loss* (2002).

Simon Shimshon Rubin, **PhD**, is a professor of clinical psychology and director of the International Center for the Study of Loss, Bereavement and Human Resilience at the University of Haifa in Israel. Chairman of the postgraduate psychotherapy program, Dr. Rubin is active as a clinician, researcher, and teacher. His most recent book, *A Clinician's Guide to Bereavement,* is due out soon and follows *Traumatic and Non-traumatic Loss and Bereavement: Clinical Theory and Practice (2000).*

Edward K. Rynearson, MD, is a semi-retired clinical psychiatrist from Seattle Washington where he founded the section of psychiatry at the Mason Clinic more than 30 years ago. In addition to full-time clinical practice, he has served on the clinical faculty of the University of Washington as a clinical professor of psychiatry. For more than 20 years, Dr. Rynearson has maintained a particular clinical and research focus on the effects of violent death on family members published in clinical papers, book chapters, and two books entitled *Retelling Violent Death* and *Violent Death: Resilience and Intervention Beyond the Crisis.*

Irwin N. Sandler, PhD from the University of Rochester, is a regents' professor of psychology and director of the Prevention Research Center at Arizona State University. His research seeks to understand factors that affect resilience in children who experience highly stressful events such as bereavement, divorce, and poverty, and to translate an understanding of resilience into programs that promote resilience for these children and their families. He has also focused on the evaluation of the long-term effectiveness of resilience promotion and disorder prevention programs for parentally-bereaved children and children of divorce. His current interest concerns understanding how to translate evidence-based programs into effective community-based practices to promote healthy outcomes for children in stress.

Alison Salloum, PhD, is an assistant professor at the University of South Florida, School of Social Work and Department of Pediatrics. She received her MSW and PhD from the Tulane University School of Social Work. She has extensive clinical experience working with children and families after trauma. Dr. Salloum is the author of *Group Work with Adolescents after Violent Death: A Manual for Practitioners* (Brunner-Routledge, 2004) and *Reactions: A Workbook for Children Experiencing Grief and Trauma* (Centering Corporation, 1998).

Diana C. Sands, PhD, the director of the Bereaved by Suicide Service in Sydney, Australia, has for more than two decades worked in community education, training and counseling and providing psycho-educational suicide bereavement group programs for adults, adolescents, and children. Dr. Sands served on the NSW Executive Committee for the National Association Loss and Grief and as NSW Representative, Suicide Prevention Australia. She has produced a film, *The Red Chocolate Elephants,* for children bereaved by suicide. Her research developed the *Tripartite Model of Suicide Bereavement* and considered implications for education, training and bereavement programs

Cynthia L Schultz, PhD from the University of Queensland, has worked with special interest in counseling, community, and health psychology. Now enjoying creative retirement as honorary associate in the Faculty of Health Sciences at LaTrobe University, she authored, taught, and coordinated undergraduate and postgraduate courses. Her research, publications, and community involvement focus on issues of loss and grief for families and parents. Dr. Schultz is the founding editor of the *Journal of Family Studies* and continues as an associate editor.

M. Katherine Shear, MD, is the Marion E. Kenworthy Professor of Psychiatry in Social Work, Columbia University School of Social Work and the Columbia University College of Physicians and Surgeons. Her recent research in bereavement and grief led to development of a novel treatment for complicated grief. This work led to a landmark randomized controlled treatment study showing efficacy published in 2005. A treatment manual is currently scheduled for publication by Guilford Press. She lectures nationally and internationally on the topic of grief and conducts training in complicated grief treatment.

Barbara E. Thompson, OTD, LCSW, OTR/L, is a licensed clinical social worker and occupational therapist with post-graduate training in the expressive arts. Barbara worked with St. Peter's Hospice in Albany, NY where she founded both the Hospice Day Program and the ALS Regional Center. Currently, she is an associate professor at The Sage Colleges in Troy, NY and a psychotherapist in private practice, integrating the expressive arts into her work as both an educator and therapist.

Eliezer Witztum, MD, is a professor in the Division of Psychiatry, Faculty of Health Sciences, Ben-Gurion University of the Negev, and is director of Psychotherapy Supervision, Mental Health Center Beer Sheva. He specializes in cultural psychiatry, trauma and bereavement, strategic and short term dynamic psychotherapy, treatment of pedophiles and the history of psychiatry. His most recent books are *Sanity and Sanctity; "Soul, Bereavement and Loss"* and *King Herod: A Persecuted Persecutor: A Case Study in Psychohistory and Psychobiography*.

Carol Wogrin, PsyD, RN, FT, is director of the National Center for Death Education, Mount Ida College. She is a licensed psychologist and registered nurse with a background in acute care, home care, and hospice, She has been working with individuals and families coping with illness and bereavement for more than 30 years. An author and educator, she is serves on the board directors of the International Work Group on Death, Dying and Bereavement, lectures nationally and internationally on care of the dying, the bereaved and the professionals who care for them. She has a private practice in Newton, Massachusetts.

J. William Worden, PhD, ABPP, is a Fellow of the American Psychological Association and holds academic appointments at the Harvard Medical School and at the Rosemead Graduate School of Psychology in California. Recipient of five major NIH grants, his research and clinical work for more than 40 years has centered on issues of life-threatening illness and life-threatening behavior. His book *Grief Counseling & Grief Therapy*, now in its fourth edition, has been translated into 14 foreign languages and is widely used around the world as the standard reference on the subject.

Emmanuelle Zech, PhD, is associate professor of psychology at the Université catholique de Louvain, Belgium. She received her doctorate at the Université catholique de Louvain in 2000. Her research interests focus on processes of coping with bereavement and trauma, the efficacy of bereavement and trauma intervention, and processes involved in the psychotherapeutic relationship. She also works as a client-centered and experiential psychotherapist in a mental health center. She is the author of a book in French, *The Psychology of Grief* (2006).

1

Introduction

The Historical Landscape of Loss: Development of Bereavement Studies

COLIN MURRAY PARKES

For most of us, the loss of a loved person is the most severe stress that we will experience, yet the majority will come through this experience without suffering lasting impairment of our physical and mental health. Copious research now enables us to understand why this is not always the case. We are all vulnerable to bereavement, but some are more vulnerable than others; all bereavements are traumatic, but some are more traumatic than others; we all enter a strange and unpredictable world when we suffer a major loss, but some worlds are more hazardous and unpredictable than others. In this volume, we begin to understand the problems that can arise and the solutions that follow from that understanding.

Those who are coming new to the topic of bereavement may find the experience bewildering. Too many theories, too many opinions, and the sheer quantity of research available leave us disoriented. In writing this chapter, I shall try to offer an historical perspective that may help to prepare the reader for what is to come.

Most of the early studies of bereavement adopted a medical viewpoint, which is a good way of diagnosing and treating some problems but runs the risk of ignoring or downplaying the importance of others and leads to charges that doctors are "medicalizing" normal life crises. After bereavement, the line between health and illness begins to blur. For many people, grief is so painful and disabling an experience that it feels like an illness. Yet doctors spend more time reassuring bereaved people of the normality of their experience than they do in diagnosing physical or mental illness.

Feelings of depression and despair are so common after bereavement that the authors of the fourth edition of the *Diagnostic and Statistical Manual of Mental*

Disorders (DSM-IV) did not permit the diagnosis of the psychiatric condition of "major depression" to be made within 2 months of a bereavement unless people are seriously impaired or at risk of suicide (American Psychiatric Association, 1994). Yet major depression is only one among several psychiatric disorders that can be triggered by bereavement. Bereavement is so painful a stress that it can contribute to a wide range of psychiatric problems. It is personal vulnerability rather than grief that determines why some bereaved people suffer anxiety and panic attacks, others suffer major depression (MD), and others take to the bottle and end up with an alcoholic psychosis. These problems were usually evident before the bereavement. Holly Prigerson and others (Prigerson et al., 1996) have confirmed, by careful research, that these disorders are not part of grief and are clearly distinguishable from grief.

Other problems are more closely linked to grief itself, and in 1703 Vogther obtained an MD degree at Altdorf University near Nuremberg, Germany, for a thesis entitled *De Morbis Moerentium*, which translates as *On Pathological Grief*, but his work was forgotten. In 1944, psychoanalyst Eric Lindemann wrote a paper that was very influential in its time. Entitled "The Symptomatology and Management of Acute Grief," it described several complications of grief and claimed that they should be treated by encouraging patients to express their grief and to "do the grief work." With only a few interviews, complicated grief could be transformed into normal grief and take its course toward resolution.

Lindemann's approach is a good example of the dangers of clinical studies that are not backed up by quantitative research. When, in the years to come, unselected bereaved people were assigned at random to counseling or no counseling and then followed up, those who received counseling were not measurably any better than those who did not (Currier, Neimeyer, & Berman, 2008; Jordan & Neimeyer, 2003; Schut et al., 2001).

Random allocation studies are, quite rightly, seen as the acid test of therapies, but we need to be careful when interpreting their findings. For instance, when a large number of people receiving therapy are compared with a similar number who do not, and no significant differences are shown between them, this lack of difference is usually assumed to mean that the therapy was ineffective. But the same result would be obtained if some of the sample were made better by the therapy and a similar proportion made worse. Lindemann had assumed that most bereaved people were repressing their grief and needed help to express it. To be fair, it may be that at that time, at the close of the Second World War, adopting a "stiff upper lip" mode of coping was giving rise to more problems than it does today. The mistake was to assume that Lindemann's method was the solution to all of the problems of bereavement.

More recent research has shown that, like childbirth, grief is a painful experience from which most people will recover with minimal help. But, also like childbirth, there is a minority of people for whom the right help, given at the right time for the right problem, will reduce the risk of lasting physical and mental damage. The solution is to match the solution to the problem. It is for this reason that we need a professional handbook like the present one that will help us to do precisely that.

Even in Lindemann's time, there were a few of us who questioned his claims. Anderson, writing in 1949, found that many bereaved people who sought psychiatric help after bereavement were not repressing their grief; far from it, they couldn't stop grieving. Encouraging such people to express their grief was more likely to harm than to help them. Likewise, in my own studies, chronic grief, now termed *prolonged grief disorder* (PGD), was more common than grief that was delayed, inhibited, or distorted (Parkes & Prigerson, 2009).

Complicated grief still hasn't made it into the DSM despite the fact that Prigerson and her colleagues (Prigerson, Vanderwerker, & Maciejewski, 2008) have shown that in its commonest form, PGD meets every criterion for a mental disorder, gives rise to great suffering, increases risks to physical and mental health, and responds to the right treatment. You can read more about that in Chapter 12.

If PGD is not caused by repression of grief, what is its cause? In the Harvard Bereavement Study (Parkes & Weiss, 1983), lasting grief was found to be associated with dependent, clinging attachments to the lost person, and this finding has been confirmed in several other studies, but that does not explain why some people are more dependent than others. An answer to that question comes from studies of the development of human attachments from childhood onward.

We shall see, in Chapter 3, how the seminal studies of Mary Ainsworth identified patterns of attachment between parents and infants that, arising in the first few years of life, predict subsequent attachments (Ainsworth & Eichberg, 1991). Among them is an insecure pattern that Ainsworth termed "anxious-ambivalent attachment," according to which these infants become severely distressed and angry during brief periods of separation from their parents. This happens in infants whose mothers are themselves anxious, overprotective, and overcontrolling of their child. It seems that these children learn that, in order to survive, you have to stay close to Mum.

My own studies of bereaved people seeking psychiatric help (Parkes, 2006) showed that those who reported anxious-ambivalent attachments in their childhood responded to bereavement in later life with severe, protracted grief and a persisting tendency to cling. Grief, it seems, is a consequence of love. You cannot have one without the other. It is by studying love and its vagaries that we begin to understand some of the problems to which it can give rise.

Other problems result from the circumstances of the death. Sudden, unexpected, and untimely deaths; multiple losses; and deaths that are manmade or associated with horrific circumstances all place an extra burden on bereaved people. Such losses are frequently found in people seeking psychiatric help after bereavement (Parkes & Prigerson, 2009). They will be considered in several of the chapters that follow.

But psychiatrists are not the only professionals with a useful contribution to make to our understanding of bereavement. Over the last few years, empirical studies by psychiatrists have gradually given place to a body of theory generated by sociologists and psychologists that opens the door to new ways of thinking about these problems.

One of the most seminal is the dual-process model (Stroebe & Schut, 1999), which recognizes two distinct but interacting psychological processes that follow all bereavements that they term the *loss orientation* and *restoration orientation*. The first process is peculiar to grief and reflects the fact that we do not cease to be attached to people when they die. Like many nonhuman animals, we are programmed to cry and to seek those we have lost, even when we know that they cannot be found. It is a paradox that our desperate struggle to get them back "out there" can blind us to the fact that we never lost them "in here"; those we love literally do "live on" in our memory. This realization is referred to as the *continuing bond* to the dead and is studied in Chapter 4.

The second dual process refers to the need to give up one set of major assumptions about the world and develop another. This is not peculiar to bereavement; it happens whenever we are faced with a major change in our lives, particularly one for which we are unprepared (Parkes, 1988). In Chapter 2, we shall explore how our assumptive world, the world that we assume to exist on the basis of our experience of life up until this moment in time, is the world that gives us a sense of direction and meaning in the narrative of our lives. We think, "I know where I'm going, and I know who's going with me," except that when we lose one we love, we no longer know where we are going or who is going with us. Important new understanding has come out of studies of the gradual process by which we rebuild our internal model of the world after bereavement and discover new meanings, a new narrative, and a new assumptive world. Just how this process plays out in the context of the treatment of complicated grief is further explored in Chapter 12.

Thus far, we have spoken of bereavement as a personal problem, but bereavement is also a family problem, and multiple bereavements may become community problems and national disasters. Human beings are social animals, and bereavements easily disrupt the social systems of which we are a part. We shall see here why some families are at special risk after bereavement (Chapter 22), how bereavement by suicide can pose a special challenge to family members (Chapter 17), and how disasters (Chapter 15) and wars (Chapter 20) can devastate communities.

By the same token, some of these social systems exist to support their members through times of trouble. We have much to learn from studying the ways in which people from cultures other than our own cope with bereavement (Chapter 26), and how spiritual and religious beliefs (Chapter 27) and rituals influence our response (Chapter 24).

Much of the early research was focused on the reaction to loss of a husband by the widow, so much so that this came to be seen as the "norm" for grief. New understandings have emerged from studies of gender differences in grieving (Chapter 7), bereaved children (Chapter 11), the loss of a child (Chapter 9), siblings (Chapter 10), gay partners (Chapter 19), and pets (Chapter 21).

Gradually a rich pattern emerges as we recognize both the common heritage that we all share, and also the subtle differences that explain why some come through grief's long valley with lasting problems while others are matured by grief. Out of this understanding new solutions are emerging, some of which are already meeting the rigorous requirements of scientific research. The many collaborative contributions of scholars and clinicians that comprise this volume should go some distance toward advancing this ongoing effort.

REFERENCES

Ainsworth, M. D. S., & Eichberg, C. (1991). Effects on infant–mother attachment of mother's unresolved loss of an attachment figure, or other traumatic experience. In C. M. Parkes, J. Stevenson-Hinde, & P. Marris (Eds.), *Attachment across the life cycle* (pp. 160–183). New York: Routledge.

American Psychiatric Association. (1994). *Diagnostic and statistical manual of mental disorders* (4th ed.). Washington, DC.

Anderson, C. (1949). Aspects of pathological grief and mourning. *International Journal of Psychoanalysis*, *30*, 48–55.

Currier, J. M., Neimeyer, R. A., & Berman, J. S. (2008). The effectiveness of psychotherapeutic interventions for the bereaved: A comprehensive quantitative review. *Psychological Bulletin*, *134*, 648–661.

Jordan, J. R., & Neimeyer, R. A. (2003). Does grief counseling work? *Death Studies*, *27*(9), 765–786.

Lindemann, E. (1944). The symptomatology and management of acute grief. *American Journal of Psychiatry*, *101*, 141–148.

Parkes, C. M. (1988). Bereavement as a psycho-social transition: Processes of adaptation to change. *Journal of Social Issues*, *44*(3), 53–66.

Parkes, C. M. (2006). *Love and loss: The roots of grief and its complications*. London: Routledge.

Parkes, C. M., & Prigerson, H. G. (2009). *Bereavement: Studies of grief in adult life* (4th ed.). London: Routledge.

Parkes, C. M., & Weiss, R. S. (1983). *Recovery from bereavement*. New York: Basic.

Prigerson, H. G., Bierhals, A. J., Kasl, S. V., Reynolds, C. F., III, Shear, M. K., Newsom, J. T., et al. (1996). Complicated grief as a distinct disorder from bereavement-related depression and anxiety: A replication study. *American Journal of Psychiatry*, *153*, 84–86.

Prigerson, H. G., Vanderwerker, L. C., & Maciejewski, P. K. (2008). A case for including prolonged grief disorder in DSM-V. In M. Stroebe, R. Hansson, H. Schut, & W. Stroebe (Eds.), *Handbook of bereavement research and practice: Advances in theory and intervention* (pp. 165–186). Washington, DC: American Psychological Association.

Schut, H, Stroebe, M. S., van den Bout, J., & Terheggen, M. (2001). The efficacy of bereavement interventions: Determining who benefits. In M. Stroebe, R. Hansson, W. Stroebe, & H. Schut (Eds.), *Handbook of bereavement research: Consequences, coping and care* (pp. 705–737). Washington, DC: American Psychological Association.

Stroebe, M. S., & Schut, H. (1999). The dual process model of coping with bereavement: Rationale and description. *Death Studies*, *23*, 197–224.

Vogther, C. B. (1703). *Disputatio … De Morbis Moerentium*. Altdorf, Germany: University Altdorf.

Section I

Current Conceptualizations of the Grief Response

2

Meaning Reconstruction in Bereavement
From Principles to Practice

ROBERT A. NEIMEYER and DIANA C. SANDS

To live is to suffer; to survive is to find some meaning in the suffering.

Friedrich Nietzsche

There is not one big cosmic meaning for all, there is only the meaning we each give to our life, an individual meaning, an individual plot, like an individual novel, a book for each person.

Anaïs Nin

To a far greater extent than other animals, we as human beings are distinguished by living not only in a present, physical world, but also in a world populated by long-term memories, long-range anticipations, reflections, goals, interpretations, hopes, regrets, beliefs, and metaphors—in a word, *meanings*. Indeed, it is this capacity to construct and inhabit a symbolic world that permits us to embroider experience with language, to speak and be heard, and to relate, revise, and resist stories of the events of our day or the entirety of our lives. In "acts of meaning," as Jerome Bruner (1990) once phrased it, we seek an order, a foundation, a plan, a significance in human existence, particularly our own.

And yet, at times the stubborn physicality of the present moment asserts itself, sometimes brutally, stressing or shredding the delicate tissue of meaning on which our all-too-vulnerable assumptive worlds depend. Never is this clearer than when these fragile expectations, understandings, and illusions meet with incompatible yet incontrovertible occurrences—the diagnosis of our own serious illness, betrayal by an intimate partner, or news of a loved one's sudden death. At such moments, we can feel cast into a world that is alien, unimaginable, and uninhabitable, one that radically shakes or severs those taken-for-granted "realities" in which we are rooted, and on which we rely for a sense of secure purpose and connection. Our intent in writing this brief chapter is to invite attention to this potential *crisis of meaning* in the context of bereavement, as well as to offer some principles and procedures for assisting with its reconstruction.

LOSS AND THE QUEST FOR MEANING

Just as philosophers, linguists, and theologians emphasize the role of meaning in human life, so too do many psychologists. In particular, both classical and contemporary constructivists (Kelly, 1955/1991; Neimeyer, 2000, 2009) have focused on the processes by which people punctuate the seamless flow of life events, organizing them into meaningful episodes, and discerning in them recurrent themes that both give them personal significance and lead them to seek validation in their relationships with others. Viewed in narrative terms, we ultimately construct a life story that is distinctively our own, though it necessarily draws on the social discourses of our place and time (Neimeyer, Klass, & Dennis, 2010). The result is a *self-narrative* (Neimeyer, 2004b), defined as "an overarching cognitive-affective-behavioral structure that organizes the 'micro-narratives' of everyday life into a 'macro-narrative' that consolidates our self-understanding, establishes our characteristic range of emotions and goals, and guides our performance on the stage of the social world" (pp. 53–54). From this perspective, identity can be seen as a narrative achievement, as our sense of self is established through the stories that we tell about ourselves and relevant others, the stories that others tell about us, and the stories we enact in their presence. Importantly, it is this very self-narrative that is profoundly shaken by "seismic" life events such as the death of a loved one, instigating the processes of reaffirmation, repair, or replacement of the basic plot and theme of one's life story (Calhoun & Tedeschi, 2006; Neimeyer, 2006).

Consider the experience of Gayle, struggling in the aftermath of the death of her son, Max, in a vehicular accident on his way back to college. As a deeply thoughtful young man exploring both Eastern and Western wisdom traditions, Max had been drawn in the months before his death to the music of Cloud Cult, whose songs, like "Journey of the Featherless," captured in a youthful, modern idiom the cosmic "flight" of sojourners skyward, beyond social convention; and in related tracks on the same CD, the voices of the performers intoned repeatedly, "I love my mother / I love my father / And when it's my time to go / I want you to know / I love you all." When Max alone died in the rollover of the SUV in which he was riding as a passenger, the singed backpack containing his reflective journal and poetry was one of the few things that escaped the flaming wreckage. As Gayle searched desperately for some meaning in the seemingly senseless death of her son, she took heart in the Cloud Cult music found in Max's CD player in his bedroom, in the philosophic tone of the poetry and prose in his miraculously salvaged journal, and in the survival of Max's girlfriend in the same accident; and the young woman herself was moved to a deep search for significance in the months that followed the tragedy. Together, she and Gayle sought and found some sense in the death through an eclectic spiritual narrative centering on their mutual "soul contracting" with Max, between incarnations, to undergo this trial together in their present lives, so that each might learn what it had to teach them in their respective journeys. Reinforced by a series of memorial services, rituals, and consultations with mediums and various spiritual guides, the new narrative of the meaning of Max's life and death consolidated into a stable resource not only for the two women but also for an entire community of relevant others, who joined in spontaneous "strike force philanthropy" in honor of Max, thereby extending the story beyond one of consolation to one fostering social action to mitigate suffering in the world, including a massive medical aid effort to survivors of the earthquake in Haiti.

In the aftermath of life-altering loss, the bereaved are commonly precipitated into a *search for meaning* at levels that range from the practical (*How* did my loved one die?) through the relational (*Who* am I, now that I am no longer a spouse?) to the spiritual or existential (*Why* did God allow this to happen?). How—and whether—we engage these questions and resolve or simply stop asking them shapes how we accommodate the loss itself and who we become in light of it. In Gayle's case, anguished and intermittent questioning impelled her forward in her search, ultimately deepening and broadening her existing sense of cosmic purpose, and galvanizing her efforts to live authentically and compassionately in relation to others who shared the same objective loss, or who faced losses and struggles in their own lives. The result was a revised self-narrative that found significance in the *event story* of her son's death, as well as in the *back story* of his life, braided together intimately with her own.

A growing body of research on meaning reconstruction in the wake of loss supports the broad outline of this model, and is beginning to add clinically useful detail to our understanding of how the bereaved negotiate the unwelcome change introduced into their lives by the loss, for both better *and* worse, and how we as professional helpers might best support their search for significance. It is worth bearing in mind at the outset, however, that loss does not inevitably decimate survivors' self-narratives and mandate a revision or reappraisal of life meanings, as many will find consolation in systems of secular and spiritual beliefs and practices that have served them well in the past (Attig, 2000). Indeed, especially when the deaths of loved ones are relatively normative and anticipated, only a minority of the bereaved report searching for meaning in the experience, and the absence of such a search is one predictor of positive bereavement outcome (Davis, Wortman, Lehman, & Silver, 2000). Even in the case of normative losses such as late-life widowhood, however, evidence suggests that a significant minority of survivors struggle to find meaning in their loss across an extended period (Bonanno, Wortman, & Nesse, 2004). Moreover, in this same prospective longitudinal study of widows and widowers, those who reported a more intense search for meaning in the loss at 6 and 18 months after the death evidenced a more painful and prolonged grief reaction across *4 years* of bereavement (Coleman & Neimeyer, 2010). Indeed, research on complicated, prolonged grief disorder documents that a struggle with meaninglessness is a cardinal marker of debilitating bereavement reactions across many populations (Prigerson et al., 2009). In a large cohort of bereaved young adults suffering a variety of losses, for example, inability to "make sense" of the death was associated with marked and preoccupying separation distress across the first 2 years of adaptation (Holland, Currier, & Neimeyer, 2006).

When losses are more objectively traumatic, data suggest that a search for sense or significance in the loss is more common, characterizing the majority of those bereaved by the sudden death of a family member, or parents who lose a child (Davis et al., 2000). Evidence demonstrates that a crisis of meaning is especially acute for those bereaved by suicide, homicide, or fatal accident, who report a far more intense struggle to make sense of the loss than do those whose loved ones died natural deaths. Moreover, the role of sense making—a key form of meaning making—is so prominent in accounting for the complicated grief symptomatology experienced by the former group that it functions as a nearly perfect mediator of the impact of violent death, accounting for virtually all of the difference between those bereaved by the traumatic as opposed to natural deaths of their loved ones (Currier, Holland, & Neimeyer, 2006).

Research on bereaved parents reinforces the powerful role of meaning making in predicting bereavement outcome. Studying a large group of mothers and fathers whose children had died anywhere from a few months to many years earlier, Keesee and her colleagues (Keesee, Currier, & Neimeyer, 2008) found that the passage of time, the gender of the parent, and even whether the child died a natural or violent death accounted for little of their subsequent adaptation, whether assessed in terms of normative grief symptoms (e.g., sadness and missing the child) or complicated grief (e.g., an ongoing inability to care about other people, and long-term disruption of functioning in work and family contexts). In contrast, their degree of sense making proved to be a potent predictor of concurrent grief symptoms, accounting for *15 times more* of these parents' distress than any of the above-mentioned objective factors (Keesee et al., 2008). A further analysis of qualitative responses to questions about the kinds of meanings made by these parents also proved enlightening. Fully 45% of the parents confessed that they were unable to make sense of their child's death even an average of 6 years later, and over 20% could identify no unsought benefits (e.g., greater personal strength) to mitigate the great pain of the tragedy. Overall, parents discussed 32 distinct approaches to finding meaning in their child's death, 14 of which involved sense making and 18 of which involved unsought benefits or a "silver lining" in the loss, each representing a means of finding meaning in a tragic experience. The most common sense-making themes involved religious beliefs (such as the conviction that the child's death was part of a divine plan, or a belief in reunion in an afterlife), and the most common benefit-finding themes entailed an increase in the desire to help and compassion for others' suffering. Parents who invoked specific sense-making themes, including attributing the death to God's will or belief that the child was no longer suffering, as well as those who reported benefits such as reordered life priorities, experienced fewer maladaptive grief symptoms (Lichtenthal, Currier, Neimeyer, & Keesee, 2010).

Finally, it is worth underscoring that bereavement adaptation entails more than simply surmounting painful symptoms of grief and depression, insofar as significant numbers of people report resilience or even personal growth after loss, outcomes that are no less important to assess and facilitate (Neimeyer, Hogan, & Laurie, 2008). Here, too, it seems likely that meaning making contributes to adaptive outcomes, as longitudinal research on widowhood demonstrates that sense making in the first 6 months of loss forecasts higher levels of positive affect and well-being a full 4 years after the death of a spouse (Coleman & Neimeyer, 2010). Fostering reconstruction of a world of meaning would therefore seem to be a therapeutic priority for many bereaved clients, one that could carry benefits not only in alleviating complicated grief symptomatology, but also in renewing a sense of hope and self-efficacy in their changed lives. The recent development of a carefully validated multidimensional measure of the extent to which a survivor can integrate his or her loss into a fuller system of personal meaning should advance this work in both clinical and research contexts (Holland, Currier, Coleman, & Neimeyer, 2010).

How might such meaning reconstruction be facilitated in support group or psychotherapy contexts? Research on bereavement professionals indicates that they routinely draw on a host of strategies to advance this goal, beginning with fostering a sense of *presence* to the needs of the grieving client, progressing to a delicate attention to the *process* of therapy, and finding ultimate expression in a great variety of specific therapeutic *procedures* (Currier, Holland, & Neimeyer, 2008). Presence, in the view of these practitioners, entails chiefly cultivating a safe and supportive relationship, one characterized by deep and empathic listening. Process goals involve psychoeducation about loss, promoting the client's telling of his or her story, exploration of spiritual and existential concerns, processing of emotions, and utilization of existing strengths and resources. And, finally, concrete therapeutic procedures include a wide range of narrative, ritual, expressive, and pastoral methods for helping clients make sense of the loss and their changed lives, which are beginning to receive support as evidence-based treatments in randomized controlled trials (Lichtenthal & Cruess, 2010; Wagner, Knaevelsrud, & Maercker, 2006). Accordingly, a good deal of attention has been paid in a meaning reconstruction framework to explaining and exemplifying these methods, in such diverse media as books (Neimeyer, 2001b, 2009), book chapters (Neimeyer, 2006; Neimeyer & Arvay, 2004; Neimeyer, van Dyke, & Pennebaker, 2009), journal articles (Neimeyer, 2001a; Neimeyer, Burke, Mackay, & Stringer, in press), training videos (Neimeyer, 2004a, 2008), and online continuing education programs (Neimeyer, 2010) for grief professionals, as well as self-help resources for bereaved clients (Neimeyer, 2002). A fuller consideration of a constructivist approach to the treatment of complicated grief can be found in Chapter 12.

VOLITION AND VIOLATION: THE TRIPARTITE MODEL OF SUICIDE BEREAVEMENT

Viewed through a meaning reconstruction lens, the deaths of significant persons in their lives through suicide poses an especially severe challenge to survivors' attempts to make sense of the event story of the death, and the back story of their relationship to the deceased. Not only does it tend to violate cherished assumptions about the safety and predictability of the world and the continued presence of their loved ones, but also the volitional nature of the act challenges core beliefs about the inherent value of life and the seemingly inscrutable explanation for the suicide victims' fatal decision. As a consequence, the question *Why?* reverberates in the survivors' self-narrative with a force that is matched by few other triggering events (Sands, Jordan, & Neimeyer, 2010). Our intent in the remainder of this chapter is to present a major clinical extension of the meaning reconstruction approach to the special problem of suicide bereavement and to sketch some of the implications for intervention it suggests.

The tripartite model of suicide bereavement (TMSB; Sands, 2008, 2009) is a meaning-making model that focuses on the distinctive themes with which those bereaved by suicide struggle in the aftermath of the death. The model (see Figure 2.1) sets out a nonlinear, 3 × 3 matrix identifying different dimensions of the grief process and the functioning of the survivors' relational world in the aftermath of the death (Sands & Tennant, 2010). The TMSB identifies how the relationships with the deceased, the self, and others change as the bereaved struggle with challenges to their assumptive world (Janoff-Bulman & Berg, 1998) and meaning reconstruction in the wake of their loss. The first phase of the model uses the metaphor of *trying on the shoes* and is concerned with the difficulties of decoding and understanding the self-volition of a suicide death. These issues are explored through a range of themes that frequently take the form of "why" questions.

The second phase of the model, *walking in the shoes*, is concerned with making sense of the pain of the life and death of the deceased. This entails attempts to understand the experience of the deceased and tends to be focused on the pain and trauma, known or imagined, of the deceased's life and death (Rynearson, 2001; Sands, 2008, 2009; Walter, 1996). During this phase, the ongoing imaginal relationship with the deceased is often maladaptive (Klass, 2006; Klass, Silverman, & Nickman, 1996) as it is constructed largely through the bereaved ruminating on the mind-set of the deceased as he or she metaphorically walks in the loved one's shoes. Significantly, the struggle in suicide bereavement to reconstruct meaning can place the bereaved in a similar position to the deceased of experiencing a challenged assumptive world, hopelessness, and vulnerability to suicidal ideation (Currier et al., 2006; Mitchell, Kim, Prigerson, & Mortimer, 2005; Runeson & Asberg, 2003). In this context, clinical interventions like the *body of trust* (which will be discussed in the following section) can facilitate meaning reconstruction to increase narrative flexibility, differentiation processes, and negotiation of the incomprehensibility or "blind spot" at the core of suicide (Sands, 2008, 2009).

The third phase of the model, *taking off the shoes*, identifies repositioning themes that surface once the bereaved has sufficiently differentiated from the deceased. Repositioning makes way for more subtle layers of grief, and it validates the suffering of the deceased but rarely the manner of the death. When successful, repositioning redeems the deceased from the suicide while also providing containment for the manner of death and associated violent and traumatic material (Sands, 2008, 2009; Sands et al., 2010). The *family snapshot* (which will also be discussed subsequently) is a clinical intervention that facilitates "taking off the shoes," repositioning themes to support growth through grief and the development of functional relationships with the deceased, the self, and others.

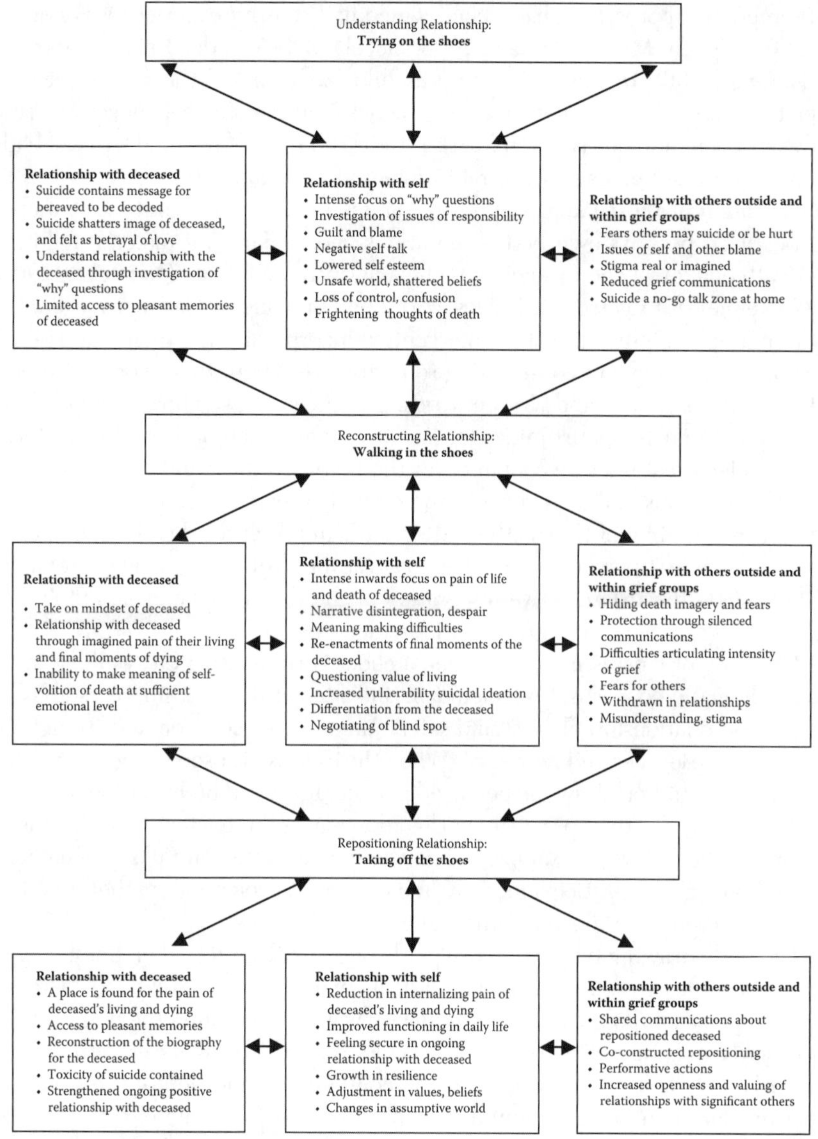

Figure 2.1 The tripartite model of suicide bereavement.

Walking in the Shoes and the Body of Trust

The TMSB suggests that the compulsion to return repeatedly to "walking in the shoes" of the loved one is an attempt to integrate disrupted meaning reconstruction in response to the self-volition of the death. Given the intense confusion, trauma, and violence often associated with a death due to suicide (Jordan, 2001), those bereaved may benefit from the application of body-focused interventions to assist narrative integration of challenging material. Researchers have noted the effectiveness of therapeutic approaches that include embodied sensory experiences (Bryant et al., 2008; Ogden, Minton, & Pain, 2006; Siegel, 1999; Van der Kolk, Weisaeth, & McFarlane, 1996). In this context, Rothschild (2000) noted the significant value after traumatic events of constructing a cohesive narrative that makes "sense of body sensations and behaviors" (p. 151). Totton (2003) also stressed the role of body-oriented processes in assisting narrative integration of traumatic events.

The *body of trust* (Sands, 2008) facilitates making sense and integration of the bereaved person's own bodily sensations and challenging material following the death of a loved one to suicide. Using a narrative approach (Neimeyer, 2001b, 2002; Neimeyer, Prigerson, & Davies, 2002), and drawing on Gardner's (1993) theory of multiple intelligences, this intervention incorporates the many ways people have of interpreting and constructing self-narratives about their world. The body of trust utilizes spoken and written words, expressive art, symbols, metaphor, and enactment to create opportunities for narrative integration of disruptive material. The clinician creates a safe container for the bereaved to sit and be with the loss, to perform actions and give voice to the embodied experience in ways not often available at the time of the death or afterward. Importantly, the bereaved person speaks from a first person perspective, to assist the shift from passive observation of the suicide toward an active integration of the death (Rynearson, 2001). This intervention can be used in groups or individual sessions.

The body of trust is indicated when a client is ruminating on "walking in the shoes" thematic concerns, and should be introduced only within an established therapeutic relationship of trust and safety and after exploration and strengthening of client resources and resilience. When the exercise is used in a group setting, other group members draw the bereaved person's life-sized body outline on a large sheet of paper; the therapist may do this drawing in the context of an individual session. In the following example, while the bereaved person talks, the clinician responds and group participants write and draw using color and symbols to reflect the bereaved person's spoken words and bodily sensations.

The body drawing becomes a bridge through which internal embodied experiences become externalized, interpreted, and woven into an expanded narrative. For example, *trembling* can be denoted with wavy lines around the body outline; *being cold* can be indicated by use of the color blue; the *presence of the deceased, internal and external resources*, and the contents or condition of the survivor's *heart* or *mind* can be represented symbolically. The following clinical example is taken from a subgroup of four participants within a larger closed group of 10 people, all of whom were grieving varied relationships of loss to suicide. The young bereaved husband was a participant in Sands's research (2008); the material included here focuses on two significant periods when he sat with his wife's body, first at the morgue and later with the open casket at her funeral.

The young man confides that he spends a lot of time thinking about the day his wife died. The clinician asks, "When you think about what happened, what parts are you thinking about?"

Crying, the young man says when he was told by the police his wife was dead, "[I] broke down and … what I couldn't believe … was that I just had spoken to her." He pauses and recalls, "I threw up.… It was the most overwhelming emotion I have ever felt—I just wanted to get the feeling out of my body." As he talks, he recalls the memory of his body's effort to cope with the shock, as a group member silently draws a twisted red mass rising from the core of his body. The husband struggles to come to terms with his sense of betrayed trust. Why, in their last phone call, did his wife not tell him she was suicidal? At the morgue, he reflected, "When she was having a good day she was incredible … [but] I saw her lying there and I just saw this body that was lifeless and I thought.… 'That is not my wife.'"

The clinician allows a lengthy pause as the man sobs quietly, and then asks softly, "What is happening in your body now?"

The young man, touching his heart, says, "I felt like it had just broken into a thousand pieces.… For days and days the pain just seemed to intensify everywhere, just everywhere."

The group members add a shattered heart to the image, and jagged purple lines of pain radiating from it, as the clinician, indicating the survivor's hunched body, asks, "And this pain now?"

The husband voices his deep regret: "If we would have got help the right way … we could have gone down another road … that might not have led to this." The bereaved walks in the shoes of the deceased, questioning his relationship with her and his relationship with himself. What was she thinking about on that day? His grief and the poignancy of their lost shared future together are captured in the metaphor of "another road," as a group member draws a brown road beneath the feet of the outline, with a branch to the left, which another labels with a yellow question mark.

After a lengthy period of reflection, the young husband recalls the funeral and the open casket: "She looked really beautiful.… But I sat with her for the whole time and it just wasn't her." The young man breaks down, crying, followed by a long pause in which the clinician asks about bodily sensations. The young man, holding his hand to his stomach, says, "In my stomach … a sort of gnawing … a weight like … I can't even explain it, maybe a combination of emptiness with something eating around the outside.… I feel like what is left inside … it doesn't matter what I do, it is not going to bring her back. Nothing I do will bring her back." The group pauses to get the sense of this, and then one member leans into the drawing and adds a dark brown, wavy void in the figure's abdomen, and another adds the word "weight" in the center.

The husband pauses his narration to sit with the enormity of his loss, and the clinician also sits, a companion in this dark and barren place, offering containment for the heavy weight of his suffering, as group members serve as attentive witnesses. Out of this space comes a moment of forgiveness and growth (Calhoun & Tedeschi, 2006), as the young man suggests, "But maybe if I can do something … for other people, maybe if they're in a position where they feel … there is nowhere to turn.… Sometimes a little bit of knowledge …

can maybe help people a long way." Gazing at the body outline filled in by the group, he explains, "Within me … my heart … I just have to live with what I'm feeling, experience the emotions.… You can't escape the feelings when you have them so you just have to live with the emotion." He adds, "You have to have pain for something to grow." Smiling tearfully, a group member adds the image of a single rose along the path. Working with his body wisdom, a moment of grace settles over the young man, and he shares his labor of love to construct the ongoing imaginal relationship to his wife (Boerner & Heckhausen, 2003). He can feel her presence: "I have overwhelming love for her.… I know her spirit or whatever it is, her energy, is I guess as real as it was when it was within the body, you know. It's not different, it's just gone to another place."

Completing the drawing, a member adds to the body outline a hovering, glowing figure of yellow light shining over him, as another writes beside it, "Overwhelming love." The group closes as the other participants speak to the feelings of respect and appreciation they experienced as a result of his disclosures, and as the young man, moved, tearfully accepts the drawing as a gift from the group with an expression of heartfelt thanks.

This clinical example illustrates how the body of trust can assist integration of embodied material to support reconstruction of an adaptive positive relationship with the deceased and oneself, at the same time that it recruits a responsive audience for the survivor's narrative of loss and transition.

Taking off the Shoes and the Family Snapshot

The family snapshot (Sands, 2008) intervention can be used in family or group sessions to facilitate "taking off the shoes" (Sands, 2008, 2009), meaning reconstruction, and repositioning the deceased within the family. Nadeau's (1998) research has demonstrated the central function of family interactions in meaning reconstruction following a significant death. The following clinical example took place in a closed suicide bereavement group of 10 people grieving different relationships of loss due to suicide. It provides insight into a bereaved mother's struggle to reconstruct meaning in the face of the pain her son endured in his life and death. The mother is a participant in Sands's (2008) research. The clinician's questions prompt the participant's attention to her visual and embodied awareness, and verbal utterances are fragmented and often broken by emotional pauses. The group members enact the roles of different family members and position themselves to create a visual snapshot, using their body postures to capture how the family is grieving. It is an enactment, with movement and minimal words. Colored materials, pillows, and other symbolic objects are also used. In the snapshot group, members may be turned away, looking backward, looking downward with arms held over their head, curled on the floor, isolated, or absent.

In this case, the onset of mental illness for her son was at age 18 years, and his functioning continued to deteriorate over the next 15 years with numerous hospitalizations and short-lived hopes, as new medications and treatment plans failed to bring improvement. At times, his behavior was violent, abusive, and threatening; the police were involved, and the family lived in fear. One day, her son decided to end it. The mother mourns for the lost years; the illness that overtook her son; and the pain, fear, and confusion suffered by her family, just as she mourns for what her son might have been. Finally, this mother mourns for her child in his aloneness, planning and implementing his death.

After hearing the mother describe the effect of the pain of her son's illness and death within the family, a subgroup of four participants from within the large group enact the family snapshot, tentatively positioning themselves to suggest the emotional distance and reaching out within the family, as well as the son's remoteness. The mother sits and considers whether the snapshot captures accurately her family as it is now, and also reflects on how she would like it to be different. The mother indicates that she wants them "not to be stepping back … to be coming forward." *Backward* suggests immersion in the sadness and pain of her son's illness. The dilemma for her is that if she steps forward, away from the illness, it feels as though she is abandoning her son and letting go of their connection forged over the years of caring for him and managing his illness. The mother says, "My son needs to be there—because he will always be," and then suggests, "Put the heart on the floor." A heart-shaped cushion is positioned in the center of the family to represent the son. The mother places a black cloth over the pillow and extends the cloth to cover other family members to represent the pain of her son's illness, his death, and their grief. It would seem that all the family members are shrouded in darkness and that this is the way the family has built their ongoing relationship with the deceased (Klass, 1999, 2006).

The facilitator asks how the family manages the weight of the sadness, and the mother indicates, "Just to stand together, closer … [long pause] … just to be there together and support each other, which is what we are doing." She indicates the black shroud, which is placed over the heart and family, and confirms, "Yes, it is shrouded in pain." The mother pauses as she struggles with her emotional response to this graphic visual representation of her family and says, "So we find comfort and healing by being together and finding…." The mother pauses, sighs, and makes a powerful relational meaning-making statement about how she wants her son repositioned in the family: "I try to remember him as he was…. It is not, not always so easy to get back to the person we like to remember…. But that's, that's how I would like it to be, that we feel sad and pained by his illness … but we remember him as he was when he was younger." The mother shifts from the singular "I try to remember him as he was" to the plural "we," indicating that she is telling the family how she wants him remembered. The mother moves over and removes the black material covering family members and, doubling over, holding it clutched in a tight ball against her stomach, murmurs, "Just keep it beside me.... Just—well I can't deny it, but.... I don't want it to be the overriding thing. I want it to recede, the sadness."

The mother looks around the room at this pivotal meaning-making juncture. If her son is to be remembered prior to his illness, what is to happen to the blackness of his pain? Will the mother carry his pain alone? A group member asks, "Is there a safe place to put it so you don't have to have it?" The mother indicates a large blue cushion that is then placed to the side of the family snapshot. The mother states, "It's an acknowledgment of his illness, and I need to...." There is a long pause as she sobs, slowly relinquishing the black cloth onto the blue cushion. The mother takes her place in the snapshot, experiencing how this feels different now, and the biological daughter, who is also a group member, moves over and they hug and sob together while other "family members" move around them to create a circle of support. At last, the son is released from his cruel illness and repositioned in a nurturing role within the family, symbolized by the heart. The family can cry and comfort each other in a new way, knowing that the chapter of looking after and fighting for help for the deceased and all the disappointment and pain that this involved has been acknowledged. Group participants cry, laugh, and hug each other, intuiting the significance of this profound moment of meaning.

REFERENCES

Attig, T. (2000). *The heart of grief.* New York: Oxford.

Boerner, K., & Heckhausen, J. (2003). To have and have not: Adaptive bereavement by transforming mental ties to the deceased. *Death Studies*, *27*, 199–226.

Bonanno, G. A., Wortman, C. B., & Nesse, R. M. (2004). Prospective patterns of resilience and maladjustment during widowhood. *Psychology and Aging*, *19*, 260–271.

Bruner, J. (1990). *Acts of meaning*. Cambridge, MA: Harvard University Press.

Bryant, R., Mastrodomenico, J., Felmingham, K. L., Hopwood, S., Kenny, L., Kandris, E., et al. (2008). Treatment of acute stress disorder. *Archives of General Psychiatry*, *65*, 659–667.

Calhoun, L., & Tedeschi, R. G. (Eds.). (2006). *Handbook of posttraumatic growth*. Mahwah, NJ: Lawrence Erlbaum.

Coleman, R. A., & Neimeyer, R. A. (2010). Measuring meaning: Searching for and making sense of spousal loss in later life. *Death Studies*.

Currier, J. M., Holland, J. M., & Neimeyer, R. A. (2006). Sense making, grief and the experience of violent loss: Toward a mediational model. *Death Studies*, *30*, 403–428.

Currier, J. M., Holland, J. M., & Neimeyer, R. A. (2008). Making sense of loss: A content analysis of end-of-life practitioners' therapeutic approaches. *Omega*, *57*, 121–141.

Davis, C. G., Wortman, C. B., Lehman, D. R., & Silver, R. C. (2000). Searching for meaning in loss: Are clinical assumptions correct? *Death Studies*, *24*, 497–540.

Gardner, H., (1993). *Multiple intelligences: The theory in practice*. New York: Basic.

Holland, J. M., Currier, J. M., Coleman, R. A., & Neimeyer, R. A. (2010). The Integration of Stressful Life Experiences Scale (ISLES): Development and initial validation of a new measure. *International Journal of Stress Management*, 17, 325–352.

Holland, J. M., Currier, J., & Neimeyer, R. A. (2006). Meaning reconstruction in the first two years of bereavement: The role of sense-making and benefit-finding. *Omega, 53*, 173–191.

Janoff-Bulman, R., & Berg, M. (1998). Disillusionment and the creation of value. In J. Harvey (Ed.), *Perspectives on loss* (pp. 33–47). Philadelphia: Bruner/Mazel.

Jordan, J. R. (2001). Is suicide bereavement different? A reassessment of the literature. *Suicide and Life-Threatening Behavior, 31*, 91–102.

Keesee, N. J., Currier, J. M., & Neimeyer, R. A. (2008). Predictors of grief following the death of one's child: The contribution of finding meaning. *Journal of Clinical Psychology, 64*, 1145–1163.

Kelly, G. A. (1991). *The psychology of personal constructs*. New York: Routledge. (Original work published in 1955)

Klass, D. (1999). *The spiritual lives of bereaved parents*. Philadelphia: Brunner-Mazel.

Klass, D. (2006). Continuing conversation about continuing bonds. *Death Studies, 30*, 843–858.

Klass, D., Silverman, P. R., & Nickman, S. L. (1996). Concluding thoughts. In D. Klass, P. R. Silverman, & S. L. Nickman (Eds.), *Continuing bonds* (pp. 349–355). Philadelphia: Taylor & Francis.

Lichtenthal, W. G., & Cruess, D. G. (2010). Effects of directed written disclosure on grief and distress symptoms among bereaved individuals. *Death Studies, 34*, 475–499.

Lichtenthal, W. G., Currier, J. M., Neimeyer, R. A., & Keesee, N. J. (2010). Sense and significance: A mixed methods examination of meaning-making following the loss of one's child. *Journal of Clinical Psychology, 66*, 791–812.

Mitchell, A. M., Kim, M., Prigerson, H. G., & Mortimer, M. K. (2005). Complicated grief and suicidal ideation in adult survivors of suicide. *Suicide and Life-Threatening Behavior, 35*, 498–506.

Nadeau, J. W. (1998). *Families making sense of death*. Thousand Oaks, CA: Sage.

Neimeyer, R. A. (2000). Narrative disruptions in the construction of self. In R. A. Neimeyer & J. D. Raskin (Eds.), *Constructions of disorder: Meaning making frameworks for psychotherapy* (pp. 207–241). Washington, DC: American Psychological Association.

Neimeyer, R. A. (2001a). Reauthoring life narratives: Grief therapy as meaning reconstruction. *Israel Journal of Psychiatry, 38*, 171–183.

Neimeyer, R. A. (Ed.). (2001b). *Meaning reconstruction and the experience of loss*. Washington, DC: American Psychological Association.

Neimeyer, R. A. (2002). *Lessons of loss: A guide to coping*. Memphis, TN: Center for the Study of Loss and Transition.

Neimeyer, R. A. (2004a). Constructivist psychotherapy. In *Series 1: Systems of psychotherapy* [DVD]. Washington, DC: American Psychological Association.

Neimeyer, R. A. (2004b). Fostering posttraumatic growth: A narrative contribution. *Psychological Inquiry, 15*, 53–59.

Neimeyer, R. A. (2006). Re-storying loss: Fostering growth in the posttraumatic narrative. In L. Calhoun & R. G. Tedeschi (Eds.), *Handbook of posttraumatic growth: Research and practice*. Mahwah, NJ: Lawrence Erlbaum.

Neimeyer, R. A. (2008). *Constructivist psychotherapy over time* [DVD]. Washington, DC: American Psychological Association.

Neimeyer, R. A. (2009). *Constructivist psychotherapy*. London: Routledge.

Neimeyer, R. A. (2010). *Strategies of grief therapy* [Online continuing education program]. Washington, DC: American Psychological Association.

Neimeyer, R. A., & Arvay, M. J. (2004). Performing the self: Therapeutic enactment and the narrative integration of traumatic loss. In H. Hermans & G. Dimaggio (Eds.), *The dialogical self in psychotherapy* (pp. 173–189). New York: Routledge.

Neimeyer, R. A., Burke, L., Mackay, M., & Stringer, J. (2010). Grief therapy and the re-construction of meaning: From principles to practice. *Journal of Contemporary Psychotherapy*, 40, 73–83.

Neimeyer, R. A., Hogan, N., & Laurie, A. (2008). The measurement of grief: Psychometric considerations in the assessment of reactions to bereavement. In M. Stroebe, R. O. Hansson, H. Schut, & W. Stroebe (Eds.), *Handbook of bereavement research: 21st century perspectives* (pp. 133–186). Washington, DC: American Psychological Association.

Neimeyer, R. A., Klass, D., & Dennis, M. R. (2010). Mourning, meaning and memory: Grief and the narration of loss. In J. Ciprut (Ed.), *On meaning*. Boston: MIT Press.

Neimeyer, R. A., Prigerson, H. G., & Davies, B. (2002). Mourning and meaning. *American Behavioral Scientist*, *46*, 235–251.

Neimeyer, R. A., van Dyke, J. G., & Pennebaker, J. W. (2009). Narrative medicine: Writing through bereavement. In H. Chochinov & W. Breitbart (Eds.), *Handbook of psychiatry in palliative medicine* (pp. 454–469). New York: Oxford.

Ogden, P., Minton, K., & Pain, C. (2006). *Trauma and the body*. New York: Norton.

Prigerson, H. G., Horowitz, M. J., Jacobs, S. C., Parkes, C. M., Aslan, M., Goodkin, K., et al. (2009). Prolonged grief disorder: Psychometric validation of criteria proposed for DSM-V and ICD-11. *PLoS Medicine*, *6*, 1–12.

Rothschild, B. (2000). *The body remembers*. New York: Norton.

Runeson, B., & Asberg, M. (2003). Family history of suicide among suicide victims. *American Journal of Psychiatry*, *160*, 1525–1526.

Rynearson, E. K. (2001). *Retelling violent death*. Philadelphia: Brunner-Routledge.

Sands, D. C. (2008). *A study of suicide grief: Meaning making and the griever's relational world* (PhD thesis). University of Technology, Sydney, Australia. Retrieved from http://handle.net/2100/777

Sands, D. (2009). A tripartite model of suicide grief: Meaning-making and the relationship with the deceased. *Grief Matters: The Australian Journal of Grief and Bereavement*, *12*, 10–17.

Sands, D. C., Jordan, J. R., & Neimeyer, R. A. (2010). The meanings of suicide: A narrative approach to healing. In J. R. Jordan & J. L. McIntosh (Eds.), *Grief after suicide*. New York: Routledge.

Sands, D., & Tennant, M. (2010). Transformative learning in the context of suicide bereavement. *Adult Education Quarterly*, *60*, 99–121.

Siegel, D. J. (1999). *The developing mind: How relationship and the brain interact to shape who we are*. New York: Guilford.

Totton, N. (2003). *Body psychotherapy: An introduction*. Philadelphia: Open University Press.

Van der Kolk, B. A., Weisaeth, L., & McFarlane, C. (Eds.). (1996). *Traumatic stress*. New York: Guilford.

Wagner, B., Knaevelsrud, C., & Maercker, A. (2006). Internet-based cognitive-behavioral therapy for complicated grief: A randomized controlled trial. *Death Studies*, *30*, 429–453.

Walter, T. (1996). A new model of grief: Bereavement and biography. *Mortality*, *1*, 7–25.

3

Attachment and Coping with Bereavement

Implications for Therapeutic Interventions with the Insecurely Attached

EMMANUELLE ZECH and CARRIE ARNOLD

Professional psychotherapeutic intervention programs for bereaved individuals are not as effective as one could expect (e.g., Currier, Neimeyer, & Berman, 2008; Jordan & Neimeyer, 2003; Kato & Mann, 1999; Litterer-Allumbaugh & Hoyt, 1999; Raphael, Minkov, & Dobson, 2001; Schut & Stroebe, 2005; Schut, Stroebe, van den Bout, & Terheggen, 2001), and this is for a complex series of reasons (see, e.g., Zech, Ryckebosch, & Delespaux, 2010). Elsewhere we have argued that, to be effective, psychotherapeutic interventions need to be individualized to the client's specific functioning. The therapist will join the clients where they are; examine their ways of being and functioning, in particular the events that cause or maintain their difficulties; and finally allow and encourage the practice of new ways of being that foster well-being and psychological development (Zech et al., 2010). In this chapter, we will address the needs of individuals dealing with bereavement according to their attachment style. The direction of this chapter will be to explore both the theoretical and clinical implications for providing therapeutic services to those bereaved individuals who are insecurely attached and therefore requiring treatment informed by their unique attachment needs, along with an understanding of the embodied nature of their grief.

TOWARD FLEXIBLE WAYS OF COPING WITH BEREAVEMENT

Until the late 1990s, most intervention programs for bereaved individuals were based on theories that were in line with the "grief work" hypothesis (e.g., Stroebe, 1992; Stroebe & Stroebe, 1991). This hypothesis postulates that bereaved individuals have to do their grief work in order to cope with bereavement. Following this, traditional interventions largely or even exclusively focused on promoting confrontation strategies and the relocation or relinquishing of the bond to the deceased (e.g., Ramsay's [1977, 1979] "flooding technique"). More recently, following inconsistencies in research findings concerning the efficacy of grief work, Stroebe and Schut (1999) developed a theoretical model, the dual-process model of coping with bereavement (DPM), which included not only confrontation with loss (termed the *loss orientation*) but also avoidant coping strategies (e.g., reinvesting in work or other roles and goals) as necessary mediators of health and well-being (termed the *restoration orientation*). In this model, the diversity of tasks and problems that individuals encounter in addition to grief over the loss of their loved one would require the use of multiple coping strategies. Most importantly, the authors hypothesized a fundamental oscillation process between these various coping strategies. Recent studies that investigated the efficacy of oscillation strategies during bereavement have begun to provide some evidence of the importance of the DPM parameters for positive outcomes (Caserta & Lund, 2007; Richardson & Balaswamy, 2001; Wijngaards et al., 2008). Psychotherapeutic interventions should thus also incorporate oscillation, and pathologically bereaved individuals should accordingly be encouraged to use other strategies than the ones they are ineffectively using. A recent intervention program developed by Shear and her colleagues (Shear, Frank, Houck, & Reynolds, 2005; see also Chapter 12) for bereaved individuals presenting complicated (i.e., chronic) grief reactions (Prigerson et al., 1995) was created to address processes postulated by the DPM, including restoration-oriented tasks. In support of the DPM, results revealed that this treatment was more effective than a control treatment (i.e., interpersonal psychotherapy) that focused essentially on loss-focused tasks (i.e., on grief, the relationship between symptoms, grief and interpersonal problems, and a more realistic assessment of the relationship to the deceased). Thus, in line with other authors (Stroebe & Schut, 1999), we propose that bereaved individuals should not all get the same intervention but, rather, an intervention that addresses the specific process that is at hand and explains or maintains their own specific difficulty (see also Zech et al., 2010). The DPM provides insight into the way in which individuals grieve, and the authors have proposed that coping with bereavement is largely influenced by the person's style of attachment (Stroebe, Schut, & Stroebe, 2005).

Next, we will present how attachment might be related to ways of coping with bereavement and, as a consequence, to (complicated) grief reactions. This carries implications for how clinicians can provide effective treatment interventions for those individuals who are anxious or avoidant in their attachment and who might present more problematic reactions than securely attached bereaved persons.

Applying Fisher's (2009) approach with traumatized clients, a case will be presented to exemplify the work on sensorimotor processes that can be used with insecurely attached bereaved clients. We then conclude with some clinical considerations.

BEREAVEMENT AND ATTACHMENT

The loss of a significant other is an event likely to activate the attachment behavioral system (Bowlby, 1969; Hazan & Shaver, 1990). The attachment system is a motivational system that regulates the proximity to attachment figures, that is, persons who provide protection, support, and care. In bereavement, this system is activated precisely because of the loss of an attachment figure, a person who would normally function as a safe haven against distress and a secure base from which to explore the environment (Bowlby, 1969). An individual's attachment style should most strongly be activated under conditions of distress (Wayment & Vierthaler, 2002), and this should particularly be so when a beloved person dies and is thus permanently lost.

Attachment theory claims that people's attachment styles evolve as a result of relationship experiences, especially with caregivers (Feeney, Noller, & Roberts, 1998). Patterns of reactions have been described initially in children, aged 12 to 18 months, temporarily separated from their mothers in a *strange situation* (Ainsworth, Blehar, Waters, & Wall, 1978). According to attachment theory, learning experiences between caregiver and infant lead to the development of mental models (representations) of others, of oneself in relation to others, and of relationships in general (Bartholomew & Horowitz, 1991). These emerge as attachment styles (e.g., Cassidy & Shaver, 1999) that remain quite stable over time and are thus also present in adulthood (e.g., Bartholomew, 1990, 1993; Main, Kaplan, & Cassidy, 1985; Reis & Patrick, 1996). A *secure* style is characterized by relative ease in closeness to others and feeling comfortable with both depending on others and having others depend on oneself (e.g., Cassidy & Shaver, 1999). Adults with an *anxious–ambivalent* or *preoccupied* attachment style see others as reluctant to get as close to them as they would like. They worry about their attachment to others, about their own desire to stay very close to them, and about the fact that this sometimes scares others away. People with a *dismissive–avoidant* attachment style present a combination of avoidant behavior and apparent lack of anxiety about abandonment. Finally, individuals classified as having a *fearful–avoidant* or *disorganized* attachment style worry about and are uncomfortable with closeness to others, find it difficult to trust others or to depend on them, and tend to avoid seeking support from others. In fact, attachment theorists have identified two dimensions, *model of self* and *model of other*, as underlying these attachment styles (Bartholomew, 1990; Bartholomew & Horowitz, 1991). The two dimensions have also been labeled *anxiety* (negative view of oneself, and worries about oneself and about relationships with others in case of need) and *avoidance* (negative view of others, difficulty to trust others or depend on them, and avoidance of interpersonal relationships) (Shaver & Fraley, 2004).

ATTACHMENT, COPING, AND OUTCOMES

In the theoretical and empirical literature, propositions have been made that (a) attachment style predicts ways of dealing with emotions and handling stressful situations, in particular ways of coping with bereavement (e.g., Fraley & Shaver, 1999; Shaver & Tancredy, 2001); and, as a consequence, (b) attachment style also predicts psychopathology outcomes (e.g., Shorey & Snyder, 2006) and grief reactions (e.g., Mikulincer & Shaver, 2008; Parkes, 2010; Stroebe et al., 2005). More specifically, the DPM proposes that the exclusive use of either loss- or restoration-oriented strategies would lead to pathological grief reactions such as chronic grief in the first case and absent or inhibited grief in the second.[1] It is also predicted that the extent to which bereaved individuals will engage in either loss-oriented or restoration-oriented processes depends on various factors, in particular their attachment styles (Stroebe et al., 2005). Securely attached individuals are expected to be able to access their attachment-related emotional memories without difficulty and to be able to discuss them coherently, and thus present normal grief reactions. Dismissing individuals would suppress and avoid attachment-related emotions and present absent or inhibited grief reactions. In this case, the bond to the deceased would be too loose or denied, and the bereaved would avoid suffering and behave as if nothing had happened. Preoccupied or anxious–ambivalent individuals are expected to be highly emotional, cling to their ties with the deceased, and develop chronic grief reactions. In this case, the bond to the deceased person would be too strong, and the bereaved would be too dependent on and cling too much to the tie to be able to recover from grief: He or she would be unable to loosen or relinquish it. Finally, disorganized individuals would be unable to coherently think and talk about attachment-related memories, and would show traumatic grief reactions (Stroebe et al., 2005).

ATTACHMENT AND THERAPY FOR THE INSECURELY BEREAVED PERSON

In practice, avoidantly attached persons are less likely to show up in consultation, particularly in individual therapy (Lopez, Melendez, Sauer, Berger, & Wyssmann, 1998). Indeed, their strategy is precisely to avoid or suppress the idea or fact that there might be a problem, and because they have a negative view of others (Bartholomew & Horowitz, 1991), they may be disinclined to seek help from another person (see Connors, 1997). On the contrary, anxiously attached persons might consult because of their intense suffering, their continued need to express their emotions and grief (Stroebe et al., 2005), and their attempts to elicit care and support from others (Mikulincer & Shaver, 2008).

The question is, then, what are the therapeutic needs of insecure bereaved people? And how can a therapist provide an effective intervention with insecurely attached individuals? In the following, along the lines developed in this chapter, we argue that the therapist should identify and work on the processes that cause or maintain the difficulties presented by the bereaved person (see also Zech et al., 2010). The therapist should thus be as flexible as possible and adapt his or her interventions to his or her client's attachment style.

In line with the DPM, Stroebe et al. (2005) have proposed that the anxious and avoidantly attached bereaved persons should be guided to oscillate between loss- and restoration-oriented strategies. Indeed, bereaved people with anxious attachment could benefit from loosening their ties to the deceased, whereas bereaved people with avoidant attachment could benefit from doing more loss-oriented tasks such as going over memories about the deceased. In a review of the efficacy of the therapeutic relationship, it has similarly been suggested that patients with preoccupied (anxious) attachment may require more supportive and containing interventions that help control overwhelming emotions, whereas patients with dismissive (avoidant) attachment may require interventions that facilitate emotional expression and connection (Meyer & Pilkonis, 2002). This suggests that oscillation in coping should be reinstated and that interventions that complement or counterbalance the natural ineffective coping strategies of the client will be necessary for therapeutic efficacy to be achieved.

In an examination of the therapeutic implications of attachment theory, Bowlby (1988) proposed that therapeutic change would need the revision of the client's insecure working models into more secure models. He had argued that the therapist should provide corrective relational experiences and thus work to become a safe haven and secure base from which clients could then explore their inner world, including painful memories and emotions, destructive defenses, and maladaptive behaviors (for an excellent review, see Mikulincer & Shaver, 2007). Thus, the therapist–client relationship should be structured so that the therapist is consistent, reliable, and emotionally available. This means that the quality of the therapeutic relationship may be crucial for efficacy in the case of grief therapy with insecurely attached people because they may have lost an attachment figure.

In the general psychotherapy literature, it is now well established that empathy and warmth are substantially and consistently associated with positive therapeutic outcomes, and congruence and acceptance are seen as being probably effective (for a review, see Norcross, 2002). It has, for example, been demonstrated that the therapist's empathic, accepting, and congruent response facilitates the client's regulation of affect (Watson, 2007). But how does this work specifically with insecurely attached patients? Indeed, the question can be raised as to how an avoidantly attached individual responds to empathic engagement. Could his or her defenses and need to resist treatment be heightened? It has indeed been shown that such individuals may be less inclined to stay in therapy because once they have talked about their problems, they tend to withdraw from the therapeutic relationship or deny they have problems, resulting in a deteriorating therapeutic alliance toward the end of therapy (Kanninen, Salo, & Punamäki, 2000; Mallinckrodt, Gantt, & Coble, 1995). Given the need for avoidant individuals to be highly independent and dismissive, would empathic engagement and unconditional positive regard then be seen as comprising an ineffective attitude? And for those who are anxiously attached, does a highly attuned and empathic therapist support and facilitate dependence and thus actually elicit negative responses from such clients?

Adequate empathy and unconditional positive regard will lead the therapist to comprehend the client's idiosyncratic frame of reference and thus recognize and respect the client's defenses against strong emotions or emotional expression in the case of avoidant attachment, and the client's fear of abandonment and need to cling to the (therapeutic) relationship in the case of anxious attachment (e.g., Elliott & Greenberg, 2007). An unconditional positive attitude will allow clients to become progressively more responsible for their personal choices (they are allowed to decide, to gain psychological freedom, to be in control, and to gain self-confidence and self-esteem). It will also decrease the possibility that the client's defenses against distress and negative states will be reinforced (e.g., Zech et al., 2010). By trying to maintain unconditional positive regard, the therapist stays flexible and adapts to the client's characteristics and state of mind moment for moment, so that the client can progressively recognize dysfunctional defenses and may be more inclined to move away from them.

This suggests that an effective strategy might require several steps and processes: first an approach that fits the client's perspective and thus does not immediately contradict it and abruptly confront the clients with new ways of being and behaving. Then, however, the client should be respectfully and gradually guided toward new and alternative ways of being, thinking, or expressing than the ones that make him or her suffer. In the following, we also suggest that prompting emotional expression and exploration may not always be indicated, as it has been shown that emotional disclosure is far from beneficial for everyone or in all cases of bereavement (e.g., Zech & Rimé, 2005; Zech, Rimé, & Pennebaker, 2007).

THERAPEUTIC IMPLICATIONS

Integrating the idea that those who are insecurely attached may be less likely to seek therapy with the concept that providing individualized treatment will be more effective, we are left with some complex clinical implications. How do clinicians attempt to meet the needs of bereaved individuals who may find a traditional therapeutic relationship overwhelming, while simultaneously providing effective treatment? Traditional psychotherapy and counseling have advocated for the "grief work" model. However, such traditional talk therapy approaches rely on language and narrative (Ogden, Pain, Minton, & Fisher, 2005), which may be more suitable for those who are securely attached. For anxious or avoidant clients, this approach may be limited, particularly as we account for the findings of Zech, de Ree, Berenschot, and Stroebe (2006), who found that in a group of bereaved patients consulting their family physician, those who demonstrated anxious attachment were more likely to seek consultation for psychological reasons, whereas those with avoidant attachment were more likely to consult for somatic concerns. Sensorimotor psychotherapy, to be discussed below, utilizes somatic awareness as the entry point (Odgen et al., 2005), which might allow for a way to engage clients that moves beyond their inability to find words to describe their grief-related distress.

In my (CAA) clinical practice with bereaved individuals, those who presented with death-related loss and nonfinite loss (see Chapter 18) have often had a history of childhood trauma as well. This intersection of being insecurely attached along with the presenting symptoms of grief and trauma meant that it was necessary to find a way in which to build rapport with such clients and provide effective treatment, while being mindful of the potential impact of emotional dysregulation. Introduction to Fisher's (2009) trauma model utilizing sensorimotor psychotherapy has provided a means by which to delicately balance the complex needs of such clients.

As this chapter has highlighted, the DPM maintains that anxiously attached individuals may engage in rumination about the deceased, whereas the avoidantly attached may be primarily focused on restorative activities and avoid thoughts related to a deceased partner. Borrowing from trauma literature, a potential way to conceptualize this is that one group is hyperaroused (i.e., experiencing emotional overwhelm, panic, impulsivity, and anger), whereas the other is hypoaroused (i.e., numb, disconnected, and shut down; Ogden, Minton, & Pain, 2006). This would subsequently impact bereavement outcomes, namely, the ability to meet the challenges in an integrated way, reflective of the DPM's oscillating framework. Encouraging either type of client to actively explore his or her deep and profound feelings of loss within an emotionally focused therapeutic encounter can potentially result in both types of clients being outside their "window of tolerance." In this secure window, both thoughts and feelings can occur simultaneously, they are tolerable, and responses are appropriate within a given situation (Fisher, 2009). Being outside this safe window can result in anxious clients experiencing an increase in rumination that becomes more difficult to contain and thus requires more therapeutic support, whereas avoidant clients tend to seek out additional ways to remain distracted from their grief or distress. At the heart of attachment is having a sense of safety; those who are insecurely attached, by definition, lack these emotional and psychological resources and therefore may be destabilized in therapy either by feeling that they are not being adequately supported (anxious) or by being flooded with unwelcome and distressing emotions (avoidant).

After learning about Fisher's therapeutic approach in her trauma model, we wondered whether an integration of the DPM with sensorimotor psychotherapy could offer a clinical intervention that supports the unique bereavement needs of insecurely attached clients. The full breadth of sensorimotor psychotherapy (see Fisher, 1999; Ogden & Minton, 2000; Ogden et al., 2006) and Fisher's trauma model (Fisher, 2009) is beyond the scope of this chapter. However, we will attempt to summarize the most salient features as they relate to the DPM and insecurely attached grieving individuals.

SENSORIMOTOR PSYCHOTHERAPY AND BEREAVEMENT

Sensorimotor psychotherapy uses the body as the primary entry point in the initial stages of therapy, to enhance the client's sense of safety and ability to be present. Traditional psychotherapy training encourages clinicians to track the narrative, establish a therapeutic alliance, monitor transference and countertransference, and skillfully listen (Ogden et al., 2005). Although the narrative approach results in greater insight, an alternative focus on the embodied nature of grief can assist in normalizing and treating the repetitive physical sensations and somatosensory experiences that accompany bereavement. As in trauma work, clients who are insecurely attached and who experience overwhelming physiological arousal and distress can benefit from a therapy that focuses on modulating such arousal.

Ogden and Minton (2000) explained that sensorimotor processing involves attention to overall body processing, namely, the fixed action patterns seen in active defenses, breathing patterns, muscular tonicity, and autonomic nervous system activation. Sensorimotor psychotherapy integrates cognitive, emotional, and sensorimotor processing in such a way that these systems support each other. As it would apply to grief, clients would be encouraged to mindfully track their physical movements such as muscular tension, breathing, heart rate, and motor impulses with the goal of distinguishing emotional grief responses from physiological dysregulation. Such bodily sensations are observed as their texture and intensity fluctuate, until the sensation has stabilized (Ogden & Minton, 2000).

As the scope of sensorimotor therapy cannot be fully addressed, the following case example may illuminate how this approach can be applied. Beth was 37 years old and had just given birth to her second child, who was her first daughter. Throughout Beth's prior pregnancy, she experienced flashbacks and memories of her childhood sexual abuse but coped primarily by using avoidance. The birth of her daughter intensified her trauma symptoms, resulting in increased hypervigilance, insomnia, nightmares, and flashbacks. Beth sought therapy following the death of her older brother in a motor vehicle accident, which occurred when Beth's daughter was 6 months old. Since her brother's death, Beth began experiencing migraine headaches along with abdominal pain. With her history of parental emotional neglect, Beth presented as dismissive in therapy, questioning its relevance in alleviating her distress and expressing mistrust of the therapist.

Such a case involves both death-related and nonfinite loss with respect to her history of abuse. Acquiring insight into the multiple ways in which her history of loss had impacted her could certainly be beneficial. However, it was evident that an insight-oriented and emotional exploration of her grief and trauma would be highly threatening and possibly destabilizing in the face of her already overwhelming emotion. In the initial stages of therapy, therefore, psychoeducation along with the sensorimotor process of observing somatic sensations was emphasized. Implementing psychoeducation in the third session, the therapist offered Beth the following information:

Your current feelings of sadness and loss have triggered past experiences in which you have felt helpless and overwhelmed. Our brain is shaped by our experiences, and therefore this stored information in your neural pathways is acting much like a domino effect with these overwhelming emotions setting others off. These deep feelings are processed in emotional, neurological, and bodily ways, and what is happening is the body's alarm system is being activated to believe that you are in danger. When grieving the death of your brother, try to be mindful and observe the other associated thoughts and feelings. If you begin to feel panic and fear, remind yourself that old experiences are being triggered, that these are symptoms of trauma and grief, and that you are not presently in danger.

Utilizing the helpful metaphor of the body's smoke alarm, Beth understood that the current feelings of sadness and loss were not reflective of any personal deficit, but rather the result of numerous negative experiences. Weeks after this information was offered, Beth was able to report that reminding herself that these symptoms were connected to old experiences proved to be extremely beneficial and assisted her in becoming more grounded in the present moment.

Within the therapy sessions, Beth was invited to "just notice" what was happening in her body when she experienced emotional distress. Gaze aversion, tense posture, and a voice choked with restrained emotions were indicators that Beth was emotionally overwhelmed. The details of what had created the arousal were not explored or interpreted at that moment; rather, Beth was cued to focus on the sensations in her body. The therapist would gently state, "Tell me what you are noticing in your body." Beth would often experience a tense pressure in her chest; as she focused on her breath and the tension, she would report this symptom decreasing after several seconds, and she would appear relieved in her relaxed posture and could resume more consistent eye contact. If the arousal reoccurred, the gentle invitation to return to her body was extended in order for her to safely attend to and track these sensations.

Beth was highly capable of observing the various symptoms, such as increased heart rate, tension, and rapid breathing, and began to differentiate the dysregulation from her emotional distress. Gradually, she disconnected the belief "I am not safe" from her hypervigilance as she became more able to identify these as symptoms reflecting her trauma and grief rather than any objective current danger. Beth became able to mindfully attend to her bodily sensations and track them until they stabilized. Such mindfulness activates the amygdala (along with other neurological processes; see Schore, 2003a, 2003b), which in turn assists in decreasing the body's alarm response (Fisher, 2009).

Over a period of months, Beth successfully identified, tracked, and attended to her somatic sensations and became more capable of regulation without the accompanying fears or shameful feelings she initially experienced. Fisher (personal communication, 2010) has contended that there are three criteria to promote neuroplasticity in the brain: (a) being mindful (not interpretive), (b) inhibiting old responses, and (c) intensely practicing new responses. When these are actively taught and encouraged in the initial stages of therapy, anxious and avoidantly attached clients can learn regulation, making them more likely to benefit from an insight-oriented, attuned therapeutic relationship and to subsequently make meaning of their loss. Beth was able to slowly begin exploring her grief regarding her brother's death and her history of childhood trauma once she had established a "window of tolerance" for managing her somatic arousal.

CLINICAL RECOMMENDATIONS

Containment

Fisher (personal communication, 2010) stated that if sharing a personal history evokes feelings of distress, she will advise her client to stop the narrative to avoid the physiological arousal that gets activated through the retelling. Initially engaging with such clients as a teacher–educator might empower the client to learn ways of implementing both internal and external safety prior to working through the delicate balance of loss and restoration that accompanies bereavement. It also allows the therapist to be flexible and to meet the unique needs of the client, who can then become a motivated participant in his or her own healing (Zech et al., 2010).

Moreover, in sensorimotor psychotherapy, Diamond, Balvin, and Diamond (1963, as cited in Ogden & Minton, 2000) suggested that the therapist act as the "auxiliary cortex." The therapist notices, tracks, and describes the sensorimotor experiences of the client until he or she is able to do this unassisted. This relational communication bears resemblance to a mother's attunement to an infant's inner processes.

Noticing and Mindfulness

Within the initial stages of sensorimotor therapy or processing, there is much focus on noticing the associations that accompany arousal, or feeling numb. The directive is often to "just notice." Invariably, when a client directs full attention to a rapid heart rate or the feeling of emptiness, he or she will report that this feeling has dissipated. To experience such sensations in the presence of a therapist and in the absence of fear helps clients learn to become more connected to their bodily processes and to regulate their experiences. What is central to this technique is attentiveness, rather than interpretation, evaluation, or judgment of one's feelings.

The Here and Now

> By focusing on the here-and-now thoughts, feelings and body sensations, whether or not connected to the narrative, the client is not unduly autonomically or emotionally activated. By letting go of the thoughts and beliefs that intensify the sensations, it is easier for the client to stay curious and in a state of dual awareness.
>
> **Janina Fishter (2003, p. 5)**

Fisher further explained that when clients are capable of parallel processing, they are not at risk of being retraumatized or, for the purposes of our discussion, experiencing grief triggers that would be too threatening.

Clinical and developmental psychologist Gordon Neufeld has stated that a fundamental tenet of attachment is extending to the other the "invitation to exist in our presence" (personal communication, 2006). For those who present for therapy with mistrust or anxiety, or who have become loosened from their moorings in some way, our role as clinicians can be to offer them such an invitation in a way that first establishes an embodied sense of safety and security, prior to engaging in the complexities of loss and restoration.

NOTE

1. Absent grief may not always reflect pathological processes; it might actually indicate that the bereaved person either does not grieve or is doing well and hence presenting no symptoms.

REFERENCES

Ainsworth, M. D. S., Blehar, M. C., Waters, E., & Walls, S. (1978). *Patterns of attachment: A psychological study of the strange situation*. Hillsdale, NJ: Lawrence Erlbaum.

Bartholomew, K. (1990). Avoidance of intimacy: An attachment perspective. *Journal of Social and Personal Relationships*, *7*, 147–178.

Bartholomew, K., & Horowitz, L. M. (1991). Attachment styles among young adults: A test of a four-category model. *Journal of Personality and Social Psychology*, *61*, 226–244.

Bowlby, J. (1969). *Attachment and loss: Vol. 1. Attachment*. London: Hogarth Press.

Bowlby, J. (1988). *A secure base: Clinical applications of attachment theory*. London: Routledge.

Brown, D., Hawkins-Rodgers, Y., & Kapadia, K. (2008). Multicultural considerations for the application of attachment theory. *American Journal of Psychotherapy*, *62*, 353–363.

Caserta, M. S., & Lund, D. A. (2007). Toward the development of an Inventory of Daily Widowed Life (IDWL): Guided by the dual process model of coping with bereavement. *Death Studies*, *31*, 505–535.

Cassidy, J., & Shaver, P. (1999). *Handbook of attachment: Theory, research and clinical applications*. New York: Guilford Press.

Connors, M. E. (1997). Renunciation of love: Dismissing attachment and its treatment. *Psychoanalytic Psychology*, *14*, 475–493.

Currier, J. M., Neimeyer, R. A., & Berman, J. S. (2008). The effectiveness of psychotherapeutic interventions for the bereaved: A comprehensive quantitative review. *Psychological Bulletin*, *134*, 648–661.

Diamond, S., Balvin, R. S., & Diamond, F. R. (1963). *Inhibition and choice*. New York: Harper & Row.

Dozier, M. (1990). Attachment organization and treatment use for adults with serious psychopathological disorders. *Development and Psychopathology*, *2*, 47–60.

Elliott, R., & Greenberg, L. S. (2007). The essence of process-experiential/emotion-focused therapy. *American Journal of Psychotherapy*, *61*, 241–254.

Feeney, J. A., & Noller, P. (1996). *Adult attachment*. Thousand Oaks, CA: Sage.

Feeney, J. A., Noller, P., & Roberts, N. (1998). Emotion, attachment, and satisfaction in close relationships. In P. A. Andersen & L. K. Guerrero (Eds.), *Handbook of communication and emotion: Research, theory, applications, and contexts* (pp. 473–505). San Diego, CA: Academic Press.

Fisher, J. (1999). The work of stabilization in trauma treatment. Paper presented at the Trauma Centre Lecture Series. Retrieved from http://janinafisher.com/pdfs/stabilize.pdf

Fisher, J. (2003, July). Working with the neurobiological legacy of early trauma. Paper presented at the annual conference of American Mental Health Counselors. Retrieved from http://janinafisher.com/pdfs/neurobiol.pdf

Fisher, J. (2009). *Psychoeducational aids for working with psychological trauma* (8th ed.). Watertown, MA: Center for Integrative Healing.

Fraley, R. C., & Shaver, P. R. (1999). Loss and bereavement: Bowlby's theory and recent controversies concerning "grief work" and the nature of detachment. In J. Cassidy & P. R. Shaver (Eds.), *Handbook of attachment theory and research: Theory, research, and clinical applications* (pp. 735–759). New York: Guilford Press.

Hazan, C., & Shaver, P. R. (1990). Love and work: An attachment-theoretical perspective. *Journal of Personality and Social Psychology*, *59*, 270–280.

Jordan, J. R., & Neimeyer, R. A. (2003). Does grief counselling work? *Death Studies*, *27*, 765–786.

Kanninen, K., Salo, J., & Punamäki, R. L. (2000). Attachment patterns and working alliance in trauma therapy for victims of political violence. *Psychotherapy Research*, *10*, 435–449.

Kato, P. M., & Mann, T. (1999). A synthesis of psychological interventions for the bereaved. *Clinical Psychology Review*, *19*, 275–296.

Lopez, F. G., Melendez, M. C., Sauer, E. M., Berger, E., & Wyssmann, J. (1998). Internal working models, self-reported problems, and help-seeking attitudes among college students. *Journal of Counseling Psychology*, *45*, 79–83.

Mallinckrodt, B., Gantt, D. L., & Coble, H. M. (1995). Attachment patterns in the psychotherapy relationship: Development of the Client Attachment to Therapist Scale. *Journal of Counseling Psychology*, *42*, 307–317.

Meyer, B., & Pilkonis, P. A. (2002). Attachment style. In J. C. Norcross (Ed.), *Psychotherapy relationships that work: Therapist contributions and responsiveness to clients* (pp. 367–382). New York: Oxford University Press.

Mikulincer, M., & Nachshon, O. (1991). Attachment styles and patterns of self-disclosure. *Journal of Personality and Social Psychology*, *61*, 321–331.

Mikulincer, M., & Orbach, I. (1995). Attachment styles and repressive defensiveness: The accessibility and architecture of affective memories. *Journal of Personality and Social Psychology*, *68*, 917–925.

Mikulincer, M., & Shaver, P. R. (2003). The attachment behavioral system in adulthood: Activation, psychodynamics, and interpersonal processes. In M. P. Zanna (Ed.), *Advances in experimental social psychology* (Vol. 35, pp. 56–152). San Diego, CA: Academic Press.

Mikulincer, M., & Shaver, P. R. (2007). Implications of attachment theory and research for counseling and psychotherapy. In M. Mikulincer & P. R. Shaver (Eds.), *Attachment in adulthood: Structure, dynamics, and change* (Ch. 14, pp. 405–432). New York: Guilford Press.

Mikulincer, M., & Shaver, P. R. (2008). An attachment perspective on bereavement. In M. S. Stroebe, R. O. Hansson, H. Schut, & W. Stroebe (Eds.), *Handbook of bereavement research and practice* (pp. 87–112). Washington, DC: American Psychological Association Press.

Norcross, J. C. (Ed.). (2002). *Psychotherapy relationships that work: Therapist contributions and responsiveness to clients*. New York: Oxford University Press.

Ogden, P., & Minton, K. (2000). Sensorimotor psychotherapy: One method for processing traumatic memory. *Traumatology*, *6*(3). Retrieved from http://www.sensorimotorpsychotherapy.org/articles.html

Ogden, P., Minton, K., & Pain, C. (2006). *Trauma and the body: A sensorimotor approach to psychotherapy*. New York: Norton.

Ogden, P., Pain, C., Minton, K., & Fisher, J. (2005, Fall). Including the body in mainstream psychotherapy for traumatized individuals. *Psychologist Psychoanalyst*. Retrieved from: http://www.sensorimotorpsychotherapy.org/article%20APA.html

Parkes, C. M. (2010). Grief: Lessons from the past, visions for the future. *Psychologica Belgica*, *50*, 7–26.

Pistole, M. C. (1993). Attachment relationships: Self-disclosure and trust. *Journal of Mental Health Counseling, 15*, 94–106.

Prigerson, H. G., Frank, E., Kasl, S., Reynolds, C., Anderson, B., Zubenko, G. S., et al. (1995). Complicated grief and bereavement related depression as distinct disorders: Preliminary empirical validation in elderly bereaved spouses. *American Journal of Psychiatry, 152*, 22–30.

Ramsay, R. W. (1977). Behavioural approaches to bereavement. *Behavioural Research Therapy, 15*, 131–135.

Ramsay, R. W. (1979). Bereavement: A behavioral treatment of pathological grief. In P. O. Sjoden, S. Bates, & W. S. Dorkens III (Eds.), *Trends in behavior therapy* (pp. 217–248). New York: Academic Press.

Rogers, C. R. (2007). The necessary and sufficient conditions of therapeutic personality change. *Psychotherapy: Theory, Research, Practice, Training, 44*, 240–248. (Original work published in 1957)

Schore, A. N. (2003a). *Affect dysregulation and disorders of the self*. New York: Norton.

Schore, A. N. (2003b). *Affect regulation and the repair of the self*. New York: Norton.

Schut, H., & Stroebe, M. S. (2005). Interventions to enhance adaptation to bereavement. *Journal of Palliative Medicine, 8*, S140–S147.

Schut, H., Stroebe, M. S., van den Bout, J., & Terheggen, M. (2001). The efficacy of bereavement intervention: Who benefits? In M. S. Stroebe, R. O. Hansson, W. Stroebe, & H. Schut (Eds.), *Handbook of bereavement research: Consequences, coping, and care* (pp. 705–737). Washington, DC: American Psychological Association.

Shaver, P. R., & Fraley, R. C. (2004, July). *Self-report measures of adult attachment*. Retrieved from http://www.psych.uiuc.edu/~rcfraley/measures/measures.html

Shaver, P. R., & Tancredy, C. M. (2001). Emotion, attachment and bereavement: A conceptual commentary. In M. S. Stroebe, R. O. Hansson, W. Stroebe, & H. Schut (Eds.), *Handbook of bereavement research: Consequences, coping, and care* (pp. 63–88). Washington, DC: American Psychological Association Press.

Shear, K., Frank, E., Houck, P. R., & Reynolds, C. F. (2005). Treatment of complicated grief: A randomized controlled trial. *Journal of the American Medical Association, 293*, 2601–2608.

Stroebe, M. S., & Schut, H. (1999). The dual process model of coping with bereavement: Rationale and description. *Death Studies, 23*, 197–224.

Stroebe, M. S., Schut, H., & Stroebe, W. (2005). Attachment in coping with bereavement: A theoretical integration. *Review of General Psychology, 9*, 48–60.

Watson, J. C. (2007). Reassessing Rogers' necessary and sufficient conditions of change. *Psychotherapy: Theory, Research, Practice, Training, 44*, 268–273.

Wijngaards, L., Stroebe, M., Stroebe, W., Schut, H., Van den Bout, J., Van der Heijden, P., et al. (2008). Parents grieving the loss of their child: Interdependence in coping. *British Journal of Clinical Psychology, 47*, 31–42.

Zech, E., de Ree, F., Berenschot, F., & Stroebe, M. S. (2006). Depressive affect among health care seekers: Who suffers most? *Psychology, Health, and Medicine, 11*, 7–19.

Zech, E., & Rimé, B. (2005). Is talking about an emotional experience helpful? Effects on emotional recovery and perceived benefits. *Clinical Psychology & Psychotherapy, 12*, 270–287.

Zech, E., Rimé, B., & Pennebaker, J. (2007). The effects of emotional disclosure during bereavement. In K. van den Bos, J. de Wit, M. Hewstone, H. Schut, & M. Stroebe (Eds.), *The scope of social psychology: Theory and applications: Essays in honour of Wolfgang Stroebe* (pp. 279–294). London: Psychology Press.

Zech, E., Ryckebosch, A-S., & Delespaux, E. (2010). Improving the efficacy of intervention for bereaved individuals: Toward a process-focused psychotherapeutic perspective. *Psychologica Belgica, 50*, 103–124.

4

The Changing Bond in Therapy for Unresolved Loss

An Attachment Theory Perspective

NIGEL P. FIELD and CAROL WOGRIN

It is widely acknowledged in the bereavement literature that a continuing bond (CB) with the deceased can be an integral part of successful adjustment to bereavement (Klass, Silverman, & Nickman, 1996). It is also clear that it is not always so, and contemporary theory and research have attempted to identify when CB is and is not adaptive (Field, 2008; Fraley & Shaver, 1999; Stroebe, Schut, & Boerner, 2010). In furthering our understanding of its place in adaptation to bereavement, it is important to situate CB within a broader theoretical framework on adjustment to interpersonal loss. In this chapter, we focus on an attachment theory perspective on CB as a comprehensive framework for understanding the nature and function of CB in bereavement that can explain normative changes in CB expression over the course of bereavement and as a means for distinguishing adaptive versus maladaptive variants of CB expression. In this context, we demonstrate its applicability in a clinical case study examining change in CB over the course of psychotherapy involving CB as a central focus of intervention. Prior to introducing the case, we first provide theoretical background on this attachment perspective.

AN ATTACHMENT THEORY PERSPECTIVE ON ADAPTATION TO BEREAVEMENT

According to attachment theory, although most self-evident in childhood, the individual never outgrows the need for supportive and nurturing relationships (Karen, 1994). In such attachment relationships across the life cycle, the experience of "felt security"—or sense of safety in knowing that a close other is physically and psychologically available if needed—is afforded through the attachment bond (Waters &

Cummings, 2000). It therefore follows that as a result of this other's death, this felt security supplied via the regulating function of the attachment bond is lost.

In the early phase of bereavement, the bereaved may engage in search efforts to recover the deceased in an attempt to restore felt security because the permanence of the separation is not yet registered at the attachment system level (Archer, 1999). Illusions and hallucinations of the deceased, and compulsive search efforts commonly displayed early on after the death of a loved one, can be understood as expressions of the attachment system's expectational set that the deceased is recoverable (Field, Gao, & Paderna, 2005). With repeated exposure to experiences of the absence of the deceased, and failed attempts to reestablish physical proximity, active search efforts shift toward more passive despair and withdrawal as it becomes increasingly more clear at the attachment system level that the separation is permanent (Bowlby, 1980). Negative emotions aroused in confronting the loss within a window of tolerance serve to motivate disengagement from unattainable goals linked to the former relationship with the deceased as part of a *reorganization* process toward constructing a new life following the loss (Bowlby, 1980). Termination of search behavior and reorientation to everyday life and its tasks are reflective of such reorganization.

REVISING THE BOND TO THE DECEASED

An important aspect of this disengagement process involves transforming the inner relationship with the deceased. Although the bereaved must give up the goal of reestablishing physical proximity to him or her, this is not tantamount to relinquishing the attachment. Rather, accommodating to the loss requires reorganizing or relocating the relationship such that it now exists at a purely mental representational level (Field, 2006). Through an active constructive process toward establishing a symbolic connection via memory and imagination, it is possible for the bereaved to experience the deceased to some degree as continuing to serve a *safe haven* attachment function, to which the bereaved can turn as a comforting presence when under stress. Similarly, when the bond is successfully reorganized, it can serve a *secure base* function, experiencing the deceased as a background presence or "holding environment" in orienting toward constructing a new life (Field, 2006). Reorganization of the relationship with the deceased may also involve *identification* with his or her values and ideals as a source of inspiration and guidance, along with *internalization* of caregiving functions previously supplied by the deceased into self-soothing capacities and self-compassion (Baker, 2001). CB may thus at least partly serve to reestablish a sense of felt security lost as a result of the death. CB expressions involving the legacy of the deceased, such as his or her function as a role model and source of inspiration, live on in the mind of the bereaved despite the loss. In this respect, the bond with the deceased continues.

CB INDICATIVE OF REORGANIZATION FAILURE

Successful reorganization following the loss of a loved one is reflected in the construction of a coherent narrative of the loss within a broader meaningful "life story" context that may include an ongoing connection with the deceased (Fraley & Shaver, 1999; see also Chapter 1). Conversely, reorganization failure at the attachment system level entails failing to revise the working model of attachment to the deceased to bring it into accord with the bereaved person's new life situation (Horowitz, 1991). The attachment literature on unresolved loss identifies a type of reorganization failure characterized by a mental schema of the relationship with the deceased that is dissociated from the knowledge that he or she is dead (for more detail, see Field, 2006). Such an outcome occurs when the loss is so emotionally overwhelming that the bereaved must resort to an extreme form of avoidance in which the implications of the loss become "defensively excluded" from experience (Bowlby, 1973; Field, 2006). CB expressions involving a lapse in reasoning that imply disbelief that the other is deceased—such as illusions and hallucinations of the deceased occurring after the death—or denial-driven fantasy of the deceased's eventual return as reflected in maintaining his or her possessions exactly as they were prior to the death are indicative of such reorganization failure. Use of "linking objects" involving special items associated with the deceased that serve to maintain the illusion of external contact with him or her, as opposed to simply serving a symbolic function of preserving the memory of the deceased (Volkan, 1981), similarly implies disbelief that the other is dead. Such CB expressions reflect both failure to relinquish the goal to regain physical proximity to the deceased and defense against acknowledging the finality of the separation (Field, 2006). A guilt-ridden connection to the deceased stemming from an irrational belief of having played a causal role in the death is also indicative of unresolved loss (Main, Goldwyn, & Hesse, 2002). CB expressions that imply such beliefs are maintained through defensive avoidance so that their irrational basis is never open to conscious scrutiny and challenge.

INTERGENERATIONAL EFFECTS OF UNRESOLVED LOSS

One of the most robust findings in the attachment research literature is the concordance between the parent and child's attachment classification (van IJzendoorn, 1995). The quality of parenting is the pivotal factor that explains these intergenerational correspondences. Securely attached parents are able to accurately read their child's attachment cues and respond contingently (Ainsworth, Blehar, Waters, & Wall, 1978). Such attuned caregiving provides a foundation for the child's healthy emotional development. Through repeated experiences of attachment figure sensitivity and responsiveness to the child's attachment needs, the child builds an internal working model that functions as an internalized secure base, involving the belief that attachment figures will be emotionally available when needed (Ainsworth et al., 1978). A working model characterizing secure attachment serves as an important inner resource for coping with stress and tolerating separation as well as for being able to make effective use of social supports. Thus, securely attached bereaved individuals have greater capacity for tolerating and working through distressing feelings and reorganizing their relationship with the deceased (this concept is also discussed by Zech and Arnold in Chapter 3 of this book).

In contrast to the above, the parenting among those who remain unresolved in regard to early losses and traumas is known to be compromised, having detrimental consequences for the child's emotional development. The sense of helplessness and loss of control activated by reminders of past losses and traumas, and defensive efforts to ward off such states, interfere with their ability to function as an effective caregiver to their child (George & Solomon, 1999). In fact, there is evidence that the child experiences parents' behavior associated with these intrusive reminders as frightening (Hesse, Main, Abrams, & Rifkin, 2003). In such circumstances where the attachment figure is the source of fear, the child cannot turn to him or her for comfort and therefore is forced to defensively exclude, or *split off*, important aspects of his or her experience as the only option. This may have long-term negative consequences such as placing the child at risk for developing later psychopathology, including dissociative disorders (Carlson, 1998).

One outgrowth of this type of parenting may be the development of a role-reversing or *parentified* attachment orientation in the child (Solomon & George, 1999). In role reversal, a parent turns to a child to have his or her emotional needs met rather than attempting to have these needs met by other adults (Chase, 1999). Here, a child feels compelled to take on the role of parent, spouse, or peer toward his or her parent, thus occupying a caregiving role in relation to the parent. In adopting this role, the child can gain a semblance of emotional security in the relationship. However, in the process the child develops inordinate responsibility for the emotional welfare of the parent and curtails his or her own attachment needs.

A role-reversing orientation may have important implications for bereavement-related adjustment and the nature of CB. In taking on inordinate responsibility for the emotional welfare of others, the bereaved may be more prone to experience guilt, in interpreting the death as the bereaved having failed the deceased. Such guilt may be even more pronounced if underlying negative feelings exist toward the deceased or if the bereaved feels relieved over the loss. This response to the loss may reflect an underlying pathogenic belief that caring for oneself is tantamount to depriving and betraying others (Silberschatz & Sampson, 1991). Although while the other was alive it was possible to maintain the belief that providing care guaranteed some semblance of having an attachment figure available, the death meant that a role-reversing strategy was no longer effective in this regard. The death may also bring to awareness the realization that the other was never satisfactorily available, thus inciting anger as well as helplessness in feeling abandoned. This intense guilt, anger, and sense of helplessness activated by reminders of the loss will, in turn, serve to motivate extreme avoidance, thus increasing the risk for unresolved loss.

The Case of Frances

We now present the case of Frances involving unresolved loss stemming from the deaths of her parents in adulthood. This case serves to illustrate both a maladaptive CB indicative of unresolved loss that led her to seek out therapy and constructive changes in the nature of CB in the course of successful treatment. In mourning the loss of a parent in adulthood, working through the loss of the attachment also entails coming to terms with preexisting hopes, goals, and beliefs linked to the relationship that have been lost (Horowitz et al., 1984). Successful mourning requires not only revising the mental schema of the past relationship with the deceased to bring it into accord with what was *actually* lost but also coming to terms with what had been expected or hoped for but never materialized in the past relationship. In effect, the hope or fantasy for what might have been realized in the relationship is no longer *possible* as a result of the death. Consequently, the bereaved must relinquish goals linked to both the actual and possible relationship with the deceased in the process of mentally reorganizing the attachment. Among those who have lost a parent who failed to provide the proper caregiving in fostering secure attachment, the mourning process will be more difficult and the bereaved will be at greater risk for unresolved loss (Hesse et al., 2003).

Background and History Frances was a 59-year-old woman who came into therapy 1½ years after the death of her father, 7 years after he was diagnosed with Alzheimer's disease. When Frances entered therapy, she was struggling with tremendous guilt, believing that she had been unable to provide her father with the care he needed in the last years of his life, when he was at his most vulnerable. As became apparent in therapy, her guilt was an outgrowth of a role-reversing orientation wherein she took inordinate responsibility for both parents' emotional welfare, leading to an irrational sense of responsibility for events linked to their deaths.

Frances was an only child whose parents had histories of significant losses. Her mother was raised by older sisters following the death of her mother in childbirth with her. Thus, her mother's older sisters were coping with the loss of their mother, which may have affected the quality of their caregiving in raising her. Frances's father's mother died when he was school age, and his father, who was reportedly alcoholic and physically abusive, died a few years later.

Frances remembers her early years as happy ones in which she was surrounded by her maternal aunts and many cousins. When she was 10 years old, her parents moved from southeastern Massachusetts to New Hampshire for her father's job. From that time on, her family was very isolated. Visits with her mother's extended family were rare, and her parents did not develop a social network in their new location. Her father had an "abrasive personality," had little trust of people outside of their nuclear family, and seemed content with the family's isolation. In her mother, however, she felt that there was always a "profound sadness" after the move. Her mother turned to Frances for comfort because her father could not tolerate expressions of grief and sadness, given his dismissive way of coping with his own past losses. She remembers going home immediately after school most days throughout high school in order to provide companionship for her mother, further promoting a parentified orientation. Frances attended a college near home but married shortly after college and moved to Florida. Eight years later, she moved back and settled about 2 hours from her parents. Her guilt over having moved away from them, which led to her eventual return to live near them, pointed toward a pathogenic belief that a move toward greater autonomy meant harming her parents.

Frances gave birth to the first of her two children, Wendy, when she was in her late 30s and her son, Michael, 2 years later. Frances chose to not follow the family tradition and use a derivative of the name Frances for her daughter. She stated that she wanted "to break the chain of loss and sadness" that accompanied this line of women. This revealed a strong identification with her mother's pain stemming from past losses and its intergenerational effect of causing her to feel burdened by a sense of responsibility for her mother's sadness, reflective of a parentified orientation.

When Wendy was 6 months old, Frances's mother was hospitalized for cardiac problems. Though her heart problems stemmed back to childhood, she avoided getting regular medical care. During this hospitalization, her physician strongly recommended surgery. Because her mother was very ill, signing the surgical consent became her father's responsibility. Instead, he asked Frances to do this. Thus, once again, Frances was thrust into a parentified role in protecting her father from having to confront his grief surrounding past losses and fear of impending loss. After Frances signed the form, her mother died in the intensive care unit 2 days after surgery. As became evident during therapy, she carried an irrational sense of having caused her mother's death that pointed to unresolved loss.

The last years of her father's life were very difficult ones. When his dementia became evident, Frances encouraged him to move in with her. He refused, but finally, after he inadvertently set a fire in his house, she had to override his wish to remain living alone. Because he was adamant that he wouldn't live with her, she moved him to an assisted living community. Frances resigned from her job and for the remainder of his life visited him every day, despite the one-hour drive in each direction—thus taking on excessive responsibility in line with her parentified orientation. His course was difficult, requiring multiple hospitalizations for complex medical issues. Two months before he died, she decided to forgo curative treatment and enrolled him in hospice. This, too, was something she later felt guilty about, wondering if she had "given up" because of her own exhaustion.

To reiterate, Frances's response to the death of her parents can be understood from a broader intergenerational perspective on transmission of the effects of their early losses. These losses had a profound influence on her—especially given that she was an only child. From early on, Frances was sensitized to her parents' emotional vulnerability linked to their past losses that instilled a parentified orientation in her in an attempt to stabilize them in their role as her primary caregivers. She thus took on inordinate responsibility for their psychological well-being that interfered with her development toward gaining psychological autonomy.

Therapy Reworking the bond with both parents was a central focus of treatment. Over the course of therapy, the nature of her bond with each parent progressed from one characterized by an enmeshed, insecure attachment orientation toward one of greater psychological autonomy. Specifically, she extricated herself from a parentification orientation toward both parents expressed in a bond based on identification with their pain stemming from their past losses toward a healthier connection via identification with their more positive qualities that were congruent with autonomous strivings. This change was reflected in a shift from the use of CB expressions indicative of unresolved loss toward a bond reflective of reorganization.

Reworking the Bond With Her Father Frances began therapy focusing on her guilt over having let down her father at the end of his life. As she explored this guilt in the safety of the therapeutic relationship, anger at her father emerged, primarily over the ways in which he had always refused to yield to the needs of others or to let other people help him, even when he clearly needed it.

As a homework assignment about a month into therapy, she wrote the first of a number of "unsent" letters to her deceased father, this one describing her anger at him. Writing the letter took her back to the move to New Hampshire when she was 10 years old. For the first time, she became aware of how pivotal that move had been in the life of the family. She realized how she had to stifle expressing sadness over being isolated from her extended family so as not to anger her father. In retrospect, Frances recognized how in silencing her own sadness over the move, she in effect was protecting her father from his own grief.

Frances wrote a second letter 2 months later, this time to "ask his forgiveness for her limitations." She began by writing about how sorry she was that she had not been able to care for him during his final years the way she thought he would have wanted at the end of his life. She also empathized with the hardships he experienced in his life, and the ways in which these had affected him. Feeling empathy, however, reignited her anger, as she became increasingly aware of the degree to which he "lived his life exclusively on his own terms."

Acknowledging and exploring her anger toward her father were pivotal in facilitating a shift from a more enmeshed attachment orientation toward a more autonomous state of mind in regard to attachment. Her anger, as an expression of voicing her needs and sense of loss over what her father never had been able to offer as a parent, served to lessen her guilt and construe him more realistically.

Frances found exploring her multifaceted experience of her father emotionally freeing, and her general level of anxiety began to noticeably diminish, although it had been present since the beginning of her father's illness. However, her gains were not linear. She would frequently slide back into her guilt and sadness. Approximately a year into therapy, she talked about her new awareness that it was hard to let go of her father's pain, stating, "He gave it to me to hold." She feared that if she let go of the pain, she would lose her relationship with him altogether. This represented an important juncture in therapy in developing a deeper understanding of her sense of responsibility for the emotional well-being of her father, whom she viewed as fragile, and in uncovering her pathogenic belief that any move toward autonomy meant harming him, ultimately threatening the attachment bond. Recognizing this paved the way for constructing a new bond with her father based on a more secure attachment organization.

Reworking the Bond With Her Mother Although Frances described her mother as having a warm and loving nature and being someone to whom she always felt close, she also recognized that her mother was timid, her world was very limited, and she was fearful of venturing out beyond her extended family. As therapy progressed, she began to explore the ways in which she had picked up her mother's anxiety. About 6 months into therapy, Frances began talking about feeling that if she changed and felt less anxious and/or guilty, she "would leave her mother behind." Using an empty chair technique, Frances had a dialogue with her mother alternating between speaking for herself and taking on the role of her mother.

"Her mother" voiced the sadness she felt in her own life, but also her love for Frances. Frances took the opportunity of this dialogue to apologize to her mother for the pain she had caused her by moving further into the world than her mother had ever been able to. She tearfully told her mother that she "didn't want to leave her behind," but, rather, her mother would continue to live "through all of her best sides." The qualities that Frances most liked in herself were the ones that she attributed to her mother. In the discussion that followed the chair work, Frances marveled at the conversation she had been able to have, and at the idea of keeping her mother with her in ways other than through the legacy of pain. She also gained insight into her pathogenic belief that moving beyond her mother's world meant betrayal and the threat of losing her. This insight was an important step toward developing a new bond with her mother through identification with the most valued aspects of her that were congruent with her autonomy strivings.

Another pivotal event later on in therapy occurred in a session where Frances explored her guilt over having signed the consent for the surgery that killed her mother. In this context, she talked about wanting to rid herself of an article she had kept in her possession for over 20 years, which she came across shortly after her mother's death. This article supported the idea that surgery was not necessarily an effective treatment for the type of cardiac problem her mother had. Keeping this article in her possession all these years could be seen as an attempt to undo the death; in effect, it represented a linking object in providing a sense of omnipotent control over the life and death of her mother (Volkan, 1981)—thus serving to defensively ward off the reality of the loss, which is indicative of unresolved loss. An irrational belief that she played a causal role in her mother's death, which was also implied here, further attested to her unresolved loss. In preparation, she wrote her mother a letter about what it was she was getting rid of: the guilt, her anger at her mother's failure to take care of herself, and the unanswerable questions about what could have been different. After the session, she placed the article and the letter into the barbeque grill in her yard and burned them. In gaining insight into the irrational nature of her guilt over responsibility for her mother's death, and through this ritual act of destroying the letter, Frances was able to accept and integrate her mother's death. The process of doing so further opened the way for constructing a new, autonomy-promoting bond with her mother.

Bond at the End of Therapy By the time Frances ended therapy, her bond with both of her parents had evolved significantly. In essence, she reorganized her bond with them such that it was possible for her to experience a positive connection based on an exclusively internalized connection with full appreciation and acceptance of their deaths. She therefore no longer needed to "keep her parents alive" through a bond based on guilt and identification with their pain, or through the use of linking objects in an attempt to undo the death, but instead was able to cultivate a connection that was integrated with moving forward in life. This newfound connection was evident in a dream that she reported near the end of therapy, in which she had been on an amusement park ride, soaring and feeling free. As she reveled in the experience, her father joined her. She later reflected on how it was he who had always encouraged her to step out into the world: go to college, move away with her new husband, and go to graduate school. She felt that developing a fuller understanding of his limitations enabled her to also understand his strengths, and was thus appreciative of what he had been able to give her.

She now saw both her parents as people who carried heavy burdens but had done their best. She no longer felt responsible for their difficulties, nor did she feel as guilty for not having been able to set things right. In this respect, she moved well beyond what her relationship with them had been prior to their deaths—it now came from a position of greater psychological autonomy. Although she still missed her parents, her mother in particular, her relationship with both of them had shifted, and she primarily felt comforted by their "presence." In this regard, her bond with them continued despite their deaths and was integral to her achievement of a coherent life narrative in the course of reorganizing these losses.

As her bond with both of her parents evolved, so too did the other relationships in her life. Her anxiety was markedly reduced, and she no longer felt as responsible for the happiness of those around her in ways that were beyond her control. As she loosened her need for control, her daughter, who was always very private and somewhat distant, began to share more with her. Finally, as her anxiety reduced, she began to entertain the possibility of returning to work. Reorganization of her continuing bonds with her parents, therefore, seemed to facilitate reorganizing her bonds with the living, allowing Frances to reopen to participation in life that had been constricted in the presence of a preoccupying double bereavement.

REFERENCES

Ainsworth, M. D. S., Blehar, M. C., Waters, E., & Wall, S. (1978). *Patterns of attachment: A psychological study of the strange situation*. Hillsdale, NJ: Lawrence Erlbaum.

Archer, J. (1999). *The nature of grief: The evolution and psychology of reactions to loss*. New York: Routledge.

Baker, J. E. (2001). Mourning and the transformation of object relationships: Evidence for the persistence of internal attachments. *Psychoanalytic Psychology*, *18*, 55–73.

Bowlby, J. (1973). *Attachment and loss: Vol. 2. Separation: Anxiety and anger*. New York: Basic Books.

Bowlby, J. (1980). *Attachment and loss: Vol. 3. Loss: Sadness and depression*. New York: Basic Books.

Carlson, F. A. (1998). A prospective longitudinal study of disorganized/disorientated attachment. *Child Development*, *69*, 1107–1128.

Chase, N. D. (1999). Parentification: An overview of theory, research and societal issues. In N. D. Chase (Ed.), *Burdened children: Theory, research, and treatment of parentification* (pp. 3–33). Thousand Oaks, CA: Sage.

Field, N. P. (2006). Unresolved loss and the continuing bond to the deceased. *Death Studies*, *30*, 739–756.

Field, N. P. (2008). Whether to maintain or relinquish a bond with the deceased in adapting to bereavement. In M. Stroebe, R. Hansson, H. Schut, & W. Stroebe (Eds.), *Handbook of bereavement research and practice: Advances in theory and practice* (pp. 113—132). Washington, DC: American Psychological Association.

Field, N. P., Gao, B., & Paderna, L. (2005). Continuing bonds in bereavement: An attachment theory based perspective. *Death Studies*, *29*, 1–23.

Fraley, R. C., & Shaver, P. R. (1999). Loss and bereavement: Bowlby's theory and recent controversies concerning grief work and the nature of detachment. In J. Cassidy & R. R. Shaver (Eds.), *Handbook of attachment theory and research* (pp. 735–759). New York: Guilford Press.

Hesse, E., Main, M., Abrams, K., & Rifkin, A. (2003). Unresolved states regarding loss or abuse can have "second-generation" effects: Disorganization, role inversion, and frightening ideation in the offspring of traumatized, non-maltreating parents. In M. Solomon & D. Siegel (Eds.), *Healing trauma: Attachment, mind, body, and brain* (pp. 57–106). New York: Norton.

Horowitz, M. J. (1991). Person schemas. In M. J. Horowitz (Ed.), *Person schemas and maladaptive interpersonal patterns* (pp. 13–31). Chicago: University of Chicago Press.

Horowitz, M. J., Marmar, J., Krupnick, N., Wilner, N., Kaltreider, N., & Wallerstein, R. (1984). *Personality styles and brief psychotherapy*. New York: Basic Books.

Karen, R. (1994). *Becoming attached: First relationships and how they influence our capacity to love*. Oxford: Oxford University Press.

Klass, D., Silverman, P., & Nickman, S. L. (Eds.). (1996). *Continuing bonds: New understandings of grief*. Philadelphia: Taylor & Francis.

Main, M., Goldwyn, R., & Hesse, E. (2002). *Adult attachment scoring and classification systems* (Version 7). Unpublished manual.

Silberschatz, G., & Sampson, H. (1991). Affects in psychopathology and psychotherapy. In J. D. Safran & L. S. Greenberg (Eds.), *Emotion, psychotherapy, and change* (pp. 113–129). New York: Guilford Press.

Stroebe, M., Schut, H., & Boerner, K. (2010). Continuing bonds in adaptation to bereavement: Toward theoretical integration. *Clinical Psychology Review*, *30*, 259–268.

van IJzendoorn, M. (1995). Adult attachment representations, parental responsiveness, and infant attachment: A meta-analysis on the predictive validity of the Adult Attachment Interview. *Psychological Bulletin*, *117*, 387–403.

Volkan, V. D. (1981). *Linking objects and linking phenomena*. New York: International Universities Press.

Waters, E., & Cummings, M. (2000). A secure base from which to explore close relationships. *Child Development*, *71*(1), 164–172.

5

The Two-Track Model of Bereavement
The Double Helix of Research and Clinical Practice

SIMON SHIMSHON RUBIN, RUTH MALKINSON, and ELIEZER WITZTUM

The most striking thing about Anna in light of the loss of her father is a kind of sadness that fills, delicately, generally invisible, her entire life—what has happened and what will happen, a kind of inner sadness that accompanies her like a shadow.

Self-report of Anna, bereaved of her father in early childhood

Life has lost its meaning. I can't stop thinking of him. I wake up in the morning and go to bed thinking about him and the life that was lost. I lost interest in life and nothing will replace it—not even my grandchildren. Most of the days I prefer to stay in bed and think about my beloved son.

Self-report of Miriam, bereaved of her son 4 years earlier

To be useful for the clinician, a model of bereavement has to address important aspects of the loss experience in such a way that conceptual, assessment, and intervention goals are served. In the present article, we use the Two-Track Model of Bereavement and its derivative, the Two-Track Bereavement Questionnaire (TTBQ), to link research and clinical practice for the clinician. To do this, we shall continue with the initial narrative material, describe the Two-Track

Model of Bereavement succinctly, and link it to the questionnaire. We then return to clinical considerations.

In the first quote, Anna shares with us that her experience of the loss of her father has left her with a sense of "inner sadness" that permeates her entire life. If her subjective experience of her sadness were reflected on objective measures as well, we would be encountering someone whose experience of bereavement had affected her way of being in the world. Indeed, the very organization of her being is described as organized around and reflecting her bereavement. Anna is one of a group of young women who lost their fathers in early childhood and participated in research that allowed us to learn from their experiences (Lampert-Tsameret, 2008). In comparison to the nonbereaved women we studied, the bereaved women function more poorly in many areas of life. When the loss occurred before the age of 3, as in Anna's case, the daughters' psychological experience of their relationships to their fathers was limited.

If Anna were to seek treatment, the clinician focused narrowly on how well she manages to function might consider any number of potential therapies that single out sadness and depression. Of course, a broader examination of her overall functioning would be in order before deciding on what assistance, if any, Anna might need. At the same time, we should ask if there are additional things we might wish to know about Anna's father and the way he is perceived and experienced by her. For example, how was and is he present in, and absent from, her life? From the minimal material included here, of course, we can know only very little. We believe that obtaining additional material about the nature of the relationship is important when seeking to determine the impact of bereavement and intervention possibilities for a client like Anna.

Our research has shown consistently that women who experience paternal loss early in life have significant difficulty in constructing and connecting to a robust sense of their deceased fathers. This was further exacerbated when the story of the deceased father and his significance was not a presence in the home (Lampert-Tsameret, 2008). A similar sense of fragility in the relationship to one's deceased parent was also noted among bereaved daughters when a mother died in childhood (Gaitini, 2009). Minimization of the significance and story of a deceased parent worked against the daughter's experience of that parent as supportive and interfered with the ability to feel the parent as a strong and available psychological resource.

In the second quote, Miriam tells us that the loss of her son has shattered her life. Here, too, we learn that the loss has affected the respondent's entire life. Changed are the ways she views herself and the world around her. There are serious deficiencies in her biopsychosocial functioning. Following the loss, her life seems to be "colored" by the death of the son; all her thoughts revolve around him, and she has lost interest in other family members and in most other sectors of life. If Miriam were to seek treatment, the clinical assessment would have to be broadened to consider what might serve best as the focus of the initial phase of treatment. Should one focus on the deficiencies of her functioning or on intervening with her preoccupation with her deceased son? Research on bereaved parents suggests that heightened involvement with the deceased child continuing for many years is common to many of them (Rubin, 1981, 1993; Rubin & Malkinson, 2001). Does Miriam's involvement with her deceased child fall into that category, or is it in and of itself too pronounced? Can we assess the levels of continuing involvement and the content as adaptive or maladaptive? What else might we wish to know when considering a treatment plan, and what might be the treatment goal? Let us turn to the bereavement model we use to assist us in our deliberations before considering this further.

THE TWO-TRACK MODEL OF BEREAVEMENT: A MODEL FOR RESEARCH AND PRACTICE

The Two-Track Model of Bereavement creates a scaffolding to address response to interpersonal loss from a bifocal perspective (Rubin, 1981, 1992, 1999). The adequacy of a bereaved individual's functioning following loss is of critical interest to the bereaved, to those who live with them, and to those who treat them. The bereavement experience influences the biological, behavioral, cognitive, emotional, intrapersonal, and interpersonal ways of one's being in the world (Bowlby, 1980; Malkinson, Rubin, & Witztum, 2000). The exploration of negative—as well as positive— changes is important here. This is the first domain or track of the model and is similar to the evaluation of all persons facing challenges to their previous mode of living in the world.

At the same time, the model builds on the core understanding that reworking the relationship to the deceased and coming to grips with grief and mourning are equally critical features in understanding bereavement (Bowlby, 1980). In accord with revisions and modifications of the psychodynamic and interpersonal approaches to loss, the second domain within the two-track framework considers the bereaved's relationship to the deceased. Here the current status of a bereavement experience is addressed through the prism of the nature of the current bond to the deceased alongside changes in the preloss tie to him or her (Rubin, 1984).

Researchers and clinicians primarily focused on the biopsychosocial responses to loss approach have often been relatively unconcerned with the significance of the character and texture of the ongoing bond to the deceased. Narrowly focusing on the extent of behavioral difficulties and symptoms of various types is valuable but limited. Similarly, by considering powerful albeit limited features of the relationship to the deceased, we are left with an understanding of how the bereaved respond, but not to whom or to what relationship they are referring (Rubin, Malkinson, & Witztum, 2003). The degree of yearning and lack of acceptance of the loss can be signs of difficulties in the extent of the mourning process, but many other aspects of the relationship to the deceased will remain insufficiently charted if we do not seek to learn more.

The importance of combining the two perspectives of functioning and relationship in broad ways formed the basis for the Two-Track Model of Bereavement (Rubin, 1981, 1984, 1992, 1999). In this model, the process of adaptation to interpersonal loss is understood as linked to the disruption of homeostatic functioning and as relating and reconfiguring aspects of the relationship to the deceased. The Two-Track Model of Bereavement advocates for the assessment of both functioning

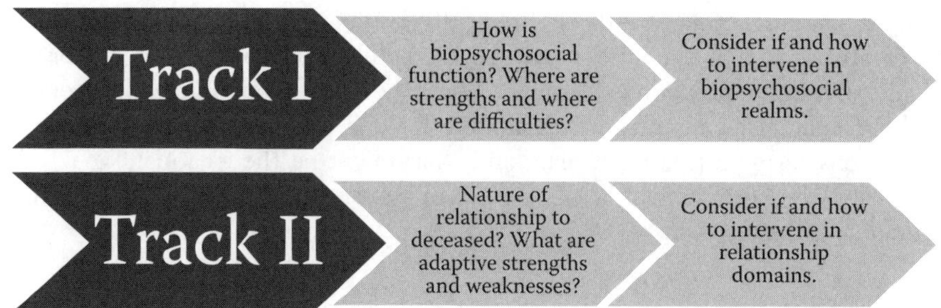

Figure 5.1 Tracking the response to loss and bereavement.

and the nature of the continuing attachment to the deceased when significant others die—and this is across the entire course of the bereaved person's lifetime. The clinical implications of the model derive directly from its binocular focus. The extent to which potential psychological interventions should privilege one or both domains of the response to loss remains an important clinical question. A visual aid to the basic assessment schema of the Two-Track Model of Bereavement is presented in Figure 5.1. A more complete description is available elsewhere (Rubin, 1999; Rubin, Malkinson, & Witztum, in press).

One of the more important questions to ask in work with this model of bereavement is the degree to which it accurately reflects clinical reality in a way that may be useful for conceptualizing and intervening with the bereaved. Although all models serve to organize a reality that is typically more complicated than the model itself, we believe that the two-track model captures distinct aspects of the response to loss that have utility. Clinical practice as well as research with the two-track bereavement model and the TTBQ may shed additional light on this point (Rubin et al., 2009). Clinical work often brings us in contact with persons for whom the focus of intervention is on regaining balanced biopsychosocial functioning. Treatment is geared to allow them to rejoin life and to renegotiate their ongoing relationship to the deceased. At the same time that the therapy may be focused on function, the process of rebalancing and reworking the relationship to the deceased may proceed outside the focus of the treatment meetings. At other times, the specific bereavement focus of therapy is on the relationship to the deceased. That focus may be what assists the bereaved to reorient to the deceased with potential implications for the biopsychosocial realm (and even without a specific focus on them). And, of course, the more balanced clinical intervention is one in which a mixture of focusing on both the function of and relationship to the deceased is a focus of concern in treatment. In such interventions, the return to more adequate function, growth, and adaptation to loss over time is most likely to occur.

Over the years, clinical and research work on bereavement with the two-track model has shown it to be a useful framework (Malkinson, 2007; Malkinson et al., 2000). In addition to continuing assessment and research activity with a variety of measures assessing functioning and relationship, there was the need for an instrument that might better address the perspective and factors contained in the two-track model. A self-report questionnaire was constructed, piloted, and validated for use with bereaved populations in research and clinical contexts. The construction of the questionnaire was predicated on the assumption that it should be relevant to clinicians as well as researchers. As such, it had to include questions related to biopsychosocial functioning, to the nature of the relationship to the deceased in past and present, and to the experience of acute grief as well as more chronic grief and mourning. The complete questionnaire is available online at http://blue.hevra.haifa.ac.il/rubin/files/TTBQ_Rubin06.pdf. Getting from initial items to final product was a long process which proved to be valuable from the clinical and research points of view (Rubin et al., 2009). In the published validation of the questionnaire, we presented five factors that accounted for a great deal of the bereavement experience. Two of the factors were related to biopsychosocial functioning, and three to the relationship to the deceased.

In the research reported in the 2009 article, we shared data that allowed the reader to see how the effects of loss for a variety of bereavements were manifest on the measure years after the deaths. This was apparent both on the total score and on the five factors of the measure. Of particular interest is the way the scales reflected the model. Of the five factors derived from the measure, two were related to Track I and three were related to Track II. The nature of the relationship was captured in the first three factors. The most prominent of all the scales was termed Relational Active Grief (RAG). It reflected the degree to which the bereaved was preoccupied with the imagery of the deceased, and was actively involved in thinking about him or her. This scale reflected a combination of functional and relational behaviors intertwined with the relationship. These affects and cognitions are prominent early in the grief response, and may continue in varying degrees for years later. The other two relational scales were more specifically related to the nature of the relationship to the deceased and the way in which the bereaved has organized it over time. The degree to which the relationship was perceived as close and positive was the second factor (Close Positive Relationship, or CP), whereas the presence of conflict and disruption in the preloss relationship emerged as the third factor (Conflict, or CN).

The significance of Track I, Biopsychosocial Functioning, was captured in the remaining two factors. The first of these factors captured the degree to which life functioning was impaired (Impaired Biopsychosocial Functioning, or F), whereas the second captured the bereaved person's ongoing perception of trauma in the loss at both cognitive and affective levels (Perception of Disruptive Trauma, or D). Figure 5.2 illustrates the five-factor structure as well as the relation to the two domains of the model.

Now let us consider in clinical terms the findings of the factor structure related to bereavement. Let us also consider Anna and Miriam on each of the factors. The first factor, RAG, is a feature of the bereavement response that is closely related to what is often meant by the term *acute grieving*. A representative item from the TTBQ that illustrates this is "I think of ______ all the time" (item II-6). The bereaved is very highly focused in thinking about the deceased, the imagery is strong, and there are strong feelings of missing and wanting to be with the deceased. At the same time, the details of the death event may be included. In some cases, there is a repetitive, sometimes ruminative experience, which mixes

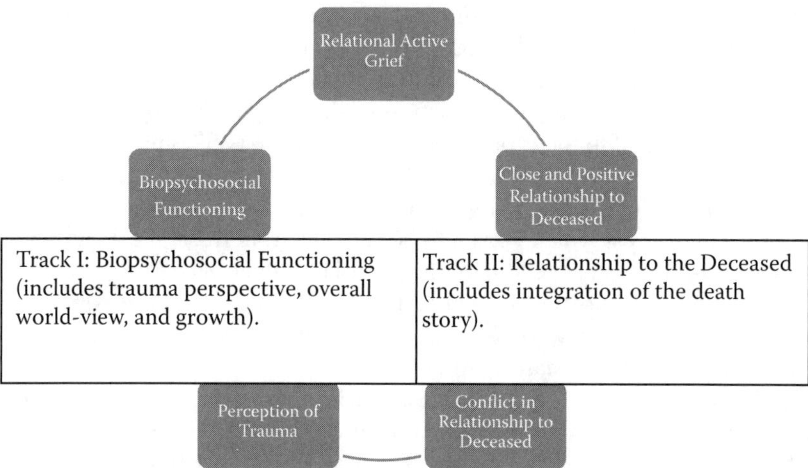

Figure 5.2 Five-factor structure of the Two-Track Bereavement Questionnaire.

the deceased and the death event. The higher the score on this item, the greater the degree of relational grief and often dysfunction.

Anna, bereaved of her father in early childhood, is likely to score very low on this scale. His death is shrouded in the past, and there is little likelihood that she would be preoccupied with the wish to be reunited with the father she barely knew. In contrast, Miriam's wish to be reunited with her son is acute, with a strong wish to be with him and recurrent and intruding thoughts of him. The continued high level of such preoccupation is a complication of bereavement, which is best understood in conjunction with the score on factor 4, Impaired Biopsychosocial Functioning.

The second factor, Close Positive Relationship to the deceased, is a factor that can be protective and a supportive source of solace for the bereaved. Yet it can serve to seduce or deflect the bereaved away from relationships with living others. An item illustrating this closeness is "My relationship with _______ was very close" (item III-1). Work with the bereaved consistently shows that it is important to supplement scores on self-report measures such as the TTBQ with examples that convey in narrative and vignette form the quality of the relationship as reflected in these stories. It is quite possible that two people may receive very similar scores on this factor on the basis of highly divergent experiences. In particular, those with response styles that maintain emotional distance between themselves and others tend to receive scores simliar to those who are intimate and close. Clinical inquiry and examples supplement the self-report and differentiate these two types of individuals (Main, Kaplan, & Cassidy, 1985).

In a similar fashion, bereaved children such as Anna may score high on this factor on the basis of their emotional and cognitive construction of the relationship as one of closeness (Gaitini, 2009; Lampert-Tsameret, 2008). The fact that much of the narrative and vignette data are often absent, however, gives such relationships an underlying dimension of fragility. Persons such as Miriam, on the other hand, are in a position to have rich and full narratives of the deceased. Not surprisingly, when they are stuck in the ruminative loop associated with Relational Active Grief, they are often unable to connect deeply with aspects of the relationship that can provide the accompaniment they are looking to regain.

The third factor, Conflict in the relationship, relays important information of the kind that is associated with ambivalence and conflict in the preloss relationship. An item illustrating this is as follows: "Our relationship was such that when I think about ______, I usually remember our disagreements" (item II-2). Scores on this factor are often associated with difficulties in grieving the death and coming to terms with the loss in salutary fashion. The fact that preloss conflict tended to differentiate itself as a separate factor dimension translates clinically into the awareness that although there may be positive features to the relationship, the attention to conflict as a separate dimension in and of itself is important. It is possible that Anna and Miriam would both score relatively low (below 2 on the 5-point scale) on this factor. Alternatively, the history of Miriam's interaction with her son would more likely yield a somewhat higher score than the history of someone like Anna. As before, the nature of the experienced, remembered, and internalized relationship differs greatly for persons bereaved very early in life as compared to parents grieving for children. In some cases, the nature of the death may also influence this score. Persons bereaved by suicide and cases where the deceased was negligent and involved in the death will often manifest heightened scores here.

By contrast to the relational factors, those associated with functioning are relatively straighforward. The higher the score, the more impaired the functioning. Determining exactly where the difficultes are is exceedingly important, however, as it is important to plan intervention with attention to what difficulties are present. Impaired Biopsychosocial Functioning reflects a range of difficulties in the somatic, emotional, intrapersonal, and interpersonal domains. Here, the self-report allows the bereaved to evaluate his or her ways of living in the world and to indicate which areas are problematic and which are not. A range of postloss growth and positive change items is often interspersed among the less salutary factors. Items in this factor span a broad range and include "My mood is very depressed" (item I-2) as well as "My values and beliefs are a significant source of support for me" (item I-18). It makes sense that the biopsychosocial factor is a quick overview of general functioning and allows the bereaved (as well as nonbereaved) individual who completes the scale to consider his or her state of functioning in the world.

Anna's sense of depression is bound up with her experience of father loss, and that item, as well as others, would allow us to compare her to what she would like to be, and allow us to conduct comparisons within groups of bereaved persons (such as those bereaved in early childhood) as well as between different groups (such as those bereaved in later childhood or adolescence). Miriam, on the other hand, would tend to score extremely high on disturbance of functioning. When this score is combined with an elevated RAG score at 4 years post loss, the picture of serious problems in working through her loss is glaringly clear.

The fifth factor, Perception of Disruptive Trauma, captures loss as a traumatic experience that continues to be shocking and disruptive at the present time. An elevated trauma and disruption score is not equivalent to posttraumatic stress disorder (PTSD), but it does convey the ongoing experience of shock and disruption that continues to operate as a core feature of the bereavement experience (Bar-Yoseph & Witztum, 1992). This can be seen clearly in the following item from the scale: "I keep on experiencing the loss as a shocking and traumatic event in my life" (item IV-7).

In the case of Anna, who has not known being with her father as a more organized experience of her mental and emotional life, his loss is a constant and is not separated sharply as an unexpected intrusion and shock to another way of being. Miriam, on the other hand, is devastated by her loss and has an experience of herself and her life as discontinuous—with the preloss and postloss worlds distinct, discrete, and disconnected. Part of an intervention plan with her would focus on softening and reconnecting these two aspects of her experience.

Finally, a number of general items included on the TTBQ were not associated with any of these five factors and yet are important for clinical usage and were very highly associated with the total TTBQ score. Among them are "Following the loss, it is fair to describe my current situation as in great need of help"; "Thinking of and remembering ______ significantly calms me"; "In facing life's difficulties, I usually trust only myself"; and more. Although responses endorsing these items at the higher levels are relatively rare, the information value for those individuals who endorse them is high. They provide information on changes of self-perception, coping styles, openness to outside help, and heightened self-reliance, which may interfere with help seeking. The total score of the TTBQ, incorporating 70 items, is a summary of the impact of bereavement. By asking clients to complete such measures during the course of our clinical work with them, we can (a) evaluate the relative and absolute state of their bereavement using their earlier self-report as a baseline, and (b) compare their responses to those of other bereaved individuals at different time points following loss. It allows us to measure the impact of time as well as other factors (including our interventions) as we seek to facilitate change, healing, and growth among the bereaved.

CONCLUDING REMARKS

The richness of clinical work provides a very human experience for working with the bereaved. Scores on bereavement measures, although informative, rarely serve to touch us in quite the same way. We are moved by human contact in ways that overshadow objective measurements of bereavement. Human stories of loss involve the bereaved, and how they were affected by the loss. Equally important are the stories of the loss and death event, which are often intertwined in the experience of loss with both the impact on functioning and the experience of the relationship to the deceased (Witztum, Malkinson, & Rubin, 2005). Sustained and careful attention to the twin domains of function and relationship captures much of the response to bereavement.

Our clients are always unique individuals. Using standardized measures that allow the bereaved to consider their current life experience, and that make room for the relationship with the deceased, provide both them and us with information that is highly relevant to our therapeutic alliance. At the same time, we recognize that standardized measures are not a substitute for the direct and powerful human connection to our clients and their unique lives. Combining the standardized format with the uniqueness of direct communication is more powerful than either approach can be on its own. The individual items on the TTBQ, the factor scores, and the total score provide additional ways of tracking the process and content of the bereavement experience over time for both therapy and research contexts.

Impaired functioning and the pain of loss motivate people to seek assistance from both professional and nonprofessional sources of support. The pain of grief and the wish to be reunited with the loved one can torment the bereaved. How these actually impact the stance of the bereaved vis-à-vis their inner and outer lives deserves careful consideration. Impairment of functioning as well as evidence of positive changes and growth following loss are addressed in the first domain of the Two-Track Model of Bereavement. The nature of the relationship to the deceased is addressed in the second domain. Research has been important in demonstrating the ongoing nature of the relationship to the deceased as a normative phenomenon. The specific construction of the ongoing relationship, however, must be understood to determine its salutary and problematic influence on the bereaved. Ongoing research with the bereaved can go much further in specifying those characteristics of bereavements and of the bereaved that facilitate and exacerbate the response to loss (Malkinson et al., 2000). Clinically using the perspective of the Two-Track Model of Bereavement allows us to focus carefully on the nature of grief and mourning. The model's consideration of behavioral outcome as well as the ongoing relationship to the deceased furthers our understanding of these domains and their interrelationship. Working clinically with this double perspective, this double helix is relevant for tailoring the goals and methods of intervention to help the bereaved live life with greater freedom and choice (Rubin et al., in press).

REFERENCES

Bar-Yoseph, T. L., & Witztum, E. (1992). Using strategic psychotherapy: A case study of chronic PTSD after a terrorist attack. *Journal of Contemporary Psychotherapy*, *22*(4), 263–276.

Bowlby, J. (1980). *Attachment and loss: Vol. 3. Loss*. New York: Basic Books.

Gaitini, M. (2009). *The dead mother: On the impact of different types of death and deadness upon the life course of adult women* (PhD dissertation). University of Haifa, Haifa, Israel.

Lampert-Tsameret, M. (2008). *"Visible" and "non-visible loss": The experience of loss in the lives of women who have lost their fathers in early childhood* (PhD dissertation). University of Haifa, Haifa, Israel.

Main, M., Kaplan, N., & Cassidy, J. (1985). Security in infancy, childhood, and adulthood: A move to the level of representation. *Monographs of the Society for Research in Child Development*, *50*(1–2), 66–104.

Malkinson, R. (2007). *Cognitive grief therapy*. New York: Norton.

Malkinson, R., Rubin, S., & Witztum, E. (Eds.). (2000). *Traumatic and non-traumatic loss and bereavement: clinical theory and practice*. Madison, CT: Psychosocial Press.

Rubin, S. (1981). A Two-Track Model of Bereavement: Theory and research. *American Journal of Orthopsychiatry*, *51*(1), 101–109.

Rubin, S. (1984). Mourning distinct from melancholia: The resolution of bereavement. *British Journal of Medical Psychology*, *57*, 339–345.

Rubin, S. (1992). Adult child loss and the Two-Track Model of Bereavement. *Omega*, *24*(3), 183–202.

Rubin, S. (1993). The death of a child is forever: The life course impact of child loss. In M. S. Stroebe, W. Stroebe, and R. O. Hansson (Eds.), *Handbook of bereavement: Theory, research and intervention* (pp. 285–299). Cambridge: Cambridge University Press.

Rubin, S. (1999). The Two-Track Model of Bereavement: Overview, retrospect and prospect. *Death Studies*, *23*(8), 681–714.

Rubin, S., & Malkinson, R. (2001). Parental response to child loss across the life-cycle: Clinical and research perspectives. In M. Stroebe, R. Hansson, W. Stroebe, & H. Schut (Eds), *Handbook of bereavement research: Consequences, coping and care* (pp. 219–240). Washington, DC: American Psychological Association Press.

Rubin, S., Malkinson, R., & Witztum, E. (2003). Trauma and bereavement: Conceptual and clinical issues revolving around relationships. *Death Studies*, *27*, 667–690.

Rubin, S., Malkinson, R., & Witztum, E. (2008). Clinical aspects of a DSM Complicated Grief Diagnosis: Challenges, dilemmas, and opportunities. In M. S. Stroebe, R. O. Hansson, H. Schut, & W. Stroebe (Eds.), *Handbook of bereavement research and practice: Advances in theory and intervention* (pp. 187–206). Washington, DC: American Psychological Association Press.

Rubin, S., Malkinson, R., & Witztum, E. (In press). *A clinician's guide to working with loss and bereavement*. New York: Routledge.

Rubin, S., Bar Nadav, O., Malkinson, R., Koren, D., Gofer-Shnarch, M., & Michaeli, E. (2009). The Two-Track Model of Bereavement Questionnaire (TTBQ): Development and findings of a relational measure. *Death Studies*, *33*, 1–29.

Witztum, E., Malkinson, R., & Rubin, S. (2005). Traumatic grief and bereavement resulting from terrorism: Israeli and American perspectives. In S. C. Heilman (Ed.), *Death, bereavement, and mourning*. New York: Transaction.

6

A Task-Based Approach for Counseling the Bereaved

J. WILLIAM WORDEN and HOWARD R. WINOKUER

I (JWW) once attended a seminar for hospice and health care professionals advertised as "new models" for understanding grief. The presenter, not knowing I was in the audience, defined the tasks of mourning as a stage theory and quickly dismissed this as an outdated and unhelpful way to think about the process of mourning. At best, this shows a lack of understanding; and at worst, ignorance.

The concept of "tasks" comes from developmental psychology and was originally defined by Robert Havinghurst at the University of Chicago (1953). Developmental tasks are important in child development as the child is required to accomplish various emotional, social, physical, and mental tasks as he or she adapts to the challenges of life. If these tasks are not mastered at lower levels of development, they can influence the mastery of similar tasks at a higher level. Borrowing from Havinghurst, I used the notion of tasks to address how people adapt to the loss of a loved one to death, one of life's major challenges. Some make a better adaptation to loss, and some adapt less well.

A colleague of mine tried to dismiss the task notion as invalid by looking up the definition of *tasks* in an unabridged dictionary and using those definitions to show that they were irrelevant to the mourning situation. By doing this, he failed to understand how tasks of mourning relate specifically to human growth and development. Human attachment is a basic developmental issue, and how one handles separation from attachment figures both before and after death can be important to growth or pathology.

I developed this task model in the early 1980s as a way to understand what grieving people were going through, as a way to conceptualize the process, and as a rationale for any interventions that might be needed. I have tweaked the definition of these tasks over the past 30 years in the various editions of *Grief Counseling and Grief Therapy* (e.g., Worden, 2009) and believe that they are still as valid and useful as when I first wrote about them. The problem with both stage theories and phase theories is their relative rigidity and the assumption of a sequential time trajectory. Task theory presents a much more fluid understanding of the mourning process. Tasks can be addressed with no special ordering, and they can be revisited and reworked over time. For most mourners, the various tasks present no special challenge. For others, some of these tasks present more of a challenge, may require more time to accomplish, and sometimes may require intervention in order to help mourners where they may be stuck.

It is important to note that the *tasks of mourning* are influenced by the various *mediators of mourning*, including who died, the nature of the attachment, the type of death, the way the loss impacts the person's sense of self, previous experiences with loss, how well these losses were handled, levels of social support, and secondary losses caused by the death, to name but a few. The counselor can*not* help people with the tasks of mourning without a thorough understanding of these multiple mediators of the process. For a current discussion of these mediators, see Worden (2009).

I have defined four tasks of mourning that I believe apply to all losses of an important person in one's life. They are as follows.

TASK 1: TO ACKNOWLEDGE THE REALITY OF THE LOSS

You need first to believe that the death happened before you can deal with the emotional impact of the loss. Seeing the body at the funeral makes it difficult to believe that the person is still alive. However, believing is more subtle than just a mental assent. Weisman (1972) spoke of "middle knowledge," defined as both believing and not believing (denial) at the same time. You can know on one level that a person is dead but still want to phone her, keep her room or closet intact, hear her driving into the driveway, reach on the other side of the bed to see if she is there, and the like. The searching behavior about which both Bowlby (1980) and Parkes (1972) wrote is a quest to be sure that the loss has or hasn't happened. Wanting to believe that the death has not happened is common and may cause some mourners to disbelieve for a long period of time until they can finally acknowledge the reality of the loss both mentally and emotionally (see Chapter 12). It is important to have both a cognitive and emotional acceptance of the death. Both of these are necessary to begin the mourning process. You must first believe that the death occurred before you can deal with emotional reality. The following two case studies will provide an understanding of the importance of helping the client actualize the death of his or her loved one.

Case Study 1: A Bereaved Mother

A 45-year-old woman came in for counseling 2 years after her daughter had disappeared. Her daughter, a senior in high school, had apparently driven with two male friends from her hometown to a beach in South Carolina. Upon completing the intake assessment, it appeared clear that the client had never acknowledged the reality of her daughter's death, even though the story had been reported in the local newspaper.

The story that appeared in the paper was as follows: On a Friday afternoon in May, three teenagers from her hometown, two boys and one girl, had been driving to the beach when they ran into an oil tanker. The tanker exploded, and the car caught fire. All of the bodies were burnt beyond recognition, although they were able to be positively identified based on medical evidence. The mother had chosen to believe that her daughter would never have left school with her friends to go to the beach. Therefore, the mother chose not to believe that her daughter was dead. She did not go to the funeral, and she continued to believe that her daughter would somehow return home and explain why she had been missing for so long.

This case was very difficult because the mother was adamant that this could not have been her daughter. However, as 4 years passed and the daughter hadn't returned, the mother reluctantly began to acknowledge that her daughter may be dead. She began to allow for the reality of her daughter's death and accept it emotionally. As therapy continued, the mother kept saying, "There has to be a way that I can know." At this point in treatment, the client was asked if she was willing to review the coroner's report. Some time passed before she agreed to read the report. After reading that the coroner was able to make a positive identification of her daughter using dental records, the client put her face on her knees, started rocking and crying, and acknowledged that her daughter was dead. This acknowledgment was the first step in this client's adapting to the death. Today, the client is living a meaningful life working as a volunteer in the court system as a child advocate.

Case Study 2: A Grieving Sister

A 37-year-old woman came for counseling after the murder of her sister. Because of the type of death, it was not difficult to understand cognitively that her sister was dead, especially given the high level of media coverage surrounding the death. But understanding the death on a cognitive level alone was not enough to help the client with her grief—she had to understand the death emotionally as well.

The day before the funeral was to be held, I (HW) was asked by the client to accompany her to the funeral home to determine whether or not it was appropriate for her to view the body of her sister. Prior to her going into the viewing room, the client asked if I would view the body and let her know what she might see and whether or not it was a good idea for her to see her sister. Understanding the value of her emotionally acknowledging the reality of the loss, it seemed like a reasonable task for her to undertake. After viewing the body, I explained to her that her sister looked peaceful, that she was under a white sheet, and that there were still very clear marks from the murder. I told the client that she could go into the room and see as little or as much of her sister's body as she chose. In the viewing room, she began by walking around the covered body. Her next action was quite interesting. She walked to the right side of the body and lifted the sheet, exposing the right hand of her sister. As she looked at the hand and held it, she said, "This is the hand of my sister." She then started crying. For her, holding her sister's hand enabled her to acknowledge the reality of the loss and begin the process of emotionally accepting her death. Seeing and grasping the hand represented an important part of the connection between the two women and acted as a catalyst for the client to begin her grieving. As therapy continued, further questions arose for her about the details of the death. The client now wanted to see the police photos, but she was afraid of what she might see. Once again, she asked me to preview the photos at the police station prior to her viewing them. Each photo was put in a manila envelope and arranged from least traumatic to most traumatic. The client then could choose what level of photo she wanted to see. She ended up looking at two of the 20 photos, and that was all she needed to have her questions answered. It is always important for us, as mental health professionals, to let the client guide us to what they need as opposed to our telling them what they should do. Our role is to accompany them through their grieving.

TASK 2: TO PROCESS THE PAIN OF GRIEF

Some deaths portend more pain than others, depending on the various mediators of mourning. And people vary in their ability to process pain in a healthy manner. Processing the pain of grief can be difficult for some, and there are those who become stuck in sadness, in anger, in guilt, and in loneliness for long periods of time. Serious difficulty in processing pain may lead to displacement of the pain into some type of somatic symptom or reappearance of the pain years later as a type of delayed grief reaction. For example, a woman was pregnant at the time her young son was killed. She was advised to limit her grieving so as not to jeopardize the pregnancy. She grieved some but held most of the feelings for her dead son in check. Years later, when her living child had graduated from high school and left for college, this woman experienced the grief she had held in all those years for her dead child.

The recently heralded diagnostic category of prolonged grief disorder (see chapter 12) is partially defined as a disorder where the person is stuck with emotions related to the loss and cannot seem to move beyond them. This "stuckness" is due, in part, to the conflicted relationship the mourner had with the deceased as well as the person's attachment style laid down early in life. Both of these are important mediators affecting a healthy accomplishment of Task 2.

There are some who tout the notion that grievers who do not experience a lot of emotion after a death make healthier outcomes than those who express a lot of feeling. This is a rather naïve and simplistic notion. The pain of grief depends on multiple mediators that influence the amount and type of pain that the death causes. The loss of one's child is often reported as a more painful loss than the loss of a sibling, parent, or even spouse (Sanders, 1979). Also, people vary in their tolerance for pain and in ways that they will allow themselves to express that pain, especially publicly.

Most people do not like to feel pain, so they avoid it by denying the degree of importance that the deceased held for them. Or they self-medicate through drugs or other substances that can blunt the pain. Distracting activities can be another way to avoid the pain of loss. In a death-denying society, feeling pain after loss can be difficult for many (Despelder & Strickland, 2009).

Case Study 3: A Worried Mother

A 46-year-old woman came in for counseling. Her presenting problem was her concern for her 13-year-old daughter. The client had just turned 46, the age at which her mother had died when she herself was age 13. Her fear was how her death might impact her daughter. This fear seemed to be unfounded as the client had recently had an annual physical and her doctor informed her that she was in excellent physical condition. The client was questioned as to what might be causing this overconcern. She was finally able to identify the root of her fear. Even though she was very close to her mother and missed her very much, she had never been able to grieve her mother's death. This prompted her to wonder what it might be like for her daughter if she herself died. The woman was not allowed to go to her mother's funeral, and after the burial, her father removed all memorabilia related to her mother. He also told her and her siblings that Mother had gone to be with God and that they were never to mention Mother's name again. Six months later, the father remarried. The client was never encouraged to feel or express her pain. The client reported a history of physiological problems that had gone undiagnosed. However, in therapy she was able to verbalize about her mother's death, and to allow herself to begin a healthy expressing of her feelings. She was able to express the sadness she had held for years, to verbalize the guilt she felt for not being at the funeral to say goodbye, and to feel the anger she had held toward her father for not allowing her to grieve. After therapy, the client was able to have a very meaningful relationship with her daughter without the anxiety or impediments of unresolved grief.

Case Study 4: A Conflicted Believer

A 47-year-old woman was referred for counseling by her gastroenterologist. The patient had been seeing this doctor for severe stomach-related problems. When a colonoscopy found no definitive causes for her stomach problems, the doctor did a preliminary psychological assessment. During that assessment, the doctor discovered that this patient had experienced the death of her 9-year-old daughter 4 years earlier.

During the initial interview, the client reported that she had a strong religious faith. She believed that her daughter was in heaven with God, so therefore there was no reason to grieve. This belief system seemed contradictory to what she was feeling. Although she knew that her daughter was in heaven, she seemed to be suffering from cognitive dissonance because she was feeling pain but not given a outlet to experience it. It appeared that that the client disenfranchised her own grief (Doka, 2002). The client then began questioning the role her faith had played in her grieving. She didn't understand why her faith belief precluded her from feeling sadness and her pain. She was having difficulty coming to terms with why certain days and times of the year triggered these very intense grief reactions. Finally, through therapy, she was able to acknowledge that she was not dishonoring her faith by grieving and that grieving her daughter's death was both a normal and healthy thing to do. The client's gastrointestinal (GI) problems continued, even after she began allowing herself to feel her pain around her daughter's death. As our sessions continued, she was able to identify her longtime practice of somaticizing feelings. A major breakthrough came in understanding her GI problems when she shared with the therapist that both her parents had been killed a few years prior to her daughter's death. As might be expected, she was never allowed to grieve her parents' death because, since they were in heaven with God, there was nothing to be sad about. Although she made progress during her therapy, she still had farther to go. Helping a client break lifetime habits can be a very difficult process.

TASK 3: TO ADJUST TO A WORLD WITHOUT THE DECEASED

Some deaths portend more changes in the mourner's life, and some deaths require less adaptation. Widows whose husbands took care of more daily life activities represent a group where the adaptation to daily life demands can be challenging. The same holds true for a parent whose spouse dies, leaving him or her with younger children. The adjustments required by Task 3 are divided into three subtypes: (a) external adjustments, (b) internal adjustments, and (c) spiritual adjustments.

External adjustments are the most obvious challenges: How do you deal with being a single parent, how do you live in an empty house, and how do you drive a car or pay bills? The external adjustments are to those activities of daily living and/or family roles that have changed significantly after the death of the loved one. One reason that grief takes time is because it takes time to realize all that one has lost when one has lost a spouse—friend, confidant, bed warmer, bill payer, social director, and more. For many, awareness of these losses does not come up until 4 to 6 months after the death, a time when the social support that was there at the funeral has started to thin out.

Add to external adjustments those *internal adjustments*: "How has the death affected the way I feel about myself?" "Who am I without him or her?" "How am I different having loved him or her?" These internal adjustments include not only social self-definitions such as "I am a widow or widower," "I am a single parent," and "I am an orphan," but also important personality variables such as self-esteem and self-efficacy. How has the death affected grievers' ability to feel good about themselves, and how has the death affected the way that people believe they can or cannot affect what happens to them? Some losses portend many more internal adjustments of self-definition.

Spiritual adjustments involve the way the death has shaken the foundations of one's assumptive world, including one's belief in the predictability of the universe and God's place in the universe and in one's life. Violent deaths like suicide, homicide, and accidents are particular challenges to belief in these areas. A mother whose 5-year-old was shot and killed while playing in the yard when gang members were shooting at each other on the street still struggled to make meaning out of this loss years later. Neimeyer (2001), Nadeau (1998), and others have pointed out the importance in finding meaning after life's important losses, and this relates directly to Task 3 (see Chapter 2).

The understanding that adjustments take place on multiple levels is critical to the process of helping clients adapt. Having a paradigm to outline these various adjustments can help both the mourner and the counselor to understand the process.

Case Study 5: A Progressive Loss

In 1979, a young couple in their 30s came to an educational program that one of the authors organized entitled "Living Till We Die." They came because the husband had severe diabetes and knew that his death was imminent. He had experienced one partial leg amputation and knew that there might be more surgery as well as other difficult symptoms. The following year, the wife came to the conference without her husband because he was in the hospital. She came so she could inform the participants about what she was learning about dying, death, and bereavement. The husband eventually returned home from the hospital, but his medical condition became progressively worse. Over the next few months, his kidneys failed, his other leg was amputated up to his knee, and both knew it was time for them to call in hospice. A year later, he had died, and she returned to the conference as a widow and shortly thereafter came for counseling. She had earlier learned about the tasks of mourning. Because of the length of her husband's illness, she didn't have any problems acknowledging the reality of his loss or difficulty processing her feelings of grief. She did, however, have difficulty adjusting to life without her husband. She lived on a golf course and reported, "I hate to see couples walking on the course holding hands because I know that I will never do that again." As the mother of five children, who ranged in age from 8 to 15, she found many family events difficult. The children's birthdays were hard, and sleeping in the same bedroom where he had died was difficult, but what appeared most difficult for her was dealing with the Christmas holiday.

Christmas was a very important holiday to the family; and, as with most families, they had their own rituals and traditions that were longstanding and meaningful. They had a lovely dinner on Christmas Eve and opened presents on Christmas morning. However, the most important ritual for the family had been the father placing the star on top of the Christmas tree after the tree was decorated. Christmas the first year after his death was so painful for her and the family that they didn't celebrate it at all. Instead, they went away on a vacation to a place where they hoped to forget that it was Christmas. Through her counseling, she learned the importance of modifying the environment and creating new rituals. The first thing that she did was redecorate her bedroom by painting the room, replacing the carpet, and moving the position of the bed. Although this was a good start, she decided that staying in that bedroom was not the right thing for her, so she moved into another bedroom that wasn't full of all of those memories. Next she was ready to tackle adjustments related to Christmas. The following year, they changed the rituals. Instead of having a large Christmas Eve dinner and opening presents on Christmas Day, they reversed their practice. They opened presents on Christmas Eve and had a lovely family dinner on Christmas Day. To resolve the issue with the placement of the star on the Christmas tree, the family decided that the best solution was to have the eldest son, who was now 17 years old, put the star up upon the completion of the tree. Changing how they did things helped move the woman, and the children through their grief and into their healing. The need to adjust to an environment without the loved one is critical to the mourning process.

Case Study 6: A Compounded Loss

Mr. and Mrs. D. were the parents of an 18-year-old boy who died in a motorcycle accident in the spring before he was to graduate from high school. As one might imagine, the details of the death were horrific, and the couple struggled greatly with his death. They began therapy approximately one year later. They had hoped through time, reinforced by the feedback they received from some of their friends, that after a year things would be better. Unfortunately, that was not the case. The statement "Time heals all wounds" is a myth, and that's why a task model is useful to help mourners understand and work through their grief.

In discussing their son's death, they reported that they had closed off his room and left it exactly the same way that it was prior to his death. Nothing was moved, and nothing was changed. It was basically set up as a shrine to their son. The death was very difficult for both Mr. and Mrs. D., and the fact that each grieved differently caused many problems in the marriage. Unfortunately, 2 years after the son's death the couple divorced. Mr. D. quit therapy, but Mrs. D. continued. Mrs. D. seemed to be stuck in her grief, and she just didn't appear open or willing to adjust to the new environment without her son. Her husband moved out of the house, complicating her grief even more. She was not only grieving her son's death but also grieving the end of her 20-year marriage. Even though Mr. D. moved out, she decided to keep the entire house intact. Her son's room continued to be a shrine. About 3 years into therapy, it was suggested to Mrs. D. that she consider going into her son's room, going into the closet, and taking the clothes that had been hanging in the closet to the cleaners. The client was told that, as long as the things were going to be hanging in the closet, they might as well be clean. The following week, Mrs. D. came to session appearing agitated and distraught. When she was questioned about what seemed to be upsetting her, she reported, "Why are you asking me to take my son's clothes to the cleaners to have them cleaned? He's dead." As she said this, she started crying uncontrollably. This appeared to be the first time she really acknowledged his death in the fullest sense. She then said, "I guess I don't need to keep his things anymore." This awareness seemed to be the catalyst for her moving forward in her grief. She then began working on other mourning tasks. It's so important to understand that the tasks are not linear and that people go back and forth between them as they adapt to the loss. By having Mrs. D. take the clothes to the dry cleaners, she was finally able to allow herself to move forward in the grieving process. Over the course of the next months, Mrs. D. cleaned her son's room, gave away many of his possessions, moved the furniture around, and then painted the room. It was not much longer until she realized that she had nothing holding her to the house, so she fixed it up, put in on the market, and sold it. She became involved in the Compassionate Friends and, having completed her grief work, has become a wounded healer and has been a helper to other parents who have experienced the deaths of their children.

TASK 4: TO FIND AN ENDURING CONNECTION WITH THE DECEASED IN THE MIDST OF EMBARKING ON A NEW LIFE

As much as one may want to, one cannot keep a dead loved one in one's life in just the same way as when that person was alive. Some try to do this and stop moving forward with life at the time the loved one died. Close to the ranch where I grew up, there was a neighboring ranch, and in the corral was a very old and gray Shetland pony. I asked my mother about this, and she told me a high school classmate of hers was killed in an accident. He was the only child of these neighbors, whose life had stopped at the time they lost their son. Now as an elderly couple, they had never changed his room, the house, or their son's pony. Everything in the house was kept just as it was when he died.

On the other hand, it is important to find a way to keep the dead loved one in one's life and memorialize that person, but in a way that doesn't keep the mourner from moving on with his or her life. An earlier notion, posited by Freud (1917), was to break the emotional bonds to the deceased so that one could move forward with one's life and make new attachments. This was an especially difficult notion for bereaved parents. How does one break the attachment to the dead child, and what does it mean to invest this energy in a new relationship? We now know that continuing bonds (Klass, Silverman, & Nickman, 1996) can be important. People do stay connected to the deceased, but they need to do it in a way that will not keep them from embarking on a life without the deceased (see Chapter 4).

This fourth task of mourning will take time, and sometimes mourners will reach out for counseling to deal with it. The counselor's task then is to help mourners find an appropriate place for the dead in their emotional lives—a place that will enable them to go on living effectively in the world.

Introducing the concept of continuing bonds is important in our work with our grieving clients. For so long, people believed that the only way to move on in one's grief was to let go. There seemed to be no place where people could hold on to the essence of their loved ones. Interestingly, in the Jewish tradition, it is believed that each time a loved one's name is mentioned, that person stays alive in the hearts of those who loved him or her.

Case Study 7: A Reluctant Widow

Ms. M. came into counseling after her fiancé died of lung cancer. This death was particularly difficult for the client because she was hesitant to get married; and by the time she had agreed, her fiancé had already been diagnosed with an advanced stage of the cancer. He died 4 months from the time of diagnosis.

This client was referred for counseling by her gynecologist, who was concerned with the physical impact the grief was having on this patient. This was a woman who was very private, had never been in therapy, and didn't know how to openly share her feelings. As her therapy began, Ms. M. didn't seem to have any difficulty with the first task of mourning. Because she was with her fiancé when he died, she was able to acknowledge the reality of the loss. However, because she was such a private person, she wasn't able to verbalize her feelings; and, indeed, this client didn't have much of a vocabulary to express her feelings. One of her first assignments was to go on the Internet and google the term *feeling words*. This helped the client have a vocabulary to express her feelings about her fiancé's death. As the course of her therapy continued, the client was able to feel the pain and adjust to the environment without her fiancé.

She also struggled with the fourth task—to find an enduring connection with the deceased in the midst of embarking on a new life. She was most reluctant to invest in a new relationship. On some level, she believed that starting a new relationship was being disrespectful to her dead fiancé. This issue was discussed, and the client was asked whether or not she thought her fiancé would want her to grieve and be sad for the rest of her life. She was quite clear that he wouldn't want that for her. However, before the client would allow herself to move on, she had to create an enduring connection with her fiancé. As a way of doing this, she stayed in contact with his sister, and with her support, they established a small foundation in his name. Because an ongoing relationship with her fiancé had been established, she began figuring a safe way to begin reinvesting in a new relationship. After reviewing a number of options, she decided to try to meet someone in an online dating service. Although she is still single, Ms. M. has met a few new men who have made her life more fulfilling, has gone back to school and completed a professional degree, and is ready to start her new life.

Case Study 8: A Doctor Seeking to Heal Himself

Dr. L., a 76-year-old male physician, came to counseling because of the death of his wife of over 50 years. Dr. L. had struggled with the death because, as a physician, he felt strongly that he should have done a better job monitoring her illness and caring for her during her dying. She died after a long battle with breast cancer. Dr. L. was a very stoic man who had little use for feelings, let alone expressing them. After his wife's death, he found himself experiencing symptoms of depression. He was very uncomfortable with these feelings and had very little experience in knowing how to process them. He didn't have a vocabulary to do so, and his pain seemed to be deeply locked inside of him. It was clear that he didn't have any difficulty acknowledging the reality of his loss, but he had no tools to enable him to express those feelings, though he needed to do so to move through the grief process. He was encouraged to write a letter to his wife telling her about how he felt about her dying, how he felt about his inability to be there for her, and how he has been doing since her death. This was a way for Dr. L. to establish an ongoing connection with his wife that he so desperately needed to make. He brought in a four-page, heartfelt letter that provided him an opportunity to share with her the thoughts and feelings he had been holding onto since her death. Dr. L. surprised himself as he read the letter out loud and began to cry. This proved to be a very effective approach to help Dr. L. express his feelings. However, he still had a great deal of guilt about the fact that he wasn't available for Mrs. L. during her dying. He was then asked to write a second letter. This time the letter was addressed to him from his wife, and it was in response to the initial letter that he had written her. When he read the letter at his next session, this three-page letter once again brought tears to his eyes. In this letter, his wife forgave him for his behavior and thanked him for the wonderful years they had together. Over the course of the next two months, six more letters were written between him and his wife: three from him to her, and three from her to him. This release of feelings and emotions was cathartic for Dr. L. Having allowed himself to feel the pain, he was now able to put his wife in a place where he could begin reinvesting himself in living. Since then, he has started working as a volunteer physician in a local long-term facility. He has gained some weight, resolved the depression, and once again found meaning in his life. This is another example of how a counselor can help a client work through the tasks of mourning and have a meaningful life in spite of a painful loss.

There are a number of other ways to look at the mourning process besides a task model. Whatever model you select, apply it to your own experiences of loss and see how it helps you understand what you went through after the death of a loved one. We suggest that the task model is a robust way to inform your own personal loss experience as well as a way to help your clients understand their mourning experience.

REFERENCES

Bowlby, J. (1980). *Attachment and loss*. New York: Oxford.

DeSpelder, L. A., & Strickland, A. L. (2009). *The last dance: Encountering death and dying* (8th ed.). New York: McGraw-Hill.

Doka, K. J. (Ed.). (2002). *Disenfranchised grief: New directions, challenges, and strategies for practice*. Champaign, IL: Research Press.

Freud, S. (1917). *Mourning & melancholia*. London: Hogarth.

Havinghurst, R. (1953). *Developmental tasks and education*. New York: Longman.

Klass, D., Silverman, P., & Nickman, S. (1996). *Continuing bonds*. Washington, DC: Taylor & Francis.

Nadeau, J. (1998). *Families make sense of death*. Thousand Oaks, CA: Sage.

Neimeyer, R. A. (Ed.). (2001). *Meaning reconstruction and the experience of loss*. Washington, DC: American Psychological Association.

Parkes, C. M. (1972). *Bereavement: Studies of grief in adult life*. London: Routledge.

Sanders, C. M. (1979). A comparison of adult bereavement in the death of a spouse, child and parent. *Omega, 10*, 303–322.

Weisman, A. D. (1972). *On dying and denying: A psychiatric study of terminality*. New York: Behavioral Publications.

Worden, J. W. (2009). *Grief counseling and grief therapy* (4th ed.). New York: Springer.

7

The Influence of Gender and Socialization on Grieving Styles

TERRY L. MARTIN and KENNETH J. DOKA

INTRODUCTION

The challenge of this book is, to say the least, daunting.[1] As authors of a chapter, we are asked to integrate our theories, research, and clinical practice in an accessible volume in order to promote a dialogue between researchers and clinicians. This is a challenge. For although our work on grieving styles heavily integrates research on gender, coping, and grief (see Doka & Martin, 2010), and has achieved a level of recognition within thanatology (Doughty, 2009; Humphrey, 2009; Machin, 2009), it has yet to generate a body of supportive evidence to validate and expand the concept.

Nonetheless, it is a challenge worth pursuing. In order to achieve it, we wish to begin to describe the underlying theoretical background of the concept of grieving styles. Following that, we will introduce a case that we believe illustrates the value of this approach. Finally, we will conclude with some implications of the conceptual model for clinical practice and research.

DEVELOPMENT OF THE CONCEPT OF GRIEVING STYLES

Corr, Nabe, and Corr (2009), in reviewing the relationship between gender and grief, noted three distinct perspectives that parallel our work. The first position, the *feminization of grief*, stressed that expressing emotion and seeking social support and help from others are critical in effectively coping with loss. A second perspective proposed that men had their own distinct patterns of grief. These patterns emphasized cognitive and active problem-solving approaches to grief. In this perspective, men might show more limited and muted emotional responses to loss such as anger or guilt. Men often valued self-reliance and solitude in coping with loss. In this perspective, men had a distinct experience of grief that was different but no less effective in coping with loss. Counseling interventions, then, should not challenge men's way of coping but rather find ways to deal with loss congruent with masculine inclinations. A third perspective placed less emphasis on gender as a critical determinant of how individuals grieve, affirming a number of influences that affected the grieving style of individuals, including culture, gender, socialization experiences, birth order, temperament, and other factors. The critical point is that gender influences but does not determine grieving styles. In this third model, there is a distinct move away from applying gender-based terminology to describe the different ways that individuals grieve.

When we began our work in this area, our focus was on men and grief. It quickly moved beyond that. At the first description of what we called *male grieving patterns*, a female colleague remarked that it had validated her own way of grieving—her pattern of adapting to loss. In fact, she had responded to her own early perinatal losses in two distinct ways. She began to do some of the basic work and research on how to best support survivors of perinatal loss. Then, once that research base was established, she became a pioneering advocate who both challenged and changed the ways hospitals dealt with such losses. Her comments were taken seriously, changing the terminology for this chapter to *masculine grief* (see Martin & Doka, 1996).

There was much to recommend the use of the term *masculine grief.* First, it allowed us to build a clear bridge to Jung on ideas of *animus–anima* (1920). Like Jung, we saw masculinity–femininity as a continuum that exists within a person as well as between individuals. Even our concept of grieving patterns is that they fall along a continuum. The use of these terms draws from that theoretical base. Second, we believe that this pattern of adapting to loss is related to gender, at least in North America and many Western cultures, even if it is not determined by it. The use of the term *masculine*, then, reaffirms that gender relationship. Third, we wished to directly challenge the notion that many men are ineffectual grievers. We asserted that "masculine" patterns of coping with grief are different but not less effective than more "conventional" or "feminine" ways of dealing with loss. Thus, there is a practical rationale for the use of the term. Because most popular literature does offer a view of the male as an ineffectual griever, we believed that only by using a gender-related term might our work be available to clinicians interested in or dealing with male or masculine grievers.

However, we ultimately decided to eschew gender-related terms for a variety of reasons. First, they caused confusion. Although we identified a pattern of grief that we believe many males use, we also sought to recognize and to validate female grievers who exhibit such a pattern. But for many, the term *masculine grief* had unfortunate baggage. This was most poignantly illustrated by a conversation with such a griever after a presentation. This woman was a pioneering female rabbi, one of the first to be so recognized. "All my life," she said, "I have tried to be perceived as not just one of the guys. You described my grieving pattern. Please, use a language to describe it that does not make me 'one of the guys' again."

It was confusing for other reasons as well. The distinction between *masculine* and *male* was often lost on readers, who kept identifying one with another.

Moreover, the use of gender-related terms created discomfort. To assert that "masculine" modes of coping with loss are cognitive and active seems to perpetuate stereotypes, only partly true, that view such responses as typical of male response to loss, and it implies that "feminine" responses to loss are more emotive.

In addition, the use of gender-related terms creates its own difficulties. If one end of the continuum is labeled *masculine*, what is the other end, the alternate pattern, called? The use of the term *feminine* has merit because it seems like the logical complement and is faithful to the theoretical base. On the other hand, the term *conventional* has merit because it reflects current conventions on grief that have tended to view seeking support and emotional responses as both desirable and normative. In addition, it avoids the further stereotyping of emotional responses as feminine. But the use of the term *conventional* also runs the risk of appearing to place negative value on the term *feminine*. In short, either term has merits and complementary disadvantages.

And that raised clinical concerns. Some men who do seek support and are comfortable with emotive responses may feel threatened to hear their mode of response described as *feminine*. And women who tend toward solitary, active, and cognitive responses may resent the label of *masculine*. In the end, use of the terms *instrumental* and *intuitive* seemed to carry far less baggage.

GRIEVING STYLES

In our model, we proposed that grieving styles range on a continuum from *intuitive* to *instrumental*. Central to this concept is that the differences in these styles are in the ways an individual *experiences* grief as well as the way grief is *expressed*. Naturally, these styles affect the ways an individual *adapts* to his or her loss.

The modalities of internal experience that are most useful in discriminating between the patterns are the cognitive and the affective. The intuitive griever converts more of his or her energy into the affective domain and invests less into the cognitive. For the intuitive griever, grief consists primarily of profoundly painful feelings. These grievers tend to spontaneously express their painful feelings through crying and want to share their inner experiences with others.

The instrumental griever, on the other hand, converts most of the instinctual energy generated by bereavement into the cognitive domain rather than the affective. Painful feelings are tempered; for the instrumental griever, grief is more of an intellectual experience. Consequently, instrumental grievers may channel energy into activity. They may also prefer to discuss problems rather than feelings.

Thus, it is the relative degree to which the griever's thoughts and feelings are affected that accounts for the differences between the patterns. However, what a griever is experiencing can never be directly observed; it only can be inferred by observing how the individual expresses his or her experience. In particular, the griever's desire for social support, the need to discuss his or her feelings, and the intensity and scope of his or her activities are varying ways of expressing grief and are often important in distinguishing between patterns. These expressions of grief usually (but not always) reflect choices, both past and present, that the griever has made or is making to adapt to the losses. These choices are the griever's adaptive strategies.

Intuitive and instrumental grievers usually choose different primary adaptive strategies. *Primary adaptive strategies* are the principal ways grievers express their grief and assimilate and adapt to their losses over long periods. These strategies tend to differ according to the pattern of grief. Grievers use additional or secondary adaptive strategies at various times and under specific circumstances. Secondary adaptive strategies are those strategies that grievers employ to facilitate the expression of the subordinate modalities of experience. For example, intuitive grievers choose additional strategies that aid them in accomplishing tasks requiring planning, organization, and activity—all expressions more common to their instrumental counterpart. Conversely, instrumental grievers need to find ways to express their feelings about their losses, and whereas intuitive grievers are quite familiar with strong feelings, instrumental grievers are less so. These secondary adaptive strategies are not as familiar or accessible as primary adaptive strategies, nor are they as critical to the individual's overall adjustment to the loss.

It also is clear that some individuals have a more *blended* style. Here the secondary adaptive strategies are strong as well. Blended grievers are able to utilize a number of strategies that encompass both the cognitive and affective.

There is one additional grieving style. Some grievers have a *dissonant* style—that is, there is dissonance between their experience and expression of grief. The choice of this term is consistent with the theorizing of Festinger (1957), who defined one's awareness of a contradiction among two or more elements of the mind and the resulting discomfort as "cognitive dissonance." In most cases, individuals are motivated to behave and think in ways that reduce dissonance. This is why most grievers experience disharmony at one time or another in their grieving, yet eventually achieve resolution through expressing their experiences of grief. Unfortunately, for some, this lack of harmony between an inner state and an outer expression persists, resulting in dissonance. These grievers are not only expressing grief differently than it is experienced; they are truly at war with themselves.

Although any significant disparity involving expressing grief in ways that are incongruent to the experience can be dissonant, the most common pattern is where an intuitive griever feels compelled to suppress the affective experience of grief. For example, male intuitive grievers are often at odds with societal norms for gender-stereotyped behaviors. For the male intuitive griever whose identity is determined solely by societal stereotypes, intense feelings of grief are more than a mere inconvenience; they represent a threat to the self. For these grievers, their need to express their feelings and share them with others is overshadowed by a rigid definition of manliness.

Because these styles exist on a continuum, they may be perceived in a number of ways. One is as a normal curve. An alternate visualization might be more a Venn diagram with two overlapping circles. The Oregon Center for Applied Science offers a nonvisual way to characterize the differences. They describe instrumental grievers as *head grievers* and intuitive grievers as *heart grievers*. Blended grievers are depicted as *head and heart*, whereas dissonant grievers are portrayed as *head versus heart*.

Only subsequent research will indicate what model best represents the distribution of grieving styles within a population. At present, despite the fact that clinicians see these styles reflected in their clients (see Doughty, 2009), there is little research that really shows how prevalent the styles are within grieving populations. In addition, it would be useful for researchers to identify the ways that gender, culture, and other variables influence this distribution.

USING THE MODEL: A CLINICAL CASE

Rob is a 63-year-old white male. He is married with two adult children. A computer engineer, he works for the government. Although he lives in New York, Rob has often traveled as part of his professional responsibilities.

Rob was excited at the prospect of flying to Texas—not for the impending business trip to Dallas, but because Kirsten, his only daughter, lived in the outskirts of the city. After a day of business, Rob rented a car and drove to her apartment.

The next day, father and daughter decided to indulge in Rob's passion and Kirsten's lukewarm interest in shooting. They went to an outdoor target range. Kirsten had her own 9-mm Ruger, and Rob was using Kirsten's roommate's (she was out of town) 40-caliber Glock. After a morning of knocking down a variety of targets, they went to lunch and then returned to the apartment. Rob asked Kirsten if she had a pistol-cleaning kit, and she said she did. She also confessed that she had never before cleaned her pistol. Rob's suspicions were confirmed when he examined a gun that had not been cleaned since its purchase. He painstakingly demonstrated how to clean the weapon. He then turned to the roommate's gun—it, too, had never been cleaned. He suggested Kirsten practice what she had just seen demonstrated. He handed her the Glock, instructing her to gently pull back on the slide to a point where the two safety releases on each side of the frame could be engaged, thus freeing the barrel for inspection and cleaning. Kirsten pulled the slide too far, and the weapon was now cocked. She handed it to Rob. At this point, one of two fatal mistakes occurred: The first mistake had Rob and his daughter sitting across from each other at her kitchen table (rather than side by side). The second and deadly mistake was Rob's. He assumed that he had cleared the gun (i.e., ejected any remaining rounds from the chamber) at the range. After all, he had followed this procedure (along with removing the magazine) dozens of times during his previous 20-plus years of target practice.

Rob pulled the trigger to release the slide. The gun bucked in his hand, and Kirsten fell to the floor. There was no blood, but she told her father that she was having difficulty breathing. Rob immediately called 911, and medics arrived within minutes. So did the police. As Kirsten was being transported to the nearest hospital, the police began questioning Rob. Although he understood the need for clarifying the event, he was desperate to get to the hospital to see his daughter. After 2 hours of questioning, he was released from police custody. When he arrived at the hospital, Kirsten was dead. Subsequently, Rob was not charged in Kirsten's death.

The police determined that the shooting was accidental and was caused by a "squib load," a firearms malfunction in which a fired projectile does not have enough force behind it to exit the barrel or, if it has just sufficient force, it will discharge but weakly. In this case, the round struck Kirsten in the side, ricocheted off a door frame, and ended up 8 feet from where Rob and Kirsten had been seated.

In counseling, Rob quickly evidenced all of the major characteristics of an instrumental griever. His affect was present but muted. His focus was on solving problems created by Kirsten's death. Initially, he contacted friends and family (including his wife and only son) about Kirsten. He arranged for the funeral after the coroner's office released Kirsten's body. He organized transportation for everyone attending the funeral from a distance. And he began working on a memorial scholarship to be given in Kirsten's name.

Rob came to counseling after he and his wife had seen another therapist. That therapist believed that Rob's wife was either unable or unwilling to talk about her feelings regarding her daughter's death with Rob present. The therapist deduced (correctly) that Rob was an instrumental griever, and his wife an intuitive one. He suggested Rob find his own therapist.

In therapy, Rob revealed himself to value mastery over his feelings as well as his environment. An engineer by training, Rob responded well to challenges. His intellectual approach to problems served him well … until now. He admitted being overwhelmed by his inability to resolve his daughter's death. Because he had few outlets to express or to understand his grief reactions, he was advised to begin some bibliotherapy.

In addition, he was instructed to find some way to reduce his sense of guilt. For Rob, in particular, guilt became a major focus of therapy. Although feelings are often muted in instrumental grievers, these feelings still exist. In Rob's case, he found it difficult to access that guilt. Although many instrumental grievers experience guilt, often a byproduct of their desire to master their world, many instrumental grievers are able to acknowledge it as part of their experience of grief. As a computer engineer, Rob was attentive to mastering small details. In this case, his daughter died because he missed one and it was difficult to acknowledge that mistake.

Instrumental grievers often best adapt to feelings, not so much by expressing them, but by responding to them in active ways. For example, therapeutic rituals of reconciliation can be one useful way to expiate guilt (Doka & Martin, 2010). A related approach may be to find active ways to make amends. In Rob's case, this alternate approach was useful. The therapist introduced the concept of doing something to redress his error. Rob embraced the notion, likening it to "penance," a practice that was a part of his past parochial education. Eventually, he began his "penance" by earning an NRA certification in pistol instruction and by volunteering at a local pistol range and providing free instruction to new shooters. He even began speaking of his experience as a cautionary tale to local gun clubs. One of the strengths of an instrumental grieving style is a predilection to the cognitive, facilitating meaning making. In Rob's case, his actions allowed a sense of "benefit finding" (Stanton, Bower, & Lowe, 2006). Though he could not change the reality of his daughter's death, he thought that his presentation could prevent future fatalities. This allowed Rob to construct some sense of meaning out of his own tragedy.

Rob's case illustrates both the strengths and weaknesses of an instrumental pattern of grieving. His initial stoicism and intellectualization allowed him to respond immediately to issues arising from Kirsten's death. He also began the work of memorializing Kirsten and achieving some sense of control of his environment.

Unfortunately, his desire to master everything about the tragedy led him to experience a profound sense of guilt: After all, it was his lack of control over details that led directly to his daughter's death. He got bogged down in his mistakes and could not forgive himself for being what every living person is—a fallible human being.

Rob's case reflects as well on the role of the therapist. With instrumental grievers, it is important to minimize the inherent hierarchy of counseling (Kiselica & Englar-Carlson, 2008). In Rob's case, the therapist reframed his role as that of an "expert consultant"—a role that resonated with Rob both professionally and personally.

CONCLUSION: CLINICAL IMPLICATIONS

The model of adaptive grieving styles has gained currency for two major reasons. First, it correlates with the observed experiences of therapists (Doughty, 2009). Second, it challenges an unspoken premise that there is only one successful way to grieve. Staudacher (1991) expressed this succinctly:

> Simply put, there is only one way to grieve. That way is to go through the core of grief. Only by experiencing the necessary emotional effects of your loved one's death is it possible for you to eventually resolve the loss. (p. 3)

In fact, there is danger in identifying grief solely with any affective expression. As Sue and Sue (2008) indicated, this reflects the inherent Western bias in counseling that tends to value affective expressiveness as inherently more therapeutic than cognitive or behavioral responses. Western counseling is "swallowed by affect." In many ways, this model affirms the many ways that grief is experienced and expressed as well as the multiple strategies that individuals may use in adapting to loss.

This, in turn, reaffirms that the grief counselor should begin with a general assessment of an individual's grieving style. This may be done by reviewing the way clients historically cope with crises as well as by using a tool such as the Grief Pattern Inventory (Doka & Martin, 2010). This allows the counselor to then develop strategies to build on the bereaved individual's historic strengths. For example, in the case of Rob, the counselor effectively employed more active and cognitive approaches. This is in line with the recent conclusion to the debate on the effectiveness of grief counseling. Grief counseling can be effective *if* the right interventions are targeted to a given individual at an appropriate time. That debate reemphasized that selective interventions are far more beneficial than universally applied strategies (Gamino & Ritter, 2009).

Although affectively orientated approaches work well with intuitive grievers, they may not only invalidate and disenfranchise instrumental grievers, but also ignore the resilience of instrumental grievers. For example, Allen and Hayslip (2001) offered a model of experienced competence that fits instrumental grievers well. Their model emphasizes that a significant loss often can necessitate the reconstruction of one's assumptive world. In that task, cognitive and active approaches work well. Moreover, past history in solving problems offers confidence that one can overcome the current crisis.

CONCLUSION: A RESEARCH AGENDA

This model, although relatively new, builds on a significant body of research on grief reactions and coping styles. However, much of that research is based on gender. Although we affirm that gender influences grieving styles, we also attest that gender does not determine grieving styles. Rather we hold that gender, culture, temperament, as well as other variables influence grieving styles. For example, based on our clinical experiences, we speculate that women who are highly instrumental are likely to be older siblings with caregiving responsibilities for their younger brothers and sisters, or, in a smaller number of cases, parentified children in a dysfunctional family. All of these assumptions need to be researched.

Furthermore, we suggest research on the developmental implications of grieving styles. At what ages do grieving styles begin to solidify? Are there periods in the developmental process when styles are likely to be modified? Are grieving styles likely to remain stable throughout life? We have speculated, based on both our clinical observations and Jung's (1920) theoretical model, that grieving styles are likely to solidify in early adolescence and remain relatively stable throughout life, perhaps moving toward a more blended style in later life. Yet, without research, these remain speculations. We also wonder about the relationship of grieving styles to personality types or attachment styles. Such speculations merit further inquiry.

The clinical strategies that emerge from this model also need to be researched. For example, should clinicians build on the historic strengths and coping mechanisms of a client or introduce new adaptive approaches? Is there an inherent desirability for more blended approaches? Schut, Stroebe, van den Bout, and deKeijser (1997) found counterintuitively that men benefitted from a more affective counseling approach, whereas women gained from a more cognitive-based therapeutic modality. These authors' research was based on gender, so it is impossible to ascertain the original grieving styles of the participants. Given the fact that the sample volunteered for therapy, one can speculate that many of the participants may have had dissonant styles. We have continually argued for a strength-based approach, noting that crisis is a poor time to teach new skills. Far more research, based on grieving styles rather than gender, is necessary before a definitive conclusion is reached.

Finally, there should be research on the outcomes based on different grieving styles—studies that explore the social, psychological, and physiological implications of these adaptations. Are varied outcomes associated with different grieving styles? Are different styles likely to result in different problematic outcomes such as increased alcohol use or substance abuse?

We have often viewed our model as a theoretical bridge—linking the concept of grief to a larger body of conceptualization on gender, the psychology of men, coping styles, and emotion regulation. Yet this theoretical bridge needs to be buttressed by supportive research. Theory only becomes potent when it directs—and, in turn, is supported by—research.

NOTE

1. Some of the material used in this chapter has been published in the authors' previous work (Doka & Martin, 2010).

REFERENCES

Allen, S., & Hayslip, B., Jr. (2001). Research in gender differences in bereavement outcome: Presenting a model of experienced competence. In D. Lund (Ed.), *Men coping with grief* (pp. 97–115). Amityville, NY: Baywood.

Corr, C., Nabe, C., & Corr, D. (2009). *Death and dying: Life and living* (6th ed.). Pacific Grove, CA: Brooks/Cole.

Doka, K. J., & Martin, T. L. (2010). *Grieving beyond gender: Understanding the ways men and women mourn*. New York: Routledge.

Doughty, E. A. (2009). Investigating adaptive grieving styles: A Delphi study. *Death Studies*, *33*, 462–480.

Festinger, L. (1957). *A theory of cognitive dissonance*. Stanford, CA: Stanford University Press.

Gamino, L., & Ritter, R. H. (2009). *Ethical practice in grief counseling*. New York: Springer.

Humphrey, K. (2009). *Counseling strategies for loss and grief*. Alexandria, VA: American Counseling Association.

Jung, C. G. (1920). *Psychological types*. London: Routledge & Kegan Paul.

Kiselica, M., & Englar-Carlson, M. (2008). Establishing rapport with boys in individual counseling and psychotherapy. In M. Kiselica, M. Englar-Carlson, & A. Horne (Eds.), *Counseling trouble boys: A guidebook for professionals* (pp. 48–68). New York: Routledge.

Machin, L. (2009). Resilience and bereavement: Part I. In B. Monroe & D. Oliviere (Eds.), *Resilience in palliative care: Achievement in adversity* (pp. 157–166). Oxford: Oxford University Press.

Martin, T. L., & Doka, K. J. (1996). Masculine grief. In K. J. Doka (Ed.), *Living with grief after sudden loss* (pp. 161–172). Washington, DC: Hospice Foundation of America.

Schut, H., Stroebe, M., van der Bout, J., & deKeijser, J. (1997). Intervention for the bereaved: Gender differences in the efficacy of two counseling programs. *British Journal of Clinical Psychology*, *36*, 63–72.

Stanton, A. L., Bower, J. E., & Lowe, C. A. (2006). Post-traumatic growth after cancer. In L. Calhoun & R. Tedeschi (Eds.), *Handbook of post-traumatic growth: Research and practice* (pp. 138–175). Mahwah, NJ: Lawrence Erlbaum.

Staudacher, C. (1991). *Men and grief*. Oakland, CA: New Harbinger.

Sue, D. W., & Sue, D. (2008). *Counseling the culturally diverse: Theory and practice* (5th ed.). New York: Wiley.

Section *II*

Contexts of Grieving

8

Spousal Bereavement in Later Life

DEBORAH CARR and JOHN SHEP JEFFREYS

Spousal loss has been described as among the most stressful of all life events, especially for older adults (Holmes & Rahe, 1967). One of the most important research discoveries in recent decades, however, is the recognition that the death of a spouse is not universally distressing. Rather, older adults' psychological adjustment to widowhood varies widely based on characteristics of the marriage, the nature of the death, the co-occurrence of other stressful events and losses, and one's personal and social resources including social support, economic resources, personality, and prior mental health. Although an estimated 40–70% of bereaved spouses experience a period of 2 weeks or more marked by feelings of sadness immediately after the loss, a substantial proportion—anywhere from 30% to 60%—withstand spousal loss with relatively few distress symptoms (see Wolff & Wortman, 2006, for a comprehensive review). Given that clinical depression is the exception rather than the norm in the face of late-life spousal loss, practitioners and researchers are devoting their efforts to identifying risk and resilience factors among the recently bereaved, and developing targeted interventions that take into account the highly individualized nature of spousal bereavement.

In this chapter, we first summarize patterns of late-life spousal loss in the contemporary United States, and then discuss recent and cutting-edge research findings documenting four important influences on spousal grief: the nature of the death (including caregiving duties prior to loss), the quality of the marital relationship, social support and integration, and the co-occurrence of other chronic and acute stressors. We then provide a list of criteria that professionals may use to identify a bereaved client's distinct risk factors (and resources) that may heighten (or protect against) symptoms of depression and grief. We conclude by providing clinical applications, arranged within each of four "tasks of mourning" (Worden, 2009); these provide a helpful guide for practitioners and caregivers who are helping older bereaved spouses to cope with their loss.

LATE-LIFE SPOUSAL LOSS: PATTERNS AND TRENDS

Spousal loss can occur at any age, yet widowhood in the United States today is a transition overwhelmingly experienced by persons age 65 and older. Of the 900,000 persons who become widowed annually in the United States, nearly three quarters are age 65 or older (Federal Interagency Forum on Aging-Related Statistics, 2010). Women are much more likely than men to become widowed, because men have lower life expectancies than women. Life expectancy at birth today is 76 for men and 80 for women, so women are much more likely to outlive their spouses.

Among persons age 65 to 74, 26.3% of women but just 7.3% of men are widowed. These proportions jump to 58.2% of women and 20.5% of men age 75 and older. This stark gender gap also reflects the fact that widowers are far more likely than widows to remarry, and thus they may "exit" the widowed category. Widows are less likely than widowers to remarry because of the dearth of potential partners. Among persons ages 65 and older in the United States, the sex ratio is 1.5 women per man. By age 85, this ratio is more than 3 women per man. As a result, few widows have the opportunity to remarry even if they would like to do so. Additionally, cultural norms encourage men to marry women younger than themselves, so widowed men may opt to remarry younger women, whereas older widows do not typically have access to a similarly expanded pool of potential spouses.

Although widowhood historically has been characterized as an *event* that occurs upon the death of one's spouse, contemporary late-life widowhood is best conceptualized as a *process*. Most deaths to older adults today occur due to chronic disease, or long-term illnesses for which there is no cure (Federal Interagency Forum on Aging-Related Statistics, 2010). The four leading causes of death to older adults today—heart disease, cancer, cerebrovascular disease, and chronic obstructive pulmonary disorder—account for nearly two thirds of all deaths to older adults; thus, most become widowed after at least one spell of caregiving for an ailing spouse. In the case of long-term chronic illness, spousal caregiving may have lasted for months or even years prior to the death. As we will discuss later in this chapter, the conditions leading up to and surrounding a spouse's death shape bereavement experiences and are important considerations when developing interventions to assist the newly bereaved.

ADJUSTING TO SPOUSAL LOSS: RISK AND PROTECTIVE FACTORS

As we noted earlier, older bereaved spouses vary widely in their psychological adjustment to loss. Some may have minor symptoms of depression and anxiety during the first 3 to 6 months following loss, whereas others may experience severe, debilitating, and persistent symptoms, including complicated and prolonged grief (Prigerson, Vanderwerker, & Maciejewski, 2008). Although myriad influences, including biological, psychological, social, and economic factors, affect one's adjustment, we focus here on four influences that recent studies have identified as particularly important and as potentially modifiable: the nature of the relationship, conditions surrounding the death, social support and integration, and other co-occurring losses and stressors.

Nature of the Marriage or Romantic Relationship

Older adults' psychological adjustment to partner death varies based on the nature of the relationship lost. Early writings, based on the psychoanalytic tradition, proposed that bereaved persons with the most troubled marriages would suffer heightened and pathological grief (Parkes & Weiss, 1983). This perspective held that persons who had conflicted marriages would find it hard to let go of their spouses, yet also feel angry at the deceased for abandoning them. However, longitudinal studies that track married persons over time through the widowhood transition find that older persons whose marriages were marked by high levels of warmth and dependence, and low levels of conflict, experience elevated grief symptoms within the first 6 months post loss (Carr et al., 2000).

Although those with high-quality marriages may suffer a greater sense of sadness within the earlier months of loss, their strong emotional ties to the late spouse may prove protective in the longer term. Recent research suggests that those in high-quality marriages may be able to draw strength from continuing bonds with the decedent. Early work on grief held that bereaved persons needed to dissolve or "relinquish" their emotional ties to the deceased and "get on" with their lives (e.g., Freud 1917/1957), yet current research suggests that maintaining a psychological tie to the deceased is an integral part of adaptation (Field, 2008). Although some aspects of continuing bonds may be problematic for adjustment, researchers point to particular scenarios where maintaining emotional ties to one's late spouse may be helpful. For instance, Rando (1993) observed that bereaved persons, when faced with a difficult decision, may think about what their late spouse might do. Others may keep alive their spouse's legacy by recognizing the continuing positive influence the deceased has on one's current life. In this way, the warmth and closeness of the relationship may continue to be protective and affirming to the bereaved spouse.

Nature of the Death

Researchers have documented that adjustment to spousal loss is affected by the timing and nature of the late spouse's death. In general, anticipated deaths tend to be less distressing than unanticipated ones. The knowledge that one's partner is going to die in the imminent future provides the couple with the time to address unresolved emotional, financial, and practical issues before the actual death. This preparation for death is believed to enable a smoother transition to widowhood. However, for older persons, "anticipated" deaths often are accompanied by long-term illness, painful images of a loved one's suffering, intensive caregiving, and neglect of one's own health concerns, thus taking a toll on the survivor's health and emotional well-being (Carr, House, Wortman, Nesse, & Kessler, 2001).

Contrary to popular lore, there is no clear-cut evidence that caregivers show greater symptoms of distress than those who did not provide direct care to their late spouses. Emerging research shows that caregivers may even experience improved psychological health following the loss because they are relieved of their stressful caregiving duties. They are no longer witnessing their loved one suffer, or they experience a sense of satisfaction, meaning, and accomplishment from caring for their loved one in his or her final days (Schulz, Boerner, & Hebert, 2008). However, family caregivers—who currently number more than 50 million in the United States alone—may require assistance prior to the death of their spouses (Caregiver Alliance, 2010). The threat of impending death, the strain of caregiving work, and the loss of personal time and activities may be distressing in the days and weeks leading up to the death. Providers should remember the strains faced by caregivers before the death as well as post loss.

Quality of end-of-life care and place of death also affect the bereavement experience. Older adults who believe that a loved one was in pain or received problematic medical care at the end of life report greater anxiety and anger post loss than persons whose loved ones had a "good death" (Carr, 2003). Use of hospice or palliative care services at the end of life is associated with better bereavement outcomes (Christakis & Iwashyna, 2003). Site of care also matters. Teno and colleagues (2004) found that family members of recent decedents who received at-home hospice services were more likely than those who died at hospitals or nursing homes to say that their loved one received high-quality care, that they were treated with respect and dignity at the end of life, and that they and the patient received adequate emotional support. Ironically, however, the vast majority of Americans (roughly 70%) currently die in institutions (Federal Interagency Forum on Aging-Related Statistics, 2010); this carries implications for survivors' well-being.

Social Support and Integration

Women's emotionally intimate social relationships over the life course are an important resource as they adjust to spousal loss. Older widows typically receive more practical and emotional support from their children than do widowers, given mothers' closer relationships with their children throughout the life course. Women also are more likely to have larger and more varied friendship networks than men, and these friendships are an important source of support as women cope with their loss (Ha, 2008). Men, by contrast, often seek social support in new romantic relationships, whether dating or remarriage. Many researchers concur that one reason why women typically adjust better psychologically to loss than men is because they have closer social ties with their children, friends, and siblings.

For both widows and widowers, however, social isolation and limited contact can impede adjustment to loss. Social isolation often is due to structural factors. Older adults living independently may lack transportation, they may have physical limitations that impair their mobility, and they may be cut off physically from loved ones following a relocation to a new home or an assisted living facility. Even those who live close to their family may feel lonely because of family conflict, or because their family does not offer support of the type or amount that the widow(er) would like. The deaths of siblings and friends also may leave older bereaved spouses feeling isolated, as they have no one with whom to reminisce or share their private thoughts and feelings. As such, practitioners should be aware of community resources that enable older bereaved persons to be with others in recreational, mealtime, education, spiritual, and support group activities.

Other Losses and Stressors

Stress researchers agree that the psychological consequences of any one stressor may be amplified when experienced in conjunction with other losses or strains. For older bereaved persons, the death of a spouse is almost always accompanied by other strains and losses which may compromise their well-being, including financial strain, the loss of work and community roles (including retirement and relocation), compromised mobility (whether walking or driving), health declines, a decline or loss of sensory functions including vision and hearing, and even the loss of daily routines that gave one's life order and meaning (Carr, 2008). Widowhood often sets off a chain of "secondary stressors," or stressors that result from the loss of a spouse; these secondary stressors, in turn, may compromise emotional and physical well-being. For widowers, the loss of a confidante, helpmate, and caregiver may be particularly harmful, whereas for widows, financial difficulties often are a source of distress (Stroebe, Folkman, Hansson, & Schut, 2006).

The well-documented effects of widowhood on mortality risk, disability and functional limitations, and depressive symptoms are consistently larger for men than women (e.g., Lee & DeMaris, 2007). Although popular myth suggests that emotionally devastated widowers may "die of a broken heart" shortly after their wives die, research shows that the loss of a helpmate and caretaker is really the culprit. Wives monitor their husbands' diets, remind them to take their daily medications, and urge them to give up vices like smoking and drinking (Umberson, Wortman, & Kessler, 1992). Widowers are more likely than married men to die of accidents, alcohol-related deaths, lung cancer, and chronic ischemic heart disease during the first 6 months after their loss, but not from causes that are less closely linked to health behaviors (Martikainen & Valkonen, 1996).

Widows, by contrast, often experience declines in their economic well-being, which may trigger anxiety and distress (Umberson et al., 1992). Within 3 years of the death of her husband, a widow's income drops by 44% on average (Holden & Kuo, 1996). More than half of elderly widows in poverty were not poor prior to the death of their husbands. Costs associated with the funeral, long-term and medical care, or estate-related legal proceedings can devastate the fixed income of older adults. Because current cohorts of older women typically tended to child-rearing and family responsibilities during their younger years, they have had fewer years of paid work experience and lower earnings than their male peers. Given their reduced work experience, they also are less likely to have private pensions. Moreover, because of their lower earnings, women have paid less into Social Security than their male counterparts, and thus receive less in public pensions.

Older widows who try to reenter the labor force also may lack the experience to secure a good job, or may face age discrimination. These financial strains may compound the emotional pain and cognitive disruption triggered by spousal loss.

DIAGNOSING AND TREATING BEREAVED OLDER SPOUSES

Many of the factors discussed above combine to affect grief and distress symptoms in bereaved older spouses. To effectively treat patients, the clinician will be initially concerned with taking a comprehensive history of the bereaved survivor (Jeffreys, 2011). The information obtained should include the following:

- Nature of spouse's death (e.g., prolonged illness or sudden death)
- Location of spouse at time of death
- Duration and nature of surviving spouse's caregiving
- Nature of marital relationship
- Medical, mood, and mental status of surviving spouse
- Hospitalizations
- Functional status and limitations
- History of other losses and stressors
- Occupational history
- Level of social, emotional, and practical support from family, friends, and professionals
- Cultural and religious information
- Contextual and economic realities: location of residence, neighborhood, residential facility, social memberships, financial status, education, and instrumental skills
- Goals: short term and long term

Developing a Course of Treatment

After completing a clinical portrait, the provider should ascertain whether treatment is necessary. Recent research suggests that clinical treatment may not be necessary or desirable for all older bereaved persons, particularly those suffering "normal" and relatively short-lived sadness over their loss (e.g., Bonanno & Lilienfeld, 2008). However, when the clinical picture of the grief response includes diagnosable psychiatric disorders such as major depression (including suicidal ideation), anxiety, thought disorder, cognitive functioning disturbance (e.g., confusion), chronic physical symptoms, social phobia, or withdrawal, then the clinician will develop a treatment plan which is in the best interest of the bereaved spouse.

Standard of care treatment for older bereaved spouses can include assessment for level of depression, including suicidal thoughts; the nature and degree of anxiety; and individual psychotherapy, group psychotherapy, referral to physician for medication evaluation, and, depending on safety concerns, hospitalization. When the clinical picture of the grief response falls into the category of complicated or prolonged grief, the bereaved spouse should be evaluated for the existence of *emotional* (e.g., deep feelings of guilt, or inability to express feeling), *cognitive* (e.g., intrusive thoughts, or feeling dazed), *behavioral* (e.g., self-destructive or compulsive behaviors), and *physical* (e.g., chronic complaints, or disrupted sleep) "danger signals" (see Chapter 12 in this book and Jeffreys [2011] for specific criteria for diagnosing complicated grief).

The practitioner should take particular care to gather information on these potential danger signals when taking a history, whether by clinical observation or from reports of family, friends, and/or other care providers. Every loss situation contains a distinctive set of influences on grief symptoms and behaviors, and these factors must be taken into consideration when assessing and drawing up a treatment plan for each case.

CLINICAL APPLICATIONS FOR OLDER BEREAVED SPOUSES

We have highlighted the sources of distress (and resilience) for older bereaved spouses, and have provided general guidelines for assessing grief symptoms among the bereaved. We now set forth a specific plan of action for structuring interventions that may help the bereaved older adult to heal. Several of these steps require no special training, whereas others should be engaged in by professional providers only. We encourage care providers to consult with a licensed mental health practitioner if they have doubts about their capacity to deliver each such action. Care providers should adapt the suggestions given here to their own level of training, as well as to the individualized needs of the bereaved. We have adapted Worden's (2009) "Four Tasks of Mourning" (see Chapter 6 in this book for further explanation and clinical examples) and added clinical interventions (Jeffreys, 2011) expressly for effective use among older widows and widowers.

Task 1: Accept the Reality of the Loss

Many bereaved spouses go through periods of denial or difficulty in accepting the death. Providers must be particularly sensitive to the widow(er)'s need to strike some balance between confronting and avoiding the loss. Some bereaved persons may experience a *head–heart split:* They may recall loss events with few or no physical or emotional reactions because the "head" knows the terrible truth but the "heart" has not yet registered it. Thus, the grieving spouse may act as though the loss had not occurred. The following activities may help the grieving spouse come to terms with the reality and finality of the loss.

Listen: The First Provider Action *The care provider* will listen first and provide ample opportunity for the grieving person to tell the story of the loss. This is the first step in the long road to acceptance. If the bereaved spouse doesn't want to talk, suggest that he or she write thoughts in a journal, speak them into a recording device, or write a new eulogy and bring it to the next appointment to share with the care provider. The client should set the pace and timing of these activities.

Revisiting the Time of Death To help a grieving client come to terms with the loss, it is important to ask questions such as "Were you there when (he or she) died?" "How did you find out about the death?" "Where were you when you found out?" "Who made the funeral arrangements?" "Was there a viewing?" "Can you describe what happened?" And "What was that like for you?"

Recall Rituals Asking questions about the death-associated rituals can also help to reintroduce the reality of loss. Consider questions like "What was the funeral like?" "Where was it held?" "What can you remember about the eulogies?" "Who gave them?" "Did you say anything at the service? At the graveside?" "Were you satisfied with the service?" And "What did you like or dislike?"

Identify Changes in Life To help a grieving spouse gain a sense of what has changed since the loss, ask questions like "What is different in your daily life now?" "What do you miss the most?" "When is the worst time for you?" And "What are some next steps for you now?"

Task 2: Experience the Feelings of Grief

If you are seeing a grieving person for a counseling session, make sure that the meeting room is private, quiet, and soundproof. Have one or two boxes of tissues within easy reach. Allow ample time for the session so that you are not tempted to look at the clock or your watch.

The goal of the care provider is to accept whatever emotions the grieving person is capable of expressing. To facilitate the expression of grief, care providers can make these suggestions.

Look at Photos Photos are a good source of background information. Old photos may provide opportunities for grieving people to talk about earlier losses and the childhood messages they received about the acceptability of expressing such feelings as sadness, anger, and fear.

Write a History Some people can better grasp the reality of their loss after they put it in historical perspective. Writing the "life history" of a relationship that has ended or some other significant loss can help individuals express feelings they are unable to verbalize.

Write Stories The grieving person may write a fictional account of his or her loss if this will help elicit feelings and expressions related to the loss.

Draw Pictures Grieving people who are more comfortable with images than words can be encouraged to draw images relating to the loss and their life now. If the care provider has no training in the interpretation of drawings, then he or she could ask the bereaved to explain the drawing.

Task 3: Adjust to a Changed Life: Creating New Meanings in the Postloss World

Acknowledge the Changes Moving from a couple to widowhood status requires a reconfigured self-concept and a new way to be seen by others. The provider can assist the grieving spouse with this transition. Grieving spouses will typically experience pain as they adjust to their new circumstances. To help grievers understand, make sense of, and adjust to their new world, practitioners can suggest the following tasks:

Compile a loss book that will describe the postloss world. Ask the bereaved to answer questions such as the following:

1. "What's different now?"
2. "Who am I now? … that I am no longer part of a couple, nor able to walk or breathe without life support…" The list can go on and on.
3. "What do I need to learn or get help with in order to make my life work now?" This list may help to identify new skills required for life in the postloss world.
4. "How are others doing it?" Support groups of people with similar losses may offer comfort, acceptance, and an opportunity to learn from others how to handle many of the concerns that are part of their new identity. The bereaved may feel a sense of normalcy when surrounded by people coping with similar challenges.

Act as Coach in the Postloss World Care providers need to help grieving people to function effectively in the postloss world, or to find resources to help with this challenge. "Lessons" might entail the following:

1. Explaining the nature and varieties of grief to surviving spouses.
2. Acknowledging and normalizing feelings and behaviors that arise in difficult situations. Widows, for instance, often report that they don't feel welcome when they are with married friends.
3. Providing decision-making support for the newly bereaved, such as advising a widow on home repairs, making financial decisions, or learning how to identify resources via the Internet.
4. Encouraging the bereaved to socialize. For example, coach a widowed man who wants to ask a woman for a date, or provide contacts for recreational activity groups.

Reenter the Social World Grieving spouses may need the care provider's assistance as they develop a new picture of themselves in the postloss world. Developing a new way of being with other people is an important part of healing. The care provider can help the newly bereaved by setting up "length-of-stay time limits" and a "back door" arrangement for easy departure if needed. For example, the care provider can suggest that a widow sit at the back of a religious service near an exit, or that she go to a party for only an hour, or take her own car so that she can leave when she wants to. Remember to respect people's own timing when they begin to reenter social life. Grieving people are creating a new narrative for living—and this takes time. For many, a gradual reentry to outer society beyond the safety and comfort of their inner social support circle is the least threatening approach.

Task 4: Reconfigure the Bond With the Lost Person

The bereaved must learn how to maintain a bond with his or her late spouse while reclaiming life in the postloss world. This often means holding onto the past while also living in the present. A grieving person may benefit from thinking, "The image of my loved one is always with me, and although I hold onto the legacy of values we shared, I don't expect him or her to be physically present as a living bond-mate."

Many bereaved spouses have benefitted by creating a new kind of bond with their deceased loved one—a *spiritual bond*. This new bond may define the loved one as gone but still available to the grieving person in his or her thoughts. In this way, the griever can feel a continued connection to the loved one. Care providers can facilitate this transition by helping to establish *personal rituals* in which the loved one is included: lighting candles, setting out fresh flowers, cooking his or her favorite foods, visiting the grave or ashes location, working with the loved one's social cause or charity, having a heart-to-heart "talk" with the loved one, and identifying and integrating the loved one's values into the bereaved spouse's own life. Prayer and meditation can be interwoven into the daily rituals if appropriate.

CONCLUSION

Spousal loss will befall nearly all married older adults, many of whom may experience symptoms of grief, distress, loneliness, and anxiety. However, such symptoms vary widely in intensity and duration, and reflect individual-level differences in the nature of the marriage, the context of the death, one's social and emotional support systems, and other stressors and resources that one faces. No two individuals grieve in precisely the same way. We hope that the general roadmap we have set out provides a useful framework as clinicians seek to understand, diagnose, and ultimately adapt appropriate clinical applications for helping the bereaved older spouses whom they encounter in their practices.

REFERENCES

Bonanno, G. A., & Lilienfeld, S. O. (2008). Let's be realistic: When grief counseling is effective and when it's not. *Professional Psychology: Research and Practice*, 39, 377–380.

Caregiver Alliance. (2010). Fact sheet on statistics. Retrieved from http://www.caregiver.org/caregiver/jsp/content

Carr, D. (2003). A good death for whom? Quality of spouse's death and psychological distress among older widowed persons. *Journal of Health & Social Behavior*, *44*, 215–232.

Carr, D. (2008). Late-life bereavement: The Changing Lives of Older Couples study. In M. Stroebe, R. O. Hansson, H. Schut, & W. Stroebe (Eds.), *Handbook of bereavement research and practice: 21st century perspectives* (pp. 417–440). Washington, DC: American Psychological Association.

Carr, D., House, J. S., Kessler, R. C., Nesse, R. M., Sonnega, J., & Wortman, C. (2000). Marital quality and psychological adjustment to widowhood among older adults: A longitudinal analysis. *Journals of Gerontology: Social Sciences*, *55B*, S197–S207.

Carr, D., House, J.S., Wortman, C. B., Nesse, R. M., & Kessler, R.C. (2001). Psychological adjustment to sudden and anticipated spousal death among the older widowed. *Journal of Gerontology Series B: Psychological Sciences and Social Sciences*, *56*, S237–S248.

Christakis, N. A., & Iwashyna, T. J. (2003). The health impact on families of health care: a matched cohort study of hospice use by decedents and mortality outcomes in surviving, widowed spouses. *Social Science and Medicine*, *57*, 465–475.

Federal Interagency Forum on Aging-Related Statistics. (2010). *Older Americans 2010: Key indicators of well-being*. Washington, DC: Government Printing Office.

Field, N. P. (2008). Whether to relinquish or maintain a bond with the deceased. In M. Stroebe, R. O. Hansson, H. Schut, & W. Stroebe (Eds.), *Handbook of bereavement research and practice: 21st century perspectives* (pp. 133–162). Washington, DC: American Psychological Association.

Freud, S. (1957). Mourning and melancholia. In *The standardized edition of the complete psychological works of Sigmund Freud* (Ed. and Trans. J. Strachey, pp. 152–170). London: Hogarth Press. (Original work published in 1917)

Ha, J. (2008). Changes in support from confidantes, children, and friends following widowhood. *Journal of Marriage and Family*, 70, 306–318.

Holden, K. C., & Kuo, D. H. (1996). Complex marital histories and economic well-being: The continuing legacy of divorce and widowhood as the HRS cohort approaches retirement. *The Gerontologist*, *35*, 383–390.

Holmes, T., & Rahe, R. (1967). The social readjustment scale. *Journal of Psychosomatic Research*, *11*, 213–218.

Jeffreys, J. S. (2011). *Helping grieving people—when tears are not enough: A handbook for care providers* (Rev. ed.). New York: Routledge.

Lee, G. R., & DeMaris, A. (2007). Widowhood, gender, and depression: A longitudinal analysis. *Research on Aging*, *29*, 56–72.

Martikainen, P., & Valkonen, T. (1996). Mortality after the death of a spouse: Rates and causes of death in a large Finnish cohort. *American Journal of Public Health*, 86, 1087–1093.

Parkes, C. M., & Weiss, R. S. (1983). *Recovery from bereavement*. New York: Basic.

Prigerson, H. G., Vanderwerker, L. C., & Maciejewski, P. K. (2008). A case for inclusion of prolonged grief disorder in DSM-V. In M. Stroebe, R. O. Hansson, H. Schut, & W. Stroebe (Eds.), *Handbook of bereavement research and practice: 21st century perspectives* (pp. 165–186). Washington, DC: American Psychological Association.

Rando, T. (1993). *Treatment of complicated mourning*. Champaign, IL: Research Press.

Schulz, R., Boerner, K., & Hebert, R. S. (2008). Caregiving and bereavement. In M. Stroebe, R. O. Hansson, H. Schut, & W. Stroebe (Eds.), *Handbook of bereavement research and practice: 21st century perspectives* (pp. 265–286). Washington, DC: American Psychological Association.

Stroebe, M. S., Folkman, S., Hansson, R. O., & Schut, H. (2006). The prediction of bereavement outcome. *Social Science & Medicine*, *63*, 2440–2451.

Teno, J. M., Clarridge, B. R., Casey, V., Welch, L. C., Wetle, T., Shield, R., et al. (2004). Family perspectives on end-of-life care at the last place of care. *Journal of the American Medical Association*, *291*, 88–93.

Umberson, D., Wortman, C. B., & Kessler, R. C. (1992). Widowhood and depression: Explaining long-term gender differences in vulnerability. *Journal of Health and Social Behavior*, *33*, 10–24.

Wolff, K., & Wortman, C. B. (2006). Psychological consequences of spousal loss among older adults: Understanding the diversity of responses. In D., Carr, R. M. Nesse, & C. B. Wortman (Eds.), *Spousal bereavement in late-life* (pp. 81–116). New York: Springer.

Worden, W. (2009). *Grief counseling and grief therapy*. New York: Springer.

9

Parenting Challenges After the Death of a Child

JENNIFER L. BUCKLE and STEPHEN J. FLEMING

In the midst of the pervasive sense of loss at the death of a child, many bereaved parents must also contend with the challenges of parenting their surviving, bereft children. Parents are not the only ones devastated by a child's death, as siblings are also deeply wounded by the loss. The unique aspects of the sibling relationship lead to wide-ranging and enduring consequences following the death of a sister or brother (Riches & Dawson, 2000). Moreover, surviving siblings suffer numerous secondary losses in the form of their parents' functional incapacity and the demise of the comforting safety, security, and predictability their family provided. Bereaved parents are confronted with the delicate, complicated task of simultaneously relinquishing their parental role with their deceased child while continuing to function in this capacity with surviving children—a phenomenon we have termed *bereaved parenting*. For parents enveloped in grief, attempts at parenting are further complicated by the reality that, not unlike themselves, their children have been fundamentally and irrevocably changed by the death.

This chapter is an abridged treatment of a more exhaustive study of the experience of parenting after the death of a child (see Buckle & Fleming, 2010). Following a brief discussion of the method, we will explore the selected topics of the challenges of parenting bereaved siblings as identified by the mothers and fathers in our study.

METHOD

Ten bereaved parents participated in this qualitative study, five mothers and five fathers. They were recruited through Bereaved Families of Ontario (BFO), a mutual help organization to assist families who have experienced the death of a child (Fleming & Balmer, 1995). The parents were all unrelated except for two married couples. Each parent (age range: 40–51 years) had at least one other surviving child who experienced the death of his or her sibling (range in number of surviving children: 1–4). Five of the children were now only children as a result of the death. All were members of intact families at the time of the death and at present, with the length of their parents' marriage extending from 13 to 31 years. The age of deceased children ranged from 1 year 6 months to 20 years 6 months. Of the deceased children, seven were male and one was female, and the time since death varied from 3 to 8 years (mean = 5.5 years). Three of the children died in fatal automobile accidents, and the other five died of illnesses.

The highest level of education ranged from completion of high school to completion of a graduate degree. Although all of the fathers worked full-time, the employment status among mothers varied (i.e., working inside the home, or working part-time or full-time outside the home). All of the participants were Caucasian and had been living in Canada for most, if not all, their lives. The data, then, are based on an in-depth analysis of those who volunteered to participate in this research; the reader is cautioned against generalizing the experiences of these bereaved parents to bereaved parents from different racial, cultural, or even socioeconomic backgrounds.

Each parent participated in an individual open-ended interview that ranged from 1.5 to 2.5 hours. Each participant was asked, "Do you feel ________'s (child's name) death has affected your parenting of your surviving child(ren)?" All participants answered "yes" to this question, which was followed by "Can you tell me about the effect on your parenting?" Subsequent questions and comments were determined by the participant's responses. Each participant consented to the interview being audiotaped and transcribed verbatim. All identifying information was altered or omitted from the transcripts, and pseudonyms were inserted.

Analysis of the transcribed interviews proceeded as per the grounded theory method (Glaser & Strauss, 1967) as understood through the methodology of methodical hermeneutics (i.e., the marriage of hermeneutics and method) (Rennie, 2000). This systematic exploration and representation of the meaning of data were accomplished through a set of procedures originally outlined by Glaser and Strauss and further clarified and refined by Rennie, Phillips, and Quartaro (1988).

The transcribed text was divided into "meaning units," or fragments of text that had a theme or coherent meaning (Rennie et al., 1988). These fragments of text were compared and grouped according to their commonalities, which were then represented by a category title. New categories were formed as often as needed to accommodate new, emerging themes in the text. In a grounded theory study, by simultaneously collecting and analyzing the data, the researcher remains grounded in the data and has the opportunity to respond, with further data collection, to any questions that may arise (Glaser & Stauss, 1967). This process continues to *saturation*, defined as the point at which relatively few new categories are required to represent the meaning units of new data (Rennie et al., 1988). Saturation was achieved in this study, which marked the end of data collection.

THE CHALLENGES OF PARENTING BEREAVED CHILDREN

Analysis of the participants' experiences revealed parenting bereaved children to be a complex and intimidating task that involved thoughtfully responding to loss-induced personality transformations; revisiting the loss over time; appreciating and adjusting to their children's differing grieving styles; grappling with the task of parenting a sole, bereaved child; enduring the powerlessness of being incapable of shielding their sons and daughters from such horrendous life experiences; and attempting to make meaning of a senseless and incomprehensible event. Each of these challenges will be discussed in turn, with direct quotes from participants to illustrate the theme and bring the depth of their experiences, in their own words, to the reader.

Changes in Surviving Children

The devastating impact of the death of a sibling has the potential to alter the personality characteristics and behavior of surviving children (Arnold & Gemma, 1983; Becvar, 2001; Fleming & Balmer, 1996; Lattanzi-Licht, 1996; Lohan & Murphy, 2002). The mothers and fathers in our study also noticed significant post-loss identity transformations in their child(ren); whereas some of these changes were considered constructive and eased parenting demands, others were viewed as troublesome or worrying and required more active, determined, and creative parenting. Regardless, the parenting challenge was to recognize these changes and respond in a manner that was attentive both to the grieving process and to the cognitive, behavioral, and affective development of childhood and adolescence (Fleming & Adolph, 1986). Bereaved mothers noticed the following:

> I think this has made them more intuitive. They understand. She'll say things at school about how kids treat other kids. She worries about those kids. That hurt, that deep hurt. I don't think that will ever go away, that's a part of her now. That's who she is. (Anna, 1-year-old child died, two surviving children)
>
> We never had a day's problem with him, he was one of those most placid children, he was so easygoing, he was the kid who always got the first student of the month because he was such a nice kid. Very placid, easygoing. Very close to [the deceased] and just snapped [at death]. It was extremely hard.… He had done some things, he was getting into fights, he was just a mess. A total mess. (Carol, 20-year-old child died, four surviving children)
>
> It's been difficult for him. He's probably more serious than a lot of children his age would be because he's gone through the experience of losing his brother and missing him, but, he's also seen the pain that it's caused us as parents I think … the element of trust I think is stronger because of the maturity that he's developed because of what's happened.… Because of the whole experience, I think he has a greater sensitivity for other children that are maybe being bullied or handicapped or any of those types of things. He seems very in tune with those less fortunate. People at school have said that he has great skills as sort of being the peacekeeper.… I think it's made him a much stronger, caring person. (Isabelle, 2-year-old child died, one surviving child)

The fathers also noticed that their bereaved children exhibited a seriousness or maturity beyond their years:

> Well, him as an individual, I find him to be very calm. He tends to be more reserved and I think that is since he lost his brother. I don't see the silliness anymore, the lack of thinking or whatever, I see a conscious effort on his part to look at what's going on.... He used to have his tantrums and stuff and he hasn't, the older he's got, those have disappeared, but, definitely since [child] died he hasn't had one. (Frank, 12-year-old child died, one surviving child)
>
> He has a grace about him that I think is really, really uncommon.... It might be manifesting itself in a determination to be perfect. I'm a little bit worried that he feels as if he must never fail at anything.... I do spend a little time looking at him and thinking, is he as poised as he appears to be, or is he forcing himself to be poised because he's concerned that he's not entitled to be any other way? (Harris, 2-year-old child died, one surviving child)

In confronting the traumatic death of a sibling, Fleming and Balmer (1996) noted resiliency to be a salient feature of adjustment. Bereaved adolescents were frequently less well adjusted than their nonbereaved peers one year post loss; however, by the second and third years the two groups were virtually indistinguishable. Moreover, many of the bereaved adolescents presented as "wise beyond their years" and attributed this perspicacity and maturity to their sibling's death. These findings are consistent with Moos and Shaefer's (1986) model that highlights the growth potential of a person who has experienced a significant life transition or crisis. There is an increasingly recognized possibility that extremely adverse life experiences can be a driving force toward posttraumatic growth (PTG). Although the majority of research has investigated PTG in adults, there is a developing literature exploring the phenomenon of children and adolescents maturing through adversity (Cryder, Kilmer, Tedeschi, & Calhoun, 2006; Milam, Ritt-Olson, & Unger, 2004). Increased maturity, improved academic performance, higher moral values, a deeper appreciation of the value of life, and a reduction in risk-taking behavior have been noted subsequent to a sibling's death (Balk, 1983; Fleming & Balmer, 1996; Forward & Garlie, 2003). Cryder et al. concluded, "Suggesting that PTG is possible and identifying factors or conditions associated with PTG among children will assist clinicians in (a) attending to and assessing positive factors and (b) pursuing means to facilitate their development or enhancement and foster PTG" (p. 68).

Despite this potential for growth and positive personality transformation, it is important not to underestimate the devastating consequences of surviving the death of a sibling. Research has shown that bereaved adolescents at risk for developing complications viewed themselves as outsiders and unpopular in social situations, held a worldview consistent with an externalized locus of control (i.e., the victim role), reported feeling disoriented, and stated they were bothered by disturbing and problematic thoughts (Balmer, 1992). In contrast to their low-risk counterparts, it is suggested that these adolescents may be susceptible to self-related cognitive distortions (e.g., "No one likes me; therefore, I am worthless"), a generalized sense of being vulnerable (e.g., "I have no control over anything that happens in my life"), and bereavement-related cognitive distortions (e.g., "I sometimes see the deceased and hear them; therefore, I must be going crazy"). The most appropriate intervention with this group involves the use of cognitive-behavioral and psychoeducational strategies (Fleming & Robinson, 2001; Malkinson, 2007).

Revisiting the Loss Over Time

Not only must parents contend with changes in their children, but also they are faced with the challenge of having to revisit the loss at various developmental stages. Time and again, the death was reviewed as bereaved siblings matured and were able to accommodate a deeper understanding of the loss and its profound impact. This was challenging for parents as they continually and painfully revisited the death and were exposed to the new levels of loss that time and maturity glaringly revealed. It was the mothers who most often mentioned this aspect of parenting bereaved children.

> Because of the developmental stages that they go through, you have to revisit this all the time. That's what I find hard too. I get tired.... Issues are going to come up and I'm going to have to deal with those and that's what's hard. (Anna, 1-year-old child died, two surviving children)
>
> I found the most interesting thing to me is ... this grieving process regarding [surviving child]. She was 8 when he [her brother] died, and she's now 15, it's changing. It's like the grief is evolving along with [her]. It's really interesting.... Because they were so close, so that's why I'm saying you know, I'm noticing her missing him in different ways [now]. It was a playmate thing before, but, it's almost like she's missing him more now I think. (Diane, 4-year-old child died, three surviving children)

Revisiting the loss at various developmental stages presented distinct and worrisome challenges, but it was the teenage years in particular that were the focus of most parental concerns. The parent–child relationship during adolescence is commonly complex; however, when the family has experienced the death of a child, this period can become increasingly complicated and sensitive for both parents and children. The majority of parents in the study discussed the intricacy of the teenage years within the omnipresent shadow of loss. Particularly, they focused on their children's difficult struggle for independence.

> She is at that age now where she is asserting her independence ... there are times when I'm just that much more overprotective. Up to now she's understood it. But, I think we're getting into some years where she might not. I think now she's at an age where she's coming out of that. (Carol, 20-year-old child died, four surviving children)
>
> I know there's a part of her that is so close to us, and is so fearful of anything happening to her mom and dad. And it's her job right now as a teenager to deny those feelings and to put that distance.... It's an interesting time with her being a teenager and trying to do what nature is telling her she should be doing and that's distancing herself. And she's working really extra hard at that. You know, because I think there's a part of her that really doesn't want to ... there's a part of her that wants a relationship with mom and dad but because

she's 15 she's got to fight that because she needs to be independent. (Diane, 4-year-old child died, three surviving children)

Bereaved fathers grappled with similar issues and, additionally, commented on the friction and disconnection they perceived in their father–daughter relationships.

> The teenager thing starting to click in and so, I'm just a stupid dad, what do I know? … It's all about pushing away, you know, "I don't want you here" but, other times she's really loving and cuddly and stuff like that.… The teen years and to lose a child at that time, the parents are going to become more, or try to be more co-dependent on the children, keep them close by. And it's the wrong time to do it. But you can't help it as a [bereaved] parent. (Elliot, 10-year-old child died, one surviving child)
>
> Especially at her age too. They don't want to be around having their parents pump them with a whole bunch of questions about what they're doing. So, that's hard too. "I want to go to university next year." It hurts, it hurts you to hear that, you know what I mean? It really hurts. I'd like her to maybe spend another year at home. She's too young to go. (Gary, 16-year-old child died, one surviving child)
>
> I think it's harder for us to let go of [surviving child]. She's becoming a teenager. Independence steps [are hard], definitely. You want to keep the family close together.… Like all teenagers she sort of rebels and says, "I don't have to report in every minute of what I'm doing." There's times when I think she does let it go but she knows deep down that it's probably concerning us but I think she's being a teenager and just doing her thing.… She's at the stage now where, I'm sure most teenage girls are like this, she doesn't like to show her emotions too much to her parents. And certainly with me now, I guess most teenage girls and fathers go through the stage where they kind of pull apart. She's not, she doesn't tell me as much as she used to. That's fine, I understand that. (Jake, 4-year-old child died, three surviving children)

Parenting bereaved adolescents involved an intensification of the issues that commonly characterize this phase of development with additional loss-specific concerns further complicating the transition. Hogan and DeSantis (1996) referred to the challenge of coping with adolescence *and* the death of a sibling as a form of double jeopardy, with each being difficult enough to adjust to on its own, but doubly so in combination. Specifically, the process of adolescents growing into greater independence and autonomy was particularly difficult for bereaved parents who were haunted by concerns for the safety and survival of their children. The clash of these two perspectives has the potential to be taxing and disruptive. In such situations, parents and clinicians alike are challenged by the complex task of distinguishing whether the adolescent is dealing with the "normal" conflicts fundamental to each developmental phase, whether he or she is grappling with conflicts essential to the grieving process, or whether there is an interaction of the two (i.e., the impact of a sibling's death affecting adolescent development and maturation).

Fleming and Adolph (1986), in recognizing that "grief responses cannot be considered in isolation; attention must be directed to the impact of loss on the conflicts and tasks of normal adolescent development" (p. 116), proposed a model of grief that combines the three tasks of adolescent development (emotional separation from parents, competency, and intimacy) with the five core issues affecting bereaved adolescents (predictability of events, self-image, belonging, fairness and justice, and mastery and control). The interaction of these two processes was apparent in varying levels in the parents' reports of their adolescents' diminishing tolerance for perceived parental overprotectiveness. This was not the complete picture, however, as parents also noted their teenagers' wavering attempts to separate and gain independence from the family. This ambivalence was illustrated in the numerous ways their children avoided age-appropriate distancing and the pursuit of independence following their sibling's death.

Differing Grieving Styles

In addition to revisiting the loss at various developmental stages, parents with more than one surviving child face the daunting challenge of differentially responding to each child's reaction to multiple levels of loss (e.g., the loss of a friend, rival, confidant, playmate, and/or role model; the "loss" of their parents in a functional sense; and the loss of their family as they knew it). Siblings' grief reactions are complex, long lasting, and highly variable. This variability requires parenting flexibility and patience, qualities that may be in short supply for parents who themselves are grieving. The mothers explained this challenge:

> She's not as apt to talk about it [as the other sibling]. See that's the difference. She won't be as quick to tell what she's feeling. I'll have to kind of watch her. (Anna, 1-year-old child died, two surviving children)
>
> At the same time, you have two children that have lived through this very differently. (Becky, 4-year-old child died, two surviving children)
>
> He was just a mess. A total mess.… He was going through some very difficult times after his brother died and I was worried.… My second son, he's the type that acts out.… He was the one that openly grieved. He was the one that was, that I worried the most about because you could see somebody grieving, but I now know enough to know that well, you are grieving, I did it myself. That's it and that's okay. He was the one you could see it. It's [those] that grieve silently that I worry more about.… I had thought it was [the] little girl that wasn't dealing with her grief. But, I now know that I have rarely, I can't say I haven't seen her cry, but, she hasn't cried very much. But, my goodness she has done so much to honour his memory. (Carol, 20-year-old child died, four surviving children)

Davies (1999) and McCown and Davies (1995) noted that reactions to the death of a sibling are a function of individual variables (gender, age, coping style, self-concept, and previous loss history), situational variables (cause of death, duration of illness, time since death, and involvement in events surrounding the death), and environmental variables (family context, parental grief, and parent–child communication). Asynchronous or incompatible grief reactions among family members have the potential to be individually or collectively problematic. For example, striking differences in grieving among family members may trigger isolation, judgmental and critical responding, and censorship of grief expression, and contribute to further disintegration of the family unit. Alternatively, incongruent grieving styles may serve to complement one another and facilitate more adaptive individual and family functioning, in families that are open to and accommodating of differences. Determining whether intermember differences in grieving styles are fractious and problematic or complementary and advantageous requires careful assessment of each member and of the family as a whole.

Now an Only Child

Although parents with one surviving child did not face the challenge of accommodating different styles of grieving, they were faced with adjusting to the experience of parenting a sole, bereaved child. Parents had to contend with the new reality of a one-child family just as their child was confronted with having lost a sibling and, consequently, the role of brother or sister. Parents commented on the unique dynamics of dealing with this change in the family constellation:

> Well, it's painful to think that he's gone through the loss of a sibling and then also painful to think that as we get older, that he will be alone. He was such a fabulous brother, that I think he would have been, it was nice to see him sort of in that mentoring type of role.… There's a lot of life skills you learn by fighting with your siblings.… I worry sometimes that he has a lot more adult contact.… I sometimes worry that he feels like he's too much under a magnifying glass. You know, because he's got two parents watching him, instead of two parents having to keep an eye on two of them. (Isabelle, 2-year-old child died, one surviving child)
>
> It was a large impact on the sibling because now she always says, "There's me, only one now." We had to fulfill that role a lot more, like playing with the child. Yeah, and play the games and do other things, so, when you come home after a hard day at the office or whatever, and then to have to sit down and play games with her all night or to keep her, it's pretty trying at times. (Elliot, 10-year-old child died, one surviving child)
>
> I have friends that have only one child and I've seen their parenting styles and different things and it seems to be very different than when you have two or more children. The only thing I didn't want to do was start to swing into looking at him as the only child.… I don't think they have the flexibility. They say only children can be spoiled, well, I don't think that's always true, but, your parent's energy is constantly always on, all over them. When you get two or more, you're spread out. (Frank, 12-year-old child died, one surviving child)
>
> He's aware of how much of our identity hinges on him. There are times when being an only child is, I mean it *hangs* about the place. He defines the family and I'm sure there are times when he feels it's a burden.… He said, "I wish I had another brother." Nothing, nothing I know of to do about it.… The poor kid, he's been denied the family that he once had. (Harris, 2-year-old child died, one surviving child)

Parental Powerlessness to Shield Children From Pain

Another challenging aspect of parenting bereaved children was the realization of the stark reality that they were powerless to shield their children from the unavoidable pain of grief. The majority of mothers and one of the fathers expressed this sense of ineffectuality.

> I think that's what was the hardest thing for me to see, [surviving child] hurting. As a parent, that's probably one of the worst things. You want to take that pain away from her because you could see she was in pain and you couldn't change it. (Jake, 4-year-old child died, three surviving children)
>
> If I have this pain, the idea that your children have that pain is overwhelming. And this is the one time you can't, you can't as a mom take away their pain. That's awful hard. (Carol, 20-year-old child died, four surviving children)
>
> Because there's nothing, you can't do anything to alleviate that. There's nothing I can say, you know, I mean as a mom, you'd do anything to make your child feel better. Anything. And in this case, there's nothing. It's really hard. You really just ache for them. So, normally we like to try and work things through and I'll usually say there's not a problem we can't fix. But this is one we can't.... That was a big thing, because as a mom, that's what you're supposed to do, is kiss it and make it all better. Well some things you just can't. (Diane, 4-year-old child died, three surviving children)

Recognizing the limits to which they could help their children, especially when witnessing their seemingly unfathomable sorrow, was particularly difficult and saddening for these parents. Unable to provide an effective antidote to dampen their children's anguish and substitute a more comforting worldview, their postloss approach to parenting was often characterized by feelings of powerlessness, frustration, and despair.

Meaning Making

The excruciating, senseless tragedy that is the death of a child left parents reflecting on the importance of providing their surviving children with wisdom, a sense of hope, or otherwise the ability to derive meaning from the death. This was a particularly daunting task because the parents themselves grappled with these very issues, and when this proved to be unattainable, they were left with feelings of guilt and sadness. They described the parenting challenge of meaning making:

> I do worry about this, where it affects my parenting is, what am I trying to convey to him in terms of faith or morality? I think I'm pretty clear on the morality part of it, but, I've always thought that morality or moral code only works in a spiritual context. So, I've had to decouple faith and morality which is something that still, intellectually, I don't think can be done. But my faith is too, sometimes it's a very black thing, whatever it is it's not something that I want to convey to my son. I can't offer him that. I can never tell him things happen for a reason. I can never tell him that things work out in the end because he knows that's not true. He can never tell himself that. And I can never say it to

> him.… One of the things I think I really owe to him is to make sense of things. And yet I'm wondering if that's going to be with us forever. The absence of an explanation, if we can't make sense of it that might linger with him. He doesn't show any signs of bitterness over it, but you know, it's one of the many things I suppose that you believe you need to do as a parent, and you can't do as a parent, and the fact that you can't do it doesn't allow you to forgive yourself for it. (Harris, 2-year-old child died, one surviving child)
>
> So, I'm thinking it's going to get better and it doesn't. I think it's just where it [grief] is. And that's where it's going to stay. It's depressing. It's very depressing. That part of it, I don't want to give to my children. Because they have a future ahead of them and they have so much to offer with what has happened to them, but it has to be in a positive way. If they don't see that from us, they could totally turn this around and use it as a detriment. Use it as "Oh, woe is me." And I don't want them to do that. So, there's that fine line. (Anna, 1-year-old child died, two surviving children)
>
> Well, you try and create some positivity in just unbearable situations. You try and do that. I've said to her, "I'm hoping that by your example, because you've got strong feelings about some things, you can influence your friends in a positive light." I'm hoping that, for me it's really important in such a bleak landscape that you can grab onto something positive and focus on that. I do that and as parents that's what we try to do in our parenting. We try, we don't always get there.… You want to impart some wisdom along the way. (Diane, 4-year-old child died, three surviving children)

Meaning making or meaning reconstruction appears to be a critical component in the grieving process (Attig, 1996; Davis, 2008; Fleming & Robinson, 2001; Nadeau, 2008; Neimeyer, 2006; Parkes, 1975; Rando, 1993; Worden, 2009; see also Chapter 2). The creation of meaning is not an effortless or straightforward endeavor; rather, it is an arduous quest demanding time, active engagement, and support. Clinicians are cautioned against attempts to rush the bereaved in the process of meaning reconstruction (Beder, 2005). The work to make meaning of a death, especially the death of a child, is ongoing and difficult, as is clear in the experiences of the bereaved parents in our study. Recognizing that their children also struggled to make sense of a reality in which their sibling could die (a reality that emphasized their own vulnerability and mortality), these parents attempted to create meaning or provide wisdom regarding the death—a task that proved to be perplexing and often inscrutable.

SUMMARY OF CLINICAL IMPLICATIONS

The challenges of parenting bereaved children are numerous, complex, and daunting, and require skill, energy, and patience that may not be readily available to most bereaved parents given the devastating impact the loss has exacted on them. Due to the intricate, pervasive nature of the loss for both parents and children, it is not uncommon for parents to seek professional help for themselves and their children. For practitioners, there are a number of clinical implications to consider when working with bereaved parents with surviving children.

- Assist parents in the task of recognizing and attending to the grieving process of their children, their developmental needs and changes (cognitive, behavioral, and affective), and the inevitable interaction of the two. The use of psychoeducational strategies may be particularly beneficial in an effort to inform parents about the multilayered grief process and the norms of development. This information may enable parents to recognize changes in their children that deviate from what would be expected in the developmental and grief contexts. Furthermore, these insights can assist parents in interpreting their own reactions to the changes they are witnessing in their children. Adolescence may need specific attention, as this transition has the potential to be particularly complicated and fractious as a result of the collision of adolescents striving for independence and autonomy and bereaved parents holding extensive and pressing concerns about safety and survival.
- Prepare parents for the challenge of revisiting the loss (often over many years) as surviving siblings mature and are able to accommodate a deeper understanding of the death and its profound, reverberating impact.
- Determine whether marked differences in grieving are evident in a family and assess (at the levels of both individual members and the family as a whole) whether these differences are problematic or complementary.
- Be attentive to the adjustments required of parents who are now faced with a one-child family. These include parenting adjustments and, frequently, role adjustments as parents attempt to fulfill some of the roles lost with the death of a sibling (e.g., playmate and confidante).
- Recognize that many bereaved parents feel powerless when witnessing the pain of their children's grief. It is important to work with parents to challenge their perception of helplessness and identify the ways in which they are effective in comforting and attending to their children's grief. This is a significant component in the overall process of rebuilding a sense of parental competence.
- Patiently support parents in the arduous pursuit of meaning reconstruction. This can be a particularly challenging endeavor for bereaved parents because the senseless tragedy of the death of a child resists meaning making, and, as parents, they feel ongoing pressure to provide their surviving children with hope, understanding, and wisdom regarding the death. With the potential to interpret the struggle to make sense of the death as parental failure, accompanied by further guilt and sadness, the clinician can play an important role in facilitating this process and challenging negative self-appraisal when difficulties are encountered.

The experiences of the bereaved parents who generously participated in our research, and the clinical implications that were derived from the data, offer insight into an aspect of the phenomenon of "bereaved parenting" and provide practitioners with a more comprehensive understanding of the nuances of treating bereaved parents with surviving children.

REFERENCES

Arnold, J. H., & Gemma, P. B. (1983). *A child dies: A portrait of family grief*. London: Aspen Systems.

Attig, T. (1996). *How we grieve: Relearning the world*. New York: Oxford University Press.

Balk, D. E. (1983). Adolescents' grief reactions and self-concept perceptions following sibling death: A study of 33 teenagers. *Journal of Youth and Adolescence*, *12*, 137–161.

Balmer, L. E. (1992). *Adolescent sibling bereavement: Mediating effects of family environment and personality* (PhD dissertation). York University, Toronto.

Becvar, D. S. (2001). *In the presence of grief: Helping family members resolve death, dying, and bereavement issues*. New York: Guilford Press.

Beder, J. (2005). Loss of the assumptive world: How do we deal with death and loss? *Omega*, *50*, 255–265.

Buckle, J. L., & Fleming, S. J. (2010). *Parenting after the death of a child: A practitioner's guide*. New York: Routledge.

Cryder, C. H., Kilmer, R. P., Tedeschi, R. G., & Calhoun, L. G. (2006). An exploratory study of posttraumatic growth in children following a natural disaster. *American Journal of Orthopsychiatry*, *76*, 65–69.

Davies, B. (1999). *Shadows in the sun: The experiences of sibling bereavement in childhood*. Philadelphia: Brunner/Mazel.

Davis, C. G. (2008). Redefining goals and redefining self: A closer look at posttraumatic growth following loss. In M. S. Stroebe, R. O. Hansson, H. Schut, & W. Stroebe (Eds.), *Handbook of bereavement research and practice: Advances in theory and intervention* (pp. 309–325). Washington, DC: American Psychological Association.

Fleming, S. J., & Adolph, R. (1986). Helping bereaved adolescents: Needs and responses. In C. A. Corr & J. N. McNeil (Eds.), *Adolescence and death* (pp. 97–118). New York: Springer.

Fleming, S. J., & Balmer, L. E. (1995). Bereaved Families of Ontario: A mutual-help model for families experiencing death. In L. A. DeSpelder & A. L. Strickland (Eds.), *The path ahead: Readings in death and dying* (pp. 281–294). Mountain View, CA: Mayfield.

Fleming, S. J., & Balmer, L. E. (1996). Bereavement in adolescence. In C. A. Corr & D. E. Balk (Eds.), *Handbook of adolescent death and bereavement* (pp. 139–154). New York: Springer.

Fleming, S. J., & Robinson, P. J. (2001). Grief and cognitive-behavioural therapy: The reconstruction of meaning. In M. Stroebe, R. O. Hansson, W. Stroebe, & H. Schut (Eds.), *Handbook of bereavement research: Consequences, coping, and care* (pp. 647–669). Washington, DC: American Psychological Association.

Forward, D. R., & Garlie, N. (2003). Search for new meaning: Adolescent bereavement after the sudden death of a sibling. *Canadian Journal of School Psychology, 18*, 23–53.

Glaser, B. G., & Strauss, A. L. (1967). *The discovery of grounded theory: Strategies for qualitative research*. New York: Aldine.

Hogan, N. S., & DeSantis, L. (1996). Adolescent sibling bereavement: towards a new theory. In C. A. Corr & D. E. Balk (Eds.), *Handbook of adolescent death and bereavement* (pp. 173–195). New York: Springer.

Lattanzi-Licht, M. (1996). Helping families with adolescents cope with loss. In C. A. Corr & Balk, D. E. (Eds.), *Handbook of adolescent death and bereavement* (pp. 219–234). New York: Springer.

Lohan, J. A., & Murphy, S. A. (2002). Parents' perceptions of adolescent sibling grief responses after an adolescent or young adult child's sudden, violent death. *Omega*, *44*, 77–95.

Malkinson, R. (2007). *Cognitive grief therapy: Constructing a rational meaning to life following loss*. New York: Norton.

McCown, D., & Davies, B. (1995). Patterns of grief in young children following the death of a sibling. *Death Studies*, *19*, 41–53.

Milam, J. E., Ritt-Olson, A., & Unger, J. (2004). Posttraumatic growth among adolescents. *Journal of Adolescent Research*, *19*, 192–204.

Moos, R. H., & Shaefer, J. A. (1986). Life transitions and crises: A conceptual overview. In R. H. Moos (Ed.), *Coping with life crises: An integrated approach* (pp. 3–28). New York: Plenum Press.

Nadeau, J. W. (2008). Meaning-making in bereaved families: Assessment, intervention, and future research. In M. S. Stroebe, R. O. Hansson, H. Schut, & W. Stroebe (Eds.), *Handbook of bereavement research and practice: Advances in theory and intervention* (pp. 511–530). Washington, DC: American Psychological Association.

Neimeyer, R. A. (2006). Re-storying loss: Fostering growth in the posttraumatic narrative. In L. Calhoun & R. Tedeschi (Eds.), *Handbook of posttraumatic growth: Research and practice* (pp. 68–80). Mahwah, NJ: Lawrence Erlbaum.

Parkes, C. M. (1975). What becomes of redundant world models? A contribution to the study of adaptation to change. *British Journal of Medical Psychology*, *48*, 131–137.

Rando, T. A. (1993). *Treatment of complicated mourning*. Champaign, IL: Research Press.

Rennie, D. L. (2000). Grounded theory methodology as methodical hermeneutics: Reconciling realism and relativism. *Theory and Psychology*, *10*, 481–502.

Rennie, D. L., Phillips, J. R., & Quartaro, G. K. (1988). Grounded theory: A promising approach to conceptualization in psychology? *Canadian Psychology*, *29*, 139–150.

Riches, G., & Dawson, P. (2000). *An intimate loneliness: Supporting bereaved parents and siblings*. Buckingham: Open University Press.

Worden, J. W. (2009). *Grief counseling and grief therapy: A handbook for the mental health practitioner* (4th ed.). New York: Springer.

10

Bereavement in Children and Adults Following the Death of a Sibling

BRENDA MARSHALL and BETTY DAVIES

ECHOES OF EACH OTHER'S BEING.
Whose eyes are those that look like mine?
Whose smile reminds me of my own?
Whose thoughts come through with just a glance?
Who knows me as no others do?
Who in the whole wide world is most like me
Yet not like me at all?
My sibling.

Faber and Mazlish (1989, p. 114)

Even from the time that a family is expecting a new baby's arrival, a special bond develops between siblings. They protect one another, support one another, and ally together against parents and others. They share bedrooms, meals, holidays, family milestones, and a way of growing up that is unique to them. Numerous shared jokes and memories form an underpinning of familiarity that can never be achieved with anyone else. "If not for death, they [siblings] would be with us longer than anyone else on earth" (Vaught Godfrey, 2006, p. 7). This relationship, unique in its longevity and intimacy, is potentially the longest one they will ever have (Gill White, 2006).

Thus, the death of a brother or sister can be traumatic for siblings at any age. In fact, siblings' stories indicate the impact of such a death lasts a lifetime, forever influencing siblings in their ways of being in the world. Although the impact of sibling death in childhood is well documented (Balk, 1990; Davies, 1991; Hogan & DeSantis, 1992; Martinson & Gates Campos, 1991; Packman, Horsely, Davies, &

Kramer, 2006; Robinson & Mahon, 1997; Walker, 1993), sibling loss in adulthood is not (Marshall, 2009a; Robinson & Mahon, 1997). In this chapter, we bring together two complementary views and approaches to the topic. One author's (BD's) experience and expertise are grounded in a background in health care with a long career in end-of-life care and bereavement, particularly in families following a child's death. The other author's (BM's) work in adult sibling loss originates from her own experience with loss and findings from her research (2009a).

CHILDHOOD SIBLING LOSS (BD)

Not all siblings are affected to the same degree by a child's death. Many factors affect children's grief responses (Davies, 1999). Characteristics of individual siblings include the child's age and gender, health status, temperament or coping style, and previous experience with loss. Situational factors refer to characteristics of the situation itself, such as duration of illness, cause of death, location of death, and the degree to which children were involved in the events pertaining to their brother or sister's illness, death, and related events, such as the funeral or memorial service. Bereaved children who were actively involved in the care of their sibling or in planning the funeral or in related events demonstrate fewer behavioral problems than children who were excluded from such activities (Davies, 1988a, 1999). Giving children a clearly informed choice about whether or not they want to be involved is of key importance. Finally, psychosocial environmental factors have an enormous impact upon sibling grief. The nature of the predeath relationship, for example, is critical. When children have shared many aspects of their lives, the loss of one child leaves a large empty space in the surviving sibling. When two children share a particularly close relationship, the empty space is even larger (Davies, 1988a, 1999). The family environment also plays a central role. For example, in families where communication is more open than closed, and feelings, thoughts, and ideas are more freely expressed, a sense of cohesion or closeness exists, and bereaved siblings exhibit fewer behavioral problems (Davies, 1988b, 1999). Because families do not live in social vacuums, their culture and community values and priorities also impact sibling bereavement. But the central critical factor influencing sibling bereavement is the nature of the interactions between the siblings and the significant adults in their lives (Davies, 1999).

Based on her research with bereaved children and adolescents, and with adults who in their childhood lost a brother or sister, Davies (1999) has characterized sibling bereavement responses using the words of siblings themselves.

"I Hurt Inside"

This response includes all the physical responses and emotions typically associated with grief that arise from the vulnerability of being human, from loving others and missing them when they are no longer with us. Bereaved siblings' hurt includes sadness, anger, frustration, loneliness, fear, irritability, and all the many other emotions that characterize grief. Unlike adults, who can verbalize and share their emotional responses, children are often unable or inexperienced at identifying what they are feeling. Instead, they express emotions through behavior. For example, some siblings hesitate to return to familiar activities, such as walking to school alone. Others act out by not listening to their parents or becoming irritable and belligerent. Some may experience sleep disorders; many experience loss of appetite or overeating. A decline in school performance may be evident, or overachievement may be a signal that a bereaved child or adolescent is trying to fulfill unrealistic self-imposed expectations. Persistent changes in siblings' behavior and a pattern of problems are significant; no one behavior or outburst alone is necessarily an indication of trouble (although it usually means some extra attention is advisable). It is important to remember that a child's death also holds potential for growth in siblings, as evidenced by increased competence in handling adversity and confidence in facing death and helping others.

For children who "hurt inside," the goal is to help children accept whatever emotion they experience and to manage those emotions in appropriate ways. This is easier said than done. Because children seldom verbalize their thoughts and feelings—at least not in adults' terms—it is important that caring adults watch for changes in the child's behavior and respond sensitively. Children who are hurting inside need comforting and consoling. They do not need lectures, judgments, teasing, or interrogations. Rather, they need someone who is consistent and honest, and who is willing to share his or her own thoughts and feelings with the child. Helping children who "hurt inside" is a two-way process, with sharing by both the children and the significant adults in their lives.

The other three response categories are rooted in a different kind of vulnerability—the kind that arises from children's dependence on adults for information, inclusion, and validation. Therefore, how adults respond to siblings' hurt contributes to the degree to which siblings experience these other responses.

"I Don't Understand"

How children begin to make sense of death depends in large part on their level of cognitive development. However, once children know about death from personal experience, their worlds are forever altered. Today's children, constantly exposed to television scenes of war and terrorism, are all too aware of the reality of death. But such awareness only compounds their confusion if they are not helped to understand and, in their own way, make sense of death and related events. As siblings grow and develop and enter new ways of understanding and approaching the world, they will have more questions about the death. Each new developmental phase will trigger additional questions and the desire to hear the story of the death yet again. This is a normal phenomenon, and not a sign that the child is "dwelling" on the death.

To help children who "don't understand," adults need to remember that confusion and ignorance are additional forms of hurting. Therefore, adults must continue to comfort and console. Adults have a responsibility to be aware of what children understand, and to offer honest explanations that fit with the children's developmental capabilities. Caregivers must be open to children's questions, giving them the freedom to ask whatever they want without fear of ridicule. Helping children understand is not just providing information about facts and events but also giving information about feelings, about what to expect, and about what not to expect. Teaching them about the reality of death and responding to their feelings and questions are of paramount importance.

"I Don't Belong"

A death in the family tears apart the normal day-to-day patterns of family life. Parents are overwhelmed with their grief; siblings are also overwhelmed with the flurry of activity and the heaviness of emotion that surrounds them. Siblings do not know what to do or how to help, and if they try, their efforts may not be acknowledged. Siblings may begin to feel as if they are not part of what is happening. Over time, as roles and responsibilities realign within the family, siblings may feel as if there no longer is a place for them. They may find solace outside of their family, but often their experience with death makes adolescent siblings in particularly feel very different from their peers. They may feel as if "I don't belong" within their family and with their friends. Encouraging children to help, even in little ways, with caring for an ill brother or sister, or involving them in the rituals surrounding death are ways of counteracting the sense of "not belonging" as long as their siblings' individual choices are also respected.

"I'm Not Enough"

Siblings typically want to alleviate their parents' despair. But, regardless of what they do, their parents' sadness persists and siblings may feel they are "not enough" to make their parents happy. Moreover, some siblings feel as if the child who died was their parents' favorite. In such cases, siblings may feel they should have been the one to die. Often, such feelings of inferiority were present before the death, but are compounded when parents direct intense emotion and longing toward the deceased child. Feelings of "not enough" may be enhanced for siblings who feel responsible for the death. Or for siblings who feel displaced by the addition of other children to the family, resulting in the siblings' conclusions that "I am not enough—otherwise, why would mom and dad need another child?" (Davies, 1999).

Helping siblings feel valued, loved, and considered special by the adults in their lives is the best way to help children avoid feeling "I am not enough." Validating their worth, not necessarily for their accomplishments, but for just being in the world, is integral to making children feel special in the eyes of the adults who mean the most to them. If adults interact with bereaved siblings in ways that comfort their hurt, clarify their confusion, and involve them in what is happening, it is unlikely that bereaved siblings will feel as if they are "not enough."

When asked what advice siblings have for adults who want to help grieving children, they inevitably respond, "Don't forget the brothers and sisters!" Their words capture well the most important message. Though sibling grief may be a difficult, long, and lonely journey, it is not one which siblings must travel alone if the significant adults in their lives acknowledge the impact of sibling bereavement and are willing to walk alongside them on their journey, comforting and consoling, teaching, involving, and validating the unique specialness of each child.

ADULT SIBLING LOSS (BM)

"And when did your brother die?" she asked.

"It's been 6 weeks," I replied.

She scribbled some notes. "Oh, that is very new. We ask that you let 4 months pass before you participate in one of our groups. You are still in shock. You haven't really started the grief process yet."

"My God, how could I feel any worse than I do right now?" I thought to myself. I began to weep. "Do you have anything I can read about siblings?" I asked.

"You know, I don't think we do. I know I have one person in our 'others' group who lost her brother—but we don't really have anything specific for siblings."

Brenda, personal story, November 15, 2006

My (BM's) brother died September 16, 2006. He was 38. I think of that date as my "last day of normal." Everything changed after—family relationships, friendships, and my academic and professional interests. And although I am now used to my new way of thinking and living, I still long for the life I had. At the time, I was a management consultant in a busy city practice, and in the midst of completing doctoral studies. My brother's death prompted an about-face from my planned thesis topic and, eventually, my career path. Finding little support material for bereaved adult siblings, I chose to conduct a narrative inquiry into this topic, which I hoped would form the basis for ongoing research. I completed 15 in-depth interviews with three bereaved adult siblings, Rena, Catherine, and Karen, chronicling their experiences and my own, in a series of stories (2009a). It is that research, and the ongoing conversations I continue to have with other bereaved adult siblings, that form the basis for this portion of the chapter.

Sibling loss is known as a disenfranchised loss (Doka, 2002; Wray, 2003; Zampitella, 2006). It is not typically recognized as being as significant as the loss felt by others who were also close to the deceased person. Amongst adults, concern is first directed toward the surviving spouse and children, and then for the deceased's parents. I saw this first hand after my brother died and heard it in the voices and stories of the participants in my study. We fielded questions about how our parents were doing, how spouses were coping, and how the children were managing. Very rarely, did someone inquire about us. In spite of years spent interacting with our siblings, we were outside the primary circle of support.

Connidis (1992) studied 60 sibling dyads aged 25 to 89 to explore the effect of life transitions on what she called the *adult sibling tie*. She reported that the majority of siblings maintained an important and valued connection throughout life. Although some participants noted there were times when they were in less frequent contact with their sibling, for the most part the closeness of the sibling tie was something that participants felt could be rekindled or mobilized when needed. "Siblings remain life long parts of most adults' social networks" (White, 2001, p. 566). Further studies have shown that the average adult has contact with a sibling once or twice a month for 60 or 70 years after leaving home (White, 2001). With today's use of social networking, text messaging, and email, it is even easier to remain in close contact. Although the strength and importance of the "living" relationship are recognized, the loss of it is not. However, just as the loss during childhood is seen as significant, the loss of a sibling in adulthood is, too. Davies's (1999) four-part model offers a useful framework for considering this loss in adults.

"I Hurt Inside"

Adults, like children, experience tremendous pain and suffering after the death of their sibling. "It was an overwhelming grief for me" (Catherine, as cited in Marshall, 2009a, p. 106). Catherine, who had previously lost a beloved parent and grandparent, found the death of her brother most difficult to reconcile. Although she acknowledged terrible pain from the previous losses, nothing prepared her for the impact and the lengthy depression that followed her brother's death. Similarly, Karen, whose brother died in a house fire at age 40, experienced significant cognitive disruptions for a year following his death. "I don't remember anything, I don't remember taking pictures at Christmas, I don't remember Christmas shopping. I was just beside myself.... It was the loneliest time of my life" (Karen, as cited in Marshall, 2009b, p. 13). Her personality changed. Previously tolerant and easygoing, she became angry and bitter, especially toward those with living siblings who did not appear to value the relationship. And although developmentally able to use language to describe what they were feeling, all of these individuals found friends, work colleagues, and family members ill prepared to offer support. They simply did not understand the pain. This lack of support, coupled with few societal resources to acknowledge the loss, led to the silencing of their stories, which had an impact upon their ability to integrate this loss into their lives.

"I Don't Understand"

Although the deaths of aging parents (and potentially spouses) seemed possible and normal, losing a sibling did not. It was out of order. As Karen remarked in referencing her father's death, "I think it doesn't break my heart as much, because that's the natural sequence of life, whereas my brother should have been beside me … and he's not" (Karen, as cited in Marshall, 2009a, p. 84). The death of a sibling in adulthood calls into question the norms of life. My sibling was meant to grow old with me. We were supposed to go away for weekends, attend our children's weddings, bury our parents, and just spend time together. How can all that be gone? Although children may turn to parents or other trusted adults to make sense of their sibling's death, as noted previously, adults do not readily find support. And, in many cases, they find themselves managing the pain of their aging parents who have lost their child. Webster Blank (1998), herself a bereaved parent of an adult child, writes about the special difficulties elderly parents face when they lose a child: "It is late; life is winding down; they have less energy, flexibility, and resiliency to cope with the tragedy" (p. 18). Almost instantly, surviving adult children feel they need to step in and take over; our parents are suddenly fragile and seemingly unable to cope. As children, we are not accustomed to seeing our parents this way.

"I Do Not Belong"

"It's like a giant hole in my life" are words I heard often. The absence of a sibling permeates all aspects of an adult's life, as if one does not belong to the "new order." Each sibling was actively involved in the funeral arrangements for the deceased brother or sister. They delivered eulogies and played the role of comforter to aging parents, bereaved spouses, and, in some cases, bewildered children who had just lost a parent. Parenting their children became more difficult. Each spoke of difficult reactions to their children's bickering, feeling disconnected from family events, and lacking energy to be the parents they were earlier (2009a). The changed structure of their family of origin was also painful. Traditional holidays that previously involved parents, siblings, and cousins were suddenly drastically different. Not only was their sibling missing, but also often their deceased sibling's spouse and children stopped coming, altering the entire family dynamic. For both Karen and me, our siblings left behind young children. We felt responsible for ensuring their well-being on behalf of our deceased siblings. Karen's brother was in the midst of a separation when he died in a house fire. Her immediate concern was for his children. "Oh my God, they'll have nothing. How will they remember their father? … I immediately started going through all of my pictures. I put together a box for each of them and shipped them out right away" (Karen, as cited in Marshall, 2009a, p. 78). In my family, I see myself as the "keeper of stories" for my brother Brent's children. I, too, have put together a memory book for them and continue to try to keep him alive through sharing stories and photographs of our lives growing up.

"I Am Not Enough"

As adults, we have the cognitive ability to understand that the death of a child is life altering. And that knowledge is painful, for we know our parents are suffering and we want to help. Karen removed a video of her brother's wedding from her parents' home, fearing that her mom would watch it over and over and fall into a deep depression. Catherine and Rena stopped mentioning their siblings in front of their parents. "You kind of feel your way around and you get to know subconsciously what you do and don't talk about" (Catherine, as cited in Marshall, 2009a, p. 109). In my family, I visit and call more frequently, trying to fill the gap created by my brother's absence. Intellectually, I know this is impossible, and yet I try. Other bereaved siblings I have subsequently met find that their parents' memorialization of their deceased sibling forces them to take on the role of listener. One noted, "There isn't a scrapbook about me." Like young children, although for different reasons, we know we are "not enough" to make our parents happy ever again. Even as adults, bereaved siblings adapt their behavior to fit with how their parents wish to remember (or not) their deceased child. When that coping method is silence, it creates a "separation from stories" that is painful.

Like children, individual, situational, and environmental characteristics interact and play a role in how an adult responds to the death of a sibling (Davies, 1999; Davies & Limbo, 2010). Individual characteristics like coping style, temperament, and previous experiences with loss influence how both children and adults cope. All participants in my study eventually turned to professionals to assist in their recovery. When siblings die suddenly, search for meaning begins with understanding the details of the death. Where did it happen? How did they die? For both Karen and Catherine, whose siblings died under traumatic circumstances, seeing coroner's reports and other data associated with the investigations was of critical importance. For Rena, who had a background in nursing and had been involved in her sister's care during her cancer treatments, that question was answered. All three described their deceased sibling as the one with whom they felt most connected, leaving an unfillable emptiness. I have also now met others who had more complicated relationships. Their sadness is over a missed opportunity to mend the relationship or get to know one another differently. For all, however, the loss is felt deeply.

As adults, bereaved siblings are not the focus of hospital workers, hospices, or funeral homes. There is an assumption that we can manage and cope with this loss independently. Perhaps this is why research on this population is limited. And yet, it is clear that the impact of losing a sibling in adulthood ripples across multiple levels. We are changed as parents, as children of aging parents, and as aunts and uncles to the children of our deceased siblings. Although not practicing as a clinician, I continually receive calls and referrals from bereaved siblings who simply want to talk. Almost universally, they acknowledge the loneliness of moving through life without their sibling.

The opportunity to tell one's story, to share feelings and to know that this loss "matters" in the greater community is important. "Our personal narratives are not merely a way of describing our lives. They are the means by which we bring order" (Gilbert, 2002, p. 224). Sharing grief with others is the underpinning of many community-based self-help bereavement groups. Adult siblings are often excluded from such opportunities, and are further excluded by the community at large, which places the loss of a sibling lower on the grief hierarchy. And, although these two "exclusions" contribute to the challenges faced by bereaved adult siblings, silencing within their family of origin is even more striking. Bereaved children, whether still children or adults, must work around grieving parents.

CONCLUSION

"The grave does not obliterate the place of the sibling in the family" (Klass, Silverman, & Nickman, 1996, p. 233). The loss of a brother or sister at any age has a profound impact upon siblings. For siblings, whether child, adolescent, or adult, bereavement is a complex process that is multidimensional in nature. All siblings share responses of hurting on the inside and feeling an indescribable emptiness, of puzzlement and confusion about so many aspects of the situation, of sensing they are now different from their friends and sometimes feeling abandoned by their peers, of feeling left out and alone and silencing their thoughts and feelings to protect their parents, and of feeling that they will never "be enough" to make their grieving parents happy again. They all report that the effects persist indefinitely. And yet, for many, growth and an expanded worldview also result.

Sibling bereavement at any age is affected by a wide range of factors—individual, situational, and environmental. For children and adults alike, family structure is a significant factor influencing how siblings respond to grief. "Our stories inform our lives and our lives, in turn, are shaped by our stories. We need to create stories to make order of disorder to find meaning in the meaningless" (Gilbert, 2002, p. 236). Part of recovering meaning is acknowledging that what was lost was meaningful. For children and adults who lose siblings, there are limited opportunities to talk through their loss with interested others. Family members are an obvious first choice, but, as noted, grieving parents of any age are typically ill equipped to assist in this role. Communication within the family of origin is significantly disrupted when a sibling dies. Whether in adulthood or childhood, the death of a sibling creates huge ripples in relationships that are difficult to navigate.

Our findings have theoretical significance in expanding knowledge about sibling bereavement and increasing awareness that bereaved siblings may share similar experiences with one another across ages than with nonbereaved individuals of the same age. Further study of bereaved adult siblings will provide more data for comparisons. Clinically, our findings emphasize that grieving siblings must not be ignored, but rather supported in their lonely journey. For clinicians who encounter bereaved adult siblings, recognizing the potential for disrupted relationships across multiple spheres is helpful. As well, understanding that simply providing an opportunity for adults to talk through the significance of a sibling's death with an interested "other" can be enormously helpful. As Karen noted in referencing her participation in Marshall's (2009a) study,

> This was better than therapy … it wasn't about fixing me or telling me to do something differently.… I got to talk about Brian and it made me remember all kinds of happy memories. Before, all I had was the funeral and his death. Now, I can think about our relationship and how lucky I was. (p. 170)

It is also helpful for clinicians to understand the many roles that grieving adults may be playing across multiple families. Within their own family, they may be struggling in their role as a parent. Within their family of origin, they may have taken on additional caregiving responsibilities with aging, and now grieving, parents. And within their deceased sibling's family, their responsibilities may have increased substantially, or decreased, depending on the reaction of the surviving spouse. Recognizing that all these changes bring additional pressures that are unique to grieving siblings is important.

Davies (1999) wrote, "Grief at the time of a child's death may cast long shadows" (p. 219). Indeed, the shadows caused by the death of a brother or sister may arise at any point in a sibling's life, but once there, they linger always. The lost opportunity to experience important milestones, celebrate successes, and grow old together is stark. Finding ways to integrate this loss into their lives is critical for siblings of any age. Having the help of loving and skilled companions who are willing to share the shadows allows sunlight to filter through the dark place.

REFERENCES

Balk, D. E. (1990). The self-concepts of bereaved adolescents: Sibling death and its aftermath. *Journal of Adolescent Research*, *5*, 112–132.

Connidis, I. A. (1992). Life transitions and the adult sibling tie: A qualitative study. *Journal of Marriage and the Family*, *54*(4), 972–982.

Davies, B. (1988a). Shared life space and sibling bereavement responses. *Cancer Nursing*, *11*(6), 339–347.

Davies, B. (1988b). The family environment in bereaved families and its relationship to surviving sibling behavior. *Children's Health Care*, *17*(1), 22–31.

Davies, B. (1991). Long-term outcomes of adolescent sibling bereavement. *Journal of Adolescent Research*, *6*(1), 83–96.

Davies, B. (1999). *Shadows in the sun: Experiences of sibling bereavement in childhood.* Philadelphia: Brunner/Mazel.

Davies, B., & Limbo, R. (2010). The grief of siblings. In N. B. Webb (Ed.), *Helping bereaved children* (4th ed., pp. 69–91). New York: Guilford Press.

Doka, K. (2002). Introduction. In K. Doka (Ed.), *Disenfranchised grief* (pp. 5–21). Champaign, IL: Research Press.

Faber, A., & Mazlish, E. (1989). *Between brothers and sisters: A celebration of life's most enduring relationship*. New York: Avon.

Gilbert, K. (2002). Taking a narrative approach to grief research: Finding meaning in stories. *Death Studies*, *26*, 223–239.

Gill White, P. (2006). *Sibling grief*. New York: iUniverse.

Hogan, N., & DeSantis, L. (1992). Adolescent sibling bereavement: An ongoing attachment. *Qualitative Health Research*, *2*, 159–177.

Klass, D., Silverman, P. R., & Nickman, S. L. (1996). Bereaved siblings. In D. Klass, P. R. Silverman, & S. L. Nickman (Eds.), *Continuing bonds: New understandings of grief* (pp. 233–234). Philadelphia: Taylor & Francis.

Marshall, B. J. (2009a). Silent grief: Narratives of bereaved adult siblings (PhD dissertation). University of Toronto, Toronto. Available from University of Toronto Research Repository. Retrieved from http://hdl.handle.net/1807/19153

Marshall, B. J. (2009b, April). Silent grief: A narrative inquiry into the meaning making processes of bereaved adult siblings, Paper presented at annual conference of the Association of Death Education and Counseling, Dallas, TX.

Martinson, I., & Gates Campos, R. (1991). Adolescent bereavement: Long-term responses to a sibling's death from cancer. *Journal of Adolescent Research*, *6*(1), 54–69.

Packman, W., Horsley, H., Davies, B., & Kramer, R. (2006). Sibling bereavement and continuing bonds. *Death Studies*, *30*, 817–841.

Robinson, L., & Mahon, M., M. (1997). Sibling bereavement: A concept analysis. *Death Studies*, *21*(5), 477–499.

Vaught Godfrey, R. (2006). Losing a sibling in adulthood. *The Forum*, *32*(1), 6–7.

Walker, C. (1993). Sibling bereavement and grief responses. *Journal of Paediatric Nursing*, *8*(5), 325–334.

Webster Blank, J. (1998). *The death of an adult child*. Amityville, NY: Baywood.

White, L. (2001). Sibling relationships over the life course: A panel analysis. *Journal of Marriage and the Family*, *63*(2), 555–568.

Wray, T. J. (2003). *Surviving the death of a sibling: Living through grief when an adult brother or sister dies*. New York: Three Rivers Press.

Zampitella, C. (2006). Using nature-based rituals as an intervention for adult sibling survivors. *The Forum*, *32*(1), 9–15.

11

Bridging the Gap
Translating a Research-Based Program into an Agency-Based Service for Bereaved Children and Families

TIMOTHY S. AYERS, C. CARYN KONDO,
and IRWIN N. SANDLER

There is growing recognition that a wide gap exists between university-based experimental trials of intervention programs and successful delivery of these interventions in community settings. The multiple reasons for this gap have been well described in prior discussions of the research-to-practice gap in treatment (Addis, 2002; Clarke, 1995; Schoenwald & Hoagwood, 2001) and preventive interventions (Biglan, Mrazek, Carnine, & Flay, 2003; Kellam & Langevin, 2003; National Advisory Mental Health Council [NAMHC] Workgroup on Prevention Research, 1998). The contexts in which interventions are delivered in community agencies differ from the context of traditional experimental research trials on many dimensions that affect their capacity to deliver highly structured, manualized interventions, including characteristics of providers, clients, and the agencies' capacity for provider training and supervision (Dobson & Craig, 1998; Duan, Braslow, Weisz, & Wells, 2001; Schoenwald & Hoagwood, 2001). The report of the NAMHC's Workgroup on Child and Adolescent Mental Health Intervention Development and Deployment (2001) concluded that reducing this gap required a new approach to intervention development in which a focus on "the final resting place for treatment or service delivery be folded into the design, development, refinement, and implementation of the intervention from the beginning" (p. 6). In the child treatment literature, Weisz and colleagues (Weisz, Chu, & Polo, 2004) have advanced a deployment-focused model in which they encourage strong clinician–researcher collaborations during many of the phases of developing and testing new interventions in treatment settings. The prevention service development model offered by Sandler and colleagues (Sandler, Ostrom, Bitner, Ayers, & Wolchik, 2005) also highlights the importance of close collaborations with end users and advocates proactively involving these users in the design and evaluation of new services. Although Sandler et al. (2005) advocated that the collaboration begin at the earliest stage of the design of the intervention, they recognized that collaboration is also needed to find ways for community agencies to optimally adapt programs that were initially tested in a research context so that they can be effectively delivered to their clients.

Such collaborations to bridge the research–practice gap are particularly important for interventions developed for parentally bereaved children for three reasons. First, there has not been a great deal of research to evaluate the effectiveness of programs for bereaved children, and recent summaries of the findings from these studies have been disappointing (Currier, Holland, & Neimeyer, 2007). Thus, it is important that intervention models with demonstrated efficacy be translated into a usable service. Second, although a large number of agencies provide services to this population, these agencies are generally not well linked to the research community (Bridging Work Group, 2005). Third, the community settings that provide bereavement services to families differ markedly in terms of resources and models of service provided, which could limit their ability to implement research-based interventions, which are often manualized and place a premium on training for fidelity of delivery.

This chapter describes a collaboration between the developers and researchers of the Family Bereavement Program (FBP), a preventive intervention for parentally bereaved families that has demonstrated positive effects in a rigorous experimental trial and a local bereavement support agency that agreed to pilot-test the delivery of the intervention within its agency. The goal of this paper is to detail this collaboration, which included an extensive process of revising the intervention from one that was used in a university-based research trial to one that could be realistically implemented in a bereavement support agency. In addition, the types of training and technical support tools that were developed to support the implementation of the intervention in a bereavement support agency will be presented. Finally, a description of the actual pilot test of the revised intervention by the community agency and the reactions of both the developers of the program (Ayers and Sandler) and the agency personnel (Kondo) of Hospice of the Valley's New Song Center for Grieving Children and Those That Love Them (NSC) regarding the implementation of this program will be offered.[1]

RISK TO BEREAVED YOUTH AND YOUNG WIDOWED PARENTS

The loss of a parent, experienced by approximately 3.5% of children (Social Security Administration, 2000) in the United States, is one of the most traumatic events that can happen to a child (Yamamoto et al., 1996). For bereaved youth, the death of a parent frequently involves additional stressors, such as relocation of the family, depression and grief of the surviving caregiver, and increased family responsibilities. In the short term, bereaved youth are at risk for a wide range of mental health problems, including depression, anxiety, externalizing problems, feelings of vulnerability, and low self-esteem (Lutzke, Ayers, Sandler, & Barr, 1997; Tremblay & Israel, 1998; Worden & Silverman, 1996). A recent study by Melhem and colleagues (Melhem, Walker, Moritz, & Brent, 2008) found that after controlling for preexisting disorders and concomitant risk factors, parentally bereaved children had higher rates of depression, PTSD, and overall diagnosed disorders, and lower levels of competent functioning as compared with nonbereaved youth. In a community sample of 360 parentally bereaved children, Cerel, Fristad, Verducci, Weller, and Weller (2006) found higher overall depression and psychiatric symptoms than a nonbereaved community comparison group over a 2-year period. Furthermore, early parental death results in an increased risk of psychological disorders over the life span (Agid et al., 1999; Luecken, 2008; Mack, 2001).

In most instances, the death of a parent also leaves a bereaved spouse as a widow or widower. Prior research has found that younger widows and widowers, those in the age range where they are likely to have children at home, are at elevated risk for multiple problem outcomes, particularly increased levels of depression, which can persist several years following the death (McCrae & Costa, 1993; Stroebe, Schut, & Stroebe, 2007; Zisook & Kendler, 2007; Zisook & Schuchter, 1993). Early widowhood has also been associated with increased risk for suicide among both men and women (Kreitman, 1988; Smith, Mercy, & Conn, 1988), but particularly for white and African American males for whom recent data suggest a 17-fold and 9-fold increase in risk for suicide, respectively, relative to their married counterparts (Luoma & Pearson, 2002).

BACKGROUND DESCRIPTION OF THE FAMILY BEREAVEMENT PROGRAM (FBP)

The FBP is a manualized program designed to prevent mental health problems among children who were parentally bereaved (Sandler et al., 2003). The FBP was designed to promote resilience of parentally bereaved children by strengthening protective factors that prior research has found to be associated with better outcomes for this population, and reducing risk factors that are associated with worse outcomes (Sandler et al., 2008). The FBP includes a group program for the caregivers and for the children and adolescents who meet simultaneously over a 12-week period. The caregiver group was designed to improve positive parenting (i.e., warmth of relationship between caregiver and child and positive discipline practices) and caregiver mental health as well as to decrease children's exposure to stressful events. The child and adolescent groups each targeted the same empirically supported correlates but differed in that the activities utilized in each group were constructed to be developmentally appropriate. The child and adolescent groups were designed to increase positive exchanges with caregivers, increase active coping efforts, and decrease negative appraisals of stressful events and the inhibition of emotional expression related to bereavement. All of the groups were 12 sessions in length with 2 individual sessions between sessions 3 and 5 and then again between sessions 7 and 9. Further description of the FBP intervention and the targets of the intervention can be found elsewhere (Ayers et al., in press; Sandler et al., 2008). Although the FBP was originally designed for delivery in an experimental trial, it should be noted that from the very beginning the content of the program was designed in a close collaboration between the research team and several clinicians who were active providers of services in community agencies. In addition, the program was subject to two pilot tests and was extensively revised based on feedback from bereaved parents and youth prior to the experimental trial.

The randomized experimental trial of the FBP demonstrated that immediately posttest, the program improved positive parenting, active coping, and caregiver mental health, and reduced children's exposure to negative events and inhibition of emotional expression. At the 11-month follow-up, the FBP was found to reduce internalizing problems (such as anxiety and depression) and externalizing problems (such as aggression and oppositionality) for girls (but not boys) who participated in the program relative to a bibliotherapy condition. In a 6-year follow-up positive program, effects were found for both caregivers and youth. Caregivers who participated in the FBP had higher levels of positive parenting and lower levels of mental health problems as compared with those in the bibliotherapy comparison group (Hagan, Tein, Sandler, Wolchik, & Ayers, 2009; Sandler et al., 2008). As compared with youth in the comparison condition, the youth who participated in the FBP had lower externalizing problems as reported by caregivers, youth, and teachers, and lower internalizing problems as reported by teachers, and by their own report had higher self-esteem (Sandler et al., in press) and lower levels of problematic grief (Sandler et al., 2010).

COLLABORATION BETWEEN FBP PROGRAM DEVELOPERS AND COMMUNITY AGENCY

The collaboration between the developers of the FBP and the local agency in the Phoenix area that agreed to conduct a pilot test of implementation of the FBP, the NSC, grew out of a 15-year relationship between the developers of the FBP and various staff members of the NSC. A past president of NSC's board of directors was a consultant on the initial development of the FBP program that was evaluated in the experimental trial. Another board member collected data for her dissertation within ASU's Prevention Research Center, and three other group leaders in the experimental trial of FBP have been paid staff at the NSC. This interplay between the developers and various staff of the NSC over the years helped to strengthen the respect and trust held between staff at the university and the agency and undoubtedly contributed to the willingness of the NSC to participate in a pilot test of implementation of the FBP.

Although the findings from the experimental trial evaluating the FBP described above are promising, it should be emphasized that the trial was conducted at

ASU's Prevention Research Center, a university-based center, under conditions in which investigators had considerable control over all aspects of implementation. Implementation conditions in community agencies are quite different. This was the case for the NSC. In our initial discussions with the NSC staff and staff of other bereavement support agencies, we learned that there is frequently less time for training and supervision than we had in the research trial. This is in part because the service providers within these agencies are often volunteers who frequently do not have mental health background and usually have limited time that they can commit on a weekly basis for this volunteer work. This was not the case in the conduct of the FBP experimental trial in which the providers were paid staff who had a master's degree or above in a helping profession and were able to commit at least 12–15 hours per week to conduct a 2-hour group. These 12–15 hours per week allow time for the group leaders to learn the session, to practice it before group, and to have supervision to review the past session and plan for the next session. Another difference between the research implementation and community agency implementation concerns eligibility criteria for participants. In the research trial, there were several issues that would make someone ineligible to participate, including age of the child, within a certain time period following the death, exceeding clinical level on one or more mental disorder diagnoses, having suicidal intent, and simultaneously receiving a different treatment. In contrast, most bereavement support agencies try to serve families who come to them and have fewer eligibility criteria for potential participants.

As a first step in planning for the implementation of the FBP, developers incorporated feedback from staff at the NSC and various other bereavement support agencies to guide the revisions to the program in order to make it more practical to implement within the context of the agency. A review of the manual by agency personnel indicated that although the FBP was more structured and used a skill-teaching model that was not currently used by the agency, the content of the FBP was appropriate for the bereaved families seen by the agency, and was consistent with their own perceptions of the needs of these families. However, the manual was overly long and was not user friendly for the agency providers. In response, the manual was simplified, reducing the amount of "scripted material," and the format and layout were changed to make it easier for facilitators to use during the actual sessions. These revisions also involved the development of PowerPoint presentations for each session of all groups, which allowed the group leaders to present most of the material from these standard slides, saving on preparation time prior to the sessions. The PowerPoint slides also replaced posters that had been used in the experimental trial, but that needed to be stored and were clumsy to use. Instructional videos were embedded within the presentation directly, again with the intention to simplify the presentation of the program, and to provide models for teaching program skills. This modeling by video reduced the need for role play modeling by the group leaders. New workbooks were developed that could be used by participants during the session itself, and the original handouts used in the trial were revised so that they could more systematically gather information about the participants' skill practice between sessions. As bereavement support agencies often use volunteer staff to help serve as leaders in their support groups, these revisions and new developments of session materials were done to reduce the "burden" on leaders both in their preparation for the session and for delivery of the FBP during the session.

One issue that arose early in the collaborative planning of the implementation pilot was whether to test delivery of all components of the program—the child and adolescent groups as well as the caregiver groups—or to deliver only one component, the caregiver group. The program developers were concerned that delivery of all program components put too great a demand on the resources and capacity of the agency in terms of available person power, aggregation of families for the groups, space, and so on, and might be overly ambitious at this stage of translation from research to practice. Driven by this concern, the original plan was for the NSC to deliver only the caregiver component of the FBP within the agency. However, following an initial training with 10 members of the NSC staff, the agency indicated a strong preference to deliver both the caregiver and the child and adolescent components of the program. This decision was made after the NSC staff heard about the positive 6-year findings of the program, its desire to maximize the potential positive impact on the families agreeing to participate in the implementation pilot, and it closely mirrored NSC's already existing program model. In keeping with the NSC preference, the program developers agreed to follow this course and delayed the initial start of the pilot in order to allow the same type of revisions to the caregiver program to be completed on the child and adolescent group materials and to allow NSC to recruit additional staff to run the child and adolescent groups. Procedures for training, monitoring implementation quality, and collecting participant data were also developed and utilized during this clinical pilot of the revised FBP and are described below.

Training of Providers

Program staff at the NSC identified 10 experienced group leaders and other key program staff whom they wanted to train in the FBP intervention and offered them an initial 16-hour training in delivering the FBP. An additional 16 hours of training was offered to six of these staff members and four additional staff that were recruited after the decision was made to deliver both components of FBP. Each of these trainings included extensive review of the program theory, as well as the structure and content of each session. Training was provided by university staff (Ayers) and focused on group processes to instill feelings of efficacy in participants, active-learning methods of teaching the program skills, and skills to develop a supportive group environment. Training also included modeling, presentation of didactic material, and role plays. Weekly group meetings were held at NSC, and Ayers provided both supervision and training to the NSC group facilitators during these weekly meetings. Although extensive training and supervision were provided, including 1½ hours each week and an additional 2 hours of preparation time by each group leader, it is notable that the amount of time allotted to training and supervision was still less than in the experimental trial.

One innovative approach to training that was developed during the implementation pilot was the use of web-based training that included the program

PowerPoints with audio overlays for both the caregiver and the child and adolescent components. The presentations for the sessions were used as the base material, and additional audio and video material was added to provide further coaching on how to implement the FBP sessions. As part of these online trainings, quizzes were integrated into the online materials in order to help facilitators review material and consolidate their learning. These web-based training programs were developed so that group facilitators could prepare for upcoming sessions at a time that was convenient for them. Feedback mechanisms were put in place to gather reactions from the NSC staff about all aspects of the training and supervision that were offered to improve future workshop and training materials.

Monitoring Quality of Implementation

In the original FBP trial, three criteria for the assessment of the quality of implementation, adherence, dosage, and responsiveness to the intervention were based on the conceptual framework of Dane and Schneider (1998). In the experimental trial, *adherence* refers to group leader completion of each action item of the intervention manual, and in the original trial the level of adherence was very high, as assessed by objective ratings of session videotapes (84% to 89%). Adherence to the manual was significantly related to improvement in the caregiver and child report of child mental health problems at 11-month follow-up (Schmiege, Ayers, & Sandler, 2003). *Dosage*, defined as the number of sessions attended, was also very high in the experimental trial (mean = 84% for caregivers, and 86% for children and adolescents). *Responsiveness* to the intervention during the experimental trial was defined as participants' reported practice of the skills taught in the program at home. Each week, the participants reported on practicing program skills at home and also provided ratings on their satisfaction with the skills and perceived efficacy in using them. The skills were classified in terms of the specific empirically correlated variable they were designed to change (e.g., positive parenting and active coping), and separate summary scores were calculated to assess skill practice and participants' satisfaction and efficacy with skills practiced. Schmiege and colleagues found that participants' reports of practice of the program skills and satisfaction and efficacy with skills predicted improvement posttest in the warmth of relationship with caregiver, active coping, and a reduction of negative appraisals of stressful events. In addition, caregiver skill practice focused on the warmth of the caregiver–child relationship was found to be related to improved caregiver warmth posttest, which in turn led to reduced internalizing and externalizing problems at the 11-month follow-up (Schmiege et al., 2003).

Motivated by these findings, the university investigators wished to develop similar, although easier to complete, measures of program implementation that could be used by a community agency. An online data entry tool was developed for this project which collected group leader and supervisor reports on these implementation measures and measures of participants' attendance and completion of homework given during the program. During the implementation, this online tool monitored both fidelity to the intervention and adaptations made by staff. Group facilitators were asked to complete these process evaluation measures after each session. The online reports were reviewed by Ayers, and problems in implementation were addressed at the weekly meetings at NSC. After program completion, participants, leaders, and the director of NSC participated in qualitative interviews on the monitoring of tasks and procedures (e.g., user friendliness of forms, respondent burden, timeliness and quality of feedback from university staff, and suggestions for improving components of monitoring tasks and procedures).

Participant Data Collection Procedures

In discussions with both the NSC and other bereavement support agencies, most agencies indicated a need to develop program evaluations and/or outcome evaluations, whose findings could be used in future fundraising efforts by the agency. However, most bereavement support agencies do not have procedures in place to conduct regular program evaluations or include standardized assessment materials as part of their normal participant recruitment procedures. There are a variety of reasons why these types of procedures do not exist within agencies, from philosophical positions regarding standardized assessment to a lack of expertise in program evaluation and/or evaluation of assessment materials. One contribution that university personnel can make is to develop a brief assessment battery that could be used by the agencies to help in their evaluation of their programs. We spent time developing a battery of questionnaires for caregivers and for children and adolescents that included general measures of symptomatology, and also had specific measures that were the target of the FBP intervention.

The resulting assessment batteries included brief but psychometrically sound versions of several of the key instruments that had been used during our experimental evaluations of the FBP. These instruments assessed key variables related to the observed FBP program effects on the targeted risk and protective factors and on problem outcomes such as mental health problems and problematic grief (Sandler et al., in press, 2003; Tein, Sandler, Ayers, & Wolchik, 2006). As an example, positive parenting has been found to mediate the relationship between the program and mental health outcomes (Tein et al., 2006). We therefore developed a shortened caregiver and child version of the Child Report of Parental Behavior Inventory (CRPBI; Schafer, 1965), which includes an assessment of acceptance, rejection, and inconsistent discipline practices. Another aspect of positive parenting from the program's perspective is creating regular positive family routines, leading us to incorporate a subscale derived from the Family Routine Inventory (FRI; Jensen, Janes, Boyce, & Hartnett, 1983; Wolchik, West, Westover, & Sandler, 1993) to assess the occurrence of positive stable events within the family from the caregiver report. Another measure that reflects children's or adolescents' sense of warmth of the relationship between the youth and caregiver was developed by the research team to assess positive sharing as reported by the youth, that is, the sense that when the youth brings problems or emotional upset to his or her caregiver, the caregiver really understands. A measure that assessed adaptive emotion expression, specifically the degree to which a youth inhibits emotional expression (i.e., active inhibition) when experiencing negative emotions, was included in the child and adolescent battery. This variable has been associated with mental health outcomes in the FBP and has been shown to be a mediator of positive program effects (Tein et al., 2006). A measure of coping efficacy, which assessed a sense that the individual believes he or she can could handle or solve problems or stressors when confronted, was included in both the caregiver and the child and adolescent versions of the assessment battery (Sandler, Tein, Mehta, Wolchik, & Ayers, 2000).

The caregiver and the child and adolescent assessment batteries also included measures of outcomes the program was designed to change. As indicated earlier, the FBP has been found to reduce "problematic grief" in youth up to 6 years after their participation in the program (Sandler et al., 2010) relative to the bibliotherapy condition. One aspect of "problematic grief" was conceptualized as the degree to which the individual experiences intrusive grief thoughts, even when they are unwanted, and this was assessed by a scale developed within the center titled the Intrusive Grief Thought Scale (IGTS; Sandler et al., 2010). We also included brief assessments of depressive symptomatology using the Children's Depression Inventory (CDI; Kovacs, 2001) for children and adolescents and the Beck Depression Inventory-II (BDI-II; Beck, Steer, & Brown, 1996) for the caregivers.

During the evaluation of the experimental trials, we administered various versions of Achenbach's Child Behavior Checklist (CBLC; Achenbach, 1991a, 1991b) to obtain the caregiver's report of symptomatology during youth. However, this instrument was too long (i.e., the average time of administration was 20 minutes) in light of the other measures that we wished to include and with the goal of keeping the assessment batteries under 1 hour for total time of administration. Investigators at ASU had administered the Strengths and Difficulties Questionnaire (SDQ; Goodman, Meltzer, & Bailey, 1998) during our 6-year follow-up of the FBP and came to learn that the SDQ was a short (average time of administration: 5 minutes) general measure of psychopathology that had good reliability and validity data (Goodman et al., 1998; Sharp, Croudace, Goodyer, & Amtmann, 2005), and that compared favorably to the CBCL (Goodman & Scott, 1999) in identifying internalizing and externalizing problems and did a better job at detecting inattention and hyperactivity. In addition, Goodman has made the SDQ and its scoring program free to use for nonprofits for parents' reports of depression and children's functioning, respectively. The separate batteries that were developed for caregiver and youth report assessed specific mediators of the FBP program and overall symptomatology in caregivers, children, and adolescents and on average took between 40 minutes to 1 hour.

Recruitment of Families for the Implementation Pilot

Families were recruited at NSC using agencies' standard intake procedures to participate in this implementation pilot. As part of these procedures, the brief assessment batteries were administered to all possible participants within the family prior to their involvement in the FBP program. During the experimental trial, participants who scored above the clinical level on mental health problems were referred for additional clinical services if they reached diagnostic levels. However, the NSC and many bereavement support agencies typically do not have formal mechanisms for screening out participants and philosophically believe that individuals should not be precluded from participating in the support groups that they offer. After much discussion, a decision was made to not use any set cut point to screen participants but that if a family member was found to have significant symptomatology or suicidal ideation, he or she was encouraged to get additional services from outside providers while involved with the FBP preventive intervention.

Feedback concerning the program was gathered midprogram (following session 6) and at the end of the program from both facilitators and the caregiver participants. In addition, focus groups were conducted with the caregiver participants during their last meeting, and with the group facilitators following the completion of the program. Transcripts from these focus groups were reviewed to help evaluate the success of the implementation and next steps in both the revision and delivery of the program. In addition, brief consumer satisfaction measures were administered posttest to the caregiver participants.

DESCRIPTION OF IMPLEMENTATION PILOT

Eight families were recruited by NSC staff to participate in the pilot (eight caregivers, nine children, and five adolescents), and all participants were administered a brief pretest battery prior to their participation in the groups. Basic demographics of the participants can be found in Table 11.1.

In terms of the type of deaths these families had experienced, three of the families had experienced murder and/or suicide, two had experienced death due to an accident, two family members died from illness, and one had died during combat. The mean time since the death of the other caregiver was 10.8 months with a range of 2–39 months.

Based on caregiver reports, we were able to use scores on the SDQ to classify children as having a possible or probable mental health diagnosis. At pretest, 36% of the youth had a probable diagnosis, and 14% of the youth had possible diagnosis based on the SDQ, for a total of 50% of the children. Using youth's own report on the CDI, a measure of depressive symptomatology and a cut point above the 95th percentile for age and gender, combined with the results from the SDQ, a total

TABLE 11.1 Demographics of New Song Center Participants

Caregivers		***N* = 8**
	Age (*M*)	42.13
	(*SD*; range)	5.99; 34–52
	Gender (% female)	87.5%
	Ethnicity (% minority)	12.5%
Children and Adolescents		***N* = 14**
	Age (*M*)	10.79
	(*SD*; range)	2.23 7–15
	Gender (% female)	50%
	Ethnicity (% minority)	7%

of 57% of the youth would be thought to have a possible or probable diagnosis of depression. Because NSC had not previously collected standardized assessment information, this figure of at least 50% of the youth referred to support groups due to a possible or probable diagnosis was a surprise to both administrative staff at NSC and university collaborators.

Caregivers and youth participated in the 12-week FBP intervention, and family members met in their own groups for 2 hours each evening, once a week. There were eight members in the caregiver group, nine in the child group, and five members in the adolescent group. Each group had two facilitators, except the child group, which had a total of three facilitators. Each group had a staff member of NSC and at least one experienced volunteer facilitating the group. On the evenings of the group, pizza was provided to the family and staff prior to the start of the group. In terms of the time that group leaders spent in the delivery of the program, on average, training and supervision (1.5 hours), preparation (2 hours), and actual group time (2.5 hours) were approximately 6 hours a week for each facilitator. During the focus groups conducted at the end of the program, facilitators reported that they believed that less time would be required the next time they ran the group because they were now familiar with the model and all group activities.

Participants at the completion of the program completed the same assessment batteries administered prior to the start of the group. This allowed us to examine in this small pilot the change experienced by the families who participated in the FBP. As can be seen in Table 11.2, based on caregiver reports there was a significant decrease in rejection and a significant increase in positive family routines. In terms of outcome as assessed with the BDI-II and the SDQ, the caregivers reported a significant reduction in emotional distress in their youth and in total symptoms on the SDQ. Based on youth reports, the children and adolescents at posttest reported a decrease in inconsistent parenting as assessed by the CRPBI and reported less problematic grief as assessed by the Intrusive Grief Thoughts Scale (IGTS). There was also a significant reduction in depressive symptomatology as reported on the CDI. Although there is no comparison group in this simple prepost design, the changes seen over the course of the program are large in magnitude and are encouraging in terms of their prospect for the benefits of implementation of the program by community agencies.

AGENCY EXPERIENCE

Einstein once said, "Without time everything would happen at once." When implementing a research-based children and family bereavement program into your community agency, it certainly feels like everything is happening at once. Closing the divide between research and the world of a real-life community agency needs commitment and stamina. Developing a strong relationship between researchers and agency is a critical component that enables this work to occur. NSC had already benefitted from knowing the FBP research group for 15 years. This longstanding collaboration allowed both agencies to work together with an unprecedented level of trust and commitment. The effort to learn the program, provide appropriate staffing, find and interview families, create enough space, and manage

TABLE 11.2 Pre and Post Test Results from New Song Center Pilot

Measures	Means		t	p
	Pre	Post		
Caregiver				
BDI-II-Total Score	.932	.524	1.86	.11
SDQ-Total Score	15.91	11.18	2.50 (d = .75)	.03*
SDQ-Emotional Distress	5.36	3.45	2.20 (d = .66)	.05*
SDQ-Conduct Problems	2.36	1.73	1.41	.19
SDQ-Hyperactivity	4.91	3.64	1.78	.10
SDQ-Peer Problems	3.27	2.36	1.66	.13
SDQ-Prosocial	7.91	8.36	–.889	.40
CRPBI-Acceptance	2.75	2.83	–.701	.50
CRPBI-Rejection	1.57	1.32	2.31 (d = .70)	.04*
CRPBI-Inconsistent Discipline	2.25	2.49	–1.44	.18
Family Routines Inventory	2.44	2.84	–3.02 (d =. 91)	.02*
General Coping Efficacy	2.69	2.97	–1.13	.30
Child and Adolescent Report				
CDI-Total Score	.414	.210	2.45 (d = .73)	.04*
Intrusive Grief Thoughts Scale	2.37	1.84	2.29 (d = .69)	.05*
Active Inhibition Scale	2.76	2.44	1.36	.20
CRPBI-Acceptance	2.44	2.61	–1.17	.27
CRPBI-Rejection	1.56	1.59	–2.78	.79
CRPBI-Inconsistent Discipline	2.44	2.04	2.32 (d = .70)	.04*
Positive Sharing of Emotions	3.75	4.13	–1.43	.18
General Coping Efficacy	2.71	3.00	–1.24	.24

Note: SDQ: Strength and Difficulties Scale (Goodman, Meltzer, & Bailey, 1998), parent report of child and adolescent symptoms. BDI-II: Beck Depression Inventory-II (Beck, Steer, & Brown, 1996), parent report of symptoms. CDI: Children's Depression Inventory (Kovacs, 2001), child report of symptoms; and CRPBI: Children's Report of Parental Behavior Inventory (Schaefer, 1965). Other measures listed developed by Arizona State University's Prevention Research Center.

many meetings all takes time. And that is even before group begins! The New Song Center quickly decided that taking on the challenge of converging research to reality was worth the effort. Some lessons we learned along the way are outlined below.

Staffing

"We've never done it like this before!" Long before families had to buy into the program, NSC needed to find the appropriate staff to understand not only the new program and structure, but also the commitment needed to bring the research to the people. As stated, 32 hours were needed for training before the group began and at least 72 hours per staff member for the duration of the 12 weeks for implementation. As a small community agency largely staffed by volunteers, we needed to search for well-trained volunteer facilitators with a clinical background and strong history of consistency. Given the additional hours needed to bring this program to the families, it was critical that all staff members believed in the importance of providing this new programming to families. Another important aspect to consider for staffing is the cost of implementation. We were fortunate enough to be able to pay staff to work on this project through grant funding as part of the research program. As future implementation is considered, funding becomes a critical factor. For the NSC staff and volunteers, letting go of the notion that there is only one way to deliver support to grieving families is essential. This process clearly takes time, effort, and thoughtfulness. The more your staff is trained and open to new ideas, the easier the path to delivery will be.

Families

"What do you mean not all families are eligible?" Most community-based grief support agencies open their doors to all children and families dealing with the grief after the death of a loved one. In the name of appropriate research methods, participants are often limited by certain "eligibility criteria" in order to rule out families who are deemed as not appropriate or as not likely to benefit from this service. New Song Center almost always serves any family whether the death was of a parent, sibling, grandparent, extended family, or friend. Limiting the families eligible to only those suffering a parent's death was a new pill to swallow. It also became apparent through the pre-interview and testing that some participants were not appropriate for group. Despite the possibility of severe mental health diagnosis, it was felt the participants scoring above clinical levels on mental health problems should still be eligible as they would have been under the nonresearch programming. The brief assessment batteries completed on all participants gave NSC better tools to provide more comprehensive services. We provided appropriate referrals to those grieving children, teens, and adults clearly needing individual clinical services to address significant symptomatology or suicide ideation. Traversing the waters of eligibility with the research staff and program staff took some time and consideration. Continuous communication between the agency providing the service and the researchers was one important key to success.

Appropriate Advertisement

"What is this group really about?" We described this program experience as a 12-week support group for grieving families after a parental death. The group structure of the FBP was very psychoeducational by design and nature. However, the reality was that during the group, participants wanted more time to process their grief and talk as they expected from a support group. This was voiced from some parents when reflecting back on their experience during the focus groups. Adequately preparing families in advance for the educational components and highly structured nature of the program could have prevented the feedback and provided for a more integrated experience that matched their expectations.

Equipment

"We're going to videotape every group!?" When learning all the equipment necessary for implementation, an important balance between content and construct became apparent. How can we conduct a group, which creates an atmosphere of safety and anonymity, while using PowerPoint and videotaping? This challenge clearly fell on the facilitators. Each facilitator had to feel comfortable being videotaped and critiqued, all the while creating comfort for the families in the midst of impersonal equipment. Group leaders needed to be vigilant about not primarily becoming teachers with the focus on them and the equipment. Bringing the group back to finding support and feedback from each other was dependent on the skills of the facilitators.

Implementation

"Are we lost in translation?" Individual groups always take on a personality of their own. Practitioners understand that the dynamics between members is unique and constantly changing. This may seem in direct opposition to staying on track with implementing the proven manualized program structure used in the research. This became quickly apparent in both the children and teen groups for different reasons. We had a large children's group (nine members) all willing to participate and share. There was so much content to the program on any given night that we couldn't get through it all. We were constantly asking the researchers, "What can we eliminate?" What sections were negotiable without destroying the integrity of the program? The teen group (five members) was much smaller and had the opposite experience. Those facilitators kept asking, "What more can we add?" They were breezing through content as the teens' participation varied. Allowing for and building in some flexibility to the content, and adding choices for the practitioner to adopt, created a more individualized and personal group experience. The goal remained to meet the unique needs of the group and its members while maintaining the researched integrity of program. Our work on content changes with the research took collaboration and compromise. We were constantly looking for revisions that maintained researched validity while increasing ease of delivery.

As practitioners, we realized that the process of adapting a research-based program to a real-world setting is less about implementation than about integration. Our program goals of providing a positive experience, offering healing tools, and creating safety are designed so that the grieving child and family can learn healthy coping skills, share their story, and ultimately process their profound grief. Our hope is that families can begin to connect despite an event that often creates chaos and division. Our belief is that experiencing a group will help ease the long-term emotional effects of grief and promote resiliency and healing. Adopting a program designed in the research setting and proven to make a difference can lend an important sense of validity to the goals and beliefs of the community agency.

As stated, the process of integrating research and agency reality can be time consuming; crossing the bridge is a long, hard journey. But in the end, despite (or because of) all the work, there are defining moments that make the effort worth every minute. Watching a family who has been greatly divided and disconnected since the suicide of the father create family fun time every week to share some laughter is one defining moment. A mother stating in her group how she had forgotten the importance of fun in a family's life and how hearing her son's laugh again was so profound is another such moment. Or a 12-year-old girl full of bravado and toughness, newly sharing in a whisper that she caused the accident ending her mother's life, is still another such moment. It was her text that her mother was reading while driving the car into an embankment that made the girl feel that it was ultimately her fault. Time does slow, as the group absorbs the information and heavy feelings without judgment or shock, and as acceptance and empathy are shared and healing begins to take place.

LESSONS LEARNED

As we move forward with our collaboration, the primary goal is to create a working balance between maintaining the fidelity of delivery of the FBP program in the realistic context of the community agency. The shared goal is to have a sustainable program that utilizes the strengths and experience of the community agency to deliver the effective components of the FBP that have been shown to have positive effects on bereaved children and caregivers. With this in mind, we propose several key takeaway messages discovered during the first implementation pilot.

Sustainability

The key factor that needs to be emphasized is sustainability of the service delivery to implement the FBP in bereavement community settings. Sustainability implies having the resources to deliver the program, including the funding and the people who have the time to devote to the program. A large majority of these agencies are small nonprofits struggling with financial stability. To meet the needs of their clients, with their limited resources such agencies often employ trained volunteers to staff groups. Integrating a manualized program such as the FBP within the agency takes money to pay people for the initial training and the preparation time. Although the implementation pilot demonstrated that the NSC staff could deliver the program with fidelity, it is still an open question as to whether the investment of added training and material costs is feasible and sustainable with a volunteer-based model. Finding a way to appropriately utilize volunteers, maintain fidelity of delivery of the program, and discover funding sources is a crucial issue that needs to be addressed. In doing this, hopefully the findings from the long-term evaluation of the program (Sandler et al., in press) might be used to attract more funding resources. Additionally, an ongoing evaluation needs to take place regarding the use of volunteers and professional staff in an optimal mix with the program tools to develop a sustainable delivery model.

Equipment

As stated, agency staff felt that the presence of technology and equipment seemed to hinder the group process. The PowerPoint presentations were designed to reduce staff training and prep time, but at what cost? In implementing the next round, we would go back to workbooks and posters for presenting material. In hindsight, this may actually reduce time in setup and cost, thus saving the agency money in the long run. Again, we need to think together about how to use the technology and the skills of agency staff and volunteers to have an optimal delivery model.

Program Content

A key question quickly emerged regarding program content and delivery. Can sections of this manualized intervention be modularized, further giving the group facilitator flexibility and choices in delivering the FBP? Providing the practitioner for each group (caregiver, children, and adolescent) content sections that can be added or deleted should be considered. This would help build on and take advantage of the skills and talents of the staff and enable them to meet the unique needs of the groups. Although this flexibility recognizes the unique nature of each group, it needs to be accomplished while maintaining the integrity and fidelity of program implementation so that we can get the same positive outcomes that were achieved in the research setting. Developing an appropriate level of flexibility challenges us to identify those components that are core and essential and that everyone should deliver, while also providing tools for flexible delivery of other components to meet the unique needs of the groups. Finding the right balance will be a challenge that can be met through continued collaborative thinking.

Crossing the divide between research and real world clearly takes thoughtful effort and collaboration. Only by taking on the journey can we better learn from each other. In reality, our goals as clinicians and researchers are parallel. We are all committed to increasing positive mental health, creating opportunities for resiliency and growth, as well as providing environments to promote healing for the bereaved. Implementing proven research-based interventions for bereaved children and families is a critical step to reaching these goals and improving services for this population in the future.

ACKNOWLEDGMENTS

The work described in this chapter was funded by NIMH Grant P30 MH068685 support and the Advanced Center for Intervention and Services Research. Readers interested in collaborating with Ayers and Sandler in their ongoing efforts of evaluating the FBP in natural service delivery settings can contact the authors at the address listed for the corresponding author in the beginning of the book.

NOTE

1. The NSC is now part of the Hospice of the Valley, the largest nonprofit hospice in the country and a leader in expanding the types of services that are delivered to the dying and bereaved.

REFERENCES

Achenbach, T. M. (1991a). *Manual for the Youth Self-Report and 1991 Profile*. Burlington: University of Vermont, Department of Psychiatry.

Achenbach, T. M. (1991b). *Manual for the Child Behavior Checklist/4-18 and 1991 Profile*. Burlington: University of Vermont, Department of Psychiatry.

Addis, M. E. (2002). Methods for disseminating research products and increasing evidence-based practice: Promises, obstacles, and future directions. *Clinical Psychology: Science and Practice*, 9(4), 367–378.

Agid, O., Shapira, B., Zislin, J., Ritsner, M., Hanin, B., Murad, H., et al. (1999). Environment and vulnerability to major psychiatric illness: A case control study of early parental loss in major depression, bipolar disorder, and schizophrenia. *Molecular Psychiatry*, *4*, 163–172.

Ayers, T. S., Wolchik, S. A., Sandler, I. N., Towhey, J. L., Lutzke Weyer, J. R., Jones, S., et al. (In press). The Family Bereavement Program: Description of a theory-based prevention program for parentally-bereaved children and adolescent. *Omega: Journal of Death and Dying*.

Beck, A. T., Steer, R. A., & Brown, G. K. (1996). *Manual for Beck Depression Inventory-II*. San Antonio, TX: Psychological Corporation.

Biglan, A., Mrazek, P. J., Carnine, D., & Flay, B. R. (2003). The integration of research and practice in the prevention of youth problem behaviors. *American Psychologist*, *58*(6/7), 433–440.

Bridging Work Group. (2005). Bridging the gap between research and practice in bereavement: Report from the Center for the Advancement of Health. *Death Studies*, *29*, 93–122.

Cerel, J., Fristad, M. A., Verducci, J., Weller, R. A., & Weller, E. B. (2006). Childhood bereavement: psychopathology in the 2 years postparental death. *Journal of the American Academy of Child & Adolescent Psychiatry*, *45*, 681–690.

Clarke, G. N. (1995). Improving the transition from basic efficacy research to effectiveness studies: Methodological issues and procedures. *Journal of Consulting and Clinical Psychology*, *63*, 718–725.

Currier, J. M., Holland, J. M., & Neimeyer, R. A. (2007). The effectiveness of bereavement interventions with children: A meta-analytic review of controlled outcome research. *Journal of Clinical Child and Adolescent Psychology*, *36*, 253–259.

Dane, A. V., & Schneider, B. H. (1998). Program integrity in primary and early secondary prevention: Are implementation effects out of control? *Clinical Psychology Review*, *18*, 23–24.

Dobson, K. S., & Craig, K. D. (1998). *Empirically supported therapies*. London: Sage.

Duan, N., Braslow, J. T., Weisz, J. R., & Wells, K. B. (2001). Fidelity, adherence, and robustness of interventions. *Psychiatric Services*, *52*, 413.

Goodman, R., Meltzer, H., & Bailey, V. (1998). The strength and difficulties questionnaire: A pilot study on the validity of the self-report version. *European Child & Adolescent Psychiatry*, *7*, 125–130.

Goodman, R., & Scott, S. (1999). Comparing the Strengths and Difficulties Questionnaire and the Child Behavior Checklist: Is small beautiful? *Journal of Abnormal Child Psychology*, *27*(1), 17–24.

Hagan, M. J., Tein, J-Y., Sandler, I. N., Wolchik, S. A., & Ayers, T. S. (2009, June). The effects of a family-based preventive intervention on the parent–child relationship six years later. Poster presented at the annual meeting of the Society for Prevention Research, Denver, CO.

Jensen, E., Janes, S., Boyce, W. T., & Hartnett, S. A. (1983). The Family Routines Inventory: Development and validation. *Social Science Medicine*, *17*, 201–211.

Kellam, S. G., & Langevin, D. J. (2003). A framework for understanding "evidence" in prevention research and programs. *Prevention Science*, *4*(3), 137–153.

Kovacs, M. (2001). *Children's Depression Inventory (CDI) Technical Manual*. North Tonawanda, NY: Multi-Health Systems.

Kreitman, N. (1988). Suicide, age and marital status. *Psychological Medicine*, *18*(1), 121–128.

Luecken, L. J. (2008). Long-term consequences of parental death in childhood: Psychological and physiological manifestations. In M. S. Stroebe, R. O. Hansson, H. Schut, W. Stroebe, & E. Van den Blink (Eds.), *Handbook of bereavement research and practice: Advances in theory and intervention* (pp. 397–416). Washington, DC: American Psychological Association.

Luoma, J. B., & Pearson, J. L. (2002). Suicide and marital status in the United States, 1991–1996: Is widowhood a risk factor? *American Journal of Public Health*, *92*, 1518–1522.

Lutzke, J. R., Ayers, T. S., Sandler, I. N., & Barr, A. (1997). Risks and interventions for the parentally bereaved child. In S. A. Wolchik & I. N. Sandler (Eds.), *Handbook of children's coping with common life stressors: Linking theory, research and interventions* (pp. 215–243). New York: Plenum.

Mack, K. (2001). Childhood family disruptions and adult well-being: The differential effects of divorce and parental death. *Death Studies*, *25*, 419–443.

McCrae, R. R., & Costa, P. T. (1993). Psychological resilience among widowed men and women: A 10-year follow-up of a national sample. In M. Stroebe, W. Stroebe, & R. Hansson (Eds.), *Handbook of bereavement: Theory, research, and intervention* (pp. 196–207). New York: Cambridge University Press.

Melhem, N. M., Walker, M., Moritz, G., & Brent, D. (2008). Antecedents and sequelae of sudden parental death in offspring and surviving caregivers. *Archives of Pediatric Adolescent Medicine*, *162*, 403–410.

National Advisory Mental Health Council (NAMHC). (2001). *Workgroup on child and adolescent mental health intervention development and deployment: Blueprint for change: Research on child and adolescent mental health*. Rockville, MD: National Institute of Mental Health.

National Advisory Mental Health Council Workgroup on Mental Disorders Prevention Research. (1998). *Priorities for prevention research at NIMH*. Rockville, MD: National Institutes of Health.

Sandler, I. N., Ayers, T. S., Tein, J-Y., Wolchik, S., Millsap, R., Khoo, S. T., et al. (In press). Six-year follow-up of a prevention intervention for parentally bereaved youths: A randomized controlled trial [referred]. *Archives of Pediatric and Adolescent Medicine*.

Sandler, I. N., Ayers, T. S., Wolchik, S. A., Tein, J-Y., Kwok, O-M., Haine, R. A., et al. (2003). The Family Bereavement Program: Efficacy evaluation of a theory-based prevention program for parentally-bereaved children and adolescents. *Journal of Consulting and Clinical Psychology*, *71*(3), 587–600.

Sandler, I. N., Ma, Y., Tein, J-Y., Ayers, T. S., Wolchik, S., Kennedy, C., et al. (2010). Long-term effects of the Family Bereavement Program on multiple indicators of grief in parentally bereaved children and adolescents. *Journal of Consulting and Clinical Psychology*, *78*, 131–144.

Sandler, I. N., Ostrom, A., Bitner, M. J., Ayers, T. S., & Wolchik, S. (2005). Developing effective prevention services for the real world: A prevention service development model. *The American Journal of Community Psychology*, *35*, 127–142.

Sandler, I. N., Tein, J. Y., Mehta, P., Wolchik, S., & Ayers, T. (2000). Coping efficacy and psychological problems of children of divorce. *Child Development*, *71*, 1099–1118.

Sandler, I. N., Wolchik, S. A., Ayers, T. S., Tein, J. Y., Coxe, S., & Chow, W. (2008). Linking theory and intervention to promote resilience of children following parental bereavement. In M. Stroebe, M. Hansson, W. Stroebe, & H. Schut (Eds.), *Handbook of bereavement research: Consequences, coping and care* (pp. 531–550). Washington DC: American Psychological Association.

Schaefer, E. S. (1965). Children's report of parental behavior: An inventory. *Child Development*, *36*, 413–424.

Schmiege, S., Ayers, T. S., & Sandler, I. N. (2003). Implementation of the Family Bereavement Program: Evaluating action theory. In J. Durlak (Ed.), *Recent developments in efficacy research/Implementation does matter: Evidence from preventive intervention studies*. Washington, DC: Eleventh Annual Meeting of the Society for Prevention Research.

Schoenwald, S. K., & Hoagwood, K. (2001). Effectiveness, transportability, and dissemination of interventions: What matters when? *Psychiatric Services*, 52, 1190–1197.

Sharp, C., Croudace, T. J., Goodyer, I. M., & Amtmann, D. (2005). The strength and difficulties questionnaire: Predictive validity of parent and teacher ratings for help-seeking behavior over one year. *Educational and Child Psychology*, *22*, 28–44.

Smith, J. C., Mercy, J. M., & Conn, J. M. (1988). Marital status and the risk of suicide. *American Journal of Public Health*, *78*, 78–80.

Social Security Administration. (2000). *Intermediate assumptions of the 2000 Trustees Report*. Washington, DC: Office of the Chief Actuary of the Social Security Administration.

Stroebe, M., Schut, H., & Stroebe, W. (2007). Health outcomes of bereavement. *Lancet*, *370*, 1960–1973.

Tein, J. Y., Sandler, I. N., Ayers, T. S., & Wolchik, S. A. (2006). Mediation of the effects of the family bereavement program on mental health problems of bereaved children and adolescents. *Prevention Science*, 7(2), 179–195.

Tremblay, G. C., & Israel, A. C. (1998). Children's adjustment to parental death. *Clinical Psychology: Science and Practice*, *5*, 424–438.

Weisz, J. R., Chu, B. C., & Polo, A. J. (2004). Treatment dissemination and evidence-based practice: Strengthening intervention through clinician–researcher collaboration. *Clinical Psychology: Science and Practice*, *11*, 300–307.

Wolchik, S. A., West, S. G., Westover, S., & Sandler, I. N. (1993). The children of divorce parenting intervention: Outcome evaluation of an empirically based program. *American Journal of Community Psychology*, *21*, 293–331.

Worden, J. W., & Silverman, P. R. (1996). Parental death and the adjustment of school-age children. *Omega Journal of Death and Dying*, *33*, 91–102.

Yamamoto, K., Davis, O. L., Jr., Dylak, S., Whittaker, J., Marsh, C., & van der Westhuizen, P. C. (1996). Across six nations: Stressful events in the lives of children. *Child Psychiatry & Human Development*, *26*, 139–150.

Zisook, S., & Kendler, K. S. (2007). Is bereavement-related depression different than non-bereavement-related depression? *Psychological Medicine*, *37*, 779–794.

Zisook, S., & Schuchter, S. (1993). Major depression associated with widowhood. *The American Journal of Geriatric Psychiatry*, *1*, 316–326.

Section *III*

Challenges in Bereavement

12

Treating Complicated Grief
Converging Approaches

M. KATHERINE SHEAR, PAUL A. BOELEN,
and ROBERT A. NEIMEYER

The death of someone close is one of the most dreaded events in the lives of most people. A painful period of acute grief typically ensues, dominating the life of a bereaved person, bringing considerable emotional anguish and a desire to retreat from ordinary life. Nevertheless, most people find a way to come to terms with the loss, accept its permanence, and restore a capacity for joy and satisfaction without needing professional help (Bonanno, Wortman, & Nesse, 2004; Currier, Neimeyer, & Berman, 2008). Through a natural integrating process, symptom intensity diminishes and grief recedes to the background. However, for a notable minority of about 10% of bereaved people, grief is complicated.

Complicated grief (CG), also termed *prolonged grief disorder* (PGD) and traumatic grief described in the published literature, is a painful and impairing condition that is under consideration for inclusion in the DSM-V (Prigerson et al., 2009; Shear et al., 2011). People with this condition experience prolonged acute grief symptoms and struggle unsuccessfully to rebuild a meaningful life without the deceased person. Typical CG symptoms include persistent feelings of intense yearning or preoccupation with the deceased, shock, disbelief, and anger about the death; feeling that it is difficult to care for or trust others; and impairing behaviors to try to avoid reminders of the loss or to feel closer to the deceased. People with CG can experience rumination over troubling aspects of the circumstances of the death or its consequences, including their own reactions (Boelen, Van den Bout, & Van den Hout, 2003, 2006; Nolen-Hoeksema, McBride, & Larson, 1997; Stroebe et al., 2007).

Risk factors for CG can be grouped into several categories. The first of these includes *personal psychological vulnerability*, such as a personal or family history of mood or anxiety disorders (Gamino, Sewell, & Easterling, 2000), avoidant or anxious attachment (Van der Houwen, Stroebe, Schut, Van den Bout, & Wijngaards-de Meij, 2010), and history of trauma or multiple losses (Gamino et al., 2000). A second category concerns *circumstances of the death* itself (e.g., untimely, unexpected, violent, or seemingly preventable death; Currier, Holland, & Neimeyer, 2006; Gamino et al., 2000). And, finally, a third category of risk factors focus on the *context in which the death occurs*, such as insufficient or toxic social support (Wilsey & Shear, 2007) or severe financial or other hardship (Van der Houwen et al., 2010). CG bears some resemblance to depression and posttraumatic stress disorder, but there is strong evidence for differences between these disorders (Boelen, Van de Schoot, Van den Hout, De Keijser, & Van den Bout, 2010; Bonanno et al., 2007; Lichtenthal, Cruess, & Prigerson, 2004; Prigerson et al., 2009; Simon et al., 2007), including lack of response to standard treatments for depression (Reynolds et al., 1999; Shear et al., 2001). CG is a source of substantial impairment in health and quality of life (Germain, Caroff, Buysse, & Shear, 2005; Hardison, Neimeyer, & Lichstein, 2005; Latham & Prigerson, 2004; Monk, Houck, & Shear, 2006; Prigerson et al., 1997) and, therefore, requires treatment.

This chapter discusses treatments developed by three research groups, each of which uses a somewhat different heuristic model derived from either attachment theory supplemented with cognitive coping propositions (complicated grief treatment, or CGT; Shear, Frank, Houck, & Reynolds, 2005), cognitive–behavioral theory (CBT; Boelen, Van den Hout, & Van den Bout, 2006), and meaning reconstruction theory (Neimeyer et al., 2010; see also Chapter 2). The models as well as the treatments have many similarities, and the current chapter focuses on these while also pointing out some differences.

HEURISTIC MODEL: CGT

The experience of grief following the loss of a loved one is an instinctive reaction, the painful manifestation of a natural healing process, rooted in the inborn neurobiological attachment system (Hofer, 1984, 1996; Shear & Shair, 2005). Complicated grief occurs when this natural instinctive process is derailed (Shear & Shair, 2005). Similar to inflammation following a physical wound, complications interfere with healing and tend to intensify and prolong the pain. Grief complications are psychological problems framed in a slightly different way in the three treatment approaches discussed in this chapter.

In CGT, psychological problems, framed as dysfunctional thoughts, maladaptive behaviors, or dysregulated emotions, emerge because circumstances related to the death or its aftermath are so troubling for the bereaved person that he or she is unable to integrate information related to the loss. Complications typically entail troubling rumination (Aldao & Nolen-Hoeksema, 2010) over a problematic circumstance, event, or interaction; impairing avoidance or compulsive proximity seeking used in a futile effort to manage pain; or inability to regulate emotions in order to process information effectively (Shear et al., 2007). People with CG are seen as preoccupied with how, why, or when the person died or with ways the death or their grief has affected their own life or their relationship with others.

The basic premise of attachment theory is that humans are instinctively predisposed to form and maintain close attachments. Support from loved ones during times of stress is seen as a natural human need, as are the ongoing confidence and support of loved ones as we pursue autonomous goals. Attachment theory posits the existence of cognitive–affective neurobiological circuitry called *working models* that contain autobiographical information about the self and attachment relationships as well as motivation for attachment-related behavior (Mikulincer, 2006). Relationship security as reflected in working models has wide-ranging effects on psychological and biological functioning (Cassidy & Shaver, 2008). Working models provide an ongoing sense of connection to a loved one, even when that person is physically absent. When activated by separation or stress, this circuitry produces feelings of yearning and longing, prominent thoughts of the attachment figure, and proximity-seeking behaviors. Activation of attachment is associated with inhibition of the biobehavioral exploratory system circuitry, and this reduces interest and sense of competence in autonomous functioning (Elliot & Reis, 2003).

When a loved one dies, the working model must be revised (Bowlby, 1980; Shaver & Fraley, 2008). However, like other mental models, attachment working models are resistant to change. Information that a death occurred is not sufficient to revise the working model. Instead, facts must be gathered, and consequences envisioned, processed, mulled over, and considered from different vantage points. To effectively revise the working model requires acknowledging the finality of the loss and its consequences. This is often difficult for a bereaved person.

Bowlby (1980) proposed that mourners are faced with a dilemma related to acknowledging of the finality of the loss and that the outcome of mourning rests upon how this dilemma is resolved. Albeit irrational, thinking the loss is not irretrievable maintains hope, but because this is at odds with reality it also engenders disappointment and frustration; whereas accepting the finality of the loss is more realistic but may seem too painful or even terrifying. Acute grief occurs during the period before a mourner resolves this dilemma. Bowlby posited that most people process such important but unwanted information by oscillating between facing it and defensively excluding it from awareness (experiential avoidance) (Hayes, Wilson, Gifford, Follette, & Strosahl, 1996). Mourning is a preoccupying and erratic process by which bereaved people come to accept their changed circumstances, revise the working models, and redefine life goals (Bowlby, 1980).

Symptoms of acute grief, such as intense yearning and longing, preoccupation with thoughts and memories of the deceased person, and diminished interest in ongoing life or other people, reflect activation of an unrevised working model. With acceptance of the painful reality and integration of information about the loss, the associated cognitive–affective response, and implications for ongoing life, grief symptoms abate, albeit leaving a permanent residue of integrated grief. Grief complications impede integration, intensify, and prolong acute grief.

Stroebe and Schut (1999) grouped coping responses into loss- and restoration-related behaviors—the various issues related to the finality and consequences of the loss, on the one hand, and redefining life goals, on the other (see Chapter 3). They made the seminal observation that coping with loss- and restoration-related stresses usually proceeds in tandem. Folkman and colleagues (Folkman, 1997;

Folkman & Moskowitz, 2000) also considered coping strategies in bereavement and underscored the role of positive emotions. Loss- and restoration-focused coping is out of balance in CG, and positive emotions are not accessed effectively. In general, transformation to integrated grief, expected by bereaved people and their friends and family, does not occur.

HEURISTIC MODEL: CBT

Based upon cognitive–behavioral approaches to psychopathology (Beck, 1976; Ehlers & Clark, 2000) more than on attachment theory, Boelen, Van den Hout, and Van den Bout (2006) developed a CBT model of CG that has similarities with CGT. This model posits that three interrelated processes maintain CG: (a) insufficient elaboration of the reality of the loss, resulting in a lack of integration of the loss with existing memory knowledge; (b) persistent negative thinking; and (c) anxious and depressive avoidance strategies.

In normal grief, the person confronts the loss and the implications of the loss for himself as he is, was, and will be in the past, present, and future. In doing so, the reality of the loss gradually gets connected with knowledge that the person has about him- or herself and the relationship with the deceased, gradually turning the loss into an experience that is painful yet acknowledged as part of the person's life story. Consistent with CGT, the CBT model proposes that this elaboration and integration do not take place sufficiently for people with CG. This has at least two consequences: (a) Because knowledge that the loved person is gone forever is disconnected from other autobiographical knowledge, it continues to erupt into awareness, causing a continued sense of shock and intrusive recollections and feelings—as if the loss happened very recently rather than months or years ago; and (b) because this knowledge is not yet integrated with the mental representation of the lost person (cf. the working model), people continue to yearn for and attempt to restore proximity to the lost person.

As a second process, the CBT model proposes that bereaved people who are prone to negative thinking will have a greater chance of developing CG. Two categories of cognitions are particularly important. The first includes *negative global cognitions* about the self ("I am a worthless person without my husband"), life ("Life has no meaning anymore"), and the future ("I will certainly never find joy again"). It is assumed that such cognitions are detrimental because they fuel the propensity to hold onto what was lost. The second category includes *catastrophic misinterpretations* of one's own reactions to the loss. People exposed to loss have to manage painful emotions, thoughts, and memories. Interpreting such unpleasant experiences as indicative of an impending mental or physical disaster (e.g., "If I will express my pain, I will go mad or lose control") is assumed to fuel distress and experiential avoidance, and to prevent the person from reviewing and adjusting to the loss's implications (Hayes et al., 1996).

Anxious and depressive avoidance represents a third key process in maintaining CG (Boelen & Van den Bout, 2010). *Anxious avoidance* refers to avoidance of confrontation with the reality, implications, and pain of the loss, driven by the fear that this confrontation will be intolerable and unbearable. It can manifest itself in situational avoidance of places, pictures, and people associated with the loss as well as in cognitive avoidance (e.g., ruminatively focusing on why the loss occurred and how it could have been prevented to avoid thoughts about the irreversibility and implications of the separation that are even more painful). *Depressive avoidance* refers to the avoidance of potentially pleasurable and meaningful activities that could foster adjustment. Both anxious and depressive avoidance are postulated to be detrimental. Among other reasons, anxious avoidance maintains CG by preventing elaboration and integration of the loss, whereas depressive avoidance blocks the correction of negative views of the self, life, and future that may develop following loss.

The three processes directly contribute to symptoms of CG but also influence each other. For instance, integrating the loss with preexisting knowledge is likely blocked when thinking about the loss brings to mind negative thoughts about the self and future. Moreover, negative thoughts about the self likely fuel the tendency to engage in depressive withdrawal and inactivity, whereas catastrophic misinterpretations of grief reactions are likely to contribute to anxious avoidance. The three processes also are assumed to mediate the impact of various risk factors for poor bereavement outcome, including personality features such as insecure attachment (see Chapter 3), characteristics of the loss event such as its unexpectedness or violence (see Chapters 14–17), and characteristics of the loss sequelae such as absence of social support. It is proposed that these factors do not cause CG directly but do so indirectly, by increasing the possibility that the person experiences difficulties integrating the loss with preexisting knowledge and by enhancing the risk of negative thinking and avoiding. The notion of mediation is important because it sheds light on changeable mechanisms (e.g., negative cognitions) that can be targeted in treatment to curb the effect of less easily changeable risk factors (e.g., personality features) on the development of CG.

HEURISTIC MODEL: MEANING RECONSTRUCTION

Neimeyer's meaning reconstruction approach (see Chapter 2) is similar to the other two models in viewing complications as arising from the mourner's difficulty in assimilating the loss experience into his or her *self-narrative*, defined as "an overarching cognitive–affective-behavioral structure that organizes the 'micro-narratives' of everyday life into a 'macro-narrative' that consolidates our self-understanding, establishes our characteristic range of emotions and goals, and guides our performance on the stage of the social world" (Neimeyer, 2006a, p. 53–54). This definition of a self-narrative is comparable to the definition of the attachment working model and autobiographical information about the self and the lost person in CBT. The self-narrative differs from the working model in placing less emphasis on the internalized representation of the loved one, and correspondingly more emphasis on the need to construct a reasonably coherent life story that renders troubling events comprehensible. Although compatible with an attachment model of CG (Neimeyer, 2006b), it differs in placing inflection on a *quest for meaning* in human experience (Neimeyer, 2001), a process not seen in other species that also respond to loss with visible separation distress. By extension, it also connects naturally to social and cultural models that analyze how the meaning of mourning is socially and historically constructed, and how tensions between a given person's, family's, or community's experience of loss and that of other systems can contribute to complications in grieving (Neimeyer, Klass, & Dennis, 2010; see also Chapters 26 and 27).

A constructivist model of psychotherapy in general (Neimeyer, 2009) and grief therapy in particular (Neimeyer, 2001) is less concerned with dysfunctional negative thoughts than CBT and more focused upon the inability to construct an alternative self-narrative that accommodates life changes. Complications arise when mourners experience profound invalidation of their current assumptive world, and struggle to reconstruct core life themes and purposes in a way that conserves some sense of coherence in their identity across time, while also projecting them into a future organized along different, but nonetheless satisfying, lines. A constructivist account focuses on the ongoing and anguishing search for meaning in the loss, a search that in the case of CG finds no satisfying answers. The result is a kind of "narrative fixation," a "broken record" retelling of the story of the loss, to oneself or to others, in a way that fails to move toward a fresh or hopeful account of the narrative of the loss and its aftermath.

A tendency on the part of the bereaved to constrict their involvement in the social world can compound this problem, depriving mourners of the validation that could result from the responsive engagement of others in the co-construction of meaning (Neimeyer, 2000). The constructivist model, like the CGT model, takes into consideration the possibility that difficulties beyond the grieving individual can aggravate this process, as when the social world of the mourner is populated by critical, blaming, or intrusive others from whom the bereaved retreats in self protection (Burke, Neimeyer, & McDevitt-Murphy, 2010). Accordingly, meaning reconstruction can be pursued in the context of family and group interventions, as well as at the level of individual clients. The CBT model focuses on the individual.

TREATMENT INTERVENTIONS: COMPLICATED GRIEF TREATMENT (CGT)

Each of the models described above guides a somewhat different treatment approach, although these nonetheless converge on some key features. CGT is a 16-session intervention developed and tested under NIMH-funded research grants (MH053817, MH052247, MH0060783, and MH070741). The objective of CGT is to treat grief complications and revitalize the natural instinctive mourning process. The treatment utilizes strategies and procedures from interpersonal psychotherapy, CBT, and motivational interviewing to achieve intervention targets related to this overarching aim. Principles of CGT are based on our understanding of complications and mechanisms of effective mourning as described above. Accordingly, four principles guide CGT: (a) successful mourning is revitalized using a balanced oscillation between thinking about the death and its consequences and setting these thoughts aside; (b) grief complications (excessive avoidance or proximity seeking, ruminative thoughts, dysregulated emotions, and social-environmental problems) can be eliminated by decreasing avoidance, and facilitating meaningful self-observation, reflection, reappraisal, and problem solving, in the context of safe and supportive companionship relationships; (c) experiencing positive emotions enhances creativity, ability to problem solve, and motivation to confront and process painful information; and (d) successful mourning is facilitated by a capacity to envision a satisfying future—a life with the potential for joy and satisfaction.

CGT is provided in 16 sessions with introductory, middle, and termination phases. In the introductory phase, the therapist establishes a supportive companionship alliance and explores current and past attachment relationships, including a history of the relationship with the deceased, the story of the death, and the course of grief. Grief diary monitoring and interval planning are introduced, and personal goals work is begun. The patient is encouraged to invite a significant other to a session, and psychoeducation is provided, including the CGT grief model and treatment approach. The middle phase is focused on relief of grief complications and facilitating the natural mourning process. Imaginal exercises are used to revisit the death and to engage in an imaginal conversation. Situational revisiting exercises are used for avoided activities and situations, and there is some structured memories work and review of pictures. Work on personal goals and current relationships is ongoing. During the termination phase, we review the treatment, discuss feelings about ending, and develop plans for the future. We illustrate some aspects of the treatment with a composite case example.

Kate is a pleasant 60-old-woman who was consumed with grief over her deceased husband, who died 5 years earlier. She sought treatment at her daughter's insistence. She had never received psychiatric treatment in the past, though she had had some intermittent problems with anxiety. Kate was married for 35 years and had three adult children. She worked as a manager for a local convenience store in a neighborhood where she had lived all her life. She saw her children regularly but no longer felt close to them since her husband died. She was slightly reserved, but appeared calm and cheerful for the first half of the initial interview. However, when the therapist asked about her husband, Kate immediately became tearful, recalling how wonderful their marriage was, how Jim was her soul mate, and how devastated she was by his death from an unusual form of cancer. Her emotions escalated, and she began to sob. Struggling to regain control, she became angry. Her husband died a horrible, senseless death. She asked if the interviewer was married and asked, "How do you think you would feel if this happened to you?" Kate had kept Jim's office and tool room intact. She refused to let anyone sit in his favorite armchair. She socialized minimally as she felt strangely incomplete when with other people, and had painful feelings of sadness, anger, and envy. She spent hours each day in reveries, imagining being with Jim.

When not daydreaming, Kate often ruminated about her failure to figure out what was wrong with Jim before it was too late. She had intrusive images of his body, ravaged by cancer. She still couldn't believe this really happened. Kate avoided places where she was afraid she would miss Jim too much. She refused to go near the hospital where he died. She thought they could have saved him if the doctors had tried harder. She visited the cemetery infrequently because she couldn't bear to think of him lying in the cold ground. Kate wished she would have died with Jim. She sometimes skipped her hypertension medication, knowing this could be dangerous. Even though she had lost much of her faith, her religious upbringing was all that kept her from trying to take her own life. She and Jim attended church regularly, but at the outset of therapy she thought, "What good is it to attend church if this is what you get? What kind of God would allow Jim to die when people who are bad continue to live?"

Kate no longer ate meals at regular times, because preparing meals, as she did every day for Jim, was too painful. She got little exercise and no longer socialized much. She felt too sad and guilty to do anything pleasant on a regular basis. As a result, she just "wandered around through life," feeling lost and empty.

Kate was the older of two children, born in the Polish Catholic neighborhood where she currently lived. Her father abandoned the family when she was six, divorced her mother, and remarried. She saw him infrequently when she was growing up and lost touch completely about 20 years ago. She described her upbringing as difficult. Her mother was forced to go to work and was often irritable when she returned. Kate said her mother was a bitter woman who was deeply hurt when her husband left. She refused to go out on dates and socialized little. Kate subsequently attended a local community college and got an associate's degree in marketing. After she graduated, she went to work at a convenience store. She quit when her first child was born, and returned to work part-time as a sales clerk when her youngest went to school. As the children grew up, she gradually increased her time on the job. She was a good worker, one who was smart and reliable. Shortly after she started back full-time, the manager retired, and Kate was promoted. This was 22 years ago.

Kate was closest to her younger brother, Jack, and they had a common group of close friends. Kate and Jack spent all of their time together and with these friends, until he died in a car accident 38 years ago. She met Jim shortly after this, and she had the "crazy idea" that Jack sent him to her. They were married at age 22. Their first child was born a year later, and two others arrived within the next 3 years. Kate described her relationship with Jim as "the best marriage that anyone could want." As a couple, they were closer than any of their friends. Jim was funny and smart and a great lover. Kate said, "Jim wasn't perfect. He was too sloppy for my taste, and he had a habit of drinking a little too much. He was a risk taker and kind of reckless, and sometimes I thought I had four children in the house. But he was my soul mate, and we were really in love." Kate had always been close to her children. She stayed home to raise them in their preschool years, wanting to avoid replicating her own experience that she called "raising myself and my brother." Kate and Jim remained close to their high school friends who also stayed in the neighborhood. They had weekly dinners at someone's house that tended to be rowdy affairs. In addition, they often got together with their children. She had not socialized with these friends since Jim died, except an occasional lunch with her best friends, Mary and Pam.

Psychoeducation focuses on explaining normal grief, acknowledging that many aspects of grief are unique for each relationship, and also that yearning and longing for the person who died, a sense of disbelief about the death, preoccupation with the deceased, an inclination to avoid painful reminders of the person, and a tendency to withdraw from usual daily activities are common. Grief never goes away after a loss like Kate's, but it usually progresses from being engrossing to being subdued, in the background and integrated into daily life. Complicated grief occurs when this transition is blocked. People with CG feel as though the death was very recent, even after years have passed. They feel a painful loss of connection to the deceased, and estranged from others in their lives as well. Often they feel hurt and misunderstood by others who are often frustrated and discouraged by what seems like "wallowing in grief." In CGT, the person is encouraged to invite a significant other to attend the third treatment session in order to educate the person and as a step in work that seeks to reestablish feelings of connectedness to others.

Kate's friends and family, initially very supportive of her painful sorrow, had long since told her that she needed to move on. In a way, Kate agreed with them. She sometimes thought she was pathetic, and that Jim would be angry with her for being so stuck. She knew he would want her to find a way to be happy again. Yet she didn't see how it was possible to live when you lose someone who is so much a part of you. Kate said she wanted help, but she didn't see how she could get it, as no one could bring Jim back.

Kate's daughter Beth came to the third session. Kate was surprised when Beth cried as she said what was really sad was that she not only lost her father, but also her mother, who was always her "rock of Gibraltar." Beth felt frustrated and hopeless. She missed her dad but she felt that she had come to terms with his death. She longed for her mother, but she couldn't get Kate to talk about anything except dad and this was disappointing and made her a little angry. This treatment was the first glimmer of hope she had had in years. She said she was more than happy to help if there was anything she could do. Kate saw that she had let her daughter down, and privately decided to work hard to get better.

Motivation can be a problem for individuals with CG (Szanto et al., 2006). As Bowlby (1980) pointed out, mourners are often ambivalent about acknowledging the finality of the loss. CGT uses a range of motivational interviewing (MI) strategies (Miller & Rollnick, 2002) to address ambivalence. One of these is a modification of MI personal goals work. Goals work is introduced at the second session and discussed in each session thereafter.

The therapist asked Kate, "If I could wave a magic wand and your grief was at a manageable level, what would you want for yourself?" Kate was surprised by this question, and said, "I don't know. I just want to feel better." The therapist waited. After a while Kate smiled slightly and said, "I always wanted to go back to school and get a degree in marketing." Then she added, "But Jim never really encouraged me to do that. He thought it was better for me to spend my time at the church. I think he was worried about the money and whether or not it would take a lot of time away from the family." She hesitated. "But now the girls are grown. He's not here…." She hesitated again, and added, "I don't know how I would feel trying to do something like that." The therapist suggested that she defer decision making and instead start to think about this. For example, how committed was she to going back to school? If she did decide to do this, what were some of the things that would tell her she was making progress? Who might be helpful? What might stand in her way? Kate said it would be interesting to think about this. She agreed to do so.

A core loss-related strategy in CGT is revisiting the death. This exercise uses a procedure similar to prolonged exposure (PE) developed by Foa and her colleagues (Foa, 1995) for posttraumatic stress disorder (PTSD), in which clients are asked to close their eyes and visualize themselves at the time of the death. They are then instructed to tell the story of what happened that day, in the present tense. The therapist monitors distress levels and makes an audio recording of the exercise so clients can take it home and listen to it again as a therapeutic homework assignment. After about 15 minutes, clients are asked to open their eyes and the therapist helps them reflect on the story. Then they do another exercise to set the story aside and focus on restoration. This *imaginal revisiting* exercise is thought to have multiple effects. In relation to trauma work, PE is a powerful tool for reducing anxiety; however, grief is a complex response, and fear is only a part. People with CG are often fearful of their own emotions upon telling the story of the death, and revisiting reduces this fear, making the "unthinkable" "thinkable." Visualization fosters integration of the death into implicit memory systems, and the narrative fosters cognitive change by reducing the person's sense of disbelief regarding death and facilitating the development of an optimally comforting narrative, as does the period of reflection after revisiting. Guilty, angry, shameful and frightening beliefs emerge and are reevaluated. Reappraisal of troubling aspects of the story is encouraged during the period of reflection.

Kate was reluctant to do the revisiting exercise, thinking it would be too hard for her. However, with the therapist's gentle encouragement, she agreed to try. She became very emotional within a few minutes of starting the visualization, and her emotions stayed high throughout. At the end she felt exhausted but relieved. In repeating the revisiting exercise over a period of about a month,

Kate's memory of Jim's death became less acutely painful, less potent, and Kate saw that she could tolerate the pain. She was no longer afraid of loss of control. She began to see that it was unreasonable to blame herself for Jim's illness and death, and also that she should be less afraid of life without him. Kate found that in listening to the tape, the reality of the death "really hit home—something about hearing myself tell that story." Kate was able to reconsider several ideas she had been holding onto, such as her thought that she did not do enough for Jim. In telling the story of his death, she began to recall how dedicated she was to Jim's comfort and care. She had thought that he died without knowing how much she loved him. This too was reappraised. Harder to achieve was the needed acceptance that though it was not really fair that he died at the time and in the way he did, she had long since understood that life is not necessarily fair. She began to feel less inclined to protest the unfairness of Jim's death, and her sense of moral indignation receded. She realized that his untimely and difficult death did not mean that it was wrong for her to enjoy life without him.

Situational revisiting exercises focus especially on doing things that the person sees as desirable, but finds too painful. Kate's situational revisiting exercises included spending time with her children, going out with her old friends, going to restaurants she and Jim liked to frequent, listening to Jim's favorite music, going out with new people, and disposing of Jim's personal items.

Very often, distressed bereaved people wish they could have one last conversation with the deceased. There are questions they would like answered and/or things they didn't get to say. CGT provides this opportunity using an *imaginal conversation*. People are invited to close their eyes, imagine that they are with the deceased shortly after the death, and also imagine the deceased person can hear and speak. They are asked to have an imaginary conversation with their deceased loved one in which they talk and then take the role of their loved one and answer.

Kate closed her eyes and imagined she was with Jim in the hospital after he died. She said she felt so sad that he was gone, that she loved him very much and hoped he was OK. She said that he meant the world to her and that she could not imagine how her life can go on without him. She said she wasn't sure if he really knew how much she loved him. Kate then took Jim's role and responded, "Gee, Kate, we always knew we loved each other more than anything. I still want so much for you to be happy—just like always. I didn't want to die, but it was God's will and I am with God now and I am at peace." Kate hesitated and then said, "I know it's wrong, Jim, but I am so angry with God. It was unfair to take you when so many wicked people are still here—and when he knew how much I need you. I know you were hoping that my faith would support me after you were gone, but I can't even go to church anymore." She began to cry, and continued, "I feel so confused—angry, guilty about not going, and afraid because it is terrible to lose your faith." She cried softly. She took Jim's role again. "Yes, Kate, it is very sad to lose your faith—especially because God never promised us anything. We used to think that if we were very good, we would get special rewards, but we learned a long time ago that this wasn't true. Remember our friends who lost a child? Remember how we talked about things that happen to people that they don't deserve? Kate, I think you should go see Father Daniel. You always liked him, and he is a very kind person. Even though he moved out of our parish, I think he would talk to you." Kate switched to her own voice, saying, "I don't know. I'll think about it." Then she said, "I love you," and switched to his voice to add, "I love you too."

Kate was relieved by the conversation and reiterated that she needed to think about getting in touch with Father Daniel. The conversation shifted to *goals work*. During the middle phase of treatment, the therapist continued work with goals during the second half of each session. Kate began thinking about her plans to return to business school. She researched schools and found one that was convenient to her home. She talked to her daughter, Beth, and her best friend, Mary, about these plans. Both were surprised and also very supportive, happy to see her interested in something new and potentially rewarding. Kate told Beth how her father had not been supportive of this idea, and they laughed together and agreed that he was not there anymore so he couldn't stop her. But Beth told her mother that she was confident that her father would support Kate's ambitions now. She said, "You always had the best ideas for advertising my school events, and you will be great at this."

The last third of CGT is used flexibly to continue revisiting or imaginal conversation, work on personal goals, and/or address an interpersonal conflict or role transition, using standard strategies from interpersonal therapy (IPT) (Weissman, Markowitz, & Klerman, 2000). The last three sessions focus on termination.

Kate's symptoms were markedly diminished at the end of the treatment. She still felt sad when she talked about Jim or when she thought about him. She still felt occasional pangs of missing him immensely when she was out with friends. But she was going out regularly with her girlfriends and had had several successful dinners with the old friends who were couples. One of them wanted to introduce her to a widower he knew, but she said she was not ready for that yet. She told the therapist that dating was probably in her future. Right now, though, she wanted to concentrate on her plans for school and on working hard to repay her boss for his "incredible understanding" over the past 3 years. She felt she owed him a great deal. Kate smiled as she shook hands with the therapist to say goodbye. "I am so grateful," she said. "You gave me my life back, and more. I feel stronger than I have ever felt. I am not quite sure how it happened, but it feels really good."

CGT has empirical support from two prospective case series (Shear et al., 2001; Zuckoff et al., 2006), one of which included people with substance use disorders. CGT was proven efficacious in a prospective randomized controlled study of 95 people with CG using a stringent comparison with IPT, a treatment that has been extensively tested and shown to be highly effective for depression and that has a grief focus. Effectiveness of CGT was demonstrated in an African American subgroup (Cruz et al., 2007). Two further NIMH-funded studies are currently underway. CGT is used by researchers and clinicians around the world.

TREATMENT INTERVENTIONS: COGNITIVE-BEHAVIORAL TREATMENT (CBT)

As with CGT, the aim of cognitive-behavioral therapy is to alleviate the acute grief symptoms and to help the person to achieve valued goals, which often include feeling happy and engaging in activities that are satisfying and meaningful. Based upon the CBT theory described above, changes needed include (a) integrating the loss with existing autobiographical knowledge, (b) changing unhelpful thinking patterns, and (c) replacing unhelpful avoidance strategies by more helpful actions and coping strategies. Various cognitive–behavioral interventions that are also used in the treatment of other forms of psychopathology, including mood and anxiety disorders, can be used to achieve these changes. Examples are described in what follows.

Facilitating Integration of the Loss

An important intervention to improve integration of the loss in CBT is *exposure*, an intervention that is similar to the revisiting interventions in CGT. During exposure in CBT, CG patients are encouraged gradually to confront the painful reality of the loss and to elaborate upon the implications of the loss for the self in the present and future. To this end, patients can be asked to tell a detailed story about the events surrounding the death, to talk or write about the most painful aspects of the loss, or to review the implications of the loss—for example, by writing a letter to the lost person in which the patient describes what is missed most. Moreover, patients can be encouraged to drop particular compulsive behaviors such as ruminating about "why" the loss occurred or paying frequent visits to the graveyard, using response prevention (an intervention frequently applied in the treatment of obsessive–compulsive disorders). Dropping these behaviors is not an end in itself; however, when they interfere with processing and adjustment, it is useful to gradually drop them. Notably, in treating CG with CBT, exposure is not used to increase "habituation" to particular emotions—as in the treatment of anxiety disorders. Instead, the aim is to facilitate connectivity of knowledge that the loss is irreversible with autobiographical knowledge about the self and the lost person and to have CG patients learn through the exposure that experiential avoidance of the grief is fruitless, that they have the strength to confront the loss, and that doing so fosters adjustment (Ehlers & Clark, 2000).

Treatment of Kate with the CBT model described here would have been comparable to CGT. In CBT, Kate would also have been asked to tell the story of Jim's death. However, they would possibly not have tape recorded the session and asked her to listen to it repeatedly in between therapy sessions. Kate and her therapist would then go on to review the implications of the loss in a detailed manner, to increase recognition of the pain and finality of the separation. While doing so, the therapist would try to identify idiosyncratic cognitions that block adjustment; specifically cognitions pertaining to Kate's view of herself, her life, and her future—and possible fear-evoking catastrophic cognitions about the consequences of truly confronting the finality of the loss. These cognitions would then be targeted in a subsequent phase of treatment.

Changing Unhelpful Negative Cognitions

A key intervention in changing unhelpful cognitions is cognitive restructuring: systematically identifying, discussing, and, oftentimes, changing them. With this intervention, it is extremely important to search for the right cognitions. Not every negative cognition can and should be changed—although it is a common misconception that this is what cognitive–behavioral therapists aim to do. Instead, the therapist looks for those cognitions that are central to the problems of the person, that interfere with the achievement of valued goals, and that are preferably relatively falsifiable. So for example, when a somber view on life is central to the person's problems, it may be tempting to try to dispute the cognition "Life has no meaning." But it will be hard to challenge the validity of such a global cognition. Instead, the therapist should focus on a more specific cognition that likely underlies that global cognition, such as "Life has no meaning now, and I probably will never find meaning in life in the future anymore," which includes an understandable but maladaptive prediction. When the right cognitions are identified, both verbal and behavioral techniques can be used to challenge and change them. An example of a verbal technique is using Socratic questioning to raise doubts about the validity and utility of the identified dysfunctional cognition (e.g., "How do you know that you won't be able to reengage in meaningful activities?" or "What's the effect when you continue to predict that you won't be able to do so?"). Behavioral techniques include *behavioral experiments*, assignments set up to test particular predictions (e.g., talking to a friend about your feelings, to test the prediction "No one is willing to listen to my story anymore").

A therapist using the CBT model would have discussed Kate's negative cognitions about life and would have explored the validity and utility of the conviction that "It is impossible to live a fulfilling life when you lose someone who is so much a part of you." In addition, a CBT therapist might have encouraged Kate to do a behavioral experiment to test the idea that other people consider her a burden and don't want to help her (e.g., by sharing feelings with a close friend and carefully monitoring this friend's responses).

Changing Maladaptive Behavioral Strategies

Changing maladaptive strategies basically means that the therapist tries to raise doubts about the usefulness of engaging in these strategies and to encourage patients to replace these with more helpful strategies to handle the pain. Anxious avoidance is actually a combination of predictions such as "When I confront my pain, I won't be able to control my feelings and will go crazy" and the actual avoidance behaviors, such as avoiding situations that remind the person of the death (behavioral avoidance) or not thinking about the implications of the loss (cognitive avoidance). The therapist uses cognitive restructuring to change such catastrophic predictions and exposure procedures to confront patients with internal and external stimuli that they tend to avoid. For instance, patients can be encouraged to face avoided situations or thoughts in order to learn that they are able to endure the pain and that confronting the reality alleviates rather than accentuates the suffering. Likewise, in targeting depressive avoidance, the therapist challenges the validity and utility of cognitions such as "Doing something that is potentially nice certainly won't make me feel better," which usually underlie this avoidance. As a next step the therapist can use behavioral activation to gradually help the patient to reengage in potentially pleasurable and meaningful activities. A key idea behind behavioral activation is that it is not necessary to feel good before one can do things that are potentially enjoyable (which is what patients with CG often think) but, instead, that action often precedes mood improvement and adjustment.

A CBT therapist would have helped Kate gradually confront situations she feared and avoided, as is done in CGT, and to restore activities that were enjoyable and meaningful before Jim's death, such as going out with friends. The impact of these activities on correcting Kate's negative cognitions about herself, her life, and her grief would be discussed explicitly.

In summary, CBT strategies are prominent in CGT and are used exclusively in Boelen's CBT treatment. Similarities in these treatments are more pronounced than differences. CBT uses a somewhat different heuristic model that is not directly linked to attachment theory. CGT includes more of a focus on interpersonal relationships and on addressing ambivalence. CBT uses standard cognitive therapy to alter maladaptive thoughts and behaviors. Both CGT and CBT encourage reflection upon the narrative of the death and upon its consequences.

CBT strategies are supported by the general efficacy of cognitive–behavioral therapy for mood and anxiety symptoms (Beck, 2005) and by the effectiveness of CGT (Shear et al., 2005). Additionally, Boelen and his colleagues found that exposure and cognitive restructuring were more efficacious than supportive counseling in a treatment study of CG (Boelen, De Keijser, Van den Hout, & Van den Bout, 2007).

TREATMENT INTERVENTION: MEANING RECONSTRUCTION

The general aim of constructivist therapy for bereavement is to alleviate acute grief symptoms and help the person to achieve valued goals, much as is the case with the other treatments. From the meaning reconstruction perspective, the therapist seeks to help the client: (a) find a meaningful place for the *event story* of the death in the client's ongoing self-narrative; (b) review and revise the *back story* of the relationship with the deceased, both to address residual concerns and to reconstruct the attachment bond with the deceased in a way that does not require his or her physical presence; (c) "revision" life and foster creative problem solving; and (d) reinforce dedicated action through legacy work. Some of the range of experiential, narrative, and action-oriented interventions that can be used to achieve these changes will be described and illustrated.

Facilitating the Integration of the Loss

As in both CGT and CBT, clients can be asked to tell a detailed story about the events that led up to the death, focusing on the painful details that are often "edited out" of the client's more public account of the loss so as to foster fuller integration. Viewed in narrative terms, a sustained engagement with the "event story" of the death fosters the recognition of previously unassimilated aspects of "plot structure" of the account, ultimately weaving a more coherent narrative of a potentially fragmenting life event (Neimeyer, 2000). As an aid to accomplishing this, the therapist might first help the person access sources of resilience through reviewing previously effective coping skills, working directly or indirectly with supportive figures in the person's family or social world, or reviewing and reinforcing features of his or her philosophic or spiritual beliefs as a prologue to a "restorative retelling" of the narrative of loss (Rynearson, 2006; see also Chapter 14). Furthermore, the therapist might promote meaning reconstruction by shifting the person into different narrative "voices" or styles, including the *external* (factual or observable), *internal* (subjective or emotional), and *reflexive* (explanatory or perspective-taking) story of the event (Neimeyer & Levitt, 2001). Such "restorying" can be undertaken in relatively brief segments of 15–20 minutes of sustained attention to the events of death and its aftermath, considered in vividly concrete detail, or can occupy whole sessions, punctuated by opportunities to "make sense" of the emotionally intense material that is related. The therapist may facilitate the latter reflective work by prompting the client with questions such as "How did you make sense of what was happening at the time?" "How do you understand it now?"

"In what way, if any, did your personal philosophy or spiritual beliefs help you find meaning in the loss?" And "How were those same beliefs challenged or changed by it, in turn?" Although this detailed sifting of the event story of the loss is commonly conducted in session, where the therapist can provide conditions of safety, respectful witnessing, and "containment" of sometimes overwhelming feelings, it can also be advanced through evocative writing about the loss to promote meaning making in any of several creative formats (Neimeyer, 2002).

Treating Kate with this approach, the therapist might have begun with a review of her spiritual and religious beliefs. This might have helped highlight the way the death seemed to invalidate the spiritual meaning of her life and led naturally to a sustained retelling of the event story of the death, beginning at the point when the hospice nurse told her the end was very near. This initial "slow motion" recounting might have lasted up to 90 minutes, as the therapist prompted Kate to "stay with" "hot spots" in the story, points of overwhelming distress, as when she observed Jim struggling for his last breath or when she had to phone Beth to tell her that Jim was gone. Combing slowly through the narrative strands of the experiences that were traumatic for Kate, the therapist might prompt her to retell certain episodes from the standpoint of what was happening in her internal world, as well as the world around her, helping her articulate and regulate (through focused breathing or repetition) previously unattended emotions they aroused, as well as to sequence the chaotic events that had been only mutely experienced, never related to others. Recording the session at the therapist's suggestion, Kate might be asked to review the account between sessions and note other memories, feelings, and observations that came to her, after she and the therapist developed a "safety plan" for stepping away from this hard work when it became too intense. This would naturally yield to a discussion of any new awareness that came to her as a result of immersion in the telling, and the sense she now made of the loss in the larger context of her life. Further integration of the loss into the client's self-narrative could be fostered by encouraging her to draft the "chapter titles" of her life story, situating the death within them, and considering how she accommodated prior significant losses and transitions in view of the key themes that underpinned them.

Reviewing and Revising the Relationship to the Deceased

In contemporary grief theory, adaptation to the death of a key attachment figure does not require that we relinquish so much as reconstruct our bond to the deceased, revising it from an attachment that requires the loved one's physical presence to one that can be sustained in emotional and practical terms in his or her absence (Klass, Silverman, & Nickman, 1996). Accessing the relationship in a vividly experiential way, as through the imaginal conversation in CGT, via an "exchange" of correspondence with the deceased or by tracing the "life imprint" of the loved one on oneself at levels ranging from mannerisms through core life purposes and values in a written homework assignment (Neimeyer, 2010), can therefore serve multiple functions: (a) restoring felt access to an attachment bond disrupted by loss, (b) permitting the person to review and redress residual difficulties in the relationship at a symbolic level, and (c) retaining the deceased as a constructive presence in the mourner's world by sharing his or her life story with others in ongoing conversations and ritual practices. To begin this process, Kate might have been encouraged to have an imaginal conversation with Jim, very similar to the one used in CGT, and to consolidate its lessons in further creative writing.

A core feature of Kate's grief was her yearning to reestablish a sense of contact with him, in part to continue in some sense their loving connection, and in part to reassure herself that he was "alright," in a place beyond pain. With the therapist's encouragement, she might address Jim symbolically in an empty chair, pouring out her longing, her grief, and her concern for his well-being. Taking Jim's chair at the therapist's suggestion, she might lend him her voice, and respond. Processing the interaction afterward with the therapist, Kate might note how helpful it had been to express her pain and concern directly "to" her husband, and to sense his compassionate response. She might accept the suggestion that she could find other times to "speak" with him, to seek his counsel about her problems, goals, and plans, and to write him in her journal, responding as if from his standpoint. She might find this exercise useful in sensing more deeply how Jim would answer her, especially as she considered changes she wished to make in her life without "abandoning" him. Tracing his "life imprint" on her own in between-session writing could further this goal of reconstructing their continuing bond.

"Re-Visioning Life" and Fostering Creative Problem Solving

A constructivist approach to working with cognition is less disputative and logical than in CBT, and more propositional and hypothetical (Neimeyer, 2009). Rather than focusing analytic attention on specific negative thought patterns, the therapist is more likely to lead clients into imaginative, "as if" engagement with the problem. For example, the therapist might invite a widow to write a letter of encouragement to a real or hypothetical mourner who had suffered a similar loss; to draft a letter to herself from the position of the person she would be in 5 years, after she had integrated the experience in a healthy way; or to permit the therapist to interview her in the role of the deceased husband, responding to queries about the signature strengths in the mourner that give the husband confidence that she would adapt to this difficult transition (Neimeyer, 2002; Neimeyer, Burke, et al., 2010; Neimeyer, Van Dyke, & Pennebaker, 2009). Similar to CGT, clients would be encouraged to envision new goals and roles that are realizable even in the wake of the loss—or, indeed, because of it—and in this way to reconstruct a more hopeful future. Finally, in the longer term aftermath of a significant loss, the bereaved might be invited to reflect on what it taught them that was of benefit, or about how it changed, challenged, or deepened his or her core spiritual or philosophic beliefs. Such prompts for ultimate meaning making typically should be offered at some considerable distance from the loss rather than in the early weeks or months of grieving, when active interventions to help modulate the person's emotional arousal and grapple with the event story of the loss are more appropriate.

Kate might have been struggling with fear that she was forever "broken" by the death of her husband, as she contended with disruption in her sleep and other daily activities. Having accessed Jim's "voice" through imaginal dialogues, the therapist might invite him into the room, and encourage Kate to speak as if she were him. The therapist might then interview Jim about their relationship, how Kate had been resilient in the face of earlier losses and stresses, and how he would continue to comfort her as she engaged the challenges of her changed life. In a further intervention, the therapist might use guided imagery to help Kate vividly imagine tending to her husband during his illness, and comforting him as he lay dying. Alternating with these experiential interventions the therapist could use reflective ones, in which Kate might be encouraged to consider her spiritual beliefs, contemplate her greater sensitivity to the suffering of others, and seek meaning in observations that seemed to affirm larger cosmological forces at work in what otherwise would be merely a cruelly random event. She might, for example, shift her thinking to conclude that she had been not so much "broken" as "broken open" by the loss, in a way that fostered in her a more profound engagement with living.

Reinforcing Dedicated Action through Legacy Work

Generally speaking, a constructivist approach to fostering behavior change focuses less on confronting maladaptive patterns than on enhancing positive ones, especially those that help the person reconstruct a world of meaning that has been challenged by loss (Neimeyer, 2002). One class of activity of high relevance to many mourners is finding some appropriate way of honoring the legacy of their loved ones, whether through constructing an online memorial, supporting a scholarship fund, launching a public safety campaign regarding a dangerous waterway or intersection, planting a tree or garden at a local school or park, or simply extending the core values of their loved ones through their own dedicated actions. Such efforts can strengthen survivors' sense of secure attachment to the deceased, while also helping them reformulate new goals appropriate to the world in which they must now live.

Finally, Kate might be encouraged to talk with some of their close friends who had experienced shared grief after Jim's death and engage in activities to honor his life. For example, she might be encouraged to start a blog about the proud and humorous moments in their lives together, inviting interested others to memorialize him in words and pictures. She might also seek to construct a positive legacy for her husband by helping organize a local walk to support the American Cancer Society, or to contribute a memorial bench to a community park in which they once spent loving hours together. Simultaneously, Kate might reengage her own long interest in marketing by returning to school and honor her loving nature by starting to date, both with a sense of Jim's support and encouragement. These would be ways to continue to honor her loyalty to Jim's memory, while also engaging new roles that are growth enhancing for her as a person.

A meaning reconstruction approach to the treatment of CG is congruent with the numerous studies that link a disruption in meaning making regarding a loss with more intense, debilitating, and prolonged grieving, and the ability to make sense of the loss with eventual well-being, efficacy, and optimism in the years to come (see Chapter 1). Moreover, it is supported by randomized controlled trials on the use of creative narrative procedures, such as Wagner, Knaevelsrud, and Maercker's (2006) study of perspective taking and loss integration assignments with 55 persons with complicated grief, or Lichtenthal and Cruess's (2010) investigation of expressive, sense-making, and benefit-finding interventions with 68 bereaved young adults. The finding that carefully focused narrative work of this kind can lead to reduction in CG as well as posttraumatic stress symptomatology suggests that explicit attention to meaning making can play a useful role in CG treatment.

CONCLUSION

Although human beings are notably resilient in the face of loss and trauma (Bonanno et al., 2004), a great deal of evidence now demonstrates that for a subgroup of about 10% of bereaved people, complicated grief can become a seemingly unending sentence. In view of this anguishing response to loss, made vivid to us in clinical practice as well as research studies, we have attempted to devise or adapt therapeutic procedures to help these people to address problems that complicate grief, to more fully integrate the reality of their loved one's death. We work with them to once more engage the world with a sense of connection, purpose, and meaning rendered largely inaccessible by the loss. Using attachment, coping, cognitive–behavioral, and constructivist models, we outlined three conceptualizations of this life-limiting condition, and described and illustrated their key procedures. Notwithstanding differences in the three approaches, we were struck by convergence in (a) fostering confrontation with the story of the death in an attempt to master its most painful aspects and integrate its finality into the mourner's internalized models of the deceased, the self, and the world; (b) encouraging engagement with the image, voice, or memory of the deceased to facilitate a sense of ongoing attachment while allowing for the development of other relationships; (c) gradually challenging avoidance coping and building skill in emotion modulation and creative problem solving; and (d) encouraging the bereaved to review and revise life goals and roles in a world without the deceased person physically in it. We believe these commonalities can serve as principles to guide clinicians and that the differences in our three approaches indicate that there is not just one way to follow these principles. We hope that therapists treating people with CG can use this information as they work to tailor interventions for individuals with complicated grief, and that researchers will find this chapter helpful as they continue efforts to refine and test treatments for this debilitating problem.

REFERENCES

Aldao, A., & Nolen-Hoeksema, S. (2010). Specificity of cognitive emotion regulation strategies: A transdiagnostic examination. *Behaviour Research and Therapy*, *48*(10), 974–983.

Beck, A. T. (1976). *Cognitive therapy and the emotional disorders*. New York: Penguin.

Beck, A. T. (2005). The current state of cognitive therapy: A 40-year retrospective. *Archives of General Psychiatry*, *62*(9), 953–959.

Boelen, P. A., De Keijser, J., Van den Hout, M. A., & Van den Bout, J. (2007). Treatment of complicated grief: A comparison between cognitive-behavioral therapy and supportive counseling. *Journal of Consulting and Clinical Psychology*, *75*(2), 277–284.

Boelen, P. A., & Van den Bout, J. (2010). Anxious and depressive avoidance and symptoms of prolonged grief, depression, and posttraumatic stress disorder. *Psychologica Belgica*, *50*, 49–67.

Boelen, P. A., Van den Bout, J., & Van den Hout, M. A. (2003). The role of negative interpretations of grief reactions in emotional problems after bereavement. *Journal of Behavior Therapy and Experimental Psychiatry*, *34*(3–4), 225–238.

Boelen, P. A., Van den Bout, J., & Van den Hout, M. A. (2006). Negative cognitions and avoidance in emotional problems after bereavement: A prospective study. *Behaviour Research and Therapy*, *44*(11), 1657–1672.

Boelen, P. A., Van den Hout, M. A., & Van den Bout, J. (2006). A cognitive-behavioral conceptualization of complicated grief. *Clinical Psychology: Science and Practice*, *13*(2), 109–128.

Boelen, P. A., Van de Schoot, R., Van den Hout, M. A., De Keijser, J., & Van den Bout, J. (2010). Prolonged grief disorder, depression, and posttraumatic stress disorder are distinguishable syndromes. *Journal of Affective Disorders*, *125*(1–3), 374–378.

Bonanno, G. A., Neria, Y., Mancini, A., Coifman, K. G., Litz, B., & Insel, B. (2007). Is there more to complicated grief than depression and posttraumatic stress disorder? A test of incremental validity. *Journal of Abnormal Psychology*, *116*(2), 342–351.

Bonanno, G. A., Wortman, C. B., & Nesse, R. M. (2004). Prospective patterns of resilience and maladjustment during widowhood. *Psychology and Aging*, *19*(2), 260–271.

Bowlby, J. (1980). *Loss: Sadness and depression* (Vol. 3). New York: Basic.

Burke, L. A., Neimeyer, R. A., & McDevitt-Murphy, M. E. (2010). African American homicide bereavement: Aspects of social support that predict complicated grief, PTSD, and depression. *Omega*, *61*(1), 1–24.

Cassidy, J., & Shaver, P. (Eds.). (2008). *Handbook of attachment: Theory, research, and clinical applications* (2nd ed.). New York: Guilford Press.

Cruz, M., Scott, J., Houck, P., Reynolds, C. F., III, Frank, E., & Shear, M. K. (2007). Clinical presentation and treatment outcome of African Americans with complicated grief. *Psychiatric Services*, *58*(5), 700–702.

Currier, J. M., Holland, J. M., & Neimeyer, R. A. (2006). Sense-making, grief, and the experience of violent loss: Toward a mediational model. *Death Studies*, *30*(5), 403–428.

Currier, J. M., Neimeyer, R. A., & Berman, J. S. (2008). The effectiveness of psychotherapeutic interventions for bereaved persons: A comprehensive quantitative review. *Psychological Bulletin*, *134*(5), 648–661.

Ehlers, A., & Clark, D. M. (2000). A cognitive model of posttraumatic stress disorder. *Behaviour Research and Therapy*, *38*(4), 319–345.

Elliot, A. J., & Reis, H. T. (2003). Attachment and exploration in adulthood. *Journal of Personality and Social Psychology*, *85*(2), 317–331.

Foa, E. B., Rothbaum, B., & Molnar, C. (1995). Cognitive-behavioral therapy of posttraumatic stress disorder. In M. J. Friedman, D. S. Charney, & A. Y. Deutch (Eds.), *Neurobiological and clinical consequences of stress: From normal adaptation to posttraumatic stress disorder* (pp. 483–494). Philadelphia: Lippincott Williams & Wilkins.

Folkman, S. (1997). Positive psychological states and coping with severe stress. *Social Science and Medicine*, *45*(8), 1207–1221.

Folkman, S., & Moskowitz, J. T. (2000). Positive affect and the other side of coping. *American Psychologist*, *55*(6), 647–654.

Gamino, L. A., Sewell, K. W., & Easterling, L. W. (2000). Scott and White Grief Study—phase 2: Toward an adaptive model of grief. *Death Studies*, *24*(7), 633–660.

Germain, A., Caroff, K., Buysse, D. J., & Shear, M. K. (2005). Sleep quality in complicated grief. *Journal of Traumatic Stress*, *18*(4), 343–346.

Hardison, H. G., Neimeyer, R. A., & Lichstein, K. L. (2005). Insomnia and complicated grief symptoms in bereaved college students. *Behavioral Sleep Medicine*, *3*(2), 99–111.

Hayes, S. C., Wilson, K. G., Gifford, E. V., Follette, V. M., & Strosahl, K. (1996). Experiential avoidance and behavioral disorders: A functional dimensional approach to diagnosis and treatment. *Journal of Consulting and Clinical Psychology*, *64*(6), 1152–1168.

Hofer, M. A. (1984). Relationships as regulators: A psychobiologic perspective on bereavement. *Psychosomatic Medicine*, *46*(3), 183–197.

Hofer, M. A. (1996). On the nature and consequences of early loss. *Psychosomatic Medicine*, *58*(6), 570–581.

Klass, D., Silverman, P. R., & Nickman, S. (1996). *Continuing bonds: New understandings of grief*. Philadelphia: Taylor & Francis.

Latham, A. E., & Prigerson, H. G. (2004). Suicidality and bereavement: Complicated grief as psychiatric disorder presenting greatest risk for suicidality. *Suicide and Life-Threatening Behavior*, *34*(4), 350–362.

Lichtenthal, W. G., & Cruess, D. G. (2010). Effects of directed written disclosure on grief and distress symptoms among bereaved individuals. *Death Studies*, *34*, 475–499.

Lichtenthal, W. G., Cruess, D. G., & Prigerson, H. G. (2004). A case for establishing complicated grief as a distinct mental disorder in DSM-V. *Clinical Psychology Review*, *24*(6), 637–662.

Mikulincer, M. (2006). Attachment, caregiving, and sex within romantic relationships: A behavioral systems perspective. In M. Mikulincer & G. S. Goodman (Eds.), *Dynamics of romantic love* (pp. 23–44). New York: Guilford Press.

Miller, W. R., & Rollnick, S. (2002). *Motivational interviewing: Preparing people for change* (2nd ed.). New York: Guilford Press.

Monk, T. H., Houck, P. R., & Shear, M. K. (2006). The daily life of complicated grief patients—what gets missed,what gets added? *Death Studies*, *30*(1), 77–85.

Neimeyer, R. A. (2000). Narrative disruptions in the construction of self. In R. A. Neimeyer & J. D. Raskin (Eds.), *Constructions of disorder: Meaning making frameworks for psychotherapy*. Washington, DC: American Psychological Association.

Neimeyer, R. A. (2004). Fostering a posttraumatic growth: A narrative contribution. *Psychological Inquiry, 15*, 53–59.

Neimeyer, R. A. (Ed.). (2001). *Meaning reconstruction and the experience of loss*. Washington, DC: American Psychological Association.

Neimeyer, R. A. (2002). *Lessons of loss: A guide to coping*. Memphis, TN: Center for the Study of Loss and Transition.

Neimeyer, R. A. (2006a). Narrating the dialogical self: Toward an expanded toolbox for the counselling psychologist. *Counselling Psychology Quarterly*, *19*, 105–120.

Neimeyer, R. A. (2006b). Complicated grief and the quest for meaning: A constructivist contribution. *Omega*, *52*, 37–52.

Neimeyer, R. A. (2009). *Constructivist psychotherapy*. London: Routledge.

Neimeyer, R. A. (2010). The life imprint. In H. Rosenthal (Ed.), *Favorite counseling and therapy techniques*. New York: Routledge.

Neimeyer, R. A., Burke, L., Mackay, M., & Stringer, J. (2010). Grief therapy and the reconstrution of meaning: From principles to practice. *Journal of Contemporary Psychotherapy*, *40*(2), 73–83.

Neimeyer, R. A., & Levitt, H. (2001). Coping and coherence: A narrative perspective. In C. R. Snyder (Ed.), *Stress and coping* (pp. 47–67). New York: Oxford.

Neimeyer, R. A., Van Dyke, J. G., & Pennebaker, J. W. (2009). Narrative medicine: Writing through bereavement. In H. Chochinov & W. Breitbart (Eds.), *Handbook of psychiatry in palliative medicine* (pp. 454–469). New York: Oxford.

Nolen-Hoeksema, S., McBride, A., & Larson, J. (1997). Rumination and psychological distress among bereaved partners. *Journal of Personality and Social Psychology*, *72*(4), 855–862.

Prigerson, H. G., Bierhals, A. J., Kasl, S. V., Reynolds, C. F., III, Shear, M. K., Day, N., et al. (1997). Traumatic grief as a risk factor for mental and physical morbidity. *American Journal of Psychiatry*, *154*(5), 616–623.

Prigerson, H. G., Horowitz, M. J., Jacobs, S. C., Parkes, C. M., Aslan, M., Goodkin, K., et al. (2009). Prolonged grief disorder: Psychometric validation of criteria proposed for DSM-V and ICD-11. *PLoS Medicine*, *6*(8), e1000121.

Reynolds, C. F., III, Miller, M. D., Pasternak, R. E., Frank, E., Perel, J. M., Cornes, C., et al. (1999). Treatment of bereavement-related major depressive episodes in later life: A controlled study of acute and continuation treatment with nortriptyline and interpersonal psychotherapy. *American Journal of Psychiatry*, *156*(2), 202–208.

Rynearson, E. K. (Ed.). (2006). *Violent death*. New York: Routledge.

Shaver, P., & Fraley, R. C. (2008). Attachment, loss, and grief: Bowlby's views and current controversies. In J. Cassidy & P. R. Shaver (Eds.), *Handbook of attachment: Theory, research, and clinical applications* (2nd ed., pp. 48–77). New York: Guilford Press.

Shear, M. K., Frank, E., Foa, E., Cherry, C., Reynolds, C. F., III, Vander Bilt, J., et al. (2001). Traumatic grief treatment: A pilot study. *American Journal of Psychiatry*, *158*(9), 1506–1508.

Shear, M. K., Frank, E., Houck, P. R., & Reynolds, C. F., III. (2005). Treatment of complicated grief: A randomized controlled trial. *JAMA*, *293*(21), 2601–2608.

Shear, M. K., Monk, T., Houck, P., Melhem, N., Frank, E., Reynolds, C., et al. (2007). An attachment-based model of complicated grief including the role of avoidance. *European Archives of Psychiatry and Clinical Neuroscience*, *257*(8), 462–472.

Shear, M. K., & Shair, H. (2005). Attachment, loss, and complicated grief. *Developmental Psychobiology*, *47*(3), 253–267.

Shear, M. K., Simon, N. M., Zisook, S., Neimeyer, R., Duan, N., Reynolds, C., et al. (in press). Bereavement and DSM-5. *Depression and Anxiety*.

Simon, N. M., Shear, K. M., Thompson, E. H., Zalta, A. K., Perlman, C., Reynolds, C. F., et al. (2007). The prevalence and correlates of psychiatric comorbidity in individuals with complicated grief. *Comprehensive Psychiatry*, *48*(5), 395–399.

Stroebe, M., Boelen, P. A., Van den Hout, M., Stroebe, W., Salemink, E., & Van den Bout, J. (2007). Ruminative coping as avoidance: A reinterpretation of its function in adjustment to bereavement. *European Archives of Psychiatry and Clinical Neuroscience*, *257*(8), 462–472.

Stroebe, M., & Schut, H. (1999). The dual process model of coping with bereavement: Rationale and description. *Death Studies*, *23*(3), 197–224.

Szanto, K., Shear, M. K., Houck, P. R., Reynolds, C. F., III, Frank, E., Caroff, K., et al. (2006). Indirect self-destructive behavior and overt suicidality in patients with complicated grief. *Journal of Clinical Psychiatry*, *67*(2), 233–239.

Van der Houwen, K., Stroebe, M., Schut, H., Van den Bout, J., & Wijngaards-de Meij, L. (2010). Risk factors for bereavement outcome: A multivariate approach. *Death Studies*, *34*, 195–220.

Wagner, B., Knaevelsrud, C., & Maercker, A. (2006). Internet-based cognitive-behavioral therapy for complicated grief: A randomized controlled trial. *Death Studies*, *30*(5), 429–453.

Weissman, M., Markowitz, J., & Klerman, G. (2000). *Comprehensive guide to interpersonal psychotherapy for depression*. New York: Basic.

Wilsey, S. A., & Shear, M. K. (2007). Descriptions of social support in treatment narratives of complicated grievers. *Death Studies*, *31*(9), 801–819.

Zuckoff, A., Shear, K., Frank, E., Daley, D. C., Seligman, K., & Silowash, R. (2006). Treating complicated grief and substance use disorders: A pilot study. *Journal of Substance Abuse Treatment*, *30*(3), 205–211.

13

Grief in the Midst of Ambiguity and Uncertainty
An Exploration of Ambiguous Loss and Chronic Sorrow

PAULINE BOSS, SUSAN ROOS, and DARCY L. HARRIS

Loss, especially through death, often occurs with startling clarity: Someone who was a key living person in our lives yesterday is not there today. At other times, loss is much more subtle, insinuating itself into our lives gradually or robbing us of someone or something of importance that we prized or had once taken for granted. This chapter is written to introduce two concepts—*ambiguous loss* and *chronic sorrow*—that help illuminate the latter circumstance, whether it is connected with the ultimate death of a loved one or any of the other uncountable ways in which loss arises in life. We hope that this opportunity to explore these constructs under one heading might provide a springboard for the discussion of bereavement from a broader perspective.

Both ambiguous loss and chronic sorrow result from losses that may not be easily defined or recognized, that are ongoing in nature, and that may be intangible in their manifestation. All of the authors of this chapter are involved in academic, research-oriented work as well as in clinical practice settings, so the blending of the research and practice in this chapter is a dialogue of professionals who represent both perspectives.

For the sake of clarity, we will start by providing a definition and overview of each concept, along with examples and descriptions. We will then discuss how these two concepts relate to and support each other in clinical practice, and then conclude with clinical implications and recommendations for working with individuals who experience ambiguous losses and chronic sorrow. In deference to our own unique perspectives on this common topic, we have chosen to preserve the writing style or voice of each author.

AMBIGUOUS LOSS

Mary came to therapy with depression and headaches. I (PB) asked about her life. She told me her 20-year-old son had been wounded in Iraq with severe traumatic brain injury. Caring for him dominated her life—and, she believed, would do so for the rest of her days. She quit her job, ignored her husband and friends, and focused on her son. No one noticed how sad she was. No one acknowledged her loss. The son she knew and her dreams for him vanished. She lost her own dreams—and her trust in the world as fair and just. Her life had become incomprehensible. Because no one had died, professionals missed the fact that Mary was grieving. Her symptoms reflected grief that was complicated by the lack of resolution or closure. She got her son back, but he was a different person now. The problem was ambiguous loss (Boss, 1999, 2004, 2006a, 2006b, 2010).

Ambiguous loss is a particularly stressful kind of loss because it is not typically officially acknowledged, and there is no possibility of closure. At times, as when someone is literally missing or is cognitively impaired, the loss remains unclear, as people don't know whether a loved one is dead or alive, absent or present (Boss, 1977, 1999, 2004, 2006a; Boss & Greenberg, 1984; Robins, 2010). Thus, there are two types of ambiguous loss. First, a loved one is *physically absent* but kept psychologically present because his or her status as dead or alive is unclear (due to, e.g., being kidnapped, lost at sea, missing, deserted, or abandoned). With the second type of ambiguous loss, a loved one is *psychologically absent* but physically present (due to, e.g., traumatic brain injury, dementia, autism, depression, addiction, or chronic mental illness).

These losses do not have to be related to external events, such as trauma or illness. For example, the physical type of ambiguous loss is often described by women in infertility treatment who feel that they "lose" a baby before there is even implantation of the embryo into their uterus, which has been termed a "pre-implantation miscarriage" by Covington (2006) or a "technical miscarriage" by Glazer (1997). The grief after an unsuccessful treatment cycle may be very difficult to describe or define, as the embryo(s) that were transferred from the petri dish after fertilization certainly occupy a profound psychological presence with these women, but when pregnancy is not confirmed after the treatment cycle ends, these women are often left to deal with the loss of a baby (or babies) whose physical presence was real, but existed only under a microscope. It is also a common aspect of my work with infertile couples to hear one partner express feelings of loss that are compatible with the psychological absence described in ambiguous loss, often associated with the emotional withdrawal by one of the partners as an attempt to cope with such an intense experience, or obsession and/or rumination about the infertility by one of the partners; in both instances, the affected partner is unavailable to address the needs and feelings of the other partner. These ambiguous losses may significantly compound the losses that are already being experienced by the couple in infertility treatment.

With either type of ambiguous loss—physical or psychological—people are confused about what to do and what role to play. The ambiguity allows hope for reunion or a shift in the circumstances, so grief is frozen (Boss, 1999), relationships are conflicted, and the uncertainty is ongoing. Importantly, both types of ambiguous loss can overlap for one individual, couple, or family. After the widespread terrorist losses of September 11, for example, a survivor I (PB) worked with had a husband who was physically missing, plus a mother with Alzheimer's disease—two ambiguous losses at the same time. Two people she loved were now absent to her (Boss, 2006a).

Because ambiguous loss is a relational loss, treatment must also be relational. It has to entail more than medication for depression. Most importantly, authentic human connection is essential to build resiliency. For example, Mary will need people who can be fully present with her to balance her diminished relationship with her son. Mourners find resiliency through fuller human connections (a friend, a therapist, and a relative), which compensate for ambiguous loss.

CHRONIC SORROW

The concept of chronic sorrow was originally based on observations of parents of children with developmental impairments. Introduced in the 1960s by Simon Olshansky (1962, 1966, 1970), a rehabilitation counselor, administrator, and researcher, its applications and intent were clearly articulated, recasting responses that had been viewed as pathological to be, in fact, normal in the situation of these parents. A paradigm shift was instigated that challenged the prevailing professional perceptions, which included stereotyping, negative labeling, and pathologizing. These parents were seen as neurotic, chronically depressed, schizophrenogenic, autistogenic, overprotective, and never satisfied. With little means of support, parents were caught in the currents of pervasive and episodic grief due to *losses that were living, ongoing, and usually disenfranchised, and that did not lend themselves to resolution or integration in the same way that many losses with finality do.* Interest was evidenced at that time by several research studies that validated the concept (Burke, 1989; Eakes, Burke, & Hainsworth, 1998; Hobdell & Deatrick, 1996).

From the 1990s, the concept has experienced a renewed interest, most notably in the field of nursing, with the establishment of a Nursing Consortium for Research on Chronic Sorrow (NCRCS), and specialized research tools have been developed by a number of professions (Burke, 1989; Casale, 2009, Damrosch & Perry, 1989; Kendall, 2005). The NCRCS conducted investigations into the presence of chronic sorrow for a variety of loss situations. Initial studies focused on adults with chronic or life-threatening conditions. Several diverse large samples of individuals diagnosed with cancer, Parkinson's disease, and multiple sclerosis, and one small sample of infertile couples, were interviewed using the Burke/NCRCS Chronic Sorrow Questionnaire for Affected Individuals as an interview guide. The outcome of this research was the identification of a common theme of pervasive sadness that is permanent, periodic, and progressive in nature (Burke, 1989; Burke, Hainsworth, Eakes, & Lindgren, 1992; Eakes, Hainsworth, Lindgren, & Burke, 1991).

These findings are consistent with those of other qualitative studies of chronic sorrow involving various sample populations (Eakes, 1993; Eakes, Burke, Hainsworth, & Lindgren, 1993; Hainsworth, 1994; Hainsworth, Eakes, & Burke, 1994). Subsequent NCRCS research endeavors have centered on family caregivers of adults, children, or spouses with ongoing disabilities. Using the Burke/NCRCS Chronic Sorrow Questionnaire (Caregiver Version) as a guide, parents of mentally ill children (Eakes, 1995), spouses of individuals diagnosed with multiple sclerosis, and parents of adult children with multiple sclerosis (Hainsworth, 1995) were interviewed. In addition, a secondary analysis was conducted on data from interviews with the wives of mentally ill husbands (Hainsworth, Busch, Eakes, & Burke, 1995). In a comparison analysis, 89% of these family caretakers were found to experience chronic sorrow (Eakes, 1995: Hainsworth, 1995; Hainsworth et al., 1995). The concept has undergone an expansion of its application to other ongoing losses, such as the effects of a wide range of chronic diseases, disabilities, and progressive deterioration of physical and mental attributes.

OVERLAPS, PARALLELS, AND DISTINCTIONS

Descriptions of ambiguous loss and chronic sorrow readily apply to many of the same experiences. Both ambiguous loss and chronic sorrow may be found in *living losses*, as the primary focus of what is lost in ambiguous loss is a discrepancy between the psychological and physical presence of someone, and the foundational losses in the descriptions of chronic sorrow relate to the loss of hopes, dreams, and certainty. The definition of *ambiguous loss* emphasizes losses that relate to another person (i.e., the psychological or physical absence of a loved one), whereas the emphasis in *chronic sorrow* may be centered on another person (i.e., loss of another due to an ongoing loss) or one's self (i.e., loss of one's faith, hope, or sense of certainty). It is apparent that situations of ambiguous loss may lead to chronic sorrow, as the lack of clarity about what has been lost can lead to an ongoing, unrelenting cycle of disequilibrium and despair, temporary adaptation, and reentry into uncertainty that is the hallmark of chronic sorrow (Peterson & Bredow, 2004).

An example of the overlap between the two constructs may be seen in situations where a loved one has been diagnosed with dementia. Family members may find that they gradually come to terms with some of the cognitive difficulties as they are confronted with the realities of their loved one's declining abilities (a time that is usually associated with difficult decision making regarding care and living arrangements), only to find that these abilities fluctuate radically from day to day. There is no ability to predict the course of the changes in cognition and functionality, and no way of knowing what will happen next, or if their loved one will recognize them or even acknowledge their presence with time. This scenario fits the description of psychological ambiguous loss, and also the ongoing loss and uncertainty of chronic sorrow. Overlaps with the descriptions of ambiguous loss and chronic sorrow can be found in some mothers who have relinquished their babies for adoption and who struggle with the inability to know what happened to these children. For some of these mothers, the baby remains psychologically present yet is physically absent, with ongoing grief and despair associated with the knowledge that their baby is still alive but will never be *their* child again. In another example, many couples who experience infertility describe the loss of a child that they have hoped for, dreamed about, and sometimes seen as an embryo under a microscope prior to its transfer into the mother's body, where it simply disappeared from existence afterward. This loss is also ambiguous and may lead to chronic sorrow, especially as the realization of involuntary childlessness begins to replace the hopes of parenthood.

Another overlap between ambiguous loss, in this case the physical type, and chronic sorrow might be seen in those with vanished loved ones whose fates are unknown, such as individuals who are missing in military action, kidnap victims, and those who have inexplicably disappeared without a trace. There are unavoidable reminders of the loss (or lost person), with no foreseeable end. In this type of ambiguous loss and in the presence of chronic sorrow, the ability to adapt or attempts at finding some form of resolution are fraught with significant obstacles. Periodic resurgence of intensity and predictable and unpredictable points of stress and renewed grief are inevitable.

It is quite likely that the prevalence of ambiguous losses and chronic sorrow is currently increasing. Those with congenital disabilities once associated with limited or precarious lives are achieving normal longevity. Technological improvements are extending the life spans of low-birth-weight infants, and lives of those with severely disabling conditions, such as amyotrophic lateral sclerosis (ALS) and major head trauma, are lengthening. Conditions once thought to be terminal are now treated as chronic life-altering conditions that may persist for years. Added to the toll are casualties of war, atrocities, and protracted large-group conflicts, with individuals surviving physically, but with chronic debilities or with significant psychological alterations. These situations and the resulting ongoing grief responses associated with them are sometimes referred to as the "new grief` phenomenon" (Okun & Nowinski, 2011). Measures of nondeath loss and the resulting grief are beginning to identify some of the unique issues associated with these types of ongoing, living losses and the impact of the unique aspects of grief that occur from nondeath losses (Casale, 2009; Cooley, Toray, & Roscoe, 2010; Kendall, 2005; Robins, 2010).

Ambiguous loss—as well as chronic sorrow—becomes problematic *structurally* when family boundaries are unclear, roles ignored, decisions put on hold, daily tasks undone, healthy members ignored, and rituals or celebrations cancelled. Ambiguous loss and chronic sorrow are problematic *psychologically* when hopelessness, depression, and feelings of ambivalence lead to guilt, anxiety, and immobilization. Grief becomes frozen, and the ongoing despair can be paralyzing; coping processes can be overwhelmed, and there are often significant blocks in cognition and stress management (Boss, 1999, 2002, 2006a; Roos, 2002).

Both ambiguous loss and chronic sorrow are akin to what is referred to as *complicated grief* (CG; see Chapter 13) or *prolonged grief disorder* (PGD; Boelen & Prigerson, 2007; Prigerson et al., 2009). As with this diagnosis, symptoms of ambiguous loss and chronic sorrow can include depression, anxiety, somatic symptoms, and relationship difficulties that are ongoing and persistent—but, unlike descriptions of prolonged grief disorder, length of time is not a credential for the signal of a disorder. Perhaps still more relevant in distinguishing the concepts is that complicated grief or prolonged grief disorder is limited in its application to circumstances of bereavement through the death of an important attachment figure, whereas the concepts central to the present chapter apply primarily when this criterion of death is not met. If, for example, clinicians saw Mary for her depression and anxiety and did not ask about her son, they would miss the reason for the chronicity of her grief symptoms and identify pathology where there was none. Symptoms need to be treated, of course, but interventions must include permission to grieve the loss of someone still here, or of a loss that is ongoing in nature and can go on for years.

Although ambiguous losses are focused upon unclear or incomplete disturbing relational changes, the experiential core of chronic sorrow is often described in more internal terms as a painful disparity between the thoughts and dreams about what should have been, might have been, and still may be hoped for—versus what actually is the present reality. Both experiences are characterized by grief responses that are normal given the context, yet frequently misunderstood or unrecognized. As the source of the loss continues, grief is continuing and resurgent, usually with no foreseeable end, as it results from attempts to cope with a loss that does not have a predictable end or resolution.

Although ambiguous losses and chronic sorrow are often disenfranchised (Boss, 1999; Casale, 2009; Doka, 1989; Roos, 2002), the ongoing grief is normal and understandable. Recognition that life as it has been or was expected to be is forever lost and has been replaced by an initially unknown, unwanted, and often terrifying and inevitable new reality is usually traumatic, forcing a new appraisal of one's assumptive world. Believing that life is predictable and fair, and a notion of justice and compensation, cannot survive in the new reality. The self and the world must be relearned. This process is often a disturbing and ongoing focus of concern. There exists a significant body of research on ambiguous loss that indicates a relationship to depressive symptoms and family conflict (Boss, 2007a, 2007b; Carroll, Olson, & Buckmiller, 2007; and see AmbiguousLoss.com, n.d., http://www.ambiguousloss.com).

CLINICAL IMPLICATIONS

In the understandings of ambiguous loss theory and in chronic sorrow, the clinical goal is to strengthen resiliency to live with—even embrace—the ambiguity surrounding a loss and the new reality that it creates. This is especially challenging in our can-do culture that likes solutions—not unanswered questions. The literature in both ambiguous loss and chronic sorrow emphasizes the potential for growth and adaptation, even while describing experiences that can be highly debilitating and heartbreaking at the same time.

The practice considerations related to both ambiguous loss and chronic sorrow underscore the importance of normalizing the ongoing grief that is present. Because these losses may have no real resolution, and may unfold as *living losses*, the grief persists for a prolonged or undetermined time. It is important to recognize that in these scenarios, the ongoing grief is a normal reaction, whether the loss is related to a person or thing that is greatly valued or to something less tangible, such as a hope or expectation. Naming the chronic sorrow that comes from ambiguous loss can be highly validating, reassuring, and comforting. As persons with the weight of chronic sorrow are more vulnerable to depression, poor self-esteem, anxiety disorders, and some stress-related physical ailments (Roos, 2002), they can be helped to prioritize preventive self-care by using techniques such as covert rehearsal, meditation, and guided imagery. It is also helpful to expect chaos in family functioning immediately following a diagnosis of severe disabilities or when there is recognition that ambiguity is present as a loss. Flexibly combining individual, couple, family, and group modalities can support those who are taking on most of the responsibilities. Finding ways to adjust and redefine roles in the family can help to minimize chaos, reduce stress, and improve relationships.

The following are meant to provide guidelines for professionals from various disciplines who work with people experiencing ambiguous losses and chronic sorrow. Even if no one has died, a loved one is gone in either body or mind, or what may be lost may not involve another individual, such as loss of health, loss of homeland, and loss of hopes and dreams. The adaptation to these types of losses comes slowly in a process that undulates like a terrible roller coaster of ups and downs. There are no linear steps, and the adjustments will vary with one's cultural beliefs and values. Various therapeutic strategies can be used (see Boss, 2006a; Harris, 2009, 2010; Roos, 2002), but what is essential is attention to ourselves—the self-awareness of the therapist. We can't help others increase their tolerance for ambiguity and uncertainty until we have attended to these experiences in ourselves (see Boss, 2006a, epilogue). In the following recommendations, we (PB) will keep Mary in mind as an example. (The following guidelines are adapted from Boss, 1999, 2006a.)

Name and Validate the Loss

Many ambiguous losses and losses that involve an ongoing, chronic process are disenfranchised in nature. Recognizing and naming these losses are cited by Doka (1989) and Boss (1999, 2006a) as the first steps in offering support to individuals who have experienced disenfranchised grief. The ability to name the experience and its unique effects that are often unacknowledged by others can provide a powerful source of strength to those who experience ambiguous loss and chronic sorrow. Clients who begin to understand the nature of these losses and receive validation for their loss(es) often experience relief and improved self-concept almost immediately (Roos, 2002). A doctoral education student with whom one of the authors (SR) consults regarding her research has reported that as a component of her scholastic work, she interviewed seven women with children who have multiple disabilities. She introduced each of them to the concept of chronic sorrow; without exception, they all experienced immediate relief, some noting that they could have been coping better had they had this information from their helping professionals when their babies were born. In a study of infertile women, Harris (2009) reported that recognition of the ongoing intense grief response to their infertility allowed participants to spend less time attempting to receive validation for their experiences in order to engage in activities that supported their resilience and innate strengths.

Find Meaning

If we go back the case of Mary, we first identify that she has an ambiguous loss and that this kind of loss is the most stressful because there is no possibility of closure. She tells the clinician (PB) that she is relieved because she now has a name for her problem—and it's not her son or herself. Labeling the experience eases her stress because she knows now what to cope with. Second, Mary is encouraged to "think both/and" (dialectically). Over time, she tries this by saying, "My son is both here and gone," "I am both his caregiver and a person with my own identity and needs," "I am both suffering loss and discovering new connections," and "I am both sad about lost hopes and dreams and happy about new ones." Third, she connects with others through social activities, rituals, and celebrations, and begins to see meaning in her relationship with her son despite its restrictions. Growing tolerance for ambiguity deepens her spirituality. Our experience from years of clinical practice demonstrates that it is common for individuals with these types of experiences to find meaning in what they have endured by reaching out to others who are just embarking on their experiences of loss, hoping that in their sharing, they make it easier for someone else who may otherwise have felt isolated or stigmatized in a similar situation. An important differentiation in this concept was found by Harris (2009), who reported that making sense (i.e., determining why something happens) is a different process from making meaning (i.e., how will I use this experience for my own betterment or toward a greater good?).

Address Trauma When It Is Present

As stated previously, many losses that are ambiguous in nature may be associated with trauma, such as in kidnappings, missing persons, and traumatic brain injuries. It has also been discussed that the beginning of chronic sorrow is often instigated by and coexists with trauma. Thus, it is important for the affected person to tell his or her story to someone who is empathic and knowledgeable. Rynearson (2001; and see Chapter 14, this volume) has developed a simple three-part model addressing this issue. It includes *restoration* of resilience, *reconnecting* with the loss and with those who care for you, and then *retelling* the personal story in a coherent manner so that it can be integrated into the entire personal narrative, rather than dissociated, revivified, or fragmented. The power of the co-creation of a coherent narrative with the client and therapist may provide a strong foundation for cultivating resilience and identifying the client's existing strengths in the midst of the ambiguity and uncertainty (see Boss, 2006a; Neimeyer & Sands; see also Chapter 2).

Temper Mastery

The more mastery oriented a culture, the more difficult it is to accept ambiguous loss and the lack of closure (Boss, 1999, 2002, 2006a). There is also the romanticized ideal of "overcoming" adversity that may be highly unrealistic for individuals who are facing ambiguous loss and experiencing chronic sorrow. To modify the need for mastery and having things go her way, Mary balanced her need for control with accepting the brain injury of her son and not feeling like she had personally failed. Echoing the Serenity Prayer, she learned to differentiate what she could control from what she could not. Her clinician (PB) talked about the world not always being fair—and that she could externalize the blame (e.g., by naming ambiguity as the culprit). When she couldn't, she learned to control her internal self. She chose playing the piano or walking with a friend. Others may choose prayer, meditation, yoga, or hobbies; but with all, connection with others is often helpful and can be encouraged.

Reconstruct Identity

One's personal identity changes in the presence of ambiguous loss and chronic sorrow. Mary reflected on these questions: Who am I now? Who is my family now? What roles have I gained—and lost? She gradually recognized that shifts in her identity and roles would be needed over time. What helped? With others, she talked about her family's gender and generational roles, being more aware of her cultural identity, broadening her family's rules for problem solving, uncovering secrets or assumptions about her family's identity, and exposing any stigma or discrimination that might block her reconstructions. Hanging onto one absolute identity would not serve her well. For the sake of her health, she needed to be more than a caregiver.

Normalize Ambivalence

It is not unusual to have mixed emotions when you don't know if someone you love is here or not here, or if a situation that seems intolerable will ever end. Mary talked with others in her group and with her therapist (PB) about the negative feelings she had. She felt guilty for being angry that she was tied down, that her son required so much care, and that she was not free at her age to do what she pleased. Eventually, she admitted to feeling both love and hate for him and for even wishing he had been killed. Once aware of her negative feelings, she could manage them. Her therapist (PB) normalized guilt and harmful feelings, but never harmful actions. Talking about conflicted emotions makes them less likely to manifest as neglect or abuse. Although not how they may have perceived themselves in the past, it is important to recognize that it can be a normal reaction to resent others who seem unaffected by the same kind of losses, or who seem protected from adverse events in life (Harris, 2009; Harris & Daniluk, 2010).

Revise Attachment

Listening to other's stories, and in individual therapy, Mary learned the dialectic of continuing her relationship with her son while also letting go of what was no longer possible. He won't play sports anymore. He will not marry or give her grandchildren. She both grieves what is lost and celebrates what she still has. He smiles at her; he knows who she is. He can now feed himself. Meanwhile, she builds new human connections in the community for support while she grieves for what is irretrievably lost. Talking with others, she learned that all human attachments are less than perfect and became more content with her compromised relationship.

Discover New Hope

As time went on, Mary found that her increased tolerance for ambiguity and uncertainty was really faith in the unknown. She gained trust and was no longer so anxious. She was even able to laugh at the absurdity of her struggle with someone being both here and gone at the same time. She gained more patience and saw both continuity and change in her life. She no longer saw suffering as punishment, but as a challenge.

People with ambiguous losses and chronic sorrow need time to discover new hope, so at first, it was important to Mary to hope for a return to the status quo, even if it seemed unrealistic. Her therapist (PB) was reminded of the early days after September 11, when many bereaved family members believed their loved ones would come walking up the sidewalk again. We suggest that therapists not interfere with such hope because for the moment, it may be all that families have to keep them going. Until people find new positive hope (and this takes time), they need their illusions a bit longer. To label such temporary denials as pathological hallucinations could interrupt the natural process of resiliency after such sudden and horrific loss. Mary, too, denied the loss at first and waited for her son to get better. Over time, although he showed some improvement, she acknowledged that his brain injury was real and very likely permanent.

Identify Resources

Helping clients with information about community resources and other supports is a high priority. Identifying potentially damaging triggers (both external and internal), and implementing strategies to reduce the effects of these triggers can be very useful. Emphasizing the highly individualized nature of grief helps to reduce self-criticism. It is also important to be aware that approaches to some conditions are inappropriate and may worsen responses to losses that are ambiguous or ongoing in nature (i.e., pushing for closure or resolution). In this regard, some therapists need to understand that these individuals may have already had destructive experiences with prior professionals (Harris, 2010). As these types of loss experiences become more commonplace in our current society, it is vitally important for helping professionals to develop a basic understanding of these phenomena in order to avoid inadvertently pathologizing a normal response to these very difficult types of losses.

Of course, further research on chronic and ambiguous losses could contribute to greater professional awareness of and responsiveness to such conditions. In particular, we would encourage researchers to look at grief from a broader perspective, and not focus singularly upon grief that occurs only after a significant death-related loss. Of interest is the recent research on the development of the Reactions to Loss Scale (Cooley et al., 2010) and the further development of the Boundary

Ambiguity Scale (Boss, Greenberg, & Pearce-McCall, 1990; Carroll et al., 2007) and our support in efforts to refine measures such as the Casale-Roos Chronic Sorrow Inventory (Casale, 2009) and the Kendall Chronic Sorrow Instrument (Kendall, 2005) in the identification of chronic sorrow in specific populations who have experienced losses that are ongoing in nature. In addition, the role of social and cultural influences on the constructs of ambiguous loss and chronic sorrow may be of benefit to identify the role of these types of loss experiences in a more global context. Research in this area has been conducted recently by Robins (2010) regarding ambiguous loss related to missing persons in Nepal. Expanding upon research in the cross-cultural applications of experiences of ambiguous loss and chronic sorrow will help to identify whether these losses do indeed cross cultural and social boundaries.

SUMMARY

Our purpose in this chapter was to merge two bodies of work—chronic sorrow and ambiguous loss—to emphasize the need to view complicated grief reactions through a more normative lens. Boss and Roos agree strongly on this. Diagnostic manuals and the professionals who use them need to take into account the context of loss. As illustrated in this chapter, assessment of pathology requires a broader and more nuanced view of loss and grief for more effective treatment.

REFERENCES

AmbiguousLoss.com. (N.d.). [Home page]. Retrieved from http://www.ambiguousloss.com

Boelen, P., & Prigerson, H. (2007). The influence of symptoms of prolonged grief disorder, depression, and anxiety on quality of life among bereaved adults. *European Archives of Clinical Psychiatry and Clinical Neuroscience*, *257*, 444–452.

Boss, P. (1977). A clarification of the concept of psychological father presence in families experiencing ambiguity of boundary. *Journal of Marriage & the Family*, *39*(1), 141–151.

Boss, P. (1999). *Ambiguous loss*. Cambridge, MA: Harvard University Press.

Boss, P. (2002). *Family stress management*. Thousand Oaks, CA: Sage.

Boss, P. (2004). Ambiguous loss research, theory, and practice: Reflections after 9/11. *Journal of Marriage & Family*, *66*(3), 551–566.

Boss, P. (2006a). *Loss, trauma, and resilience: Therapeutic work with ambiguous loss*. New York: Norton.

Boss, P. (2006b). Resilience and health. *Grief Matters: The Australian Journal of Grief and Bereavement*, 9(3), 52–57.

Boss, P. (Ed.). (2007a). Ambiguous loss and boundary ambiguity [Special issue]. *Family Relations*, *56*(2).

Boss, P. (2007b). Ambiguous loss theory: Challenges for scholars and practitioners. *Family Relations*, *56*(2), 105–111.

Boss, P. (2010). The trauma and complicated grief of ambiguous loss. *Pastoral Psychology*, *59*(2), 137–145. doi: 10.1007/s11089-009-0264-0.

Boss, P., & Greenberg, J. (1984). Family boundary ambiguity: A new variable in family stress theory. *Family Process, 23*(4), 535–546.

Boss, P., Greenberg, J., & Pearce-McCall, D. (1990). *Measurement of boundary ambiguity in families* (Minnesota Agricultural Experiment Station Bulletin No. 593-1990; Item No. Ad-SB 3763). St. Paul: University of Minnesota.

Burke, M. (1989).*Chronic sorrow in mothers of school-age children with a myelomeningocele disability* (PhD dissertation, University Microfilms No. AAD89-20093). Boston University, School of Nursing.

Burke, M., Hainsworth, M. L., Eakes, G. G., & Lindgren, C.L. (1992). Current knowledge and research on chronic sorrow: A foundation for inquiry. *Death Studies*, *16*, 231–245.

Carroll, J. S., Olson, C. D., & Buckmiller, N. (2007). Family boundary ambiguity: A 30-year review of theory, research, and measurement. *Family Relations*, *56*(2), 210–230.

Casale, A. (2009). *Distinguishing the concept of chronic sorrow from standard grief: An empirical study of infertile couples* (PhD dissertation, University Microfilms No. UMI3353016). New York University, Silver School of Social Work.

Cooley, E., Toray, T., & Roscoe, L. (2010). Reactions to loss scale: Assessing grief in college students. *Omega*, *61*, 25–51.

Covington, S. N. (2006). Pregnancy loss. In S. Convington & L. Hammer Burns (Eds.), *Infertility counseling: A comprehensive handbook for clinicians* (2nd ed., pp. 290–304). New York: Cambridge University Press.

Damrosch, S., & Perry, L. (1989). Self-reported adjustment, chronic sorrow, and coping of parents with children with Down syndrome. *Nursing Research*, *38*(1), 25–30.

Doka, K. (Ed.). (1989). *Disenfranchised grief: Recognizing hidden sorrow*. Lexington, MA: Lexington.

Eakes, G. G. (1993). Chronic sorrow: A response to living with cancer. *Oncology Nursing Forum*, *20*, 1327–1334.

Eakes, G. G. (1995). Chronic sorrow: The lived experience of parents of chronically mentally ill individuals. *Archives of Psychiatric Nursing*, *9*, 77–84.

Eakes, G., Burke, M., & Hainsworth, M. (1998). Middle-range theory of chronic sorrow. *Journal of Nursing Scholarship*, *30*(2), 179–184.

Eakes, G. G., Burke, M. L., Hainsworth, M. A., & Lindgren, C. L. (1993). Chronic sorrow: An examination of nursing roles. In S. G. Funk, E. M. Tornquist, M. T. Champagne, & R. A. Wiese (Eds.), *Key aspects of caring for the mentally ill: Hospital and home*. New York: Springer.

Eakes, G. G., Hainsworth, M. A., Lindgren, C. L., & Burke, M. L. (1991). Establishing a long-distance research consortium. *Nursing Connection*, *41*, 51–57.

Glazer, E. S. (1997). Miscarriage and its aftermath. In S. R. Lieblum (Ed.), *Infertility: Psychological issues and counseling strategies* (pp. 230–245). New York: Wiley.

Hainsworth, M. A. (1994). Living with multiple sclerosis: The experience of chronic sorrow. *Journal of Neuroscience Nursing*, *26*(4), 327–240.

Hainsworth, M. A. (1995). Chronic sorrow in spouse caregivers of individuals with multiple sclerosis: A case study. *Journal of Gerontological Nursing*, *21*, 29–33.

Hainsworth, M. A., Busch, P., Eakes, G., & Burke, M. (1995). Chronic sorrow in women with chronically disabled husbands. *Journal of the American Psychiatric Nurses Association*, *7*, 120–124.

Hainsworth, M. A., Eakes, G. G., & Burke, M. L. (1994). Coping with chronic sorrow. *Issues in Mental Health Nursing*, *15*, 59–66.

Hammer-Burns, L., & Covington, S. (Eds.). (1999). *Infertility counseling: A comprehensive handbook for clinicians*. New York: Parthenon.

Harris, D. (2009). *The experience of spontaneous pregnancy loss in infertile women who have conceived with the assistance of medical intervention* (UMI no. 3351170). Ann Arbor, MI: Proquest Digital Dissertations.

Harris, D. (2010). *Counting our losses: Reflecting on change, loss, and transition in everyday life*. New York: Routledge.

Harris, D., & Daniluk, J. (2010). The experience of spontaneous pregnancy loss for infertile women who have conceived through assisted reproduction technology. *Human Reproduction*, *25*(3), 714–720.

Hobdell, E., & Deatrick, J. (1996). A content analysis of parental differences. *Journal of Genetic Counseling*, *5*, 57–68.

Kendall, L. C. (2005). *The experience of living with ongoing loss: Testing the Kendall Chronic Sorrow Instrument* (PhD dissertation, No. AAT 3196497). Virginia Commonwealth University, School of Nursing.

Okun, B., & Nowinski, J. (2011). *Saying goodbye: How families can find renewal through loss*. New York: Berkley.

Olshansky, S. (1962). Chronic sorrow: A response to having a mentally defective child. *Social Casework*, *43*(4), 21–23.

Olshansky, S. (1966). Parent responses to a mentally defective child. *Mental Retardation*, *4*, 21–23.

Olshansky, S. (1970). Chronic sorrow: A response to having a defective child. In R. Nolen (Ed.), *Counseling parents of the mentally retarded*. Springfield, IL: Charles C. Thomas.

Peterson, S. J., & Bredow, T. S. (2004). *Middle range theories: Applications to nursing theory*. Philadelphia: Lippincott Williams.

Prigerson, H., Horowitz, M., Jacobs, S., Parkes, C., Aslan, M., Goodkin, K. et al. (2009). Prolonged grief disorder: Empiric validation of criteria proposed for the DSM-V and the ICD-11. *PLOS Medicine*, *6*(8). Retrieved from http://www.ncbi.nlm.nih.gov/pmc/articles/PMC2711304/pdf/pmed.1000121.pdf/?tool=pmcentrez

Robins, S. (2010). Ambiguous loss in a non-Western context: Families of the disappeared in postconflict Nepal. *Family Relations*, *59*(3), 253–268.

Roos, S. (2002). *Chronic sorrow: A living loss*. New York: Brunner-Routledge.

Rynearson, E. K. (2001). *Retelling violent death*. New York: Brunner-Routledge.

14

Restorative Retelling
Revising the Narrative of Violent Death

EDWARD K. RYNEARSON and ALISON SALLOUM

The objective of this chapter is to clarify the disruptive effects of violent killing on the narrative processing of bereavement and grief in children and adults.

Violent dying, an unanticipated and external event, is portrayed as a spectacled enactment of the killing, an imaginary portrayal of what the deceased experienced while dying. Because few violent deaths occur with a family member or loved one in attendance, this imaginary drama offers no comforting role for the bereaved in the retelling. The compulsory and sometimes compulsive retelling of this surreal act of violent killing is a fundamental narrative aftermath of bereavement and grief.

Fortunately, violent dying is comparatively infrequent. Although over 2.6 million people die each year in the United States, 7% of those deaths are violent. To be more specific, of the approximately 160,000 violent deaths in the United States each year, 115,000 or 70% are caused by accidents (most frequently motor vehicle fatalities), 38,000 or 20% by suicide, and 17,000 or 10% by homicide (National Centers for Disease Control, 2009). If we extrapolate that each of these violent deaths impacts at least four or five primary family members and loved ones, then 600,000 to 800,000 individuals are forced to accommodate to the psychological effects of violent death each year. Although comparatively infrequent, violent dying remains the leading cause of death before age 40, so young family members and children remain challenged by its retelling for many years.

Clinical reports suggest that grief after violent death is associated with specific responses to killing—accompanied by higher levels of traumatic distress with reenactment recounting and heightened victimization. Because killing is socially and psychologically abhorrent, there are additional demands for reciprocity (retaliation, retribution, and punishment) to restore the honor of the deceased and their families. Further, research has clearly demonstrated the high risk of mental health problems experienced by children (Nader, Pynoos, Fairbanks, & Frederick, 1990; Pfefferbaum et al., 1999) and adults who have had a loved one die violently (Currier, Holland, & Neimeyer, 2006; Murphy et al., 1999; Zinzow, Rheingold, Hawkins, Saundors, & Kilpatrick, 2009).

THE PSYCHOLOGICAL PURPOSE OF NARRATION

Humans process and share all sorts of conscious experience as stories because the "structuring" of experience as a story promises coherence. By ordering a series of events on a storied template of time, space, and action, an understanding is established of what transpired—the story becomes an illumination we can "stand under."

Stories play a vital function in consolidating many experiences during psychological development. The continuous narrating of attachment is chronologically the first and most primary narrative—who we are close to and care for is pivotal and remains fundamental to each of us, whether these stories are spoken or private. This attachment narrative begins during early childhood as a formative model of relational security challenged by themes of frustration and separation and rejection. Attachment stories maintain psychological security, continuity, and durability in the context of past and present as well as promise future relational fulfillment.

Our earliest stories of attachment as preschoolers were highly imaginative and magical, intensely heroic and romantic during latency and adolescence, and finally more measured and rational as we mature—but are arranged upon the same elements of time, space, and action with a beginning, middle, and ending. Most endings match our expectations of attachment narratives. Stories that fail to end in harmony with our assumptions of attachment are disruptive, puzzling, unpleasant, and even possessive if they end in horror and helplessness.

Dying and death are timeless triggers for a compensatory story of interrupted attachment called *bereavement*. The inevitable death of someone intrinsic to one's private self—a parent, sibling, spouse, child, intimate, best friend, or even pet—someone to whom we are intimately attached—begins a private, cascading narrative of shared living. The thematic purpose of the bereavement narrative is of revitalization and reunion with the dead figure and motivates bereavement and grief as integral facets of a reorganizing pattern or "syndrome" after death.

THE NEUROBIOLOGY OF BEREAVEMENT NARRATION

The "cascade" of the living, narrative remembrance of someone amputated from us by death undoubtedly has a neurobiological correlate. Before clarifying the narrative structure of bereavement after violent death, we present a brief review of the neurobiological effects of physical amputation because the loss of a part of our body is roughly analogous to the loss of a part of our self:

If your arm were amputated, you would maintain a "phantom limb"—an active, somatosensory representation of your arm—evoking not only its illusory presence, but also its movements and sometimes pain.

In simplest terms, following amputation of an arm, subcortical and cortical neural patterns representing the arm in your brain would undergo a predictable reactivation, continuing to evoke the arm's presence as *phantom limb* sensations. Fortunately, because of its substantial "plasticity," the brain's neural patterning of the arm would reorganize over time and the phantom limb sensations would diminish, but never disappear.

Like the amputation of a limb, the death of a stabilizing "other" is followed by a "phantom presence." The neural circuitry of attachment figures is probably based upon similar principles of neural patterning and stabilization. However, different from the somatosensory representation of the body, the human mental representation of self and attachment relationships is primarily conveyed through narrative memory expressed in storied form. After death, the living representation of an attachment figure (a part of self "dismembered" rather than a part of body amputated) is predictably "remembered" and experienced as a "phantom" presence. The psychological representation of the attachment figure in the cortex and subcortex continues to signal his or her presence as mental projections produced by our brain in an involuntary effort to remain psychologically connected with someone we love. Similar to the process of reorganization after the physical amputation of an arm, the presence of the "dismembered" loved one would be "remembered" as a narrative of revitalization—recontextualized over time to diminish but never disappear. Recent neuroimaging studies (with small sample sizes and uncontrolled design) suggest hyperreactivity in subcortical areas (amygdala, limbic system, and nucleus accumbens) after viewing pictures of the deceased in patients with prolonged grief (O'Connor et al., 2008). These findings suggest glimmerings of a complex neural system of narrative representation, and although suggesting a neurophysiologic correlate of prolonged grief, at this early stage of research these studies have no clinical relevance. Unfortunately, the neuroimaging findings lack requisite specificity or sensitivity for diagnostic validity or demonstrate mechanisms for neurophysiologic treatment. There is no neurological diagnosis, "pill," or biological treatment for prolonged grief.

Now, let's introduce the dimension of violence to make this neurobiological model more inclusive. What if the amputation of a limb occurred without emotional preparation—blown away in an explosion or broken, mangled, and torn off through intentional torture? Phantom limb phenomena would then be accompanied by a horrific narrative memory of the external events of the amputation.

And so, too, would the memory of an attachment figure who died violently be accompanied by the tortured story of the violent dying. The collective reorganization of attachment and dying and its retelling would contain the disparate narrative elements of caring and killing—caring with the living narrative and killing with the dying narrative.

From this premise it follows that with bereavement and grief, not only may the narrative remembrance of the living of the deceased be absorbing and prolonged, but also the narrative of their dying may be even more so:

- When a loved one dies from a disease or some "natural" cause, there is time, space, and opportunity to share a dying narrative enactment with proximity, caring, respect, and finally relinquishment. There is a place for loved ones in the unfolding dying narrative, painful but meaningful, because natural dying is an anticipated ending to our own life narrative.
- If that same loved one is strangled to death after being raped and sodomized, those bereaved are traumatized and outraged as well as bereaved. There was no time, space, or opportunity for them to stop or rescue their loved one from the dying. The narrative reenactment of violent dying is a solitary enactment of horror and helplessness isolated from the care, respect, and protection we normally enact with dying from a natural cause. This narrative is retold as an alienated event, a surreal story that loved ones cannot "own" because they played no role in its unfolding, and is rendered meaningless because it never should have happened.

These contrasting illustrations of dying highlight the narrative dilemma of retelling the life and death of a loved one after their violent death—how to maintain a coherent narrative of the memory of someone loved through and around the storied chronicle of the killing, because a killing is an antinarrative, a black hole of a story eclipsing the meaning and light of the loved one's life. A killing proscribes a storied spectacle, spotlighting a lethal external act of human intention or neglect, victimizing and dishonoring the memory of the deceased and those who are bereaved—a dying that never should have happened.

THE COMPLICATED NARRATIVE OF VIOLENT DEATH

Without participating in a death, it is more difficult to realize and accept. There would be opportunity to engage in the dying story from a natural cause. That story could follow a linear interaction that included the time and attention of many. There is an inherent restorative theme in such a dying. When natural death finally occurs, each family member has opportunity to play a final role as comforter and protector so whoever dies will not die alone. Retelling the dying narrative of a natural death leaves sorrow, but not the insoluble dilemma of recounting a story that reenacts events of impotent terror and helplessness. Without opportunity to intervene during dying—to protect or rescue, or "be present" by holding, respecting, and finally relinquishing the loved one as he or she died—the violent dying story leaves family and loved ones with a narrative dilemma: How can we retell this dying story drawn from media and police descriptions and further distorted by the imaginary reenactment of terror and hopelessness?

Natural and violent dying stories also contain different terms. The narrative terms of dying from a disease are microscopic and molecular, retold as a medical narrative that unfolds in the discovery and progress of physical signs and symptoms, abnormal laboratory values, radiology reports, pathology findings, medical and surgical interventions, prognosis, and palliative care. Violent dying is more horrific because of its vivid terms of enactment as tangible, human acts in ordinary time and space. Unlike the medical narrative, the narrative terms of violent dying are visible, dramatic, intentional, or negligent: Someone is at fault.

Finally, there is an inherent instability in the retelling of the violent death of a loved one because of narrative dissonance. The simultaneous retelling of the events of the violent dying and imagined agony of the loved one cannot contain the simultaneous dramas of killing and caring (Rynearson, 2001). The action of violent dying distorts the coherent and linear drama of caring. Because of its instability, the narrative structure of violent dying is pulsating and intrusive (the story of the dying) rather than linear and progressive (the story of the caring). Initially the reenactment of the dying image is at the very center. Stories of remorse, retaliation, and protection are secondary themes that tightly surround it as compensatory dramas.

COMPULSIVE REENACTMENT RETELLING

The central narrative structure of violent dying as spotlighted killing subsides within weeks in the great majority of resilient children and adults. Presumably the majority maintain resilience with the support of remaining family, friends, spiritual community, and work, enabling them to reengage with their own living, valued relationships, and activities. However, the relentless reenactment of the violent dying story may remain preoccupying and enervating for 20–30% of mothers bereaved by the violent death of a child (Murphy et al., 1999). It is not stabilizing to repeat a violent dying story of senseless and meaningless disintegration that collapses in chaos. There is an implicit ruination that fixation on retelling cannot escape—trapped in a narrative labyrinth—a metaphor for the hopeless confusion of finding a "way out" of the chaos of the story of violent dying through aimless and repetitive retelling.

The Narrative Labyrinth of Violent Dying

The primary purpose of any psychotherapeutic intervention of prolonged grief after violent dying is to release fixated survivors from the labyrinth of overidentifying with their narrative reenactment of the dying.

A preliminary model of intervention termed *restorative retelling* suggests that prolonged grief after violent death is associated with fixating narrative representations (possessions), and from this premise a therapeutic corollary follows—that possessive representations can be modified through a therapeutic procedure of reconstructive narration.

The narrative of reenactment may be viewed as a caricatured semifiction with overelaborated actors, overplayed motivations, and actions distorted by an incomplete scenario. The goal of restorative retelling is not to extinguish this semifiction but to encourage its retelling between clinician and patient in a shared perspective of time, space, and action. The retelling can include speaking, writing, drawing, and playing with dolls—whatever method(s) of expression are deemed appropriate by the teller. Once shared, the fixation is suspended between the teller and listener, and once external becomes less literal. What was intensely private and unedited is now open for commentary and revision. The goal of restorative retelling is to revise the narrative memory of reenactment through a collaborative, corrective retelling, so that in its modified form the memory remains but no longer demands reenactment and restitution.

FROM MYTH TO METHOD: CLASSIC ILLUSTRATIONS OF RESTORATIVE RETELLING

Before presenting preliminary evidence of the effectiveness of restorative retelling and a clinical case study, it would be judicious to consider the restorative principles embedded in the narrative genre of violent dying in myths.

One of the timeless and universal purposes of myths is to provide coherent explanations of life and death and offer guidelines for dealing with the most basic existential dilemma of all—our helplessness in confronting our own dying. Although nearly every myth contains some mention of violent dying, the myth of Theseus and the Minotaur includes not only the basic narrative ingredients—love and hate, good and evil, violent dying, and vivid reenactment—but also the feature that it is enacted in a labyrinth. It ends in heroic mastery, with a metaphorical theme of release and transformation. Telling and interpreting this myth highlight a reconstructive theme that has restorative utility for family members and loved ones lost in the self-created labyrinth of retelling (Rynearson, 2005).

In mythic antiquity, every 9 years Athens was forced to send a tribute of seven maidens and seven male youth to Crete to be sacrificed to the Minotaur, a half-human, half-bull monster. To add to the specter of horror and helplessness, the Minotaur was confined in the Labyrinth from which there could be no escape. Theseus insisted that he be sent, for without such rashness there would be no heroic story. As the young victims arrived in Crete and were publicly paraded to the Labyrinth, the daughter of King Minos, Ariadne, saw Theseus and they fell in love. In her determination to save Theseus from his inevitable death and disappearance in the Labyrinth, Ariadne gave him a golden cord to unravel as he descended into the maze. Theseus killed the Minotaur, but mere triumph over violent dying could not serve as an ending, for the retelling would leave him and his companions stranded in dark limbo with nothing but the corpse of the Minotaur and the inevitability of their own deaths. By following and rewinding the golden cord, Theseus, and those who followed him, were able to retrace their steps and return into the world of the living.

1a. *Restorative principle*: The love and support of Ariadne as well as the tool of the golden cord provided Theseus with the strength he needed to be resilient and to have the desire to reengage with the living. Having a supportive person and ways to moderate distress is an essential ingredient before engaging in the violent dying narrative.

1b. *Therapeutic strategy*: The first stage of restorative retelling involves stabilizing the patient by promoting ways for the patient to moderate the distress. This includes strategies such as mobilizing supportive people for the bereaved, and reviewing stress management skills.

2a. *Restorative principle*: It was the maintenance of connection with love (Ariadne) and life (the outer world) that transported and transformed Theseus safely to his former self. This principle, the maintenance of hopeful, coherent imagery (a golden thread), is an important resource of psychological resilience and is an early ingredient of various trauma treatments, including restorative retelling.

2b. *Therapeutic strategy*: The initial stage of restorative retelling will be to establish an enduring connection with the patient's narratives of meaning, hope, and love shared with the deceased to counterbalance the violent imagery of the reenactment story. The last stage involves a positive reconnection with the deceased and a reconnection to self and others.

3a. *Restorative principle*: Theseus' simple retelling of the violent killing would have left him saturated with images of the threat of his own death and images of the corpse. Instead, following Ariadne's thread, his story of violent killing was transformed into one of love and living. In restorative retelling, immersion in traumatic grief imagery aims for more than exposure and extinction. Retelling and revising the traumatic grief story through generative metaphors transform the telling from oracle to narrative—a story with coherence and meaning.

3b. *Therapeutic strategy*: The second stage of restorative retelling involves witnesses who serve as supportive allies and guides, who accompany the teller into his or her immersion (exposure) into the violent dying story, in order to revise and reframe it through retelling. Restorative retelling counterbalances the "dark and wordless" imagery of violent death by encouraging and summoning unique imaginative and generative metaphors with the teller. The goal is not to deny the story, but to create a role for the teller within the story—a poetic revision—so the story now "belongs" to the teller.

These three restorative principles and therapeutic strategies provide the framework for the restorative-retelling intervention: (a) resilience and safety, (b) restorative retelling, and (c) reconnecting (Herman, 1997; Rynearson, 2001).

PRELIMINARY EVIDENCE OF RESTORATIVE RETELLING AND CLINICAL ILLUSTRATION

Recently, there has been controversy about the definition of and criteria for a grief disorder or condition (i.e., traumatic grief, complicated grief, or prolonged grief disorder) for both children and adults (for more about the proposed definitions and criteria, see Cohen, Mannarino, Greenberg, Padlo, & Shipley, 2002; Nader & Layne, 2009; Prigerson, Vanderwerker, & Maciejewski, 2008). Despite the inconsistent definitions of clinically significant bereavement, there is mounting evidence that interventions such as restorative retelling that involve stress management (e.g., relaxation, resilience, safety, and reengagement) and some type of bereavement and trauma narration (e.g., exposure, meaning making, and narrative transformation) help decrease distress for children, adolescents (Cohen, Mannarino, & Staron, 2006; Layne et al., 2008; Salloum, 2008; Salloum & Overstreet, 2008), and adults (Rynearson, Correa, Favell, Saindon, & Prigerson, 2006; Shear, Frank, Houck, & Reynolds, 2005) who suffer from violent dying grief.

Restorative retelling with children and adults: Restorative retelling with children, known as Grief and Trauma Intervention (GTI) for children, and restorative retelling with adults, are time-limited interventions that are typically used in group treatment, although both may be used with individuals and families. Restorative retelling focuses on reinforcement of resilience, retelling of the life and dying of the deceased, and reengagement with living. These interventions have been tested with children and adults who have had someone close die due to all types of deaths, and treatment manuals are available (Rynearson et al., 2006; Salloum, 2008; Salloum & Overstreet, 2008).

Brief clinical illustration: Shanika is an 11-year-old African American girl whose family home was destroyed during Hurricane Katrina, which hit the Gulf Coast area in the United States in 2005. The family had left the area before the storm. Upon driving back to the city after the storm, Shanika's 16-year-old sister, who was in a separate car from Shanika and her family, was killed in a car accident. Five months later, Shanika participated in a GTI group at her school. A structured process to help children create a coherent bereavement and trauma narrative is part of GTI. The process involves children drawing their imagery, engaging in a restorative discussion, writing the child's narrative, and having witnesses (such as the therapist, other children in the therapy group, and the child's supportive person) listen to the child share his or her story and empathetically respond. The structured narrative process provides a method to develop the child's story in a limited time frame. Following are excerpts from the drawing, discussion, writing, and witnessing (DDWW) narrative process with Shanika, which was repeated several times across the course of the intervention to capture various aspects and episodes of her story of living and dying.

Supportive People

Drawing: In session 1, Shanika was asked to draw "My Supportive People." Shanika drew a picture of her mom and her dad, and then added a picture of her sister.

Discussion: The therapist then asked, "So tell me about your drawing?" Shanika explained who the supportive people are to her, and she then wrote on the drawing, "My mother, my father, and my sister." Discussion followed about how these people are supportive to her, and about her sister,

Toni. For example, the therapist asked, "How do they help you when you feel upset? What is your sister's name? How would she help you now?"

Writing: The therapist then worked with Shanika to write her story about the drawing: "My supportive people are my mom, dad, and my sister. My sister's name is Toni. Every time I talk to them they help me to feel better. Toni would always give me things like candy, clothes, and whatever I asked for. She would tell me that everything is going to be OK."

Witnessing: Shanika shared her drawing and written story with the other children in the group.

After five sessions that primarily focused on resilience building, the next sessions were geared toward a restorative retelling that helped Shanika create a beginning, middle, and ending to her narrative. After each drawing, the therapist asked, "So tell me about your drawing?" After listening to her story, the therapist followed up by asking selected questions to help Shanika explore, expand, and at times revise her narrative in a way that provided time and space and that allowed Shanika a role in her story.

Before the Accident

Drawing: For her "Before It Happened" drawing, Shanika drew a picture of her mom, dad, brother, and herself getting in a car getting ready to drive back to their home in New Orleans.

Discussion: "What was the car ride like for you?" Shanika shared how much fun she had in the car listening to music and talking.

Writing: She wrote about her family being together before driving back and about the fun she had with her father and brother while in the car.

Witnessing: Shanika shared her drawing and story with the other children, who listened and asked her questions such as what music they were listening to in the car.

The Accident

Drawing: For her "When It Happened" drawing, she drew a car upside down and her sister with a sad face laying on the ground next the car.

Discussion: Two questions were asked: "Who do imagine was with your sister?" and "How do you imagine she got to the hospital?" Shanika was not completely sure about how her sister got to the hospital, but she imagined that the other cars stopped and people got out to be with her sister on the road and then the ambulance came to help her. Another question was "If you were there, what do you wish you could have said?" Though she had drawn her sister alone on the road, she was able to revise her story to include people being with her sister. She and the therapist also talked about what she would have said if she had been there with her sister.

Writing: The therapist wrote Shanika's story of how others helped her sister and that she told her sister she loved her very much.

Witnessing: Shanika shared her revised story with the group members and told them that she felt much better thinking about people being with and helping her sister.

The Worst Moment

Drawing: For her "Worst Moment" drawing (which was performed in an individual session), she drew her sister lying on a hospital bed with "her bone sticking out of her chest." Shanika had not actually witnessed her sister dying or seen her at the hospital, but she often had this horrifying imagery of her sister with blood pouring out of her chest and seeing her bones.

Discussion: Shanika had never shared with anyone the horrific image that intrusively replayed in her mind. The therapist asked questions about what she was thinking and feeling, as well as how it was for her to draw this picture.

Writing: The therapist listened to Shanika describe this horrific image and helped her to put words to the imagery as well as to acknowledge her reactions to this imagery.

Witnessing: Together, the therapist and Shanika reviewed her drawing and writing. Shanika was able to moderate her distress during this time by using the relaxation techniques she had learned in previous sessions.

After the Accident

Drawing: For her "After It Happened" drawing, Shanika drew a picture of herself with tears streaming from her eyes with a thought bubble from her head that stated, "I heard that my sister died."

Discussion: Shanika discussed the shock and aloneness that she felt when her father told her that her sister had died. The therapist asked more contextual questions about that moment, such as "Where were you when you heard this news, and who else was in the room?" The therapist then asked a reconnection question: "If your sister were in the room, what would she have said to you?" Shanika stated that her sister would have told her that she was all right and with God in heaven, and that she, Shanika, was going to be OK too. She continued to discuss the funeral and that she felt safe that night because her mother let her sleep with her.

Writing: Shanika was able to write a more complete story that contained a place, her family, and a sense of comfort.

Witnessing: Shanika shared her story with the other group members and was able to tell them not only when she remembered hearing that her sister had died but also her belief that her sister is in heaven and that she and her sister are all right.

In the next two sessions, Shanika continued with the narrative process and was able to draw, discuss, write, and share about a happy time with her sister as well as things that she likes now about her life. At the end of the 10 weeks of GTI, Shanika shared all of her drawings and writings with her mother and father at home. Shanika learned to moderate her distress (symptoms of posttraumatic stress, depression, and traumatic grief had all significantly decreased), and was able to talk about the positive memories of her sister without the intrusive dying imagery.

SUMMARY

Violent death presents a more complex challenge for narrative reconstruction than the natural death of a loved one. After violent death, the narrative includes the processing of aversive trauma imagery to the violent dying act simultaneous with the processing of alluring separation imagery to the irrevocable separation from someone loved. The internalized memory of the deceased (when alive) is a restorative focus dynamically opposed by the memory of the external trauma (the violent dying act), and the clinical task of revising the internalized relationship with the deceased and the way he or she died (alone and unprotected) may be paramount. Accommodation to violent dying may be complicated by waves of disparate images and narrative themes—the memory of the life of the deceased may have been all but eclipsed by the fantasy of the dying. Preliminary empirical studies with children and adults in group and individual therapy document improvement associated with a staged protocol, restorative retelling, for reconstructing a narrative that includes hopeful and purposeful imagery as a basis for stabilization preparatory to reexposure to the imagery and narrative of violent dying.

REFERENCES

Cohen, J. A., Mannarino, A. P., Greenberg, T., Padlo, S., & Shipley, C. (2002). Childhood traumatic grief: Concepts and controversies. *Trauma, Violence and Abuse, 4*, 307–327.

Cohen, J. A., Mannarino, A. P., & Staron, V. (2006). A pilot study for modified cognitive-behavioral therapy for childhood traumatic grief. *Journal of the American Academy of Child and Adolescent Psychiatry, 45*, 1465–1473.

Currier, J. M., Holland, J. M., & Neimeyer, R. A. (2006). Sense-making, grief, and the experience of violent loss: Toward a mediational model. *Death Studies*, 30, 403–428.

Herman, J. L. (1997). *Trauma and recovery*. New York: Basic.

Layne, C. M., Saltzman, W. R., Poppleton, L., Burlingame, G. M., Pasalic, A., Durakovic, E., et al. (2009). Effectiveness of a school-based group psychotherapy program for war-exposed adolescents: A randomized controlled trial. *Journal of the American Academy for Child and Adolescent Psychiatry, 47*, 1048–1062.

Murphy, S., Braun, T., Tillery, L., Cain, K. C., Johnson, L. C., & Beaton, R. D. (1999). PTSD among bereaved parents following the violent death of their 12 to 28 year old children: A longitudinal prospective analysis. *Journal of Traumatic Stress, 12*, 273–291.

Nader, K., & Layne, C. (2009). Maladaptive grieving in children and adolescents: Discovering developmentally linked differences in the manifestation of grief. *Traumatic Stress Points*, 23(5), 12–16.

Nader, K., Pynoos, R. S., Fairbanks, L., & Frederick, C. (1990). Children's PTSD reactions one year after a sniper attack at their school. *American Journal of Psychiatry, 147*, 1526–1530.

National Centers for Disease Control. (2009, April 17). *Vital Statistics Report, 57*(14).

O'Connor, M. F., Wellisch, D. K., Stanton, A. L., Eisenberger, N. I., Irwin, M. R., Lieberman, M. D. et al. (2008). Craving love? Enduring grief activates brain's reward center. *Neuroimage, 42*, 969–972. doi: 10.1016/j.neuroimage.2008.04.256.

Pfefferbaum, B., Nixon, S. J., Tucker, P. M., Tivis, R. D. Moore, V. L., Gurwitch, R. H., et al. (1999). Posttraumatic stress in bereaved children after the Oklahoma bombing. *Journal of the American Academy of Child and Adolescent Psychiatry, 38*(11), 1372–1379.

Prigerson, H. G., Vanderwerker, L. C., & Maciejewski, P. K. (2008). A case for inclusion of prolonged grief disorder in DSM-V. In M. S. Stroebe (Ed.), *Handbook of bereavement research and practice advances in theory and intervention* (pp. 165–186). Washington, DC: American Psychological Association Press.

Rynearson, E. K. (2001). *Retelling violent death*. New York: Brunner Routledge.

Rynearson E. K. (2005). The narrative labyrinth of violent dying. *Death Studies, 29*, 351–360.

Rynearson, E. K., Correa, F., Favell, J., Saindon, C., & Prigerson, H. (2006). Restorative retelling after violent dying. In E. K. Rynearson (Ed.), *Violent death: Resilience and intervention beyond the crisis* (pp. 195–216). New York: Taylor & Francis.

Salloum, A. (2008). Group therapy for children experiencing grief and trauma due to homicide and violence: A pilot study. *Research on Social Work Practice, 18*(3), 198–211. doi: 10.1177/1049731507307808.

Salloum, A., Garfield, L., Irwin, A., Anderson, A., & Francois, A. (2009). Grief and trauma group therapy with children after Hurricane Katrina. *Social Work With Groups, 32*(1–2), 67–79. doi: 10.1080/01609510802290958.

Salloum, A., & Overstreet, S. (2008). Evaluation of individual and group grief and trauma interventions for children post disaster. *Journal of Clinical Child and Adolescent Psychology, 37*(3), 495–507. doi: 10.1080/15374410802148194.

Shear, M. K., Frank, E., Houck, P., & Reynolds, C. F. (2005). Treatment of complicated grief: A randomized controlled trial. *Journal of the American Medical Association, 293*, 2601–2608.

Zinzow, H. M., Rheingold, A. A., Hawkins, A. O., Saundors, B. E., & Kilpatrick, D. G. (2009). Losing a loved one to homicide: Prevalence and mental health correlates in a national sample of young adults. *Journal of Traumatic Stress, 22*, 20–27. doi: 10.1002/jts.20377.

15

Bereavement and Disasters
Research and Clinical Intervention

PÅL KRISTENSEN and MARIA-HELENA PEREIRA FRANCO

Disasters are commonly divided into natural and human-induced or man-made types (Norris et al., 2002). Although natural disasters are perceived as unavoidable and usually develop more slowly, human-induced disasters are unnatural, typically strike more suddenly without forewarning, and are caused by a failure in control systems (Weisæth, 2006). Subsequently, human-induced disasters are preventable, and someone will be held responsible and may be blamed. Although most people seem to cope well with the stresses associated with disasters (Bonanno, 2004), for many survivors disaster losses are associated with long-term mental health problems such as posttraumatic stress disorder (PTSD), depression (MDD), and prolonged grief disorder (PGD) (Green et al., 1990; Kristensen, Weisæth, & Heir, 2009; Kuo et al., 2003). Moreover, the differences between the two kinds of disasters may influence the psychological reactions seen among the bereaved. For example, deaths that are perceived as preventable due to negligence or human callousness may lead to more excessive anger and bitterness (Kristensen, Weisæth, Herlofsen, Langsrud, & Heir, submitted; Parkes, 2008).

THE UNIQUE STRESSES OF DISASTER LOSS

Disaster losses are often characterized by a set of unique stresses or circumstances that alone or in combination can prolong and/or complicate the course of bereavement (Parkes, 2008; Raphael, 1986). The suddenness of disaster loss is not unique, as it shares with any other sudden death the difficulty for relatives to grasp the reality that one or several close family members have died. The suddenness also hinders bereaved relatives from bidding a final farewell and carrying out last services for the loved one. The violent nature of disaster losses can result in bodies being severely mutilated and disfigured. This can hinder relatives from the opportunity to view the deceased, which is considered important in confronting the reality of the loss (Paul, 2002; Worden, 2009). Moreover, intrusive images of the death scene can occur regardless of whether the bereaved were present when death occurred or not (Rynearson, 2001). Search for meaning and a sense of helplessness can also be found among the experiences of bereaved relatives due to disasters (Rando, 1993; see also chapter 15).

After disasters, there is often a period of waiting before all bodies are found and identified and death can officially be confirmed. This is a period of great stress, with relatives oscillating between feelings of hope and despair. The uncertainty can sustain denial of the loss and fantasies about the missing not being dead, which can delay or prolong the grieving process (Kristensen, Weisæth, & Heir, 2010). The need for information about what has happened and what is being done to rescue or locate missing family members is imminent, especially in the early hours and days after the disaster. Anger is a common reaction in the absence of clear and factual information, and is often directed toward authorities or helpers for not responding fast enough or for not handling the situation adequately. Later in the bereavement phase, information about the cause of death, injuries that the deceased has sustained, where the deceased was found, and whether he or she died instantly or suffered will be important for many in order to make sense of what has happened. For some, questions such as "What did the deceased think before he or she died?" or "Was he or she afraid?" may lead to relentless ruminations after the loss (Lehman, Wortman, & Williams, 1987; Winje, 1998).

Bereaved relatives may either be survivors of the disaster themselves or reside far from the disaster site. Bereaved survivors are often exposed to other potentially traumatic events such as threats to their own lives and having witnessed horrific events, which can affect their mental health (Kristensen et al., 2009; Wang, Zhang, Shi, & Wang, 2009). The combination of trauma and loss can lead to both stress reactions and grief (Raphael, 1997), which can be either intertwined or fluctuating with one condition dominating over the other. PTSD symptoms, such as reliving the scene of the death, may hinder the resolution of normal grief. Survivor guilt or guilt for not having done enough to save those who died is also common among bereaved survivors (Hull, Alexander, & Klein, 2002). Being far from the disaster area can pose a different set of challenges for the bereaved. The high level of uncertainty and low level of control of the situation may lead to high-intensity stress reactions (Weisæth, 2006).

When death finally is confirmed, the uncertainty and despair are replaced by feelings of sadness as well as relief. Finding the deceased gives relatives the opportunity for a proper burial and a grave to visit, which can promote closure. Unfortunately, large-scale disasters often result in bodies not being recovered. These losses, also termed *ambiguous losses*, can induce feelings of helplessness, depression, somatization, and relationship conflicts (Boss, 2002; and see Chapter 13). Finally, another consequence of disasters is persons experiencing multiple losses. Losing several family members simultaneously deprives the bereaved of their natural support systems, and can leave them feeling overwhelmed with grief, also referred to as *bereavement overload* (Neimeyer & Holland, 2004). Moreover, children and adolescents have specific grief reactions to the loss of parents in disaster because of their developmental level and special attachment relationship (Adams, 2002; Stevenson, 2002; and see Chapters 3 and 11).

Together with the private experience of loss, which can be extended to the family circle and to a small community, this century offers opportunity for what is called "the new public mourning" (Walter, 2008). This gives rise to three special groups of mourners: the bereaved who are prevented from grieving in private due to the public nature of an event, those who are not so close to the bereaved but join the public mourning, and those who witnessed the death.

One important question is "How we best can assist and support those who are bereaved by disasters?" A second important question is "What have research and clinical practice taught us in order to provide helpful interventions in the aftermath of disaster losses?"

INTERVENTIONS FOR BEREAVED FAMILIES AFTER DISASTER LOSS

In the acute phase after a sudden and violent loss, a primary aim is to help bereaved families to grasp the reality of the loss and to facilitate an acceptance of the loss (Weisæth, 2006). During the last two decades, a certain practice, termed *confrontational support*, has been developed in Norway after disasters and large-scale accidents involving multiple deaths (Winje & Ulvik, 1995). Counter to a tendency to protect the bereaved from the hard facts of the circumstances of the death and painting a more comforting picture (e.g., "He died during his sleep" or "She most likely experienced no pain"), confrontational support can be described as a strategy by which bereaved families are confronted with the brutal reality of death in a caring and supportive manner. This strategy has been implemented during various phases after disaster losses, such as when the message of death is conveyed, when information is given concerning the circumstances and cause of death, when the family is offered to visit the site of death, and when the family is invited to view the deceased loved one. After large-scale accidents, such interventions have been conducted from the disaster information and support center. The center brings together all parties who can contribute to an accurate and comprehensive picture of the event for those affected, including the bereaved (Weisæth, 2004).

In Brazil, a similar approach has been developed (Franco, 2005), with results that show the importance of capacity building (or reconstruction) together with emotional disclosure. A team of psychologists also has training in critical incident stress management (CISM) and debriefing (Mitchell, 1983), a technique that has been widely used in the last decades of the 20th century (Everly & Boyle, 1999). However, it has been decided not to use this technique in the immediate response to two of the disasters mentioned in this chapter. The reason is the lack of evidence that such a technique would be useful and effective for the general population (Bonanno, 2009; McNally, Bryant, & Ehlers, 2003). Instead, the group decided to work with the approach used by Young (1998) also recommended by Hodgkinson and Stewart (1998), with active listening and cognitive reappraisal. Instead, grief therapy has been guided by the dual-process model of coping with bereavement (Stroebe & Schut, 1999, 2001; see also Chapter 3) together with a meaning-making perspective (Nadeau, 2001; Neimeyer, Keesee, & Fortner, 2000; see also Chapter 1).

In the next section, different disasters involving multiple deaths will be described to demonstrate how collective and individual interventions can be organized to assist bereaved families after disaster loss.

THE DISASTERS

THE 2004 ASIAN TSUNAMI

On the morning of December 26, 2004, a tsunami hit the coast along the Indian Ocean and more than 220,000 people died. The majority of casualties were from the local populations. Still, a large number of tourists traveling for the Christmas holidays also died in the tsunami disaster, and among them were 84 Norwegians. Both children and adults were among the deceased, and several families experienced multiple losses. Some of the bereaved survivors had to struggle for their lives; others had been staying far away from the disaster area. All deceased Norwegians were located, but for some bereaved it took nearly 7 months before the deaths of their family members finally could be confirmed. Few had the opportunity to view their deceased loved ones.

The 2004 tsunami disaster affected families from all over Norway. Subsequently, a nationwide follow-up had to be organized. Each bereaved family was allocated a police liaison officer who had the responsibility for continually informing them about the progress in the rescue work and to notify them when death was confirmed. Another outreach strategy included the general practitioners, who were charged with a special responsibility for contacting patients who were directly affected by the disaster in order to screen for mental health problems.

As part of the follow-up, bereaved families and individuals directly or not exposed to the disaster were offered the opportunity to travel to the disaster area and visit the site where their loved ones had died. Although this was designed primarily for families of the deceased, the trips also included several experts such as representatives from the police identification squads, physical and psychiatric health care, and the Seaman's Church. Two commemoration journeys were held, one in May 2005 and one in October 2005, and both trips included a memorial service with the possibility of talking to police and rescue personnel in order to get a better informed picture of what occurred when the tsunami struck.

Two years after the tsunami, an evaluation of 130 bereaved persons aged 18–80 who had lost close family members revealed that 87% of them had visited the site of death either as participants on the commemoration journeys or by independent travel (Kristensen et al., 2010, in press). Visiting the site of death was highly valued by the families, and the single most important effect of the visits was gaining an increased understanding of what had happened as reported by 61% of the participants. Feeling closeness to the deceased loved one (21%) and togetherness with family or other bereaved families (8%) were also considered important with the visit. Those who had visited the site of death reported lower avoidance behavior and a higher degree of acceptance of the death than those who had not visited the site of death after the disaster.

A Norwegian Avalanche

On March 5, 1986, while taking part in the NATO exercise entitled Anchor Express, a platoon of 31 Norwegian soldiers (3 noncommissioned officers and 28 conscripted men) was hit by a snow avalanche in Vassdalen, northern Norway, and 16 soldiers, aged 19–24 years, died. In the aftermath of the accident, an investigative committee concluded that a combination of circumstances contributed to the tragic outcome. Among these were the weather conditions of heavy snowfall and wind, and the underestimation by military leaders of the potential risk associated with conducting exercises under difficult conditions in that mountainous region.

The avalanche disaster in 1986 affected soldiers in the Norwegian Army and the families of the dead soldiers. After the parents (n = 32) were informed of their sons' deaths, they were offered transportation to the military camp close to the disaster area. The bereaved parents attended a memorial service, and viewing of their deceased sons was held in a local church. It was also possible for parents to meet with military leaders, survivors, and comrades of their deceased sons in order to receive firsthand information about their loved ones. Autopsies of the deceased soldiers were performed to establish the cause of death, and this information was voluntarily presented to the parents by health personnel. Three months after the disaster, all parents were flown into the disaster area by helicopter to get a closer look at where the avalanche had happened and to be informed about where their sons' bodies had been found.

A recent 23-year follow-up study (n = 16) revealed that most parents felt that the deaths should have been prevented and that there was a lack of information about who was responsible for proceeding with the military operation under the dangerous conditions (Kristensen et al., 2010). Although this experience had a profound impact on the bereaved parents' mental health, they expressed that they were pleased and thankful for the opportunity to be transported to the disaster area shortly after the avalanche. All but three of the parents had viewed their dead sons, and no one regretted the viewing. About half of the parents had asked for information regarding the cause of their sons' deaths. In the majority of the cases, asphyxia was the main cause (Rostrup, Gilbert, & Stalsberg, 1989).

All the bereaved parents revealed that visiting the site where death occurred had been important. Convergent with what was found after the tsunami disaster, the parents' responses to what had been most important with the visit fell into three categories. First of all, seeing the area where the avalanche had happened was important to get a better picture of what happened. Second, some emphasized the feeling of closeness to their sons when they visited the site. Third, most parents reported that it had been helpful to meet with the other bereaved parents, and some of them still held contact with each other over 20 years after the disaster. Some had established a bereavement support group which was considered important in working through their loss. Several of the parents had also revisited the site of death in the years following the accident. However, contrary to what was found after the tsunami, the visit did not seem to increase the acceptance of the loss. Some even reported that visiting the site of death had made the loss more difficult to accept, because it was even more obvious to them that their sons should not have been sent into the area at the time. Some had also been given wrong information regarding where their sons were, which had created unnecessary confusion and distress. Still, no parent regretted the visit, and the collective intervention was reported to have been helpful.

Comments

Clinical and research experience has shown that collective interventions such as visiting the site of death, when conducted in a supportive environment, can be beneficial for bereaved families after disaster losses. Several factors can account for this. First of all, collective family-based interventions can be important after disaster losses. Obviously, losses do not affect individuals alone, but whole families. Visiting the site of death may be one way to help families and individuals put fragmented pieces of information together to create a common understanding or narrative of what happened when a loved one died, also termed *family meaning making* (Nadeau, 2001; Walsh, 2007). This may be particularly important when some family members are directly exposed to the disaster themselves while others are not. Being together at the site of death can also facilitate the sharing of grief and loss. The collective aspect of visiting the site of death may involve bereaved families connecting with each other, which can promote the feeling of togetherness (Dyregrov, Straume, & Sari, 2009).

Another important aspect of visiting the site of death is cognitive coping with the loss (Winje, 1998). It is essential for those who are bereaved by disasters to try to make sense of what happened (see Chapters 1 and 6). In the early phases of bereavement, this often involves a need to understand what caused the death, why the loved one did not survive, and whether the death could have been prevented (Rando, 1996). Visiting the site of death may facilitate a more precise understanding of what occurred, can reduce confusion and uncertainty, and can lead to a more unambiguous picture of the scene of loss and trauma. After the tsunami disaster, many of the bereaved reported that the visit to the site had contributed to a realization that death was inevitable given the circumstances, subsequently leading to a greater cognitive acceptance of the loss (Kristensen et al., 2010, in press).

Enhancing the continuing bond or attachment to the deceased seems to be another valuable part of visiting the site of death (see also Chapter 24). The site of death is often experienced as a sacred place where symbolic rituals such as paying their final respects and bidding a final farewell can be conducted in order to achieve a form of closure (Clark & Franzmann, 2006). A commitment or sense of duty toward the deceased to visit the site where death occurred may also be guilt relieving. Finally, although the research is scarce, the mental health effect of traveling to the disaster area and visiting the site of death may be significant (Kristensen et al., 2010, in press). Direct exposure to the disaster area has been shown to alleviate anxiety symptoms and avoidance behavior among disaster survivors (Heir & Weisæth, 2006). Visiting the site of death can be an important confrontational strategy in overcoming some of the potentially negative consequences of disaster losses such as avoidance of the reality of the loss (Gray & Litz, 2005; see also Chapter 6).

Although there are many potential beneficial effects to visiting the site of a death, both professionals and survivors must be aware that these visits can be experienced as painful reminders of the loss and trauma and may reactivate or exacerbate distress in the bereaved (Layne et al., 2006). Consequently, good preparation beforehand is essential. First of all, the timing of the visit may be important. Some may want to visit the site of death soon after the disaster in order to see the area while the disastrous impacts still are evident. Others may want the reconstruction to be underway to mute the visual impact of the disaster. In either case, it is necessary to ensure that the site is safe to visit and that all human remains are recovered that can be (Johnson, 2008). Bereaved relatives should have the opportunity to ask questions regarding the circumstances of death, and it is important to ensure that factual information such as where the deceased's body was located is correct.

A Brazilian Airline Disaster

In July 17, 2007, while landing at the busiest airport in São Paulo, Brazil, an airplane with 181 passengers and 9 crew members hit a commercial building where 20 employees were working. The building caught fire, 8 employees died immediately, and one severely burnt employee died 2 days later in hospital. All in the airplane were killed. As the accident happened in rush hour, the city stopped, and it was very difficult for rescuers and fire brigade workers to get quickly to the crash site. A group of psychologists was called into action by the airline so that family members who were already at the airport and airline ground staff employees could be assisted that same evening by the use of an emergency response protocol. This disaster was the biggest one with a Brazilian airline to date, and journalists and media were everywhere. As the building affected was the cargo headquarters of the same airline, the employees who witnessed the accident lost friends and colleagues. Three bodies were not identified when search operations ended 3 months later.

Initial intervention: Grief support given to the bereaved was divided into two phases. The first, in the immediate aftermath, lasted for one month and involved home visits, official presence during funerals and/or at body identification, accompanying family members for collection of personal belongings at the crash site, looking after their specific needs, and storytelling and playing with children as a means to address their grief reactions. In this phase, the group of psychologists worked in many different places (family homes, hotels, the morgue, a cemetery, an airport lounge, a crisis room, and the crash site), in long-time shifts, and not only with family and employees, but also with fire teams, nurses and doctors, and volunteers. Special attention was given to the families of victims whose bodies were not positively identified.

Subsequent intervention: In the second phase, for as long as 36 months, a significant number of family members and employees were offered grief therapy, not only in São Paulo but also in Porto Alegre (the departure airport) and 20 other Brazilian cities. The age range for those in psychotherapy varied from 2 to 90 years old. Partners, grandparents, widows and widowers, siblings, children and grandchildren, fiancé(e)s, a son-in-law, and a mother-in-law were in psychotherapy that, although consistent with various theoretical approaches, had a focus on disaster loss, coping with the reality of the loss, meaning reconstruction, and attention to social and health problems. At or after 36 months, the monthly clinical reports showed some difficulties related to history of previous losses, family dysfunctions, and health problems. Among those who witnessed the accident, evidence of PTSD was found and addressed with the use of eye movement desensitization and reprocessing therapy (EMDR) techniques (Shapiro, 1995) or the dual-process model (see Chapter 3).

During the second phase, the family members held a monthly reunion at which they requested the presence of the psychologists. The task of the psychologist was just to be there and reachable in case of need. The meeting was held in São Paulo or Porto Alegre, and the airline covered all the costs of transportation, hotel, meals, medical needs, and psychological support. On many occasions, the families required psychological support during the meetings. One important matter that required psychological assistance was what to do with the human remains that were found at the crash site some 9 months after the disaster. These reunions also made it possible to support the families in dealing with issues related to the rituals, particularly those related to the first anniversary. The group of psychologists actually also had an important role in the monthly reunions and at the anniversary rituals, both as facilitators and as support figures for family members.

Many issues were raised by this disaster and its consequences regarding the grief process, psychological support, and the role of psychotherapy. This study is ongoing, and it is expected that a broader and more in-depth view will arise from its results. In assisting the survivors, psychologists had to learn to negotiate with insurance companies or to defend the needs of a client-patient within the boundaries of ethical considerations. This meant developing skills that were not in their formal education at the university or in any professional experience.

Among the lessons learned from this experience, three can be stressed. The first is related to the specific needs of the bereaved group in a disaster. They differ from other bereaved groups because they do not know whom they can trust in view of all the help that is offered, especially because human-induced disasters naturally invite the attribution of blame and suspicion, and the tendency of responsible people, organizations, and even government bureaucracies is to diffuse and delay identification of the guilty parties. The second lesson concerns the need for training of psychologists in disaster work. Obviously this training requires knowledge in grief and bereavement as much as in features of trauma and stress and the possible connections among them. The third lesson bears on the relation among governmental and nongovernmental agencies, volunteers of the community, insurance companies, and many others that may have an interest in the disaster. This is a genuine multicultural issue when the community affected is diverse, and can even carry international implications for coordination of efforts among many agencies. In such cases, it is critical to collaborate to develop clear lines of authority and jurisdiction if chaos is to be avoided, especially for bewildered and angry survivors and those who have been bereaved.

An Atlantic Oil Rig Explosion

In March 15, 2001, an oil rig—the largest in the world—200 km off the coast of Rio de Janeiro, Brazil, caught fire and one of its four columns exploded. Nine workers were missing. Only one body was found, 2 days later. Five days later, the oil rig collapsed and sank to 1800 m in the Atlantic Ocean, with no chance of recovering the bodies. Five days after the explosion, a psychologist was called to go to Macae, the coastal city where the oil company had its offices. By the time she got there, the oil rig was already submerged and the family members of the missing employees were demanding information and were in denial that their family members were dead, despite the evidence that the missing relatives could not be found. The following day, it became clear that there were no survivors and the family members, supported by the trade union, put pressure on the company to go to the site and recover the bodies.

In a meeting with human resources and safety–security staff, the psychologist suggested procedures for a ritual at the disaster site, so that family members could have something to remember in the absence of bodies. Also, measures for a memorial ceremony were planned, including writing the speech of the president of the oil company, so that specific conditions of bereaved families would be addressed. The main concern of the psychologist was not to turn that memorial service into a political gathering and not to make the bereaved families actors in that scenario. The meeting lasted for 6 hours and included information regarding the effects of violent and unexpected death, bereaved family needs, normal grief responses, and common physical, mental health, social, and psychological reactions to traumatic loss. During the meeting, all the details and decisions were explained to the families.

As the families put pressure on the company to go to the area where the oil rig had sunk, it was suggested by the psychologist that a ritual could be performed there. In collaboration with family members, it was decided to scatter petals of white roses (symbolic of love and purity of spirit) on the sea from a helicopter. Because of the fragile psychological state of the bereaved, extra safety procedures were used on the helicopter.

A visit to the place suggested for the memorial service was made, and a moving ritual was performed. Late in the afternoon, when the families came back from the ceremony at the sea, a meeting with them was organized. The aim of this meeting was to offer them active listening, support, answers to practical questions, and guidance regarding what could be expected for the next days or weeks. They were concerned with how to explain the disaster and death to children, social support from the company, survivor guilt, and fear for the future. Previous to that meeting, a long talk with the social workers of the oil company was held to discuss with them the provision of grief psychotherapy in the cities of origin of the families, with remote follow-up by the psychologist. That follow-up was not conducted as regularly as the psychologist considered desirable, due to circumstances beyond her control. The main difficulties arose when families were assisted by psychologists without training to work with bereavement, underscoring the need for much wider training in this demanding and specialized type of service.

CONCLUSIONS

As evident in these disasters, whether natural and human induced, both early and long-term assistance may be needed for bereaved relatives due to the unique stresses or circumstances of disaster loss. Several interventions such as providing timely and accurate information, organizing gatherings of survivors so that they can give and receive peer support, visiting the disaster site, assisting in commemorative activities, and offering professional psychotherapy—especially focused on trauma and grief—may be indicated at different times during the follow-up, in roughly the order listed. We also consider it important to balance collective approaches with individualized services for high-risk persons and groups, several examples of which are suggested in other chapters of this volume. We are encouraged by the preliminary support that research is providing for such disaster intervention, and hope this brief chapter encourages fuller training and involvement of helping professionals in this specialized form of assistance to those communities that may one day need it.

REFERENCES

Adams, D. W. (2002). The consequences of sudden and traumatic death: The vulnerability of bereaved children and adolescents and ways professionals can help. In G. R. Cox, R. A. Bendiksen, & R. G. Stevenson (Eds.), *Complicated grieving and bereavement* (pp. 23–40). Amityville, NY: Baywood.

Bonanno, G. A. (2004). Loss, trauma, and human resilience: Have we underestimated the human capacity to thrive after extremely aversive events? *American Psychologist, 59*, 20–28.

Bonanno, G. A. (2009). *The other side of sadness: What the new science of bereavement tells us about life after loss*. New York: Basic.

Boss, P. (2002). Ambiguous loss in families of the missing. *The Lancet, 360*(Suppl.), s39–s40.

Clark, J., & Franzmann, M. (2006). Authority from grief, presence and place in the making of roadside memorials. *Death Studies, 30*, 579–599.

Dyregrov, A., Straume, M., & Sari, S. (2009). Long-term collective assistance for the bereaved following a disaster: A Scandinavian approach. *Counselling and Psychotherapy Research, 9*, 33–41.

Everly, G. S., & Boyle, S. H. (1999). Critical incident stress debriefing (CIDS): A meta-analysis. *International Journal of Emergency Mental Health, 1*, 165–168.

Franco, M. H. P. (2005). Apoio psicológico para emergências em aviação: A teoria revista naprática [Psychological support for emergencies in aviation: Theory revised by practice]. *Estudos de Psicologia, 10-2*, 177–180.

Gray, M. J., & Litz, B. T. (2005). Behavioral interventions for recent trauma. *Behavior Modification, 29*, 189–215.

Green, B. L., Lindy, J. D., Grace, M. C., Gleser, G. C., Leonard, A. C., Korol, M., et al. (1990). Buffalo Creek survivors in the second decade: Stability of stress symptoms. *American Journal of Orthopsychiatry, 60*, 43–53.

Heir, T., & Weisæth, L. (2006). Back to where it happened. Self-reported symptom improvement of tsunami survivors who returned to the disaster area. *Prehospital and Disaster Medicine, 21*, 59–63.

Hodgkinson, P. E., & Stewart, M. (1998). *Coping with catastrophe: A handbook of post-disaster psychosocial aftercare*. London: Routledge.

Hull, A., Alexander, D. A., & Klein, S. (2002). Survivors of the Piper Alpha platform disaster: A long-term follow-up study. *British Journal Psychiatry, 181*, 433–438.

Johnson, E. (2008). Memorial services, site visits, and other rituals. In S. Roberts & W. Ashley (Eds.), *Disaster spiritual care: Practical clergy responses to community, regional, and national tragedy* (pp. 196–208). Burlington, VT: Skylight Paths.

Kristensen, P., Tønnessen, A., Weisæth, L., & Heir, T. (In press). Visiting the site of death: Experiences of the bereaved after the 2004 Southeast Asia tsunami. *Death Studies*.

Kristensen, P., Weisæth, L., & Heir, T. (2009). Psychiatric disorders among disaster bereaved: An interview study of individuals directly or not directly exposed to the 2004 tsunami. *Depression and Anxiety, 26*, 1127–1133.

Kristensen, P., Weisæth, L., & Heir, T. (2010). Predictors of complicated grief after a natural disaster: A population study 2 years after the 2004 South East Asian tsunami. *Death Studies, 37*, 134–150.

Kristensen, P., Weisæth, L., Herlofsen, P. H., Langsrud, Ø., & Heir, T. (Submitted). Parental mental health after the accidental death of a son during military service: 23-year follow-up study.

Kuo, C. J., Tang, H. S, Tsay, C. J., Lin, S. K., Hu, W. H., & Chen, C. C. (2003). Prevalence of psychiatric disorders among bereaved survivors of a disastrous earthquake in Taiwan. *Psychiatric Services*, *54*, 249–251.

Layne, C. M., Warren, J. S., Saltzman, W. R., Fulton, J. B., Steinberg, A. M., & Pynoos, R. S. (2006). Contextual influences on posttraumatic adjustment: Retraumatization and the roles of revictimization, posttraumatic adversities and distressing reminders. In L. Schein, H. I. Spitz, G. M. Burlingame, P. R. Muskin, & S. Vargo (Eds.), *Psychological effects of catastrophic disasters: Group approaches to treatment* (pp. 235–286). New York: Haworth Press.

Lehman, D. R., Wortman, C. B., & Williams, C. F. (1987). Long-term effect of losing a child or spouse in a motor vehicle crash. *Journal of Personality and Social Psychology*, *52*, 218–231.

McNally, R. J., Bryant, R. A., & Ehlers, A. (2003). Does early psychological intervention promote recovery from posttraumatic stress? *Psychological Science in the Public Interest*, *4*, 45–79.

Mitchell, J. T. (1983). When disaster strikes: The critical incident stress debriefing process. *Journal of Emergency Medical Service*, *8*, 36–39.

Nadeau, J. W. (2001). Meaning making in family bereavement. In M. Stroebe, R. O. Hansson, W. Stroebe, and H. Schut (Eds.), *Handbook of bereavement research: Consequences, coping, and care* (pp. 329–348). Washington, DC: American Psychological Association.

Neimeyer, R. A., & Holland, J. (2004). Bereavement overload. In N. Salkind (Ed.), *Encyclopedia of human development*. Thousand Oaks, CA; Sage.

Neimeyer, R. A., Keesee, N. J., & Fortner, B. V. (2000). Loss and meaning reconstruction: Propositions and procedures. In R. Malkinson, S. S. Rubin, & E. Witzum (Eds.), *Traumatic and non-traumatic loss and bereavement* (pp. 197–230). Madison, WI: Psychosocial Press.

Norris, F., Friedman, M. J., Watson, P. J., Byrne, C. M., Diaz, E., & Kaniasty, K. (2002). 60,000 disaster victims speak: Part 1. An empirical review of the empirical literature, 1981–2001. *Psychiatry*, *65*, 207–239.

Parkes, C. M. (2008). Bereavement following disasters. In M. S. Stroebe, R. Hansson, H. Schut, & W. Stroebe (Eds.), *Handbook of bereavement research and practice* (pp. 463–484). Washington, DC: American Psychological Association.

Paul, R. J. (2002). Viewing the body and grief complications: The role of visual confirmation in grief reconciliation. In G. R. Cox, R. A. Bendiksen, & R. G. Stevenson (Eds.), *Complicated grieving and bereavement* (pp. 255–274). Amityville, NY: Baywood.

Rando, T. A. (1993). *Treatment of complicated mourning*. Champaign, IL: Research Press.

Rando, T. A. (1996). Complications in mourning traumatic death. In K. J. Doka (Ed.), *Living with grief after sudden loss* (pp. 139–160). Washington, DC: Taylor & Francis.

Raphael, B. (1986). *When disaster strikes: How individuals and communities cope with catastrophe*. New York: Basic.

Raphael, B. (1997). The interaction of grief and trauma. In D. Black, M. Newman, J. Harris-Hendricks, & G. Mezey (Eds.), *Psychological trauma: A developmental approach* (pp. 31–43). London: Gaskell.

Rostrup, M., Gilbert, M., & Stalsberg, H. (1989). The avalanche in Vassdalen: Medical experiences (in Norwegian). *Tidsskrift for Norsk Lægeforening*, *109*, 807–813.

Rynearson, E. K. (2001). *Retelling violent death*. New York: Brunner Routledge.

Shapiro, F. (1995). *Eye movement desensitization and reprocessing: Basic principles, protocols and procedures*. New York: Guilford Press.

Stevenson, R. G. (2002). It's never easy! Children and adolescents and complicated grief. In G. R. Cox, R. A. Bendiksen, & R. G. Stevenson (Eds.), *Complicated grieving and bereavement* (pp. 275–287). Amityville, NY: Baywood.

Stroebe, M. S., & Schut, H. (1999). The dual process model of coping with bereavement: Rationale and description. *Death Studies*, *23*, 197–224.

Stroebe, M. S., & Schut, H. (2001). Meaning making and the dual process model of coping with bereavement. In R. A. Neimeyer (Ed.), *Meaning reconstruction and the experience of loss* (pp. 55–73). Washington, DC: American Psychological Association.

Walsh, F. (2007). Traumatic loss and major disasters: Strengthening family and community resilience. *Family Process*, *46*, 207–227.

Walter, T. (2008). The new public mourning. In M. S. Stroebe, R. Hansson, H. Schut, & W. Stroebe (Eds.), *Handbook of bereavement research and practice* (pp. 241–262). Washington, DC: American Psychological Association.

Wang, L., Zhang, Y., Shi, Z., & Wang, W. (2009). Symptoms of posttraumatic stress disorder among adult survivors two months after the Wenchuan earthquake. *Psychological Reports*, *105*, 879–885.

Weisæth, L. (2004). Preventing after-effects of disaster trauma: The information and support centre. *Prehospital and Disaster Medicine*, *19*, 86–89.

Weisæth, L. (2006). Collective traumatic stress: Crises and catastrophes. In B. Arentz & R. Ekman (Eds.), *Stress in health and disease*. Weinheim, Germany: Wiley-VCH.

Winje, D. (1998). Cognitive coping: The psychological significance of knowing what happened in the traumatic event. *Journal of Traumatic Stress*, *11*, 627–643.

Winje, D., & Ulvik, A. (1995). Confrontation with reality: Crisis intervention services for traumatized families after a school bus accident in Norway. *Journal of Traumatic Stress*, *8*, 429–443.

Worden, J. W. (2009). *Grief counseling and grief therapy: A handbook for the mental health practitioner* (4th ed.). New York: Springer.

Young, M. A. (1998). *The community crisis response teams training manual*. Washington, DC: National Organization for Victims Assistance.

16

Grief After Terrorism
Toward a Family-Focused Intervention

GRACE H. CHRIST, DIANNE KANE, and HEIDI HORSLEY

A question frequently asked when we present our bereavement program developed for widows and children of New York firefighters killed in the World Trade Center attacks on September 11, 2001, is whether there are differences in the grief associated with that form of traumatic loss and grief associated with other sudden, traumatic forms of death. The literature suggests there are more similarities than differences between the processes of recovering from a terrorist attack and from a natural disaster (Herrmann & Anders, 2006; U.S. Department of Health and Human Services [DHHS], 2004). The authors have typically recommended analyzing every disaster in relation to its unique characteristics of onset, duration, scope, and degree of impact. Suggested differences are often subjective. Relative to natural disasters, terrorist attacks engender more fear, ongoing feelings of threat, anger, desire for revenge, and sense of the disruption of the social order.

We developed the family-focused intervention in close collaboration with the Counseling Service Unit of the New York City Fire Department (FDNY-CSU) for the wives and children of the 343 firefighters killed on September 11, 2001. Most of them were married men with young families, which included 387 minor children plus 10 to 15 yet to be born.

One of us (DK) found that after the deaths of these first responders, the most frequently vocalized concerns and requests for help came from their widows, especially from those with young children. The widows' concerns ranged from "How do I tell my 2-year-old that Daddy is not coming home?" to the long-term effects of the death and the disaster on their children. Recognizing that they could not handle those concerns alone, the CSU staff reached out to form a partnership with child bereavement specialists. The goal was to design an intervention that would be responsive to the widows' pressing concerns while also taking advantage of the opportunity offered by this large cohort of families to learn more about the trajectory of recovery for widows and children after a terrorist attack (Christ, 2006).

CSU's request for intervention programs converged with the interests of another author (GC), who shortly after 9/11 sought a population of families who had lost a first-responder father during the World Trade Center terrorist attack. This interest followed the recent completion of a randomized clinical trial of a parent guidance intervention for families with dependent children who lost one parent to cancer (Christ, 2000; Christ, Raveis, Siegel, Karus, & Christ, 2005). The purpose of the practice research that was proposed to CSU was to provide services to women and children and to understand the similarities and differences in the experiences of families affected by expected and unexpected deaths—a good meeting of perspectives and expertise. The CSU sought an intervention that would offer psychoeducation and support based on the understanding that traumatic grief reactions were normal, understandable, and manageable. In addition, the unit wanted the intervention to support the widow's role as a competent head of household who, though grieving, was able to be a caring, available single parent to each of her children (Greene, Kane, Christ, Lynch, & Corrigan, 2006). Particularly supportive to this collaboration was that the FDNY-CSU had a long history of effectively providing firefighters' widows and children with an extremely important and trusted supportive community environment that could reduce the fear and mistrust commonly reported after a terrorist attack.

THE CSU–COLUMBIA UNIVERSITY ASSESSMENT AND GUIDANCE PROGRAM

Interventions for at-risk children and adolescents after disasters generally focus on identifying and alleviating symptoms of posttraumatic stress disorder (PTSD), major depression, anxiety disorders, and traumatic grief (Brown & Goodman, 2005; Cohen, Mannarino, & Gibson, 2006; Layne et al., 2006; Pfeffer, Altemus, Heo, & Jiang, 2007). Although this approach is warranted, researchers have cautioned that such a narrow focus on diagnosable disorders "does not provide a comprehensive … frame to define the spectrum of needed strategies to serve the wide population of children, adults and families" affected by disasters (Pynoos, Steinberg, Schreiber, & Brymer, 2006, p. 89). Many children who could benefit from professional guidance and support will not exhibit disorders that can be diagnosed with the *Diagnostic and Statistical Manual of Mental Disorders* (American Psychiatric Association, 2000; Layne et al., 2006). Most children will experience significant distress and confront the surviving parent or caregiver with major parenting challenges (Masten, 1999; Pfeffer et al., 2007; Pynoos et al., 2006; Yehuda, 1999). The surviving caregiver's critical role in promoting children's adaptation and reducing adverse consequences after the parent's death is supported across studies of bereaved children (Dowdney, 2000; Haine et al., 2006; Kwok et al., 2005; Raveis, Siegel, & Karus, 1999; Saler & Skolnick, 1992; Sandler, Wolchik, & Ayers,

2008; Siegel, Mesagno, & Christ, 1990; Tremblay & Israel, 1998). Studies of interventions that provide parent education, support, and empowerment for parentally bereaved children have provided an evidence base for the efficacy and effectiveness of these approaches.

An Intervention Model for Parent Guidance

The proposed model for parent guidance was an individual family-focused intervention provided for the bereaved families. The model had been evaluated previously with families in which a parent died of cancer (Christ, 2000; Christ et al., 2005). It also was replicated with adolescents experiencing an accidental traumatic loss, such as drowning or an automobile accident (Horsley & Patterson, 2006). Results from the cancer study provided support for the intervention's acceptance and efficacy with distressed families. Communication between children who participated in the intervention and their surviving parents improved significantly over the 14 months between the assessments before and after the intervention compared with families that had been randomized into a less intensive telephone comparison intervention. The majority of families participating in the cancer-related intervention said they found it accessible and helpful during the parent's terminal illness and after the death. The families also suggested several areas for improvement. Specifically, they recommended more direct work with their children and greater flexibility in the intensity and frequency of services over a longer period of time.

Although the participants in the CSU–Columbia University partnership initially considered group interventions, a number of factors worked against the use of parent groups for our families. Unlike bereaved families who are isolated in their loss, our families experienced the opposite situation: they were overwhelmed with people who wanted to interact with them about their loss, which burdened the families with overexposure and constant reminders. Although the widows wanted to interact with other women in the same situation, the fact that the FDNY families were spread out over a wide geographic area in the New York metropolitan area and many had several children meant that traveling to weekly meetings was difficult for all of them and unappealing to most of them. These factors were especially relevant because the women were working hard to maintain their children's routines.

Therefore, the proposed family intervention was an individual family assessment and guidance model that incorporated modifications suggested by participants in the earlier, cancer-related study. Time would be provided for direct assessment and counseling of the children, and mothers would receive feedback on the results of the assessments gathered for clinical purposes as well as for research. The CSU's desire for a "nonpathology psychoeducational" perspective was compatible with our experience with the previous parent guidance intervention. In addition, trauma-specific assessments and interventions were integrated into the parent guidance model.

Two or more family consultants were assigned to each family, depending on the number of children who would be participating. One consultant was designated as the lead, who would coordinate all communication and work with the mother.

During the first months of contact with each family, four biweekly therapeutic interviews in the home were proposed to obtain preliminary information, establish rapport, gauge the needs of the mother and each child, and complete a battery of psychological measures. In the third month, the mother and the children would receive a verbal preliminary assessment to respond to the question "How are my children doing?" This assessment would be followed by monthly therapeutic interviews with each family for the first 2 years and at a more varied frequency as needed or requested in the third to fifth years. Because many of the families lived 50 to 70 miles from the city, individual family members who required more intensive contact would be referred to an appropriate local provider. We would offer to continue in-home interviews with the other members of the family and with the referred child or parent if a collaborative arrangement could be worked out with the local therapist.

Goals of the Parent Guidance Program

The goals of the intervention were to educate and empower the bereaved mothers with knowledge of their children's stresses and grief experiences, to suggest ways they could support the children's coping, to encourage and enhance empathy between family members, and to offer solutions for the unique problems confronting the family. Therapeutic goals were to be achieved by promoting open family *communication* about the death and its impact on the family, facilitating the mother's *competence* in parenting her grieving children, and supporting *consistency* in her parenting in relation to caregiving, education, discipline, and decision making (Sandler et al., 2008; Siegel et al., 1990). The children would be helped to express their emotions and reactions, understand grief and trauma reactions, and develop skills in managing intense emotions and ongoing reminders of the traumatic loss as well as in coping with changes in the family caused by the loss. The family consultants would help both parents and children to manage stress behaviors through education about the traumatic grief process, normalization of their reactions, and interpersonal support with ongoing screening for pathological symptoms. An additional goal was to learn about expected trauma-related components and external ongoing stressors that might interfere with the mourning processes of both mothers and children.

We recognized that many aspects of this specific traumatic bereavement situation were unknown and that there was much we needed to learn from the families while providing approaches based on existing trauma and bereavement research and practice. For example, how would the interplay of indirect trauma and grief affect the responses of bereaved widows and children? Although they were not present at the traumatic event or did not witness the violent deaths, they were likely to be traumatized by a number of factors: constant televised images of the airliners striking the Twin Towers that subsequently collapsed on their husbands or fathers, the sudden unanticipated deaths of the parent and multiple friends and colleagues, the prolonged and often unsuccessful recovery of remains, exposure to ubiquitous traumatic reminders of the disaster, and the global and historic impact of the event.

Data Collection and Analysis

Concurrent collection of qualitative and quantitative data for the research included the family members' scores on standardized measures plus the transcribed therapeutic interviews and the consultants' on-site observations and field notes.

Standardized measures: The results of the standardized measures administered to the mothers and children (see Table 16.1) served to achieve both clinical and research goals. The mothers' most pressing concerns about their children would be addressed by combining the results of the children's clinical measures with our clinical assessments. The results of both mothers' and children's clinical measures were also used to assure the comprehensiveness of the assessment process and, over time, to measure changes in the child's and parent's functioning. Each child received $25 on completing the measures. The Child Behavior Check List (CBCL) had a form for teachers as well as for parents. We planned to have the child's teacher fill it out, which would provide an important perspective on the child's functioning in the school environment as well as within the home environment.

Interviews with surviving family members: With parents' consent and children's assent, individual and family interviews were audiotaped and transcribed. We explained that to review our work, we needed an ongoing record of the interviews. We also explained that so little is known about the processes of recovery over time that sharing this experience with other professionals might be invaluable. The interviews were organized first into NVivo projects by family, then within each project by individual family members, and finally by date of interview (QSR International, 2002).

Recording and transcribing consultants' analyses and debriefings: On the 50–70-mile car trip back from the families' homes, the consultants reviewed each interview and discussed their formulations and personal

TABLE 16.1 Primary Standardized Clinical Measures Used in Assessments

Measure	Age (years)	Source
Child Behavior Check List (CBCL)		Achenbach & Rescorla, 2001
Parent Report of Child Behavior	6-18 & 1½–5 years	
Teacher's Report Form	6-18 & 1½–5 years	
Youth Self-Report Form	11–18 years	
Brief Symptom Inventory (BSI)	11 years–adult	Derogatis, 1993
Children's Depression Inventory (CDI)	Children	Kovacs, 1992
Expanded Grief Inventory	All ages	Layne, Sayjak, Saltzman, & Pynoos, 1998
State Trait Anxiety Inventory (STAI)	11 years–adult	Spielberger et al., 1983c
State Trait Anxiety Inventory for Children (STAIC)	Up to age 11	Spielberger et al., 1983

and professional reactions. Because consultant's thoughts about how the interventions were taking shape, the successes, the failures, and insights about alternative approaches seemed important enough to be audiotaped, these discussions were transcribed and entered into the family's NVivo project.

Data analysis: The ongoing development of the intervention required an iterative and interactive process that took into account the individual family's expressed needs and concerns. However, we also needed research methods that would enable us to evolve and monitor a consistent intervention that not only incorporated the ongoing experiences of all the participating families but also provided knowledge about coping patterns and the trajectory of recovery in these circumstances in the aftermath of 9/11.

Staffing, Supervision, and Support of Intervention Teams

The challenge for team members working with the bereaved families was considerable because of the travel time that limited more frequent visits, the exposure to the family's intense emotions in the home setting, the process of engaging often mistrustful and angry family members, and the difficulty of assessing how adaptive the family members' behavior was in relation to the totally abnormal situation in which they found themselves.

The CSU had agreed that at least two professionals would enter the home at each visit. This procedure was designed to assure the consultants' ability to interview each family member with limited disruption of ongoing family life. The visits generally lasted no more than 2½ hours. Having two professionals in the home also enabled them to monitor each other as a means of assuring that appropriate boundaries were maintained and that at least two different professional observations of family functioning would be available.

Team members included doctoral students from the Columbia University School of Social Work and social work faculty who had a minimum of 5 years of clinical experience with children and adults as well as experience working in research programs. Several faculty members had more than 10 years of clinical experience. The team also was interdisciplinary; it included educational psychologists, a nurse, and a child psychiatrist.

All team members found that the weekly supervisory discussions held in a faculty member's living room over lunch were a critical learning and emotionally restorative experience. All members, including the senior staff members, brought up the most challenging issues that had occurred with families. The group then provided thoughtful reactions and possible therapeutic approaches. Team members also shared their emotional responses and ways of coping with their own reactions. During this group supervision, the additional insights provided by in-depth discussion of a particularly vexing problem added greatly to gradual clarification and consistency in the content of the intervention.

Finally, team members also found that describing and recording their reviews and analyses of the often highly emotional interviews while traveling back to the city was extremely supportive because it helped them to discuss intense emotional reactions as well as develop a shared case formulation and clarify the next steps in the intervention with a given family. As often happens when working in emotionally intense environments, team members naturally developed a "buddy system" that offered easy access to discussion of challenging case situations on a one-on-one basis (Herrmann & Anders, 2006).

IMPLEMENTATION OF THE PROGRAM IN THE FIRST YEAR

For the current purposes, we will focus on families' responses, interventions, and therapeutic challenges that occurred during the first year after 9/11. Families indicated they especially wanted their children to be evaluated and the family to receive supportive counseling. The women had signed up for the family guidance program by faxing their names, the names and ages of their children, and their preferences for the site of the intervention to the Columbia University family program.

As we implemented the intervention during the first year, we confronted some situations that were completely unexpected, some that were expected but often were more complex than situations involving families that had lost a parent to illness, and situations involving issues that were similar to those confronting families bereaved from an expected loss. The most unexpected losses were the ongoing external trauma-inducing events that took precedence over families' experience of grief and constantly made them feel threatened and overwhelmed. Their struggle with intense anger, mistrust, and withdrawal were consistent with the responses described for families after other terrorist attacks (DHHS, 2004). Priority had to be given to helping families cope with these events, to helping them achieve a sense of safety and calmness, and to building a "protective shield."

Examples of stressful events that confronted the bereaved families after 9/11 were the multiple memorial services and commemorative events, especially those of the husband-father's close friends and many colleagues. Also stressful were the constant public discussions about remains of body parts; the constant exposure to television pictures of the planes flying into the Twin Towers; the 6-month anniversary events; then the closing of the site around the ninth month, although more than half of the grieving families still awaited news regarding the remains of their loved one; and, finally, the intense first-anniversary celebration geared to honor the dead and bring closure to the city, state, and nation. Most mothers agreed that although the celebration honored the firefighters' sacrifice appropriately, it was too public and intense for many of the widows and children. Furthermore, there were threats of more terrorist attacks and the corresponding development of a well-publicized system of red and orange alerts. Though necessary to assure vigilance during this period, the alerts retraumatized the bereaved. For example:

One family meeting concerned 12-year-old Patrick's meltdown on the baseball field the previous week. But when the consultants arrived at the house, 14-year-old Patsy told them there had been a "lockdown" at school that day related to a terrorist threat, "just like what happened on 9/11," when no one was allowed in or out of the classroom. On 9/11, a neighbor had gone to the school to ask that Patsy be allowed to come home because her mother was stuck in the city, and her father's whereabouts were still unknown. Patsy's two younger siblings remembered how angry they had been because they had not been allowed to go home to see what had happened and wait there for their mother. All of them had reexperienced their original anxiety for hours after the school lockdown on the day of the family interview and needed to be debriefed and regain a sense of safety. Few other issues seemed relevant that day. Patsy said she noticed that while other students returned to their classes and resumed their activities, she felt upset for the rest of the day.

Children learned to anticipate and normalize their reactions to these events by asking their teachers to provide them with any additional information that was available and by debriefing with their mothers when they returned home.

During the first year, the interventions were dominated by a need to help families manage stressful aspects such as those described here. Some families turned off their televisions. canceled their newspaper and magazine subscriptions, and covered their windows to keep people from peering in at them. Other families changed the stores where they shopped for food so they would not be confronted constantly by well-wishers who were motivated by a genuine desire to help but, instead, served as unrelenting reminders of the family's tragic loss. However, families that withdrew to a serious degree limited their access to the information and clarification they desperately needed. The family consultants provided the families with information about the kinds of experiences that were evoking stress reactions in other bereaved families. They also encouraged the widows to take advantage of sources of trustworthy information and to participate in FDNY events and support groups.

Engaging Traumatized Families in the Helping Process

Engaging traumatized bereaved families in an intervention program is challenging, and such attempts after terrorist attacks were reported to be unsuccessful (Allen, Whittlesey, Pfefferbaum, & Ondersma, 1999; Pfefferbaum, Call, & Sconzo, 1999; Pfefferbaum et al., 2003). Even the mothers who had requested our parent guidance program struggled with accumulated anxiety, anger, mistrust, and feeling overwhelmed, which made them hesitant to engage. Despite their need for help, they were afraid of losing control and being overwhelmed by powerful feelings of weakness and vulnerability at a time when they needed courage to meet the many demands made on them in their sudden, new roles as single parents.

The mothers were reassured by the comprehensive assessments of the children, the review of each child's grief process, and how they were handling the loss of their father, and the plan developed to manage targeted problem areas. For example, many children slept with their mother or another sibling for months after the disaster. Normalizing this behavior and thinking about how to provide the children with a greater sense of security and reassurance that met the needs of all family members were constant preoccupations of the mothers. Families needed multiple services and resources for different children. The family consultants referred children who required more intensive therapy for elevated symptoms to local therapists. However, the consultants continued their consultant role with a family even if individual family members were receiving services from a local therapist. Thus, coordinating the care provided by multiple sources was another important function of the family consultants.

Most family members were eager to describe how they had learned about the death of their husband or father and how they handled the memorial events. Although it was important for both mothers and children to express their reactions and emotions, the family consultants helped them to normalize their reactions and to develop their capacity to move toward or away from emotionally intense situations when appropriate. We often had to remind mothers that children's capacity to sustain intense sad emotions was limited—that children needed to experience positive emotions and activities much sooner than bereaved parents and other bereaved adults did.

Shaping the Trauma Narrative

The mothers' descriptions of their experiences provided the consultants with the opportunity to begin helping the mothers organize and shape the various components of the narrative of their grief and trauma in a way that facilitated their ability to engage in more adaptive thinking about what had occurred and would help them move forward (Cohen, Mannarino, & Deblinger, 2006; Neimeyer, Burke, Mackay, & Stringer, in press; Neimeyer, Prigerson, & Davies, 2002).

Families that have lost a family member to a terminal illness often express relief because the patient's pain and suffering have ended, whereas the families who experienced the sudden devastating loss of a firefighter husband and father on 9/11 experienced powerful and disturbing images of their loved one dying afraid and in pain:

One mother reported having difficulty sleeping at night because of images of her husband huddled with two friends in the stairwell of the second tower (where their bodies had in fact been found). She thought of them as being frightened and in pain. When she was able to reframe the original images into images in which the men prayed together and had a moment of peace, as brave people often do when faced with their imminent death, her sleeping problem was immediately alleviated.

Children also struggled with powerful images such as these. For example:

Two adolescents visited the disaster site with their mother before the site was closed 9 months after 9/11. No remains of their father had been found, and their mother heard them ask the firefighter guide taking them through the site, "Do you think our father felt pain?" The guide held up his watch and had the teenagers count out 7 seconds. Then he said, "That's how long it took from the time the tower began to come down till it hit the ground. There was no time for pain." The teenagers were greatly relieved.

While listening to a mother's narrative about the loss and its aftermath, the family consultant helped her to reframe her reactions in the context of a completely abnormal situation. In addition, the consultant provided critically important support by helping the mother focus on the strengths, accomplishments, coping abilities, and parental commitment she was exhibiting while dealing with the ongoing stresses and problems she faced every day. Some mothers began to feel proud of what they had accomplished and, although still fearful and subject to anxiety and sadness, were optimistic about being able to manage effectively as a single parent. As one mother said proudly, "My kids seem surprised at how well I have done in managing things and keeping the family going."

The trauma of the husband's death reactivated widows' memories of earlier stressful events and losses. Some of them needed to mourn earlier losses, but these memories could increase their feelings of victimization and helplessness. In the first year, it was important for the women to acknowledge these intrusive memories, separate past fears from current realities, and identify positive attributes they had developed in response to earlier traumas that were applicable to their current situation. For example, one widow had developed a tremendous capacity to function independently during a previous stressful situation; another had developed resilience while learning to accept and live with a disability.

Identifying the Impact of Concurrent and Cumulative Stresses

One risk factor associated with a sudden traumatic loss is lack of time to prepare for the experience of concurrent and cumulative stresses (Melhem, Moritz, Walker, Shear, & Brent, 2007; Sandler et al., 2008). Although a family member's illness can, in itself, have traumatic aspects (Saldinger, Cain, & Porterfield, 2003), the illness does provide the family with opportunities to prepare for the loved one's death in their day-to-day lives by absorbing and integrating information in small doses over time (Christ, 2000).

As a result of the World Trade Center attack, the bereaved families lost not only firefighter husbands and fathers but numerous family friends as well. Listening to the families recount the details of these stories provided the family consultants with opportunities to assure the families that their intense reactions were appropriate responses to a horrific situation, to help the families understand the traumatic elements of the situation that were most distressing for them, and to identify previous and current stresses that were likely to be contributing to the complexity and intensity of the emotions they were experiencing. Many of these stresses surfaced during the initial assessment interviews. For example, one mother's firefighter husband was the beloved stepfather to her two teenage children. Three months after 9/11, his best friend, a fellow firefighter who survived the event and was attempting to be a substitute father to the children, suddenly died of a heart attack. The effect of this abrupt loss, on top of all the accumulated losses, which were far more stressful than any one of them alone, naturally created more attachment anxiety in the children, who understandably required more time to accommodate the latest loss.

Other examples of families experiencing accumulated losses included a widow whose son remained an active duty firefighter after his father's death and whose parents died in the year after the death of her husband. Another widow gave birth to her fourth child a week after her husband's death, the eldest son of a third widow had suffered a traumatic brain injury 2 years before his father's death, and a fourth widow struggled with a genetic condition that would eventually result in blindness.

Mothers often underestimated how previous losses and current stresses affected their reactions to the traumatic loss of their husband because all the other losses seemed to pale in comparison. In these situations, mothers tended to fear their reactions were pathological, rather than the result of cumulative stresses. Clarifying these situations for the women helped to reduce their anxiety and enabled them to develop more realistic expectations about the intensity and complexity of the recovery process and the time required to complete it.

Coordinating Care and Case Management

The family consultants helped families resolve a number of practical problems that emerged during the first year after the disaster. Identifying a family's immediate needs and facilitating its access to services helped to relieve the mother of worry and increased her confidence in the consultant as a person who was willing to address the family's urgently felt needs. *The LINK*, the FDNY-CSU's monthly newsletter for bereaved families, became an invaluable and trusted source of information about current coping issues and available resources. The family consultants contributed information and articles to *The LINK* about complex topics, such as finding ways to integrate the reality of the death when no bodily remains were found.

By serving as case managers, the consultants were able to help families gain access not only to other FDNY-CSU services but also to community sources of financial advice, school-based counseling and tutoring, art therapy groups, bereavement programs, and neuropsychiatric assessments when necessary. In addition, the family consultants offered to communicate with schools and other service providers when needed. For example, one consultant attended a school meeting concerning a 6-year-old boy who became distraught by a life-sized picture of a firefighter on the classroom wall. As a result of the meeting, the teachers increased their sensitivity to the retraumatizing effects of such pictures and classroom discussions about 9/11 on bereaved students. For example, the teachers quickly learned to prepare students ahead of time about imminent discussions focused on sensitive subjects so that bereaved students could engage in other activities, such as meeting with a school counselor.

Many mothers sorely needed household help with child care and cleaning because they were overburdened with the mountains of paperwork required to obtain financing and the need to respond to well-wishers, attend memorials, and participate in a broad range of activities scheduled for bereaved families. However, if an overburdened widow hired outsiders to help with housework, she risked criticism from FDNY families who viewed the practice as a sign of negligence. If grandparents were not available for babysitting, most widows refused to have anyone else care for their children. Many couples had regarded paying for child care as unacceptable. After 9/11, widows were afraid their children would be injured or killed in an accident or they would be accused of negligence and the children would be taken away from them. For example, some mothers who hired a cleaning service asked the workers to park around the corner from the home so their neighbors would not criticize them for using these services.

Handling Child-Related Problems and Fears

The four-session assessment process, followed by feedback, proved to give the mothers a great sense of relief. For example, the results of the CBCL were informative because the mothers were able to review their children's scores regarding a broad range of behavioral symptoms. Thus, although most of their children had elevated scores on symptoms of distress, as would be expected following a devastating loss, the mothers were gratified to find that the scores fell below the borderline or clinical range. As they completed the CBCL, they were relieved by the symptoms their children did *not* exhibit and were better able to focus on behaviors that did require their attention. Another source of relief was the fact that the children who made up the control groups that provided average scores for comparative purposes had been drawn from a normal, average population of children who had not experienced the traumatic loss of a parent.

Because the children's teachers also completed the CBCL, the mothers were able to compare the teachers' assessments with their own assessments. Such comparisons helped them focus on their disciplinary practices, help their children with homework, and engage in ongoing communication with school personnel. In addition, the mothers were relieved to learn that, in general, their children's ability to control their behavior at school was a positive sign of adjustment and that their tendency to exhibit regressive behavior at home was not a negative sign. It was more likely to be an indication that the children were able to control or put aside their grief where it mattered most—at school. However, the teachers' reports also clarified the academic challenges some children were experiencing after months of preoccupation with the disaster and its aftermath.

Pervasiveness of Grief

Extremely striking was the difference in the pervasiveness of the children's grief. During the first year after 9/11, most children were able to escape from the pervasive heaviness of their grief at school or with their friends. Although they found it difficult to concentrate on their schoolwork, some children elected to go to school the day after 9/11 because contact with their friends was a distraction and provided a sense of support. Children who were younger or shy found that the special attention they received as the children of heroes, though surprising, was especially supportive.

For the mothers, on the other hand, such moments were rare or nonexistent. Toward the end of the first year, however, some found that being with other widows "who understood without having to talk about it" provided a sense of respite.

Exposure to Repeated Emotionally Intense Experiences

It was difficult for many mothers to set limits on their children's exposure to emotionally intense burials and memorials. Before 9/11, all firefighters attended the funerals of fellow firefighters who had died in the line of duty. After 9/11, widows believed it was their responsibility to fulfill their husband's obligation by attending the memorial services of the men who had been their husband's friends.

Some mothers asked their older children to attend the memorial services with them. Finding that people cared about their family and their father's friends proved to be both supportive and reassuring for some children, whereas the experience was overwhelming for other children. Most families agreed that the first-year anniversary services were able to engage a distant public but were too intense and too long for many bereaved families, especially for the children, as illustrated by the following vignette:

> One 17-year-old standing in the ceremonial line to receive her father's flag at this first-year event suddenly turned her back in anger and refused to accept it. Her mother, who was standing behind her, filled in, realizing the emotion of the moment was way too much for her daughter.

Hoping for a Miracle

Children were devastated, first by the shocking news that their father was missing, then again when they were told he had died. They continued to hope during the first year that somehow he had survived. There were many moments of hope against hope, followed by disappointment and despair. For example:

> Twelve-year-old Kenneth saw his father's car coming down the street 2 weeks after 9/11. Excited, he ran down the street with joy, only to fall to his knees in despair when he recognized that his father's best friend was driving the car home from the train station where it had been left two weeks before. "It was awful," said his mother, still reacting to the poignancy of that moment 8 months later.

Effect of the Firefighter Father's Sudden Disappearance

John had a miserable time in Little League the first summer after his dad died because baseball reminded him of all the times his dad had coached him and sat in the stands watching him play. One day, after repeatedly striking out during practice, John had a major meltdown on the field, lashed out in anger at his coach, then dissolved in tears, unable to imagine how he would ever achieve his dad's dreams for him or his own dreams without his dad's day-to-day presence.

Impact of Gruesome Details and Permanent Loss of a Family Advocate

As the following vignette illustrates, the gruesome details being discussed as part of the identification of body parts were upsetting to parents and children alike:

One mother described how, when she received a phone call from the fire department, she asked, "Is this call for business or pleasure?" Business meant they were calling because they had found an arm with a tattoo and wondered if her husband had a tattoo like that on his arm. If the purpose was pleasure, the department was calling to ask, "How are you doing?" As she said, "Those are two very different conversations, and I needed to prepare myself for one or the other."

Some children felt that their father understood them in a way that no one else in the family did. For those children, the loss was extremely traumatic:

Ten-year-old Lisa was finding it very difficult to accept that her father, her primary champion in the family, was no longer there for her. She felt overshadowed by her two older siblings, and she was struggling to discover how to shine in the family. Sitting on Dad's lap in his chair at the kitchen table, she felt he understood and valued her and she had a special place. She struggled to comprehend the meaning of body parts and dust. One day the teacher called her mother to say Lisa refused to watch a video on menstruation that was given to all 10-year-old girls. Later Lisa explained that she thought they were going to show blood and body parts in the movie, and this would remind her of what happened to her father.

Identifying Differences in the Mothers' and Children's Needs and Grief

Because of the mothers' overwhelming emotions and the many demands on them in their new role as single parents, they often found it difficult to be empathic about their children's needs. The children were so afraid of upsetting their only remaining parent even further that they were reluctant to make demands. Instead, they sometimes expressed their emotions through angry, stubborn, or regressive behavior. Discussions with mothers about understanding their children's needs and developing different ways of meeting their needs and providing an environment in which the children could express their emotions and concerns was a continuing therapeutic challenge.

As an expression of this difficulty, family members resisted family group or subgroup meetings in the first years. Pushing beyond the parent's or children's reluctance and having a meeting sometimes resulted in the families withdrawing. For the monthly interviews, each person wanted individual time in a private place, and with children that generally meant their bedrooms. Children expressed fear of saying things that would upset their distressed mothers, and mothers were afraid they would cry or say things in a family group that would upset their children even more. The very gathering of the family together as a group, especially around the kitchen table, could be a powerful reminder of who was not there. Who would sit in Dad's chair? For children, this kind of confrontation could be overwhelming.

During the first year, most of the widows became involved in using some of the donated funds to make improvements in their homes that they and their husbands had planned long before 9/11 but that generally had been put on hold for lack of funds. To the mothers, the renovations felt like a fulfillment of their husband's wishes and provided a sorely needed uplift to the family. Lisa's mother decided to replace the kitchen furniture, and later learned that Lisa was angry and upset because her mother had given away the chair she sat on with her dad. For a Christmas present, her mother tracked down the old chair through the shop that had sold it for her and put it under the tree with a ribbon on it. Lisa was thrilled.

Handling the Expected and Unexpected

Traumatized families often express a need for outreach, consistency, and a structured intervention (Dyregrov & Dyregrov, 2010). Continuous outreach to families was essential to keep them engaged. Although at times the team members felt that their phone calls and reminders amounted to "harassing" the families, most families said they usually appreciated the calls. Other families described feeling numb, disorganized, and overwhelmed because of all the demands on them and even had difficulty answering the phone for long periods.

The consultation and collaboration approach described here was the only viable one that would engage the widows, given their need to control the topics discussed, and would enable the family consultants to understand the widows' unique concerns and ways of coping. Until proved to be otherwise, the widows' coping behaviors were viewed as normative and necessary. Helping mothers and children to learn to expose themselves to intense overwhelming emotions in small doses and to develop ways to contain, compartmentalize, calm, and distract themselves was necessary to prevent them from withdrawing from the program altogether. Finally, given the families' heightened attachment fears following the firefighter's death, the team members realized the importance of being clear and consistent about appointments and of giving families direct, honest reasons for any unavoidable changes.

CONCLUSIONS AND LESSONS LEARNED

Overall, integration of the practice and research components of the family-focused intervention was mutually enhancing, although challenging to implement. The feedback and follow-up regarding the results of the standardized measures were highly valued by the mothers and led naturally to a strong therapeutic alliance; they also added a psychoeducational component to the program. Maintaining the same lead consultant for each family also facilitated continuity and engagement. However, the large geographic area in which the firefighters' families lived presented a challenge to ongoing problem solving when more intense follow-up was indicated, especially during the first year and with highly distressed families. Building in interim phone sessions as a regular part of the intervention and using more recent technological interventions, such as Skype telephone calls, should be tested to address this need in a cost- and time-effective way.

During the first year after the World Trade Center attack, dealing with the severe confluence of external stressors took precedence over pursuing indications of more intrinsically troubling components and risk factors that had the negative potential to affect families' responses to the intervention. However, we were able to address these factors in the later years of the program.

The severe emotional responses of the widows and some children 6 months after 9/11 were difficult to assess, given the horrific characteristics of the situation. Yet, in retrospect, it was clear that most of the severe responses were transient, seemed to be specific to the situation, and were responsive to the psychoeducational, cognitive, and supportive interventions used in the first year after the disaster.

The collaboration between the FDNY's Counseling Service Unit and the Columbia University Family Program not only provided the bereaved families with a secure community context but also gave the families access to a broad range of resources as well (Hobfoll et al., 2009; Lynch, 2006). It also helped both the CSU and the university program to understand the families' trajectory of recovery as a group as well as their individual needs and concerns.

In many ways, it demonstrates an ideal. We believe the project is a strong example of how public health guidelines can be used to support recovery through the building and rebuilding of trusted community contexts. It is hoped that this summary of our experiences provides encouragement and direction for other services that may be called on to provide large-scale support services for families in the wake of mass terrorism and trauma.

REFERENCES

Achenbach, T. M., & Rescorla, L. A. (2001). *Manual for the ASEBA school-age forms and profiles*. Burlington, VT: ASEBA.

Allen, J., Whittlesey, S., Pfefferbaum, B., & Ondersma, M. (1999). Community and coping of mothers and grandmothers of children killed in a human-caused disaster. *Psychiatric Annals*, *29*(2), 85–91.

American Psychiatric Association. (2000). *Diagnostic and statistical manual of mental disorders* (4th ed., text rev.). Washington, DC.

Brown, E. J., & Goodman, R. (2005). Childhood traumatic grief: An exploration of the construct in children bereaved on September 11. *Journal of Clinical Child and Adolescent Psychology*, *34*(2), 248–259.

Christ, G. (2000). *Healing children's grief: Surviving a parent's death from cancer*. New York: Oxford University Press.

Christ, G. (2006). Providing a home-based therapeutic program for widows and children. In P. Greene, D. Kane, G. Christ, S. Lynch, & M. Corrigan (Eds.), *FDNY crisis counseling: Innovative responses to 9/11 fire fighters, families and communities*. New York: Wiley.

Christ, G., Raveis, V., Siegel, K., Karus, D., & Christ, A. (2005). Evaluation of a bereavement intervention. *Social Work in End-of-Life and Palliative Care*, *1*(3), 57–81.

Cohen, J., Mannarino, A., & Deblinger, E. (2006). *Treating trauma and traumatic grief in children and adolescents*. New York: Guilford Press.

Cohen, J. A., Mannarino, A. P., Gibson, L. E., Cozza, S. J., Brymer, M. J., & Murray, L. (2006). Interventions for children and adolescents following disasters. In E. C. Ritche, P. J. Watson, & M. J. Friedman (Eds.), *Interventions following mass violence and disasters* (pp. 227–256). New York: Guilford Press.

Derogatis, L. (1993). *Brief Symptom Inventory (BSI): Administration, scoring and procedures manual* (3rd ed.). Minneapolis, MN: National Computer Systems.

Dowdney, L. (2000). Childhood bereavement following parental death. *Journal of Child Psychology & Psychiatry & Allied Disciplines*, *41*(7), 819–830.

Dyregrov, K., & Dyregrov, A. (2010). Helping the family following suicide. In B. Monroe & F. Krause (Eds.), *Brief interventions with bereaved children*. New York: Oxford University Press.

Greene, P., Kane, D., Christ, G., Lynch, S., & Corrigan, M. (2006). *FDNY crisis counseling: Innovative responses to 9/11 firefighters, families, and communities*. New York: Wiley.

Haine, R., Wolchick, S., Sandler, I., Millsap, I., Roger, E., & Tim, S. (2006). Positive parenting as a protective resource for parentally bereaved children. *Death Studies*, *30*(1), 1–28.

Herrmann, J., & Anders, P. (2006). *Disaster mental health: A critical response, a training curriculum for mental health and spiritual care professionals in healthcare settings*. Rochester, NY: University of Rochester.

Hobfoll, S. E., Watson, P., Bell, C. C., Bryant, R. A., Brymer, M. J., Friedman, M. J., et al. (2009, Spring). Five essential elements of immediate and mid-term mass trauma intervention: Empirical evidence. *Focus*, *7*, 221–242.

Horsley, H., & Patterson, T. (2006). The effects of a parent guidance intervention on communication among adolescents who have experienced the sudden death of a sibling. *American Journal of Family Therapy*, *34*(2), 119–137.

Kovacs, M. (1992). *Children's Depression Inventory: CDI manual*. North Tonawanda, NY: Multi-Health Systems.

Kwok, O., Haine, R., Sandler, I., Ayers, T., Wolchik, S., & Tein, J. (2005). Positive parenting as a mediator of the relations between parental psychological distress and mental health problems of parentally bereaved children. *Journal of Clinical Child and Adolescent Psychology*, *34*(2), 260–271.

Layne, C. M., Pynoos, R. S., Savjak, N., & Steinverg, A. M. (1998). *Grief Screening Scale*. Unpublished psychological test, University of California, Los Angeles.

Layne, C. M., Warren, J. S., Saltzman, W. R., Fulton, J. B., Steinberg, A. M., & Pynoos, R. S. (2006). Contextual influences on posttraumatic adjustment: Retraumatization and the roles of revictimization, posttraumatic adversities, and distressing reminders. In L. A. Schein, H. Spitz, G. M. Burlingame, & P. R. Muskin (Eds.), *Psychological effects of catastrophic disasters: Group approaches to treatment*. New York: Haworth Press.

Lynch, S. (2006). Understanding culture. In P. Greene, D. Kane, G. Christ, S. Lynch, & M. Corrigan (Eds.), *FDNY crisis counseling* (pp. 33–67). New York: Wiley.

Masten, A. (1999). Resilience comes of age: Reflections on the past and outlook for the next generation research. In M. Glantz & J. Johnson (Eds.), *Resilience and development* (pp. 281–296). New York: Kluwer Academic/Plenum.

Melhem, N. M., Moritz, G., Walker, M., Shear, M. K., & Brent, D. (2007). Phenomenology and correlates of complicated grief in children and adolescents. *Journal of the American Academy of Child & Adolescent Psychiatry*, *46*(4), 493–499.

Neimeyer, R. A., Burke, L., Mackay, M., & Stringer, J. (In press). Grief therapy and the reconstruction of meaning: From principles to practice. *Journal of Contemporary Psychotherapy*. doi: 10.1007/s10879-009-9135-3.

Neimeyer, R. A., Prigerson, H., & Davies, B. (2002). Mourning and meaning. *American Behavioral Scientist*, *46*(2), 235–251.

Pfeffer, C., Altemus, M., Heo, M., & Jiang, H. (2007). Salivary cortisol and psychopathology in children bereaved by the September 11, 2001 terror attacks. *Biological Psychiatry*, *61*(8), 957–965.

Pfefferbaum, B., Call, J. A., & Sconzo, G. M. (1999). Mental health services for children in the first two years after the 1995 Oklahoma City terrorist bombing. *Psychiatric Services*, *50*(7), 956–958.

Pfefferbaum, G., Sconzo, G. M., Flynn, B. W., Kearns, L. J., Doughty, D. E., & Gurwitch, R. H. (2003). Case finding and mental health services for children in the aftermath of the Oklahoma City bombing. *Journal of Behavioral Health Services and Research*, *30*(2), 215–227.

Pynoos, R. S., Steinberg, A. M., Schreiber, M. D., & Brymer, M. J. (2006). Children and families: A new framework for preparedness and response to danger, terrorism and trauma. In L. A. Schein, H. Spitz, G. M. Burlingame, & P. R. Muskin (Eds.), *Psychological effects of catastrophic disasters: group approaches to treatment*. Binghamton, NY: Haworth Press.

QSR International. (2002). *NVivo qualitative data analysis software* (Version 2). Melbourne: Author.

Raveis, V. H., Siegel, K., & Karus, D. (1999). Children's psychological distress following the death of a parent. *Journal of Youth and Adolescence*, *28*(2), 165–180.

Saldinger, A., Cain, A., & Porterfield, K. (2003). Managing traumatic stress in children anticipating parental death. *Psychiatry: Interpersonal and Biological Processes*, *66*(2), 169–181.

Saler, L., & Skolnick, N. (1992). Childhood parental death and depression in adulthood: Roles of surviving parent and family environment. *American Journal of Orthopsychiatry*, *62*(4), 504–516.

Sandler, I. N., Wolchik, S. A., & Ayers, T. S. (2008). Resilience rather than recovery: A contextual framework on adaptation following bereavement. *Death Studies*, *32*(1), 59–73.

Siegel, K., Mesagno, R., & Christ, G. (1990). A prevention program for bereaved children. *American Journal of Orthopsychiatry*, *60*(2), 168–175.

Spielberger, C., Gorsuch, R., Lushene, R., Vagg, P., & Jacobs, G. (1983). *STAI: State Trait Anxiety Inventory*. Redwood City, CA: Mind Garden.

Tremblay, G. C., & Israel, A. C. (1998). Children's adjustment to parental death. *Clinical Psychology: Science and Practice*, *5*(4), 424–438.

U.S. Department of Health and Human Services (DHHS). (2004). *Mental health response to mass violence and terrorism: A training manual.* Rockville, MD: Center for Mental Health Services, Substance Abuse and Mental Health Services Administration.

Yehuda, R. (Ed.). (1999). *Risk factors for posttraumatic stress disorder*. Washington, DC: American Psychiatric Association.

17

Is Suicide Bereavement Different?

Perspectives From Research and Practice

JOHN R. JORDAN and JOHN L. MCINTOSH

The question whether and in what manner the mode of death changes the nature of the bereavement experience has a long and sometimes contested history in thanatology, including in our area of interest, which is survivorship after the loss of a loved one to suicide. The question has important research and clinical implications. For example, if the bereavement experience of the bereaved after suicide is reliably different from that of other loss survivors, then suicide survivors may do better in support groups that are homogeneous as to cause of death, or they may require specialized types of interventions that target their unique problems. Recently, we have devoted an entire chapter to addressing this important issue in our new book on the subject of grief after suicide (Jordan & McIntosh, 2010a).[1] In the present chapter, we try to accomplish several goals. First, we briefly summarize the research literature that bears on the subject of differences between bereavement after suicide and after other modes of death, and we offer an abbreviated summary of our recent thinking about how we might resolve the many contradictory findings in the empirical literature on this matter. Second, we present a case example of the suicide of a young adult and some of the clinical work done by the first author with the deceased's father and his family. And, last, we illustrate how the research literature can inform our understanding of the experience of losing a child to suicide and the clinical work that flows from that understanding.

THE RESEARCH ON DIFFERENCES

Historically, the problems of suicide survivors have received comparatively little attention within suicidology. The first focused consideration of the sequelae of suicide was the pioneering book *Surviving Suicide*, edited by Albert Cain (1972). Although groundbreaking, the book had little research or even clinical foundation upon which to build. Over time, research evidence slowly grew, with some reviewers arguing that qualitative differences in bereavement existed between suicide and other types of death (e.g., Clark & Goldney, 2000; Ness & Pfeffer, 1990), whereas others concluded that mode of death was not the most salient dimension for bereavement differences (e.g., Cleiren, Diekstra, Kerkhof, & van der Wal, 1994).

McIntosh's (1993) analysis of primarily quantitative studies that included comparison groups led to the interpretation that suicide bereavement is generally nonpathological, and that the research evidence shows more similarities than differences between suicide survivors and the survivors of other modes of death, although some aspects of grieving may differ for suicide survivors. In contrast, Jordan's review (2001) identified specific "thematic" aspects of suicide bereavement that differentiate it sufficiently from other modes of death to warrant continued research and clinical programs for suicide survivors. These themes included a greater need to make sense of or find meaning in the loss; greater feelings of guilt, responsibility, and blame; and heightened feelings of abandonment or rejection by the deceased, often coupled with greater anger at the deceased.

In the most recent and comprehensive review of studies of suicide survivors that included a comparison group, Sveen and Walby (2008) conducted a qualitative analysis of the results of 41 quantitative studies. Their analysis categorized measured outcomes of the studies of mental health variables and grief reactions. The authors identified only a small number of studies that found differences in mental health variables, and concluded that it has not been established that there are any clear differences between suicide survivors and survivors of other modes of death on most mental health variables (i.e., overall general mental health indices, depression, suicidal ideation, symptoms of posttraumatic stress disorder [PTSD], or anxiety). The exception to this is that there is clear evidence that exposure to suicide does confer a small but nonetheless elevated risk of attempt and death by suicide in survivors (Jordan & McIntosh, 2010b).

In contrast to mental health variables, Sveen and Walby's (2008) analysis did reveal evidence for some differences between suicide survivors and other loss survivors for a limited number of grief variables. These included higher levels for suicide survivors for feelings of rejection, shame, or stigma; for concealment of the cause of the death as suicide; and for blaming with respect to the death. Also, on measures that were specific to grief after suicide, they found greater levels of grief distress in survivors. Interestingly, conclusions of no differences between suicide survivors and other causes of death were found for feelings of anger, loneliness, relief, acceptance, or shock. Ambiguous results were found for differences in the grief variables of social support, family functioning and adjustment, searching for an explanation for the death, and guilt and responsibility.

It should be noted that although many studies examined by Sveen and Walby did not observe differences on grief variables, a minority of studies did find differences between suicide survivors and others losses on many variables. Moreover, those studies that showed differences almost always found more grief distress in the suicide survivors than in the nonsuicide survivors. Virtually the only exceptions to this trend occurred when comparisons were made with survivors of accidental or homicide death—also forms of sudden and usually violent death. It is also important to note that the Sveen and Walby review considered only outcomes that were assessed using quantitative outcome measures, rather than qualitative research methods. The latter tend to show more complex and nuanced responses among suicide survivors, although they also typically lack control groups of nonsuicide survivors for comparison.

To summarize this section, although the body of current research-based evidence remains inadequate to provide definitive evidence of clear and consistent differences or unique features associated with suicide bereavement, we believe that the empirical research evidence is relatively convincing regarding a small number of reactions and aspects of bereavement after suicide. Again, Jordan (2001) has conceptualized these as prominent themes in the subjective experience of survivors. Thus, when we consider the available empirical research (quantitative and qualitative), clinical experience, and personal accounts of survivors, the following are the likely candidates as common features of suicide bereavement—that is, we believe that many (but not all) suicide survivors will manifest many (but not all) of these themes, reactions, and features in their grief reactions.

Features supported by the existing quantitative research evidence—elevated levels of the following:

- Abandonment and rejection
- Shame and stigma
- Concealment of the cause of death as suicide
- Blaming
- Increased self-destructiveness or suicidality

Features supported by qualitative studies, clinical experience, and survivors' anecdotal accounts—elevated levels of the following:

- Guilt
- Anger
- Search for an explanation or desire to understand why and "make meaning"
- Relief
- Shock and disbelief
- Family system effects, social support issues, and/or social isolation
- Activism, obsession with the phenomenon of suicide, and involvement with prevention efforts

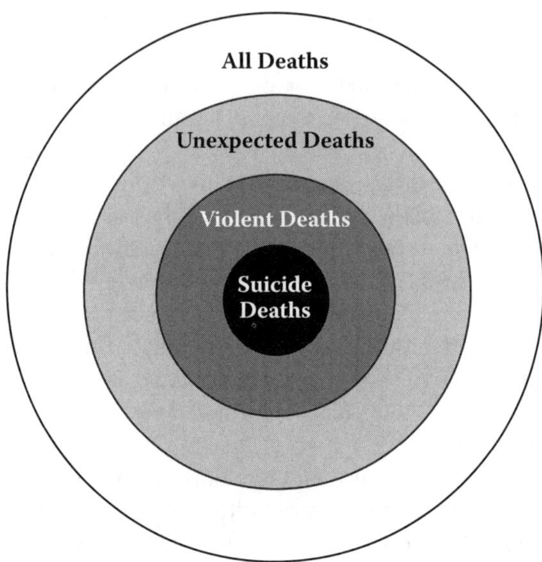

Figure 17.1 Differential response to loss and mode of death. Source: Copyright 2010 from *Grief After Suicide: Understanding the Consequences and Caring for the Survivors*, edited by John R. Jordan and John L. McIntosh. Reproduced by permission of Taylor & Francis Group, LLC, a division of Informa plc.

A Framework for Understanding the Differences

Having presented common features of suicide bereavement and current evidence regarding whether and how suicide bereavement differs from other modes of death, we now propose a framework to conceptualize the issue of differences within a broader context. As Figure 17.1 illustrates, some aspects of bereavement can be understood as nearly universal, regardless of the mode of death. For example, feelings of sorrow at the loss and the yearning to have the loved one return are extremely common in almost all bereavement situations, including, of course, after suicide (Balk, Wogrin, Thornton, & Meagher, 2007; Stroebe, Hansson, Schut, & Stroebe, 2008). We might call these the normative and universal aspects of the grief response. On the other hand, the grief responses and resulting processes associated with unexpected and sudden death—as well as with sudden, violent death—are perceived as nonnormative (i.e., not universal) in most societies. For instance, the loss of a loved one to most illnesses allows for some degree of psychological preparation or anticipatory mourning for what life will be like without the loved one. Conversely, the loss of a loved one in a sudden manner may lead to a heightened experience of shock and a sense of unreality about the loss. There is empirical support for the idea that unexpected losses tend to increase distress in mourners and may produce more complicated grieving pathways (Miyabayashi & Yasuda, 2007).

Additionally, the sudden and violent death of a loved one—whether to accident, natural disaster, homicide, or suicide—carries with it an even greater risk of a complicated bereavement trajectory and a higher potential for depression, PTSD, other anxiety symptoms, and complicated or prolonged grief disorder (Armour, 2006; Currier, Holland, Coleman, & Neimeyer, 2007; Murphy et al., 1999; Murphy, Johnson, Chung, & Beaton, 2003; Rynearson, 2006), as mourners react to the horrific nature of the dying process itself.

Of equal importance are the attributions made by the mourner about the responsibility for and preventability of a violent death that are generally not present when a loved one dies from an illness, even a sudden one. Traumatic losses appear to present a much greater challenge to the assumptive world of the survivor (Kauffman, 2002). They require considerable time and psychological effort to "make meaning" of the death or, alternatively, to come to terms with the perceived senselessness of the event (e.g., Currier et al., 2008; Currier, Holland, & Neimeyer, 2009; Holland, Currier, & Neimeyer, 2006; Neimeyer, 2005; Neimeyer, Prigerson, & Davies, 2002; Sands, Jordan, & Neimeyer, 2010; see also Chapter 1). When viewed from this more complex perspective, bereavement after a suicide can be understood as containing elements from all four types of losses represented in Figure 17.1.

We can summarize this thinking by stating that there seem to be elements of the response after unexpected deaths and after sudden violent deaths that are likely to be more or less universal, whether the cause of death is an accident, a homicide, or a suicide. When compared "head to head," these different modes of death may not typically show many unique responses for suicide survivors. Generally speaking, it appears that suicide bereavement is most different from mourning after death from natural causes; is somewhat different from other sudden, unexpected deaths; and is most similar to loss after other types of sudden and violent causes. It is also important to note that suicides are not all the same; thus, the impact on survivors is not always the same. Finally, it must be emphasized that the individual course and intensity of grief and bereavement experiences are complex and are affected by many potential variables, only one of which is the mode of death.

A CASE EXAMPLE

A 52-year-old man (Dan) sought help for himself and his family, consisting of his ex-wife (Sue) and adult son (Jeff), and stepson (Al), after the suicide of their son/brother (Tim) at college. Tim had been having difficulty adjusting academically and socially to his first year away from home. He had become involved in fairly heavy marijuana usage, and was having problems in a relationship with a girlfriend. Although Dan was in frequent contact with Tim at the start of the winter semester and knew that his son was having some difficulty, neither he nor anyone else in the family knew the extent of Tim's suicidality. Thus, family members were stunned and distraught upon hearing of Tim's suicide by hanging.

Shortly after Tim's death, Dan sought therapy for himself and his family, and was eager to have everyone receive information and support from the clinician. Thus, the initial sessions were a combination of conjoint family sessions and individual meetings with each family member. They were used to provide a forum for family members to share and compare their confused understandings about the factors that had contributed to Tim's death. The meetings also served to make available information about what to expect in the weeks and months to come, ways that family members could support one another, and concerns that family members had about the impact of the suicide on each other. Family members were particularly worried about the surviving biological brother, Jeff, because he had experienced a close but conflictual relationship with Tim and, in hindsight, probably had the most indicators that Tim was suicidal. Family members were concerned about whether Jeff might become suicidal in response to his grief and guilt over his brother's death. The initial work with the family, both conjointly and individually, included assessment about the potential suicidality of each member and contracting with the clinician to work to assure the safety of all family members. Following these initial conjoint sessions, the work consisted primarily of individual therapy sessions with Dan, and occasional individual sessions with Jeff when he was in town, as well as medication and therapy referral for Jeff to be followed individually in his home city.

In addition to the concerns over other family members, Dan struggled with many issues in his own grief. Dan had been the protector and provider for the family all of their life together, even through his divorce from the boys' mother. Therefore, he felt a great sense of failure at not foreseeing the suicide, and for not being more proactive about Tim's distress. Dan felt an intense need to make sense of what had happened, trying to puzzle together Tim's state of mind at the end of his life, reviewing his last contacts with his son in the days leading up to the suicide, and attempting to understand how his son could have chosen to end his life rather than ask for help. Dan also had a recurrent "flashback"-type experience in which, at the time and day of the week at which Tim took his life, he would find himself experiencing intense waves of grief, anxiety, and visual images of what his son might have experienced as he died. Dan was tormented with the thought that perhaps Tim had changed his mind at the last minute, but found it too late to save himself from being asphyxiated. Perhaps in contrast to this, on the night of Tim's death, Dan had an experience while drifting off to sleep of a golden cloud entering his room and surrounding his bed, and he had an extremely strong sense of the presence of his son hovering near him. Dan, who was basically agnostic about religion and the question of an afterlife, wondered often about the meaning of this experience. In the months following Tim's death, Dan also became preoccupied with and actively involved with suicide prevention efforts in the local community where Tim and Jeff had grown up. He has continued to be an activist in reaching out to other parents in the community to warn them about teenage depression, drug usage, and suicidality. Lastly, Dan simply has felt great yearning and sorrow for Tim, missing the close relationship they had and grieving intensely for the now shattered future that he had always envisioned with his sons as they matured into adult manhood.

How Is Suicide Bereavement Different?

Congruent with the literature reviewed previously, Dan shows many of the reactions of people who are bereaved by a loss to suicide (Jordan, 2008, 2009; Jordan &

McIntosh, 2010c). These include shock and horror at the manner of death, intensified guilt and responsibility for the death (particularly for a perceived failure to foresee the suicide and intervene to prevent it), and a globally anxious disorientation that is characteristic of people whose assumptive world has been shattered by a death (Currier et al., 2008; Kauffman, 2002). These characteristics reflect a combination of an intense grief response overlaid with a trauma response. They signal the profound physiological and psychic dysregulation that occur when people have experienced a massive threat to their sense of psychological safety, control, and well-being following the sudden, violent death of a loved one.

For example, even though he was not an eyewitness to his son's death, Dan was haunted by a form of traumatic reliving of the death scene that involved vicarious traumatization and reexperiencing of his son's suffering at the end of his life. This focus on the "death narrative" is a hallmark of traumatic grief and quite different from the experience of most mourners whose loved one died of less violent and more natural causes (Rynearson, 2006). Likewise, hypervigilance about the possibility of another trauma (in this case, the possible suicide of his other son and of other young people in the community) is characteristic of the trauma response in general and of traumatic grief in particular. As a third example, Dan's intense need to conduct what Jordan (2008, 2009, 2010) has called a personal psychological autopsy of the deceased, attempting to make sense of his son's state of mind and motivations for ending his life, as well as his own role in failing to foresee and prevent his son's suicide, reflects the profound challenge to the mourner's assumptive world that suicide presents (Sands et al., 2010). In a somewhat different way, Dan's experience with the "golden cloud" the night of his son's suicide is an example of the potentially transformative nature of traumatic loss. It has led Dan to reexamine his beliefs about the boundaries between life and death, and what the possibilities are for ongoing connection with the dead—issues which heretofore have had no personal relevance for Dan. All of these responses, if they are present at all after natural, nonviolent modes of death, are typically more attenuated and transitory. Some of Dan's responses, such as the focus on Tim's suffering during the dying process, are probably common to all violent modes of death. Others, such as the intense need to understand Tim's state of mind at the time of the death, are probably unique to suicide survivors. And still others, such as the search for the "whys" of life and death, and the reasons for the timing of people's exit from life, are perhaps more universal to most "off-cycle" losses such as the death of a child. These losses challenge our assumptions about the "natural order" of the universe and our assumptions about the script for our particular life trajectory.

IMPLICATIONS FOR INTERVENTION

The issues identified in Dan's grief have also required the use of interventions that are not typical for most grief-counseling situations. Dan's trauma response of shock and horror at the manner of Tim's death, and the involuntary reliving of the experience, are indicative of PTSD. As it became clear to the grief therapist and to Dan that these responses were not going to be "self-limiting" over time (as is more often the case with trauma symptoms), the therapist and Dan jointly decided to take a more proactive stance toward them, and the therapist suggested eye movement desensitization and reprocessing therapy (EMDR; see Shapiro & Forrest, 2004, for more detail on this trauma reduction technique). On his own, Dan found an EMDR therapist with considerable experience with whom he could work, and it was mutually agreed that he would see this clinician for several sessions of EMDR to work specifically on his imaginal images of Tim's death. In consultation with this EMDR practitioner, it was also agreed that the grief therapist would attend the first of those sessions to provide support and "bear witness" to the process. The EMDR therapist, Dan, and the grief therapist all agreed that what transpired was a remarkable and cathartic transformation in which Dan confronted the "demons" of his son's death, his fears about what his son endured as he died, and his own guilt about not being able to stop his son. At the end of the session, Dan remarked that he felt that he now understood that his son had actually chosen to die, and that although he still felt great sadness over the death, he no longer felt so much anguish over the way that he had died. That feeling of release has persisted to the present time, as has an absence of the weekly flashbacks of the death scene.

Second, the grief therapist has been active in encouraging Dan's attempts to make sense of and find meaning in the seeming senselessness of his son's suicide (see also Chapter 1). For example, the therapy has included considerable psychoeducational work about the complex "perfect storm" of factors that generally contribute to suicide, and how some of those factors may have been at play in Tim's situation (Jordan, 2008). Dan has worked hard to educate himself about suicide and suicide prevention, and he has become a strong activist in his community about reaching out to other parents and youth in the community, telling his story at public meetings, and helping with the organizational work of the suicide prevention coalition within his town. This has helped Dan to feel that "Tim's death was not in vain" and that he is finding some redemptive good in the death of his son, a very important healing task for many survivors of traumatic loss. The grief therapist has encouraged this involvement with the larger suicide prevention movement, and has attended several of the community events where Dan has spoken.

Third, the grief therapist has introduced a concept that Dan has found very helpful in learning to manage his sometimes overwhelming grief and trauma responses. Rooted in both trauma therapy approaches and the dual-process model of the grieving process (see Chapter 3), *dosing* involves learning skills to voluntarily move toward and away from one's grief, at points of one's own choosing (Jordan 2009, 2010). For example, the therapist has helped Dan learn distraction skills to use when he is about to go to work, or is home alone and is not wanting to think about Tim's death. These involve providing himself active permission to not think about Tim or his death without feeling guilty or disloyal, to engage in distracting activities (e.g., playing pool with friends and watching television), and to engage in activities that help to compartmentalize his feelings, such as journaling only for time-limited periods of time and then literally and symbolically "putting the grief and writing away." In contrast, Dan has also been supported in activities that psychologically move him directly "toward" his grief, even when it was difficult to do. For example, in one session Dan briefly mentioned in passing that the family home where Tim had lived most of his life was about to be sold, now that his ex-wife was moving out. Dan wanted to move on to another topic, but the therapist noted that this was probably going to be a difficult transition to make, and asked Dan to stay with the topic and describe some of his memories of the house and raising his children there, an activity that brought a flood of cathartic tears to Dan's eyes. It was followed by a suggestion that in the coming week Dan "visit" each of the rooms in the house to say goodbye before leaving the house for the last time. Dan noted afterward that both of these activities, although very difficult, also felt very meaningful to him. He observed that "learning to dose myself" (language the therapist had explicitly presented to Dan as a skill to learn) had given him a sense of control over his grieving that had allowed him to break it into bearable segments that he could address when he was ready to do so.

Last, the therapy has made room for Dan to explore the existential issues raised by the suicide of his son. These issues reflect Dan's assumptive world of meaning, his characteristic ways of making sense of his own experience, and the ways that Tim's death has challenged those assumptions. In the process, Dan has found himself rethinking his beliefs about life and death, about his purpose and role in relationship with others, and about his goals for his own life. For example, with the help of the therapeutic conversations, Dan has begun exploring the limits of his caretaking role in life, a role that had been central to both his family and work identities. The suicide of his son has been a profound confrontation with the limitations of his ability to protect and take responsibility for other people, even those in his family. Dan now wonders if people are only "on loan" to the living—here on earth for a short while until their "mission" is accomplished and it is their time to leave. This evolving frame for understanding Tim's passing puts his suicide in a perspective that is larger than just something that is a result of parental mistakes or youthful impulsivity.

The therapeutic exchange has also included a review of previous important losses in Dan's life, including the loss of his mother at an early age, and the ways that loss helped set the stage for his subsequent "caretaker" role in life with others, and the loss of his father as an adult, an important reminder of the lost future that Dan grieves with the death of Tim. As the therapy provides a unique setting for Dan to explore the larger meaning of Tim's death in terms of his own life narrative, Dan is beginning to gain a sense of perspective and a measure of acceptance about his son's suicide that was impossible in the nightmarish days and weeks immediately following Tim's death. This difficult work of meaning reconstruction (Neimeyer, 2001, 2005; see also Chapter 1) is a central part of the healing process for survivors of suicide and other traumatic losses, who find their personal world of meaning and security shattered by this most disturbing and confusing of modes of death.

CONCLUSION

Each loss and each mourner is unique. Dan shows many, but not all, of the responses that are common to suicide survivors. For example, he has experienced very little of the shame and stigma felt by many survivors. And unlike some survivors, who report that bereavement support group involvement has been literally a "life saver" for them (McMenamy, Jordan, & Mitchell, 2008), Dan's brief participation in a survivor support group has been a relatively minor component of his healing process. Looking at the particulars of Dan's mourning process, and the therapeutic approaches used with him, we can see that research plays a valuable role in informing one's understanding of his experience and the choice of interventions for him, but it cannot dictate a universal path to follow with all survivors. The work of the therapist in walking this difficult journey with Dan has at its core the art of empathic attunement to his pain, along with compassionate and collaborative problem solving with his efforts to rebuild his life (Jordan, 2010). The problems that Dan has encountered are both identified in the research on this population and yet are unique to Dan's specific personality and history, and the circumstances of his son's suicide. Thus, we believe that the art of doing skillful clinical work with survivors involves combining a broad knowledge of the research on these common problems of survivors with a deep understanding of the particular challenges faced by the individual client with whom one is working. We hope that this chapter has illustrated the balanced blend of perspectives from research and practice that, in our opinion, provides the optimal opportunity for healing for suicide survivors.

NOTE

1. Parts of this chapter are drawn from Jordan and McIntosh (2010a), with additional material added for this chapter.

REFERENCES

Armour, M. (2006). Violent death: Understanding the context of traumatic and stigmatized grief. *Journal of Human Behavior in the Social Environment*, *14*, 53–90.

Balk, D., Wogrin, C., Thornton, G., & Meagher, D. (Eds.). (2007). *Handbook of thanatology: The essential body of knowledge for the study of death, dying, and bereavement.* New York: Taylor & Francis.

Cain, A. C. (Ed.). (1972). *Survivors of suicide*. Springfield, IL: Charles C. Thomas.

Clark, S. E., & Goldney, R. D. (2000). The impact of suicide on relatives and friends. In K. Hawton & K. van Heeringen (Eds.), *The international handbook of suicide and attempted suicide* (pp. 467–484). New York: Wiley.

Cleiren, M. P. H. D., Diekstra, R. F. W., Kerkhof, A. J. F. M., & van der Wal, J. (1994). Mode of death and kinship in bereavement: Focusing on "who" rather than "how." *Crisis: The Journal of Crisis Intervention and Suicide Prevention*, *15*, 22–36.

Currier, J. M., Holland, J. M., Coleman, R. A., & Neimeyer, R. A. (2008). Bereavement following violent death: An assault on life and meaning. In R. G. Stevenson & G. R. Cox (Eds.), *Perspectives on violence and violent death* (pp. 177–202). Amityville, NY: Baywood.

Currier, J. M., Holland, J. M., & Neimeyer, R. A. (2009). Assumptive worldviews and problematic reactions to bereavement. *Journal of Loss & Trauma*, *14*, 181–195.

Holland, J. M., Currier, J. M., & Neimeyer, R. A. (2006). Meaning reconstruction in the first two years of bereavement: The role of sense-making and benefit-finding. *Omega: Journal of Death and Dying*, *53*, 175–191.

Jordan, J. R. (2001). Is suicide bereavement different? A reassessment of the literature. *Suicide and Life-Threatening Behavior, 31*, 91–102.

Jordan, J. R. (2008). Bereavement after suicide. *Psychiatric Annals, 38*(10), 679–685.

Jordan, J. R. (2009). After suicide: Clinical work with survivors. *Grief Matters: The Australian Journal of Grief and Bereavement, 12*(1), 4–9.

Jordan, J. R. (2010). Principles of grief counseling with adult survivors. In J. R. Jordan & J. L. McIntosh (Eds.), *Grief after suicide: Understanding the consequences and caring for the survivors* (pp. 179–223). New York: Routledge.

Jordan, J. R., & McIntosh, J. L. (2010a). Is suicide bereavement different? A framework for rethinking the question. In J. R. Jordan & J. L. McIntosh (Eds.), *Grief after suicide: Understanding the consequences and caring for the survivors* (pp. 19–42). New York: Routledge.

Jordan, J. R., & McIntosh, J. L. (2010b). Suicide bereavement: Why study survivors of suicide loss? In J. R. Jordan & J. L. McIntosh (Eds.), *Grief after suicide: Understanding the consequences and caring for the survivors* (pp. 3–17). New York: Routledge.

Jordan, J. R., & McIntosh, J. L. (Eds.). (2010c). *Grief after suicide: Understanding the consequences and caring for the survivors*. New York: Routledge.

Kauffman, J. (2002). *Loss of the assumptive world: A theory of traumatic loss*. New York: Brunner-Routledge.

McIntosh, J. L. (1993). Control group studies of suicide survivors: A review and critique. *Suicide and Life-Threatening Behavior, 23*, 146–161.

McMenamy, J. M., Jordan, J. R., & Mitchell, A. M. (2008). What do suicide survivors tell us they need? Results of a pilot study. *Suicide and Life-Threatening Behavior, 38*(4), 375–389.

Miyabayashi, S., & Yasuda, J. (2007). Effects of loss from suicide, accidents, acute illness and chronic illness on bereaved spouses and parents in Japan: Their general health, depressive mood, and grief reaction. *Psychiatry and Clinical Neurosciences, 61*, 502–508.

Murphy, S. A., Das Gupta, A., Cain, K. C., Johnson, L. C., Lohan, J., Wu, L., et al. (1999). Changes in parents' mental distress after the violent death of an adolescent or young adult child: A longitudinal prospective analysis. *Death Studies, 23*, 129–159.

Murphy, S. A., Johnson, L. C., Chung, I-J., & Beaton, R. D. (2003). The prevalence of PTSD following the violent death of a child and predictors of change 5 years later. *Journal of Traumatic Stress, 16*, 17–25.

Neimeyer, R. A. (2001). *Meaning reconstruction & the experience of loss*. Washington, DC: American Psychological Association.

Neimeyer, R. A. (2005). Tragedy and transformation: Meaning reconstruction in the wake of traumatic loss. In S. C. Heilman (Ed.), *Death, bereavement, and mourning* (pp. 121–134). New Brunswick, NJ: Transaction.

Neimeyer, R. A., Prigerson, H., & Davies, B. (2002). Mourning and meaning. *American Behavioral Scientist, 46*, 235–251.

Ness, D. E., & Pfeffer, C. R. (1990). Sequelae of bereavement resulting from suicide. *American Journal of Psychiatry, 147*, 279–285.

Rynearson, E. K. (Ed.). (2006). *Violent death: Resilience and intervention beyond the crisis*. New York: Taylor & Francis.

Sands, D. C., Jordan, J. R., & Neimeyer, R. A. (2010). The meanings of suicide: A narrative approach to healing. In J. R. Jordan & J. L. McIntosh (Eds.), *Grief after suicide: Understanding the consequences and caring for the survivors* (pp. 249–281). New York: Routledge.

Shapiro, F., & Forrest, M. S. (2004). *EMDR: The breakthrough therapy for overcoming anxiety, stress, and trauma*. New York: Basic.

Stroebe, M. S., Hansson, R. O., Schut, H., & Stroebe, W. (2008). *Handbook of bereavement research and practice: Advances in theory and intervention*. Washington, DC: American Psychological Association.

Sveen, C-A., & Walby, F. A. (2008). Suicide survivors' mental health and grief reactions: A systematic review of controlled studies. *Suicide and Life-Threatening Behavior*, *38*, 13–29.

18

Giving Voice to Nonfinite Loss and Grief in Bereavement

CYNTHIA L. SCHULTZ and DARCY L. HARRIS

Michael sat at his desk and read the words he had carefully typed. He could no longer live his life as a lie, and as much as he cared about the well-being of the people in the parish where he was the priest, he could no longer be a representative of a religious tradition that he now found to be oppressive and rigid to many of the individuals he cared about deeply. The change had occurred over a long period of time. He'd tried to ignore the inner discomfort at first, assuming it was just a "phase" he was going through as he reached midlife. Gradually, the discomfort turned into a painful loneliness and cynicism that robbed him of the very parts of himself that drew him to the church—compassion, a desire to serve, and a sense of divine purpose. Now, he just felt empty and tired. And he knew the cure was to leave what was once a home to him, but which now felt like a prison. From the moment this letter of resignation left his hands, his life would be forever changed … or was he already changed, and the letter just a reflection of what he had now become? He thought of his parents, and how hard this news would be for them. He wondered how he would survive financially, as a degree in theology didn't offer much for job prospects in the secular world. Many people in his parish would feel that he betrayed them, and he would be unable to explain that he felt like he was betraying them by mouthing words that were now empty to his heart. This was not how he envisioned his life to be. None of his hopes and dreams when he was younger included the possibility of losing his faith, his community, and the support of his family and friends who were all firmly rooted in the church's teachings. He wondered how God would weigh in on all of this … and yet, he wasn't even sure that he really even knew God at all now.

In this chapter, we invite our readers to reflect upon an aspect of loss that represents a departure from previous literature related to death and bereavement. We explore loss experiences that are ongoing and often intangible in their nature, with the resulting grief response that also continues in an ongoing manner. We begin this chapter by exploring the context from which the term *nonfinite loss* emerged, describing a scientifically based seeding and germination period by one of the authors, with examples and explication by both authors regarding the hallmark of nonfinite loss, which is the sense of an *ongoing presence* of the loss and accompanying grief response. A clear definition of nonfinite loss precedes a diagrammatic explication of the spectrum of loss and the place of nonfinite loss within that spectrum. Finally, we address the challenge that the concept of nonfiniteness presents for existing bereavement theory and associated clinical practice.

THE RESEARCH

One morning, over 20 years ago, I (CLS) was introduced to a doctoral candidate by the coordinator of postgraduate studies at Latrobe University in Melbourne, Australia. Elizabeth Bruce was seeking a research supervisor, and I was delighted to oblige. Joint interest in the study of the grief of parents of children with disabilities was quickly established. The insight gained from this research led to the coining of the term *nonfinite loss* to describe the loss encountered by these parents and their abiding grief. However, it soon became apparent to both of us that the nonfinite loss and grief experience applied to innumerable situations where significant loss occurs and that, in actual fact, it is an umbrella term for a whole range of loss experiences. Hence, the book published in 2001, *Nonfinite Loss and Grief: A Psychoeducational Approach*, covers all manner of loss and change in life and not only the grief of parents of children with disabilities. A follow-up book, *Through Loss* (Bruce & Schultz, 2004), is far less theoretical than the first and is designed to reach out at a basic level. Numerous publications since that time are a testimony to the realization of the goals of that partnership (e.g., Bruce & Schultz, 2001, 2002, 2004; Bruce, Schultz, & Smyrnios, 1996; Bruce, Schultz, Smyrnios, & Schultz, 1994; C. Schultz & Schultz, 1997, 1998; Schultz et al., 1993; N. Schultz & Schultz, 1997).

A related concept to nonfinite loss is that of *chronic sorrow*, a term that was first proposed by Olshansky (1962) after his observations of parents whose children were born with disabilities. He noticed that these parents experienced a unique form of grieving that never ended as their children continued to live, and the hopes that they had for these children were repeatedly dashed as time went on. Chronic sorrow may be seen as a common response to nonfinite losses, as the identifying feature is a response to a loss that has no ending, with lost hopes and dreams and ongoing uncertainty frequent companions to the loss experience. This and related concepts are discussed further by Boss, Roos, and Harris in Chapter 13 in this volume.

A CLINICIAN'S PERSPECTIVE

In my private therapy practice, I (DLH) often work with women and couples who are infertile and going through medical treatment for infertility. My background as a bereavement specialist gives me a lens whereby I see the many losses that occur as a result of going through the process of infertility treatment and involuntary childlessness; however, most of the theories of bereavement have been gleaned from working with individuals who have experienced the loss of a loved one through death. My observations of these infertile clients led to the recognition of a profoundly complex grieving experience that was ongoing in nature.

When I listen carefully to these clients, many will share about the loss of their hopes and dreams, loss of roles that are socially significant, loss of one's self, loss of how life was supposed to be, loss of control over their lives, and loss of friends and family members who have had children and moved on in their lives. Questions about their purpose in life and their identity as women in the absence of the role of motherhood frequently arise. Many of these women have always wanted children, had assumed they would have children, and did not know how to move forward in their lives if they were living without children. They frequently describe the *ongoing sense of absence of the presence* of their much wished-for children. What I have also found especially interesting is that aspects of the grief continue with these women even after they have children through success in the infertility treatments or by adoption. So, even though they become mothers through these means, their view of the world and themselves is often never the same again.

Because infertility counseling is a highly specialized area of practice, there were few clinicians to draw upon for insight into this work. I therefore went to the literature, hoping to find illumination about the ongoing aspects of the experience of infertility, and some therapeutic suggestions that would assist me to become more adept in my support of these clients. I stumbled upon the book *Nonfinite Loss* (2001) by Elizabeth Bruce and Cynthia Schultz, and I read the material with great interest. The "aha" of having someone describe in words what I saw in these clients was very affirming and provided me with additional insight into this aspect of ongoing loss with my clients. Many of these infertile women in my practice have grief experiences that are nonfinite in nature, and the ongoing adjustments and grief are both profound and pervasive in all aspects of their lives.

DEFINITION AND DESCRIPTION OF TERMS

In Figure 18.1, loss is depicted as comprising the three identified types: common, uncommon, and nonfinite. Note how the arrows trace the pathways by which the shift into nonfiniteness can occur. In drawing attention to the potential for individuals to be overwhelmed via either route, the unique effects of the experience are reiterated here.

Losses we have *in common* with most other persons are the kinds of experiences every one of us is likely to encounter. They are inseparable to growing up and growing old. They can be salutary, unremarkable, or even ultimately rewarding. For instance, a promotion may call for celebration, but in the process there may well be an element of loss and grieving for previous colleagues and relationship with the same, a customary workplace environment, and so on. Common losses can also be positive learning experiences, enabling an empathic connection with others.

Nevertheless, this common type of loss *can* leave an indelible mark that in turn slides into nonfiniteness characterized by a *continuing presence of the loss*

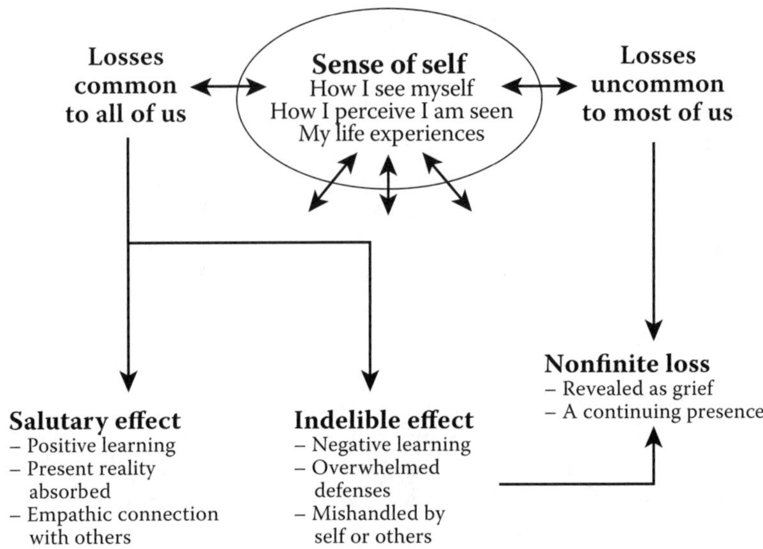

Figure 18.1 The spectrum of loss. Source: Bruce, E. J., & Schultz, C. L. (2004, p. 99). *Through loss*. Melbourne: ACER Press. Reproduced by permission of the Australian Council for Educational Research.

itself, and not simply the ongoing presence of the individual's grief. This ongoing sense of the loss is particularly poignant when one's sense of self is undermined and defenses are overwhelmed. We elucidate this concept further as we go, but consider the example of the postparental transition, also referred to as the *empty nest period* when children leave home. Mothers especially often find this to be a bittersweet time, as the normal developmental milestones are celebrated, but there is also often sadness in these transitions that is less openly acknowledged or discussed, and is thus less understood (Lewis & Gorman, 2011). For some, developmental transitions present deeply held and often silently acknowledged feelings of loss and upheaval, internally constructed demands for personal adaptation, and a recognition that life will never be the same as it has been in the past. In this example, it is known that many mothers' lives revolve around their children's lives and activities, and once these children are no longer living at home, there may be a sense of being lost, unneeded, or empty.

Uncommon losses are those not experienced by the majority of us, even though their rate of occurrence within the general population may be alarmingly high. Table 18.1 provides examples, all of which may or may not be generally recognized as loss experiences. It is important to emphasize that nonfiniteness can be the outcome of any loss experience, due either to the uncommon nature of the loss itself or to other determining factors surrounding a common loss.

Nonfinite loss is best described in terms of a *continuing presence of the loss.* This presence may be physical, psychological, emotional, or all of these, as is the case, for example, in infertility or sexual abuse. As in ambiguous loss (Boss, 2007), the loss itself may be difficult to articulate precisely because it may not involve

TABLE 18.1 Examples of Uncommon Loss

Abandonment	Injury to self, child, or significant other
Adoption; fostering	Life-threatening illness
Alcoholism; drug dependency	Lifestyle change
Chronic unemployment	Loss of childhood (e.g. caring for parents; work)
Degenerative condition in self, partner, parent, or child	Migration
Developmental anomalies	Psychiatric illness in self, partner, or child
Disability in self, partner, parent, or child	Psychic loss of father or mother
Disappearance of a loved one	Reason for being
Disfigurement	Relinquishment of a child or grandchild
Disenfranchisement	Separation or divorce affecting spouse, children, or grandparents
Dislocation; refugee status; breakdown of cultural heritage	Sexual abuse
Emotional or physical abuse	Suicide
Failure at lifelong vocation or "groomed-for" goal (e.g., ballet, gymnastics, sport, or a profession)	Untimely bereavement
Gender dysphoria or sexual identity	Victim of crime, terrorism, war, or natural disaster
Infertility; impotence	Violent death

Source: Bruce, E. J., & Schultz, C. L. (2004, p. 19). The spectrum of loss. In *Through loss*. Melbourne: ACER Press. Reproduced by permission of the Australian Council for Educational Research.

a death, or it may not be recognized by others as a loss, such as in the previous example of the postparental transition, when others are congratulating the parents and the young adult who is embarking upon a new era of life. The presence is often difficult to describe precisely and is complicated by the specific circumstances and context of the loss. For example, the mother of the young adult who leaves home for college may feel this absence as she walks past her child's room in the home, now void of the child's presence. A woman who has completed a treatment cycle for infertility may mourn the absence of a baby within her body, especially if she saw the developing embryo under a microscope just prior to it being transferred into her uterus with hopes of a pregnancy. In both of these examples, the loss is real, but it is often hidden from view and ongoing in nature, and may be experienced with overt or covert grief. However, it is always there, even if it is actually an absence of a presence—blatantly obvious or shadowy—above or just below the surface. It should be noted that loss and grief are counterparts in this continuing presence.

It may readily be stated that loss is a part of life, and that some of these experiences are simply normal developmental milestones that involve adaptation and adjustment. However, the definitive aspects of nonfinite loss and the resulting ongoing grief usually involve many of the following:

- Shattered hopes and dreams.
- The individual feels compelled to engage in a significant search for meaning.
- The loss itself gathers significance over time.

- The loss involves a significant attachment.
- The loss is ongoing in nature, with no clearly marked conclusion.

The experience of the ongoing sense of loss may also be exacerbated because the circumstances surrounding the loss result in recurrent pain, grief, or intense distress involving, for example, shame, self-consciousness, or social isolation. It may be traced to a lost sense of self, or the loss of a significant person, object, or lifestyle. This lost sense of self takes center stage in Figure 18.1. It is defined for the present purposes as an evolving and blending of life experiences with the knowing of "who I believe I am," and "how I perceive that other people see me." For further exploration and examples of nonfinite losses, the reader may be directed to material that has been recently published on this topic by Harris (2011).

In these examples of nonfinite loss and grief, it is important to note the difference between acceptance and adaptation. A loss may never be emotionally acceptable due to the deep wound created in the core of one's assumptive world when it occurs. However, inability to accept the loss does not preclude the ability to adapt to and accommodate the loss experience. In this instance, the concept of adaptation means working toward the best possible outcome, and it is incredibly hard work. Adaptation involves conquering fears and dreads, redefining or modifying hopes and dreams, and asserting control in the face of extreme difficulties and vulnerability. It also means bridging the gaps and filling the voids. Finally, adaptation means respecting the place that grief will always have as counterpart to the loss from its onset, but in which the loss itself does not necessarily have to be accepted.

THE CHALLENGE OF THE CONCEPT OF NONFINITENESS TO BEREAVEMENT THEORY AND PRACTICE

It is important to note that most bereavement theories are focused upon experiences after the death of a significant person. With the exception of the constructivist focus on the need for meaning making after the experience of significant life-altering events (see Neimeyer & Sands, Chapter 1, this volume), most theories of bereavement have not been readily applied to grief that results from a nondeath loss. However, we can extrapolate how some of these theories may be applied to nonfinite losses.

Klass, Silverman, and Nickman (1996) proposed the concept of the continuing bond with the deceased individual as a normative response to the death of a significant person. This theory is discussed in Chapter 4 of this book, but the basic implication is that grief may never really end, and that bereaved individuals frequently access their bond and associated relationship with their deceased loved ones internally. This ongoing aspect of their grief is often a conscious choice that provides comfort and reassurance. Nonfinite loss certainly implies that there is ongoing grief and adaptation to the loss that may also never really end. However, the focus in the continuing bonds theory is upon the continuation of the relationship with the deceased and the accompanying triggers of grief that may occur at specific times, and not upon the continuation of the loss experience itself.

The dual-process model of bereavement (Stroebe & Schut, 1999), which also is discussed in detail in Chapter 3 of this book, describes the unfolding of one's grief experience as an oscillation between focus upon the relationship with the deceased individual (loss orientation) with an alternate focus upon tasks of everyday life and distractions (restoration orientation). Although this model is built upon the experiences of individuals who are bereft after the death of a loved one, there are implications for how one may cope with losses that are less tangible as well. Instead of a focus upon a person or a relationship, the focus in the loss orientation may be upon the loss itself and the implications of that loss, whether it is a person, a role, an object, or some intangible aspect of one's life. This model allows for a wide range of diversity within responses to loss, including a model of coping with loss that may be compatible with nonfinite losses.

Another area of interest in regard to bereavement research and the description of nonfinite loss is related to the more recent research by Boelen and Prigerson (2007) and Prigerson et al. (2009) on prolonged grief disorder (PGD), also discussed in Chapter 12 of this book. The comparison here is relevant to the ongoing nature of the grief that is part of the definition of nonfinite loss. For example, is the long-term, ongoing experience of grief in nonfinite loss similar to what is described in the diagnostic criteria for PGD? The first criterion indicates that the event must be the death of a significant other. Thus, nonfinite losses that are intangible or non-death-related would not fit into this diagnostic category. The focus in nonfinite loss is upon the ongoing presence of the loss that requires continued adaptation and accommodation, whereas the literature that sets out the criteria for PGD focuses on the interruption in daily functioning for individuals thus diagnosed. One further distinction between these two entities is that in nonfinite losses, the loss itself may be ongoing and not a definitive event, such as what is implied in PGD.

One further theoretical comparison is to examine the constructivist view of grief as a springboard to rebuild one's assumptive world and life narrative by making meaning of what has and is occurring through the loss experience (Neimeyer, 2001). Certainly, meaning making as a form of coping with a significant loss experience that is nonfinite in nature would readily be identified in many instances. For example, in interviews with infertile women who described their experience of childlessness in ways that would be consistent with nonfinite loss, many participants cited their ability to make meaning as a comfort during a very dark and painful time in their lives (Harris, 2009).

We earlier made the comparisons of nonfinite loss to chronic sorrow and to ambiguous loss. One additional comparison to be made is with disenfranchised grief, which was developed by Doka (1989, 2002). Disenfranchised grief is described as grief that is not socially recognized or sanctioned, nor is the individual who is associated with these types of losses. Because the core of disenfranchised grief is the lack of social recognition or the stigmatization of the loss in some way, many nonfinite losses would also fall into the category of disenfranchised loss, as these losses are often not recognized because they are intangible, expected, or part of normal, anticipated developmental milestones (such as the example given with the postparental transition).

In summary, it is the *continuing presence* of the loss that is the hallmark of what is encapsulated in the term *nonfinite loss* and its underlying conceptualization. We would argue that it is imperative for those individuals who are haunted by such a presence to be assured that their ongoing grief is legitimate. Thus, the continuing element can actually be that of an absence in one form or another. The analogy of the ghost child comes to mind. What a relief, an unburdening, to know that it *is* legitimate to feel that way; that this ongoing grief is an entirely personal and unpredictable matter, and an understanding that there is no return to the world as it used to be or to the person one was before; and that closure may well be an unreasonable expectation. However, there is a realistic possibility of adaptation to the changed view of the world and self that emerges in an ongoing way. The grief response in this context will be ongoing, but it will not be abnormal because the experience of loss is ongoing as well.

COMPLICATING FEATURES

The following factors are important to consider in relation to nonfinite losses:

- There is ongoing uncertainty regarding what will happen next. This uncertainty may lead to exhaustion and "burnout" of supports that may have been available for a limited period of time.
- Nonfinite losses may be tangible or intangible.
- There is often a sense of disconnection from what is generally viewed as "normal" in human experience.
- The magnitude of the loss is frequently not acknowledged by others. There is a high likelihood that the assault on one's assumptive world that occurs as a result of the loss may not be validated, either due to the ongoing nature of the loss experience (and assumptions that the person should "move on" from the grief) or due to the intangible nature of a loss (which is difficult to quantify or validate by external sources).
- There is an ongoing sense of helplessness and powerlessness associated with the loss, which can further complicate the adaptation process.
- Nonfinite losses may be accompanied by shame, embarrassment, and self-doubt that further complicate existing relationships, thereby adding to the struggle with coping.
- There are often no rituals that assist to validate or legitimize the loss, especially if the loss was symbolic or intangible.

Jones and Beck (2007) further added to this list a sense of chronic despair and ongoing dread, as individuals try to reconcile the world that is now known through this experience and the world in the future that was hoped for prior to the realization of the loss. In short, the person who experiences nonfinite loss is repeatedly required to adjust and accommodate to the loss in an ongoing way. At the same time, because nonfinite loss is often not well understood, the experience may generally be unrecognized or acknowledged by others. Support sources may tire of attempting to provide a shoulder to lean on when there is an ongoing need for their assistance without letup, or if the person experiencing nonfinite loss is consumed by the loss experience over a long period of time.

CLINICAL RECOMMENDATIONS

Name and validate the loss(es). Validation of the experience and the perceptions of the affected individual(s) are very important so that the loss is recognized for the significance it has to the person(s) involved. There may also be "layers" of loss present as the experience takes its toll on family members physically, cognitively, behaviorally, and emotionally (Betz & Thorngren, 2006).

Normalize the ongoing nature of the loss. The inability to resolve the grief is not due to personality defects or deficiencies, but due to the situation that has been created by the loss itself.

Find supports and resources. Tapping in to groups, networks, information, and ongoing therapeutic support may be an essential component of adaptation for individuals who must live in the shadow of losses that are unending. The ability to share common experiences with others helps to normalize the person's reactions and responses in the context of what has happened instead of placing undue blame for lack of recovery on some flaw or weakness in the individual person. There is strength in finding good support and in being able to identify with the experiences of others facing nonfinite losses.

Recognize the loss(es) and identify what is not lost. It is easy to focus on the loss and how it has negatively affected the world of that individual. However, there are aspects of life and the person that have not been lost. This aspect of intervention focuses on the innate strengths of an individual that are not lost as a result of the experience. Focusing on what is still present and what has not been lost is not meant as a form of distraction or negation of the heavy toll that the loss has taken on the individual or family. Rather, the focus is upon identifying innate strengths and abilities that are apparent and that provide a foundation upon which healing can occur.

Allow for the possibility of meaning making and growth. Times of great pain and despair are also times when we identify what is most important in our lives and when we also recognize positive aspects of ourselves that we may have never known before. Although it would be highly insensitive for a therapist to ask a client in the midst of an excruciatingly painful experience about the meaning she or he has attached to that experience, clients will often reflect back upon their experiences and identify positive aspects of themselves or things they have learned from going through such an arduous event. Many clients will speak of being more sensitive to others who are facing similar losses, or of increased awareness that even when they may not be able to make sense of what has happened, they will somehow use this experience to help others or to have a view of the world that is more accommodating to a diverse range of human experiences. The concept of the "wounded healer" refers to the condition of having to tend to one's own wounds during a very painful time, and then using this experience to help others.

Initiate rituals where none exist. Rituals give symbolic meaning and validity to significant events in life. Clients may be able to identify rituals that symbolize the loss they have experienced or give validation to the importance of the experience. For example, a client in my (DLH) practice who went through several years of infertility treatment made a clay model of her uterus and then formed several small balls of clay that represented the embryos that were transferred into her body during the various infertility procedures. She initially placed each "embryo" into the clay uterus and then took each one out, one by one, and said goodbye to the children that she would never bring into the physical world with her. She then buried each of these clay balls to symbolize a funeral for them.

SUMMARY

Although nonfinite losses are certainly not new to the human condition, our attention to and better understanding of loss experiences that have an ongoing presence comprise an important addition to the current bereavement literature. Studies that explore losses that are nonfinite may yield further depth to our knowledge in this area, and we hope that research and clinical practice narratives may help to distinguish the normal ongoing grief of nonfinite loss from grief that is seen as pathological in some way. We hope to see measures emerge that are sensitive to nonfinite loss and that will provide new insights into this loss experience. Individuals who experience nonfinite losses require a great deal of ongoing support to manage the uncertainty, social stigma, and layers of loss that accompany this experience. We hope that this chapter can be a start for further dialogue and exploration of this topic.

ACKNOWLEDGMENT

The authors wish to dedicate this chapter to the memory of Dr. Elizabeth Bruce, whose groundbreaking research and extensive experience as a clinician led to the development of the term *nonfinite loss and grief*.

REFERENCES

Betz, G., & Thorngren, J. M. (2006). Ambiguous loss and the family grieving process. *The Family Journal: Counseling and Therapy for Couples and Families*, *14*(4), 359–365.

Boelen, P., & Prigerson, H. (2007). The influence of symptoms of prolonged grief disorder, depression, and anxiety on quality of life among bereaved adults. *European Archives of Clinical Psychiatry and Clinical Neuroscience*, *257*, 444–452.

Boss, P. (2007). Ambiguous loss: challenges for scholars and practitioners. *Family Relations*, *56*(2), 105–110.

Bruce, E. J., & Schultz, C. L. (2001). *Nonfinite loss and grief: A psychoeducational approach*. Baltimore: Paul H. Brooks.

Bruce, E. J., & Schultz, C. L. (2002).Nonfinite loss and challenges to communication between parents and professionals. *British Journal of Special Education*, *29*(1), 9–13.

Bruce, E. J., & Schultz, C. (2004). *Through loss*. Melbourne: ACER Press.

Bruce, E. J., Schultz, C. L., & Smyrnios, K. X. (1996). A longitudinal study of the grief of mothers and fathers of children with intellectual disability. *British Journal of Medical Psychology*, *69*, 33–45.

Bruce, E. J., Schultz, C. L., Smyrnios, K. X., & Schultz, N. C. (1994). Grieving related to development: A preliminary comparison of three age cohorts of parents of children with intellectual disabilities. *British Journal of Medical Psychology*, *67*, 37–52.

Doka, K. J. (1989). *Disenfranchised grief: Recognizing hidden sorrow*. Lexington, MA: Lexington.

Doka, K. J. (2002). *Disenfranchised grief: New directions, challenges, and strategies for practice*. Champaign, IL: Research Press.

Harris, D. (2009). *The experience of spontaneous pregnancy loss in infertile women who have conceived with the assistance of medical intervention* (UMI No. 3351170). Ann Arbor, MI: Proquest Digital Dissertations.

Harris, D. (2011). *Counting our losses: Reflecting on change, loss, and transition in everyday life*. New York: Routledge.

Jones, S. J., & Beck, E. (2007). Disenfranchised grief and non-finite loss as experienced by the families of death row inmates. *Omega*, *54*(4), 281–299.

Klass, D., Silverman, P., & Nickman, C. (1996). *Continuing bonds*. New York: Basic.

Lewis, L., & Gorman, E. (2011). Loss related to developmental milestones: An analysis of the post parental transition. In D. Harris (Ed.), *Counting our losses: Reflecting upon change, loss, and transition in everyday life*. New York: Routledge.

Neimeyer, R. (2001). The language of loss: Grief therapy as a process of meaning reconstruction. In R. A. Neimeyer (Ed.), *Meaning reconstruction & the experience of loss* (pp. 261–292). Washington, DC: American Psychiatric Association.

Olshansky, S. (1962). Chronic sorrow: A response to having a mentally defective child. *Social Casework*, *43*(4), 190–192.

Prigerson, H., Horowitz, M., Jacobs, S., Parkes, C., Aslan, M., Goodkin, K., et al. (2009). Prolonged grief disorder: Empiric validation of criteria proposed for the DSM-V and the ICD-11. *PLOS Medicine*, *6*(8), Retrieved from http://www.ncbi.nlm.nih.gov/pmc/articles/PMC2711304/pdf/pmed.1000121.pdf/?tool=pmcentrez

Schultz, C. L., & Schultz, N. C. (1997). *Care for caring parents*. Melbourne: ACER Press.

Schultz, C. L., & Schultz, N. C. (1998). *The caregiving years*. Melbourne: ACER Press.

Schultz, C. L., Schultz, N. C., Bruce, E. J., Smyrnios, K. X., Carey, L., & Carey, C. (1993). Psychoeducational support for parents of children with intellectual disability: An outcome study. *International Journal of Disability, Development and Education*, *40*, 205–216.

Schultz, N. C., & Schultz, C. L. (1997). *Care for caring parents: Leader's manual*. Melbourne: ACER Press.

Stroebe, M., & Schut, H. (1999). The dual process model of coping with bereavement: Rationale and description. *Death Studies*, *23*, 197–224.

Section IV

Specific Populations

19

Grief in GLBT Populations
Focus on Gay and Lesbian Youth

LINDA GOLDMAN and VINCENT M. LIVOTI

The researcher–practitioner dialogue within this chapter explicates the sociocultural underpinnings of bereavement, depression, and suicide in gay and lesbian youth populations. Through an examination of both the causal factors and the subsequent therapeutic responses, we will explain how the "coming-out" experience for many gay and lesbian youth is both a literal and symbolic grieving process largely established and reinforced through the mechanisms of contemporary Western media. This dialogue will conclude with approaches to personal empowerment and counseling for gay and lesbian young people as they strive to positively embrace their identity.

As a caveat, the chapter will focus exclusively on the developmental experience of gay and lesbian and questioning youth in the United States and Canada. Though social stigma is present across Westernized cultures, and the issue of homosexuality continues to be a matter of life and death in some parts of the world,[1] the writers' experiences and research foci center primarily on the psychosocial dynamics of homosexuality in these two countries. Although the grief issues facing transgendered, intersexed, and bisexual youth are equally as important, the writers are conscious that treatment of those diverse perspectives from this standpoint would be projective at best.

GRIEF AMONG GAY AND LESBIAN YOUTH: STATISTICAL ANALYSIS AND MEDIA EXPLICATION

Although perspectives on grief and grieving processes are typically explored from a psychological lens, there are many sociocultural factors contributing to the perception, framing, and understanding of grief. Amongst gay and lesbian youth, grief is a socially directed issue because the cyclical outcomes of social rejection, born and reinforced from cultural constructions, create the very climate that leads to and perpetuates the alienation, depression, and violence that have often, unfortunately, become associated with the gay and lesbian identity.

GLSEN's (Gay, Lesbian, and Straight Educators' Network) 2007 *School Climate Survey* polled 6,209 middle and high schoolers. The findings showed that 9 out of 10 gay and lesbian students experienced harassment at school, three fifths felt unsafe at school because of their sexual orientation, about a third skipped a day of school in the past month because of feeling unsafe, more than 73% heard derogatory remarks such as *faggot* or *dyke* frequently at school, over 86% reported being verbally harassed, over 44% reported being physically harassed, and over 22% reported being physically assaulted at school in the past year (p. 2). This troubling paradigm spurs two separate, but interrelated, manifestations within the demographic group: depression and suicide (including tendencies, ideation, and attempts).

Meyer's (2003) meta-analysis determined that the likelihood of mood and anxiety disorder was twice as high for lesbians and gays than for their heterosexual counterparts (p. 689). In tandem with these findings, Hershberger, D'Augelli, and Pilkington's (2002) study of 350 gay and lesbian students in the United States and Canada determined that 42% of gay and lesbian youth had suicidal ideation, and an additional 33% reported at least one suicide attempt (p. 365). These circumstances characteristically followed an awareness of same-sex feelings and preceded disclosure of sexual orientation. A follow-up study by the same team showed that the earlier these students identified their sexual orientation, the more they were victimized (Hershberger, Pilkington, and D'Augelli, 2002). Conversely, GLSEN (2007) reports that students in schools with a gay–straight alliance report decreases in homophobic remarks, harassment, and assault (GLSEN, 2007, p. 8). Although there is a valid preoccupation with bullying and bullying prevention, particularly at school and in social media interaction, there has been limited focus on the documented difficulties confronting gay and lesbian youth—who may face potential prejudice not only in school, but also at home and within their respective religious communities: "adjustment problems for gay youth emerge from the interpersonal stressors associated with coping with sexual orientation in society, rather than being a characteristic of gay, lesbian, and bisexual identities" (Feldman, 2001, p. 1). Moreover, research conducted by the Gay and Lesbian Taskforce suggests that between 320,000 to 640,000 of America's 1.6 million homeless youth are gay, lesbian or questioning (Ray et al., 2006, p. 2). This indicates that a significant proportion of homeless youth are without familial or community support because of their sexuality.

Collectively, these aforementioned circumstances are too often correlated to the societal consequences of nonnormative expressions of identity: "Blaming the child for their failure to adapt to traditional gender norms is easy.... [These] behaviors are often taken as further evidence that something is wrong with the child, rather than a normal response to attempting to accommodate oneself to a hostile environment" (Mallon & De Crescenzo, 2006, p. 219).

Although the aforementioned statistics indicate a pervasive social concern for today's homosexual youth and their allies, it is equally important to note that this issue impacts us all. It connotes a cultural practice of ostracism for any child who does not fit into the limiting boundaries of Western norms—norms that are ubiquitously presented as objective reality. Every person, and therefore every child, deserves access to safe public expression and models of behavior that mirror their lived experiences. Lacking such models, individuals are left to absorb the skewed depictions and reactions that do exist. In therapeutic contexts, this transaction is classified as *internalized homophobia*, wherein members of the gay and lesbian community ingratiate and embrace the very biases that debase them (Russell & Bohan, 2006, p. 344). The primary delivery system for this inaccurate worldview is mass media.[2] The imagery presented in books, as well as in film and television, will be the basis of our applied analysis. A sampling of these representations and the power structures that drive them will be explored through the lens of *symbolic annihilation*.

Initially developed by Gerbner and Gross, *symbolic annihilation* is a conceptual framework highlighting the underrepresentation of sexual minorities in media (Means Coleman & Yochim, 2008, p. 4922). It decodes the way media treatment contributes to social disempowerment and how "symbolic absence in the media can erase groups and individuals from public consciousness" (Means Coleman & Yochim, 2008, p. 4922). Tuchman later modified the theory by establishing three distinct applications for cultural scripting: symbolic omission, symbolic condemnation, and symbolic trivialization (Means Coleman & Yochim, 2008, p. 4922). Given the burgeoning formation of a homosexual text in mainstream cultural perception, trivialization and condemnation as forms of annihilation are particularly applicable. Richard Dyer (2002) asserted that "representations here and now have real consequences for real people, not just in the way they are treated … but in terms of the way representations delimit and enable what people can be in any given society" (p. 10). The social vilification of homosexuals greatly impacts personal and societal perception.

Developing qualitative and neurobiological research illustrates that the formation and recognition of sexual identity begin earlier than traditionally thought. In 2005, neuroendocrinologists uncovered the trigger for puberty: the KiSS-1 gene, which initiates a chemical onset as early as age 8 (Kaufman, 2007, p. 511). Social scientists also confirm that gender identity, a construction influenced by sociological and biological factors, becomes emergent in human beings by the age of 3 (Fausto-Sterling, 1999, p. 52). Especially in the context of these considerations, there is a dearth of factual, humanizing representations in media regarding identity for this population, and many of the resources established for children about gays and lesbians are censored.

Multicultural theorists claim that children's media should "be transformative, or life—and culture—affirming. As a result, it must act as both mirror—allowing students to reflect on their own experiences—and as window, providing the opportunity to view the experiences of others" (Glazier & Seo, 2005, p. 688). Although there is a clear warrant here for the inclusion of homosexual culture under the umbrella of multiculturalism, integration has been slow coming.

The Office of Intellectual Freedom at the American Library Association (2010) has compiled statistics on banned and challenged[3] books since 1980. Between 2001 and 2008, sexually explicit, homosexual, or "anti-family" content motivated nearly 1,600 challenges (American Library Association, 2010). Within this context, it is unsurprising that children's picture books offering affirming portrayals of gay families, such as *And Tango Makes Three* and *Heather Has Two Mommies*, have dominated the list since its inception.

In 2005, U.S. Secretary of Education Margaret Spellings denounced an episode from the popular children's program *Postcards From Buster*, causing PBS to pull the episode "Sugartime" from its 350 affiliates (Gaffney, 2006). The show was largely funded by a $5 million grant from the Department of Education's *Ready to Learn* program. The episode followed the life of a Vermont girl who collects maple sugar with her same-sex parents. As a direct result of Spellings's objections, the federal grantor withdrew funding and rewrote its criteria—ultimately eliminating its central goal of representing cultural diversity (Gaffney, 2006). Neither the Corporation for Public Broadcasting (which is regulated by the U.S. Congress) nor any of the mainstay corporate sponsors of children's programming at PBS would underwrite the episode. WGBH-TV, Boston's PBS affiliate, broke from national offices by distributing the episode on its own (Gaffney, 2006).

In depriving developmental youth of resources with affirming portrayals reflecting their reality, our gay and lesbian family members, neighbors, civic leaders, and friends become invisible. For homosexual children and their allies, nearly all the windows have been bricked up, and the mirrors have been broken. This pattern of fragmentation—in schools, in media, and, worst of all, at home—establishes a cycle that perpetuates into adolescence and on through to adulthood for too many. Although conventional wisdom continues to falsely suggest that children have no sexual identity, an early interventionist approach is arguably needed to curb pervasive sociocultural prejudices before they (internally and externally) become manifest.

In media created for teenage audiences, we see an explosion of "coming-out" narratives both textually and visually. In many instances, these stories arrive too late. Unlike children, teenagers are given more entrée to communicate the disjunctions they have been conditioned to feel about their sexual identities. The experience of embracing one's sexuality, although unique for each individual, can be a process of grief and a process of transcendence. Although the sociocultural undergirding of gay and lesbian disenfranchisement (and the alienation it perpetuates) is a well-worn trope in American culture, there are limited models for empowerment.

The majority of developmental youth who have been denied positive or realistic representations of behavior for their entire lives, and otherwise inundated with two-dimensional stereotypes, are left to blindly sort the claiming of personal identity without constructive charters. Even formalized approaches to the experience of coming out have been systematized to prepare the individual for feelings of anger, bereavement, rejection, and self-loathing (Grov, Bimbi, Nanin, & Parsons, 2006). Before youth can grow beyond the recognition of a sexual identity, they must first process the grief of annihilation. Recent mass market publications like Brent Hartinger's *Geography Club* (2003) reinforce themes of stigmatization. Stigmatization then becomes a signifying trait for the homosexual experience. Protagonist Russell Middlebrook confides,

> The fact that I even thought about getting naked with a guy in a sexual way was something that Kevin and Leon and Brad and Ramone would never understand.... I wasn't the most popular.... But one *sure* way to become unpopular was to have people think you might be gay.... I wasn't one of them, I didn't fit in, but they didn't need to know that.... I desperately wanted to be somewhere where I could be honest about who I was. (Hartinger, 2003, pp. 3–11)

Despite being credited as a progressive GLBT ethnography for teens, the message here is clear: Sexual shame should be not only tolerated but also expected. This is a dangerous cultural construction, particularly when the narrative is contextualized within the realm of related statistical analysis. With the exception of character arcs like the one written for Justin Suarez on ABC's *Ugly Betty* (2006–2010), there remains a sensibility in teen-centered coming-out stories that has not left popularized culture since the after-school specials of the 1980s.

In 2010, homosexual youth continue to be overwhelmingly characterized as outsiders of culture, rather than proponents of culture. Mentally, socially, and emotionally, gays and lesbians are saliently presented as tragic heroes, with a flamboyantly tragic flaw. Even the critically lauded and wildly popular teen melodrama *Glee*, which (in addition to several industry nods) received both a Peabody Award and a GLAAD (Gay and Lesbians Alliance Against Defamation) Media Award (IMBD.com, 2010), has sustained this worldview through the tribulations of its Emmy-nominated, tragic gay character Kurt. Kurt, a male soprano who kicks for the football team (while shimmying to Beyonce's *Single Ladies*) and eventually becomes the school's only male cheerleader, is constantly harassed and bullied without consequence or adult intervention. Though the creator himself is gay, he chose to fashion Kurt in a dull pastiche of traditional identity norms.

At the end of season 1, Kurt takes on the mantle of predatory manipulator. He contrives a relationship between his widower father and a heterosexual love interest's widowed mother in the hopes that the two boys will have to share a bedroom. The results are calamitous, and Kurt's father paternally bonds to Kurt's target of infatuation—effectively removing Kurt from their interactions. Amid dating chatter and sports on television, the audience sees Kurt watching the pair through a living room window. In true melodramatic fashion, it is pouring outside and a drenched Kurt is crying.

Although Kurt's father evidently loves and supports his son (a brief departure from the archetype of the withholding parent), the grief Kurt expresses as a direct result of his nonnormative lifestyle is palpable. The coding of behaviors and behavioral consequences is underscored: not only is Kurt literally an outsider, but also he is mentally compromised, emotionally unstable, and morally conniving. Though it could be argued that the show's entire cast is at one time or another manipulative, Kurt's portrayal is connected to a tradition of pervasive one-dimensional characterization. Although other characters, such as differently abled Artie Abrams, present a contemporary reframing of a historically marginalized population within media, the cultural script for Kurt is, sadly, nothing new. In 2010, *Glee* averaged 9.77 million viewers each week—the most devoted of which refer to themselves as *gleeks* (see IMBD.com, 2010). When considering its live tours, downloadable songs, and extensive merchandising, the show has tremendous social influence yet does nothing to drive the consciousness of teen sexuality in mainstream perception forward. As a model, Kurt has the potential to leave many young homosexuals out in the rain.

As with recent cinematic portrayals of the gay and lesbian life for adults, *Glee* sugarcoats the poison pill. With commercially and critically successful films like *Boys Don't Cry* (1999), *The Hours* (2002), *Monster* (2003), *Brokeback Mountain* (2005), *Milk* (2008), and even *A Single Man* (2010), we see more of the same sociocultural coding. These purportedly sympathetic and humanizing depictions of the homosexual experience only continue the long-standing tradition of equating sexuality with mental illness, social rejection, personal tragedy, and moral deviance, as first explicated by Vitto Russo in *Celluloid Closet: Homosexuality in the Movies* (1987).

Although not the entire story, there appears to be a cyclical pattern of omission, condemnation, and trivialization of gay people at every developmental stage of existence, both close to home and in the popular imagination. The questions remain, "What can be done to reclaim personal truth for homosexual youth and their families?" And "How can the grievous process of annihilation and tumult of personal discovery become an agent for change through counseling approaches to intervention, affirmation, and empowerment?"

COUNSELING APPROACHES TO INTERVENTION, AFFIRMATION, AND EMPOWERMENT

Now that a basic understanding of the social issues faced by gay and lesbian youth has been codified and the sociocultural framing of this population in media depictions has been explicated, a series of directives can be set forth that strive to make the therapeutic environment a productive oasis of safety. Grieving the loss of an idealized self, family, and future is a central aspect in the counseling of homosexual adolescents. Teens may grieve the loss of being a part of a heteronormative social structure. Although some may feel relieved to abandon the charade, most may grieve the relationships they thought they had with friends and loved ones. Many are equally saddened by the limitations or the lack of unitive rights afforded to GLBT families.

A therapeutic environment must incorporate knowledge of the loss of the idealized self and future, the internalization of homophobia, the complex minority struggles, and the inherent possibilities of depression, high-risk behaviors, suicide ideation, and suicide attempts. The counselor can best serve the homosexual adolescent by helping to separate stereotyping from self-identity, providing fact-based information, offering resources and mentorship, and allowing expression of all feelings and thoughts without judgment.

The following goals, adapted from *Coming Out, Coming In: Nurturing the Well-Being and Inclusion of Gay Youth in Mainstream Society* (Goldman, 2007), create a framework for deepening the therapeutic relationship. They (a) emphasize that stereotypical prejudice is a function of society and not the individual, (b) stress the importance of helping lesbian and gay adolescents process thoughts and feelings about gender identity and sexual orientation, and (c) require the creation of safety in the homes, schools, and communities for these young people. The foundation of all counseling is the principle that every individual is entitled to equal rights, privileges, and respect.

Goal 1 is the recognition that this is a societal problem, an imposed prison of bigotry that is manifested by the injustice of not seeing gay and lesbian adolescents or their families as typical people who should be respected as human beings for their ability to love. Enhancing self-image is possible when young people begin to separate stereotyping from self-identity. Clearly the first step in self-acceptance is developing a positive inner stance against the backdrop of social contradiction.

In the continuously evolving development of self-acceptance, gay and lesbian teens can demonstrate positive behaviors and actions in society. This expressive exhibition of accomplishment reinforces self-empowerment on many levels. These levels include forming new friendships, creating deep community bonds, and gaining a sense of partnership with "a larger whole" working toward a common cause. An important piece of the counseling process is blending the cultural and political constructs.

It is also essential to support the innate spiritual belief system of the individual and provide welcoming spiritual communities to aid in resolving religious conflict. The following is an example of this religious conflict shared by a young woman in clinical practice. Doris, a 17-year-old teen, explained her deepest fear after coming out: "I wasn't scared that people would hate me; I was scared God would hate me." She struggled with the messages from a strong fundamentalist background. Her parents rejected Doris after she disclosed her sexuality. Through supporting her innate spiritual belief system, she reframed her concept of God as one of a purely loving and accepting being. Internalizing this image of God, she experienced more self-love and acceptance. Through exploring the support of her extended family of friends, Doris began to realize that she was not alone in the world. Although saddened by the estrangement, she even began to have compassion for her family's difficulty in accepting her. Her parents' rejection was a function of their homophobia and fear.

Doris also missed her spiritual community and began investigating welcoming religious affiliates for gay and lesbian youth. Attending services and volunteering at a nearby religious youth group led by a gay male clergy with both lesbian and gay and straight membership were affirming. A new sense of community and spirituality surfaced as Doris was able to create another piece of a larger extended family. Research from Caitlin Ryan and her team at the Family Acceptance Project has documented the role of religion and other key issues in the family life of LGB youth. More than 100 specific behaviors that parents and caregivers use to express acceptance and rejection of their LGBT adolescents have been identified and linked to health and mental health concerns of young people (http://familyproject.sfsu.edu/publications).

Goal 2 is to help gay and lesbian youth process the myriad feelings that can come with the recognition of their gender identity or sexual orientation. By creating methods that provide a safe passage for them to "come out," they can share themselves in the most protected way. "Parental responses to a child's disclosure as gay or lesbian can range along a continuum from complete rejection to extreme activism. Points on this continuum vary, grow and evolve as the nature of the relationship and deeper understandings emerge" (Goldman, 2008, p. 23).

All too often, a parent's initial reaction can lead to the loss of a relationship. Amelia was extremely close with her mom. She grew up thinking she was different but could never find the words to explain her feelings. When she finally could articulate her attraction to other females, she was excited to share this discovery with her mother. To her astonishment and devastation, her mom was enraged and angry. They became distant from that point on, and the loss of Amelia's idealized mother created deep wounds and intense suffering.

Brian confided to his older sister, Amy, that he was gay as they were driving home from dinner. He asked Amy to tell his parents, and if they were "OK" with that, to light the porch light as a signal. Brian drove around the block many times and finally called his sister. Amy explained, "Mom and Dad are doing something. It will take a few more minutes." Brian's mother and father decided to go to every room in the house, from the third floor to the basement, and light each light, so that their son would know how very much they embraced him in every way.

Counseling support for parents can help with processing new and complex feelings and free hidden prejudice and misconceptions. Findings from the Family Acceptance Project (2010) underscore LGB young adults who report high levels of specific family rejection behaviors during adolescence (such as blocking access to a gay friend or LGBT resource, or telling a child that you are ashamed because of the child's gay or lesbian identity) have poorer health than peers from families that are not rejecting (Ryan, Huebner, Diaz, & Sanchez, 2009).

Goal 3 is to establish safe homes, schools, and communities. This offers the GLBT youth all the rights, privileges, and respect afforded to any other adolescent group.

An important intervention to enhance self-esteem and create resilience is active engagement in activities promoting education, demonstrating advocacy, and protecting civil liberties.

Michael, a college freshman, felt disconnected from his parents. His father was enraged and he would not go to therapy to help Michael "change his mind about being gay." Michael began to find other young people who did understand him through becoming more politically active by joining clubs on campus and national organizations that supported GLBT students. He actively participated in promoting movements that curbed sexual harassment and promoted marriage equality: "I felt inspired to be a part of a cause I could put energy into and believe in."

Michael had become proactive. When GLBT youth feel their voice is heard within school systems, communities, religious affiliations, and political venues, they are able to incorporate self-expression as a viable means to create change.

COUNSELING TECHNIQUES

The following techniques are suggestions for helping professionals build a positive therapeutic framework for the personal empowerment of gay and lesbian youth; they are also adapted from *Coming Out, Coming In: Nurturing the Well Being and Inclusion of Gay Youth in Mainstream Society* (Goldman, 2007). They incorporate providing accurate information, creating support systems, enhancing client self-esteem. All techniques emphasize separating external homophobic assumptions from the client's inner identity. These interventions can be understood in terms of practitioner accountability, communication strategies, and broad self-concept exploration.

Practitioner Accountability

1. Actively gain knowledge and education about LGB issues from informed LGB youth and adults and their allies.
2. Use the terms *lesbian*, *gay*, *bisexual*, *intersexed*, and *transgendered* positively in general conversation.
3. Do not assume fixed sexual or gender identities in your clients.
4. Explore your comfort with your own sexuality as well as any internalized homophobic judgments or prejudices that you may have.
5. Identify and challenge negative and dehumanizing stereotypes about LGB people in conversational English, and create language that welcomes open discussion.
6. Become aware of the many issues involving gay youth, and the tremendous amount of energy these young people expel in dealing with coming out, dating, partnering, discrimination, and acceptance.

Communication Strategies

1. Allow gay or lesbian youth to take the lead on the issues they need to deal with, and resist projecting your own values or "quick fixes" in a patronizing or overly inquisitive style.
2. Communicate an atmosphere of acceptance and respect that encourages spontaneous expression of many repressed, denied, or uncomfortable feelings and thoughts.
3. Offer community supports and resources for the client as well as his or her family to create a network of support, understanding, and normalization.
4. Maintain an environment that includes language conducive to sharing sexuality. Asking whether the person is dating allows for an open-ended response. Johnson and Johnson (2000, p. 632) suggested that "even small things, such as inquiring whether the client has a partner rather than a boyfriend or a girlfriend, can indicate it is safe to open up about oneself."
5. Provide information and resources on prominent LGBT role models.

Broad Self-Concept Exploration

1. Provide affirming narrative devices, including role-play and storytelling.
2. Remember that all youth have issues appropriate to their developmental age. Everyday problems may be those naturally attributed to young people and may not necessarily be exclusively "gay" concerns.
3. Neutrally educate youth on the cautions, preventions of safe, and responsible sex practices in both physical and virtual environments.

Society can no longer continue to maintain the burden of *compulsory heterosexuality* in our homes, schools, communities, or media. North America is making strides in amalgamating the concepts of a humanity that expresses a wide continuum of gender identities and sexual orientations, yet the structuring of prejudicial stereotyping for our lesbian and gay youth still perpetuates the internalization of culturally sanctioned homophobia. As a result, this population is too often forced outside the parochial borders of the "acceptable mainstream."

Understanding the basic nature of adolescence is inherent to understanding the challenges faced by our gay and lesbian children. Teenage years are a time when peer support is paramount. Sustained sexual harassment and homophobic slurs hinder evolving self-identity. This becomes increasingly difficult for a gay or lesbian youth as he or she struggles with sexual orientation in the midst of pervasive vilification of natural sexual expressions. Living in fear about one's sexuality in an exclusionary world with few affirming guideposts causes too many young people to hide and distort essential pieces of themselves.

Similarly, the already bewildering task of preparing for a committed future is thwarted by constraining gender norms and volatile legalities. The acceptance of same-sex partnership, marriage equality, and a nonprejudicial worldview (as it relates to personal expression) is still too limited. By-products of internalizing sociocultural judgment include the inability to visualize a comfortable future and an increased likelihood of rejection from family and peers, both of which can demonstrably lead lesbian and gay youth into feelings of grief, depression, and suicide. Fortunately, these detrimental paradigms can be substantively curbed when practitioners and researchers collaborate to positively impact the framing of representation and the fostering of personal empowerment for our at-risk children.

NOTES

1. Homosexuality is currently illegal and punishable by jail and, in some cases, torture and death in Afghanistan, Algeria, Antigua and Barbuda, Bangladesh, Barbados, Belize, Bhutan, Botswana, Brunei, Burundi, Cameroon, Comoros, Cook Islands, Dominica, Eritrea, Gambia, Ghana, Guinea, Guyana, Grenada, Iran, Jamaica, Kenya, Kiribati, Kuwait, Lebanon, Lesotho, Liberia, Libya, Malawi, Malaysia, Maldives, Mauritania, Mauritius, Morocco, Myanmar, Namibia, Nauru, Nigeria, Oman, Pakistan, Palau, Palestinian Territories, Papua New Guinea, Qatar, Saint Kitts and Nevis, Saint Vincent, Samoa, Sao Tome, Saudi Arabia, Senegal, Seychelles, Sierra Leone, Singapore, Solomon Islands, Somalia, Sri Lanka, Sudan, Swaziland, Syria, Tanzania, Togo, Tonga, Trinidad and Tobago, Tunisia, Turkmenistan, Tuvalu, Uganda, United Arab Emirates, Uzbekistan, Yemen, Zambia, and Zimbabwe.
2. For the purposes of this dialogue, the term *mass media* encompasses any nonrhizomic product created by, and disseminated to, a culture.
3. A *challenge* is an attempt to remove or restrict materials, based upon the objections of a person or group. A *banning* is the removal of those materials.

REFERENCES

American Library Association. (2010, August 1). Banned and challenged books. Office of Intellectual Freedom, ALA.com. Retrieved from http://www.ala.org/ala/issuesadvocacy/banned/index.cfm

D'Augelli, A. R., Pilkington, N. W., & Hershberger, S. L. (2002). Incidence and mental health impact of sexual orientation victimization of lesbian, gay and bisexual youths in high school. *School Psychology Bulletin*, *17*, 148–167.

Dyer, R. (2002). *The matter of images: Essays on representation*. New York: Routledge.

Family Acceptance Project. (2010). *Marian Wright Edelman Institute (MWEI)*. Retrieved from http://www.familyproject.sfsu.edu

Fausto-Sterling, A. (1999). Is gender essential? In M. Rottneck (Ed.), *Sissies and tomboys: Gender nonconformity and homosexual childhood* (pp. 52–57). New York: New York University Press.

Feldman, M. J. (2001). *Fact sheet on suicidal behavior in GLB youth*. San Francisco: AGLP.

Gaffney, D. (2006, December 16). Censored PBS bunny returns, briefly. *New York Times*, pp. E1(L) 12–18.

Glazier, J., & Seo, J. A. (2005). Multicultural literature and discussion as mirror and window? *Journal of Adolescent & Adult Literacy*, *48*(8), 686–700.

GLSEN. (2007). *Executive summary: The 2007 national climate survey: Key findings on the experiences of lesbian, gay, bisexual and transgender youth in our nation's schools*. New York.

Goldman, L. (2007). *Coming out, coming in: Nurturing the well-being and inclusion of gay youth in mainstream society*. London: Taylor & Francis.

Goldman, L. (2008, Spring–Summer). Parenting gay youth: Creating a supportive environment. *Healing Magazine*, pp. 23–24. Retrieved from http://www.childrensgrief.net

Grov, C., Bimbi, D. S., Nanin, J. E., & Parsons, J. T. (2006). Race, ethnicity, gender and generational factors associated with the coming-out process among gay, lesbian, and bisexual individuals. *Journal of Sex Research*, *43*(2), 115–121.

Hartinger, B. (2003). *Geography club*. New York: HarperTeen.

Hershberger, S. L., Pilkington, N. W., & D'Augelli, A. R. (1998). Lesbian, gay, and bisexual youths and their families: Disclosure of sexual orientation and its consequences. *American Journal of Orthopsychiatry*, *68*, 361–371.

IMBD.com. (2010). *Glee*. Retrieved from http://www.imdb.com/title/tt1327801/

Johnson, C., & Johnson, K. (2000), High-risk behavior among gay adolescents: Implication for treatment and support. *Adolescence*, *35*(140), 619–837.

Kaufman, A. S. (2007). Emerging ideas about kisspeptin-GPR54 signaling in the neuroendocrine regulation of reproduction. *Trends in Neurosciences*, *30*(10), 504–511.

Mallon, G. P., & De Crescenzo, T. (2006). Transgender children and youth: A child welfare practice perspective. *Child Welfare*, *85*(2), 215–241.

Means Coleman, R. R., & Yochim, E. C. (2008). *The international encyclopedia of communication*. Malden, MA: Wiley-Blackwell.

Meyer, I. H. (2003). Prejudice, social stress, and mental health in lesbian, gay, and bisexual populations: Conceptual issues and research evidence. *Psychological Bulletin*, *129*(5), 674–697.

Ray, N., Berger, C., Boyle, S., Callan, M. J., White, M., McClelland, G., et al. (2006). *Lesbian, gay bisexual and transgender youth: An epidemic of homelessness*. Washington, DC: National Gay and Lesbian Taskforce.

Russell, G. M., & Bohan, J. S. (2006). The case of internalized homophobia: Theory and/as practice. *Theory Psychology*, *16*(3), 343–366.

Russo, V. (1987). *Celluloid closet: Homosexuality in the movies*. New York: HarperCollins.

Ryan, C., Huebner, D., Diaz, R. M., & Sanchez, J. (2009). Family rejection as a predictor of negative health outcomes in white and Latino lesbian, gay and bisexual young adults. *Pediatrics*, *123*(1), 346–352.

20

Traumatic Death in the United States Military
Initiating the Dialogue on War-Related Loss

JILL HARRINGTON-LaMORIE and
MEGHAN E. McDEVITT-MURPHY

For over two centuries, young men and women have served in the U.S. military in defense, support, and protection of its Constitution from enemies, both foreign and domestic. In its lifetime, the United States has participated in 12 wars resulting in approximately 1.1 million accountable American death casualties (Congressional Research Service, 2010). However, the toll of death casualties does not end at the reportable number of the deceased, as it is magnified exponentially by its impact on survivors affected by each individual loss.

American society has been forged on the loss of its youth in defense of the nation. Yet, how does this society accord for the loss of its youth in the care and treatment of those left behind in its wake? There exists a cavernous gap in the research literature on those affected by the death of a loved one, friend, or comrade in the U.S. Armed Services, as there are few studies on military-related death loss. With approximately 5,400 death casualties associated with the wars in Iraq and Afghanistan, the study of the impact of war-related death should emerge as a health care priority to provide informed care to this population of traumatic death survivors.

DEATH IN THE U.S. MILITARY

In peacetime and at war, the U.S. military suffers death casualties. There are many occupational hazards associated with serving in the military that can lead to deadly physical and psychological injuries. In 2009, there were 2.4 million Americans serving in the U.S. Armed Forces (U.S. Department of Labor, 2010), and in the past 10 years there have been an average of 1,500 active duty military deaths annually (U.S. Department of Defense, 2010).

Most deaths during active duty are sudden, traumatic, and violent in nature and involve an adolescent or young adult. Classified circumstances of death include accidents, hostile action, homicide, illness, self-inflicted, terrorist attack, and undetermined. In the past 10 years, accidents and hostile deaths have been the leading causes of death, followed by illness and self-inflicted deaths (U.S. Department of Defense, 2010).

Operation Iraqi Freedom (OIF) and Operation Enduring Freedom (OEF)

The U.S. Department of Defense (DoD) classifies war-related deaths into two different casualty types: nonhostile (e.g., due to nonhostile accidents, homicide, suicide, and illness) and hostile (e.g., due to enemy gunfire, improvised explosive device, torture, sniper fire, rocket-propelled grenades, suicide bombers, and air losses). Improvised explosive devices have been responsible for almost half the death casualties of coalition forces in Iraq and currently two thirds in Afghanistan. Multiple service members are also killed together in mass casualties through incidents such as suicide bomber attacks, air crashes, and ambushes.

Each branch of the U.S. Armed Services has incurred death casualties associated with military action in Iraq and Afghanistan; however, the Army and the Marine Corps have endured the brunt of the battle. Current data show that casualty deaths connected with OEF (1,142) and OIF (4,264) total 5,406 (U.S. Department of Defense, 2010).

WAR AND DEATH: THE CONSEQUENCES TO SURVIVORS

Death is an inherent part of war. The inevitability of the death of military service members generally does little to mitigate the overwhelming burden of grief that may face survivors following this catastrophic type of traumatic loss. For every military casualty, the loss ripples through multiple social networks, including comrades-in-arms, military leadership and personnel, surviving immediate and extended family members, friends "back home," as well as American society more broadly. To each of the affected persons, different aspects of the death likely resonate; however, there is a high likelihood for fellow service members and families who struggle in the aftermath of these violent deaths to be exposed to the biopsychosocial impacts of both grief and trauma.

Survivors: OIF and OEF

Women and men service members have died in casualties associated with the wars in Iraq and Afghanistan. The majority of deaths have been of young, enlisted men between the ages of 18 and 30 (U.S. Department of Defense, 2010). Many are survived by a young family, extended family, and friends.

Military deaths have a broad effect. Recognized primary grievers usually include spouses, children, and parents. The acute influence of grief upon fellow service members is typically quickly addressed by a unit memorial service, and the implicit message for the soldiers is that their grieving process is at an expected end, although loss-related feelings continue to resonate. The mission must continue, and service members go right back to duty. The study of the effects of traumatic death loss (acute and long term), intervention strategies, and risk and resiliency in both these populations is immensely underrecognized.

The military formally focuses its resources and support on the *primary next of kin* (PNOK) and *secondary next of kin* (SNOK) listed by service members on their personnel paperwork, most commonly spouses, parents, children, and sometimes siblings. However, survivors may include ex-spouses, fiancé(e)s, grandparents, cousins, aunts and uncles, friends, significant relationships, lovers, and same-sex partners. The grief and pain of these survivors are often unrecognized, hidden, stigmatized, or not acknowledged by society, which can lend itself to a more complicated and disenfranchised grief process.

War, Death, and Comrades-in-Arms: What We Know

For fellow service members who may have witnessed the death or learned of it soon after, the trauma of the event itself may reverberate in the form of distressing images or nightmares. Negative emotional responses to combat have been acknowledged for some time (e.g., having been referred to as *shellshock* or *combat neuroses* following previous wars), prior to the formal recognition and codification of posttraumatic stress disorder (PTSD) in the psychiatric nosology in the third edition of the *Diagnostic and Statistical Manual of Mental Disorders* (American Psychiatric Association, 1980). Since the formal recognition of PTSD as a response to combat and other traumatic events, research on the predictors, correlates, and effects of this disorder has proliferated. PTSD has been linked to high rates of co-occurring disorders, including other anxiety disorders, mood disorders, and substance abuse as the most commonly co-occurring conditions, and much of this research has been conducted with veterans (e.g., Kulka et al., 1990). Despite the attention to the diverse effects of trauma among war veterans, the related subject of grief (particularly complicated grief) has received little attention.

Although complicated grief has been measured only infrequently in this population, some evidence about the impact of traumatic death loss in this population may be gathered from the extant literature. For example, in an analysis of a large database of Vietnam veterans, Papa, Neria, and Litz (2008) found that more than three quarters of the sample had known an American soldier who was killed, and just over half reported the death of a close friend in combat and these veterans reported higher levels of symptoms suggestive of complicated grief and PTSD. Another study investigated experiences of war-related bereavement symptoms of PTSD, depression, and grief in a sample of Vietnam veterans who were enrolled in inpatient therapy for PTSD (Pivar & Field, 2004). That study reported that grief-related symptoms were distinct from PTSD and depression in this population. Moreover, the data suggested that grief symptoms were more strongly associated with attachment to the military unit, closeness with military buddies, and number of losses experienced, when compared to symptoms of PTSD and depression. These findings highlight the importance of assessing a range of clinical syndromes in combat veterans because some aspects of combat may result in symptoms of complicated grief, rather than or in addition to PTSD.

Although most of the research on the psychological sequelae of combat has had a primary focus on PTSD, it is clear that returning service members may also experience symptoms of other anxiety and mood disorders, as well as substance abuse (Hoge et al., 2004). Traumatic brain injuries have also been diagnosed frequently among veterans of the current wars in Iraq and Afghanistan (Vasterling, Verfaelle, & Sullivan, 2009). It is difficult to estimate the rate of complicated grief among veterans who may present for clinical services given the paucity of data bearing on this issue. But, given the relatively high rate of psychological distress among returning OEF and OIF service personnel, particularly among those presenting for medical care at U.S. Veterans Administration medical centers (VAMCs), and the high rate of comorbidity of psychological disorders in the wake of trauma, it is likely that complicated grief may be present alongside other disorders that are more readily acknowledged by VAMC providers. Thus it is advisable that clinicians screen for distress related to death losses sustained in war that may take the form of complicated grief, as treatments targeted at PTSD symptoms may not be sufficient.

The assessment and treatment of complicated grief may be addressed within the case conceptualization model proposed by Meichenbaum (2009; see also Chapter 12). Using this model, Meichenbaum advocated taking a detailed history that includes assessment of predeployment factors (e.g., developmental trauma and education level), military history (e.g., the number and length of deployments, nature of any injuries sustained, deaths of battle buddies, perceptions of military leadership, and experiences as a prisoner of war), postdeployment experiences (e.g., time since deployment, adjustment difficulties across domains, and medical history since returning from combat), as well as the specific reasons for referral for psychological services. The case conceptualization model then guides the clinician through the assessment of presenting problems and common symptoms among returning service members including PTSD symptoms, cognitive problems, and relationship difficulties. Also addressed in the model are contextual factors such as current strengths and barriers, as well as past experiences with treatment. Meichenbaum's model provides a comprehensive approach to understanding a veteran's problems and to developing a treatment plan. Although complicated grief was not specifically addressed in Meichenbaum's (2009) description of this approach, it would be a relevant clinical syndrome to include in this population.

Wartime Death and Bereavement in Families: What We Know

What we know about the impacts of active duty military death and wartime bereavement in surviving families comes from studies conducted in Israel (Rubin, Malkinson, & Witztum, 1999). Born in the aftermath of the Holocaust, Israel's

63 years of independence have been marked by conflict with neighboring Arab and Palestinian-Arab states. The impact of military loss has been a principal area of bereavement research in Israel, particularly since the 1973 Yom Kippur War, which lasted 20 days and resulted in the death casualties of approximately 2,600 young adult Israeli military servicemen, wounding just over 7,200.

In a pioneering anthropological work, Palgi (1973) observed the grief and bereavement reactions of parents whose sons died in military service during the Yom Kippur War and noticed discernable responses of bereaved fathers, who seemed to be experiencing a deep sense of loss, accompanied by intense feelings of deprivation. These fathers seemed to age prematurely. Subsequent research on parents bereaved by military loss suggested that social withdrawal and isolation were common consequences. Purisman and Maoz (1977) studied parents who had an adult son killed during the War of Attrition (1969–1970). Their study showed higher levels of depression and somatic complaints and poor self-concept among bereaved Israeli parents. Gay (1982) measured the self-concept of parents who lost their adult sons in the 1973 Yom Kippur War. She compared grief and adjustment scores of bereaved Israeli parents with the scores of nonbereaved Israeli adults in general society. Her findings suggested that bereaved parents ranked poorly in measures of self-concept and had higher incidences of somatic complaints and depression.

Rubin (1990) investigated Israeli parents who had lost an adult son in a war, with time since loss at an average of 9 years, compared to parents who had lost a 1-year-old child to illness around the same time. He discovered that parents who had adult sons who had died in war demonstrated higher levels of current grief as well as higher levels of recalled grief than parents who had suffered the death of an infant to illness. His research brought into question how the circumstances of death, age of the deceased, and age of the bereaved parent may predispose parents to potentially more intensified grief reactions as well as complicated and enduring bereavement. As a follow-on to his findings, Rubin (1992) studied 102 Israeli parents who had suffered the death of their sons to war in the past 4–13 years. In this second study, Rubin found that bereaved parents of fallen wartime sons showed higher levels of grief and anxiety than did the control group of 73 nonbereaved Israeli adults. This study proposed that despite the length of time since the death loss, there may be a more long-lasting impact of wartime death to parents, whose grief is less inclined to subside over time.

Florian (1989–1990) aimed to investigate the perception of the meaning and purpose of life in 52 bereaved parents whose sons died during active duty military service 2 years to 11 years earlier. Florian compared scores on both measures to a control group of 50 nonbereaved parents. The findings of the study indicated that the bereaved couples experienced less meaning and purpose in life compared with nonbereaved couples as well as suffered poorer health and mental problems over time. This research began to identify bereaved parents as a group "at risk" for a longer, intensified, and more prolonged bereavement with a predisposition for developing impairments to their physical and mental health. Based on these findings, Florian (1989–1990) suggested that in order to promote well-being of bereaved parents and improve their quality of life, mental health practitioners should seek using therapeutic interventions to help them regain meaning in life, encourage bereaved parents to participate in peer support self-help groups, and follow-up with bereaved parents to check on both their health and mental health status in an attempt to prevent pathological conditions.

The legacy of this loss seems to persist into late life. Malkinson and Bar-Tur (1999) reported on a focus group study of 29 bereaved older-adult parents, ages 60 to 87 years, whose sons were killed in Israeli military service 11 to 33 years earlier. The predominant theme that emerged from parents was that "grief is a private, isolating inner process" (Malkinson & Bar-Tur, 1999, p. 425). They also observed that the grief of these parents continued along their life span, seemingly unaffected by other developmental processes or life events, and that their inner attachment to the deceased child had not been relinquished.

These studies have begun to elucidate the bereavement and the impact of sudden, often violent deaths of young adult children serving in the military upon parents. The results of their findings begin to raise essential questions regarding the impact of war on the bereaved, although there are limitations to their findings and limited generalizability across cultures and nations.

Each war or conflict is a unique historical event, influenced by factors such as time, era, economics, technology, and culture. Surprisingly little research has explored the experience of bereavement among surviving families of service members who die in U.S. active duty military. Anecdotal reports are available in the popular press. In spite of this, the United States can begin to draw inferences from the findings of this primary research to begin to conduct vitally needed studies of a population at risk for exposure to trauma and grief.

Grief and Bereavement

Death is a universal, natural part of the human experience. Grief and bereavement following loss through death comprise a normal, highly individualized human process (Worden, 2009). The death of a loved one, friend, coworker, or attached relationship is considered to be one of life's most distressing events. The majority of individuals accommodate to death loss in their lives and find a way of adaptive, resilient healing (Neimeyer & Currier, 2009). However, research suggests that 10% to 20% of bereaved persons suffer from complications which can prolong acute grief reactions, impair mental and physical health, as well as prohibit an adaptive course of healing (Shear, Frank, Houck, & Reynolds, 2005; see Chapter 12).

Research has identified factors that influence the extent, intensity, and manner in which individuals grieve (Worden, 2009). These factors include relationship to the deceased, nature of the attachment, circumstances of death, history of coping with prior loss, personality, social variables, and coexisting stressors.

Sudden and violent deaths predispose survivors to the collective influences of both trauma and grief (see Chapters 14, 15, and 16). The literature suggests that those affected by sudden, violent deaths caused by accidents, suicide, homicide, acts of terrorism, and war are highly exposed to these dual influences and are at greater risk for the potential of developing complicated grief (Doka, 1996). There is mixed opinion in the field as to when a clinician should assess for prolonged, complicated grief, and this question is yet to be answered. Six months to after the first anniversary of the death have been proposed (Prigerson et al., 2009; Worden, 2009). However, it is highly important for the clinician to monitor and assess traumatic death loss survivors for potentially serious complications, such as suicidal ideation and intent, substance abuse, engagement in high-risk and self-destructive behaviors, symptoms of major depression and PTSD, as well as failure to thrive. These signs and symptoms should be addressed immediately as they can be life-threatening to the survivor.

Military deaths and the consequences for those affected involve mediating factors that may predispose survivors to complicated grief. Given these mediating factors, clinicians and researchers should explore the likelihood that survivors of a military death may experience a more complex and complicated grief process.

Complicating Factors in Wartime Deaths

There are complexities to wartime deaths unlike those seen in the civilian world (Carroll, 2001), which may compound the loss and contribute to a more distressing grief process for survivors. Wartime deaths can involve a long period of separation from the service member before the death occurs, due to training and deployment. In addition, other factors that may compound wartime losses include the sudden, traumatic, and violent nature of the death; the transfer of remains; the circumstances surrounding the death; death notification; the geography of the death; the age of the decedent; the age of the survivor(s); the condition and existence of bodily remains; military rites and rituals; death investigations; the service member's commitment to his or her duty; the survivor's view of war and military service; dealing with military and government bureaucracy; and media involvement.

Survivors are also immediately confronted with making complex decisions in the face of traumatic loss. The primary next of kin must navigate through numerous decisions involving voluminous paperwork associated with disposition of the remains of the service member, personal effects, insurance, entitlements, and benefits. These tasks often involve interfacing with multiple highly bureaucratic systems of the DoD and Department of Veterans Affairs.

Surviving U.S. Military Families Just as the definition of *survivor* is broad, so too is the definition of what constitutes a military family. In this section, we describe some considerations for working with children, spouses, parents, and siblings whose service members died as a consequence of current U.S. wars.

Spouses The death of a spouse in active duty U.S. military service confronts the surviving spouse with a series of compounding, multiple losses associated with the death. After the loss, spouses often feel the loss of an identity as a "military spouse," loss of a way of life as a "military family," loss of housing (if on base or post), loss of friends through the unit or command, and a loss of feeling connected to the greater military community. Members of the U.S. military and their dependent families live and function in the culture of the military, which has its own customs, laws, hierarchal structure, bureaucratic systems, health system, educational systems, codes of conduct, rituals, and housing. For spouses, many were afforded little opportunity to develop their own careers, hobbies, and support networks outside of the military due to frequent moves and the demands of the military occupation on the family. This adds to the emphasis of the idea of having to find a new identity. For many surviving spouses of regular, active duty personnel, the death of their spouse service member is an involuntary, immediate, abrupt transition from the identity of a "military" family and way of life to a "civilian" one.

Clinicians should be aware of a widow or widower's potential for complex and mixed feelings regarding their spouses' commitment to duty. These feelings may be quite definitive or a mixture of both pride and anger for the deceased spouse's willingness to be placed in harm's way, which may contribute to a sense of personal rejection.

The face of OIF or OEF surviving spouses is young. Many are in their twenties. Young adult loss presents challenges to the survivor. Inexperience with previous deaths, coping with extreme life stressors, as well as a lack of a similar peer group who have endured the death of a spouse at a young age are complications faced by OIF or OEF surviving spouses.

If the couple has children, the surviving spouse is now confronted with what to tell the children, how much to tell the children, raising children affected by traumatic grief in the midst of his or her own trauma and grief, as well as the challenges posed by single parenting.

Spouses must often make immediate decisions under complex grief and trauma regarding housing and moving (where to live or relocate), benefits, schooling for children, insurance, and future employment. The military system is not always easy to navigate or compassionate in assisting with the transition of care to the survivor.

Children

The loss of a parent through war may be particularly traumatic for a child. Children may exhibit symptoms of *childhood traumatic grief*, which is characterized by symptoms similar to PTSD, including intrusive imagery related to the death (as children imagine the details of the death or have recollections about the notification) and avoidance of reminders of the death, which may include avoiding military events or military peers. Also like PTSD, childhood traumatic grief may be associated with increased arousal, such that a child may have difficulty sleeping or concentrating.

The most common interventions accessed by children suffering the loss of a parent in combat are peer support groups where they may work through their trauma and grief reactions with children who are experiencing similar losses and who also share the military background and culture. The Tragedy Assistance Program for Survivors (TAPS, n.d.; www.taps.org), which was founded in 1994 by a military widow, provides peer-based emotional support programs for adults and children, such as Good Grief Camps for children and adolescents grieving the loss of a loved one in U.S. military service.

Parents

The death of a child, at any age, is considered to be one of life's most devastating losses, whose impacts can be pervasive and prolonged (Worden, 2009). Data document that grief is more complicated and intense for parents when their child's death is sudden, untimely, and violent (Keesee, Currier, & Neimeyer, 2008). Strong feelings of guilt coupled with inability to protect their child can be particularly challenging for parents whose children die young and unexpectedly. Very little attention has been paid in the literature to the impact of the loss of a young adult child.

The majority of OIF and OEF deaths have been sudden, often violent, and of young service members whose surviving parents are often younger adults themselves. Parents may have had little experience with the military and have difficulty dealing with or understanding military culture, rites, rituals, and bureaucracies. They also may have agreed or disagreed with their child's choice to serve in the military, especially in a time of war. Surviving parents are often confounded with the experience of confusing, conflicting emotions. Combat-related, wartime deaths present unique challenges to surviving parents. Society may assume these deaths should be "anticipated" by the family because of their child's given line of work (Spungen, 1998) and may not be understanding of their grief.

Paradoxically, due to the highly publicized nature of the death, parents may find themselves in the role of "professional grievers" who live with the chronic spotlight of their child's death at many public services, memorial events, holidays, plaque unveilings, and ceremonies. The parent's viewpoint of whether this is comforting or distressing is essential. The public label of *hero* may add to a sense of emotional confusion for parents, who may feel pride in their children's service and sacrifice, yet anger at the fact that they died.

Parents whose children die as a result of war and who are not afforded what they feel is due recognition by the military or government may need further support by clinicians to help them process these feelings. Parents may not understand, and are often surprised at, their own needs and responses after a child dies. Intensified feelings of guilt, anger, and blame are frequently present. Anger and blame may be a reaction of bereaved parents, whether the causes justifying this reaction are real or perceived. Parents may displace their feelings on the military and personnel, surviving children, other family members, and marital partners or intimate others.

Reaching out to others who understand this type of loss can be a helpful and nurturing process for bereaved parents. Peer support groups have been found to be effective in aiding parents in maintaining more positive memories of their deceased child (Klass, 1988).

Siblings

Bereaved siblings are often an unrecognized and disenfranchised group of survivors, who cope to survive in the shadow of their service member sibling's death. Even though bereaved siblings experience profound loss, they are often overlooked in their grief (Godfrey, 2006). Society often does not recognize siblings as primary grievers, nor acknowledge the death of an adult sibling as a significant loss (Godfrey, 2006).

This can also hold true for sibling survivors of wartime deaths. Because the military focuses its resources and supports on the primary and secondary next of kin, who are typically spouses and parents, siblings who are not these designees may feel further disenfranchised in their grief from both the military and society at large. Social and emotional supports for siblings who have lost a young adult brother or sister are limited.

As with all mediating factors, how the sibling died, the nature of the sibling relationship, and the dynamics of the family are also important factors in working with siblings. The death of a brother or sister during wartime can add another level of challenge to surviving siblings. If the death is deemed heroic, the sibling must contend with the influence this has on his or her own role and status in the family. The "hero child" who dies young may eclipse the status of other children in the family. Siblings may have difficulty processing their own feelings about their sibling's involvement and service in the war. If the death is stigmatized, this can further compound grief for siblings.

SUGGESTED INTERVENTIONS AND NEED FOR FUTURE RESEARCH

There is a small but growing body of evidence to inform our care of surviving veterans, families, and service members affected by the traumatic war-related death of a friend, comrade, or loved one serving in the U.S. Armed Forces. The dual exposure of both grief and trauma to these survivors leaves them at risk for the development of complicated grief and PTSD. The need for the study of grief in the context of traumatic military death loss is critical for this vastly neglected population of traumatic loss survivors.

If a survivor is a parent, spouse, or child of a U.S. Armed Service member, reservist, or National Guardsman who died in the line of duty, he or she is eligible for bereavement counseling through the Department of Veterans Affairs Vet Center (www.vetcenter.va.gov). Referrals for therapists and counselors who specialize in working with traumatic loss survivors can be obtained through the Association for Death Education and Counseling (www.adec.org) as well as the International Society for Traumatic Stress Studies (www.istss.org).

Finally, the power of peer support is an underutilized but highly recognized area of healing and support to bereaved survivors. The validation and support of similar others who can uniquely understand one's suffering are powerful, long-term healing components for most survivors who struggle to make meaning of the death in their lives and live in a new assumptive world (see Chapter 1). The peer connection and cultural understandings of the military and veterans community are strong. These related connections, as well as identification with a survivor community that has suffered the loss of a U.S. military service member during wartime, may be vastly beneficial for survivors. Groups such as TAPS, which was founded in 1994 by a military widow and provides peer-based emotional support programs for adults and children, are considerable sources of care for the short- and long-term bereavement needs of survivors of a military death, regardless of the circumstance of the death and relationship to the deceased. We hope that this chapter will encourage further research efforts to document the impact of military bereavement and the construction and validation of interventions for this vulnerable population of survivors.

REFERENCES

American Psychiatric Association. (1980). *Diagnostic and statistical manual of mental disorders* (3rd ed.). Washington, DC.

Carroll, B. (2001). How the military family copes with a death. In O. D. Weeks & C. Johnson (Eds.), *When all the friends have gone: A guide for aftercare providers* (pp. 173–183). Amityville, NY: Baywood.

Congressional Research Service. (2010). *American war and military operations casualties: Lists and statistic* (Report RL32492). Retrieved from http://www.fas.org/sgp/crs/natsec/RL32492.pdf

Doka, K. (Ed.). (1996). *Living with grief after sudden loss: Suicide, homicide, accident, heart attack, stroke*. New York: Routledge.

Florian, V. (1989–1990). Meaning and purpose in life of bereaved parents whose son fell during active military service. *Omega Journal of Death and Dying*, *20*, 91–102.

Gay, M. (1982). The adjustment of parents of wartime bereavement. In N. A. Milgram (Ed.), *Stress and anxiety* (Vol. 8). New York: Hemisphere.

Godfrey, R. (2006). Losing a sibling in adulthood. *The Forum: Association of Death Education and Counseling*, *32*(1), 6–7.

Hoge, C. W., Castro, C. A., Messer, S. C., McGurk, D., Cotting, D. I., & Koffman, R. L. (2004). Combat duty in Iraq and Afghanistan, mental health problems, and barriers to care. *New England Journal of Medicine*, *351*, 13–22.

Keesee, N. J., Currier, J. M., & Neimeyer, R. A. (2008). Predictors of grief following the death of one's child: The contribution of finding meaning. *Journal of Clinical Psychology*, *64*(10), 1145–1163.

Klass, D. (1988). *Parental grief: Solace and resolution*. New York: Springer.

Kulka, R. A., Schlenger, W. E., Fairbank, J. A., Hough, R. L., Jordan, B. K., Marmar, C. R., et al. (1990). *Trauma and the Vietnam War generation*. New York: Brunner/Mazel.

Malkinson, R., & Bar-Tur, L. (1999). The aging of grief in Israel: A perspective of bereaved parents. *Death Studies*, *23*, 413–431.

Meichenbaum, D. (2009). Core psychotherapeutic tasks with returning soldiers: A case conceptualization approach. In S. M. Freeman, B. A. Moore, & A. Freeman (Eds.), *Living and surviving in harm's way* (pp. 193–210). New York: Routledge.

Neimeyer, R., & Currier, J. M. (2009). Grief therapy: Evidence of efficacy and emerging directions. *Current Directions in Psychological Science*, *18*(6), 352–356.

Palgi, P. (1973). The socio-cultural expressions and implications of death, mourning, and bereavement arising out of the war situation in Israel. *Israel Annals of Psychiatry and Related Disciplines*, *11*(4), 301–329.

Papa, A., Neria, Y., & Litz, B. (2008). Traumatic bereavement in war veterans. *Psychiatric Annals*, *38*, 686–691.

Pivar, I. L., & Field, N. P. (2004). Unresolved grief in combat veterans with PTSD. *Journal of Anxiety Disorders*, *18*, 745–755.

Prigerson, H. G., Horowitz, M. J., Jacobs, S. C., Parkes, C. M., Aslan, M., Goodkin, K., et al. (2009). Prolonged grief disorder: Psychometric validation of criteria proposed for DSM-V and ICD-11. *PLoS Medicine*, *6*(8): e1000121, 1–12.

Purisman, R., & Maoz, B. (1977). Adjustment and war bereavement: Some consideration. *British Journal of Medical Psychology*, *50*, 1–9.

Rubin, S. (1990). Death of a future: An outcome study of bereaved parents in Israel. *Omega*, *20*(4), 323–339.

Rubin, S. (1992). Adult child loss and the two-track model of bereavement. *Omega*, *24*(3), 183–202.

Rubin, S., Malkinson, R., & Witztum, E. (1999). The pervasive impact of war-related loss and bereavement in Israel. *International Journal of Group Tensions*, *28*(1–2), 139–151.

Shear, K., Frank, E., Houck, P. R., & Reynolds, C. F. (2005). Treatment of complicated grief: A randomized controlled trial. *Journal of the American Medical Association*, *293*(21), 2601–2608.

Spungen, D. (1998). *Homicide: The hidden victims*. Thousand Oaks, CA: Sage.

Tragedy Assistance Program for Survivors (TAPS). (N.d.). [Home page]. Retrieved from http://www.taps.org

U.S. Department of Defense. (2010). *Procurement reports and data files*. Retrieved from http://siadapp.dmdc.osd.mil/personnel/CASUALTY/Death_Rates.pdf

U.S. Department of Labor. (2010). *Occupational outlook handbook*. Retrieved from http://www.bls.gov/oco/ocos249.htm

Vasterling, J. J., Verfaellie, M., & Sullivan, K. D. (2009). Mild traumatic brain injury and posttraumatic stress disorder in returning veterans: Perspectives from cognitive neuroscience. *Clinical Psychology Review*, *29*, 674–684.

Worden, J. W. (2009). *Grief counseling and grief therapy: A handbook for the mental health practitioner* (4th ed.). New York: Springer.

21

Pet Loss
The Interface of Continuing Bonds Research and Practice

BETTY J. CARMACK and WENDY PACKMAN

> This is the most terrible pain I have ever had, and I feel like I will never be the same person I was before my pet passed. It felt like someone ripped my heart out of my chest when he died and a scream came out of me that was from some place unknown. I feel like I cannot go on and have lost my best friend who loved me without conditions or expectations.
>
> **Research participant**

INTENSITY OF LOSING A LOVED ANIMAL COMPANION

The death of a pet induces grief responses of comparable severity to the loss of human relationships (Archer, 1997; Carmack, 2003; Clements, Benasutti, & Carmone, 2003; Field, Orsini, Gavish, & Packman, 2009). "The emotional attachment which many humans develop for their pets … frequently transcends the emotional attachment which they form with humans" (DeGroot, 1984, p. 283). In fact, people often describe being more emotionally attached to their pets than to humans in their lives (Barker & Barker, 1988; Carmack, 1985). Animal companions provide emotional qualities—a sense of security and well-being, unconditional love, and acceptance—that are difficult to attain or sustain in relationships with people (Sharkin & Knox, 2003).

A large number of pet owners describe their pets as family members or consider pets as children (Cowles, 1985; Toray, 2004; Voith, 1985). Such perceptions of pets as members of the family have been reported across the life span—by children (Kaufman & Kaufman, 2006; Ross, 2005), adolescents (Brown, Richards, & Wilson, 1996), and adults (Ross & Baron-Sorensen, 2007). Thus, it is not surprising that research has demonstrated strong ties between pets and humans and profound reactions to loss (Archer & Winchester, 1994; Carmack, 2003).

Similarities in bereavement following the death of a significant human relationship are comparable to those following the loss of a pet. Similarities are reported in terms of sleep loss, days missed from work, and other psychological and social difficulties (Quackenbush, 1985). Gerwolls and Labott (1994) assessed whether the loss of a pet was different from the loss of a human companion. At 2 and 8 weeks post loss, the grief scores of those who had lost a pet were similar to those who had lost a human companion. At 8 weeks and 6 months post loss, there were no statistically significant differences in grief scores between the two groups. These findings of comparable grief severity were substantiated in later research (Field et al., 2009).

Archer and Winchester (1994) also found that following the loss of a pet, there are grief reactions parallel to those following the death of a human. Over half of the respondents reported that their initial reactions were numbness and/or disbelief. Greater than half endorsed preoccupation with thoughts about the pet and felt that "a part of them had gone" when their pet died (p. 267). About one fourth endorsed anger and negative affect (depression and anxiety).

CONTINUING BONDS WITH BEREAVED PET OWNERS

There is growing attention in bereavement literature about the function of a "continuing bond" in relation to coping (Field & Friedrichs, 2004; Field, Gao, & Paderna, 2005; Stroebe, Gergen, Gergen, & Stroebe, 1992) and adaptation following the death of a loved one (Klass, Silverman, & Nickman, 1996; see Chapter 4). Despite the permanence of physical separation, the bereaved can be emotionally sustained through a continuing bond to the deceased (Field, Nichols, Holen, & Horowitz, 1999). Thus, resolving grief does not involve ending a relationship, but instead involves a reorganization of the relationship with the deceased (Field, 2008).

The concept of *continuing bonds* (CB) has not been labeled as such in the pet bereavement literature, although similar phenomena have been described in relation to pet loss (Carmack, 2003; Cowles, 1985; Podrazik, Shackford, Becker, & Heckert, 2000; Weisman, 1990–1991). Individuals describe illusory phenomena in which they seem to hear or feel the presence of their deceased pet (Carmack, 2003). Cowles reported that bereaved pet owners experienced an ongoing attachment with their deceased pet in two major ways. First, memories of the deceased pet were reported by all participants. Although painful at first, most owners eventually derived comfort from recalling "special times" with their pet. Second, the majority retained special items as remembrances of their deceased pet (e.g., collars, food dishes, and favorite toys).

Research Program: Continuing Bonds and Pet Loss

Our current research program is a systematic attempt to examine and quantify continuing bonds expressions (CBE) experienced by bereaved pet owners. Participants who had lost a dog or cat within the past year completed a set of measures that assessed psychosocial adjustment (grief, symptoms, and growth) and CBE. The measures consisted of the Inventory of Complicated Grief (ICG), the Brief Symptom Inventory (BSI), the Post-Traumatic Growth Inventory (PTGI), and projective drawings. For the drawing task, participants were asked to depict how they are now using the time they would have spent with their pet, that is, "How have you changed the ways in which you use your energy and time since your pet's death?" This drawing focuses on future orientation and shows the extent to which the participant has integrated the loss (Long, 2004).

The Continuing Bonds Interview (CBI) of Field, Packman, and Carmack (2007) was used to evaluate the degree of connection that the bereaved maintains with the deceased pet and how that bond affects functioning. This interview-based CB measure is designed to investigate the different facets of CB and goes well beyond simply assessing extent of CB usage to distinguish whether the CB expressions are indicative of poor versus successful adaptation to the loss (Field, 2008). In the CBI, participants were asked whether they had any of the following experiences in the past month: (a) sensing the presence and a continuing connection with their deceased pet; (b) holding onto or using special belongings of their pet in order to feel close; (c) being drawn to places associated with their pet; (d) recalling fond memories; (e) dreaming of the pet; (f) having thoughts of being reunited with their pet; (g) attempting to carry out or live up to their pet's wishes; (h) being influenced by the pet in making everyday decisions and choices; (i) reminiscing with others about pet; (j) creating memorials or shrines, or attending special events in tribute to their pet; (k) thinking they heard or felt their pet's sounds or movements (i.e., intrusive symptoms); and (l) learning lessons from their pet (i.e., the positive lasting influence of a deceased pet). If the participants endorsed CBE, they were asked to describe and rate whether the experience was comforting, distressing, or both and the degree to which this occurred.

Participants

A total of 33 individuals between the ages 25 and 79 (*MN* = 45.57 years) participated in the study. The sample included 27 females and 6 males; 82% (n = 27) of the sample were Caucasian. In terms of household yearly income, 30% reported an income greater than $100,000. The sample was highly educated (55% had attended graduate school and 30% attended college). Of the total sample, 58% (n = 19) lost their dogs, whereas 42% (n =14) lost their cats. The deceased pet's age ranged from 3 to 20 years (*MN* = 12.79 years). The majority of participants (70%; n = 23) lost their pets due to major illness.

TABLE 21.1 Continuing Bonds Expressions (CBE)

	Pet Loss (N = 33)			Spousal Loss (N = 24)		
Continuing Bonds Expression[a]	**%**	**Comfort**	**Distress**	**%**	**Comfort**	**Distress**
Fond Memories Focus on fond memories of deceased	85	3.54** (1.07)	2.32 (1.52)	92	3.23*** (1.07)	1.45 (.86)
Belongings Use of deceased's belongings for comfort	79	3.42*** (1.21)	1.73 (1.15)	75	3.05*** (1.13)	1.74 (.99)
Reminisce Reminisce with others about deceased	79	3.46** (1.27)	1.88 (1.31)	96	3.39*** (1.08)	1.43 (1.08)
Lessons Learned and Positive Influence Positive lasting influence of deceased	76	3.64*** (1.11)	1.56 (1.15)	63	3.33*** (1.18)	1.60 (1.18)

[a] Endorsed in the past month.
*$p < .05$; **$p < .01$; ***$p < .001$.

RESULTS: PRESENCE AND PREVALENCE OF CONTINUING BONDS

As shown in Table 21.1, the most frequently endorsed CBEs about the pet were recalling fond memories (85%), holding onto or using belongings (79%), reminiscing with others (79%), and lessons learned and/or positive influences (76%) (Packman, Field, Carmack, & Ronen, in press). In order to investigate the similarities in the incidence of different types of CBE in pet loss and human loss, we compared our sample with a spousal loss sample involving the loss of a husband between 1 and 2 years ago (Field, 2010). It is noteworthy that both groups are similar in terms of relative frequency of endorsement of each CBE. For example, both samples have high endorsement of reminiscing with others, focusing on fond memories, and using the deceased's belongings (Table 21.1).

Because our previous research highlighted the importance of the comforting and distressing dimensions of CB (Field, 2010; Hsu, 2008; Ronen et al., 2009), we used this dimension in our current investigation. A mean score was derived for the extent of comfort and the extent of distress reported across the CBE. Both the pet loss and spousal loss groups show an overall tendency to experience a CB as more comforting than distressing (Packman et al., in press) (Table 21.1).

It is also noteworthy that 58% reported thoughts of being reunited, 52% had dreams involving their pet, 48% endorsed a sense of the deceased pet's presence, and 48% reported being drawn to places associated with the deceased. Thirty-nine percent endorsed the following: living up to the ideals or wishes of the deceased, creating memorials, and intrusive sights or sounds of the deceased. The least endorsed was influence by the pet in making everyday decisions and choices (18%) (Packman et al., in press).

In our statistical analyses, we assessed whether the comfort and distress mean score ratings moderated the relationship between the Continuing Bond Ongoing

Connection (CBOC) factor (composed of five of the CBE) and the psychosocial adjustment measures. Whether or not CBEs are associated with better adjustment may be contingent on the extent to which they are experienced as comforting or distressing. Therefore, there may be a significant interaction between the CBOC and comfort versus distress variables in predicting psychosocial adjustment.

Our analyses revealed that the comfort variable does moderate the relationship between the CBOC and grief, as well as between the CBOC and symptoms. Significant trends were found for the moderating role of comfort on the relationship between the CBOC and posttraumatic growth and drawing measures. Importantly, our research suggests that the relationship between CBE and grief and the relationship between CBEs and symptoms is contingent on comfort: Those who use more CBEs and derive comfort from them experience less grief and fewer symptoms. In addition, those who use CBEs and derive comfort from them experience growth. On the other hand, these relationships do not hold for the distress variable (i.e., individuals who report using many CBEs accompanied by distress experience more grief and symptoms).

CLINICAL IMPLICATIONS

High Endorsement of CBE

Our results confirm that individuals experience dimensions of the phenomenon of CB following the deaths of their beloved companion animals. Thus, one of the first steps in recognizing the interface of CBE research and practice is to acknowledge that those grieving the death of a loved animal companion do experience CBE. This is confirmed by our research as well as from previous professional writings cited in our literature review, in addition to verification from clinical experience. Table 21.1 documents the high percentages of participants reporting CBE. Those in practice must recognize this as a fairly common phenomenon and assess for their presence in those individuals with whom they are working. At a recent pet loss support group, three participants spontaneously described CBE and the comfort they received from their particular experiences. For example, a woman whose cat had died within the past month touched her chest describing how she carries her cat there in her heart. She expressed gratifying surprise that her cat was "still in my heart—that's been a revelation to me."

Assessing a client's experience in the area of CB is essential in determining the degree of value of their experiences. One could say to a client something like "We're finding that often when one loses a loved animal, that person feels or senses his pet's presence or continues to use the pet's belongings or something similar to try to keep and feel an ongoing connection. I wonder if any of that is happening for you." Or one could simply ask, "Do you still feel his presence?"

Establishing an environment that makes it safe and acceptable to acknowledge CBE is primary. Clinical experience suggests that those grieving for their pets are hesitant to bring up these experiences for fear that the helping person will think them "weird" or "crazy." Yet, when a counselor gently and nonjudgmentally prompts this area of discussion, clients often readily acknowledge the experiences and are relieved to be able to speak of it. One of the authors (BC) consistently sees this occurrence in her monthly pet loss support groups—when one person describes feeling as if the deceased pet can be felt or heard, others nod their heads in agreement and understanding. To see that such statements are accepted and invited decreases group participants' initial hesitation about reporting such an experience. To normalize and legitimize a person's experience helps decrease reservations to disclose the experiences.

Evolving Nature of CBE

Second, just as grief is continually changing and evolving, so appears to be the experience of CBE. Our findings indicate that people's experiences of CBE shift and evolve. Those in practice must acknowledge the evolving nature of CBE with their potential for comfort and/or distress. A young man whose Boston terrier, Baxter, died 6 months ago had come each month to the pet loss support group. He was in anguish because he was unable to have any good memories of Baxter. Instead, all he thought of was the last day when the death occurred and he kept telling the group, "I just want to be able to remember our good times." At the sixth month, he came to the group and described a dream he recently had about Baxter and how much comfort he received from the dream: "It was like I visited with him, like I had time with him." The young man's demeanor and affect were considerably different that evening. The dream, with the comfort he got from it, was a turning point in his grief processing. To inform clients of the possibility that what they are currently experiencing—both in type of CBE and in intensity and frequency—may change over time seems to be a requisite part of the educative component of grief.

In our interviews with participants, we limited our questions to CBEs solely within the past month, but it soon became clear that this was only one piece of the temporality of CBE. Many of our participants shared that they had experienced CB throughout the previous weeks and months and that the expressions continually shifted in intensity and frequency. In our view, if researchers focus on only a limited time frame, they risk missing the richness and uniqueness of each person's total experience of CBE. For some clients CB may develop over time, while for others they may develop immediately after the death. On the other hand, it is important that clinicians do not burden bereaved pet owners with expectations that they should or will develop CB. Such bonds may develop and change over time and are unique to each person.

Degree of Comfort and/or Distress of CBE

Third, it is not whether a person experiences CB that is most important. What matters is the degree of comfort or distress that is experienced from a particular CB. Our research instructs us that whether CBE result in better adjustment, growth, and/or decreased grief scores appears to depend on the degree to which CBE are felt as comforting or distressing. As an example from clinical practice,

Jane described the comfort she felt a short time after her cat's euthanasia: "[I]t felt good … like he was right here in my arms, like he was there."

Michelle, a 28-year-old woman whose dog died 12 months prior to the interview, derives considerable comfort from her use of the two CBs of attempting to live up to the ideals or wishes of her dog and being drawn to places associated with her deceased dog:

> Yeah, I think Teton is proud of me and the choices I'm making in my life now in terms of serving others and having a deeper sense of compassion for others. It's really about her and I think she would want me to continue caring for people, caring for Canyon [her new dog] and other animals.

And,

> I feel like she's always telling us what to do. Ever since she died, it seems she is guiding us on this path that's helping us make choices of who we are as people. Being back and surrounded by mountains … that is who we are, where we met as a couple.

The comfort Michelle receives from these CBEs moderates her grief and facilitates her growth. She had a low score on a measure of complicated grief, and her drawing showed positive adaptation and integration of loss.

Contrast Michelle with Greta, a 57-year-old woman whose cat died 4 months prior to the interview. She had a high score on the measure of complicated grief, and her drawing showed both lack of adaptation and minimal integration of loss. On the CBE for dreams, Greta described her dreams as both "very comforting" and "extremely distressing." She described her dreams in terms of "reliving all the bad things that had happened and dreaming that my cats were biting me. The nightmares were coming back." She reported that her feelings of distress were more intense and lasted considerably longer than her feelings of comfort. It is noteworthy that as part of our research program, Hsu (2008) used six case studies from our larger participant pool and split participants into high- or low-grief groups based on scores on the ICG. Hsu reported that the quality and duration of pain (i.e., comfort and/or distress) differentiated the high-grief group from the low-grief group.

It is also important to note that within the same person, a CB can be experienced as both comforting and distressing either at the same time or at a later time. As an example, clients may experience a dream as comforting when the deceased pet visits and lets the person know he or she is in a good place and is healthy and well. Yet, when the person wakes up and has to acknowledge once again that the pet is no longer present, feelings of distress can quite readily arise. For Harriet, age 42, the CBE of fond memories is more distressing than comforting:

> It's really distressing because … oh, just everything … going to the market, not having him here, I can't go to the beach yet but going to the park, even walking down the street was hard. I think about him all the time and every-

> thing is a memory. And it's distressing because he's not there.… So no, it's not good or happy. It's good happy memories, but it's also upsetting.

Harriet's description shows the complexity of experience, the different layers of emotions, and the reason why clinicians cannot generalize or assume they know what someone is saying. What became apparent from these data is the importance of understanding a grieving pet owner's total experience. Thus, to make an assumption based only on high or low scores on objective grief or symptom measures is to run the risk of missing what is actually happening. For example, one could have a high score on a measure of grief but actually be functioning quite well because of the CBE utilized. Because of the uniqueness of each person's experience, it is not the number of CBEs but the degree of adaptability that is most significant. By using one or more particular CBEs that provide comfort, a client may be able to regulate his or her emotions so that the intensity of grief, although deep, is not overwhelming the person. Our research, which supports the evolving nature of CBEs as well as the evolving nature of the comfort and distress dimensions, suggests clients' need for ongoing assessment as well as the changing type and frequency of therapeutic assistance needed from those in practice.

Rituals and Memorials

Fourth, because CBEs have the potential to comfort, those persons who are not using CBEs might be encouraged to consider their use. Such an intervention optimally would be made within the context of a discussion with the person about using CBEs for the comfort they might bring. For example, of our 33 interviews, 20 respondents (61%) described creating, holding, or attending a ritual or memorial for their pet. Of these, 15 (46%) described them as comforting. Five described feelings of both comfort and distress.

Podrazik et al. (2000) described the importance of rituals as a way to maintain a connection with a deceased pet, serving to "unite and mold the significance of the decreased within their life. By using such rituals, the attachment bonds can be reworked to transform the deceased pet into an internal representation that is based on meaning, memory or emotional connection" (p. 381).

Clinicians appreciating the value of rituals and memorials might consider exploring with their clients their willingness or resistance to create a ritual. For those who fear they may lose the relationship or lose the feelings for their animal, a discussion about how relationships can, in fact, continue through a memorial might be appropriate. For those persons who have no knowledge of how to create a memorial, numerous examples are available (e.g., creating a home altar, making a scrapbook, or scattering the pet's ashes at a favorite place).

This is only one example of initiating a conversation to describe the potential comfort one might get from using CBEs. Clinicians cannot generalize but must individualize a client's potential or actual use of CBEs based on that particular person's needs, current intensity of grief, availability of additional supports, and general level of functionality.

Thoughts of Being Reunited

Fifth, there is widespread disagreement on whether people and their animals will be reunited. Interestingly, 21 (64%) of our participants have thoughts about being reunited in some way with their animal. Fourteen of those 21 reported the thoughts as being comforting. Our results related to this particular CBE have clear implications for clinicians as well as those in pastoral and spiritual roles. One's theological or spiritual perspective appears to be a contextual factor influencing one's response to this particular CB.

For those clients who have been taught they will never see their animal again, the finality of their loss can be overwhelming. A woman came for counseling for her grief related to her cat's death. When asked, "Do you think you'll be reunited with your pet?" she said "No" because of her religious teachings. When asked if she thought it would make a difference in her grief if she would be reunited, she said, "Yes, because it wouldn't be so final." The finality of never seeing her animal again was exacerbating her grief experience. Another client, who is Jewish, said, "I don't care what Judaism teaches, it is not clear, and I don't care. I find the Rainbow Bridge much more helpful and comforting." The Rainbow Bridge describes a person being reunited physically with a beloved animal companion at the time of the person's death. In fact, in our interviews several participants talked about the Rainbow Bridge when asked about being reunited with their beloved pets and said they drew considerable comfort from this image.

Clinicians and those in pastoral or spiritual roles must find some way to support clients who want to believe or do believe that they will be reunited with their animals, yet they have been taught that such cannot happen. How do pastoral staff and clinicians support someone who presents in this way, especially in a denomination in which he or she is expected to respond in a particular way or one comes from a faith in which what is taught is unhelpful to the client? Clinical and pastoral work is about helping people. This is a sensitive yet significant area that both deserves and requires discussion among those of us working with those grieving the loss of a pet.

Disenfranchised Grief

Sixth, those grieving the death of a pet often feel invalidated and unsupported because of their loss. They are reluctant to speak of the intensity of their grief or any experiences of CBE because of either previous rejection or fear of their grief being disenfranchised. Statements such as "It was just a dog" or "What's the big deal—there are lots of cats who need homes"—comments often directed to those in grief—reinforce feelings of disenfranchisement and invalidation. Unfortunately, "[S]ociety generally does not acknowledge pet loss as a significant loss, which alienates those who grieve. Clinicians must not fall into the same category" (Podrazik et al., 2000, p. 377). Encouraging clients to seek out supportive situations (e.g., pet loss support groups) helps them learn what other bereaved individuals do to manage their grief and learn to share their own feelings and coping strategies.

CONCLUSION

There is a clear interface between research and clinical practice in relation to CBE and pet loss. Both our research and clinical practice emphasize that a majority of pet owners do maintain ongoing, meaningful ties with their pet and with the parts of their lives they shared together. Our findings also reflect the comfort that individuals often receive from their CBEs. These findings corroborate the earlier literature related to this topic as well as our clinical experiences.

Certainly more needs to be done. Clinical practice suggests that the evolving nature of CBEs, in both intensity and duration, needs additional exploration. How CBEs change through the course of grief is a fruitful area for study and can influence clinical practice. The identification of other possible CBEs can be explored. Clinical practice is also in need of knowing if or how CBEs are experienced similarly or differently in various demographic groups (e.g., children and adolescents as well as adults). Knowledge about multicultural and different spiritual experiences of CBEs is lacking. Because of this lack, our ongoing international cross-cultural research related to CBE and pet loss is significant. Those of us in clinical practice need knowledge about different cultural, spiritual, and religious responses to pet loss and the interaction of CBEs with these experiences of grief.

Coursework and curricula should seriously consider including information about CBEs and pet loss. For too long, those in grief were not encouraged to speak of their CBEs. Just as grief related to pet loss has been disenfranchised, so has the experience of CBE.

CBEs are unique to each person—differences exist in type as well as intensity and duration. Clinicians can affirm and normalize the experiences of CB. Clients deserve and need that. As clients increasingly share their experiences of CBE with us, our understanding of the phenomenon will grow. As we understand more and understand better, we can contribute to the knowledge base. Our shared conversations can change in focus and depth. The interface can strengthen our resolve to remember and our ability to put into practice our growing knowledge of CBEs.

REFERENCES

Archer, J. (1997). Why do people love their pets? *Evolution and Human Behavior, 18*, 237–259.

Archer, J., & Winchester, G. (1994). Bereavement following death of a pet. *The British Journal of Psychology*, *85*, 259–271.

Barker, S., & Barker R. T. (1988). The human–canine bond: Closer than family ties? *Journal of Mental Health Counseling*, *10*, 46–56.

Brown, B., Richards, H., & Wilson, C. (1996). Pet bonding and pet bereavement among adolescents. *Journal of Counseling and Development*, *74*, 505–509.

Carmack, B. J. (1985). The effects on family members and functioning after the death of a pet. *Marriage & Family Review*, *8*(3–4), 149–161.

Carmack, B. J. (2003). *Grieving the death of a pet*. Minneapolis: Augsburg.

Clements, P. T., Benasutti, K. M., & Carmone, A. (2003). Support for bereaved owners of pets. *Perspectives in Psychiatric Care*, *39*(2), 49–54.

Cowles, K. V. (1985). The death of a pet: Human responses to the breaking of the bond. *Marriage & Family Review*, *8*(3–4), 135–148.

DeGroot, A. (1984). Preparing the veterinarian for dealing with the emotions of pet loss. In R. K. Anderson, B. L. Hart, & L. A. Hart (Eds.), *The pet connection: Its influence on our health quality of life. Proceedings of the Minnesota–California conferences on the human–animal bond* (pp. 283–290). Minneapolis: University of Minnesota.

Field, N. P. (2008). Whether to relinquish or maintain a bond with the deceased. In M. S. Stroebe, R. O. Hansson, H. Schut, & W. Stroebe (Eds.), *Handbook of bereavement research and practice: Advances in theory and intervention* (pp. 113–132). Washington, DC: American Psychological Association.

Field, N. P. (2010). [Continuing bonds in coping with the loss of a husband]. Unpublished raw data.

Field, N. P., & Friedrichs, M. (2004). Continuing bonds in coping with the death of a husband. *Death Studies*, *28*(7), 597–620.

Field, N. P., Gao, B., & Paderna, L. (2005). Continuing bonds in bereavement: An attachment theory based perspective. *Death Studies*, *29*, 277–299.

Field, N. P., Nichols, C., Holen, A., & Horowitz, M. (1999). The relation of continuing attachment to adjustment in conjugal bereavement. *Journal of Consulting and Clinical Psychology*, *67*, 212–218.

Field, N. P., Orsini, L., Gavish, R., & Packman, W. (2009). Role of attachment in response to pet loss. *Death Studies*, *33*(4), 332–355.

Field, N. P., Packman, W., & Carmack, B. J. (2007). *Continuing bonds interview*. Unpublished data.

Gerwolls, M. K., & Labott, S. M. (1994). Adjustments to the death of a companion animal. *Anthrozoös*, *7*(3), 172–187.

Hsu, M. (2008).*Continuing bonds expressions in pet bereavement* (PhD dissertation). Pacific Graduate School of Psychology.

Kaufman, K. R., & Kaufman, N. D. (2006). And then the dog died. *Death Studies*, *30*, 61–76.

Klass, D., Silverman, P., & Nickman, S. L. (Ed.). (1996). *Continuing bonds: New understanding of grief*. Philadelphia: Taylor & Francis.

Long, J. K. (2004). Medical art therapy: Using imagery and visual expression in healing. In P. Camic & S. Knight (Eds.), *Clinical handbook of health psychology* (2nd ed., pp. 315–341). Seattle, WA: Hogrefe & Huber.

Packman, W., Field, N. P., Carmack, B. J., & Ronen, R. (In press). Continuing bonds and psychosocial adjustment in pet loss. *Journal of Loss and Trauma*.

Podrazik, D., Shackford, S., Becker, L., & Heckert, T. (2000). The death of a pet: Implications for loss and bereavement across the lifespan. *Journal of Personal and Interpersonal Loss*, *3*, 361–395.

Quackenbush, J. E. (1985). The death of a pet: How it can affect owners. *The Veterinary Clinics of North America: Small Animal Practice*, *15*, 395–402.

Ronen, R., Packman, W., Field, N. P., Davies, B., Kramer, R., & Long, J. (2009). The relationship between grief adjustment and continuing bonds for parents who have lost a child. *Omega*, *60*(1), 1–31.

Ross, C. (2005). *Pet loss and children*. New York: Routledge.

Ross, C., & Baron-Sorensen, J. (2007). *Pet loss and human emotion* (2nd ed.). New York: Routledge.

Sharkin, B. S., & Knox, D. (2003). Pet loss: Implications for the psychologist. *Professional Psychology: Research and Practice*, *34*, 414–421.

Stroebe, M., Gergen, M. M., Gergen, K. J., & Stroebe, W. (1992). Broken hearts or broken bonds: Love and death in historical perspective. *American Psychologist*, *47*, 1205–1212.

Toray, T. (2004). The human–animal bond and loss: Providing support for grieving clients. *Journal of Mental Health Counseling*, *26*, 244–259.

Voith, V. L. (1985). Attachment of people to companion animals. *Veterinary Clinics of North America: Small Animal Practice*, *15*, 289–296.

Weisman, A. D. (1990–1991). Bereavement and companion animals. *Omega*, *22*(4), 241–248.

Section V

Specialized Therapeutic Modalities

22

Family Therapy for the Bereaved

DAVID W. KISSANE and AN HOOGHE

Sharing grief generally aids its healing. Sharing emotions within a family brings reflection on the meaning of valued relationships, helping to activate coping and restoration processes through the most natural source of support, the family. Although both individual and group therapy approaches to bereavement care have been the dominant paradigms historically, use of family therapy bridges across generations, makes use of what is often a very accessible source of support, and permits the cultivation of relational meaning as a key dimension of adaptation. Given such logic, it is surprising that systemic therapies have been overlooked for so long among models of grief therapy.

Family therapy in bereavement care has obvious applicability following the death of a child or the death of a parent leaving bereaved children and adolescents. In working with the elderly, family care connects the surviving widow(er) with the support of their children and grandchildren. Indeed, there are few instances where a family is not accessible for support—perhaps the most isolated or alienated individuals cut off from others, the migrant whose family resides in another country, and the single child who has never reproduced and has deceased parents. For the vast majority of cancer and palliative care patients, relatives can be identified to enable therapy to be commenced preventively before the death of the index patient and then continued into bereavement. Or, once bereaved, use of the family reinforces the most natural form of support to foster dialogue and harness mutual support as a pathway to healing.

For most families, their natural resilience serves the needs of the mourning process admirably (Kissane & Bloch, 1994; Kissane, Lichtenthal, & Zaider, 2007). Supportive families comfort one another, recognize and respond to needs, and encourage healthy adaptation among their members. For therapists, then, the challenges arise with families in need of specialized help, or families struggling to go on after the loss because of injured relationships, competing ways of coping, or lack of mutual support, which potentially handicaps healthy mourning. The development of therapeutic models that aim to reinforce the natural support system for the bereaved and/or optimize relationships, enhance the functioning of the family, and use these very processes to facilitate the sharing of grief can direct the family and its members down a restorative pathway (Kissane et al., 2006).

In this chapter, we first explore an approach to engage families in therapy starting during palliative care. We describe its techniques and strategies, offer guidance about the challenges that arise, and review the empirical evidence for the efficacy of this approach. Second, we explore an approach that relies on the natural support resources of the bereaved to engage families in therapy after the death. In this way, we highlight the fundamental value that a systemic perspective brings. Moreover, we seek to deepen appreciation for relational meaning through the active sharing of vulnerability, the fostering of tolerance and respect, the nurturance of generosity, and mutual care provision; in short, we focus on the family grieving together as an efficient and cost-effective path to a creative outcome, despite loss and change.

ENGAGING FAMILIES IN THERAPY: FAMILIES AT RISK IN A PALLIATIVE CARE SETTING

In the palliative care setting, before a patient with cancer dies, family members can be invited to complete a Family Relationships Index (FRI) (Moos & Moos, 1981), a 12-item true–false scale, which informs about family cohesiveness, expressiveness of thoughts and feelings, and conflict resolution, and has good sensitivity to identify families at risk of psychosocial morbidity during bereavement (Edwards & Lavery, 2005; Kissane et al., 2003). Those families considered at risk are invited to attend a family meeting, where their issues and concerns about caring for the dying family member can be appraised and continuing family therapy contracted with the members (Kissane, 2000). Therapy readily continues into bereavement once a therapeutic alliance is established.

Predicting How Much Therapy Any Family May Need

Repeated studies have confirmed a typology of families based on their relational functioning as defined by the FRI (Kissane et al., 1996, 2003). Two types of families are well functioning. The first is termed *supportive*: These families are highly cohesive, communicate readily, comfort and support one another, and are free of conflict, and their resilience protects their membership from psychiatric disorders and complicated grief. The second well-functioning type is termed *conflict resolving*, because their open communication and high cohesion protect their members from difficulties, despite prominent differences of opinion. They are also free of psychiatric disorder during bereavement. Neither *supportive* nor *conflict-resolving* families are in need of preventive family therapy.

Three types of families have reduced cohesiveness and communication, and are troubled by conflict. *Intermediate* families have mild reductions in communication and teamwork, carry some members in need of psychological help, and are readily amenable to being engaged in therapy. Generally 6–8 sessions of therapy over as many months will help intermediate families share their grief and protect members from adverse psychiatric outcomes (Kissane et al., 2006).

Of the more dysfunctional family types, *sullen* families have poor communication and cohesion, but muted anger; they carry the highest rates of depression (anger turned in) and accept help, generally needing 8–12 sessions of therapy over 12–18 months to prevent complicated grief (Kissane et al., 2007). In contrast, *hostile* families are fractured by conflict, use distance as their means of survival, and may not be willing to come together for therapy. If they can be engaged, therapists may be wise to set more modest goals, but can expect 12–16 sessions of therapy over 18 months to be needed to prevent adverse outcomes for those families engaged in treatment (Kissane et al., 2006). An acceptable compromise is to work with an accessible part of such a family and help those open to this assistance.

The empirical typology delineated above helps conceptually to recognize families where attachment processes are more disturbed and accurately predicts rates of psychiatric disorder (Kissane & Bloch, 2002). However, we avoid classifying families by these names clinically, lest harm be done by pejorative labeling. It is sufficient to say to families with *intermediate*, *sullen*, or *hostile* levels of functioning that experience teaches us the value of meeting with the family-as-a-whole to help patients and their caregivers manage the illness and care provision.

Conducting Therapy in the Home

Arranging therapy in the home of the primary caregiver is common in the hospice setting. This practice increases the ability of the ill patient to take part in early sessions despite his or her frailty and thus become known to the therapist before death intervenes (Kissane & Bloch, 2002). Families are very appreciative of this, and the therapist is better able to bring the deceased back figuratively into the therapy, given his or her personal knowledge of the person. The wishes and hopes of the lost relative can be powerfully used to motivate the family to sustain efforts at mutual support. When high conflict is recognized in families, therapists are wise to conduct the initial assessment sessions on neutral territory rather than in the home, until confidence develops about the safety of therapy in the home.

Once families become bereaved and return to their communities, more barriers emerge to engage the family than are seen within a hospice program, because the relatives disperse to their various homes across cities or states and geographic impediments arise. Telephone linkage to a family meeting is manageable if one sibling lives distantly, but it becomes impractical if several are scattered.

The more dysfunctional or fractured the family is, the more difficult it becomes for a willing therapist to engage members, who fear rekindled conflict, may doubt the capacity of the therapist to facilitate anything beneficial, and prefer to assume the solution of distance as their coping response to their differences of opinion and relational style (Zaider & Kissane, 2009). There may be great wisdom in the solution already adopted by such a family. Miracles cannot be worked, and without the opportunity for healing engendered by having a relative dying, the motivation is often absent to reconsider this modus operandi.

Sometimes one family member serves as the symptom bearer and rationale for a reluctant group of relatives to come together. Here the therapist plays actively on the needs of a psychiatrically ill relative, whether the symptom cluster is a clinical depression or another variation of reduced coping. The invitation to assist a clinician in helping someone who is acknowledged to be ill serves the systemic function of avoiding any blame on the family-as-a-whole. This constellation helps to convene and engage the family in therapy. Nevertheless, therapists need to actively reach out to all family members and invite them to attend, lest the hesitancy to get involved prevails strongly for the majority. A wise therapist works with whoever is available and later invites outliers to attend, telling them something of the dynamics discovered and emphasizing the role they could take up to the benefit of the family or ill family member. A letter from the therapist summarizing what has been understood of the family's strengths and challenges can serve as a vital inducement to draw together reluctant participants. Often, early separations, divorces, or conflicts have left unfinished business, which can serve as motivations for the family to reconvene in the hope of resolution of hurts from long ago.

Susan and Bill were often asked by their father to make excuses on his behalf as teenagers when they recognized his infidelity, an alliance that cast them into unwelcome awkwardness with their mother. His advanced illness and an associated family meeting provided them with an unanticipated opportunity to revisit ambivalent feelings and gain an apology from their dying parent before it was too late. The active sharing of these feelings facilitates grief resolution, rather than leaving anger repressed and more likely to persist chronically as prolonged grief disorder (see Chapter 12).

Goals of Therapy

Therapists work to facilitate a constructive process, wherein families grapple with both enabling and restrictive choices that flow from a deepened understanding of who they are and where they might go to accomplish the following goals:

1. To recognize that illness, loss, and change bring normal human emotions of grief (their mourning) alongside a transition point of opportunity for review, reconnection, and reconfiguration, flowing from choices about relational life (their coping)
2. To make explicit the family's relational pattern of valued and meaningful connections (their strengths) that invariably sit in balance with differences in interests, temperament, and goodness of fit, the latter creating tension and disagreement in family life (their vulnerabilities)
3. To foster acceptance of their heritage, who they are and can choose to become, while clarifying the potential pathways of mutual respect and care, recognition of similarity and difference (their acceptance of reality),

and adoption of celebration and commitment, tolerance and forgiveness, and closeness or distance that flow as choices in continuing relational life (their constructive choice of outcome)

4. To support them through a period of revisiting, reconnecting, reconciling, and reconfiguring as they mourn and adapt to their choice of future family life

This therapeutic process is consistent with theoretical constructs of dual process (oscillation between loss orientation and restoration orientation) (Stroebe, Schut, & Finkenauer, 2001), attachment theory (Ainsworth & Eichberg, 1991; Bowlby, 1977), social-cognitive reframing of assumptive worlds (Janoff-Bulman, 1989; Parkes, 1972; see also Chapter 1), and processes of group adaptation (Whitaker & Lieberman, 1964). These therapeutic objectives benefit from being modest in their ambition to effect change, respectful of personal autonomy and choice, and wise about the systemic forces that operate at any given time, struggling between maintenance of what is familiar and growth through novelty and creativity.

Techniques Used by Therapists

The goals of therapy are accomplished through the establishment of a trusting alliance, the creation of a safe environment for exploration and growth in understanding, a curiosity fostered by skillful questions, and eventually an integrated understanding by the family through the process of balanced summaries. Traditional principles of family therapy are represented by circularity, neutrality, and hypothesizing (Cecchin, 1987). Each of these merits brief definition.

Although the therapist's natural warmth, interest, enthusiasm, and compassionate care must shine through, avoidance of being drawn into any alliance with an individual or subgroup is essential to serve the good of the family-as-a-whole: *neutrality*. This stance is made possible through asking naturally inquisitive questions, but also through posing these sequentially to different family members to gain varied perspectives that make explicit the dynamic forces operational within the system: *circularity*. Such inquiry is driven by wisdom and insight, which permits the therapist to recognize the potential competing views and to respect the family's ability to make constructive choices when its relational processes are made explicit: *hypothesizing*.

The questioning technique needs to be facilitative as its circular process of moving around the room unfolds. Much use is thus made of the diverse views of family members, helpfully placed in tension, one with another, to emphasize the richness and variety of family life, and especially the blending of backgrounds that marriage creates. Construction of a genogram across three generations usefully highlights relational patterns that repeat themselves from generation to generation, together with patterns of coping with loss and death, especially when these can be contrasted with adaptive and maladaptive features (Kissane, Bloch, McKenzie, McDowall, & Nitzan, 1998). Such exposition of transgenerational patterns maintains respect and avoids blame through the family's recognition of inherited dispositions.

Tomm's (1988) model of investigative and facilitative questions casts the therapist's role as catalytic, yet nondirective, through the framing of words that invite reflection (reflexive questions) or consideration of choice (strategic questions) (Dumont & Kissane, 2009). Many opinions, intriguing stories, and much confounding material inevitably emerge, necessitating the vital skill of constructing integrative summaries that clarify the group's mutual understanding and foster its coherent recognition for all involved. The active naming of patterns, relational dynamics, similarities and differences, tensions and balances, and coping response styles is grist for the mill. Importantly, affirming what robustness and resilience are present counters any awkwardness for the family in naming their vulnerabilities. Linking the latter to transgenerational patterns increases acceptance and tolerance, while also inviting choice over whether the family repeats or varies any behavioral response to key events that disrupt ordinary life.

Structuring all of the above within a framework of focused therapy helps the family make sense of any plan to accomplish achievable goals of family therapy. This negotiation needs to be both explicit and achieve consensus to ensure cooperation and commitment to the potential work that can be pursued. Movement must occur from the perspective of attending as a care provider to assist (or simply a bystander who watches) the sick person, to ownership of family membership in a team that wants to realign its shared direction to collectively and collaboratively work toward the mutual benefit of all. Unless members can recite their goals—to communicate feelings more openly, to cooperate more generously, and to respect differences of opinion more thoughtfully—the holding frame of therapy has not been established to create shared confidence about the objectives pursued together. Making a commitment to attend four or six sessions over as many months necessitates working through ambivalence about these collective pursuits. Considerable therapist skill underpins any agreement reached by the family to continue to work together in a mutually supportive manner to achieve overtly shared goals.

Themes Met within Oncology and Palliative Care

In the cancer setting, talk about death and dying proves an obstacle for many families wanting to avoid distress and to protect patients from becoming demoralized about their plight (Zaider & Kissane, 2010). For patients accepting their reality, however, its acknowledgment begins the conversation about farewell, with its accompanying expressions of gratitude and future hopes and dreams for the survivors. For those unable to acknowledge the finitude of their life, avoidant coping blocks any sharing of anticipatory grief; therapy is often sought by some relatives wanting more open communication about end-of-life preparation. Families in these predicaments often want to know from a potential therapist whether he or she will collude with their protective stance before agreeing to meet as a group.

Once death has occurred, the story of illness and its diagnosis and treatment, mired with myriad complications and challenges along the way, becomes the essential narrative for the family to share and integrate into its history. Conflict over the medical approach, caregiving roles, and the distribution of tasks and responsiveness of those involved are common themes that replicate relational dynamics from years earlier. Therapists strive to move beyond the concrete facts to better recognition of patterns of relating and responding; relatives often prefer to battle on about the minuscule details. Nevertheless, most therapy makes progress when deeper understanding emerges about interactional styles and related choices.

Unresolved conflicts, affairs, or family secrets present barriers to open communication across the generations, whether such perceived wrongs involved a criminal, sexual, homosexual, or mentally ill dimension and occurred in the context of abuses, thefts, bankruptcies, gambling debts, drunken violence, or contagious disease. Issues of shame, hatred, vengeance, violation, or complicity impact the related emotions that coexist with these complex issues. Sometimes the truth must emerge for the healing of complicated grief, but the family needs time to establish trust and confidence that a safe environment can be maintained to work through the associated affects.

Cultural and ethnic traditions and religious beliefs form another constellation of issues that may influence the course of the therapy and themes needing to be discussed (see Chapters 26 and 27). Blended families that create a mixture of backgrounds bring considerable diversity to the work, sometimes with reasons for migration, divorce, or separation never having been fully explained. Sensitivity, patience, and wisdom are crucial therapeutic attributes.

Evidence for Efficacy of Family Therapy Commenced Preventively during Palliative Care

A randomized controlled trial has demonstrated the ability of family therapy commenced during palliative care and continued into bereavement to protect families from complicated grief and depressive disorders (Kissane et al., 2006). Smaller effect sizes were evident for more dysfunctional families (Kissane et al., 2007), leading to dose intensity studies now being conducted with support from the National Cancer Institute in the United States. We anticipate that families with only mild or *intermediate* disturbance in their functioning will gain from relatively brief periods of intervention, whereas *sullen* and *hostile* types will need more prolonged support over 18 months.

Illustrations of Challenging Cancer Families

Mild family dysfunction can become quickly responsive to improved communication when protective barriers have been well intentioned yet not conducive to adaptive outcome.

> I remember—my mother died of cancer … it was so difficult for everybody and … somehow I want to make it a little better for us … we would talk to each other about my mother, but she was the one dying and nobody talked to her about what they were experiencing.

> There are things that I feel we don't talk about and I understand why … but I feel like it's something I'd like to do if it's appropriate … [pause]. We don't talk about me dying and I'd like to.

More severe family dysfunction can mask and perpetuate clinical depression unless the relational issues are defined and understood as necessary therapeutic targets.

Daughter 1: How are we all going to deal with Brenda's depression?
Brenda: I wish my old therapist was still practicing.
Therapist: Who in the family could Brenda pick up the phone to and say, "It's been a month since Mommy died and I'm really missing her? Who would Brenda be likely to turn to first?"
Daughter 1: I think she's most comfortable confiding in our brother, Don.

A therapist used to the individual setting will typically feel the urge to respond empathically to distress voiced by a family member. Yet more powerful support can come from relatives around the circle. Questions to others about the tears seen in one party can facilitate the development of compassion and mutual support, with the capacity for it to be sustained beyond the therapy. Key differences in therapeutic style are paramount for effective family work.

Joe had spent 10 years in an orphanage as a child, leaving him with a vulnerability to abandonment that had been assuaged by his marriage to Sheila. Her death cast Joe back into a lonely state, despairing, "It feels like a flood and I have to swim through it, and I cry and feel ashamed of this. My uselessness! A timeless life! I am withered up. I have nothing. I think of suicide." The daughter, Maureen, was also bereft as the remaining woman of the household. Both sons, Peter and Chris, had created independent lives away from the family home. Therapy gave them insight into the need to support Joe and Maureen, visiting regularly and engaging with them until the pain of grief began to ease. The therapy contained their distress, and although Joe and Maureen declined referral for individual treatment, the family sessions guided them supportively across 18 months until they both reengaged in life.

Dependence on alcohol, profound aloneness, suicidal thoughts to achieve reunion, preoccupation with physical symptoms and personal health, traumatic memories of the death, guilt over unresolved wrongs, blame and criticism of others, spiritual doubt, and despair: Many forms of distress are seen in the bereaved (Kissane & Bloch, 2002). A family approach can helpfully deepen the support and rally the family's assistance when the pain of loss seems devastating.

In very different, noncancer settings of bereavement or traumatic grief consequent upon family violence, the collective experience of members constitutes an important reason to grieve together. When suicide or homicide has happened within the family, revisiting the violence in the safety of a contained therapeutic environment can be restorative to members unable to otherwise express their rage at the deceased.

ENGAGING BEREAVED FAMILIES IN THERAPY: RELIANCE AND REINFORCEMENT OF NATURAL SUPPORT RESOURCES

When confronted with the loss of a loved one, most people rely on their own strengths and those of the social network they live in to face the challenges of grief (Bonanno, Wortman, & Nesse, 2004; Boss, 2006; Shapiro, 2008). However, some search for more support or professional guidance. As therapists, we can only offer a temporary connection. Therefore, we emphasize the importance of connecting the bereaved with their own natural support network, where many people receive the ongoing human connection needed for resiliency (Boss, 2006). Inspired by Boss's concept of the "psychological family" and Landau's (2007) construct of "network therapy," we broaden the conception of "family" within this model to persons who are perceived as supportive, concerned, and willing to help.

In the following, we describe a case to illustrate how we can help the bereaved by optimizing reliance on and reinforcement of their natural support resources. From a collaborative approach to psychotherapy (Anderson & Gehart, 2007), we aim to make space for stories to be shared. At the same time, we want to attend to the possible tensions and hesitations involved in this exchange (Hooghe, 2009; Hooghe, Neimeyer, & Rober, in press; Rober, 2002), and the possible value of silence, for the individual as well as for the system (Baddeley & Singer, 2010).

Inviting Other Family Members: A Dialogue Between Different Voices

When someone seeks individual therapy, the therapist can immediately encourage his or her attendance with other family members. Thus,

---

Mieke, age 42, sought psychotherapy following the loss of her 16-year-old son, Pieter, who died 10 months ago. During the first few months after his death, she had "coped quite well," but now she felt "stuck in her grief" and wanted someone to talk to. As her appointment was arranged, she was asked if she could bring others from her family who could help the therapist to better understand her "stuckness." She seemed surprised by this request, stating that she had assumed she would come alone, but immediately added that she could ask her husband to come along. Her husband, Koen, aged 47 years, was recently diagnosed with a brain tumor and was currently receiving chemotherapy.

Inviting other family members to the therapy sessions generates multiple perspectives and brings varied meanings into the conversation. In the dialogue, new meanings are interactively produced between all those who are present in the therapy room (Bakhtin, 1981; Seikkula, 2002; Seikkula & Arnkil, 2006). Additionally, already existing or sometimes new support resources are enforced.

Talking About Talking

As therapists, we don't want unilaterally to promote the expression of grief, but rather to create a space and opportunity to explore with family members the possibility of sharing their grief experiences with others.

For the first session, Mieke and Koen come together as a couple. From the very beginning, it is obvious that Koen, the father, attended because his wife had invited him and not because he personally wanted to talk. While Mieke began by telling the story of their son's death, Koen looked around and appeared somewhat anxious. As his wife described the haunting images of Pieter hanging with a rope around his neck in his bedroom, the therapist wondered how it was for Koen to listen to this. Koen replied firmly, "I came because Mieke said I needed to come along. I will surely not come along each time." Then he added, "I don't have a lot to say; I'll listen. There is nothing we can do about this. Pieter won't come back by talking about it." Immediately, Mieke pointed to their very different ways of coping with their loss. Quite often, she wondered if Koen cared about having lost his son. This comment caused Koen to be even more upset. The therapist expressed curiosity about Koen's way of dealing with the death of his son, highlighting that the difference between bereaved mothers and fathers is a common challenge in bereaved couples. Bereaved fathers might avoid therapy in which they would be invited to talk or listen. The therapist also added that she had learned from many bereaved fathers that sharing their grief is not always experienced as helpful. She wondered, "How is this for you?" Koen explained, now less defensively, that he usually "takes things as they come" and does not feel the need to talk about the loss. "This is how I am: It passed, leave it quiet, it will go away." Remarkably, he added, "But perhaps for Mieke, this is different," and Mieke replied, "Well, Pieter was that way too, like his father."

As marital and family therapists, we want to foster tolerance for the different meanings attributed to the loss, for different views and ways of understanding what happened, together with recognition of the varied coping styles of partners and family members who are grieving (see Chapter 7). In this case, the therapist's acknowledgment of the challenge posed by each parent having different response styles created some space for a less argumentative atmosphere. It then became possible to learn more about their unique ways of coping. Not only the tendency to share grief with others, as in the case of Mieke, but also the ambivalence to talk and desire to "leave it alone," as in the case of Koen, are considered to be coping styles with equal value. Through a collaborative approach, we explore how they each experience such talking about the pain of their loss. This "talking about talking" (Fredman, 1997; Hooghe, 2009) is somewhat different from the dominant approach in individual psychotherapy, and more specifically in grief therapy, where the emphasis is usually put on the importance of sharing grief in order to create a stronger bond, a sense of togetherness and relational intimacy (Cook & Oltjenbruns, 1998; Gottlieb, Lang, & Amsel, 1996; Hagemeister & Rosenblatt, 1997; Sedney, Baker, & Gross, 1994). Some authors in the bereavement literature have advocated for a balanced view about the degree to which talking or not talking is beneficial for individual couples or families (Couper et al., 2006; Hooghe et al., in press; Rosenblatt, 2000a, 2000b). For the father, Koen, his reluctance or hesitation not only concerned *talking* about the loss in the context of this therapy but also *listening* to his wife's stories. Listening brings a distressing confrontation with the loss, which for some can be experienced as painful, useless, or too disruptive (Hooghe, 2009).

Engaging Possible Resources of the Bereaved

In the initial phase of therapy, and also during the whole therapy process, we can explore possible support resources with our clients.

Toward the end of the first session, the therapist and the couple talked about Koen's choice not to come along subsequently. The therapist asked Mieke if she would invite somebody else whom she thought would prove supportive of her grief. Mieke commented that their 19-year-old daughter was also unlikely to come. Lovingly, she mentioned that their daughter is like her father and brother, mainly wanting to push forward and not dwell on what had happened. Encouraged by the therapist, she decided that she would ask her daughter nevertheless. Furthermore, Mieke thought that her own sister, Greet, who lives in the same village, would be most willing to accompany her.

Sometimes there is a thin line between being respectful of patient's choices (e.g., choosing not to attend, or preferring to come alone) and our own therapeutic objective to strengthen possible connections in the natural network (Hooghe, 2009). This can be a real dilemma. Empowering the bereaved to choose who attends, rather than assuming that it should be the whole family or particular family members (e.g., both bereaved parents as partners, and the children of the widow), honors the bereaved as experts on their own life situation and their resourcefulness. Often, the bereaved do not want to be a burden to others by inviting them to therapy. If so, the therapist can help to explore any ambivalence to invite these relatives. Although we want to respect their choices, we also want to keep in mind the close relational network in which the bereaved is embedded in daily life. We can do this by frequently inquiring about them, for example by asking about the impact of the grief process and the therapy on them. Sometimes we don't know whether a particular relative refuses to come, or whether he or she was never invited. Encouraging the bereaved to bring their relatives at least once can give us a better understanding of their relational network and possible support resources. Often, an initially reluctant relative decides to take up a genuinely supportive role for the good of the family.

Sharing Grief Creates New Meaning

During collaborative narration, or joint storytelling, families engage in sense making (Koenig Kellas & Trees, 2006; see also Chapter 1). Or, as Nadeau (2008), puts it, "Out of their conversations, threads of meaning start to emerge and, over time, these threads become woven into a tapestry of family meanings." Hence, shared meaning making within the family is both encouraged and actively facilitated.

For the next seven sessions, Mieke attended with her sister, Greet. First, they talked about Koen's absence. Mieke accepted his decision, noting that her husband was content to have met the therapist and to appreciate where she would be going for future sessions. For Mieke, it was important that he came initially. She reflected, "I always thought he didn't care much, but now I understand that he is just too afraid to talk about it. And, you know, he came because he loves me." Now, she also felt thankful toward her sister Greet, who attended willingly, and with whom Mieke thought she might be able to share a lot of her grief.

During subsequent sessions, they talked a lot about Pieter, who he was, how he had been confronted with identity struggles, how Mieke found his dead body and tried to resuscitate him, and how she had been trying to go on with daily life since his death. In the presence of her supportive sister, an atmosphere emerged to comfortably share these stories, some that had never been told before. The therapist was privileged to hear their stories as they, at times, expressed surprise about their somewhat different experiences. They brought up a lot of memories together; they laughed sometimes, cried often, and comforted each other frequently.

Although most of the time Mieke's experiences remain central, Greet's both similar and diverse perspectives about life enrich the conversation, bring new meanings and new stories, and, perhaps most importantly, create an experience of shared grief.

Reinforcing Human Connection in the Natural Context

As therapists working with grief and bereavement, we can feel powerless in the face of devastating and irreversible loss. However, from a family or network perspective, we aim to strengthen the competencies and resiliency of the survivors through their family, thus reinforcing human connection in its most natural context. As was the case for Mieke, faced with inconceivable losses, coming to the sessions with her sister clearly deepened the connection between them.

As family therapy progressed, Koen's brain tumor worsened and his chemotherapy did not hold his illness at bay. Sadly, he began to decline quickly, became frailer and dependent, and needed much help from his family. Mieke stopped working and took care of him in a loving way. She knew he would die soon. The therapy sessions served as a sporadic but helpful respite while her husband was cared for at home by a nurse. Gradually, stories about Pieter's death transitioned to Mieke's grief over Koen's cancer, stories of the care he needed, and his pending death. With her sister Greet, she shared her loneliness and fears, and even began to plan for Koen's funeral. Often, the therapist inquired about Mieke's daughter, Veerle, who would soon lose her father, only one year after she had lost her brother. Although Mieke had frequently invited her daughter to attend therapy, Veerle preferred the support of her boyfriend, and reassured her mother that she would come if she felt the need.

The therapist discovered that these two sisters developed their own ritual while driving to therapy. Although the actual journey took only 20 minutes, they allowed a full hour. Laughingly, they admitted that they have their "own secret spot, somewhere down the road," to talk together on the way. After each session, they regularly treated themselves to an ice cream as a reward for their hard and emotional work. In this way, they connected for more than 3 hours during each evening they came to therapy.

One week after the seventh session, Mieke called the therapist to say that Koen had died. The last days of his life had been "horribly painful, but also very connected and loving." At the funeral, Mieke expressed appreciation not only for the therapy but also especially for the wonderful connection with her sister, who had been beside her, often silently, in these last days of Koen's life.

This illustration highlights poignantly not only how these sisters could be a rich support for each other in the sessions but also, and even more importantly, how their relationship served them deeply in the real world. The therapist felt quite powerless to lighten the pain of these cruel losses, but the model of therapy fostered enhanced connections with relatives that could be relied on. Family resources can be creatively harnessed to good effect through such deeper connection, mutual support, and the therapist's confidence in the robustness that emerges despite great adversity and grief.

INTEGRATIVE CONCLUDING THOUGHTS

When illness, death, and grief enter our lives, not only are we deeply moved emotionally, but also these experiences inevitably challenge our beliefs, our worldview, who we are, and whom we relate to. We need to reconstruct our individual sense of identity, as well as our family's sense of identity as a whole. We feel intense pain, perhaps a sense of devastation or suffering, alongside other potential feelings of love and gratitude. Each loss impacts all of our relationships, and these, in turn, can be an important resource of support. From a family therapy perspective, the value of the relational network in which the bereaved is embedded is paramount. As professionals working with palliative care and bereavement services, we can create the opportunity to join with the families of those dying, thereby utilizing the natural continuity that exists between palliative care and subsequent bereavement. For families "at risk" of increased challenges in their grieving processes, we can initiate a shared family process, in which meanings can be exchanged and created anew through the family's shared dialogue.

Of course, some of the bereaved only reach us long after death has occurred, presenting for therapy at different times in the grieving process. Although the majority might initially contact professionals expecting individual assistance, this individual therapy approach for the bereaved potentially neglects the natural resources available through their family, friends, and local community. Here we have presented a systemic model of bereavement care, one that can be applied preventively to those deemed at some risk, or one applied acutely for those with emerging or established complications of grief. Recognition of the family as an ally to the therapist has the potential to shorten the overall requirement for bereavement care and lessen its intensity through having family members join as a supportive network for those most deeply affected by the loss.

ACKNOWLEDGMENTS

David Kissane acknowledges the research support of the National Cancer Institute (Grant R01-CA115329) in the United States, and An Hooghe thanks her colleagues at Context, Peter Rober and Lieven Migerode, for the many years of inspiring dialogue that continues.

REFERENCES

Ainsworth, M. D. S., & Eichberg, C. G. (1991). Effects on infant–mother attachment of mother's experience related to loss of attachment figure. In J. Stevenson-Hinde & P. Marris (Eds.), *Attachment across the life cycle* (pp. 160–183). New York: Routledge.

Anderson, H., & Gehart, D. (Eds.). (2007). *Collaborative therapy: Relationships and conversations that make a difference*. New York: Routledge.

Baddeley, J., & Singer, J. A. (2010). A loss in the family: Silence, memory, and narrative identity after bereavement. *Memory*, *18*(2), 198–207.

Bakhtin, M. (1981). *The dialogic imagination*. Austin: University of Texas Press.

Bonanno, G. A., Wortman, C. B., & Nesse, R. M. (2004). Prospective patterns of resilience and maladjustment during widowhood. *Psychology of Aging, 19*(2), 260–271.

Boss, P. (2006). *Loss, trauma and resilience: Therapeutic work with ambiguous loss*. New York: Norton.

Bowlby, J. (1977). The making and breaking of affectional bonds. II. Some principles of psychotherapy. The fiftieth Maudsley Lecture. *British Journal of Psychiatry, 130*, 421–431.

Cecchin, G. (1987). Hypothesizing, circularity, and neutrality revisited: An invitation to curiosity. *Family Process, 26*, 405–413.

Cook, A. S., & Oltjenbruns, K. A. (1998). *Dying and grieving: Lifespan and family perspectives* (2nd ed.). Fort Worth, TX: Harcourt Brace.

Couper, J., Bloch, S., Love, A., Macvean, M., Duchesne, G. M., & Kissane, D. (2006). Psychosocial adjustment of female partners of men with prostate cancer: A review of the literature. *Psychooncology, 15*(11), 937–953.

Dumont, I., & Kissane, D. (2009). Techniques for framing questions in conducting family meetings in palliative care. *Palliative Support Care*, 7(2), 163–170.

Edwards, B., & Lavery, V. (2005). Validity of the Family Relationships Index as a screening tool. *Psychooncology, 14*, 546–554.

Fredman, G. (1997). *Death talk: Conversations with children and families*. London: Karnac.

Gottlieb, L., Lang, A., & Amsel, R. (1996). The long-term effects of grief on marital intimacy following infant death. *Omega, 33*, 1–19.

Hagemeister, A. K., & Rosenblatt, P. C. (1997). Grief and the sexual relationship of couples who have experienced a child's death. *Death Studies, 21*, 231–251.

Hooghe, A. (2009). Talking about talking, hesitations to talk and not talking. *Context Magazine, 101*, 33–35.

Hooghe, A., Neimeyer, R. A., & Rober, P. (In press). The complexity of couple communication in bereavement: An illustrative case study. *Death Studies*.

Janoff-Bulman, R. (1989). Assumptive worlds and the stress of traumatic events: Applications of the schema construct. *Social Cognition*, 7, 113–136.

Kissane, D. (2000). Family grief therapy: A model for working with families during palliative care and bereavement. In L. Baider, C. Cooper, & A. De-Nour (Eds.), *Cancer and the family* (pp. 175–197). Chichester: Wiley.

Kissane, D., & Bloch, S. (1994). Family grief. *British Journal of Psychiatry, 164*, 728–740.

Kissane, D., & Bloch, S. (2002). *Family focused grief therapy: A model of family-centred care during palliative care and bereavement*. Buckingham: Open University Press.

Kissane, D., Lichtenthal, W. G., & Zaider, T. (2007). Family care before and after bereavement. *Omega (Westport), 56*(1), 21–32.

Kissane, D., McKenzie, M., Bloch, S., Moskowitz, C., McKenzie, D., & O'Neill, I. (2006). Family focused grief therapy: A randomized controlled trial in palliative care and bereavement. *American Journal of Psychiatry, 163*, 1208–1218.

Kissane, D. W., Bloch, S., McKenzie, M., McDowall, A. C., & Nitzan, R. (1998). Family grief therapy: A preliminary account of a new model to promote healthy family functioning during palliative care and bereavement. *Psychooncology*, 7(1), 14–25.

Kissane, D. W., Bloch, S., Dowe, D. L., Snyder, R. D., Onghena, P., McKenzie, D. P., et al. (1996). The Melbourne family grief study I: Perceptions of family functioning in bereavement. *American Journal of Psychiatry, 153*, 650–658.

Kissane, D. W., McKenzie, M., McKenzie, D. P., Forbes, A., O'Neill, I., & Bloch, S. (2003). Psychosocial morbidity associated with patterns of family functioning in palliative care: Baseline data from the family focused grief therapy controlled trial. *Palliative Medicine, 17*(6), 527–537.

Koenig Kellas, J., & Trees, A. R. (2006). Finding meaning in difficult family experiences: Sensemaking and interaction processes during joint family storytelling. *Journal of Family Communication*, *6*(1), 49–76.

Landau, J. (2007). Enhancing resilience: Families and communities as agents for change. *Family Processes*, *46*(3), 351–365.

Moos, R. H., & Moos, B. S. (1981). *Family Environment Scale manual*. Stanford, CA: Consulting Psychologists Press.

Nadeau, J. W. (2008). Meaning-making in bereaved families: Assessment, intervention and future research. In M. Stroebe, R. Hansson, H. Schut, & W. Stroebe (Eds.), *Handbook of bereavement research: 21st century perspectives* (pp. 511–530). Washington, DC: American Psychological Association.

Parkes, C. M. (1972). Components of the reaction to loss of a limb, spouse or home. *Journal of Psychosomatic Research*, *16*(5), 343–349.

Rober, P. (2002). Some hypotheses about hesitations and their nonverbal expression in the family therapy session. *Journal of Family Therapy*, *24*, 187–204.

Rosenblatt, P. C. (2000a). *Parent grief: Narratives of loss and relationships*. Philadelphia: Brunner/Mazel.

Rosenblatt, P. C. (2000b). *Help your marriage to survive the death of a child*. Philadelphia: Temple University Press.

Sedney, M. A., Baker, J. E., & Gross, E. (1994). "The story" of a death: Therapeutic considerations with bereaved families. *Journal of Marital and Family Therapy*, *20*, 287–296.

Seikkula, J. (2002). Open dialogues with good and poor outcomes for psychotic crises: Examples from families with violence. *Journal of Marital and Family Therapy*, *28*(3), 263–274.

Seikkula, J., & Arnkil, T. E. (2006). *Dialogical meetings in social networks*. London: Karnac.

Shapiro, E. R. (2008). Whose recovery, of what? Relationships and environments promoting grief and growth. *Death Studies*, *32*(1), 40–58.

Stroebe, M., Schut, H., & Finkenauer, C. (2001). The traumatization of grief? A conceptual framework for understanding the trauma-bereavement interface. *Israeli Journal of Psychiatry and Related Sciences*, *38*(3–4), 185–201.

Tomm, K. (1988). Interventive interviewing: Part III. Intending to ask lineal, circular, strategic or reflexive questions? *Family Process*, *27*, 1–15.

Whitaker, D., & Lieberman, M. (1964). *Psychotherapy through the group process*. New York: Atherton Press.

Zaider, T., & Kissane, D. (2009). The assessment and management of family distress during palliative care. *Current Opinion and Support of Palliative Care*, *3*(1), 67–71.

Zaider, T., & Kissane, D. (2010). Psychosocial interventions for couples and families coping with cancer. In J. Holland, W. Breitbart, P. Jacobsen, M. Lederberg, M. Loscalzo, & R. McCorkle (Eds.), *Psycho-oncology* (2nd ed., pp. 483–487). Oxford: Oxford University Press.

23

Grief and Expressive Arts Therapy

BARBARA E. THOMPSON and JOY S. BERGER

On this given day and at this moment, mourners are gathered at vigils, deathbeds, wakes, and funerals throughout the world. The bereaved are giving expression to the meaning of the deceased person's physical absence and ongoing presence in their lives through acts of remembrance. The words, images, stories, music, cultural adornments, and movements these mourners select reenact rituals from their past attachments and losses, yet with a new impact and interpretation for this loss. Sights, sounds, touch, and tone can reveal veiled emotions and can tap into otherwise inaudible questions about living and dying (Berger, 2006).

Fresh markers stake grief into the soul's ground. Memories of these expressions will be revisited for years to come, whether physically at a gravesite or emotionally within one's being. Mourners often replay and "re-search" their experiences for a greater understanding of their relationship with the deceased, while learning how to live with their absence and create a new life with the living (Stroebe & Schut, 2001).

Although this book focuses on grief and bereavement in contemporary society, extensive examples exist in virtually all prior civilizations, geographical areas, cultures, and faith systems. Ancient shamans sang, drummed, created body paintings and masks, and danced for the ill, the dying, and the mourners (Goss & Klass, 2005; Morgan & Laungani, 2002). Artisans crafted pyramids, gold-laden tombs, Stonehenge-like burial grounds, and statued homages for the dead. Through the ages, these expressions have been congruent with the creator's historical and geographical contexts (Berger, 2006; Small & Walser, 1996).

Moving forward, today's globalization awakens us to deeply rooted similarities and unique distinctions in our cultural and religious or spiritual modalities for expressive mourning and healing (Irish & Lundquist, 2003). This chapter will explore use of the expressive arts by contemporary clinicians working with people experiencing grief, loss, and bereavement in clinical practice and community settings in today's society.

WHAT IS EXPRESSIVE ARTS THERAPY?

Expressive arts therapy is a distinct discipline that is part of the larger creative arts therapy community, which includes music, art, drama, poetry, and dance therapies, as well as psychodrama and bibliotherapy (McNiff, 2009). It is philosophically aligned with phenomenology in its emphasis on prereflective awareness and expression of the lived experience through art making. In some traditions, images that emerge during art making are assigned meaning or used diagnostically (Malchiodi, 1998). The alternative view of expressive arts therapy is that the image, in all of its sensory immediacy and "thingliness," reveals its latent meaning to the receptive witness with no need to impose additional meanings (Levine, 2009). This way of setting aside presuppositions and "moving forward" through the senses is suggested in Rilke's (1902–1906/1981) poem of the same name, where he described seeing "farther into paintings" and feeling "closer to what language can't reach" (p. 101). Phenomenological description is used to heighten awareness of sensory experience and reduce an inclination to focus on the skill-oriented aspects of art making or a tendency to think about rather than sense the work. This approach, referred to by Paolo Knill as "low skill-high sensitivity," needs to be particularly emphasized when working with adolescents and adults who may view themselves as "not creative" (McNiff, 2009).

In expressive arts therapy, an attitude of openness and receptivity invites images to appear and allows them to find their appropriate forms. In order to stay in an imaginative mode, responses are kept aesthetic and metaphoric, such as a poetic response to a painting rather than reductive interpretation or analysis. This allows stories to emerge in new and unanticipated ways, freshened and fashioned through embodied forms that can be sensed and shared (Levine, 2009; Romanoff & Thompson, 2006). Moreover, the metaphoric and mythic dimensions of the artwork can be apprehended as stories take shape through the art-making process, and through responsive engagement with the artwork itself (McNiff, 2009). Asking an image in a painting what it has to say or teach, or what it wants to know, helps to elicit dialogue that engages both artist and therapist in a playful mode of discovery (Romanoff & Thompson, 2006). McNiff (2004) suggested that if interpretation is seen as a storytelling process, then we are able to see the "inevitable multiplicity of meanings that an image suggests" (p. 81). For instance, 23.1 is a black-and-white reproduction of a color painting entitled *The Never Ending Path*. A young man named Michael who attended a workshop run by the first author rendered this painting in response to the September 11, 2001, World Trade Center attack. Though none of Michael's immediate family died in the attacks, family members of friends and colleagues died that day. Michael spoke of a loss of innocence and safety as well as grief for a city he once called home. Animated figures, connected by a line that weaves its way through the center of the painting, move toward an uncertain future that is represented by a red question mark embedded in a series of staccato dark gray marks at the right border of the painting. Michael's poetic response to the painting describes a range of emotions in response to September 11 concomitant with an underlying belief in the potential to create a positive future as expressed by the closing lines to his poem, "Move into the unknown future with

Figure 23.1 *The never ending path* (2001), acrylic on paper.

optimism and love. We are our world." Michael said that he had not painted since childhood and that this was his first poem. Several years later, Michael continued to write poetry as a way to narrate his experiences and create a worldview.

Expressive arts therapy, unlike some creative arts therapies that focus primarily on one mode of artistic expression, integrates multiple modes of expression in order to deepen and widen the range of expressive and imaginative possibility (McNiff, 2009). Images of grief and loss are allowed to take shape in whatever artistic medium is indigenous to the experience and consonant with the particular circumstances and needs of the individual or community. This freedom to move from one expressive mode to another prompts shifts in the articulation and elaboration of images as more of the senses are engaged. Moreover, transformations can occur as images of grief and loss in pictures, words, movements, sounds, or dramatic enactment are formed, reformed, and reimagined through responsive, inquiring engagement. These acts of "making" and sensing, or "sense making," are ways of knowing, shaping, and storying grief and loss. This way, experiences do not remain "sense-less," silenced, unseen, immovable, or untouchable. The arts are also ways of learning from or through grief. In the first poem in his series on *The Book of Poverty and Death*, Rilke (1903/1981) spoke of "not having much knowledge yet in grief" (p. 55). Though he longed for a "great transforming" to happen, he was at the beginning, "pushing through solid rock" with "no space" to see a way through "this massive darkness" (p. 55). For Rilke, poetry was a "way through," not "to accomplish something, to become a better person, to achieve salvation, or to publish a book," but rather to "be alive" (p. 187), to learn through grief and to praise life, while trying to "understand when it is time to do either" (p. 190).

The arts also offer opportunities for the communalization of grief and loss, providing necessary structures and modes of expression for experiences that are difficult to convey in conventional language or for which there are no words (J. S. Rogers, 2007; Romanoff & Thompson, 2006). For example, therapeutic theater, using approaches drawn from expressive arts therapies and psychodrama, provides structured support for participants to express and experience the truth of their stories through the primary medium of the body. Through role-playing, dramatization, and empathic witnessing, participants "discover the deep meaning of his/her own history of experiences and their influence upon his/her decisions and acts in life" (Naor, 1999, p. 223).

Levine (2009) suggested that we "make art not to be saved but to be seen" (p. 11). Expressive arts therapy is a way of being present to suffering by letting it find its artistic form. Through the arts, we can "respond to and change the world through the act of shaping what is given to us" (p. 25). If *transform* means to "change the form of; to change into another shape or form; to metamorphose" (Oxford English Dictionary, 1989) the expressive arts offer ways to literally and metaphorically transform experiences of grief and loss so that they can be borne differently.

DEEP PLAY

Along with phenomenology, expressive arts therapy has roots in "therapies of the imagination" such as archetypal and Jungian psychology (McNiff, 2009, p. 42). Carl Jung was the "first psychotherapist to fully integrate the arts into everything he did" (p. 44). During a period of disorientation and turmoil, Jung discovered a method for his own self-healing that became known as "active imagination" (Jung, 1997). According to Jung, active imagination involves "letting the unconscious come up" by being mindful of moods, bodily sensations, or images that arise, and "coming to terms with the unconscious" by giving images physical expression through dance, painting, sculpture, music, or other artistic forms (Jung, 1997, p. 19). These approaches have been likened to deep play.

The concept of "play" is central to expressive arts therapy (McNiff, 2009). Therapy becomes a place and time "in-between" worlds, where different possibilities can be "played out" without censure, and with the necessary structure and containment offered by the therapeutic relationship, setting, and particularities of the artistic medium. Simple approaches can be used to stimulate a creative process that is exploratory and experimental. For instance, "jump-off lines" can be used to start a writing process (J. E. Rogers, 2007, p. 60). This approach was used with a 16-year-old client named Helen, whose mother had died 2 months earlier from a long-term illness. Helen wanted to visit her mother's grave on her mother's birthday but "didn't know what to say or do." Though generally comfortable with writing as a mode of expression, she "couldn't find the right words." To help her begin, Helen was asked to complete a series of sentences beginning with lines such as "I want you to know …" "I will always remember …" "I never told you …" and "I remember when …" The sentence openings were repeated multiple times, which encouraged Helen to become more spontaneous and playful in her successive responses. Eventually, Helen began to tell stories that communicated the depth of her relationship with her mother. Having shifted into an imaginative mode, Helen was then able to create a plan for a ceremony honoring her mother's upcoming birthday.

There are various ways to introduce art into a session. You can ask whether the person or people you are working with are willing to try something new. If so, you might invite them to make marks with various drawing materials using the nondominant hand while paying attention to the range of possibilities inherent in the materials. Another popular approach is the use of D. W. Winnicott's squiggle drawings, which involves the therapist and client taking turns making squiggles with a pencil on paper for the other to complete. Exchanges of images are typically followed by narrative. Various types of drawing material can be used to expand on this approach and stimulate creativity (Rubin, 2005). Although initially developed for use with children, squiggle drawing with adults can be a nonthreatening way to facilitate a shift from more linear, rational modes of knowing to ways of knowing that are more intuitive and imaginative. These types of simple "warm-ups" or "decentering activities" provide a helpful beginning to lengthier expressive arts therapy sessions. They can also be used within the context of more traditional psychotherapy to reanimate sessions that have relied too heavily on cognitive processes and have become "stuck" or devitalized (Eberhart, 2002; McNiff, 2009; Wood & Near, 2010). According to Jung, what the therapist "does is less a question of treatment than of developing the creative possibilities latent in the patient himself" (Jung, 1954/1985, p. 41).

TRANSFORMATION

Bereavement shatters ways of being in the world that were once sustaining. It deprives us of the presence of loved ones and disrupts daily rhythms, roles, and routines that shape daily life, a sense of self, and structures of meaning (Thompson, 2003). *Therapies of the imagination* such as the expressive arts may be of particular value in helping people to transform and revision their lives in the aftermath of traumatic loss. In their study of suicide bereavement, Sands and Tennant (2010) noted the importance of interventions such as "drawings, psychodrama, re-enactments, and mime" to help clients to "draw together inchoate, tacit, preverbal feelings and thoughts about the death" that are laden with emotion (p. 115). Deconstructing the loss through cognitive processing or "meta-cognitive reasoning" is insufficient in addressing intentionality in suicide, how the bereaved construct meaning around this issue, and how they develop the death story (p. 115).

The expressive arts, because of their capacity to engage people on an emotional or bodily level, can help people to put into words and convey more fully the meaning of experiences. In working with communities experiencing traumatic loss as a result of political violence, Kalmanowitz and Lloyd (2005) learned that the use of expressive arts therapy helped people "unravel their internal responses to traumatic experiences," "reveal the unspeakable," and contain the intensity of experiences that might have otherwise been overwhelming (p. 31). Byers and Gere (2007) described use of the expressive arts and "honoring rituals" with children and grandchildren of Holocaust survivors who expressed an interest in finding ways to "move with" communally held grief so that it didn't become "frozen in time," mourned in isolation, or passed on silently and invisibly to future generations (p. 389).

Levine (2009) suggested that traumatic experiences that we seek to avoid can be a source of transformation. Through the arts, there is the possibility of "conscious enactment" or the "dramatic re-presentation of the traumatic event" in artistic form (p. 61). The experience of trauma, reimagined and embodied through the arts, can be witnessed, responded to, played out in different ways, enacted differently, learned from, and faced so that "suffering is not eliminated, but given meaning and value through a transformative act of poetic imagination" (p. 86).

BETH'S STORY: EXPRESSIVE ARTS IN CLINICAL PRACTICE

Beth's mother was concerned because 10-year-old Beth was becoming increasingly "angry and uncontrollable" at home, "hitting herself, throwing things, and slamming doors" for no apparent reason. Beth had also begun bedwetting. Her teacher noted withdrawal, inattention, and difficulty with schoolwork. Beth's mother did not associate these changes with Beth's history of loss.

The holidays were approaching and Beth had begun crying, looking through family photo albums, and asking about her biological father, who had left the family before Beth was born. Her mother described him as a short-tempered alcoholic who visited sporadically and unreliably. Beth was "often moody" after contact with her father and would attempt to engage her mother in conversation about him. Beth's mother said she was uncomfortable talking about Beth's father, adding "I wish [Beth] could look at what she has and the positive things in her life." This was also the one-year anniversary of the precipitous departure of Beth's stepfather, who left without saying goodbye to her even though he had known Beth since she was 2. Beth's mother described him as "short-tempered, moody, and verbally abusive at times." Though there were no reports of physical or sexual abuse, he was often critical of Beth. After his departure, Beth was "upset for 2 weeks and then seemed to get over [his] absence, expressing no desire for further contact."

Beth's great-grandfather, with whom she and her mother were close, had died 8 months earlier. Beth was asking to visit his gravesite, but her mother was reluctant to do so, admitting that she was "not good at talking about feelings" or "dealing well with death."

Initial sessions with Beth's mother helped her to develop an understanding of Beth's history of loss and ways of responding, such as providing reassurance, validating feelings, listening actively, and modeling a language and behavioral repertoire for grief and mourning. We also discussed the multigenerational impact of alcoholism on the family's functioning. After several visits with Beth's mother, Beth was invited to attend therapy. Beth agreed, because she "was curious about therapy" and thought it was a way to "get negative thoughts out of your head."

The First Nine Sessions: Setting the Stage

Beth and her mother were seen together for the opening of each session, which usually consisted of shared storytelling about the week. Then, Beth would excuse her mother and engage in symbolic play using a variety of expressive media. Consistent with an expressive arts therapy approach, there was no direct interpretation of symbolic material presented by Beth through her imaginative stories, drawings, or enactments. Although verbalization was encouraged, Beth was permitted to choose when and how to talk about her experiences during the art-making process and what she wanted to share with her mother after the therapy session.

After the third session, I asked Beth to keep a "drawing diary" during the week and, if she liked, to bring it to therapy each week. She created "All About Bethany," which she subdivided into chapters entitled "home," "friends," "school," and "me." Eventually, Beth began to share excerpts with her mother, which facilitated more regular and responsive communication between them around topics of concern for Beth, such as her father's absence in her life, her great-grandfather's death, and the funeral she planned for her recently deceased pet guinea pig.

By the sixth session, Beth's mother said that "things had gotten better at home," there had been "no angry outbursts," and Beth's enuresis had resolved. Beth and her mother had visited the great-grandfather's gravesite, and they were now sharing stories about him. Beth was also spending time with her younger stepbrother and stepsister, and was less withdrawn at school.

On the ninth session, Beth revealed that for years she had kept a journal of letters written to her father that expressed her anger at him for abandoning her. She had burned the journals a year ago when she was feeling particularly angry with her father. Now, with the approach of her birthday, Beth was feeling a resurgence of anger toward him. At home, her mother said that Beth was "yelling and slapping herself," exhibiting more distress than she had for some time.

The Final Six Sessions: Once Upon a Time in the Land of One-Eyed Giants

At our next session, Beth opened with an elaborate "dream" and asked me to transcribe while she painted images from the story. For the next four sessions, Beth began with a sequel to the dream. As the story developed, Beth moved from creating two-dimensional depictions of the characters to three-dimensional mask making and costume design. Eventually, Beth decided to stage a performance of the dream for her mother and myself. Here, in abbreviated form, is the story that unfolded.

> I was lost in a strange land of gray Cyclops that were very big and mean, with the exception of one friendly, turquoise-colored Cyclops named Jupiter. The biggest and meanest of the Cyclops has black warts on his face, a straight red mouth, and sawed-off fangs for teeth. He tried to stomp on me because he hates people. I was as tiny as a mouse. He hates people because his father was even bigger and meaner, and that's how he learned to be so mean. Also, someone killed his mother. I was very scared. Jupiter saw me, scooped me up, put me in his pocket which was as big as this room, and took me to his cave where

I would be safe. I was the first person he had met. He offered me food because I was really hungry, and I stayed.

Jupiter had a nice papa, but the Big Mean Cyclops ate him and used his rib bone as a toothpick. Jupiter has to act tough now so that the bully giants will leave him alone. Jupiter secretly tries to rescue the little kids when they are captured. One day Jupiter was caught and they tortured him. Jupiter had to give himself stitches and put a bandage over his wound. He's still a good Cyclops, though. One day, he rescued me and flung me to safety.

Jupiter has no family. The Big Mean Cyclops ate them all. A little girl lives with him now. She is about 4 years old. Her mother and father were eaten by one of the giants when she was 2 years old. After her parents were eaten, she was in a bad orphanage where they fed her hot mush when they were good to her and cold mush when they were mean to her. She ran away because she hated it there and she went to the land of the Cyclops, which was known as the Land of Mystery.

The little girl stayed with Jupiter. He was able to corral three or four of the big mean Cyclops and put them in a pit. There's been an increase in the number of big friendly Cyclops. Sometimes the big mean Cyclops still get out at night and eat people, but they don't like to eat good people now because then they begin to feel good and they don't want to do that. The end.

EPILOGUE

Beth's mother was visibly moved by the dream performance and its implicit meanings. After the performance, Beth continued to make masks at home, eventually making a turquoise Cyclops mask for her mother's new boyfriend. In contrast to previous years, "Beth was enjoying everything about school this year" and had made the honor roll for the first time. Additionally, she was now participating in a variety of extracurricular activities with her peers. According to her mother, Beth was beginning to use language to more directly convey a range of feelings. Beth also reported various methods to self-soothe when she was "stressed." Beth's father continued to be an erratic presence in her life. Her mother said that Beth was speaking directly about her experience of his behavior and was continuing to draw and write in her journal on a regular basis. We concluded after meeting for 15 sessions over the course of one year.

Meaning Making Through Use of the Arts and Ritual at Community Commemorations

> Artists reach areas far beyond the reach of politicians. Art, especially entertainment and music, is understood by everybody, and it lifts the spirits and the morale of those who hear it.
>
> **Mandela (2005)**

Crisis, disaster, and loss can challenge the core meanings of any community. Journalists, community leaders and members, musicians, and artists create soulful ways to respond to tragedies in meaningful, participative ways, such as videography, visual arts, music, and dance. Often, multiple mediums interweave, and bring the broken community together in developing rituals and commemorations or memorials. The arts engage individuals and communities in making new meanings. A few examples are listed below. Readers are invited to remember any of their own experiences at these pivotal, communal events of grief as nations, cultures, and all facets of humanity joined together when facing an uncharted future ahead:

- Grief-laden, symbolic moments at President John F. Kennedy's funeral, like the riderless horse, Little John's salute, the bugler's "Taps," and the eternal flame
- The Vietnam Memorial's healing meeting ground for veterans, families, and adversaries
- South Africa's Apartheid revolutionary arts, such as Vusi Mahlasela's ballads, Masekela's "Stimela," and the poetry of Mzwakhe Mbul
- The AIDS Quilt's homemade stitches and panels of remembrance and advocacy
- The flooding of flowers and notes when Princess Diana died, culminating with her sons' "Mum" card on her casket; and solemn royal pageantry paired with Elton John's "Goodbye, England's Rose" for the people
- Music concerts to engage communal relief efforts for African famines, America's Farm Aid, September 11, the 2004 Southeast Asian Tsunami, Hurricane Katrina, Afghanistan's 2005 earthquakes, Rwanda's children in 2006, the 2010 Haiti earthquakes, and the 2010 Gulf Coast crisis, as well as relief concerts yet to be, for global tragedies yet to unfold

Community-based, therapeutic programs that use the expressive arts are impacting history. War-torn Angola began to be pieced back together by an extensive peace program for 320,000 traumatized children and youth. They engaged and trained 4,000 local adults to assist. The curriculum focused on children's psychological development, the impact of war on children, rites of death and mourning, the arts for healing, and nonviolent conflict resolution (Christie, Wagner, & Winter, 2001). Similarly, a network of music therapists responded to September 11 with the New York City Music Therapy Relief Project's healing interventions for children, seniors, professional relief workers and therapists, and families of the victims (Loewy & Hara, 2002).

More personally, families and communal groups have told ancestral stories through song and art at tribal fires and on front porches. Now, in the virtual world, the bereaved share photos, Facebook walls, and blogs that memorialize and pay tribute to the deceased. Faster and broader than ever possible before, personal accounts are now recorded on cell phones and disseminated across the globe in an instant. New forms of social networking that incorporate the arts provide avenues of support and additional forms of expression for those who are grieving.

CLOSING CONSIDERATIONS

Training programs and resources are available for therapists interested in integrating the expressive arts into practice through organizations such as the following: the Applied Arts and Health Network at http://appliedartsandhealth.ning.com, the International Expressive Arts Association at http://www.ieata.org, the National Coalition of Creative Arts Therapies Association at http://www.nccata.org, and the Society for Arts in Healthcare at http://www.thesah.org. Collaborations between trained expressive art therapists and psychotherapists can also be fruitful. As a leader in the field of the arts and medicine suggested, however, "One does not have to be specially trained to offer a poem, song, meditation or reflection question" in response to art making with the bereaved (Bertman, 2010, p. 275). What is critical is an attitude of nonjudgmental openness and appreciation for what is expressed. To discount the person's artistic expression, whether song, dance, or painting, can be to discount the person. Professionals must tune into their own artistic biases and filters. Simple acronyms can guide professionals' responses to another's art and music: the CORE principles of **C**are, **O**wnership, **R**espect, and **E**mpowerment, and the HEALing techniques to actively **H**ear, **E**xplore, **A**ffirm, and **L**earn from the other's art and music (Berger, 2006). Expressive therapies can connect us with personal, familial, and community histories and engage imaginative, healing transformations. Further research and practice expectantly await.

REFERENCES

Berger, J. S. (2006). *Music of the soul: Composing life out of loss*. New York: Routledge.

Bertman, S. (2010). [Review of the book *The art of grief: The use of expressive arts in a grief support group*]. *Death Studies*, *34*, 274–288.

Byers, J. G., & Gere, S. H. (2007). Expression in the service of humanity: Trauma and temporality. *Journal of Humanistic Psychology*, *3*, 284–391.

Christie, D. J., Wagner, R. V., & Winter, D. A. (Eds.). (2001). *Peace, conflict, and violence: Peace psychology for the 21st century*. Englewood Cliffs, NJ: Prentice Hall.

Eberhart, H. (2002). Decentering with the arts: A new strategy in a new professional field. In S. K. Levine (Ed.), *Crossing boundaries: Explorations in therapy and the arts* (pp. 123–136). Toronto, Ontario: EGS Press.

Goss, R. A., & Klass, D. (2005). *Dead but not lost: Grief narratives in religious traditions*. Walnut Creek, CA: AltaMira Press.

Irish, D. P., & Lundquist, K. F. (2003). *Ethnic variations in dying, death and grief: Diversity in universality*. Philadelphia: Taylor & Francis Group.

Jung, C. G. (1985). *The practice of psychotherapy: Essays on the psychology of the transference and other subjects* (2nd ed.). New York: Princeton University Press. (Original work published in 1954)

Jung, C. G. (1997). *Jung on active imagination: Key essays selected and introduced by Joan Chodorow*. London: Routledge.

Kalmanowitz, D., & Lloyd, B. (2005). Art therapy and political violence. In D. Kalmanowitz & B. Lloyd (Eds.), *Art therapy and political violence with art, without illusion* (pp. 14–34). New York: Routledge.

Levine, S. K. (2009). *Trauma, tragedy, therapy: The arts and human suffering*. London: Jessica Kingsley.

Loewy, J. V., & Hara, A. F. (Eds.). (2002). *Caring for the caregiver: The use of music and music therapy in grief and trauma*. Silver Spring, MD: American Music Therapy Association.

Malchiodi, C. A. (1998). *Understanding children's drawings*. New York,: Guilford Press.

Mandela, N. (2005). Nelson Mandela: Mandela music. Retrieved from http://www.mandela.tv/mandela_story9.html

McNiff, S. (2004). *Art heals: How creativity cures the soul.* Boston: Shambhala Press.

McNiff, S. (2009). *Integrating the arts in therapy: History, theory and practice*. Springfield, IL: Charles C. Thomas.

Morgan, J. D., & Laungani, P. (Eds.). (2002). *Death and bereavement around the world. Volume 1: Major religious traditions*. Amityville, NY: Baywood.

Naor, Y. (1999). The theater of the Holocaust. In S. K. Levine & E. G. Levine (Eds.), *Foundations of Expressive Arts Therapy: Theoretical and clinical perspectives* (pp. 223–239). London: Jessica Kingsley.

Oxford English Dictionary. (1989). S.v. Transform. *Oxford English Dictionary online*. Retrieved from http://dictionary.oed.com

Rilke, R. M. (1981). Moving forward. In *Selected poems of Rainer Maria Rilke: A translation from the German and commentary by Robert Bly* (Ed. R. Bly, p. 101). New York: Harper & Row. (Original work published in *The book of pictures*, 1902–1906)

Rilke, R. M. (1981). *The book of poverty and death*. In *Selected poems of Rainer Maria Rilke: A translation from the German and commentary by Robert Bly* (Ed. R. Bly, p. 55). New York: Harper & Row. (Original work published in 1903)

Rogers, J. E. (2007). The written story: Creative writing, journaling, and poetry. In J. E. Rogers (Ed.), *The expressive arts and grief: Use of the expressive arts in a grief support group* (pp. 59–68). New York: Routledge.

Rogers, J. S. (2007). Grief and the sacred art of ritual. In J. E. Rogers (Ed.), *The expressive arts and grief: Use of the expressive arts in a grief support group* (pp. 129–149). New York: Routledge.

Romanoff, B., & Thompson, B. (2006). Meaning construction in palliative care: The use of narrative, ritual, and the expressive arts. *American Journal of Hospice and Palliative Medicine*, (4), 309–316.

Rubin, J. A. (2005) *Artful therapy*. Hoboken, NJ: Wiley.

Sands, D., & Tennant, M. (2010). Transformative learning in the context of suicide bereavement. *Adult Education Quarterly*, *60*(2), 99–121.

Small, C., & Walser, R. (1996). *Music, society, education* (Rev. ed.). Middletown, CT: Wesleyan University Press.

Stroebe, M. S., & Schut, H. (2001). Meaning making in the dual process model of coping with bereavement. In R. A. Neimeyer (Ed.), *Meaning reconstruction & the experience of loss* (pp. 55–73). Washington, DC: American Psychological Association.

Thompson, B. (2003, April–June). The expressive arts and the experience of loss. *The Forum*, 29(2), 1–2.

Wood, D. D., & Near, R. L. (2010). Using expressive arts when counseling bereaved children. In C. A. Corr & D. E. Balk (Eds.), *Children's encounters with death, bereavement and coping* (pp. 373–393). New York: Springer.

24

Bereavement Rituals and the Creation of Legacy

LAURA LEWIS and WILLIAM G. HOY

The death of a loved one radically sculpts the emotional frontiers of any person's experience. In Western culture, those who experience such a death often encounter a challenging journey of private suffering, forging ahead with lives that have been dramatically altered and changed by their losses. For individuals who have loved dearly, emotional tides run high, with affective experiences of anxiety, despair, sadness, guilt, and even relief being potential currents in the emotional swirl that is grief.

One way the bereaved may find some solace amidst the affective torrents of loss is through the use of rituals and the creation of legacy. Bereavement rituals and legacy are inextricably linked concepts as often the use of rituals by mourners assists in the consolidation of the legacy of the one mourned. Rituals may inform the construction of a deceased's legacy, and one's legacy may also inform the creation of appropriate rituals. Understanding these interconnections is important to revealing how one influences and is influenced by the other. Yet, ritual and legacy are also distinct concepts requiring necessary elaboration for clarity and consideration.

RITUALS

Rituals can be understood as those actions that the bereaved construct and repeatedly participate in which provide some kind of necessary gratification of need. Vale-Taylor (2009) defined *ritual* as a specific behavior or activity that gives symbolic expression to certain feelings or thoughts. Romanoff and Terenzio (1998) defined *rituals* as cultural devices that provide ways to comprehend the complex and contradictory aspects of human existence within a given social context. Though in many societies, bereavement rituals are thought to benefit the dead, Western thought essentially views these ceremonies as beneficial primarily for the living.

They provide varied means whether through words, objects, or actions to represent the emotion or ideas that a death induces in those who remain. They may also be vital vehicles to maintaining attachment and internally accessing the deceased (Lewis, 2003; Lewis & Brown, 2008).

Moving forward in life without those we have loved can mean many things to many people, and as such, rituals in bereavement can be highly varied in their presentation. Some people may wear the deceased's clothing in efforts to remain close in some tangible way. Some may light a candle in their loved one's memory, and others may, like Queen Victoria upon the death of her beloved husband Albert, have the deceased's clothing laid out every day for ensuing years. There is no limit to the creativity and ingenuity of ritualized acts as a response to human need born from loss and grief.

According to Vale-Taylor (2009), ritual activities may include such diverse actions as visiting the grave, displaying photographs of the deceased, showing photos and speaking about the loved one to others, taking up an interest the deceased enjoyed, writing letters to the loved one, watching a particular TV program that evokes memories, creating something, wearing or interacting with something that belonged to the deceased, attending a particular event because the loved one would have attended it, creating a memorial of some kind, or even planting something in memory of the deceased. This list is by no means exhaustive because the rituals in which people participate are unique to themselves. The list, however, does exemplify some of the activities that can become ritualized in death. We are complex and varied beings, and our consequent ritualized responses are always unique to the needs of the self or the self in community with others.

Participation in bereavement rituals is a personal response by mourners to individualized needs embedded in their grief. As such, the same ritual may be carried out by two different people for entirely different reasons (Vale-Taylor, 2009). This suggests that although some ritual actions may look the same, one is not able to make generalized assumptions about how the ritual itself meets the unique personal needs of the mourner. For example, for those who tend to visit a grave site, the action may provide a feeling of emotional connection to the deceased for one person, whereas for another it is the place where he or she connects spiritually to a higher power. The action is the same, but how the action is experienced and what personal needs the action gratifies are quite different. For those who use rituals in grief, an understanding of both dimensions—the action and the felt need that the action attempts to meet—is worthy of consideration and reflection.

What is the purpose of ritualized behavior, and to what end does such behavior serve in mourning? Jordan and Ware (1997) suggested that rituals assist in the transformation of the relationship that is lost from one of physical contact with the deceased to one of symbolic and spiritual connection through ritualized means. Their statements reveal rituals as vital vehicles to symbolic and spiritual connection. Vale-Taylor (2009) suggested numerous purposes for ritual. Such actions are identified as providing a source of emotional comfort, creating a bond with or sense of the presence of the deceased, or taking an action that relieves tension and provides balance against the pain of life in the present. Rituals may also allow the mourners access to a broader community, as exemplified in annual remembrance gatherings.

For others, rituals may evolve from a sense of obligation or doing what is right or expected of them. Rituals may also be vital to the preservation of dimensions of ongoing attachment to the deceased and the construction of an internalized presence of the deceased in the psychological life of the mourner (Lewis, 2003; Lewis & Brown, 2008). These findings are consistent with recent developments in therapeutic counseling practice, which advocates for assisting the bereaved in finding a manner in which the deceased can continue to be held within and the relationship maintained although transformed (Jordan & Ware, 1997; Klass, Silverman, & Nickman, 1996; Valliant, 1985). (The idea of maintaining a transformed internalized relationship is often referred to in the bereavement literature as "continuing bonds"; this concept is discussed more fully in Chapter 4.)

Rituals may allow people to be in touch with the essential essences of the deceased's being that are longed for at particular times of developmental transition. Akhtar and Smolar (1998) suggest that individuals have an internal desire for continuity with deceased loved ones, particularly evidenced at the junctures of major developmental milestones (e.g., graduations, marriages, and the birth of a grandchild). These longings for internal continuity can be assisted by interacting with objects that belonged to the deceased and as such can assist and facilitate the developmental transition in the loved one's absence.

In their study on grief rituals, Castle and Phillips (2003) found that bereavement could be positively facilitated through appropriate postfuneral rituals. In this study of 50 participants, the vast majority engaged in at least one ritual activity in order to help them with their grief, with the majority identifying a positive attitude toward ritual use. In their study, "[T]he ritual activity that was rated as most helpful was a remembrance ceremony or celebration designed by the bereaved person" (p. 53). Castle and Phillips noted that rituals performed in an emotionally safe environment, rituals that were personally meaningful, and rituals that inspired a sense of the sacred were identified as being most helpful. Using symbolic objects, such as photos or mementos of the deceased, was also helpful. This study identified important outcomes of ritual use, such as facilitating the acceptance of grief as an ongoing process, as well as assisting in the reevaluation of life priorities. Other benefits to ritual use included assisting in the acceptance of the death, and enhanced feelings of personal power over grief.

In summary, the Castle and Phillips (2003) study confirms that bereavement can be facilitated through appropriate postfuneral rituals. These research conclusions mirror many years of clinical observation by grief counselors, which support the use of postfuneral rituals in their counseling practices, and suggest that rituals, however varied, provide mourners with a positive way of being in the presence of their grief and facilitate their unique mourning processes (Hunter, 2007–2008; Vale-Taylor, 2009).

LEGACY WORK

An old worn shovel stood at the entrance of the church as mourners approached. Though many did not know the shovel's significance, during the funeral service, they learned the meaning. The deceased had volunteered his time and shovel to till the flower beds and dig foundation trenches for the church. The stories their pastor told joined with the symbolic shovel at the church entrance to illustrate the legacy of this man's life—his contributions, his faith, his family, and his friends. Together, family and community mourned his death and celebrated his legacy.

The word *legacy* is commonly used to denote an inheritance of high value received from an ancestor. Ask around at a memorial service, and one usually hears stories about the deceased person's character and the intrinsic qualities worthy of imitation. Family and friend tributes posted to online obituary websites exemplify this legacy consolidation by tangibly noting the deceased's character qualities that were worthy of identification and adulation. Legacy characteristics chosen by tribute writers in one study included *compassionate, brave, respectful, enthusiastic, fun loving, humorous, positive, warm, polite, peace loving*, and *heroic* (Hoy, 2010). These words are frequently spoken aloud in eulogies at memorial services and funerals as well.

As these character qualities are written down or spoken aloud in the hearing of a gathered community, they are "recorded for posterity." Such narratives define the essential essences of the deceased and are vital to the emerging construction of the deceased's legacy. The efficacy of memorial ceremonies for bereaved people is well documented (Doka, 2002; Fristad, Cerel, Goldman, Weller, & Weller, 2000–2001; Rando, 1993; Sanders, 1999). In part, this effectiveness grows out of mourners articulating, even in the very earliest days of their bereavement, the deceased's unique features—of personality and character, accomplishment, human passion, and contribution—that create his or her legacy.

In *Grief Counseling and Grief Therapy: A Handbook for the Mental Health Practitioner*, Worden (2009) wrote,

> The funeral service can give people an opportunity to express thoughts and feelings about the deceased. Earlier we saw how important it is to verbalize thoughts and feelings about the dead person. In its best tradition, the funeral can provide this opportunity. However, there is a great tendency to over-idealize and over-eulogize a person at a funeral. The best situation is one in which people can express both the things that they are going to miss about the lost loved one and things that they are not going to miss, even though some may consider this inappropriate. The funeral service can help the grief process, as it allows people to talk about the deceased. (pp. 118–119, cited with permission of the Springer Publishing Company)

Symbols have been used by mourners to mark the deaths of their loved ones since time immemorial. Some symbols are ancient; holy water, earth, candles, and mourning colors provide a few examples. In addition to these symbols, contemporary mourners often employ objects to represent the attributes of the deceased most remembered by the bereaved. Garden tools, musical instruments, a doll collection, sports equipment, or books from the deceased's personal library are a few of the ways that mourners use symbols in contemporary funerals and memorial services.

Symbols effectively draw together the diverse communities in which an individual participated, with each mourner drawing slightly customized meanings from the symbols that are accessible and displayed. At the funeral of one cowboy, the funeral director rested the casket on two bales of hay for the funeral home visitation and the deceased's favorite saddle sat astride the casket instead of the spray of flowers familiar to North Americans. Apparently the symbolism worked, because many people were heard to say as they entered the room, "That's *so* Bob!" Here symbolic objects assisted in constructing one dimension of personal legacy.

The creation of legacy is not confined to the time frame of the traditional funeral. Legacy often extends beyond this ceremony and may enter into facets of community that were important to the deceased. In one community, the parents of a boy who died at age 10 presented a substantial scholarship to every senior in their son's memory 8 years later when his class graduated. Many parents of bereaved teens have marked the legacy of their children with similar gestures. One widowed mother used her daughter's college fund to endow a permanent scholarship at the high school she was attending when she was killed during her junior year.

Mourners plant trees, endow community gardens, grant funds for school or hospital construction, and erect monuments—all in an attempt to establish the legacy of their dead in the minds and hearts of current and future generations. Although additional empirical research is needed to test the efficacy of such behavior on bereavement outcomes, clinicians attest anecdotally to the powerful sense of "settledness" for mourners in knowing their loved ones are remembered in such public ways. The construction of the deceased's legacy, both in the elaboration of features of the deceased's identity and personhood, and as a living remembrance in the communities of the living, proves vital and necessary to many mourners as they negotiate the trajectories of their grief.

LEGACY—FROM THE PERSONAL TO THE SOCIETAL

Legacies not only are the purview of the individual but also are passed from one generation to the other, creating vital contributions to the identity of the next generation. The erection of war monuments and subsequent pilgrimages to them by former soldiers and families of the dead are an important way in which social legacy is established. The Canadian war monument on the site of the Battle of Vimy Ridge in France commemorates the united effort of all four Canadian expeditionary forces in France during World War I. The dedication of the monument in 1936 was attended by more than 100,000 people, including more than 6,000 Canadians who traveled aboard five chartered steamships from the Port of Montreal (Veterans Affairs Canada, 2007). The 10-story white limestone memorial was rededicated in 2007 after a 3-year restoration effort to commemorate the 90-year anniversary of this heroic battle in Canadian history, and it was attended by dignitaries and thousands of Canadian mourners who had affiliated familial connections to this tragic and triumphant place. Here we see the social and historical legacy of a tragic place, instilled in the intrapsychic being of generations removed, who remain compelled to visit and remember those who lost their lives in this place.

In much of the world, shrines arise near the location where people die or at sites most associated with the deceased's life. Thousands of candles, stuffed animals, and bouquets of flowers were deposited by mourners at the gates of Kensington Palace following the death of Diana, Princess of Wales. Roadside memorials, often accompanied by crosses or other faith symbols, are maintained by families and friends at the sites of fatal automobile crashes. In their research into roadside memorials, Clark and Tidswell (2010) found that such memorial markers served to make visible and tangible a mourner's great loss and sorrow. These memorial markers may be a means to "assuage grief—to work through suffering, to focus on something material to explain the unexplainable, —yet, still grief continues to haunt" (p. 25). This is consistent with Collins and Opie (2010), who suggested that "although the pain persists, the roadside memorial offers a potential means to healing, albeit the process itself may be difficult to negotiate, and impossible to regulate" (p. 117). What is evidenced here may be the need of mourners to create a social beacon that evidences the anonymous and nameless suffering of mourners who are now bound to the tragic and unexplainable.

Mourning is social. In his perspective on "mediators of mourning," Worden (2009) suggested that perceived social support is integral to bereavement adaptation. It can be inferred that gathering with others in ritual acknowledgment of death and celebration of the deceased's legacy helps solidify this social support, a point that is noted by many researchers and clinicians in their perspectives on the value of rituals like funerals and memorial services (Rando, 1993; Sanders, 1999; Worden, 2009).

A few years ago, while visiting the World War II Memorial in Washington, D.C., I (WGH) observed how ritual and legacy can intersect across generations. As occurs many days of the week, an "honor flight" of veterans from that war, all undoubtedly in their 80s, was visiting on the same day as a large group of high school students. I watched as the veterans made their way down the ramp to the "Gold Star Wall," near where the students were sitting on benches and talking together. One student must have spied the veterans slowly making their way down the ramp, spontaneously rose to his feet, and began to applaud. He was immediately joined by his fellow students and teachers, and soon the entire plaza was filled with students and adults reverently standing and applauding the large contingent of elderly soldiers.

As I have reflected on the experience, I realize more happened in that plaza than just a group of students acknowledging a group of older adults. Rather, what occurred was that a group of students "received the legacy" from a group of patriots, all more than six decades the students' senior. Not a dry eye remained in the plaza that morning, and no words defined the moment as legacy was passed—from one generation to the next—through a national symbol of solidarity, patriotism, and ritual.

CLINICAL UTILITY OF RITUALS AND LEGACY: APPLIED COUNSELING PRACTICE

Related to rituals and legacy work, therapeutic responses to the bereaved need to be considered in terms of the unique individual with whom one is working. Individuals have their own ways of working through private suffering, and many do not require therapeutic intervention. Yet, when grief counselors are sought out or called to assist, it is incumbent upon them to do so from a position that is informed from both research and applied therapeutic practices. Rituals that are the most successful (those that maximally assist mourners) often come from and are suggested by the client, or are co-created in counseling with the counselor acting as a guide to ideas that may assist.

Clinicians will want to remain alert to various opportunities for ceremony, especially during the first year of bereavement. Many faith communities, for example, regularly observe a memorial service in the fall. Hospices and funeral homes often coordinate remembrance services as the holidays approach, and the traditional observances surrounding Memorial Day, Remembrance Day, Anzac Day, and Veterans Day can be very meaningful to bereaved family members. Participation in these rituals, although potentially very comforting, can also stir sadness and other expressions of affect not previously disclosed or that the bereaved thought he or she "was already past." Clinicians intervene appropriately by referring appropriate clients to community ceremonies.

Because one purpose of rituals is the establishment of new roles for the bereaved (Romanoff & Terenzio, 1998), clinicians can inquire about the meanings attached to the use of various ongoing rituals. During the history-taking and rapport-building phases of a therapeutic relationship, clinicians can inquire about the mourner's participation in various memorial or ritualized events and practices. Say to the client, "Bereaved people attend funerals, make financial contributions to charity, plant trees, or participate in other activities to remember their loved one. Have you found any of these to be helpful to you? How?" Gently guiding clients to the possible ways that ritualized and memorial acts can assist them in their bereavement is good therapeutic practice.

The ritualized, predictive behavior surrounding holidays and special events may partially contribute to what Rando (1993) classified as *subsequent temporary upsurges of grief*, or STUG reactions, even many years after a death. Christmas carols playing in a shopping mall in late November can create a flood of memories and emotion for bereaved people. The sight of children in costumes trick or treating on Halloween can create a STUG reaction for parents or grandparents years after a child's death. Many experienced therapists have been consulted by a parent in anticipation of a high school commencement at which their child would have graduated, even though she died years earlier. As a matter of practice, clinicians will want to anticipate and work to prepare clients for the various rituals, ceremonies, and events that will likely pose significant challenges during the early years of bereavement. Even inquiring early in the therapeutic relationship with a lead such as "Tell me about your favorite holidays when you were together," and "What were some of the special times to which you were looking forward?" can provide important insights to the counselor about ritual-related challenges ahead.

Clinicians must also be acutely aware of the possibility for disenfranchisement in the client's bereavement experience, perhaps pointing to social prohibition on participating in formal rituals (Doka, 2002). One client's divorce had been finalized just days before her ex-husband's suicide. His family blamed the client for his death and forbade her to attend the memorial service. Because they were divorced, she had no legal claim to control the funeral arrangements, but she felt she had clearly missed the opportunity to say goodbye. Together with her counselor, she constructed a ritual to complete this part of her grief process. She and her therapist went to a park the client and her ex-husband had frequented during their early marriage, where the client read a letter aloud near a favorite spot. Her words were not angry but, rather, filled with sadness at missed opportunities and regret that their relationship had ended this way. Even though his abusive behavior had made it impossible to remain married to him, the client still loved the man deeply. With her therapist bearing witness to the event and hearing both the positive and negative characteristics of the man, the client found that her words helped to establish her perception of his individual legacy in her life.

Finally, any ritualized behavior has the possibility of revealing compulsive features, so attuned, clinical experience is necessary in approaching the assessment and evaluation of any ritualized behaviors. Some behaviors are potentially rooted in unbearable anxieties, and counseling interventions might profitably explore, expand, and reveal other self-soothing and cognitive-reframing options. Though a thorough exploration of compulsive disorders manifesting as ritualized behavior is beyond the scope of this chapter, clinicians must evaluate ritualized bereavement behaviors for self-destructive tendencies as well as for behaviors that impair functional daily living (Rando, 1993; Volkan, 1981).

Consolidating the legacy of a loved person's life is essential work, often aided by the appropriate use of funeral and postfuneral rituals. Their use frequently assists the mourning process by providing comfort, if not solace, in the early and ongoing years of the loss experience. Postfuneral rituals and rituals of legacy construction confirm the earthly existence of the deceased. They may help in necessary role transitions or in the redefinition of self without the living presence of the loved one. Rituals may also act as repositories of meaning, whereby legacy continues to be constructed and integrated into the identity of those who remain here in this world. Although rituals and legacy construction are all of the above, perhaps most importantly they exist to reaffirm our most vital connections and allow some modicum of accessibility to those who have offered one of life's most treasured gifts—the gift of love.

REFERENCES

Akhtar, S., & Smolar, A. (1998). Visiting the father's grave. *Psychoanalytic Quarterly*, *67*, 474–483.

Castle, J., & Phillips, W. L. (2003). Grief rituals: Aspects that facilitate adjustment to bereavement. *Journal of Loss and Trauma*, *8*, 41–71. Excerpt reprinted by permission of the publisher, Taylor & Francis Ltd, http://www.informaworld.com

Clark, J., & Tidswell, T. (2010, Autumn). Roadside mourning: Exposing the grief behind roadside memorial construction. *Grief Matters*, 22–26.

Collins, C. A., & Opie, A. (2010). When places have agency: Roadside shrines as traumascapes. *Continuum: Journal of Media and Cultural Studies*, *24*(1), 107–118. Excerpt reprinted by permission of the publisher, Taylor & Francis Ltd, http://www.informaworld.com

Doka, K. J. (Ed). (2002). *Disenfranchised grief: New directions, challenges, and strategies for practice*. Champaign, IL: Research Press.

Fristad, M. A., Cerel, J., Goldman, M., Weller, E. B., & Weller, R. A. (2000–2001). The role of ritual in children's bereavement. *Omega*, *42*(4), 321–339.

Hoy, W. G. (2010). The funeral as social stabilizer. Paper presented at the 32nd annual conference of the Association for Death Education and Counseling. Retrieved from http://www.adec.org/distance/recordings_sessions.cfm?session=stabilizer

Hunter, J. (2007–2008). Bereavement: An incomplete rite of passage. *Omega*, *56*(2), 153–173.

Jordan, J., & Ware, E. (1997). Feeling like a motherless child: A support group model for adults grieving the death of a parent. *Omega*, *35*, 361–376.

Klass, D., Silverman, P. R., & Nickman, S. (1996). *Continuing bonds: New understandings of grief*. Washington, DC: Taylor & Francis.

Lewis, L. (2003). The use of physical objects in mourning by mid-life daughters who have lost their mothers (UMI No. 307805). *Dissertation Abstracts International*, *65*(11A), 4348.

Lewis, L., & Brown, J. B. (2008). Accessing mother within: A study of midlife daughters' use of maternal belongings in mourning. *Journal of the Association for Research on Mothering*, *10*, 134–145.

Rando, T. A. (1993). *Treatment of complicated mourning*. Champaign, IL: Research Press.

Romanoff, B. D., & Terenzio, M. (1998). Rituals and the grieving process. *Death Studies*, *22*, 697–711.

Sanders, C. M. (1999). *Grief: The mourning after—dealing with adult bereavement*. New York: Wiley.

Vale-Taylor, P. (2009). "We will remember them": A mixed-method study to explore which post-funeral remembrance activities are most significant and important to bereaved people living with loss, and why those particular activities are chosen. *Palliative Medicine*, *23*, 537–545.

Valliant, G. (1985). Loss as a metaphor for attachment. *American Journal of Psychoanalysis*, *45*, 59–67.

Veterans Affairs Canada. (2007). Dedication of the Canadian National Vimy Memorial, July 26, 1936. Retrieved from http://www.vac-acc.gc.ca/remembers/sub.cfm?source=feature/vimy90/media/backgrounders/1936dedication

Volkan, V. (1981). *Linking objects and linking phenomenon*. New York: International Universities Press.

Worden, J. W. (2009). *Grief counseling and grief therapy: A handbook for the mental health practitioner*. New York: Springer.

25

Bereavement Services Provided under the Hospice Model of Care

STEPHEN R. CONNOR and BARBARA MONROE

Hospice, as a philosophy of care, has always considered the provision of bereavement support to be a key characteristic or standard of practice. Since the International Work Group on Death, Dying and Bereavement (1979) published *Assumptions and Principles Underlying Standards of Care for the Terminally Ill*, virtually all hospice standards have included an expectation that bereavement services be provided to families usually for a minimum of one year after the death of the patient.

In this chapter, the provision of bereavement services through American hospice programs will be examined with a focus on the types of services that are commonly offered to both hospice families and those in the community who have suffered a death-related loss. Also discussed will be the impact of recent bereavement research on the provision of bereavement services by hospice providers. A case description of bereavement service offered through St. Christopher's Hospice in the United Kingdom will be used to highlight some of the challenges and opportunities faced by hospices providing bereavement services.

HOSPICE BEREAVEMENT SERVICES IN THE UNITED STATES

The services typically provided by a hospice bereavement program may include the following:

- Individual grief counseling
- Various types of bereavement support groups
- Educational interventions
- Social support programs

- Specialized programs for bereaved children
- Expressive therapies (art, music, movement, and play)
- Grief camps
- Family bereavement programs

INDIVIDUAL GRIEF COUNSELING

Individual counseling varies considerably among hospice programs. Such counseling can range from informal visits to listen to the bereaved person "tell the story" of the circumstances surrounding the death to formal weekly therapy directed to helping the bereaved person return to some previous level of higher functioning. Outcomes in bereavement counseling are thought to be better when individuals self-select to receive counseling than if they are recruited, as is the case in all mental health treatments. There remains a lack of evidence for the effectiveness of various forms of bereavement counseling (Forte, Hill, Pazder, & Feudtner, 2004); however, neither is there support for the suggestion that grief counseling may be harmful to individuals (Larson & Hoyt, 2007), an issue of importance to hospices delivering services to the bereaved.

VARIOUS TYPES OF BEREAVEMENT SUPPORT GROUPS

Hospice programs that have run general bereavement support groups have found that, when possible, it is useful to have different types of support groups for different bereaved populations. For instance, those who have experienced sudden traumatic deaths may find it difficult to relate to a spouse whose partner died of cancer over an extended period. Similarly, those who have experienced stigmatized deaths from HIV, suicide, or drug overdose may have difficulty sharing their experiences with others who experienced a death that was more socially accepted. In general, where possible, having groups for individuals with similar losses will usually be more effective, such as for bereaved parents or siblings or children of different ages.

Educational Interventions

A mainstay for hospices providing bereavement follow-up is to provide educational resources that help family members to gain a perspective on what to expect during the bereavement period. Mailing information at intervals during the year following the death often does this. The initial mailing usually focuses on common reactions and feelings and what is "normal" grief. Later mailings may address ways of coping with grief, including topics such as journaling, poetry, building self-esteem, and coping with holidays.

Social Support Programs

Social support has been found to be an important component to successfully coping with bereavement (Holtslander, 2008; Schulz, Hebert, & Boerner, 2008). Many hospices, sometimes as an outgrowth of bereavement groups, sponsor or encourage bereaved persons to network together to go on outings, to have potluck dinners, to attend sporting events, to attend cultural events, or to travel together. It is not unusual for new relationships and sometimes marriages to result from these activities.

Specialized Programs for Bereaved Children

Surviving parents are frequently concerned for the health of children who have lost a parent or sibling. (Candle, the children's bereavement service at St. Christopher's Hospice, is an exemplar program discussed later in this chapter.) Specialized programs for bereaved children include the use of expressive therapies for children to express grief both verbally and nonverbally through art projects, musical expression, dance and other forms of movement, and—especially for younger children—play therapy.

Family therapy may be indicated in some circumstances as well as individual counseling. A well-researched intervention called the Family Bereavement Program (Sandler et al., 2003, 2010) is available to use for parentally bereaved children (see chapter 11). The Family Bereavement Program consists of 14 sessions (12 classes and 2 individual sessions) and aims to increase positive affect, positive coping, and positive parenting while decreasing active inhibition and negative events. Hospices also sponsor periodic camps for bereaved children that feature many positive experiences with other grieving children to counteract the perception that a bereaved child is alone and without support.

In general hospice bereavement follow-up, clinical staff assigned to the case visit the family to say goodbye and to attend funeral or visitation. A staff member or specially trained volunteer is assigned to contact the family at some regular intervals in the year after the death. Additional contacts are through regular mailing of educational materials on aspects of grief. Hospice staff or volunteers are assigned to visit or call families at intervals determined by need. For those families without special needs, contact is often after 1, 3, 6, 9, and 12 months. For families having trouble coping with grief, contact may be more frequent or, if requested, may require referral to a competent mental health professional with expertise in grief and loss. Regular grief support groups are usually held, and all families are invited. These groups may include emotional support, educational components, or both, and some programs also include a social component (Connor, 2009).

Bereavement follow-up services should be based on need. Families requesting services should be given priority for access to bereavement support. Similarly, families opting out of receipt of bereavement follow-up should be accommodated, though it is generally considered a good idea to check back with a family declining services following death a few months later to make sure they have not changed their minds. It is not unusual for such families to say, "Thank you for calling. This is harder than I realized, and I would appreciate someone to talk with."

The identification of families at risk for poor outcome in bereavement is challenging. Tools that have been developed lack predictive validity. The majority of bereaved families are resilient enough to not need much in the way of follow-up services. Experience has shown that about 39% of hospice families seek additional support services after death (Gamino & Ritter, 2009). A small percentage of these, perhaps 5–10%, develop significant problems related to the death and may be depressed or in rare cases suicidal. Hospices need to develop their capacity to identify those who are really doing poorly and bridge them to competent mental health treatment.

PROLONGED GRIEF DISORDER

Several authors have proposed the inclusion of a new disorder in the DSM-V (Prigerson et al., 2009) that is currently referred to as *prolonged grief disorder*. This condition is thought to be distinct from clinical depression and to have unique features that are directly related to the loss (see Chapter 12). Some of the proposed diagnostic criteria for prolonged grief disorder include the following:

- A significant loss of a loved one through death that involves the experience of yearning (e.g., physical or emotional suffering as a result of the desired, but unfulfilled, reunion with the deceased).
- At least five of the following nine symptoms experienced at least daily or to a disabling degree:
- Feeling emotionally numb, stunned, or that life is meaningless; experiencing mistrust; bitterness over the loss; difficulty accepting the loss; identity confusion; avoidance of the reality of the loss; or difficulty moving on with life.
- Symptoms must be present at sufficiently high levels at least 6 months from the death and be associated with functional impairment.

There is continuing debate in the hospice and palliative care field on the wisdom of pathologizing grief by including it as a disorder (Breen & O'Connor, 2007). Although this would move grief from a normal human experience to an illness model, others argue that it may also help to facilitate the delivery of care to individuals who are experiencing significant emotional distress and functional impairment.

A decision on the inclusion of prolonged grief disorder in the DSM-V is forthcoming, as is a recommended change to the criteria for major depressive disorder. Currently one cannot be diagnosed with major depressive disorder if a recent death has been experienced. A proposal is under consideration to remove this disqualifier so that someone grieving could receive a diagnosis of major depressive disorder.

COMMUNITY-WIDE BEREAVEMENT SUPPORT AND USER EVALUATION

A significant proportion of U.S. hospice programs now offer bereavement support programs to the entire community, not just those who have received hospice services. According to the National Hospice and Palliative Care Organization (2010), 98.3% of hospices provide bereavement services to the community and 17.1% of bereaved clients were not users of hospice services.

Many U.S. hospice programs evaluate the effectiveness of their one-year bereavement follow-up services by using the National Hospice and Palliative Care Organization's Family Evaluation of Bereavement Services questionnaire. Overall, 76.7% of users rated *how well services met the need of the bereaved client* as *very well.*

DIFFERENCES BETWEEN HOSPICE BEREAVEMENT SERVICES IN THE UNITED KINGDOM AND UNITED STATES

Historically bereavement services in the United States developed quite differently from those in the United Kingdom. There was a lesser tendency in the United Kingdom to focus on psychological services, with more focus on support from communities and volunteers, whereas in the United States there was a belief that bereaved persons needed to grieve and often needed assistance in doing so. This idea has changed considerably in recent years with a new paradigm that grief work is not always necessary, that continuing bonds with the deceased are normal, and that the bereaved person should seek support when needed rather than be recruited to bereavement services (Klass, Silverman, & Nickman, 1996; see also Chapters 4 and 25).

ST. CHRISTOPHER'S HOSPICE BEREAVEMENT SERVICES

St. Christopher's Hospice has been providing care to an ethnically, culturally, and socially diverse population of about 1.5 million people in South East London since Dame Cicely Saunders founded it in 1967. Widely recognized as the first "modern" hospice, its early work inspired rapid developments across the world, changing the way dying people were cared for and extending that care to families and friends during the illness and into bereavement. In the United Kingdom, the challenges of an aging population and the economic recession have brought an increasing recognition that the aspiration to ensure good care to all dying people and the bereaved cannot be met by hospices alone, or simply by efforts to improve individual welfare. Cost-effective approaches are required that seek to integrate health and social care, recognizing that death, dying, and bereavement are primarily social experiences in which good symptom control and physical care remain very important. The expertise of hospices must be used to support the development of competent and confident generalists, and the relative richness of hospice resources made to work harder in outreach to local communities beyond their direct patient populations (Monroe, 2010). With their strong local community roots and significant and long-term volunteer contributions, hospices are well placed to support the development of "compassionate communities" where citizens are less afraid of loss and are empowered to offer one another sensitive and individually appropriate help.

Early on, hospice philosophy emphasized the importance of working with the strengths and resources of individual families and community networks, rather than simply identifying problems and associated risks and generating a professionally defined prescription to "solve" them (Monroe, Hansford, Payne, & Sykes,

2007). More recently, this approach has been extended by an interest in the concept of "resilience" and services designed to sustain and promote it (Bonanno, 2008; Monroe & Oliviere, 2007; Stroebe, 2009). Recent years have seen an important debate about the efficacy of bereavement interventions (and their costs) and the definition of those most likely to benefit from them. One of the difficulties with the debate in terms of children is that measures tend to focus on outcomes defined in terms of psychiatric symptoms and behavioral disorders (Currier, Holland, & Neimeyer, 2007), which may not capture the most relevant outcomes for children and families.

THE CANDLE PROJECT

Candle, the children's bereavement service at St. Christopher's Hospice, will be used as an exemplar of a service based on a public health model using a quality-of-life rationale that seeks to prevent or mitigate the potential negative consequences of bereavement for children and young people and to promote stress-related growth (Penny, 2010; Stokes, Pennington, Monroe, Papadatou, & Relf, 1999). A multisystem approach has been adopted with a wide range of interventions focused on the individual child, the family, communities, agencies, and national policy development. Such an approach does more to maximize possible benefits than a sole focus on symptom reduction. The relationship with families is designed to be collaborative, and many services have been developed through listening carefully to their feedback. Such services need to fit with the culture and individual situation of each family if they are to prove acceptable, particularly to those hardest to reach. In common with all St. Christopher's services, the project is free to children and families.

By the early 1990s, St. Christopher's had developed an expertise in working with bereaved children that was widely recognized by local professionals. As there was no other service to support bereaved children in the area, St. Christopher's received regular requests to provide bereavement support for children unrelated to its patient population. In response, a needs assessment was conducted in 1995 with all local agencies involved with children. A steering group of local stakeholders and parents was formed, and in 1998 Candle was launched after having attracted funding from a charitable trust and an appeal in the local community. The aim was to offer a service to any child bereaved through death in the South East London area.

Candle now has a full-time equivalent clinical staff of three who support about 250 children and their families each year. Referrals are accepted from parents, carers, and professionals. Flexible and accessible short-term services delivered at the right time can underpin the strength of children and their families, supporting their coping by boosting confidence in their own skills. To avoid waiting lists, it was decided that the pattern for individual work would be a maximum of six sessions linked to an opportunity to return briefly to the service at a later date. Individual and family work is linked to a group work program and a telephone advice service.

Individual and Family Support

Research on whether bereaved children and young people as a group are at greater risk of negative life consequences is not easily summarized because a wide range of factors moderate and mediate the impact of bereavement. However, those who experience bereavement alongside other losses or preexisting disadvantages seem to be at increased risk of negative outcomes in areas such as education, emotional, and mental health and risk-taking behavior (Ribbens-McCarthy, 2006). There is a sense in which all bereaved children and young people face disadvantages. This is particularly so for those bereaved by a sudden death and those living in areas of social deprivation. Of the families seen by the Candle Project, 80% live in areas identified as below the halfway mark in the government's index of multiple deprivation, and two thirds of the children come from nonwhite British families, demonstrating the trust in which the project is held by local communities. Some families who attend Candle indicate that they would refuse a referral to a statutory agency such as a child and adolescent mental health service or a social care team, fearing that this would "label" their children. Last year, 65% of the children referred to the Candle Project had experienced the sudden and often violent death of someone close to them: 11% were bereaved through murder, 7% through suicide, 11% through road traffic accidents, and 23% through heart attack.

Following an assessment meeting with the parent or carer of the child, up to six sessions of individual or family work are offered. These sessions are held at the hospice in order to maximize professional resources by avoiding travel time. Volunteer transport is provided as appropriate to make it easy for families whose lives may be seriously disrupted to attend meetings. Parents report the value of brief interventions because work and home demands are immediate and pressing, and commitment to counseling can rank low in terms of day-to-day priorities. The short-term approach also means that children miss few classes at school and parents do not have to ask for much time off work. The aim is to normalize the bereavement process and empower the parent with information and knowledge to help his or her child. A variety of therapeutic approaches are used in the intervention, which is an introduction to a way of approaching and managing a process that will continue for a long time (Way & Bremner, 2010). The final session includes a review with child and parent that reinforces learning and a sense of achievement. The message is one of confidence in their ability to carry on with their life, using the things they have done in the sessions to support them and with the offer of returning if they need to. This concept is known as the *extended warranty* and serves as an insurance policy for bereaved families who are facing a changed world with many new challenges. Interestingly, no family has ever complained about the limit on sessions. There seems to be solidarity in suffering, and the public are more realistic and aware of resource limitations than professionals and politicians give them credit for, fully understanding the argument about maximizing equity of service allocation. About 10% of families make contact again each year, with some maintaining sporadic contact over a number of years. When families come back, they are offered a maximum of two follow-up sessions to examine strategies for coping with the bereavement-related issue that has arisen, such as school transition or a parent finding a new partner.

All children, young people, and families are also offered the opportunity to attend a group day. The ongoing groups and family workshops offer a mechanism for maintaining a low-key connection with the project. The Candle clinical team delivers all individual and family interventions at Candle but the group work program has always relied on additional support from trained volunteers. Most groups are held on weekend days, when children, families, and volunteers are more available. Twenty-four group events are offered per year, and the group work has developed to meet different needs (Way, Kraus, & the Candle Team, 2010):

- *Children's Days for 3–7-year-olds.* Parents attend with their children but also have an opportunity to talk separately to each other over lunch (three per year).
- *Children's Days for 8–12-year-olds* with a separate group for parents and carers (three per year).
- *Young People's Evenings*, for those aged over 13 and ongoing until they reach their 19th birthday. These are run three times a year, between 6:30 and 9:00 p.m. on a weekday evening because young people reported that they preferred not to meet on weekend days when they are busy with part-time jobs and other activities. The groups are open, and young people attend for as long as they like.

Other groups have developed in response to user feedback:

- *Monthly bereavement support groups for parents and carers*, facilitated by staff and volunteers. This group was initiated following requests from parents for a regular group for those in the early stages of bereavement
- *Self-help group for parents and carers.* This meets three times a year, and volunteers provide child care. Two former service users lead the group. It is an open group that parents can attend for as long as they wish.
- *Sibling Carer Group* is for bereaved young people bringing up their siblings following parental death. Child care is provided (three per year).
- *Family Workshop days* explore issues around parenting for parents and children. This occurs twice a year. These days began in response to requests from parents and are adapted from the well-researched family-based interventions of Sandler et al. (2003, 2010).

Numbers and a desire to avoid delays mean that children and families bereaved by murder or suicide are integrated into standard groups. Despite concerns about the effects on others of hearing family stories of murder and suicide, parents and children seem to take it in their stride. Some separate group events are delivered—for example, a group day for children and their carers from all over the United Kingdom who had experienced bereavements in the South East Asian tsunami.

Outreach, Training, and Community Development

Candle provides a telephone advice service during working hours. It receives calls (often multiple) from about 500 individuals each year: professionals, parents, and carers. Most calls involve giving advice and information followed up by sending relevant literature, much of it produced by Candle. The service was externally audited in 2001 (Levy, 2004). Results of this audit indicated that most callers felt that the advice and resources supplied had increased the confidence with which they could provide support to bereaved children without the need of a formal referral to a bereavement service. Project staff have also edited a widely used textbook published by Oxford University Press, now in its second edition, and produced a range of journal articles including the underexplored area of work with under-5-year-olds (Way, 2006). In addition, efforts to maintain good links with the media, national and local, including newspapers and magazines focused on black and minority ethnic communities, are continuous.

Training and raising awareness are integral to the Candle service. From the outset, it was clear that a small project could not deliver a direct service to every bereaved child in the catchment area. Therefore, about a third of project professional resources are dedicated to training, to disseminate the knowledge and experience gained to the many professionals and volunteers whose work brings them into contact with bereaved children on a daily basis, such as teachers, nursery staff, and health care professionals. If professionals and volunteers working in relevant agencies receive basic training, they will be able to support many children through bereavement. The project runs over 50 training events each year, ranging from one-day courses for professionals in education, health, and social care, to the first university-validated courses in childhood bereavement in the United Kingdom at undergraduate and postgraduate levels, which began in 2004. Students' backgrounds have been varied: Some work in or have established child bereavement projects, and others work in schools, secure units, and the police force.

Candle has also developed a training initiative with the Metropolitan Police Service, which began in 2000 with the first pilot training programs for *family liaison officers*. These police officers work closely with families who are bereaved where an investigation is necessary around deaths, including suicide, road traffic accidents, and homicides. Nearly 2,000 officers have been trained. Each officer receives an information pack including Candle literature and an invitation to contact Candle for advice in the future. This relationship ensures early contact with particularly vulnerable children. The program has now been rolled out nationally. Candle also partners with the British Army in training service volunteers to support bereavement-focused activity holidays for service families bereaved by the fighting in Afghanistan.

The St. Christopher's Schools Project began in 2006 as a partnership between the hospice and Candle. The project has been highlighted by the Department of Health as an example of good practice in public information and education and an information resource for other agencies, and supports the rollout of the program on a national basis (Hartley & Kraus, 2008). The project has so far worked with 9–10- and 15–16-year-olds from 30 local schools. The children are invited to the hospice to take part in joint artistic projects with hospice patients. At the end of the project, there is a celebration at the hospice where the children's families are invited to attend with the children to see the jointly completed work. The South East London area we cover has significant problems with gang-related violence and crime, and we are keen to support these children and young people to learn more about the importance of life through talking to those with an awareness of the reality of death. The project also allows families who would otherwise have no reason for contact with the hospice to understand more about the issues surrounding terminal illness. Evaluation of the project indicates that children, families, and teachers all value the experience. Teachers also report increased confidence to approach the subject of loss, which is part of the national curriculum.

Consultancy

Candle provides a training and consultancy service to the government department responsible for helping families bereaved through disasters and terrorist attacks. Candle staff members also provide clinical supervision for a number of volunteers from other agencies working with bereaved children and supervision or telephone support to professionals who encounter bereaved children, and agree to work with them as part of their daily contact role. The project hosts an informal support group for leaders of children's bereavement projects across the South of England. It also plays a part in the government-level advocacy and policy development work of the national Childhood Bereavement Network (n.d.; *www.childhoodbereavementnetwork.org.uk*).

Demonstration of Need and Evaluation

In 2010, we conducted a brief stakeholder survey of 50 agencies that had referred children to us in the last year. Thirty-six replies covered responses from schools, child and adolescent mental health teams, hospital teams, social services, GPs, health care agencies, and local bereavement services for adults. All (100%) replied that there was still a need for the Candle Project. No other service for children has been established in the area, and Candle remains the only open access service. Eighty percent had used the training, advice, and consultancy provided by Candle as well as made referrals for individual children.

All service interventions include a feedback response sheet. As is often the case, these are overwhelmingly positive. There have been difficulties in finding an acceptable tool for more formal evaluation (Stokes, Wyer, & Crossley, 1997). Since April 2010, Candle has been testing the use of two measures recommended by the Child and Adolescent Mental Health Services Outcome Research Consortium: The Experience of Service Questionnaire (Barber, Tischler, & Healy, 2006) and Goal Based Outcomes, which permits clients to set their own goals (see Child and Adolescent Mental Health Services, n.d., for more information). The results will be analyzed and reviewed after a year.

It is hoped that Candle demonstrates that a small project with very limited resources can have a significant, cost-effective impact if focused on integration and capacity building. There is no simple recipe for support to bereaved children and their families. All should have the opportunity to access appropriate, culturally sensitive information and support. A few will need considerably more, and Candle's close links with other agencies facilitate rapid specialist referral routes including the Child Trauma Stress Clinic at the Maudsley Hospital in London. We also cowork cases with the clinic, exposing our staff to new techniques such as the use of the Children and War Foundation's Writing for Recovery, a short-term, structured approach to narrative work with young people (Yule et al., 2005).

Conclusion

Hospices are in the forefront of development of community-based and -owned bereavement service delivery that serves as an important link in the primary public health care system. Common service elements were described, and some of the implications of recent research on practice were discussed. The clear definition of anticipated outcomes and evidence about the extent to which they are achieved remain significant challenges for bereavement services, as does the need to provide interventions that are informed by research. The bereavement program at St. Christopher's Hospice was profiled with a focus on Candle, the children's bereavement program, which is an exemplar for hospices seeking to expand or deepen the community bereavement services they provide.

ACKNOWLEDGMENTS

Barbara Monroe gratefully acknowledges the contributions of Frances Kraus and the Candle Team.

REFERENCES

Barber, A. J., Tischler, V. A., & Healy, E. (2006) Consumer satisfaction and child behaviour problems in child and adolescent mental health services. *Journal of Child Health Care*, *10*(9), 9–21.

Bonanno, G. A. (2008). Grief, trauma and resilience. *Grief Matters: The Australian Journal of Grief and Bereavement*, *11*, 11–17.

Breen, L. J., & O'Connor, M. (2007). The fundamental paradox in the grief literature: A critical reflection. *Omega*, 55(3), 199–218.

Child and Adolescent Mental Health Services Outcome Research Consortium. (N.d.). CORC measures. Retrieved from http://www.corc.uk.net/index.php?contentkey=81#goals

Childhood Bereavement Network. (N.d.). [Home page]. Retrieved from http://*www.childhoodbereavementnetwork.org.uk*

Connor, S. R. (2009). *Hospice and palliative care: The essential guide*. New York: Routledge.

Currier, J. M., Holland, J. M., & Neimeyer, R. A. (2007). The effectiveness of bereavement interventions with children: A meta-analytic review of controlled outcome research. *Journal of Clinical Child and Adolescent Psychology*, 3(2), 253–259.

Forte, A, L., Hill, M., Pazder, R., & Feudtner, C. (2004). Bereavement care interventions: A systematic review. *BMC Palliative Care*, 3(1), 3. Retrieved from http://www.ncbi.nlm.nih.gov/pmc/articles/PMC503393/

Gamino, L. A., & Ritter, R. H. (2009). Ethical controversies in grief counseling. In *Ethical practice in grief counseling* (pp. 237–259). New York: Springer.

Hartley, N., & Kraus, F. (2008). *The St Christopher's Schools Project*. London: St Christopher's Hospice.

Holtslander, L. F. (2008). Caring for bereaved family caregivers: Analyzing the context of care. *Clinical Journal of Oncology Nursing, 12*(3), 501–506.

International Work Group on Death, Dying and Bereavement. (1979). Assumptions and principles underlying standards for care of the terminally ill. *American Journal of Nursing, 79*, 296–297.

Klass, D., Silverman, P., & Nickman, S. (Eds.). (1996). *Continuing bonds: New understandings of grief*. Washington, DC: Taylor & Francis.

Larson, D. G., & Hoyt, W. T. (2007). What has become of grief counselling? An evaluation of the empirical foundations of the new pessimism. *Professional Psychology: Research and Practice, 38*(4), 347–355.

Levy, J. (2004). Unseen support for bereaved families. *Bereavement Care*, 23(2), 25–27.

Monroe, B. (2010). Driving improvements in hospice care—beyond the walls. In *Delivering better care at end of life: The next steps* [a King's Fund Report from the Sir Roger Bannister Health Summit at Leeds Castle, November 9–12, 2009]. London: King's Fund.

Monroe, B., Hansford, P., Payne, M., & Sykes, N. (2007). St Christopher's and the future. *Omega, 56*(1), 63–75.

Monroe, B., & Oliviere, D. (2007). *Resilience in palliative care: Achievement in adversity*. Oxford: Oxford University Press.

National Hospice and Palliative Care Organization. (2010). *NHPCO Facts and Figures: Hospice Care in America (2009 Edition)*. Retrieved from http://www.nhpco.org/i4a/pages/index.cfm?pageid=5994

Penny, A. (2010). Childhood bereavement: The context and need for services. In B. Monroe & F. Kraus (Eds.), *Brief interventions with bereaved children* (2nd ed., pp. 129–134). Oxford: Oxford University Press.

Prigerson, H. G., Horowitz, M. J., Jacobs, S. C., Parkes, C. M., Aslan, M., Goodkin, K., et al. (2009). Prolonged grief disorder: Psychometric validation of criteria proposed for DSM-V and ICD-11. *PLoS Med, 6*(8), e1000121.

Ribbens-McCarthy, J. (2006). *Young people's experiences of loss and bereavement: Towards an interdisciplinary approach*. Berkshire: Oxford University Press.

Sandler, I. N., Ayers, T. S., Wolchik, S. A., Tein, J. Y., Kwok, O. M., Haine, R. A., et al. (2003). The family bereavement program: Efficacy evaluation of a theory-based prevention program for parentally bereaved children and adolescents. *Journal of Consulting and Clinical Psychology, 71*(3), 587–600.

Sandler, I. N., Ma, Y., Tein, J. Y., Ayers, T. S., Wolchik, S., Kennedy, C., et al. (2010). Long-term effects of the family bereavement program on multiple indicators of grief in parentally bereaved children and adolescents. *Journal of Consulting and Clinical Psychology, 78*(2), 131–143.

Schulz, R., Hebert, R., & Boerner, K. (2008) Bereavement after caregiving. *Geriatrics, 63*(1), 20–22.

Stokes, J., Pennington, J., Monroe, B., Papadatou, D., & Relf, M. (1999). Developing services for bereaved children: A discussion and the theoretical and practical issues involved. *Mortality, 4*(3), 291–307.

Stokes, J., Wyer, S., & Crossley, D. (1997). The challenge of evaluating a child bereavement programme. *Palliative Medicine, 11*, 179–190.

Stroebe, M. (2009). From vulnerability to resilience: where should research priorities lie. *Bereavement Care, 28*(2), 18–24.

Way, P. (2006). Recalling little memories: On including pre-schoolers in co-remembering someone who has died. *Human Systems: The Journal of Systemic Consultation and Management*, *17*, 3–14.

Way, P., & Bremner, I. (2010). Therapeutic interventions. In B. Monroe & F. Kraus (Eds.), *Brief interventions with bereaved children* (2nd ed., pp. 67–86). Oxford: Oxford University Press.

Way, P., Kraus, F., & the Candle Team. (2010). Groupwork. In B. Monroe & F. Kraus (Eds.), *Brief interventions with bereaved children* (2nd ed., pp. 87–106). Oxford: Oxford University Press.

Yule, W., Dyregrov, A., Neuner, F., Pennebaker, J. W., Raundalen, M., & van Emmerick, A. (2005). *Writing for recovery: A manual for structured writing after disaster and war*. Bergen, Norway: Children and War Foundation.

Section VI

Grief in a Global Perspective

26

Culture and Ethnicity in Experiencing, Policing, and Handling Grief

DENNIS KLASS and AMY YIN MAN CHOW

Our assignment in this chapter is to think about grief in terms of culture and ethnicity. After defining these terms, we discuss grief's relationship to culture and ethnicity within three general themes. First we note that that bereavement is experienced within a cultural framework, even at the level of words. We show, for example, that introducing Chinese words for *grief* was a key part of the movement to bring Western understandings of grief into Chinese culture. Second, we show that culture polices grief, especially with rules about how the emotions of grief may be expressed and how continuing bonds with the dead are to be managed. Third, we discuss how culture affects the ways the bereaved handle grief, that is, how coping styles and grief trajectories may be different in different cultural settings.

The book's method of pairing authors from disparate backgrounds has resulted in an interesting and sometimes surprising dialogue between the two of us. We are very pleased that so much of the illustrating material is from China, taking it as a case study of a non-Western society that exemplifies the cultural factors at work in constructing the experience and expression of grief.

DEFINITIONS

As we are using the terms *ethnicity* and *culture*, they largely overlap. That is to say that in bereavement studies, they refer to the same thing. The members of an *ethnic group*, as we are using the term, identify with each other as sharing common genetics, history, religion, language, geographic origin, governmental organization, or physical appearance. Each of those elements may be flexibly applied and can change, sometimes rapidly, over time.

Culture is from the Latin "to cultivate." The word has many uses we do not include in our chapter, for example in the original meaning of farming, and then extended to such practices as culturing pearls. The word has social class connotations, as when cultured people have nurtured socially superior behaviors or tastes. This connection of culture and social power often finds its way into bereavement literature in the form of unexamined social class values, for example that it is better to express than to contain emotions.

As we use the term, *culture* is how a people or groups of peoples construe their world. Culture provides the templates for how people represent their experience and is, thus, the basis for their actions. In his definition of the humanist tradition, Gadamer (1993) found the German word *Bildung* helpful. The root *Bild* is a picture, an image, a representation. Thus, our culture is literally our picture of our world.

BEREAVEMENT IS EXPERIENCED WITHIN A CULTURAL FRAMEWORK

We cannot experience our world outside the cultural framework we bring to it. This understanding provides a good corrective to a distinction often drawn in bereavement studies between *grief* as an inner process and *mourning* as its social expression. We will note that the distinction was unknown until recently in China. As Fontana and Keene (2009) noted, "It is really difficult to provide specific examples of grief, since the moment it is expressed it becomes mourning" (p. 162). Thus there is no death that is not experienced within cultural categories and no grief that is not felt and expressed within cultural guidelines and expectations.

T-Shirts, Fast Food, and Grief

The attempt to include culture in the study of death and dying cannot be a simple enumeration of grief guidelines and the ways grief is experienced and expressed within different cultures, because cultures are always interacting with each other and changing in response to political and economic realities. The rise of an international culture is apparent in the spread of U.S, fast food and dress as well as in Bauhaus architecture. Part of that internationalization has been the spread of the Western definitions of *mental health* and *illness*. Watters (2010) has recently continued an argument that Szasz (1961) and Foucault, Khalfa, and Murphy (2006) began. Szasz and Foucault et al. argued that definitions of mental illness are cultural artifacts that reinforce the social arrangements of political and economic power. Watters showed that along with the spread of blue jeans and Bauhaus architecture, Western psychiatric definitions of aberrant behavior have been adopted and adapted by cultures around the world. As the definitions of mental illness have been taken up by the professional and intellectual classes in diverse nations, common people have adjusted how they express inner difficulties. That is, a repertoire of symptoms ranging from depression and posttraumatic stress disorder to anorexia are now found in cultures that previously had different definitions and symptoms that expressed inner and interpersonal disharmony.

A Concept of Grief Imported from the Western World

There seems to be good evidence that the definition of grief that gradually developed in the middle of 20th-century Europe and North America is part of the spread of the Western idea of mental health and illness. One implication of this development is that cross-cultural studies of grief may well be reporting only on how European and North American ideas are assimilated into Asian, South American, Middle Eastern, or African cultures.

Recent developments in China seem to support Watters's thesis. Chinese had no word for *grief* until recently. An old word, *bei shang*, denotes only the emotion of sorrow or sadness (Chow & Chan, 2006, p, 254). There is a proper term, *shou xiao*, that loosely corresponds to "mourning" as that term is often used in bereavement literature. It literally means expressing *filial piety*, a core value in traditional China. *Xiao* is the correct attitude that will be expressed in my acting, thinking, and feeling in the proper manner toward the person now dead, toward my family, and toward the rituals, customs, and obligations I must now fulfill. Customs based in *shou xiao* mandated that bereaved adult children should live simply—with simple food, with simple clothing, and in a plain hut—for 3 years. They had to stay away from any cerebration ceremonies, such as birthdays or weddings, during the first year of bereavement.

The problem, as Chinese bereavement clinicians and researchers see it, is not that ideas about grief have spread from the West. The cultural assimilation is clear to them. The problem they see is that *shou xiao* seems to have very limited meaning to contemporary Chinese people. Further, *shou xiao* supports gender and age discrimination that are no longer acceptable. Confucian beliefs emphasize hierarchical relationships. There is a saying that "the white-haired should not say farewell to the black-haired" (Koo, Tin, Koo, & Lee, 2006, p. 269). In keeping with this precept, parents might not attend their child's funeral. Given the difficulties that contemporary bereavement workers observe among Chinese bereaved people, the Western way of understanding grief often seems like a workable substitute. Indeed, one of the tasks for leaders in work with Chinese bereaved people has been to develop and introduce words that describe grief as an individual, inner experience. *Bei shang* (sadness) counseling portrayed an image that sadness in grief is problematic and needs to be fixed. Thus, a new term, *shan bei*, meaning good separation, was introduced (Chow & Chan, 2006). Such linguistic innovation to support new understandings and practices clearly reveals the role of the social construction of meaning in the cultural (re)framing of bereavement (Neimeyer, Klass, & Dennis, 2011).

Because Chinese bereaved are familiar with *shou xiao*, but are less familiar with terms describing grief, we find that they emphasize behaviors and actions over emotion. When Chinese do express how they feel, the most frequent is *sei bu de*, which is difficult to translate directly in English. It literally means missing him or don't want to abandon or let go of him. It also carries a connotation of being very sad (Ho, Chow, Chan, & Tsui, 2002). It is possible that *sei bu de* corresponds to the English word *yearning* that Stroebe, Abakoumkin, and Stroebe (2010) recently noted is more characteristic of grief than the depression usually used as a measure in bereavement research. Thus, this typical Chinese description of feelings might be useful in understanding typical, but often ignored, feelings in Western bereaved people.

CULTURE POLICES GRIEF

Our first theme, then, is that culture is how people construe their world. Culture provides the templates for how people represent their bereavement and, thus, the basis for their feelings and actions. Culture provides the words by which people recognize and articulate their experience.

Our second theme in culture's role in grief is that culture *polices* grief. In the radical individualism of contemporary consumer culture, it appears that grieving has few limitations placed on it. The mantra often heard among bereavement counselors is that "there is no right way to grieve." The present individualism, however, is deceptive. Individuals grieve and continue their bonds under the watchful eyes of their family and neighbors as well as those who hold religious and political power.

All cultures regulate the mourning of their members, subtly or overtly, and implicitly or explicitly. In the terminology of Neimeyer's constructivist model of bereavement (see Chapter 1), individual grief narratives are subjected to a dominant narrative of grief (Neimeyer, 2001). As Walter (1999) said, society polices bereavement. It controls and instructs the bereaved how to think, feel, and behave. Those who do not conform to social expectations are labeled aberrant. In contemporary psychotherapeutic culture, aberrant grief is termed *complicated*, a term that emerged when the former term *pathological* made some bereavement counselors uncomfortable. Complicated grief can be applied to those who are seen as grieving too long, grieving at the wrong time, or not grieving at all. In other times and other cultures, the labels would be different.

We see policing most clearly in two elements of grief: how grief's emotions are expressed and how continuing bonds with the dead are managed.

Policing Grief's Emotions

Emotions must be expressed in ways that are congruent with larger behavioral codes. Across cultures, we find a wide spectrum in which emotions are acceptable and in how overtly emotions may be expressed.

How, or how much, emotional expression is "appropriate" is often tied to gender roles. In a review of anthropological reports, Rosenblatt, Walsh, and Jackson (1976) concluded that "where there are differences, women seem to cry, to attempt self-mutilation … more than men; men seem to show more anger and aggression directed away from self" (p. 24).

Shou xiao carried with it complex rules on emotional expression, in which gender roles, context, and to whom it was to be expressed determined the level and style of expression. The power relationship between male and female was acted out in the funeral. The male was *yang*, associated with the enduring aspects of the body, the bones. The female was *yin*, associated with the flesh, with decomposition, and thus with pollution. One of the purposes of the rituals was to remove the corpse's pollution from contact with the living and to reduce the corpse to the nonpolluting bones. Women wailed and lamented at funerals while the men sat silently (Martin, 1988).

On the other hand, some Chinese funeral rituals, like the soul flag ritual and the purifying wash ritual, have to be carried out by men, preferably the sons of the deceased (Lai, 2006). Even though much of its meaning has been lost, we find that *shou xaio* is often the background of thoughts and feelings. If there are no sons in today's smaller families, a nephew or son-in-law might take up the duty. Widows who have no sons often feel guilty for not having a male offspring to perform the rituals (Chan, Chow, & Ho, 2005).

Jie ai shun bian ("Save the tears and follow the flow") is the commonly used condolence phrase at Chinese funerals. Some families believe that excessive expression of emotion is hazardous to health. On the other hand, some traditional Chinese families believe that wailing shows their level of filial piety. If they do not cry on their own, they can hire professional mourners to wail on their behalf.

In a quantitative study among bereaved persons in Hong Kong, only 10% said they did not share their bereavement experiences with anyone else. This implies that the majority of Chinese bereaved are ready to express and share their grief, despite cultural proscriptions on such expression. More surprisingly, the study found that those with whom they shared were not restricted to family members. They also shared with friends and professionals. The choice to express feelings to outsiders rather than family members can be explained by the good intention of preventing the overburdening of other grieving family members (Chow, Chan, & Ho, 2007).

Although the scripting of gender roles is the most obvious example of how emotional expressions are policed, national character may also be at stake (Walter, 1997). In a Western example, after the death of Diana, princess of Wales, media commentators were ambivalent about an un-British expressiveness that seemed to be replacing the stiff-upper-lip mode. The Windsor family followed the casket showing almost none of the deeply conflicting feelings her death must have evoked, whereas Diana's admiring commoners, for whom she was the queen of their hearts, wept and hugged openly (Biddle & Walter, 1998).

Local variations of religious beliefs are also reflected in the rules of how emotions are to be expressed. We find in Buddhism, for example, a wide spectrum of how grief's emotions are regarded. Though the majority of Hong Kong Chinese do not have any religious affiliations, some Buddhist beliefs are deeply rooted. Hong Kong widows say that they tried to contain their emotions at the moment of their husband's deaths because overtly expressed emotions disturb the deceased's transition to the new world (Chow et al., 2006). A similar prohibition on expressing emotions is found in Tibetan Buddhism. Mourners' tensions, attachments, and discomfort can generate negative emotions that can push the deceased in the afterlife toward a less than favorable rebirth. On the other hand, in traditional Japanese Buddhism, there could be quite emotionally fraught interactions among the survivors and between the survivors and the deceased as conflicts and difficulties in the relationship were resolved, so that the deceased could assume a positive role in the family as an ancestor and not become a wandering spirit that could cause bad things to happen to the survivors. American converts to Tibetan Buddhism have almost completely adopted contemporary psychological culture's positive view of emotion. Indeed, in interviews they said that deeply feeling grief is also deeply realizing the core Buddhist teaching of impermanence (Goss & Klass, 2005; Klass & Goss, 2006).

Policing Continuing Bonds

The second aspect of grief that displays strong policing is in the management of continuing bonds that the living maintain with the dead. In some cultures, continuing bonds are important and pervasive. In traditional Japanese ancestor rituals, bonds with the dead are a normal part of everyday life. In common speech, the dead are in *ano yo* ("that world") as opposed to *kono yo* ("this world"). The dead pass easily from one world to another. They are both there and here. They can be contacted easily at the household Buddha shelf on which their tablets stand and at which they are offered food each morning. They return for a yearly visit in the summer *bon* festival, yet after the festival, they are seen off as if they are embarking on a long journey back (Plath, 1964).

Chinese culture has a similar sense of ancestral bonds, though in China it is more based in Confucian beliefs. In the past, families placed tablets of their ancestors in their houses and offered incense joss sticks, food, and flowers. They reported important events to the ancestors and asked for their blessings. Although nowadays many families place the tablets of their ancestors at temples, monasteries, or cemeteries rather than at home, people still place photographs of the deceased at home and regularly talk to the photographs. On festival days, the birthday of the deceased, or the death anniversaries, people go to the cemeteries to be with their ancestors. It is not uncommon for younger generations to be pushed on these designated dates to visit the graves of their great-great-grandparents who died many decades ago.

The continuing bond can be initiated by the bereaved, as they talk to the tablets and photographs of the deceased or visit the cemetery to make offerings to the deceased. Influenced by Daoism, many Chinese burn paper offerings to transmit them to the ghosts of their dead, including money, houses, cars, cell phones, or even a maid, to improve the quality of their afterlife. Such expressions of continuing bonds, of course, are not part of most bereavement counselors' Westernized model of grief. Still, Chinese counselors see them as therapeutic, especially in dealing with guilt. Burning a paper house is cheaper than offering a real house, but can fulfill the unfinished business of supplying a good environment for the deceased (Chan et al., 2005).

Interaction between the living and the dead can also be initiated by the deceased. Reports of hearing, feeling, and seeing the deceased after the death or in dreams are described as soothing and reassuring. There is a common belief that the deceased can return in the form of insects like moths, butterflies, and even cockroaches. These encounters are usually extraordinary: the insect landing on a place where the deceased often sat, a cockroach that is not afraid of light, or an exceptionally big butterfly in a high-rise building with no natural environment nearby.

Over the course of the 20th century, the American and Western European popular and professional cultural grief guidelines changed from an emphasis on continuing bonds, to breaking bonds, and then back to continuing bonds. Among the middle and upper classes in the Victorian period, elaborate mourning customs channeled the sentimental attachment between the living and the dead. The mass deaths of the First World War overwhelmed Victorian ideals (Stroebe, Gergen, Gergen, & Stroebe, 1992). As the war ended, grief began to be regarded as an individual interior process with few social customs to support it. The idea of "decathexis" or withdrawing emotional energy from the deceased articulated by Freud (1917/1961) assumed that bonds to the dead served no healthy psychological purpose. For most of the 20th century, then, both mental health professionals and laypeople believed that the goal of grief was to reconstitute the autonomous individual who would sever bonds with the dead in order to form new bonds that facilitated adaptation to the changed social environment. Pathological grief was conceptualized as failing to relinquish the now useless attachment to the deceased.

Data from and about bereaved people, however, showed that many—perhaps most—people continue their bond with the deceased in a way that does not admit any diagnosis of pathology (Klass, Silverman, & Nickman, 1996). Today, most psychological bereavement theories maintain a place for continuing bonds in individuals and families. Field, Gal-Oz, and Bonanno's (2003) continuing bond measure includes focusing on fond memories, keeping items as reminder, sensing the deceased presence, identification with the deceased's wishes, use of the deceased's viewpoint in decision making, and reminiscing with others about the deceased (see also Chapter 4). At this time, however, continuing bonds in popular opinion, counseling guidelines, and empirical scales do not include listening to insects or the family performing prescribed rituals. Any provision for the dead contacting the living or the dead's need for help or support from the living is defined as merely something in the bereaved's symptoms or beliefs, not as ontologically real or empirically measurable. That is, in contemporary North American and Western European culture, continuing bonds are restricted to the private sphere, and grief remains defined as an internal psychological process (Goss & Klass, 2005; Klass, 2000).

Historically, the most common continuing bonds are within ancestor rituals that create family identity and define the values by which the family lives. At critical times in history, however, as the arrangement of political power changes, loyalty to the family dead detracts from the individual's allegiance to the new order (Goss & Klass, 2005). Family bonds are subversive in that they detract from allegiance to emerging political power. "This new loyalty—to God or the Church, to the Nation, to the Party or ideology—awards maximum points to those who forsake all other ties" (Mount, 1992, p. 6). When power arrangements change, continuing bonds with ancestors are recast into narratives that more directly support those who now claim political and economic power. A few examples will illustrate this widespread phenomenon.

In ancient Israel, monotheism finally overcame Baalism in the Deuteronomic reform under King Josiah (621 BCE). Before the reform, "to appeal to the dead meant basically to call upon lost relatives residing in Sheol to aid the living. From these dead relatives the living expected personal protection and, more importantly, numerous offspring" (Lang & McDannell, 1988, pp. 3–5). Under Josiah, family graves, where ancestor rituals were performed, were destroyed and the bones dumped on the altars of other gods. Communications with the dead were forbidden (Bloch-Smith, 1992). Although the reform was short lived, the Israelites who went into the Babylonian Exile used Josiah's reform as a template as they reformulated the religion into book-based Judaism, thus setting the pattern that would be adopted in Christianity and Islam.

In the mid-20th century, a very similar change happened in China. In the Communist narrative under Mao Zedong, individuals were no longer to regard themselves as family members, but rather to define themselves as workers, members of the proletariat. Funeral reform was high on the Communist Party's agenda. Ancestor rituals were suppressed (Whyte, 1988). Filial piety was converted into loyalty to the state, and then to loyalty to Mao himself. The dead were eulogized as exemplars of dedication to Mao and to newfound zeal in production. As a way of consolidating the new cultural narrative, the Communists created new ancestors (Wakeman, 1988). In an antique Chinese house last inhabited in 1982, now at the Peabody Essex Museum near Boston, Mao's name heads the list of ancestors above the ritual table. After Mao's death, his preserved body in a tomb on Tiananmen Square became a pilgrimage site. In all of these developments, mourning and memory were assigned new meanings in keeping with the emergent dominant narrative of the state (Neimeyer et al., 2011).

CULTURE AFFECTS HOW GRIEF IS HANDLED

Our third theme is that culture affects how grief is handled. Bereavement disrupts daily functioning. Stroebe and Schut's (1999) dual-process model looks to a balance in the oscillations between loss-oriented coping and restoration-oriented coping. Some observations in China seem to indicate that instead of maintaining a balance in both domains, there recently has been a disproportionate emphasis on restoration. After the earthquake in Sichuan in May 2008, tens of thousands of widows and widowers remarried shortly after their spouses' deaths. A significant number of middle-aged mothers whose only child died used reproductive technology to get pregnant soon after. Among Chinese widowers (Woo, Chan, Chow, & Ho, 2008–2009), one of their greatest concerns was to fulfill their duty to their children. They attributed their ability in managing their children's grief to their postbereavement self-esteem.

This inclination toward the restoration orientation can be further seen in Chinese individuals in coping with cancer. Ho, Wong, Chan, Watson, and Tsui (2003) suggested that fatalism was positively correlated with maintaining a fighting spirit among cancer patients. Fatalism is not resignation but rather an acceptance of *yuan* (predestined power which is external and stable). Though they accept the unchangeable fact of illness, they reserve energy and resources for managing what is changeable. Without further study, it is hard to comment on whether more balance of the two coping styles or a bias toward restoration-orientated coping is better for Chinese bereaved people, or how different Chinese coping is from the coping of Western bereaved people. Here, practice-based observations could help set an agenda for further research.

There are some recent cross-cultural studies among bereaved persons in China and the United States that shed light on cultural differences in grief management. Pressman and Bonanno (2007) found that Chinese bereaved persons score higher in avoiding thinking about the deceased and higher in searching for meaning in the bereavement process. Avoiding thinking about the deceased can help the bereaved focus on the daily tasks within the pattern of reserving energy and resources in managing that which is changeable. Searching for meaning is related to restoration and functionality as it gives new direction for how to live after the death (see Chapter 1).

Lalande and Bonanno (2006) found different trajectories of handling grief in Chinese and U.S. subjects. Chinese had more acute distress in the first few months but a quicker improvement. This relatively more "efficient" way of grieving might be related to the cultural value of pragmatism, the notion of moving on with life, and participation in ancestor rituals that contain overt grieving to specific prescribed dates. In bereavement counseling with Chinese individuals, then, it might be worthwhile to explore the practical matters of daily life first.

CONCLUSION

No individual or community grief can be fully understood without considering its cultural setting. In this short chapter, we have tried to sketch and illustrate three themes in the relationships of culture to grief. First, bereavement is experienced within a cultural framework, especially in language. Second, culture polices grief, especially in the expression of emotions and the management of continuing bonds. Third, culture affects how grief is handled. A good way to look for cultural differences in handling grief is to examine the balance between loss-oriented coping and restoration-oriented coping.

We hope that by using contemporary Chinese culture for many of our examples, we have given readers a broad enough understanding to help Chinese bereaved people whom they may try to help, and to make comparisons between the bereaved in China and other cultures with which readers are familiar.

From Knowing to Acting

What are the clinical implications of these three themes? It would be misleading to offer guidelines for particular cultures, because many clinical cases show a mix of cultures and each element of that mix has a deep history that may be expressed in surprising ways. We will attempt, then, to briefly point to some areas that we think might be helpful for clinicians. The suggestions that seem most important to us have to do with clinicians themselves, not with the bereaved whom they would help.

First, the theories in which we understand grief, the ways we think grief is resolved, and the techniques by which we help are as culturally bound as the Confucian values and rituals embodied in *shou xiao*. Just as English speakers often expect that others should learn to understand them rather than learn the languages of other peoples, they often expect that others should operate in the words, concepts, and feelings of the Western definitions of mental health and illness. Because those Western notions are spreading as part of international culture, it is often easy to be lulled into a false sense of security when we hear a few concepts that we recognize and forget that the concepts are now part of a cultural framework that has its own assumptions and values.

Second, just as self-awareness of the counselor's own thoughts, emotions, and personal history is a necessary component of effective clinical work, cultural self-awareness is increasingly a necessary component. Often we mistakenly think we understand our own culture without making the effort to locate the philosophical, historical, or literary roots of how grief is experienced, expressed, and resolved in our culture. A thoroughgoing review of the cultural background we bring to our practice is a good orientation for clinicians who work with bereaved persons in their own or different cultural backgrounds.

With this background, clinicians can, instead of passively receiving the information, also critically examine the applicability of the historical prescription of grieving and mourning in the modern world. For example, *jie ai shun bian*, the Chinese common condolence statement, has been critically reexamined in the community death education program. Though the cultural prescription might not be changed after this movement, the increase of awareness and reflectivity toward these prescriptions is already a valuable outcome of death education. Similarly, these discussions can further be extended to definitions of appropriate grief or appropriate mourning from an *emic* rather than an *etic* point of view.

Third, the cultural function of policing grief has critical implications for clinical practice. Whether they want to be or not, grief counselors are grief police. Even if they do not say it aloud, if the therapist thinks the client's grief is out of the normal range, the client will respond to that judgment. The client's family and community will also come to see things that way. As part of the cultural self-awareness we recommend, clinicians owe it to themselves and those they would help to rigorously test their ideas about complicated or dysfunctional grief in the light of what they learn about their own and other cultures.

Fourth, policing grief also plays a role in problems that clients bring to the counseling room. What emotions the bereaved express and the modes by which they express those emotions are often topics of judgmental conversation in the clients' family and community. How the bereaved continue or do not continue their bond with the dead is also a frequent subject of conversation about them. Often, then, the problem bereaved people bring to counseling is not how the bereaved are doing, but how others judge how they are doing. When family members or neighbors hold negative views of the bereaved persons, the level of social stress might be as high as the stress brought by the death itself. One study showed that negotiating their way through "the dominant grief discourse was a significant component of the bereaved participants' experience of grief" (Breen & O'Connor, 2010, p. 33).

Thus in working with bereaved persons, in addition to the pain of bereavement, the secondary stresses induced by how peers and family are judging the bereaved might also be an important area of work.

Finally, we would like to comment on the implications of the finding that Chinese, and perhaps people from other cultures, tend more toward restoration-oriented coping than loss-oriented coping. Instead of promoting an even balance between loss-oriented and restoration-oriented coping, clinicians can explore whether the bereaved need the optimal balance between the two. For example, in working with Chinese bereaved persons, starting with the restoration-oriented coping can be a good entry point. As reflected in the clinical experiences of the second author, groups which focused on restoration like Communication With Your Children After the Death of Your Wife, Management of Household Chores, and Financial Arrangements DIY are perceived as important and useful issues by Chinese bereaved persons.

REFERENCES

Biddle, L., & Walter, T. (1998). The emotional English and their queen of hearts. *Folklore*, *109*, 96–111.

Bloch-Smith, E. M. (1992). The cult of the dead in Judah: Interpreting the material remains. *Journal of Biblical Literature*, *111*(2), 213–224.

Breen, L. J., & O'Connor, M. (2010). Acts of resistance: Breaking the silence of grief following traffic crash fatalities. *Death Studies*, *34*, 30–53.

Chan, C. L. W., Chow, A. Y. M., & Ho, S. M. Y. (2005). The experience of Chinese bereaved persons: A preliminary study of meaning making and continuing bonds. *Death Studies*, *29*, 923–947.

Chow, A. Y. M., & Chan, C. L. W. (2006). Bereavement care in Hong Kong: Past, present and future. In C. L. W. Chan & A. Y. M. Chow (Eds.), *Death, dying and bereavement: A Hong Kong Chinese experience* (pp. 253–260). Hong Kong: Hong Kong University Press.

Chow, A. Y. M., Chan, C. L. W., & Ho, S. M. Y. (2007). Social sharing of bereavement experience by Chinese bereaved persons in Hong Kong. *Death Studies*, *31*, 601–618.

Chow, A. Y. M., Chan, C. L. W., Ho, S. M. Y., Tse, D. M. W., Suen, M. H. P., & Yuen, K. F. K. (2006). Qualitative study of Chinese widows in Hong Kong: Insights for psycho-social care in hospice settings. *Palliative Medicine*, *20*, 513–520.

Field, N. P., Gal-Oz, E., & Bonanno, G. A. (2003). Continuing bonds and adjustment at 5 years after the death of a spouse. *Journal of Consulting and Clinical Psychology*, *71*(1), 110–117.

Fontana, A., & Keene, J. R. (2009). *Death and dying in America*. Cambridge: Polity Press.

Foucault, M., Khalfa, J., & Murphy, J. (2006). *The history of madness*. New York: Routledge.

Freud, S. (1961). Mourning and melancholia. In J. Strachey (Ed.), *The standard edition of the complete psychological works of Sigmund Freud* (Vol. 14, pp. 243–258). London: Hogarth Press. (Original work published in 1917)

Gadamer, H. G. (1993). *Truth and method* (Trans. J. Weinsheimer & D. G. Marshall, 2nd ed.). New York: Continuum.

Goss, R., & Klass, D. (2005). *Dead but not lost: Grief narratives in religious traditions*. Walnut Creek, CA: AltaMira.

Ho, S. M. Y., Chow, A. Y. M., Chan, C. L. W., & Tsui, Y. K. Y. (2002). Assessment of grief among Hong Kong Chinese: A preliminary report. *Death Studies*, *26*(2), 91–98.

Ho, S. M. Y., Wong, K. F., Chan, C. L. W., Watson, M., & Tsui, Y. K. Y. (2003). Psychometric properties of the Chinese version of the Mini-Mental Adjustment to Cancer (Mini-MAC) scale. *Psycho-Oncology*, *12*(6), 547–556.

Klass, D. (2000). Continuing bonds in the resolution of grief in Japan and North America. *American Behavioral Scientist*, *44*(5), 742–763.

Klass, D., & Goss, R. (2006). Buddhisms and death. In K. Garces-Foley (Ed.), *Death and religion in a changing world* (pp. 69–92). Armonk, NY: Sharpe.

Klass, D., Silverman, P. R., & Nickman, S. (Eds.). (1996). *Continuing bonds: New understandings of grief*. Washington, DC: Taylor & Francis.

Koo, B. W. S., Tin, A. F., Koo, E. W. K., & Lee, S. M. (2006). When East meets West: The implication for bereavement counselling. In C. L. W. Chan & A. Y. M. Chow (Eds.), *Death, dying and bereavement: A Hong Kong Chinese experience* (pp. 216–272). Hong Kong: Hong Kong University Press.

Lai, C. T. (2006). Making peace with the unknown: A reflection on Daoist funerary liturgy. In C. L. W. Chan & A. Y. M. Chow (Eds.), *Death, dying and bereavement: A Hong Kong Chinese experience* (pp. 87–92). Hong Kong: Hong Kong University Press.

Lalande, K. M., & Bonanno, G. A. (2006). Culture and continuing bonds: A prospective comparison of bereavement in the United States and the People's Republic of China. *Death Studies*, *30*(4), 303–324.

Lang, B., & McDannell, C. (1988). *Heaven: A history*. New Haven, CT: Yale University Press.

Martin, E. (1988). Gender and ideology. In J. L. Watson & E. S. Rawski (Eds.), *Death ritual in late imperial and modern China* (pp. 164–179). Berkeley: University of California Press.

Mount, F. (1992). *The subversive family: An alternate history of love and marriage*. New York: Free Press.

Neimeyer, R. A. (2001). Meaning reconstruction and loss. In R. A. Neimeyer (Ed.), *Meaning reconstruction and the experience of loss* (pp. 1–9). Washington, DC: American Psychological Association.

Neimeyer, R. A., Klass, D., & Dennis, M. (2011). Meaning, mourning and memory: Grief and the narration of loss. In J. V. Ciprut (Ed.), *On meaning*. Boston: MIT Press.

Plath, D. W. (1964). Where the family of god is the family: The role of the dead in Japanese households. *American Anthropologist*, *66*(2), 300–317.

Pressman, D. L., & Bonanno, G. A. (2007). With whom do we grieve? Social and cultural determinants of grief processing in the United States and China. *Journal of Social and Personal Relationships*, *24*(5), 729–746.

Rosenblatt, P. C., Walsh, R. P., & Jackson, D. A. (1976). *Grief and mourning in cross-cultural perspective*. New York: Human Relations Area Files Press.

Stroebe, W., Abakoumkin, G., & Stroebe, M. (2010). Beyond depression: Yearning for the loss of a loved one. *Omega—Journal of Death and Dying*, *61*(2), 85–101.

Stroebe, M. S., Gergen, M. M., Gergen, K. J., & Stroebe, W. (1992). Broken hearts or broken bonds: Love and death in historical perspective. *American Psychologist*, *47*(10), 1205–1212.

Stroebe, M. S., & Schut, H. (1999). The dual process model of coping with bereavement: Rationale and description. *Death Studies*, *23*, 1–28.

Szasz, T. (1961). *The myth of mental illness: Foundations of a theory of personal conduct*. New York: Harper & Row.

Wakeman, F. (1988). Mao's remains. In J. L. Watson & E. S. Rawski (Eds.), *Death ritual in late imperial and modern China* (pp. 254–288). Berkeley: University of California Press.

Walter, T. (1997). Emotional reserve and the English way of grief. In K. Charmaz, G. Howarth, & A. Kellehear (Eds.). *The unknown country: Death in Australia, Britain and the USA* (pp. 127–140). New York: St. Martin's.

Walter, T. (1999). *On bereavement: The culture of grief*. Buckingham: Open University Press.

Watters, E. (2010). *Crazy like us: The globalization of the American psyche*. New York: Basic.

Whyte, M. K. (1988). Death in the People's Republic of China. In J. L. Watson & E. S. Rawski (Eds.), *Death ritual in late imperial and modern China* (pp. 289–316). Berkeley: University of California Press.

Woo, I. M. H., Chan, C. L. W., Chow, A. Y. M., & Ho, R. T. H. (2008–2009). Management of challenges of conjugal loss among Chinese widowers: An exploratory study, *Omega*, *58*(4), 275–297.

27

Religion and Spirituality in Adjusting to Bereavement

Grief as Burden, Grief as Gift

CRYSTAL L. PARK and ROSHI JOAN HALIFAX

Both religion-spirituality and death play central roles in the human experience (Wuthnow, Christiano, & Kuzlowski, 1980). Accordingly, religious traditions and academic disciplines such as theology and philosophy have long featured death as a central theme, and have long considered ways to deal with the burden of grief, which is an unavoidable aspect of existence. *Grief* refers to the deep sorrow following significant losses, the experience of mourning. This burden is the psychological weight experienced by the loss of a loved one, the loss of identity or status, the loss of relationship, the loss of place or thing, and the loss of capacity. These are the five great territories of grief (Halifax, 2008).

Grief can be an underlying mental process that flavors a life continuously or an experience that one passes through and is resolved in a positive manner, bringing about a greater sense of humanness, compassion, and wisdom. Grief is a multivalenced experience that can include shock, denial, numbness, anger, longing, yearning, searching, disorganization, despair, and potential reorganization. The burden of the loss can be carried over a lifetime or laid down. Grief can be seen as a natural human process giving rise to one's basic humanity, yet it can also be a potential trap, a no-exit, a source of chronic suffering.

Grief, of course, is a profound and often complex response for those who have been left behind by the dying. Survivors are often broken apart by the knowledge that they cannot bring back that which has been lost. The sense of irrevocability leaves them often helpless and sad, sometimes cognitively impaired, and sometimes socially withdrawn. And then there is the taste of grief in the landscape of Western culture, which is conditioned to possess and not let go; and yet beings and things are inevitably lost as we live our lives in this all-too-transient world. All human beings face loss, moment by moment; there is nothing that we can fully possess forever, even our own minds.

Often we associate grief only with the experience of loss that family members and friends go through upon the death of a loved one. But grief touches others as well. For example, dying people also can grieve before they die. They can grieve in anticipation of their death for all they will seem to lose and what they have lost by being ill. Such losses can include that of control, identity, wellness, healthy appearance (loss of hair, for example), energy, psychosocial engagement, and relationships, finally touching on the future loss of life. Anticipatory grief is a fairly normal response to upcoming loss and death, and the symptoms that one experiences in mourning are parallel to the symptoms of anticipatory grief, including a dying person feeling shock, denial, profound sorrow, withdrawal from the world, depression, anger, alienation, and physical and mental pain.

The resolution of grief is important. If grief is not been sufficiently attended to after the loss of a loved one, it may remain unresolved for a long period of time. For example, family and friends of the deceased can become consumed by the busyness of the business that happens right after someone dies. This is one of the great problems that one faces in the Western way of dying: that business is so much a part of the experience of dying and death. Survivors often face a complex situation on the material level in the after-death phase. They find themselves looking for a funeral home, letting friends and family know that a death has happened, and creating a funeral service. Unraveling health insurance, taxes, and the last will and testament also takes time and energy at this stage. Later there is cleaning up, dividing and giving away the deceased's property, and other seemingly endless chores of closure. Resorting to the business and busyness of death can be a way for survivors to avoid or be taken away from the depth of their own loss.

Bereavement is universally recognized as a critical life experience with which humans must grapple, as is its potential for strong positive and negative implications that reverberate throughout the lives of those who remain behind. Religious and spiritual answers are universally applied to the problems presented by bereavement (Wuthnow et al., 1980). Curiously, however, relatively little social science research has addressed the role of religion or spirituality in adjusting to the death of a loved one. This lack of empirical attention may reflect a reluctance of mainstream social scientists to examine metaphysical constructs (Paloutzian & Park, 2005). In the remainder of this chapter, we review empirical research and theoretical perspectives on religion and spirituality in the context of bereavement and then illustrate these linkages with examples from Christian and Buddhist traditions. The chapter concludes with a Buddhist practice offered as a means to work with grief.

EMPIRICAL RESEARCH ON RELIGION, SPIRITUALITY, AND ADJUSTMENT TO BEREAVEMENT

In spite of the tremendous advances in science and technology and a cultural thrust toward secularity, religion and spirituality continue to thrive throughout the world and there is little evidence of its abatement (Park, Edmondson, & Hale-Smith, in press). For example, in a recent nationwide poll in the United States, 56% of adults said that religion is *very important* to them, and an additional 25% said it is *somewhat important* to them; 63% reported being a member of a church or synagogue, whereas 42% reported having attended services there in the past week, numbers that are consistent with, and even somewhat higher than, those in polls from earlier decades (Gallup, 2009). The pervasive presence of religion and spirituality over time and place is likely due, at least in part, to the provision of meaning that they provide, particularly in times of high stress (Park et al., in press; Wuthnow et al., 1980). Recent years have seen a renewed empirical interest in religiousness and spirituality (Paloutzian & Park, 2005), such that academic disciplines seem to be finally acknowledging the influence of religion and spirituality that is well established in the broader culture.

One result of this increased research focus on religiousness and spirituality is the emerging consensus that religion and spirituality comprise myriad dimensions (Wortmann & Park, 2008). For bereavement research, this recognition of the complexity of religiousness and spirituality is important because it allows researchers to delve much more deeply into these phenomena, producing a much more nuanced body of literature. However, it also means that researchers must strive to look beyond simplistic assessments such as service attendance or denomination, taking into account religious and spiritual aspects such as relationships with God and congregation, religious emotions and attachments, views of God, experiences of the transcendent, beliefs, commitment, meaning, and many others. For example, a bereaved individual's denomination may inform the impact of the loss and his or her way of grieving with it, but so might many other aspects of his or her religious and spiritual life (Wortmann & Park, 2008).

At present, the body of empirical literature addressing religious and spiritual influences on psychological adjustment following bereavement must be interpreted with caution because nearly all of the studies on this topic suffer serious methodological limitations. For example, many studies that have attempted to determine how religiousness or spirituality influence adjustment to loss of a loved one assessed both religious or spiritual variables and adjustment variables at the same time. Findings from studies using such cross-sectional designs cannot determine whether there is a causal relationship and, if so, its direction. If a positive association is found between religion and grief, it may mean that those who are suffering more turn more to their faith to help them through, or that something about religion or a particular type of religion leads people to suffer more, or that some underlying third variable (e.g., personality) is influencing measures of both religiousness and grief. All of these interpretations of cross-sectional correlational findings are plausible, but none is conclusive. In addition, most studies have not included a control group of individuals who are not bereaved. Thus, it is unknowable whether any links found between aspects of religion-spirituality and adjustment to bereavement are specific to the context of bereavement or simply reflections of the relationship between religion–spirituality and well-being found in the population at large (Stroebe, 2004).

With these caveats, what conclusions can we draw from extant empirical studies? Three recent systematic reviews (Becker et al., 2007; Hays & Hendrix, 2008;

Wortmann & Park, 2008) have usefully aggregated the literature on these linkages. The majority of the studies reviewed reported generally positive relationships between religion or spirituality and some aspects of adjustment to bereavement, particularly if observed over time. For example, in a study of bereaved elderly adults, most of whom had lost a spouse, higher levels of religious coping were related to more functional disability at baseline (Pearce et al., 2002). However, at follow-up, higher use of religious coping was associated with improved physical health, whereas lower use of religious coping was associated with decreased health status, even controlling for other explanatory variables such as age, health, and health-promoting behaviors.

All three reviews noted that although studies often reported some positive relations between religion or spirituality and some indicator of well-being, they typically failed to find consistent effects. For example, studies often report a favorable relationship for one dimension of religion or spirituality but not for others or for one aspect of adjustment but not for others (e.g., Park & Cohen, 1993). Thus, the reviews were remarkably consistent in concluding that the studies do not provide conclusive evidence regarding relations between religion or spirituality and adjustment in bereavement. For example, Hays and Hendrix (2008) noted, "[C]onclusions concerning the role of religion in coping with bereavement remain elusive because study designs generally lack rigor" (p. 341), and Becker et al. (2007) concluded that "no statistically significant findings could be reported in the studies. Most studies reported positive effects of spiritual or religious beliefs on bereavement. However, there is a lack of evidence because of weaknesses in design and methodological flaws" (p. 215). All three reviews noted the difficulties and complexities in conducting this research and ended with calls for better research designs to more definitively address these critical questions.

THEORETICAL MODELS OF RELIGION AND SPIRITUALITY: ADJUSTMENT TO LOSS

People often report that their religion or spirituality was helpful or even essential for getting through and recovering from their grief (see Wortmann & Park, 2008, for a review) in spite of the lack of solid empirical evidence that this is so. Indeed, there are strong theoretical rationales for positing that religion and spirituality can strongly impact the process of grieving. For many individuals, religion or spirituality underlies their general approach to life and forms the system of meaning through which they experience and understand the world and operate on a daily basis, making the universe seem benign, safe, just, coherent, and, ultimately, controllable (Park et al., in press). Clearly, when facing highly stressful experiences such as the death of a loved one, this meaning system will influence their responses to it.

Religious and spiritual perspectives provide many resources for understanding and coping with loss. Many traditions provide perspectives on death, such as viewing loss as illusory rather than real or as a necessary step toward a more glorious future. Several predominant religious belief systems hold out possibilities for everlasting life and for reunification with the lost loved one after one's own death (Greeley & Hout, 1999). Beliefs in a soul that is separate from and persists after the death of the physical body also allows for the possibility of remaining in contact with the deceased (Benore & Park, 2004), a commonly reported experience in the United States (Klugman, 2006).

In addition, religious and spiritual traditions offer a panoply of coping resources for dealing with death. These resources include social support from pastors and fellow congregants, and many rites and rituals to assist mourners through the process of grieving. For example, all religious traditions prescribe specific prayers, behaviors, and funeral ceremonies to deal with death, which comfort mourners and give them a sense of structure and a sense of belonging to a broader community (Wuthnow et al., 1980). Through these resources, individuals may find solace and comfort and, over time, work through their grief in ways that allow them to find peace and acceptance and to return to their normal daily lives (Halifax, 2008). Of course, normal life is forever changed with the loss of a loved one, and people often carry a lingering sense of sadness and longing for the lost person (Stroebe, Abakoumkin, & Stroebe, 2010).

Importantly, mitigating negative outcomes is not the only possibility represented by religious and spiritual approaches to bereavement. In fact, many religious and spiritual traditions hold that the suffering experienced through bereavement can be an impetus for transformative spiritual experience. Such a perspective holds that to deny grief is to rob one of the heavy stones that will eventually be the ballast for the two great accumulations of wisdom and compassion. Indeed, grief is a vital part of our very human life, an experience that can open compassion, and an important phase of maturation giving depth and humility to life; it can be regarded as a gift. Grief can ruin or mature us. Like the mother who bathed her dead baby in her breast milk, grief can remind us not to hold on too tightly as it teaches us tenderness and patience with our own suffering. Many bereaved individuals report extensive personal growth following bereavement, including increased appreciation for life, enhanced spirituality, and closer interpersonal relationships, and religious and spiritual pathways commonly lead to this transformative growth (Park, 2005).

CHRISTIAN PERSPECTIVES ON BEREAVEMENT

Christianity comprises an array of denominations that vary widely in many ways, including their views of God and human nature as well as their views of death and the possibilities of life after death. Thus, generalizations about Christian perspectives on bereavement can only approximate any particular strain of Christianity. Nonetheless, most Christians hold the pursuit of eternal life as central, and see human existence as a prelude to this everlasting life (Engelhardt & Iltis, 2005; Greeley & Hout, 1999). According to the General Social Survey (GSS) conducted in the United States, nearly all Christians believe in an afterlife consisting of union with God, peace and tranquility, and reunion with loved ones (Greeley & Hout, 1999).

Christian beliefs generally provide comfort for the bereaved (Wortmann & Park, 2008). For example, in a qualitative study of adult daughters describing the loss of their mothers, one participant stated,

> The body goes away but the spirit lives on, you know. I often picture her [mother] in my mind because you will meet your loved ones again. I said, "Oh God, she's with her mother, her father, my sister, her brothers and her sisters." If I live right, I'll meet them there too. At death, you know, you're going on to a better place. (Quoted in Smith, 2002, p. 317)

However, Exline (2003) noted that the GSS revealed that beliefs in hell as well as in heaven were common among Christians; she speculated that, particularly for those who are bereaved, the specific content of afterlife beliefs may influence their impact on the process of bereavement. For example, depending on the specific features of the deceased's life and death, concerns may arise about the loved one being in danger of going to hell. Exline gave the example of a bereaved Catholic who was concerned that her sister, who had committed suicide, might be eternally damned.

BUDDHIST PERSPECTIVES ON BEREAVEMENT

Buddhism emphasizes that death is an unavoidable and natural part of life, and focuses on how the principles of compassion and respect for all living beings can be carried out in all contexts, including bereavement (Keown, 2005). Buddhists explicitly acknowledge the impermanence of the world and the nonreality of the individual ego, positing that suffering is caused by attachments to particular people or objects that are fleeting or illusory. Insights into the Buddhist approach to loss can be gleaned from some of the stories of the first nuns of Gautama Buddha, 2,500 years ago. These accounts are rendered by Susan Murcott (2006) in *The First Buddhist Women*.

In one story, Ubbiri, one of the first women Buddhists, was drowning in grief as a result of the death of her daughter. Through the help of the Buddha, she discovered truth from within the experience of her own suffering. Ubbiri came from a high family in Savatthi. She was beautiful as a child, and when she grew up she was given to the court of King Pasenadi of Kosala. One day she became pregnant by the king and gave birth to a daughter whom she named Jiva, which means "alive." Shortly after being born, however, Jiva died. Ubbiri, wounded by grief, went every day to the cremation ground and mourned her daughter. One day, when she arrived at the cremation ground, she discovered that a great crowd had gathered. The Buddha was traveling through the region, and he had paused to give teachings to local people. Ubbiri stopped for a little while to listen to the Buddha but soon left to go to the riverside and weep with despair. The Buddha, hearing her pain-filled keening, sought her out and asked why she was weeping. In agony she cried out that her daughter was dead. He then pointed to one place and another where the dead had been laid, and he said to her,

> Mother, you cry out "O Jiva" in the woods.
> Come to yourself, Ubbiri.
> Eighty-four thousand daughters
> All with the name "Jiva"

Have burned in the funeral fire.
For which one do you grieve?

Murcott (2006, p. 94)

Grieving is a landscape that is so varied and so vast that it can be discovered only through one's own most intimate experience. It touches the one who is dying, those around a dying person, and those who survive. No one escapes its touch, nor in the end should we. The river of grief pulses deep inside all human beings, hidden from view, but its presence informs one's life at every turn. It can drive a person into the numbing habits of escape from suffering or bring an individual face-to-face with his or her own humanity.

When the 18th-century Japanese Haiku master Issa lost his baby daughter, he wrote,

The dewdrop world
is the dewdrop world
and yet—and yet.

Issa (1994, p. 191)

Issa has not yet been released by the anguish of grief. But the hand is beginning to open. And like the transiency of his precious daughter's life, one hopes his grief also passed.

The Zen nun Rengetsu expresses the poignancy of loss and impermanence in this way:

The impermanence of this floating world
I feel over and over
It is hardest to be the one left behind.

Rengetsu (2005, p. 117)

Buddhism holds that grief can be a pathway for spiritual transformation. An old woman once told a caregiver that wisdom and compassion are not given to us; they can only be discovered. The experience of discovery means letting go of what one knows. When an individual moves through the transformation of the elements of loss and grief, he or she may discover the truth of the impermanence of everything in life and, of course, of this very life itself. This is one of the most profound discoveries to be made. In this way, grief and sorrow may teach gratitude for what one has been given, even the gift of suffering. From grief, one can learn to swim in the stream of universal sorrow. And in that stream, one may even find the gift of joy.

A BUDDHIST PRACTICE FOR TRANSFORMING GRIEF

This practice, based on the Buddhist practice of the Boundless Abodes, consists of phrases that can help us swim the waters of grief until grieving is transmuted into compassion and equanimity (Halifax, 2008, p. 195). In this practice, we are guided again and again toward the arms of grief. Transformation comes when we are touched by loss, come to know it, and experience purification through being fully washed in its waters. When practicing these phrases, let the body settle; you can either sit or lie down. Remember why you are practicing; cultivate a tender heart. Then find the phrase or phrases appropriate to you, practice them with the breath, or let your attention rest gently with each phrase as you work with it.

- May I fully face life and death, loss and sorrow.
- May I be open to the pain of grief.
- May I find the inner resources to be present for my sorrow.
- May loving kindness sustain me.
- May I accept my sadness, knowing that I am not my sadness.
- May I accept my human limitations with compassion.
- May I accept my anger, fear, anxiety, and sorrow.
- May I forgive myself for not meeting my loved one's needs.
- May I forgive myself for mistakes made and things left undone.
- May sorrow show me the way to compassion.
- May I be open with others and myself about my experience of suffering and loss.
- May I receive the love and compassion of others.
- May I find peace and strength that I may use my resources to help others.
- May all those who grieve be released from their sorrow.

CONCLUDING THOUGHTS

Although the empirical research has not (yet) convincingly demonstrated the helpfulness of religion in dealing with loss, most people will continue to turn to their religious or spiritual beliefs and practices for solace, comfort, and understanding in the midst of their bereavement. In this chapter, we have illustrated several different religious and spiritual approaches to coping with grief; there are many others. Through these different religious and spiritual pathways, grievers may find their way through their burdens and, perhaps, transform them into compassion and a deeper way of living.

REFERENCES

Becker, G., Xander, C., Blum, H., Lutterbach, J., Momm, F., Gysels, M., & Higginson, I. (2007). Do religious or spiritual beliefs influence bereavement? A systematic review. *Palliative Medicine*, *21*, 207–217.

Benore, E. R., & Park, C. L. (2004). Religiousness and beliefs in continued attachment after death. *International Journal of the Psychology of Religion*, *14*, 1–22.

Engelhardt, H. T., & Iltis, A. S. (2005). End-of-life: The traditional Christian view. *The Lancet*, *366*, 1045–1049.

Exline, J. J. (2003). Belief in heaven and hell among Christians in the United States: Denominational differences and clinical implications. *Omega: The Journal of Death and Dying*, *47*, 155–168.

Gallup. (2009). *Religion*. Retrieved from http://www.gallup.com/poll/1690/Religion.aspx

Greeley, A. M., & Hout, M. (1999). Americans' increasing belief in life after death: Religious competition and acculturation. *American Sociological Review*, *64*, 813–835.

Halifax, J. (2008). *Being with dying: Cultivating compassion and fearlessness in the presence of death*. Boston: Shambhala.

Hays, J. C., & Hendrix, C. C. (2008). The role of religion in bereavement. In M. S. Stroebe, R. O. Hansson, H. Schut, W. Stroebe, & E. Van den Blink (Eds), *Handbook of bereavement research and practice: Advances in theory and intervention* (pp. 327–348). Washington, DC: American Psychological Association.

Issa, K. (1994). *The essential haiku* (Trans. and ed. Robert Haas). New York: Ecco Press.

Keown, D. (2005). End of life: The Buddhist view. *The Lancet*, *366*, 952–955.

Klugman, C. M. (2006). Dead men talking: Evidence of post death contact and continuing bonds. *Omega: The Journal of Death and Dying*, *53*, 249–262.

Murcott, S. (2006). *The first Buddhist women*. Berkeley, CA: Parallax Press.

Paloutzian, R. and Park, C. L. (Eds.) (2005). *Handbook of the psychology of religion and spirituality*. New York: Guilford Press.

Park, C. L. (2005). Religion as a meaning-making framework in coping with life stress. *Journal of Social Issues*, *61*, 707–730.

Park, C. L., & Cohen, L. H. (1993). Religious and nonreligious coping with the death of a friend. *Cognitive Therapy and Research*, *17*, 561–577.

Park, C. L., Edmondson, D., & Hale-Smith, A. (In press). Why religion? Meaning as the motivation. In K. Pargament (Ed.), *Handbook of the psychology of religion and spirituality*. Washington, DC: American Psychological Association.

Pearce, M. J., Chen, J., Silverman, G. K., Kasl, S. V., Rosenheck, R., & Prigerson, H. G. (2002). Religious coping, health, and health service use among bereaved adults *International Journal of Psychiatry in Medicine*, *32*, 179–199.

Rengetsu. (2005). *Lotus moon: The poetry of the Buddhist nun Rengetsu* (Trans. John Stevens). Buffalo, NY: White Pine Press.

Smith, S. H. (2002). "Fret no more my child … for I'm all over Heaven all day": Religious beliefs in the bereavement of African American, middle-aged daughters coping with the death of an elderly mother. *Death Studies*, *26*, 309–323.

Stroebe, M. S. (2004). Religion in coping with bereavement: Confidence of convictions or scientific scrutiny? *International Journal of the Psychology of Religion*, *14*, 23–26.

Stroebe, W., Abakoumkin, G., & Stroebe, M. (2010). Beyond depression: Yearning for the loss of a loved one. *Omega*, *61*, 85–101.

Wortmann, J. H., & Park, C. L. (2008). Religion and spirituality in adjustment following bereavement: An integrative review. *Death Studies*, *32*, 703–736.

Wuthnow, R., Christiano, K., & Kuzlowski, J. (1980). Religion and bereavement: A conceptual framework. *Journal for the Scientific Study of Religion*, *19*, 408–422.

28

Technology and Grief Support in the Twenty-First Century
A Multimedia Platform

KATHLEEN R. GILBERT and GLORIA C. HORSLEY

The dramatic increase in access and use of the Internet and other electronic technologies has expanded the availability of information to the bereaved and their families. In addition, and possibly more significantly, the Internet provides opportunities for interaction with others around the topics of loss and grief. Because it is such a recent phenomenon, research on the use of technology in relation to grief and grieving has been limited. It is, however, growing.

In this chapter, we will first review existing research literature on the use of technology (primarily the Internet) as a tool for dealing with a loss. Following that, we will present an existing complex, multifaceted website designed to help people find hope after a loss. The Open to Hope website (www.opentohope.com) is a unique "open platform" to support those who are grieving. The content-driven site includes a combination of articles written by grief experts, radio programs, and video clips, and it provides an opportunity to grievers to write about their experiences and connect with others who have had similar losses.

We recognize that other electronic technologies are used by the bereaved to deal with loss, cope with and/or process grief, or maintain a connection to the deceased. These include a range of websites, the major ones being www.legacy.com, www.griefnet.org, www.compassionatefriends.org, and www.aarp.org/relationships/grief-loss/, among others. Research on the use of nonnetworked technologies is extremely limited. One study (Massimi & Baecker, 2010) asked about technologies used, and among them was only one nonnetworked technology (using digital pictures in frames in the home), so we will restrict this chapter to networked electronic technologies, primarily the Internet. In addition, although questions have been raised about the use of the Internet for therapy, we will focus primarily on the supportive and informational functions of the Internet.

ONLINE INTERNET COMMUNITY FOR THE BEREAVED

The process of grieving a loss and recovering a sense of normalcy in life can be challenging, and resources may not be readily available to the bereaved. Healing and grief reconciliation to loss occur in *years*, not weeks or months (Heinz, 1999). Widows, for example, take approximately 4 years to begin to resolve loss; the loss of a child can result in parents taking as much as 8 years to integrate and begin to heal from the loss (McBride & Simms, 2001). In addition, those who are bereaved may find that resources immediately available to them may not adequately meet their needs. At the same time, the bereaved may feel out of control after a loss (Gilbert, 1996). Aspects of Internet community, identified by McKenna (1998), may be especially appealing to those who are grieving. These aspects are anonymity, the absence of traditional gatekeeping processes on nonmonitored sites, a higher degree of control over relationships, and ease of finding others who share interests.

Anonymity. Anonymity is the ability to regulate how much information about oneself a person is willing to share with others (McKenna & Bargh, 2000). In fact, anonymity and the related absence of such social markers as age and race might allow individuals to be more open in their communication (Miller & Gergen, 1998). It is possible to create a screen name and to protect one's personal identity so that people who interact regularly on the Internet can meet in another context and not know that they have met and shared personal information on the Internet. The downside of this aspect of the Internet is that others can do the same and may have less than pure intentions that are shielded by their anonymous screen names. The ability to create a virtual identity was seen as a benefit to women in an online perinatal loss support group (Capitulo, 2004).

An absence of traditional gatekeeping processes. Traditional gatekeepers like families and friends and other social arbiters may be absent on the majority of nonmonitored sites on the Internet. All that is needed is a shared interest and an Internet connection. Those who are bereaved may see this as empowering in that they can sidestep or avoid the interference of traditional gatekeepers so that they might find others who share their focus. The bereaved may be at risk, though, especially early on in their bereavement when they are emotionally vulnerable and lack the protection of traditional gatekeepers who might screen mail or phone calls from insensitive or abusive outsiders. With the Internet, that filter may be sporadic on unmonitored sites, and even sometimes on monitored sites.

Higher degree of control over relationships. Users of the Internet, especially those using an anonymous screen name, are able to maintain a higher degree of control over their communication with others. As long as the relationship remains virtual, they can choose to communicate or not to communicate with others. Alternatively, the other person in the virtual relationship also has this ability, and the sudden end of a supportive relationship may be troubling to a vulnerable bereaved person, just as it can be when nonvirtual relationships end abruptly.

Ease of finding others who share interests. Finding others online who have had similar losses can provide opportunities for grievers to validate their developing narratives (Gilbert, 1996). Each loss has its unique aspects, and the ability to interact with someone who has "walked the same walk" can be very beneficial. Not having to tell one's story in great detail, while also feeling that the person to whom the story is told understands, has great power. In the study of an online perinatal support group (mentioned above), women were seen to extend this shared interest to create a common culture of shared metamorphosis (Capitulo, 2004).

THE INTERNET AS A SOURCE OF SOCIAL SUPPORT

In a study of social support and technological connectedness for the bereaved, Vanderwerker and Prigerson (2004) studied the use of technologies, specifically the Internet (which the authors did not specifically defined), e-mail, and cell phones. They found that almost 60% of their respondents used the Internet, and almost half specifically reported communicating by e-mail as a type of social support. Although not conclusive, their results indicated a potential protective effect of the use of the Internet and e-mail with regard to more severe depressive disorder, posttraumatic stress disorder, and chronic grief, and their use was associated with a better quality of life.

Sofka (1997) identified, in an early examination of thanatology-related Internet resources, three forms of social support—informational or guidance support, emotional or affective support, and instrumental or material support—on the web. She found these resources on "stand-alone" sites or, more typically, as a part of a comprehensive website. Since that time, these three continue to serve as the forms of support provided on the Internet.

The most essential aspect of social support via the Internet is its potential to provide a community of supporters who legitimize the griever, the loss, or both. As demonstrated by Hollander's (2001) study of suicide survivors, who are often disenfranchised publicly in their grief, the Internet serves as "a kind of refuge from the larger social order where grieving was perceived as unwelcome" (p. 140). Hollander's study provides an example of how e-mail support groups for suicide survivors can provide a cyber community where discussion of deceased loved ones is not just tolerated but also encouraged. Although suicide survivors may be disenfranchised by the larger culture, cyber communities can create a refuge where suicide survivors can discuss their grief openly and without fear of prejudice. As Hollander described in her study, "They [suicide survivors] understand themselves as outcasts, and they speak and write and confer most of all with one another, on the fringes of the larger society that frowns upon them" (p. 142).

Supportive, interactive Internet resources cover a tremendous range: Hollander's (2001) findings are echoed by those of Fiegelman, Gorman, Beal, and Jordan (2008). In a comparison of face-to-face and Internet-based support groups,

Fiegelman and his colleagues found that those who chose Internet-based groups did so because of uniquely appealing factors associated with the Internet: the group's "24/7" (i.e., 24 hours each day, 7 days each week) availability and the ability to spend extensive amounts of time participating on the site. Consistent with McKenna's (1998) description of the strengths of the Internet, two aspects of the Internet stood out for their respondents: the ability to maintain privacy (i.e., anonymity) and having the source of help available whenever problems arose (i.e., ease of finding others with shared interests). Additionally, a study of telephone support groups, conducted in Australia, found that the phone support may provide benefits not present in face-to-face support (Nair, Goodenough, & Cohn, 2006).

Online bereavement support mirrors that found in face-to-face groups in several ways. First, members can identify with each other in the group because others share their experiences. Members may bond with one another and find that they are not alone in their grief experience. Although grief is, in many ways, a unique and individual experience, common reactions and experiences contribute to a degree of universality in the grief experience. Finally, groups provide a safe place in which to express feelings and thoughts (Corr, Nabe, & Corr, 2006; Yalom, 1995).

THE INTERNET AS A SOURCE OF GRIEF EXPRESSION FOR GRIEVERS

This form of Internet resources includes commemorative, expressive, and experiential functions that provide opportunities for grievers to describe personal stories, express thoughts and emotions, create memorials, and, occasionally, conduct rituals in a supportive environment. Examples of these kinds of sites include "cyber cemeteries," poetry and prose sites, web memorials, and online blogs.

Rituals followed closely after death can help the bereaved acknowledge their losses personally. The Internet has no cultural boundaries or rules that govern how the deceased are memorialized. Freedom of expression through poetry, art, music, and writing is unrestricted. Anonymity of the person posting to the site is most likely ensured if it is desired. Also, expressive sites such as the creation of a web memorial, unlike most postdeath rituals, can be created at one's own pace (Roberts, 2004).

Web memorials have become very popular venues for grief expression. They can be created by anyone, including the surviving family members as well as friends and others who were not included in standard mourning rituals. For instance, in a study on web memorials (Roberts & Vidal, 2000), friends and pets often were mentioned as survivors of the deceased. Web memorials allow the bereaved to honor their dead in their own way and at their own time, to visit the memorial whenever they choose, and to share with others their memories and information about the deceased person (Roberts, 2004). Also, web memorials can be updated and changed continuously to reflect evolving grief.

Social networking sites offer unique opportunities for survivors to use the deceased's personal web page as a personal memorial after the death (Hieftje,

2009) by leaving comments and writing blogs on the deceased's personal web page. Writing messages to the dead functions as either a substitute for or an enhancement of the experiences obtained in traditional postdeath rituals and may be particularly helpful to those experiencing disenfranchised losses (Kollar, 1989).

THE OPEN TO HOPE WEBSITE

The Open to Hope website was established by psychotherapists Dr. Gloria C. Horsley and Dr. Heidi Horsley in memory of their deceased son and brother, Scott. The founders are published authors on grief and loss and are cohosts of the weekly *Open to Hope* radio show (Horsley & Horsley, 2007, 2008, 2011, in press). The website follows the mission of the Open to Hope Foundation, which is based on the belief that despair and suffering, although painful, are all part of the normal process of grief and adaptation to loss, and that the technology of the Internet is the perfect forum to reach bereaved individuals throughout the world. The website was designed with web agency Wheel Media with the purpose of empowering the griever and to make each feel as if his or her own unique needs are not only heard but also understood. (See Figure 28.1.)

The Open to Hope site offers users the opportunity to explore and understand their own experiences with loss in a safe, caring online community. Resources on the site are wide, varied, and constantly being expanded. Visitors to opentohope.

Figure 28.1 The www.opentohope.com website was designed to enable visitors, including grief professionals and the bereaved, to intuitively access the information they need on grief and loss.

com are invited to "write your story" and respond to articles, video, and radio shows. Content on the site addresses not just the immediate aftermath of loss but also grief over the long term. This content is provided by grief professionals, as well as survivors of loss, with a growing collection of over 2,000 original articles, 300 radio shows, and more than 75 videos.

Available 24/7, visitors to the site can shape their use of the site to best fit their own needs, and at their own convenience, while also recognizing that one's grief is as unique as one's fingerprints. The Internet offers intimacy, as well as safety at a distance. Because the site is a passive medium, visitors can compartmentalize their grief and visit the site, or choose not to visit it, as they wish. As noted above, the unlimited availability allows for access for any length of time and at any time of day. Phil, one opentohope.com site visitor, wrote,

> I felt depressed at work today and I left early, when I got home I typed the following into my computer's Google search, 'My son died and I need help.' The Open to Hope site came up and I knew that I was not alone.

The Open to Hope site is organized to help grievers more easily access resources that will be helpful to them. Searches can be organized around type of loss, the nature of their relationship, and the concern with which they are dealing. Special topics focus on particular concerns like "For Men Only." One of the site visitors, Peter, wrote,

> I'm 25 and none of my friends has ever lost a parent. It hurts to know I'm so alone in that sense. But it is a relief to know there are others out there in similar situations, and others who understand why the little things can be the biggest triggers.

As is evident from the screen shot of the homepage, opentohope.com is a multifaceted site that offers users a multitude of Internet modalities. As well as providing easy access to information about grief in a centralized source, the site also offers numerous possibilities to engage users—whether those in grief, or professionals who are seeking information—even further. These include becoming an author on the site, listening to archived streaming audio radio shows, viewing video clips created for Open to Hope television, and being involved with social media like Facebook and Twitter.

Articles authored and available on the site are written by both grief professionals and the bereaved. Open to Hope Radio is podcasted weekly, and each show features diverse guest speakers, all of whom are either survivors of loss or experts on the topic. Open to Hope Television consists of brief video segments that feature interviews with both grief experts and individuals who have experienced a loss, and are also available on youtube.com.

Personal stories of loss can be shared in a number of ways on the Open to Hope website. Throughout the site, users are encouraged to provide their own story and insights by responding to the articles, stories of others, radio shows, or videos. These postings may take on the character of memorials and may at times include an announcement of funeral or memorial service arrangements. Overall, they are heartfelt and very personal, and many site visitors post supportive comments responding to the plights of others. In the following exchange, "Big B" posted, "My son died, recently of cancer. I am in living hell." In response, Phil wrote, "Dear Big B: I don't know you but my son died of cancer also. I know your pain." Virtual conversations and friendships are common, and for those who wish to continue further connections with other grievers beyond the boundaries of the opentohope.com site, visitors have the opportunity to check a box and include their personal email addresses.

Although one might expect some misuse of a site like this, it is surprisingly free of typical website "flaming" or harsh treatment of other users, which is rife on other sites. This may be because the users feel a part of a larger community of caring and shared pain. Site visitors seem extremely reluctant to abuse those who are in grief. To ensure that improper content is not posted, the site is monitored by professional opentohope.com staff, and all new content that is inappropriate is immediately removed. Because the site has experienced so few problems with this issue, visitors' comments and stories appear on the site immediately after being posted, thus validating the value of the visitors' words as they are posted without delay, in contrast to other sites where all new content is first vetted before being available online.

The Open to Hope Foundation also hosts a Facebook page and Twitter channel. Facebook is a place where current events, radio show guests, upcoming articles, and current news and events related to the website's authors and other grief-related organizations are posted and shared. Twitter is used when a show is being broadcast, and participants are "tweeted" with the web address to make it easy to connect. Additionally, Open to Hope disseminates a monthly newsletter with highlights from the radio programs, new website articles, and invitations for website visitors to write about specific topics relating to grief and loss. The newsletter provides an important additional opportunity to support the Open to Hope community with news about fresh information that supports them in their grief and healing.

CONCLUSIONS

The Internet can provide a supportive environment for individuals who are coping with grief. It is possible to find information on a wide variety of losses, and to find others who are coping with the same or similar losses and emotional experiences. Resources that provide for interaction and information, and that offer the opportunity to express emotions, are available in increasing numbers.

The studies discussed above as well as information drawn from the Open to Hope website suggest that the Internet serves a positive function for those coping with grief. Grievers may utilize the Internet as a source of general or specific information about grief and loss, as a tool to communicate with others who have had similar experiences, or as a venue for grief expression, memorialization, or both (Sofka, 1997). Websites function as a resource for understanding the grief process, and as a venue to connect with others. They allow bereaved individuals to feel less alone in their grief, and they also serve to normalize the grief experience.

The quality of sites is an issue for those who are grieving as well. Inaccurate or biased information or poorly designed sites can certainly add to the stress, if not the grief, of the bereaved who are searching for support. Most bereaved individuals have only their own personally generated search terms and may not find websites and other resources that could be helpful. Open to Hope serves as a model for providing high-quality information and communication possibilities to those who are grieving and their family and friends.

Communities and relationships that form in cyberspace have proven to be as deep and personal as face-to-face relationships (McKenna, 1998; Wellman & Gulia, 1999). Critics have argued that life on the Internet can never be meaningful because it lacks face-to-face interaction (Bell, 2007). Those in support of the Internet have argued that it allows individuals to interact who might not otherwise because of such things as race, gender, and age; these cannot be seen online and therefore are not barriers to overcome (Wellman & Gulia, 1999). Roberts and Vidal (2000) supported the latter opinion, reporting that bereaved individuals felt that support received from other people online was more valuable than traditional bereavement support groups. Similarly, Wagner, Knaevelsrud, and Maercker (2006) found that an Internet-based (e-mail) cognitive–behavioral treatment approach was effective for bereaved individuals experiencing complicated grief. A follow-up (Wagner & Maercker, 2007) demonstrated that posttreatment reduction in symptoms was maintained 1.5 years after the e-mail treatment had been completed.

As can be seen in opentohope.com, it is possible to maintain a multifaceted website for those who are coping with their grief and trying to find hope in the process. Consistent with Yalom's (2009) view of the curative influence of group process, people in groups produce a ripple effect through their good works. It is clear that Open to Hope is having a strong ripple effect, not only by helping the grieving find hope but also by informing the general public about the challenges faced by those who suffer loss.

REFERENCES

Bell, V. (2007). Online information, extreme communities and Internet therapy: Is the Internet good for our mental health? *Journal of Mental Health*, *16*, 445–457.

Capitulo, K. L. (2004). Perinatal grief online. *MCN: The American Journal of Maternal/Child Nursing*, *29*, 305–311.

Corr, C. A., Nabe, C. M., & Corr, D. M. (2006). *Death and dying, life and living* (5th ed.). Belmont, CA: Wadsworth.

Fiegelman, W., Gorman, B. S., Beal, K. C., & Jordan, J. R. (2008). Internet support groups for suicide survivors: A new mode for gaining bereavement assistance. *Omega*, *57*, 217–243.

Gilbert, K. R. (1996). "We've had the same loss, why don't we have the same grief?" Loss and differential grief in families. *Death Studies*, *20*, 269–283.

Heinz, D. (1999). *The last passage: Recovering a death of our own*. New York: Oxford University Press.

Hieftje, K. D. (2009). *The role of social networking sites as a medium for memorialization* (PhD dissertation). Indiana University, Bloomington.

Hollander, E. M. (2001). Cyber community in the valley of the shadow of death. *Journal of Loss and Trauma, 6*, 135–146.

Horsley, G., & Horsley, H. (2007). *Teen grief relief: Parenting with understanding, support and guidance*. Highland City, FL: Rainbow.

Horsley, G., & Horsley, H. (2008). *Real men do cry: A quarterback's inspiring story of tackling depression and surviving suicide loss*. Naples, FL: Quality of Life.

Horsley, G., & Horsley, H. (2011). *Open to hope: Inspirational stories of loss and recovery*. Dallas, TX: Brown Books.

Horsley, G., & Horsley, H. (In press). Open to Hope: An online bereavement resource community. In C. Sofka, K. Gilbert, & I. Noppe (Eds.), *Dying, death, and grieving: The new science of Thanatology*. New York: Springer.

Kollar, N. R. (1989). Rituals and the disenfranchised griever. In K. J. Doka (Ed.), *Disenfranchised grief: Recognizing hidden sorrow* (pp. 271–286). Lexington, MA: Lexington.

Massimi, M., & Baecker, R. M. (2010). A death in the family: Opportunities for designing technologies for the bereaved. Paper presented at CHI 2010: Death and Fear, Atlanta, GA.

McBride, J., & Simms, S. (2001). Death in the family: Adapting a family systems framework to the grief process. *The American Journal of Family Therapy, 29*, 59–73.

McKenna, K. Y. A. (1998). The computers that bind: Relationship formation on the Internet. *Dissertation Abstracts International, 54*, 07.

McKenna, K. Y. A., & Bargh, J. A. (2000). Plan 9 from cyberspace: The implications of the Internet for personality and social psychology. *Personality and Social Psychology Review, 4*, 57–75.

Miller, J. K., & Gergen, K. J. (1998). Life on the line: The therapeutic potential of computer-mediated conversations. *Journal of Marital and Family Therapy, 24*, 189–202.

Nair, K., Goodenough, B., & Cohn, R. (2006). Telephone support groups for isolated bereaved parents: A review of the literature and an example from Australian paediatric oncology. *Illness, Crisis & Loss, 14*, 319–336.

Roberts, P. (2004, Summer). Here today and cyberspace tomorrow: Memorials and bereavement support on the web. *Generations, 28*, 41–46.

Roberts, P., & Vidal, L. (2000). Perpetual care in cyberspace: A portrait of memorials on the web. *Omega, 40*, 521–545.

Sofka, C. (1997). Social support, "Internetworks," casket for sale, and more: Thanatechnology and the information superhighway. *Death Studies, 21*, 553–474.

Vanderwerker, L., & Prigerson, H. (2004). Social support and technical connectedness as protective factors in bereavement. *Journal of Loss and Trauma, 1*, 45–57.

Wagner, B., Knaevelsrud, C., & Maercker, A. (2006). Internet-based cognitive behavioral therapy for complicated grief: A randomized controlled trial. *Death Studies, 30*, 429–453.

Wagner, B., & Maercker, A. (2007). A 1.5 year follow-up of an Internet-based intervention for complicated grief. *Journal of Traumatic Stress, 20*, 625–629.

Wellman, B., & Gulia, M. (1999). Net surfers don't ride alone: Virtual communities as communities. In B. Wellman (Ed.), *Networks in the global village* (pp. 331–367). Boulder, CO: Westview Press.

Yalom, I. D. (1995). *The theory and practice of group psychotherapy* (4th ed.). New York: Basic.

Yalom, I. D. (2009). *Staring at the sun: Overcoming the terror of death*. San Francisco: Jossey-Bass.

29

"The Remedy Is Not Working"

Seeking Socially Just and Culturally Conscientious Practices in Bereavement

VALARIE MOLAISON, TASHEL C. BORDERE,

and KATHLEEN FOWLER[1]

The following is a dialogue between Dr. Valarie Molaison, a clinical psychologist who presents the case study (based on a client she counseled in the late 1980s), and Dr. Tashel Bordere and Dr. Kay Fowler who responded in light of current research on socially just and culturally competent practice.

CASE STUDY: SETTING THE STAGE

"The remedy is not working," she mumbled, eyes averted. "You can see him today and that's it." She looked up, a direct, protracted gaze. "*The remedy is not working.*"

I scanned my mind. How could there have been such a disconnect between her perceptions and mine? I thought I had communicated reasonable expectations about what therapy could (and could not) do, and yet, she was looking for a "remedy." Was she seeing therapy as akin to medicine, or did she envision it as similar to a spiritual intervention, where through the mystery of prayer or ritual one seeks strength or inspiration? Or had *I* missed something along the way? I looked at her son, Darien. He stared at the floor. No surprise on his pensive

---

[1] Valarie Molaison (noted hereafter as VM) offers the case study based on a child she counseled in the late 1980s. All identifiers have been removed or changed. Throughout the chapter, Tashel Bordere and Kay Fowler respond in light of current research on socially just and culturally competent practice.

face—a face I would see only a few more times, and mostly from a distance. "Can you join us today to review what Darien and I have been working on, and so I can address your concerns better?" "No. Saturday is my only free day. I don't have time for all these appointments, and Darien is still not helping enough with his brother and still failing sixth grade." "What would it look like for you to have the remedy working?" "Listen, just finish with him today." My marching orders.

So I did what I could to review with Darien what we had learned during therapy. He now recognizes that he *feels* chronically unsafe because he *is*. Despite challenges, he has interests, goals, skills, and needs. He now knows basic first aid. He takes pride in being a good singer and a great father figure to his 6-year-old brother, Marvin. Academics are not exciting or easy for him, but he now recognizes that he is an insightful thinker. He has learned how to breathe deeply and exercise to soothe his anxiety. How could his mother not see that he is calmer, less reactive, and more interested in living? I was not to know, but that phrase "The remedy is not working" is emblazoned in my mind and serves as an iconic refrain in my pursuit of cultural competence and sensitivity.

Here we explore "the remedy" and what Darien, Ms. Jones, and I each thought it was. I want you to know what happened over time so we can all learn, as I did as a young psychologist, from this remarkable young man and his story. I invite us to consider not only the person-to-person implications of a case like Darien's, but also the implications for social justice in bereavement.

COMMENT: BRIDGING RESEARCH AND PRACTICE (TB & KF)

Darien's case illustrates the complexity of the social context in counseling and the challenges and opportunities of engaging in "culturally conscientious" (Bordere, 2009a) and socially just practice. Dr. Molaison brought to this case compassion, commitment, keen listening skills, creative approaches, experience with counseling distressed children, and a willingness to take risks in order to help Darien. Simultaneously, Dr. Molaison faced the challenges of time constraints, absence of pay, parameters set by an insurance company, and scant research and theory (at that time) to draw upon regarding socially just counseling practice[2] and social justice issues in grief counseling. Fortunately, this past decade has seen increasing attention to social justice issues among counselors. The American Psychological Association's (2010) website now specifies "Social Justice, Diversity and Inclusion" as core values. The Counselors for Social Justice (2010) website noted,

> Social justice counseling includes empowerment of the individual as well as active confrontation of injustice and inequality … as they impact clientele as well as those in their systemic contexts … social justice counselors direct attention to the promotion of … equity, access, participation, and harmony … focus[ing] on … cultural, contextual, and individual needs.

Recent books (Aldorando, 2007; Constantine, 2007; Ellis & Carlson, 2009; Hayes, 2007; Sue & Sue, 2006; Toporek, Gerstein, Fouad, Roysircar, & Israel, 2006) present insights and resources on culturally competent and socially just practice from multiple researchers and practitioners. Socially just practice is interwoven with *culturally conscientious practice*, which "entails meeting the diverse needs of families through an understanding of their social locations (e.g., family structure, ability, sexuality, class, nationality, ethnicity, spirituality)" (Bordere, 2009b, p. 1). Fowler (2008) observed that

> death and grieving, are … situated in, mediated by, and filtered through cultural, social, and historical contexts.… Attending to [these] contexts encourages[2] us to work … to promote equity, collaboration, community-centered practice, human rights and dignity, and social justice in our society and in our world. (p. 55)

Keeping these concepts in mind, we return to Darien's case.

CASE STUDY: DARIEN (VM)

Darien was referred by an attorney representing Ms. Jones's car insurance and warned that payment would be contingent on an insurance settlement. An inattentive driver had rear-ended the family several months earlier, causing bumper damage and a broken collarbone for 6-year-old Marvin. At the scene, when the driver spoke to Ms. Jones, Darien was furious, "Don't talk to my mom! Leave her alone!" His first instinct was to call on friends to beat the man up. He was dumbfounded that no one even asked, "Are you OK?" Subsequently, Darien was reluctant to ride in a car, and when required, was vigilant and continually pressed imaginary brakes. Though he had experienced some low-level behavioral issues prior to the accident, he now had headaches and outbursts of rage.

Initial Assessment

Darien was an edgy, beleaguered 12-year-old African American living in a high-crime neighborhood in a medium-sized midwestern American city. His mother worked second shift (3:00–11:00 p.m.) as an administrative assistant. Darien provided after-school care for his younger brother. Unlike his upbeat and self-assured brother, Darien was quiet, had few friends, did not have contact with his own father or father's family, and had enduring signs of heightened arousal and reactivity seen in traumatized children. He was struggling with mostly "Ds" in the sixth grade at a rundown urban school known for violence.

The accident had precipitated anxiety specific to motor vehicles, as well as generalized anxiety related to fear of being a crime victim, fear of death, fear a family member would be hurt, and fear related to living in an unsafe neighborhood. These feelings were masked; indeed, during the assessment, Darien completed the

---

[2] Most of what had been discussed of socially just practice by the 1980s was in the social work area rather than in counseling psychology. See the useful history given by Aldorando (2007).

sentence stem "I'm afraid ..." with "... of nothing." Rather than express his feelings more directly, Darien tended to lash out. Darien's mother expressed fear that if Darien did not learn to control his anger, he would get into legal trouble. Darien himself completed the stem "I need ..." with "... a job to stay out of trouble." Ms. Jones was bright and responsible, and worked hard to provide a better life for her children than she had lived. Nonetheless, she was raising two children alone, struggling to make ends meet, and had little breathing space for repose.

Concerns and Goals

After a brief clinical assessment, I met with Ms. Jones to explain my impressions and to present treatment ideas. I hoped Ms. Jones would engage in family therapy, but she saw Darien as the person needing a "remedy," and her time and energy were in high demand. I feared that any gains with Darien would be circumscribed if she did not engage, but not wishing to stress her further, I hoped she would see changes in him and increase her involvement over time. It was clear that the concept of therapy was foreign to her, and that the initial motivation had come from the insurance company.

Remembering my training and special interest in providing culturally competent care, I wondered if I could bridge the abyss between us. I was white, female, and highly educated, and had a nice suburban office. I tended to approach therapy through experimentation and tinkering, and tried to foster enjoying learning about oneself and the world's possibilities. I was terribly peppy and upbeat, and subscribed to concepts such as strengthening children by showing them their value and competence and rejoicing in it. How could I join this family in a way that I could get buy-in from Darien and from Ms. Jones, who subscribed to a more pragmatic, no-fluff, authoritarian parenting model? Reasoning there was no one in my community more competent who would work for free, I forged ahead, trusting the process and always inviting mom to join. Although she usually declined, she did bring Darien on time every Saturday morning for 4 months.

Darien's personal risk factors were ever present, and his resilience skills limited. Knowing resilience can be learned, I sought to create a rapport, and to create greater empowerment through enhanced self-awareness (including building a "feelings vocabulary," and observing his thoughts, feelings, body, and behaviors under stress). I also aimed to enhance Darien's stress management and self-care skills, positive internal dialogue, and ability to view his situation realistically without losing hope.

Treatment Highlights

Darien quickly settled into having a place to bring his stressors and to ponder the meaning of the injustices he observed. Ever-present examples included drug dealing on the corner, unclean and harsh conditions at school, cars speeding down his narrow street, pressure to care for his brother, academic struggles, and inability to connect easily with others.

As we worked, I saw transformation, and Darien's concept of "the remedy" came to life. He recognized that his circumstances were unfair, that he was not the culprit, and that multiple forces were bearing down on him. Nonetheless, he recognized more and more of his personal power and started to imagine a realistic and positive future. His internal dialogue was less angry and scared; he became more determined and felt more competent. His curiosity about human nature and social injustice, quest to understand and master himself in his environment, and openness to exploration were remarkable. For example, Darien was keenly interested in a packet of highway safety education materials for which I had sent: "Just how powerful can seatbelts be in reducing injury?" And "How frequently is alcohol a factor in driving incidents?" This was a great opportunity to model seeking information from experts, and to recognize that learning new information can be interesting, practical, and empowering. Later, we explored a first aid kit Darien had spotted in my office. "What does the alcohol wipe do?" "How old should a child be in order to use basic first aid?" And "How should a burn be treated?" He uncoiled the Ace bandage™ repeatedly and practiced wrapping arms and legs, wondering just how tightly to wrap a limb and how much pain relief it could bring to a sprain.

On another occasion, Darien arrived in heightened distress and spewed his horror at witnessing a toddler struck and killed by a car on his street the prior day. He was so flooded I decided to slow him down and let him tell the story from the beginning. I suggested we might want to write it. "Yes! The newspaper needs to know!" Here is part of the news article he scribed:

Baby Killed by Drunk Driver

> About 3:22 p.m. at 236 Pine Road, a baby was coming up [the street], and a little girl called him across the street. Before he reached the other side he was hit by a blue Nissan. He flew 5 feet and then the guy ran over him with all 4 tires. People had to flag him down; he finally stopped. His mom came … and an uncle came to him as he was laying on the ground and took his pulse. He said he had a very low pulse and told somebody to call the ambulance. Blood was coming from his mouth and nose. His face was puffed up. They finally got there, and a lady said she had just gave him a popsicle, and then she started crying. The baby's mom said, "He's not gonna make it." A lady said, "Allah will be with him." Then they put him in an ambulance.… They [the police] marked the [blood] spots with yellow ribbons. The blood was still in the street. Nobody cleaned it up! They said he died before he got to the hospital. The driver of the car went to prison. The baby, known as "Speedy," was a nice little boy who liked to ride his big wheel. The only thing left that his mother might have is his sneaker, clothes, and toys.

Darien asked his mother and brother to witness his reading of the article. We continued with a family conversation about whether to attend the funeral, and respect for individual differences in grief. I was amazed at how willing Ms. Jones was to have this conversation and to allow Darien to make his own decision about how to show his respects. At the next meeting, Darien brought in news clippings about the incident, recognizing that there are many stories to be told. This was extended when an older African American celebrity was murdered a few weeks later, leaving Darien to question why even wealth and maturity cannot protect us.

The Firing

I was optimistic after Ms. Jones's thoughtful engagement in our conversations regarding the deaths and how people cope with and understand them. Meanwhile, Darien grew more comfortable with the power of his own voice. We role played conflict resolution, and he successfully resolved a conflict with a friend he had been willing to "disown" after a relatively minor slight. Given his interest in sports, we used game rules and sportsmanship to discuss how people can show one another respect. Darien came to trust me, and relied on our meetings. We settled into finding that sweet spot of empathizing with daily difficulties and keeping him focused on envisioning a future.

Soon Darien asked for help discussing with his mother his frustration and anxieties in caring for Marvin. He was especially concerned about whether and how to keep his brother indoors to protect him from motor vehicles and crime. Darien was respectful, skillful, and nondemanding in this conversation with his mother, which I had prefaced with the concept that sometimes just giving voice to a concern (even if there is no viable solution) reduces the chance of anger mounting and being acted upon. Ms. Jones responded impatiently, accusing Darien of selfishness. Though I reiterated the purpose of Darien's remarks, and reinforced the message that she was a hardworking and competent parent, our next meeting started with the firing.

I persuaded Ms. Jones to allow three more sessions to review our work and Darien's progress, and to reflect on Ms. Jones's strength and resolve as a mother. I wanted to install a model for saying goodbye that respected the power of relationship and did not wrench people apart. I was grateful for those final meetings. Darien reflected that he was glad to end therapy because he was starting a sport soon. This decision itself was a victory; his mother had consented to an extracurricular activity even though it would complicate child care. Darien knew that something of worth had happened through our work, though it had not changed his outer circumstances much.

Later Sightings

I always felt sad and unfinished with Darien, and indeed I had more to learn from him. At age 16, Darien ran into juvenile trouble and the attorney, wanting to make a case for mitigating factors, requested my treatment records. I reread every note in that file before forwarding it. I was sad and angry that Darien continued to struggle, though not surprised. His mother declined additional treatment but was thankful for the records. Soon after, I was excited to spot Darien hawking sodas at a local stadium. He did not notice me, and I imagine would not have recognized me. No matter; I was relieved to see him well and employed.

Finally, one morning years later, I turned the newspaper page and saw that familiar face looking square at me. The caption read, "Jones Found Guilty in Fatal

Stabbing." It was Darien at age 23—a mug shot on the police blotter. He looked angry and sad. My heart fell. He had been in an altercation with another young man, and with one stroke had ended his life. Darien pled guilty to second degree murder and is serving life in prison. How was I to make sense of this? He had been so angry that people disregarded human life, and now he had taken the life of another.

COMMENT: SOCIOCULTURAL CONTEXT (TB & KF)

From the outset, Dr. Molaison is clearly conscious of the intricate and weighty impact of Darien's sociocultural context—what Bronfenbrenner (1977) termed the nested "ecological environment" (p. 514). Powerful social constructions of race, class, gender, adolescence, and so on operate in the macrosystem that Darien inhabits. A long and vexed history shapes expectations for adolescent urban African American males and affects interactions in the community, school, and larger environment. Pinderhughes (2004) addressed the cumulative impact of prolonged historical oppression:

> Living with chronic anxiety, fear, and high levels of tension, because of racism and entrapment in the societal projection process for so many generations[,] undermines physical and mental health and creates a vulnerability for African Americans, where any further stress may take them over the edge. (pp. 161, 171)

Cultural Dissonance

Both Ms. Jones and Dr. Molaison had Darien's best interests in mind. They shared a desire to equip Darien with the tools necessary to ensure his survival and competence. Where they diverged was in their philosophies and methods. It is important to allow those we help to be experts on their own grief. That requires trusting families to "tell" us what they need and how their needs can best be addressed. In this case, Dr. Molaison had wanted Darien and his mother to "buy in" to what she thought they needed, and what she thought would be functional based on her social location (training, experiences, upbringing, parenting philosophy, etc.). Unfortunately, the resulting cultural dissonance may have ultimately led to Ms. Jones's conclusion that "the remedy is not working."[3] Culture is largely unconscious, and cultural dissonance is inevitable when entities come from vastly different experiences within their social locations.

In keeping with her social location and training, she employed an *authoritative* approach consistent with her goals and beliefs about the survival tools Darien needed: self-expression, independent thinking, and negotiated decision making (see Baumrind, 1968). Her approach was quite appropriate in the sense that this style is thought to enhance self-competence and, consequently, raise self-esteem and sense of worth. Yet, in other ways, this approach was incongruent with survival in Darien's cultural context. The promotion of *generalized* negotiation posed not only a direct threat to parental authority but also, actually, a threat to survival in his primary settings (e.g., neighborhood and school) and even within the larger culture. For example, efforts at negotiating and expressing one's views during a robbery attempt could potentially lead to Darien's death. Along these lines, self-expression and negotiation among young black males in the school setting are often taken as aggression and defiance.

Dr. Molaison's *authoritative* approach with Darien contrasted starkly with the *authoritarian* ("no-nonsense") parenting style of Darien's mom and of many other parents living in environments permeated by violence and crime. Darien's mother was caring, conscientious, intelligent, responsible, and strong, but multiple responsibilities and limited time and resources made it impossible for her to participate fully in therapy and difficult for her to reduce Darien's family responsibilities.

Like Dr. Molaison's goals, Ms. Jones's goals were also consistent and functional given her social location. Acutely aware of the challenges of raising two African American boys in a macrosystem that sets up powerful obstacles to their survival and success, her characteristic parenting approach reflects her understanding of the multiple risk factors facing them. To help Darien survive and thrive, Ms. Jones wanted him to stay close to home, contribute to family functioning through caring for his younger brother,[3] and succeed academically. Notwithstanding Baumrind's (1968) critique, authoritarian parenting, in this cultural context, serves a critical survival function in keeping youth safe and in warding off the negative impacts of racism and discrimination (Halgunseth, Cushinberry, & Bordere, 2003).

Authoritarian parents are, in fact, nurturing to their children and do engage in communication and compromise. Although some issues, especially those related to safety, are not negotiable, others are likely to be open for discussion. Ms. Jones's readiness to discuss the toddler's death and to allow Darien to make his own decision about funeral attendance is consistent with parallel discussions in many African American families. Recent research finds that African American parents are particularly communicative about violence in the community, losses, grief, and mourning (Barrett, 1996; Bordere, 2009b; Holloway, 2003). Further, Ms. Jones's respectful listening to Darien's written account also accords with her goal of enhancing his academic skills, including his writing skills. Here, Dr.Molaison and Ms. Jones are very much on the same page.

Developmentally, adolescents are concerned with identity development, and have an increased need for independence and control over their lives (Erikson, 1968). Yet African American teens often face the dilemma of finding ways to exert control over a mesosystem that is at once chaotic and controlling. In the United States, the violent death rate remains highest among Black males ages 15–24 (Centers for Disease Control and Prevention, 2010), which raises troubling questions about factors contributing to perpetration and the paradigmatic and behavioral shifts of Black male youth during mid- to late adolescence and early adulthood. Black youth and their families are keenly attuned to this alarming statistic; the heightened awareness of injustice and violence found through conversations with Darien resonates across the literature in studies of black male youth negotiating

[3] Ms. Jones's doubts about therapy are consonant with a frequently observed distrust of health and mental health systems based on a history of mistreatment and even abuses of African Americans within them (see, e.g., Martin, 2007).

their lives in similar settings. Teens enact various strategies to try to stay alive. Dr. Molaison observed that Darien was "quiet" and had few friends. If Darien is like his agemates in similar social locations, we find a consistent shift in the behavior of black male youth during the early to mid-adolescent period (i.e., ages 12–15). They tend to have smaller friendship groups and minimize other contacts in order to limit unwelcome social situations (Howard, Kaljee, & Jackson, 2002).

Ironically, the literature related to supporting youth in violent areas has largely focused on *violence* (e.g., McMahon, 2009) and given little attention to *death and grief* as by-products of violence. Further exploration is needed about the connection between victimization and later perpetration of violence and homicide. Valadez-Meltzer, Silber, Meltzer, and D'Angelo (2005) noted a correlation between a sense of hopelessness and high-risk behaviors. Literature exploring the experiences of African American youth grieving violent death is growing but still limited (e.g., Barrett, 1996; Bordere, 2009c; Currier, Holland, Coleman, & Neimeyer, 2007).

Dr. Molaison identified early that Darien's anxieties, fears, and grief around violence were "masked" in angry displays. Chronic losses and a consistent absence of socially sanctioned support for grief lead to what Bordere terms "suffocated grief,"[4] which goes beyond current understandings of "disenfranchised grief" (e.g., Attig, 2004; Doka, 1989, 2002).[5] Young African American males often find their grief multiply disenfranchised—by gender messages that undermine instrumental grieving (Doka & Martin, 2010), by the circumstances of the death (especially when violent; Doka, 2002) and by the larger society's tendency to devalue the lives of African Americans—what Holloway (2003) called "color-coded death" (p. 57). Spaces and opportunities (e.g., parks, playgrounds, and jobs) to channel grief instrumentally are sorely needed.

Denied opportunities to express grief in a way functional to them, they must "suffocate" and silence their grief (see Bordere, in preparation). Young African American males are often faced with powerfully negative societal responses to their natural outpourings of grief and coping strategies. Certain expressions of mourning (e.g., rap music, tattoos, graffiti, and mourning T-shirts) may be actively rejected, and even condemned as inappropriate or "dysfunctional" to the mourner or "offensive" to others (see also Barrett, 2009a, on street memorials).

Goodman's Model of Social Justice Counseling

Goodman et al. (2004) identified six recurring … principles of social justice counseling: (a) ongoing self-examination, (b) sharing power, (c) giving voice, (d) facilitating consciousness raising, (e) building on strengths, and (f) leaving clients with the tools for social change" (p. 798). We believe that this model can serve as a gut check for counselors seeking culturally conscientious practices in whatever role

[4] The concept of "suffocated grief" (discussed briefly here) was introduced in Bordere (2010) and will be fully explored in Bordere (in preparation).

[5] Attig (2004) came closest to Bordere's concept of "suffocated grief" when he focused on the way that disenfranchisement can "actively undermine efforts to reach through suffering and affirm life.… It invalidates, discourages, hinders, even blocks hopeful striving for meaning, value, and love" (p. 209).

or corner of the globe they find themselves. As we analyzed my engagement with Darien, it became obvious that I had carefully and thoughtfully enacted each of their principles.

Ongoing self-examination: Dr. Molaison engages in reflection throughout the case and in the sightings that followed it. Many years later, she continues to reflect on this case and to learn from it. Her very decision to reexamine it here in light of more recent research reflects her eagerness to keep learning and honing her culturally conscientious practices.

Sharing power: Dr. Molaison sought actively to share power with Darien in the direction and design of his treatment. That process required a good deal of flexibility and spontaneity on both their parts, and it is clear that a great deal of trust was built. Dr. Molaison was less successful in sharing power with Ms. Jones despite their shared overall goals. An APA report released in 2008 stresses the vital role that African American parents play in fostering their children's resilience. One recommendation reads, "Promote collaborative decision making among providers, parents, and youth (as developmentally appropriate), involving a careful risk–benefit analysis and informed treatment decision-making" (p. 101). Dr. Molaison also regrets not having the opportunity to reach out to community leaders and resources to engage them as allies for Darien, another recommendation in the same report.

Giving voice and facilitating consciousness raising: Ironically, Dr. Molaison's very success to some extent ran counter to the parenting style of Ms. Jones, who recognized the real risks involved in such empowered speaking up by young African American males.

Building on strengths: Dr. Molaison capitalized on Darien's many strengths: his curiosity, realism, sense of justice, empathy, "openness to exploration," and determination to resist being helplessly swept along in a particular direction.

Tools: Darien had begun to reframe and reinterpret what he was already hyperconscious of—the pain and injustice of his everyday world. Dr. Molaison helped Darien connect his empathy for the dead toddler with his concerns for Marvin. Darien carried away with him, as tools for social change, his new sociocultural understanding and his strengthened empathy. He also took with him tools for personal growth in his stress management and self-care skills.

CASE STUDY: FINAL THOUGHTS ABOUT SOCIAL JUSTICE AND "THE REMEDY"

There were three deaths in this story: the toddler, the African American celebrity, and the young man my client killed. All crimes, all violent, all tragic. Yet, there were many more untold losses in the lives and deaths of these people and those involved in their lives. It is critical that we understand the context of our clients' lives—their personal and family losses, as well as their triumphs, goals, and aspirations. And we must seek to understand their larger historical and cultural contexts. In our personal and political lives, we must continue to work to change societal structure and systemic injustices.

It can be daunting to step into situations rife with natural and unnatural trauma and losses. Nonetheless, I am ever grateful for having said "yes" when asked to take on a likely pro bono case that initially appeared bleak. Barrett (2009b) wisely urged those engaged in cross-cultural counseling,

> Be yourself, be honest, be real, and be open to and teachable about aspects of a person's experience that may be different from your own. Have faith in our common humanity to connect and support one another … in spite of our separateness and apparent differences. (p. 89)

It is perhaps in these words that we find the essential ingredients for "the remedy." The fact that this admixture is complex and sometimes beyond our power to fully realize should not stand in the way of our efforts.

I have used what I have learned to deepen my personal understanding of the clinical work in which I engage, and to remind myself that attaching and engaging are gifts. I urge all clinicians to muster up the stamina and hope to take on painful loss-filled cases that may be viewed by some as "failures." I urge us to consider mindfully our role, however big or small, whether through research or practice—or ideally both—in moving humanity forward toward social justice in all manner of human endeavor and suffering.

REFERENCES

Aldorando, E. (Ed.). (2007). *Advancing social justice through clinical practice*. Mahwah, NJ: Lawrence Erlbaum.

American Psychological Association (APA). (2010). About APA: Core values. Retrieved from http://www.apa.org/monitor/2010/04/council-action.aspx

American Psychological Association (APA) Task Force on Resilience and Strength in Black Children and Adolescents. (2008). Executive summary. *Resilience in African American children and adolescents: A vision for optimal development*. Washington, DC.

Attig, T. (2004). Disenfranchised grief revisited: Discounting hope and love. *Omega*, *49*(3), 197–215.

Barrett, R. K. (1996). Adolescents, homicidal violence, and death. In C. A. Corr & D. E. Balk (Eds.), *Handbook of adolescent death and bereavement* (pp. 42–64). New York: Springer.

Barrett, R. (2009a). Emerging and universal trends in urban memorials. *The Forum*, 35(4), 17–18.

Barrett, R. (2009b). Sociocultural considerations: African Americans, grief and loss. In K. J. Doka & A. S. Tucci. (Eds.), *Diversity and end-of-life care* (pp. 79–91). Washington, DC: Hospice Foundation of America.

Baumrind, D. (1968). Authoritarian vs. authoritative parental control. *Adolescence*, *3*(11), 255–272.

Bordere, T. C. (2009a). Culturally *conscientious* thanatology. *The Forum*, *35*(2), 1–4.

Bordere, T. C. (2009b). Culturally sensitive approaches to support grief in the classroom. Retrieved from http://www.education.com/reference/article/cultural-approaches-support-grief/

Bordere, T. C. (2009c). "To look at death another way": Black teenage males' perspectives on second lines and regular funerals in New Orleans. *Omega*, *58*(3), 213–232.

Bordere, T. C. (2010, July 21). Violent death and culturally sensitive strategies for outreach and practice with youth. Association for Death Education and Counseling (ADEC) Webinar.

Bordere, T. C. (In preparation). *Suffocated grief: Black adolescent males and violent death in New Orleans*.

Bronfenbrenner, U. (1977). Toward an experimental ecology of human development. *American Psychologist*, *32*, 513–530.

Centers for Disease Control and Prevention. (2010). Surveillance for violent deaths: National violent death reporting system, 16 states—2007. *Morbidity and Mortality Weekly Report*, *59*(4), 1–56.

Constantine, M. G. (Ed.). (2007). *Clinical practice with people of color*. New York: Teacher's College Press.

Counselors for Social Justice. (2010). Advocacy competencies. Retrieved from http://www.counselorsforsocialjustice.com/advocacycompetencies.html

Currier, J. M., Holland, J. M., Coleman, R. A., & Neimeyer, R. A. (2007). Bereavement following violent death: An assault on life and meaning. In R. Stevenson & G. Cox (Eds.), *Perspectives on violence and violent death* (pp. 175–200). Amityville, NY: Baywood.

Doka, K. J. (1989). *Disenfranchised grief: Recognizing hidden sorrow*. Lexington, MA: Lexington.

Doka, K. J. (Ed.). (2002). *Disenfranchised grief: New directions, challenges, and strategies for practice*. Champaign, IL: Research Press.

Doka, K. J., & Martin, T. L. (2010). *Grieving beyond gender: Understanding the ways men and women mourn* (Rev. ed.). New York: Routledge.

Ellis, C. M., & Carlson. J. (Eds.). (2009). *Cross-cultural awareness and social justice in counseling*. New York: Routledge.

Erikson, E. H. (1968). *Identity: Youth and crisis*. New York: Norton.

Fowler, K. L. (2008). "The wholeness of things": Infusing diversity and social justice into death education. *Omega*, *57*(1), 53–91.

Goodman, L. A., Liang, B., Helms, J. E., Latta, R. E., Sparks, E., & Weintraub, S. R. (2004). Training counseling psychologists as social justice agents: Feminist and multicultural principles in action. *The Counseling Psychologist*, *32*(4), 793–837.

Halgunseth, L., Cushinberry, C., & Bordere, T. C. (2003). Race, ethnicity, and parenting styles. In M. Coleman and L. Ganong (Eds.), *Controversial relationship and family issues in the 21st century*. Los Angeles: Roxbury.

Hayes, P. A. (2007). *Addressing cultural complexities in practice: Assessment, diagnosis, and therapy* (2nd ed.). Washington, DC: American Psychological Association.

Holloway, K. (2003). *Passed on: African American mourning stories: A memorial*. Durham: Duke University Press.

Howard, D., Kaljee, L., & Jackson, L. (2002). Urban African American adolescents' perceptions of community violence. *American Journal of Health Behavior*, *26*(1), 56–67.

Martin, J. K. (2007). African American populations. In M. G. Constantine (Ed.), *Clinical practice with people of color* (pp. 33–45). New York: Teacher's College Press.

McMahon, S. (2009). Community violence exposure and aggression among urban adolescents: Testing a cognitive mediator. *Journal of Community Psychology*, *37*(7), 895–910.

Pinderhughes, E. (2004). The multigenerational transmission of loss and trauma: The African American experience. In F. Walsh & M. McGoldrick (Eds.), *Living beyond loss: Death in the family* (2nd ed., pp. 161–181). New York: Norton.

Sue, D. W., & Sue, D. (2006). *Counseling the culturally diverse: Theory and practice* (5th ed., pp. 287–311). Hoboken, NJ: Wiley.
Toporek, R. L., Gertstein, L. H., Fouad, N. A., Roysircar, G., & Israel, T. (Eds.). (2006). *Handbook for social justice in counseling psychology: Leadership, vision, and action.* Thousand Oaks, CA: Sage.
Valadez-Meltzer, A., Silber, T. J., Meltzer, A. A., & D'Angelo, L. J. (2005). Will I be alive in 2005? Adolescent level of involvement in risk behaviors and belief in near-future death. *Pediatrics, 116*(1), 24–31.

30

Grief Dimensions Associated with Hastened Death

Clinical and Ethical Implications

LOUIS A. GAMINO and CLINT MOORE III

When it comes to end-of-life decision making by medical patients with terminal illness, Welfel (2006) summarized ethical controversies that arise when patients approaching the end of life encounter pain and suffering that lead them to consider "hastening" their own deaths:

> Professionals faced with this circumstance are facing one of the most complex and troubling ethical dilemmas in practice—are they obligated to intervene to prevent the [patient's] actions in the same way they would be obligated to prevent a suicide for an individual at a different point in the lifespan? Does the proximity of a painful and difficult death of a competent person change in any way the clinician's duty to prevent suicide? Does the consideration of suicide in itself indicate the presence of a depressive disorder in a person nearing death from illness or injury? (p. 87)

Situations of hastened death raise clinical questions as well, such as how the mental state of the patient, including grief factors, affects the calculus of decision making. In this chapter, we explore the clinical and ethical problems involved in evaluating and treating an individual contemplating hastened death when faced with the prospect of a potential life-threatening malignancy, using a case study.

In regard to grief issues that influence the patient's clinical state, we consider the nature of the patient's losses and how the associated grief potentially impacts the refusal of life-sustaining treatment. We also conduct an ethical inquiry of the end-of-life decision-making processes by providing "working consultations" from our respective positions within the field of thanatology. Louis A. Gamino writes from the perspective of a licensed mental health professional whose practice encompasses grief counseling, and Clint Moore writes as an ordained priest practicing as a hospital-based clinical ethicist. Our intentions are to "present various views of a death-related question, indicating the [professional's] own values if appropriate, [while] respecting the [patient's] choice among alternatives" (Association for Death Education and Counseling, 2006, Basic Tenets 6), and highlight the need for thanatologists to operate from "a credible model of decision-making that can bear public scrutiny and its application" (American Counseling Association, 2005, p. 3).

CASE HISTORY

Lorrie is a 50ish white female diagnosed with recurrent major depressive disorder with some paranoid features. She attempted suicide by overdose 5 years ago resulting in admission to a psychiatric hospital. Two years ago, she sought psychotherapy and described herself with the following metaphor: "I am a basket that needs weaving."

Developmentally, Lorrie's mother was cruel and abusive, whereas her father was nurturing but rarely home. She was singled out for abuse and rejection by her mother, who viewed her as "different" from her siblings in appearance (i.e., hair and eye color) and temperament (i.e., stubborn). Lorrie's siblings adopted the mother's demeaning attitude toward her and called her derisive names such as "mutton head."

Lorrie has lost two career positions because of problems with coworkers. Her paranoia emerged in thinking that she was being systematically persecuted by fellow staffers. Subsequently, she applied for and received Social Security disability benefits based on her psychiatric condition.

Family relations have been a major disappointment for Lorrie. After two divorces, her treasured son was killed in a head-on car crash 10 years earlier. Lorrie describes her daughter as "mean-spirited," much like Lorrie's mother, because she has cut off all contact with Lorrie, preventing her from having a relationship with the 13-year-old grandchild who, until the estrangement, was favored by Lorrie as "my light." Now, Lorrie feels "unloved and unneeded."

Lorrie finds her life meaningless. In a "quest for significance," she completed paperwork to donate her body to medical science in order to "be important to somebody." She rationalized that there would be no funeral expenses or obligation for her family. She relishes the fact that medical students form a "personal relationship" with and always remember their cadavers. She desires that kind of legacy. However, Lorrie read the "fine print" and realized that her body may not be accepted for medical science if she dies by suicide. This presents an ironic, antisuicide incentive for her.

Recently, Lorrie discovered a golf ball–sized mass in her neck and fears that it may be lymphoma, especially in light of a family history of cancer in her father (lung) and sister (breast). She is awaiting the results of a CAT scan but is determined to accept "no treatment" if it is cancer. Because she has little reason for living, she is disinclined to treat a disease that might be fatal.

Lorrie's case presents a novel clinical challenge in understanding how grief factors may moderate her appraisal of her life's worth and thus influence her attitude toward life-prolonging treatment. It also poses a vexing ethical question of whether her anticipated treatment refusal, which could potentially lead to a hastened death, constitutes a form of passive suicide (i.e., ending her life indirectly by not taking active steps to preserve or prolong it).

MENTAL HEALTH PROFESSIONAL'S PERSPECTIVE

Encountering Lorrie's story, I am struck by the overwhelming amount of loss she has endured, which includes the loss of legitimacy in her family of origin as she was ostracized for being different; loss of career; loss of partner relationships; tragic loss of her son, who died in a wreck; "loss" of her daughter and granddaughter due to estrangement; and now, loss of health and potential loss of her own life. This inventory of profound losses illustrates many of the concepts introduced in previous chapters of this text. Although an argument could be made that the losses of Lorrie's career and her marriages—two endeavors of her life now relegated to the past—are "completed," there may be continuing dreams connected to these losses that represent "nonfinite" loss (see Schultz & Harris, Chapter 18). Likewise, the loss of belonging and legitimacy within her family of origin has a nonfinite, ongoing quality. Lorrie's loss of her son constitutes traumatic loss (see Rynearson & Salloum, Chapter 14). The suspended nature of the estrangement from her daughter and granddaughter who, although physically absent from her life, remain in psychological relationship to her fit the definition of ambiguous loss (see Boss, Roos, & Harris, Chapter 13). Her potential loss of health (and life) is an anticipated loss.

From a clinical perspective, these multiple types of loss generate difficult and complex grief responses. Lorrie can be seen to experience anticipatory grief with regard to her possible cancer, complicated grief in response to the life-vitiating death of her son (see Buckle & Fleming, Chapter 19), ambiguous grief (Boss, 2007), and chronic sorrow (Roos, 2002; see also Boss et al., Chapter 13) pertaining to her nonfinite losses, especially the ongoing estrangement from her daughter and granddaughter. Grief therapy (cf. Worden, 2009) that addresses this matrix of intricate dynamics seems indicated to help Lorrie with the deleterious psychological effects accumulated from her multiple losses.

Considering the ethical conundrum of Lorrie's end-of-life decision making, my first thought is to weigh the difference between electing to forgo treatment for a potentially fatal lymphoma (i.e., *passive suicide*) and contemplating a leap from a high bridge in order to die (i.e., *active suicide*). Researchers have designated these two categories as either *preemptive*, referring to terminally ill individuals who choose to forgo life-extending treatment, or *ordinary* (i.e., clinical), referring to medically healthy persons who choose to end their lives (Cohen, Dobscha, Hails, Pekow, & Chochinov, 2002).

In the scenario of a fatal jump, I would take immediate steps to dissuade or intervene so as to prevent, if possible, a suicidal action that is imminent, highly lethal, and irreversible. I would alert and involve others (e.g., emergency personnel or law enforcement) in the effort. My (reflexive) rationale would assume some degree of ambivalence in the potential victim, and my obligation would be to provide an opportunity to reconsider, as well as place basic value on human life. In the scenario with the possible lymphoma, where imminence and irreversibility do not apply, I would more likely pursue a dialectical approach of exploring the individual's decision making in hopes of influencing her toward living. It would be more akin to encountering someone with advanced lung disease who is disinclined to stop smoking.

Kitchener (1984) admonished practitioners to go beyond immediate, intuitive ethical judgments, based on the facts of the situation and one's ordinary moral sense, to a "critical evaluative" level, incorporating professional codes of ethics, laws, and moral principles. She invoked the now familiar ethical principles of *nonmaleficence*, *beneficence*, *autonomy*, *justice*, and *fidelity* (cf. American Psychological Association, 2002; Beauchamp & Childress, 2008) and argued for the use of a systematic theory to achieve higher order reasoning. Writing specifically for the practice of grief counseling, Gamino and Ritter (2009) proposed a Five P Model for ethical decision making that accounts for *person*, *problem*, *place*, *principles*, and *process* to achieve a thoughtful, systematic analysis of any ethical dilemma.

Person

It seems clear that Lorrie is a depressed and bereft person who finds little meaning or value in her current life. Yet, despite a lifelong history of devaluation, rejection, and loss, she is still searching for meaning as evident by her decision to donate her body to medical science to achieve "significance" in death she did not find in life. Potentially, reunion with her daughter and granddaughter, if ever accomplished, would resuscitate her vapid existence. Even reaching out electively for psychotherapy and persisting in treatment indicate she has not given up completely. Dejected as she is, Lorrie still appears to hope that things can get better. To use her metaphor, if the "strands" of her existence can be "woven" into a coherent whole, the "basket" of her life may be rendered useful and meaningful. This is *not* the picture of a person with a unitary drive toward dying.

Problem

Questions abound in this case. Is Lorrie able to make informed, reasoned, and "competent" decisions about her health care? Does depression impair her judgment? Do multiple losses and complicated grief erode her will to live? Is treatment refusal an expression of her "right to die," or is "hastening death" a form of suicide? Can a decision for suicide ever be "rational," or is it always "irrational"? What is the health provider's ethical obligation toward Lorrie, specifically, is there a "duty to protect" (Werth, 1999) and does her contemplated course of action (i.e., no treatment) constitute a condition for breaching confidentiality and involving others to avert a collision course with death?

Place

Although the action in this drama occurs in an "outpatient" setting, Lorrie maintains maximum autonomy as an independent agent with executive capacity. Only a court of law could restrict her freedoms. Should the situation move to an emergency department or hospital inpatient setting, the medical institution itself, together with its providers, has an obligation to protect and preserve the patient's life (and avoid potential liability for failing to treat or for discharging a "dangerous" person). Thus, risk managers and an ethics committee may become involved. Werth and Richmond (2009) astutely identified that the clinical and ethical issues for nonmedical practitioners who provide only assessment and therapy differ from the issues for medical personnel who may actually play a role in implementing a person's decision to hasten death.

Principles

Giving consent for diagnosis and treatment is based on the ethical principle of *autonomy*—the right of a person to self-determination. In our society, an adult is presumed to have the capacity to exercise autonomy (over health care options) unless demonstrated in a court of law that such capacity is lacking or limited. Although one may not agree with how Lorrie estimates the value (or not) of her life, respect for autonomy demands listening carefully to how she makes this appraisal.

When considering whether Lorrie can make an informed, reasonable decision about forgoing life-prolonging treatment, one may ask whether it is truly her wish to die or, invoking the disease model of mood disorder, "Is it the 'depression talking'?" In her state of depression, Lorrie's cognitive and executive functions may be dysfunctional or impaired in a way that undermines her ability to experience any positive emotion (cf. Beck, 1995) or, through "affective distortion," to appreciate the potential outcomes of various possible courses of action (Leeman, 1999).

Leeman (2009) suggested considering the motives of the person in trying to evaluate the rationality of such a request. He believes "rational" motives for hastening death include escaping intolerable pain, asserting control, avoiding inevitable decline, and retaining dignity and independence. Conversely, depression, hopelessness, and despair constitute "irrational" motives because these conditions may be "reversible" with adequate treatment. Empirical studies with terminally ill cancer patients demonstrate that the presence of depression and hopelessness (Breithart et al., 2000), as well as lower family cohesion and perceived burden on others (Kelly et al., 2004), correlate with a desire for hastened death. Hopelessness, loss of dignity, and perceiving self as a burden to others undermine the "will to live" (Chochinov et al., 2005). These latter findings introduce the role of family members and loved ones whose potential survivors' grief (or survivors' guilt) may affect Lorrie's decision. Admonitions of love or assurances of caregiving—elements sorely missing in Lorrie's everyday existence—may alter Lorrie's calculation of her life's worth (Dyck, 2002).

However, evaluating the extent to which depression influences end-of-life decision making may not be so straightforward. Sullivan and Youngner (1994) argued that assessing depression in medically ill patients who refuse life-extending treatment is problematic because depression may be camouflaged as a "reasonable" response to serious medical illness, or depression may affect subtle distortions of decision making by preserving comprehension of medical facts while impairing the appreciation of their personal importance. Leeman (1999) reminded practitioners that their viewpoint matters—the provider's "lens" about life choices may refract the perceived reasonableness of the patient's decision. Finally, Muskin's (1998) psychodynamic view of a request to die interprets it as a communication inviting interaction with the professional and warranting an exploration of multiple potential meanings, such as experiencing the self as already dead, that could be embedded in the request.

A second principle of *beneficence*—the professional obligation to help or serve the patient—requires acting in a responsible manner to assist Lorrie. Considering that there is at least enough hope in the scenario to keep Lorrie coming for psychotherapy, engaging her in a therapeutic discussion about the possible current or future value of her life seems a mandatory step to discharging an obligation of beneficence. Identifying "reasons for living" would be an important component of that discussion. Likewise, psychotherapy that targets Lorrie's complicated grief, incorporating rubrics specifically designed to redress loss and bereavement that go beyond standard protocols for treating clinical depression (cf. Shear, Frank, Houck, & Reynolds, 2005; also see Shear, Boelen, & Neimeyer, Chapter 12), could prove vital in helping Lorrie achieve a new psychological position from which to survey her life and its significance. Again, beneficence demands doing something salutary for Lorrie whenever possible.

A key aspect of beneficence is to determine whether "helping" Lorrie means "protecting" her from her own inclination not to preserve or prolong her life. An interesting counterpoint to the studies of terminally ill cancer patients cited earlier (Breithart et al., 2000; Chochinov et al., 2005; Kelly et al., 2004) is an investigation of patients with end-stage renal disease who electively discontinued life-sustaining dialysis (Cohen et al., 2002). The overwhelming majority of these patients were *not* depressed (86%), were *not* recently suicidal (100%), and did *not* consider dialysis discontinuation to be the equivalent of suicide (87%). The authors took a provocative position that dysphoria among the dying may be better conceptualized as anticipatory grief rather than depression. Because anticipatory grieving contains many of the same elements as postloss bereavement, such considerations underscore the earlier recommendation for grief-specific psychotherapy for Lorrie.

James L. Werth Jr. and colleagues (Werth, Burke, & Bardash, 2002; Werth & Richmond, 2009; Werth & Rogers, 2005) acknowledged a clinician's obligation to do something (beneficial) when a patient considers hastening death but proposed that a "duty to assess" would satisfy the need for intervention typically assumed to be mandated under "duty to protect" requirements. The American Psychological Association's Working Group on Assisted Suicide and End-of-Life Decisions (2000) identified several factors to assess, such as decision-making capacity, influence of pain and suffering, cultural factors, quality of life, level of social support, and possible coercion. Exploring these factors as they apply to Lorrie's contemplated treatment refusal would appear to be at least a minimum application of the principle of beneficence.

Process

Engaging Lorrie in a thoughtful discussion about her various treatment options following a possible cancer diagnosis would, of course, have to include delineation of the severity of cancer, its prognosis with and without treatment, and the benefit–risk profile of proposed treatment courses. Of all the "voices" to be heard in this conversation, hers clearly has primacy. Because Lorrie is an outpatient in control of her own destiny whose death is not imminent, the "resolution" of this dilemma will emerge from sensitive questioning and careful listening by all the providers involved in her care. As Graybar and Leonard (2005) so eloquently stated, "Being listened to allows us to be understood in all our complexity. It allows our experiences to count and ourselves to matter" (p. 3). This is the basic dignity owed to Lorrie as a person and a fundamental expression of the ethical principle of *fidelity*—exercising loyalty to the patient in the context of a fiduciary relationship. In this process, sound ethical practice and good counseling technique converge into a synonymous enterprise (Gamino & Ritter, 2009).

Following the leads provided by Muskin (1998), a psychotherapeutic dialogue with Lorrie aimed at discovering possible latent meanings in her quest to die could proceed down several trails. She may have a "split" in her experience of self so that the wish to be dead actually constitutes a wish for the "bad" or unworthy part of self to die, leaving the healthy part to "survive." Or, out of rage incited by a lifetime of abuse and mistreatment, Lorrie may seek revenge against the perpetrators in a psychologically "inverted" manner by channeling her hostility toward others into a death wish: "I'll show you how worthless I am (by ending my life)." Or, she may have adopted a position of self-loathing and equate death with punishment deserved to atone for guilt.

Lorrie's multiple losses (e.g., completed, nonfinite, traumatic, ambiguous, and anticipated) and the corresponding complications in her grieving may influence her inclination toward hastened death. For example, due to parental bereavement, Lorrie may desire death hoping that she will be rewarded by reunion with her treasured (deceased) son in the afterlife.

By listening attentively throughout this dialogue, the provider's obligations are to identify what may be multiple motivations layered into Lorrie's predetermination to forgo medical treatment, assist her in evaluating the merits (or lack thereof) for each dimension affecting her choice, and thus help her decide between prolonging life and hastening death. Carried out conscientiously, such an effort would meet applicable clinical and ethical obligations to the patient in the spirit of the "duty to assess" criterion (Werth & Richmond, 2009) evidenced in

> demonstrating to the [patient] that one has not only a technical understanding and relevant experience related to the [patient's] condition but also a will-

ingness to appreciate the [patient's] life circumstances that may make death appear to be a better option that continuing to live. (p. 199)

HOSPITAL-BASED CLINICAL ETHICIST'S PERSPECTIVE

As a hospital-based clinical ethicist, I provide ethics consultations according to guidelines promoted by the American Society for Bioethics and Humanities (Society for Health and Human Values—Society for Bioethics Consultation Task Force on Standards for Bioethics Consultation, 2010):

> [T]o help patient, families, surrogates, health care providers, or other involved parties address uncertainty or conflict regarding value-laden issues that emerge in health care. This uncertainty or conflict may have both cognitive and affective dimensions.... These issues have moral and legal dimensions that may involve, among other things, patient autonomy, informed consent, competence, health care provider rights of conscience, medical futility, resource allocation, confidentiality, or surrogate decision making. (p. 3)

For purposes of this chapter, two caveats come to mind about my role as ethics consultant. First, I describe my responses as if I were providing counsel to the clinicians treating Lorrie based on the facts of the case presented to me, not as if I have had any direct contact with Lorrie or spoken with her. Second, I am continually cognizant of an important injunction by one of my mentors *not* to be a "two-handed ethicist" who concludes consultations equivocally by telling people, "You could do this *or* you could do that." Instead, after thoughtfully considering the various issues involved, I try to reach a definite point of view about the question before me. I would approach Lorrie's case in this way and focus on the adequacy of her decision-making capacity.

Evolution of Biomedical Ethics

The growing use of ethical principles in health care in general and the pervading domination of individual patient autonomy in particular frequently demand an ongoing evaluation of the decisions made by a patient as well as those made by health care providers. Decision making in health care has moved away from centuries of physician paternalism to recent decades of individual autonomy and codified ethical principles. In approximately 400 BCE, Hippocrates offered the initial declaration of beneficence and nonmaleficence, "As to diseases, make a habit of two things—to help, or at least to do no harm" (Jones, 2004, p. 165). The National Research Act of 1974 (Pub. L. 93-348), partly a response to the disastrous Tuskegee syphilis study (Jones, 1981), created the National Commission for the Protection of Human Subjects of Biomedical and Behavioral Research (the "Commission") to oversee and regulate the practice of human medical experimentation. In *The Belmont Report*, the Commission (1979) identified three basic principles—respect for persons (autonomy), beneficence (including nonmaleficence), and justice—to guide the resolution of ethical problems arising from research with human subjects.

Implementation of these ethical principles throughout health care was solidified by publication of *The Principles of Biomedical Ethics* in 1979, now in its sixth edition (Beauchamp & Childress, 2008), authored by two key members of the Commission. One of the best known and most challenging claims made by this framework of principle-based ethics is respect for autonomy, which finds its everyday expression through the action of an autonomous agent. Showing respect for persons as autonomous agents means

> to recognize with due appreciation their own considered value judgments and outlooks even when it is believed that their judgments are mistaken. To respect them in this way is to acknowledge their right to their own view and the permissibility of their actions based on such beliefs. And to grant them this right is to say that they are entitled to such autonomous determination without limitations on their liberty being imposed by others. (Beauchamp & Childress, 2008, p. 58)

Capacity

In the context of hospital-based health care, the term *capacity* refers to whether a person is capable of making decisions about medical treatment. Although there is not a single, clinically accepted standard for what constitutes decision-making capacity, Miller and Marin (2000) proposed four criteria: understanding one's medical condition specifically, in terms of diagnosis and prognosis; comprehending the treatment options available and appreciating the consequences of each option; making a reasoned choice based on personal values or beliefs; and communicating a choice that is consistent over time.

Reviewing Lorrie's case in the context of the Miller and Marin (2000) criteria, it would seem that she is aware of her overall condition and the possible prognoses, for her mental as well as physical health. Although it is difficult to address how well Lorrie understands her condition without speaking to her directly, her statement "I am a basket that needs weaving" implies some level of understanding that her mental health has unraveled. Regarding her possible cancer, Lorrie understands that this condition may carry a fatal prognosis because she anticipates refusing any aggressive life-prolonging treatment.

Lorrie exhibits comprehension of the options available for treatment and the consequences of each. For her mental health issue, Lorrie sought out psychotherapy. For me, this shows that she made some assessment of seeking treatment versus no treatment. Obviously she also could have demonstrated the same comprehension by rejecting psychotherapy as a realistic option. Continuing that treatment implies a value assessment of its consequences—finding some benefit.

In terms of her possible medical condition, Lorrie plans to refuse any life-prolonging treatment. Clearly she comprehends there is an option for cancer treatment; she has weighed the consequences of accepting treatment (e.g., the rigors of therapy, and possible extension to her life) against refusing treatment (e.g., certain decline, and natural death). Although some might claim that Lorrie's decision shows some form of suicidal ideation inferred to be, de facto, irrational, I find no evidence in the case scenario indicating impairment in her rational decision making.

When the criterion of making a "reasoned choice" is considered, one may wonder why questions about decision-making capacity arise when Lorrie stated that she would refuse any life-prolonging treatment. Jones and Holden (2004) declared, "Most often, physicians question patients' decision-making capacity when patients disagree with the physician; however, agreement with the physician does not imply that this capacity is intact" (p. 972). Would anyone be concerned if Lorrie were to tell those involved in her care that she wished to pursue aggressive treatment if her biopsy showed a malignant process? Obviously, the value systems of Lorrie's providers, and of society at large, can come into play and potentially conflict with her stated values.

In my opinion, this disparity illustrates the problems associated with the criterion that the patient makes a reasoned choice. If one disagrees with the patient's value or belief system, then that system may be seen as irrational or illogical, as will any choice that emanates from it. My goal in consultation would be to assure, to the degree possible, that the patient's value or belief system does not have some foundational flaw and that the system is applied in some "reasoned" way. Taking stock of a family network may validate the patient's stated value system (as well as help detect possible coercion), although this does not seem applicable in Lorrie's case. Also, inquiry about the operation of spirituality or faith beliefs may clarify matters but, at the same time, openness is needed to a variety of perspectives, or none at all, regarding this dimension.

Finally, the criterion of consistency in decision making is difficult to apply in the course of a single consultation. Nonetheless, vacillation on Lorrie's part could signal some level of uncertainty so continued vigilance is required throughout the deliberation process.

In conclusion, Lorrie appears to meet full criteria for decision-making capacity; therefore, her wishes for treatment refusal should be honored. Her original statement, "I am a basket that needs weaving," began her journey, and it could also end her journey as she weaves a design that seems intended to bring significance, and perhaps meaning, in death that she did not find in life.

CASE POSTSCRIPT AND CONCLUSION

In the actual patient case on which the hypothetical scenario of "Lorrie" was based, additional tests proved the mass in her neck to be "fatty tissue" rather than any type of malignancy. Therefore, she was spared the dilemma of having to make a decision about accepting or forgoing life-extending treatment. Nonetheless, her "story" provided an interesting heuristic for exploring the grief dimensions associated with her wish for hastened death and examining the clinical considerations and ethical principles pertinent to her end-of-life decision making. Lorrie's case illustrates how grief therapy and ethical practice go hand in hand when working with complex bereavement problems.

REFERENCES

American Counseling Association. (2005). *ACA code of ethics*. Retrieved from http://www.counseling.org

American Psychological Association. (2002). *Ethical principles of psychologists and code of conduct*. Retrieved from http://www.apa.org/ethics/

American Psychological Association Working Group on Assisted Suicide and End-of-Life Decisions. (2000). *Report to Board of Directors*. Washington, DC: American Psychological Association. Retrieved from http://www.apa.org/pubs/info/reports/aseol.aspx

Association for Death Education and Counseling. (2006). *Code of ethics*. Retrieved from http://www.adec.org/about/ethics.cfm

Beauchamp, T. L., & Childress, J. F. (2008). *Principles of biomedical ethics* (6th ed.). New York: Oxford University Press.

Beck, J. S. (1995). *Cognitive therapy: Basics and beyond*. New York: Guilford.

Boss, P. (2007). Ambiguous loss: Challenges for scholars and practitioners. *Family Relations*, *56*, 105–110.

Breitbart, W., Rosenfeld, B., Pessin, H., Kaim, M., Funesti-Esch, J., Galietta, M., et al. (2000). Depression, hopelessness, and desire for hastened death in terminally ill patients with cancer. *Journal of the American Medical Association*, *284*, 2907–2911.

Chochinov, H. M., Hack, T., Hassard, T., Kristjanson, L. J., McClement, S., & Harlos, M. (2005). Understanding the will to live in patients nearing death. *Psychosomatics*, *46*, 7–10.

Cohen, L. M., Dobscha, S. K., Hails, K. C., Pekow, P. S., & Chochinov, H. M. (2002). Depression and suicidal ideation in patients who discontinue the life-support treatment of dialysis. *Psychosomatic Medicine*, *64*, 889–896.

Dyck, A. J. (2002). *Life's worth: The case against assisted suicide*. Grand Rapids, MI: Eerdmans.

Gamino, L. A., & Ritter, R. H., Jr. (2009). *Ethical practice in grief counseling*. New York: Springer.

Graybar, S. R., & Leonard, L. M. (2005). In defense of listening. *American Journal of Psychotherapy*, *59*, 1–18.

Jones, J. (1981). *Bad blood: The Tuskegee syphilis experiment: A tragedy of race and medicine.* New York: Free Press.

Jones, R. C., & Holden, T. (2004). A guide to assessing decision-making capacity. *Cleveland Clinic Journal of Medicine*, *71*, 971–975.

Jones, W. H. S. (Trans.). (2004). *Hippocrates*. In *Loeb Classical Library* (Vol. 1). Cambridge, MA: Harvard University Press.

Kelly, B. J., Burnett, P. C., Pelusi, D., Badger, S. J., Varghese, F. T., & Robertson, M. M. (2004). Association between clinician factors and a patient's wish to hasten death: Terminally ill cancer patients and their doctors. *Psychosomatics*, *45*, 311–318.

Kitchener, K. S. (1984). Intuition, critical evaluation and ethical principles: The foundation for ethical decisions in counseling psychology. *Counseling Psychologist*, *12*, 43–55.

Leeman, C. P. (1999). Depression and the right to die. *General Hospital Psychiatry*, *21*, 112–115.

Leeman, C. P. (2009). Distinguishing among irrational suicide and other forms of hastened death: Implications for clinical practice. *Psychosomatics*, *50*, 185–191.

Miller, S. S., & Marin, D. B. (2000). Assessing capacity. *Emergency Medicine Clinics of North America*, *18*, 233–242.

Muskin, P. R. (1998). The request to die: Role for a psychodynamic perspective on physician-assisted suicide. *Journal of the American Medical Association*, *279*, 323–328.

National Commission for the Protection of Human Subjects of Biomedical and Behavioral Research. (1979). *The Belmont report: Ethical principles and guidelines for the protection of human subjects of research*. Retrieved from http://www.hhs.gov/ohrp/humansubjects/guidance/belmont.htm

Roos, S. (2002). *Chronic sorrow: A living loss*. New York: Brunner-Routledge.

Shear, K., Frank, E., Houck, P. R., & Reynolds, C. F. (2005). Treatment of complicated grief: A randomized controlled trial. *Journal of the American Medical Association, 293*, 2601–2608.

Society for Health and Human Values—Society for Bioethics Consultation Task Force on Standards for Bioethics Consultation. (2010). *Core competencies for health care ethics consultation: The report of the American Society for Bioethics and Humanities*. Glenview, IL: American Society for Bioethics and Humanities.

Sullivan, M. D., & Youngner, S. J. (1994). Depression, competence, and the right to refuse lifesaving medical treatment. *American Journal of Psychiatry, 151*, 971–978.

Welfel, E. R. (2006). *Ethics in counseling & psychotherapy: Standards, research, and emerging issues* (3rd ed.). Belmont, CA: Thomson Brooks/Cole.

Werth, J. L., Jr. (1999). Mental health professionals and assisted death: Perceived ethical obligations and proposed guidelines for practice. *Ethics & Behavior, 9*, 159–183.

Werth, J. L., Jr., Burke, C., & Bardash, R. J. (2002). Confidentiality in end-of-life and after-death situations. *Ethics & Behavior, 12*, 205–222.

Werth, J. L., Jr., & Richmond, J. M. (2009). End-of-life decisions and the duty to protect. In J. L. Werth Jr., E. R. Welfel, & G. A. H. Benjamin (Eds.), *The duty to protect: Ethical, legal, and professional considerations for mental health professionals* (pp. 195–208). Washington, DC: American Psychological Association.

Werth, J. L., Jr., & Rogers, J. R. (2005). Assessing for impaired judgment as a means of meeting the "duty to protect" when a client is a potential harm-to-self: Implications for clients making end-of-life decisions. *Mortality, 10*, 7–21.

Worden, J. W. (2009). *Grief counseling & grief therapy: A handbook for the mental health practitioner* (4th ed.). New York: Springer.

Section VII

Conclusion

31

Building Bridges in Bereavement Research and Practice
Some Concluding Reflections

ROBERT A. NEIMEYER and DARCY L. HARRIS

Upon reading the contributed chapters to the present project, we had a gratifying sense of just how much has been discovered about the "new territory" of bereavement research and practice. Not only have our understandings of bereavement deepened over the past several decades, but also they have broadened, resulting in a much greater awareness of the impact of qualitatively different types of losses within diverse populations of the bereaved. Whereas Freud (1917/1957) and Lindemann (1944) mostly described the intrapsychic processes of individuals who experienced the death of a loved one, current bereavement research and practice have expanded this early work to explore the grief response with multifaceted lenses that focus upon intrapersonal, interpersonal, sociological, political, and spiritual dimensions of individuals, communities, and even nations after losses of all kinds. Clearly, the scope of bereavement research and practice now encompasses a diverse array of experiences and populations, which are amply surveyed in this volume.

Our goal in this closing chapter is to reflect on the range of current work in bereavement as reflected in this book, with an emphasis on four general issues: (a) current models of bridging science and practice evidenced in the foregoing chapters, (b) points of substantive convergence and divergence of contributors that invite closer consideration, (c) practical implications for clinicians that arise across chapters, and finally (d) recommendations for future research suggested by the current bridging effort. We recognize that the scope of these considerations—not to mention the number and richness of the chapters on which we provide commentary—precludes any exhaustive summary and analysis, which could probably fill a volume of comparable length. Instead, our hope is to spark interest in each of the foregoing topics, and invite readers to join us in extending the already lively dialogue between bereavement research and application.

MODELS OF BRIDGING

The effort to "close the gap" between bereavement researchers and practitioners does not originate with this volume. Indeed, in 2005 the Bridging Work Group of the Center for the Advancement of Health published the results of a qualitative and quantitative study focused on the lack of integration of scholarly and applied communities concerned with grief and loss, yielding several recommendations to advance their more meaningful dialogue.[1] Construing the traditional schism between these two communities as a problem of "cross-cultural communication," the group noted the rather different sources of authority endorsed by the two cultures (e.g., clinical experience with bereaved clients versus statistical results), the distinctive constraints and inducements in each setting (e.g., reward for reducing human suffering and completion of paperwork versus emphasis on peer-reviewed publication and success in finding funding), and the characteristic reliance on different outlets in the two groups, with books being the most important source of new knowledge used by practitioners, whereas they were among the least likely outlets to be utilized by researchers. Without seeking to reiterate the multifaceted recommendations for both communities propounded by the Bridging Work Group, we hope to make a modest contribution to the effort by reflecting in these closing pages on the patterns of bridge building observed in the present volume. Indeed, we conceived this project partly as a response to the needs identified in their report, including the clear imperative to offer field-changing developments and refinements in the form of a book that would be of broad interest to clinicians as well as researchers. Our goal in so doing was more than simply disseminating promising theoretical and empirical contributions to applied readers, as it extended to the intent to foster a genuine dialogue between the two perspectives by pairing authors from the two "cultures." Thus, in its format as well as its content, we hoped the book would represent an experiment in bridging.

How did this experiment fare? As editors, we, by and large, have felt enriched by the efforts of our contributing authors to boldly venture into dialogue with counterparts who shared their interest in a specific area or topic, but from varying perspectives as researchers or clinicians. Ultimately, we hope that the interplay between the two will allow readers who are practitioners to explore the application of research to practice, and those who are scholars to immerse themselves thoughtfully in case study material and clinical implications of scientific work. In this fashion, we hope that the book reflects the spirit of "bi-directional interchange" endorsed in the Bridging Work Group's (2005) recommendations.

It is worth emphasizing that the unique format of the volume encouraged bridging as a *process* as well as an *outcome*, as the pairing of coauthors for most of the chapters was something of a "blind date," in the sense that we suggested collaborations between prominent theorists or scientists on the one hand and practicing professionals on the other, many of whom had never met prior to being invited to write together. As a result, the effort to coauthor a substantive chapter in itself entailed a serious effort at bridging, and it is important to acknowledge candidly that not all of these arranged marriages worked out amicably! Some authors approached seemed astonished and leery of working alongside someone who was not already a trusted colleague, and a few of them declined participation on these grounds. Interestingly, suspicions arose on both sides of the dialogical divide, with some researchers incredulous at the suggestion that they collaborate with a less well-published practitioner, and some practitioners voicing skepticism about the relevance of a suggested coauthor's research for their practice. Considered as a bold social experiment in its own right, our effort to facilitate such pairings and the occasional reluctance or refusal of invited authors to do so highlight the challenge of fostering dialogue across communities that differ in style, focus, institutional context, "closeness" to the reality of human suffering and resilience, and even basic epistemology. Simply stated, some attempted dialogues were insufficient in their scaffolding to span the divide.

In the great majority of cases, however, collaborators eagerly rolled up their sleeves and got on with the business of bridge building, with encouraging results. Although a few of these coauthor teams had enjoyed a long-standing history of collaboration—especially in the work of large and well-funded programs like those associated with the Family Bereavement Project and interventions for families suffering loss as a result of the 9/11 terrorism—most were minimally acquainted prior to the current project, and the resulting chapter might be viewed more as an initial icebreaker or brainstorming session than as a report of a final consensus. Moreover, although all chapters included strong clinical and scientific "voices," these were occasionally represented *within* each coauthor rather than *between* them, when both contributors were scientist-practitioners "bilingual" in both perspectives (as in the chapters on meaning reconstruction, complicated grief, nonfinite loss, ambiguous loss and chronic sorrow, and suicide bereavement). Finally, the very different types and contexts of bereavement, different styles and forms of scholarship (theoretical, quantitative, and qualitative), and different levels of development of research and practice addressed in the various chapters further contribute to the variety of forms of bridging—some tentative and provisional, others extensive and thoroughgoing—represented in the volume. Here we will remark on some of the resulting differences in the form of dialogue observed, and some possible next steps to advance each.

Theoretical Implications for Practice

Perhaps the most germinal form of dialogue occurred in those chapters in which a novel conceptual framework that was not yet supported by an extensive empirical literature was illustrated by brief practice vignettes. This form of preliminary bridging occurred, for example, in chapters concerned with grieving styles associated partly with gender as well as in those conveying an influential theory of grief (such as the task model) and its practical implications. Attempts to explore a heuristic understanding of various types of grief associated with ambiguous loss, chronic sorrow, and nonfinite loss might also fit in this category. Here, the points of contact between theory and application suggested by the authors might be read as an invitation to consider the clinical or conceptual utility of the model propounded, as well as a call for more scientific research on the processes or issues described.

Clinical Practice Inviting Research

The inverse situation also obtained in some chapters, such as those detailing a novel hospice program or a set of practice techniques drawing on rituals or the expressive arts. Here, innovative methods have to date attracted little empirical documentation of their efficacy with the bereaved, although this would be highly desirable and informative. In fact, one is tempted to conclude that the more creative the intervention, the less likely it is to derive from psychological theory, and hence the less likely it is to have drawn significant research attention. This could reflect a dominant trend in attempts to bridge science and practice by seeking merely to apply the lessons of the former to the domain of the latter, in the place of a more bilateral exchange that could enliven research, while at the same time disciplining practice. We will return to this point below.

Surveys of Empirical Literature Relevant to a Particular Population, Topic, or Type of Loss

More empirically grounded but less theoretically focused were those chapters that reviewed a sometimes diffuse or suggestive literature concerned with a particular group such as bereaved siblings, persons who have lost same-sex partners, military personnel, and widows and widowers, as well as those summarizing what is known about a particular cause of death, as through suicide, catastrophe, or other forms of traumatic loss. To a considerable extent, the survey of research on the use of ritual in bereavement also fits this pattern. Perhaps in part because these chapters attempted to draw together a variegated literature that rarely was integrated by a comprehensive model, they less often provided detailed clinical case studies, and more commonly attempted to offer principles to guide intervention with a particular population or problem. As such, they frequently suggested a trove of implications for underresearched topics that invite further empirical assessment.

Focus on a Particular Research Project and Its Clinical Implications

In some chapters, authors offered a succinct review of existing research, but concentrated particularly on a detailed presentation of a single research project with practical relevance, whether that project was qualitative (as in the chapter on parental grief) or quantitative in nature (as in those on pet loss or the two-track model). An advantage of this style of bridging is that it conveys the strengths as well as limitations of a given study in a form accessible to an applied readership, which often complains that research articles in the peer-reviewed literature are inscrutable or offer little of practical value to clinicians (Bridging Work Group, 2005).

Generation of Novel Interventions Suggested by Basic Scientific Research

A more developed form of bridging seemed to occur in cases of progressive research programs with substantial empirical evidence regarding factors associated with bereavement outcome, such as work in meaning reconstruction, continuing bonds, or attachment from the standpoint of the dual-process model. Although each of these frameworks certainly invites further empirical attention and documentation, each has generated a sufficiently large literature that it is beginning to suggest novel strategies and techniques for grief therapy beyond the emphasis on empathic witnessing, normalization, and psychoeducation that have long been mainstays of bereavement intervention. Next steps would logically entail rigorous scientific assessment of such methods as therapeutic tools, a step now being taken in the case of meaning reconstruction techniques, as noted below.

Randomized Clinical Trials and Case Illustrations

As the research literature in bereavement has matured, it has reached the point of generating a growing body of well-controlled research on carefully developed therapeutic interventions, evaluating their efficacy against no-treatment or contrasting treatment conditions (Currier, Neimeyer, & Berman, 2008). In the present volume, these are most clearly represented in the chapters on therapy for complicated grief from attachment and coping, cognitive, and narrative and meaning reconstruction orientations, as well as in the chapter on family therapy. In each case, specific and clearly delineated procedures have been offered to an indicated or at-risk group of mourners (e.g., those suffering prolonged and debilitating grief or loss of a loved one to cancer), and their efficacy established by comparison to other conditions. Such research obviously carries strong practice implications, as illustrated in case studies or qualitative research that affirms or qualifies its particular findings. Though a strong form of bridging the sometimes antagonistic cultures of research and practice, it is worth underscoring that even the most promising laboratory studies require replication outside the university or research hospital in the domain of typical clinical practice in order to test how robust their methods might be in the "real world." The approaches detailed in these chapters would seem to be prime candidates for such evaluation.

Field Trials of Evidence-Based Interventions

Only two chapters in this volume report the results of stringent attempts to implement empirically evaluated interventions in field settings, namely, the chapters focusing on children's loss of a parent and the death of family members (typically husbands and fathers) as a result of terrorism. Such attempts clearly underscore the critical necessity of research–practice dialogue *for clinical scientists*, as they make necessary and occasionally substantial adjustments to their laboratory-based interventions in light of user feedback and real-world constraints. These same chapters also hint at different processes by which such modifications can be approached deliberately and planfully in the case of progressive research programs that develop on an academic timeline, as opposed to being accommodated in a more improvisational style when the service program is implemented in response to urgent social need, as in the wake of September 11. Norwegian research on "confrontational coping" in response to natural catastrophe represents something of an intermediate case, with certain principles of practice formulated in response to one crisis, and then evaluated, at least in a preliminary fashion, in subsequent disasters.

Scholarly Advocacy for Broader Frameworks

A final form of bridging evident in this volume is the exploration of broader trends, issues, or frameworks that carry implications for bereavement practice, though they are less easily reducible to specific theories or methods of a kind that could be evaluated in clinical trials or manualized interventions in field settings. Chapters devoted to such themes as spirituality, culture, technology, ethics, LBGT issues, and social justice fall into this category. Although each might suggest testable hypotheses in the usual tradition of positivist social science (e.g., that spiritual coping promotes adaptation to loss, or that people in Eastern and Western cultures construct continuing bonds with the deceased differently), they also function as embracing contexts that condition, challenge, and critique the more narrow concerns of bereavement research and practice. Ultimately, they suggest the relevance of other disciplines (e.g., sociology, anthropology, philosophy, religious studies, gender studies, and technology studies) in framing the human response to loss, offering vantage points from which mortality and transition can be understood, and services devised with greater awareness of their role in a larger frame.

Too often, discourse addressing the gap between research and practice merely advocates *that* the two worlds be brought together, and stops short of addressing *what* the necessary dialogue might look like. If the various chapters of this book are read as answers to this question, it is evident that any of several forms of collaborative conversation are possible between members of the two "cultures," to the extent that they are disposed to such contact. This can range from practitioners straightforwardly taking direction from existing theory or research to dialogues in which they take the lead through crafting practices or services that invite deserved evaluation of their efficacy. More complex iterations of research and application are also possible, as when creative clinicians "riff" in an improvisational manner off of the central themes of a research program by devising techniques in keeping with the spirit of the underlying theory, or when applied researchers seek the systematic feedback of practitioners in modifying evidence-based practices in response to clinical wisdom or real-world contingencies. Especially for "bridge leaders" who are themselves scientist-practitioners (Bridging Work Group, 2005), this weaving of the two cultures may even occur seamlessly in the same individual, although the principles that guide this practice are mostly implicit and require greater explication. Ultimately, we hope that the work in this volume takes a step toward the fuller integration of science and practice in the field of bereavement, in a way that moves beyond the veiled admonition that unmotivated or uncritical clinicians step out of the darkness of personal prejudice into the cold, clear light of science. If anything, we believe that this dominant, if disguised, narrative has done more to frustrate genuine bridging than to promote it.

CLINICAL CONVERGENCE AND DIVERGENCE

Whatever the form of bridging attempted in the various chapters, what was the practical yield across them for both the serious scholar and the concerned clinician? In this section, we draw attention to some illustrative trends that merit the attention of both communities.

Duration of Grief

One initial area of comparison is in the area of length of time that grief can be expected to last—a common concern of the bereaved themselves. Although most of the chapters do not address specific time frames to demarcate when grief is considered adaptive or problematic, one implication of research on complicated grief (CG) or prolonged grief disorder (PGD) is that there is indeed a timeline involved in adaptation to loss. Specifically, mounting evidence demonstrates that if a mourner's grief remains disabling and preoccupying for 6 months, a year, or more beyond a death, then intervention may be indicated—perhaps especially when his or her trajectory seems to be going in a downward direction. In this book, the chapter that describes CG and PGD focuses upon the stunting of adaptive processes of grieving more than the persistence of symptomatology over time. However, there is an understanding that ongoing obsessive rumination and persistent symptoms of acute grief in the presence of one's inability to begin the process of rebuilding after a loved one has died signify that adaptation has become stalled in some way and specific therapy may be necessary to help the mourner move forward. In contrast, in discussion of nonfinite or ambiguous losses, where the loss itself is ongoing in nature, no assumption is made that ongoing grieving is maladaptive. This is clearly an area that merits further research, to consider whether indeed there are pathonomic indicators of difficulty in adapting to chronic losses in a way that would necessitate more active intervention, rather than simple normalization or reassurance that some form of chronic sorrow is to be expected.

Styles and Types as Mediators of Grief

Clearly, if the work in this volume is representative of contemporary professional opinion, any "uniformity myth" that once haunted the bereavement field has been effectively dispelled, as the variety of ways people grieve is emphasized by numerous authors. For example, several of the chapters described specific relational factors that moderate the grief response. For instance, the chapter on attachment style and coping explores responses to grief based upon lifelong tendencies in how individuals relate to the world and others. The main focus of this chapter is upon the difficulties that individuals with an insecure attachment style may have after the loss of a significant person. This chapter identifies how anxious or dependent attachment may interfere with the grieving process, and suggests ways to engage with insecurely attached individuals to enable them to find a secure base within the therapeutic context in order to better adapt to the presence of that loss in their lives. Congruent with this thinking is the chapter on restructuring the continuing bond, which addresses similar issues in the context of ongoing attachment to the deceased, a topic we discuss further in the next section.

Another example of grieving styles arises in the chapter on family therapy, where specific family types are discussed in the context of how a system, rather than an individual, responds to the loss of one of its members. These family types are discussed in terms of interventional needs, identifying some families (supportive and conflict resolving) that require very little professional support, whereas other types of families (intermediate and sullen) need professional support and intervention to manage the effects of grief. Moreover, in one of the rare concessions to the limitations of grief therapy, the authors underscore their observations that some families, such as those marked by high levels of anger and conflict (identified as *hostile family type*), tend to deteriorate in family interventions and perhaps are best seen individually.

In contrast, the chapter on gender socialization differentiates grieving styles that were formerly assigned by gender stereotyping and that are now identified by patterns of behavior that may characterize both men and women in varying degrees. Whereas the chapter on attachment style focused on the potentially problematic aspects of insecure attachment in bereavement, and the chapter on family therapy identified family styles that are also seen as problematic, the grieving styles that are identified in this particular chapter are descriptions of responses that are considered normal and congruent for specific individuals, and the intent is to normalize diversity within responses and not to identify problematic responses that require intervention. Clearly, establishing the assets and liabilities of different grieving styles should be a priority of research, and one with high clinical relevance.

Restructuring the Continuing Bond

Some of the authors describe a process of readdressing the relationship with the deceased individual in order to facilitate healthy adaptation to loss. For example, the chapter on restructuring continuing bonds uses an attachment-based model to focus not simply upon the attachment style of the bereaved individual but also upon the attachment relationship that existed between the bereaved person and the deceased. The intervention suggested in this chapter strives to alter the character of the ongoing attachment to permit the relationship to evolve posthumously, allowing the healthy aspects of grief to become more prominent. Likewise, the coverage of spousal loss in later life also mentions the importance of finding ways to enable bereaved individuals to create an ongoing spiritual bond with the deceased in a way that facilitates the adaptation of the surviving partner.

The description of complicated grief therapy also makes reference to reconnecting the bereaved individual with the deceased through the use of an imaginal conversation to prompt reaffirmation of the bond on the part of both living and dead, and to address lingering concerns, such as survivor guilt, that might interfere with adaptive grieving. Similarly, restorative retelling interventions that invite the bereaved to visualize themselves providing some form of comfort to their dying loved one that was denied them in the actual circumstance of their violent dying might be considered a specific imaginal reenactment of the relationship that contends against the helplessness felt in the aftermath of traumatic death. The effect, in essence, is the development of a loving bond with the deceased individual that is readily accessible and competes with the narrative of separation and powerlessness to engage the deceased in healthy ways. Finally, the section on meaning making in complicated grief treatment addresses the need to review and revise the underlying story of the relationship with the deceased, in order to reconstruct the attachment bond with the deceased and with it provide the attachment security required to allow the bereaved individual to move forward in life. A closer understanding of the strategies by which this is accomplished—perhaps by close process analysis of successful realignment of the relationship in grief therapy—would make an important contribution to future practice.

Importance of Ritual, Legacy, and Meaning Making

Finally, several chapters make reference to the importance of rituals, legacies, and meaning making for bereaved individuals as part of the grieving process. For example, the discussion of ritual and legacies offers specific descriptions of various rituals and legacies used by bereaved individuals to foster connection to the deceased, to attach meaning to the life that has concluded, and to highlight the significance of their loss experience. The descriptions of such practices are numerous and may involve individuals, families, communities, and even countries. Examples from the various chapters include revisiting the site of a disaster or place of death of a loved one and marking it in some way to have its significance recognized; implementing a meditative practice for dying and bereaved individuals; developing a scholarship fund in memory of a loved one, exploring the use of linking objects to the deceased; forming and passing down the narrative of a relationship, person, or family; creating a piece of art or clothing that relates to the deceased individual; and personal rituals such as lighting candles, cooking certain foods, and honoring significant dates.

It is clear from the many references in the chapters to the importance of ritual, legacies, and the story of the bereaved individual that human beings actively seek out meaning in the context of significant losses, and this effort to find meaning can play a constructive role in the grieving process. Just how various practices contribute to people's attempt to make sense of an unwelcome transition, whether in spiritual or secular terms, deserves more attention and warrants further exploration by grief therapists.

IMPLICATIONS FOR PRACTICE

Although it is daunting to tease out implications for clinicians that cut across chapters—though easy enough to discern countless such implications within them—we will mention a few themes that emerged that deserve special emphasis.

The Individuality of Grief

It is clear from the writings in this book that grief is a complexly personal, multi-faceted experience. Clinicians who work with bereaved individuals are reminded of the importance of many factors to take into consideration in their practices. For example, it is apparent from several of the chapters that an understanding of the attachment system and the different attachment styles would be highly relevant to therapeutic practice with bereaved individuals, as are numerous other factors (e.g., the mode of death of the loved one, and the positive or conflictual nature of the prior relationship to the deceased) that can influence their adaptation to bereavement. Moreover, one corollary of the foregoing discussion of grieving styles is that no "one-size-fits-all" model of grief will be sustainable in a treatment setting, a recognition that in itself challenges psychoeducational models that offer formulaic depictions of the typical course through bereavement. One is left with the recognition that *who we are shapes how we grieve*, and who we are is a function of the many personal, historical, and developmental factors that give rise to our individuality. This implies that, to be maximally effective, therapy must be tailored to the uniqueness of the person, relationship, and circumstances that characterize a specific client, at a specific moment, grieving a specific loss. Logical though this conclusion may be, its use in the therapeutic context will rely on informed clinical wisdom for implementation, insofar as the research literature does not come close to specifying the full range of person variables (much less their interaction) of relevance to a given client's unique strengths and vulnerabilities in adapting to loss.

Grief in the Social Field

As important as it is to recognize the individuality of grief, it would be a serious mistake to simply locate grief *inside* persons, rather than seeing it as a process that also unfolds *between* them. That is, it is apparent that bereaved persons are highly influenced by their family systems and the social and political structures in which they live; within these contexts, assumptions about the world and about what is meaningful in life are made and sustained, challenged and revised, and negotiated and contested.

The chapter on gender socialization and grieving styles opens the possibility that gender stereotyping in grief may marginalize individuals who do not "fit" into social expectations of grief based upon rigidly defined criteria for each sex. Similarly, the discussion of grief in LGBT youth highlights the role of social messages in media and institutions in the formulation of norms governing perceptions of what is regarded as "deviant." The coverage of social justice and cultural awareness identifies situations in which "mainstream" therapy may fail to assist individuals who do not share the same social or cultural values as the therapist. In addition, the chapter on ethical implications for individuals who are bereaved in the context of multiple losses gives further consideration to the complexity of the impact of grief in people's lives. In all of these cases and more, therapists are challenged to assess and often intervene at levels that range from the intimate communication (or noncommunication) occurring between members of a couple following the death of their child to broad social discourses governing the recognition and validation of some forms of loss (or some mourners) and not others. Clearly, these distinctively social dynamics give rise to potential problems not reducible to individual psychopathology, such as the hostile or nonsupportive reactions that can follow stigmatizing deaths or the sullen withdrawal of overwhelmed families contending with the pending death of a family member. But just as evident are the resources resident in the social field, from the prospect of mobilizing emotional and instrumental support between the surviving parent and child after the death of a parent to broad group rituals to promote healing within a community after a shared loss. In the latter case, therapists function as genuine agents of social change, helping to construct systems that are more responsive to the needs of the bereaved people within them.

Grief Defined in a Broader Perspective

Although the majority of the chapters in this book describe losses that result from death, several chapters also identify the presence of grief in response to nondeath, nonfinite, and intangible losses. This exploration of grief from a broader perspective opens up doors for the exploration of clients' life experiences as they have been shaped by loss in its many forms. The chapter on the ethical considerations for care in a woman with multiple death and nondeath losses identified the importance of acknowledging the presence of all of these losses in her life and their impact upon her current decision-making capacity. Similarly, astute clinicians may begin to observe how these types of losses affect their clients in day-to-day functioning, and apply some of the suggested therapeutic interventions in this book to these clients in order to assist their emergence from the more debilitating effects of ongoing or intangible losses.

Many of the therapeutic suggestions in the sections on cognitive–behavioral therapy (CBT) and meaning making from the chapter on complicated grief may be readily adapted to other types of loss situations, where the focus might be upon rebuilding one's assumptive world rather than reworking one's relationship with a deceased individual. Certainly, the use of rituals and legacies may be of benefit in nondeath and nonfinite losses as well, where the focus is upon finding meaning after a significant life event. With the rise in treatments that prolong the lives of individuals who might have died previously, more individuals are living longer with chronic medical conditions and changes in their living circumstances. The "new grief" (Okun & Nowinski, 2011) that results from such changes needs to be recognized and supported in the same way as traditional grief that occurs after the death of a loved one.

RECOMMENDATIONS FOR RESEARCH

It is tempting to conclude this book with the hackneyed recommendation that "more research is needed," supplemented by the well-worn advocacy of research with applied relevance and the necessity of randomized controlled trials as the guarantor of secure causal inference about treatment efficacy, perhaps with a few predictable ideas thrown in about partnering with practitioners or agencies to get feedback on laboratory-tested protocols prior to field trials. Equally unenlightening would be a recitation of the trove of topical research implications resident in the foregoing chapters, which could of course be consulted as easily by readers as by editors, and which in any case will be read closely by any aspiring researcher seeking inspiration or direction concerning a particular theory, population, or problem. The reader can therefore be assured that we will do neither of these things, and that we will try instead to transcend the obvious and close with seven suggestions concerning the research process itself, concentrating on the form of partnership implied by full bridging between science and application in the pursuit of a deeper engagement with loss and grief.

1. *Deconstruct the dominant narrative of research and practice*: Any serious student of bridging cannot fail to notice that what is advocated in most discussion forums—which are, of course, dominated by academics—is hardly a dialogue of equals. Beneath the thin veneer of egalitarianism is all too often the strongly hierarchical implication that the goal of bridging is to bring scientific Enlightenment to benighted practitioners worshiping at the altar of their customary prejudices and self-serving illusions. From this implicit standpoint, practitioners are being prodded into constructing a bridge that will carry the armamentarium of efficacious techniques to the front of practice—even if the conscripted practitioners view this as inimical to their interests. The unequal power relationship undergirding this image is reminiscent of the classic 1957 film *Bridge on the River Kwai*, in which British prisoners of war ultimately join their Japanese captors in constructing the span over the waterway to transport war materiel, only to have the structure dramatically destroyed by Allied saboteurs at the proud moment of its completion. If bridging efforts in thanatology (or psychotherapy more generally) are to meet with more auspicious outcomes, a genuine negotiation of goals and methods is necessary that presupposes the dignity and needs of both parties.
2. *Cultivate a stance of not knowing*: As a corollary to the above principle, researchers who are genuinely interested in dialogue would do well to approach their practitioner partners in a spirit of humility, cultivating genuine curiosity about the exigencies of practice and the delicate art of facilitating growth in the midst of grief. Whatever the researcher's preferred theory, its empirical assessment would only be informed by a deepened familiarity wrought by immersion in intervention, whether as a participant or an observer. This might take the form of logging a few dozen hours respectfully witnessing the functioning of support groups for the bereaved, carefully studying training videos by respected master therapists, or, perhaps still more radically, participating as clients in the very interventions whose efficacy he or she wishes to test, given the ubiquity of loss in all our lives. It is a reasonable bet that the ensuing dialogue would be more reciprocal, as engaged researchers asked better informed questions of their clinical colleagues, sought consultation about their attempts

to understand the subtleties of therapy process or client resistance, and in general respected practitioners as potential mentors rather than merely students to be enlisted in research programs they had no serious hand in designing.

3. *Become closet epistemologists*: Contemporary social science is dominated by the mantra of logical empiricism, that branch of metascience generated especially in Anglo-American and Viennese circles in the early 20th century. With its strict puritanical obsession with objectivity, deduction, operationalism, quantification, control, and hypothesis testing, it stands in opposition to the quite different "ways of knowing" associated with a continental hermeneutic tradition, with its invitation to phenomenology, induction, credulity, qualitative methods, "letting the data speak," and the development of grounded theory (Radnitsky, 1973). However, as philosophic training has waned in the social sciences, and especially in psychology, whole generations of researchers may be substantially unaware that the paradigm they inhabit is simply one means of pursuing understanding, one with its own distinct advantages and limitations, and not necessarily one that speaks to practitioners. Fortunately, researchers need not become fully conversant in alternative idioms of investigation to communicate more meaningfully with the contrasting culture of clinical practice, as acquiring some working level of competence in a "second language" can go a fair distance toward building bridges of understanding. But the effort to do so is not trivial, and might justifiably be compared to an effort to develop greater bilingualism in a spoken language. If our intent is to do more than colonize the field of practice, it is an effort worth expending.
4. *Mix methods*: A practical entailment of the above emphasis on bilingualism in bereavement research is the suggestion to traffic in mixed methods, combining numbers and narratives in a single study so as to develop a fuller grasp of the phenomena associated with grief and grief therapy (Neimeyer & Hogan, 2001; Neimeyer, Hogan, & Laurie, 2008). Fortunately, the interdisciplinary nature of thanatology encourages just this sort of cross-fertilization, as the dominant quantitative traditions in psychology and medicine can be usefully supplemented by qualitative methods more extensively developed in sociology and nursing. Although perusal of the content of major journals in the field such as *Death Studies* and *Omega* will yield an abundance of research of both kinds, it is striking how seldom the same team of investigators will make use of both methodologies in tandem. Instead, proponents of each perspective will simply persevere in the use of their preferred methods, often even failing to cite relevant research deriving from the complementary tradition. A pragmatic contribution to overcoming this methodological myopia would be to comprise research teams with strong representation of both approaches, with greater equity of funding for both than is typically the case, particularly in the United States. As a single example of a topic that invites such an integration, one might consider the utility of a study that begins by using quantitative, diagnostic criteria for distinguishing two sets of

mourners, one characterized by adaptive and the second by complicated or prolonged grief over an "objectively" comparable loss, and then using grounded theory to better appreciate differences in their lived experience of bereavement. Such an approach, combining richness and rigor, might arguably extend the more rarefied statistical treatment of complicated grief featured in the burgeoning scientific literature on the topic, as well as the common but repetitive qualitative studies of groups of widows and bereaved parents without respect to the level of their distress or resilience.

5. *Practice falsificationism*: Ironically, despite the strong emphasis on falsifiability in the long tradition of logical empiricism (Popper, 1963), bereavement researchers (and social scientists in general) rarely design their studies in a way that attempts to invalidate predictions derived from their favorite theories, except in the trivial sense of testing the "no difference" conclusion implied by the null hypothesis. Instead, they carefully construct their studies to maximize support for their preferred models rather than to challenge them. The result is a literature that even in the rigorous form of controlled outcome studies of bereavement interventions is often marred by substantial investigator allegiance effects, whereby the researcher's pet model is supported vis-à-vis other carefully neutered comparisons (Currier, Holland, & Neimeyer, 2010). Beyond the obvious threats to validity associated with such practices, the failure to critically test the limits of preferred models restricts the practical yield of research in applied settings. Consider, for example, the usefulness of studies that demonstrated when psychoeducation about bereavement might be a *contraindicated* intervention, or when fostering a group climate of expression of emotion might do more harm than good. Identifying the "boundary conditions" of any popular theory or method could go some distance toward highlighting areas in which different models or approaches are needed, moving one long step closer to the contextualized knowledge of a concept or technique's applicability sought by practitioners.
6. *Engage in member checking*: In the field of qualitative research, it is common to conclude a study by feeding back the results of research to the data contributors, not in a simple pedagogical exercise of "debriefing," but rather to solicit their feedback about the understandings generated by the study, which are then used to temper, frame, or critique its conclusions (Strauss & Corbin, 1990). Needless to say, such procedures are nearly unheard of in quantitative studies of bereavement. Implementing such member checking need not imply regarding research participants (whether the bereaved or the clinicians who serve them) as the ultimate authority on what is true and valid, but it does imply genuine interest in fostering dialogue about the accuracy and significance of the results rather than merely an interest in their dissemination. Viewed holistically, "closing the loop" in this fashion would signal a fuller integration of the voices of practitioners (and ultimately the bereaved themselves) and scientists in the conduct of research, from its inception at the stage of question

or hypothesis generation through its ultimate interpretation and publication. Having greater voice in the design, implementation, and analysis of studies would almost certainly contribute to greater interest on the part of clinicians in supporting them and utilizing their results to shape their practice.

7. *Pursue principles rather than rules*: The goal of clinical science in the logical empiricist mold too often seems to be the generation of strict and decontextualized rules about what constitute "best practices," which ironically are rarely derived from a close study of "best practitioners"! The result tends to be sweeping pronouncements regarding the efficacy of preferred procedures, typically carefully manualized to minimize variability in their implementation. Yet this rule-bound, formalistic approach stands in stark contrast to the improvisational, contextual character of counseling, which is by its nature responsive to subtle variations in client presentations not only at the level of one client as distinct from another, but also at the level of nuanced signals of receptivity or resistance to a particular point or procedure on a moment-to-moment basis in the therapeutic interaction (Neimeyer, 2000). One lesson from the debate on empirically supported treatments in psychotherapy is that although prescriptive *rules* (e.g., "avoid sex with clients" or "evaluate suicide risk in the presence of implied threats") function adequately when the behaviors to be regulated are simple and clearly defined, descriptive *principles* function better as the behaviors in question grow more complex (e.g., "provide greater direction when clients feel overwhelmed" or "follow the client's affective lead") (Levitt, Neimeyer, & Williams, 2005). Generally speaking, research that contributes to a principled rather than rule-bound practice will prove more congenial to clinicians, giving them the compass they need to adapt particular techniques and strategies to the unique demands of a given person or problem.

CODA

Although contemporary research and practice in the area of bereavement are of fairly recent advent, we, as well as our colleagues on the editorial team for this project, find ourselves encouraged by the scope and depth they have achieved. Indeed, all of us recall a time when professionals spoke with conviction of "the stages of grief," and practiced as if the same "grief work" were necessary across persons, cultures, and losses, largely in keeping with empirically untested psychodynamic assumptions. As a survey of the content of this volume will attest, that time is long gone, and in its place is a much richer and variegated appreciation of the landscape of loss, one for which the contributors to this book offer an atlas of maps varying in their projection, detail, and geographical focus. Our hope is that they collectively provide useful orientation for the further cartographic efforts of bereavement researchers as well as the clinical exploration of practitioners. We look forward to the ongoing synergy between these communities, and trust that the present project has given impetus to this effort.

NOTE

1. Chaired by Irwin Sandler, the group included David Balk, John R. Jordan, Cara Kennedy, Janice Nadeau, and Ester Shapiro. The useful report they generated (Bridging Research Group, 2005) represented a companion piece to the substantive review of bereavement research drafted by a second work group empaneled by the Center for the Advancement of Health (CAH), chaired by Robert A. Neimeyer (CAH, 2004).

REFERENCES

Bridging Work Group. (2005). Bridging the gap between research and practice in bereavement: Report from the Center for the Advancement of Health. *Death Studies*, *29*, 93–122.

Center for the Advancement of Health. (2004). Report on bereavement and grief research, *Death Studies*, 6, (Special Issue), 489–575.

Currier, J. M., Holland, J. M., & Neimeyer, R. A. (2010). Do CBT-based interventions alleviate distress following bereavement? A review of current evidence. *International Journal of Cognitive Therapy*, *3*, 71–95.

Currier, J. M., Neimeyer, R. A., & Berman, J. S. (2008). The effectiveness of psychotherapeutic interventions for the bereaved: A comprehensive quantitative review. *Psychological Bulletin*, 134, 648–661.

Freud, S. (1957). Mourning and melancholia. In J. Strachey (Ed.), *The complete psychological works of Sigmund Freud* (pp. 152–170). London: Hogarth Press. (Original work published in 1917)

Levitt, H. M., Neimeyer, R. A., & Williams, D. C. (2005). Rules versus principles in psychotherapy: Implications of the quest for universal guidelines in the movement for empirically supported treatments. *Journal of Contemporary Psychotherapy*, *35*, pp. 117–129.

Lindemann, E. (1944). Symptomatology and management of acute grief. *American Journal of Psychiatry*, *101*, 141–148.

Neimeyer, R. A. (2000). Research and practice as essential tensions: A constructivist confession. In L. M. Vaillant & S. Soldz (Eds.), *Empirical knowledge and clinical experience* (pp. 123–150). Washington, DC: American Psychological Association.

Neimeyer, R. A., & Hogan, N. (2001). Quantitative or qualitative? Measurement issues in the study of grief. In H. Schut, M. Stroebe, S. R. Hansson, & W. Stroebe (Eds.), *Handbook of bereavement research* (pp. 89–118). Washington, DC: American Psychological Association.

Neimeyer, R. A., Hogan, N., & Laurie, A. (2008). The measurement of grief: Psychometric considerations in the assessment of reactions to bereavement. In M. Stroebe, R. O. Hansson, H. Schut, & W. Stroebe (Eds.), *Handbook of bereavement research: 21st century perspectives* (pp. 133–186). Washington, DC: American Psychological Association.

Okun, B., & Nowinski, J. (2011). *Saying goodbye: How families can find renewal through loss*. New York: Berkley.

Popper, K. R. (1963). *Conjectures and refutations*. London: Routledge.

Radnitsky, G. (1973). *Contemporary schools of metascience*. Chicago: Henry Regnery.

Strauss, A., & Corbin, J. (1990). *Basics of qualitative research*. Newbury Park, CA: Sage.

Author Index

E

F

G

K

L

S

T

X

Y

Z

Subject Index

D

N

S

T